D1126495

THE LOEB CLASSICAL LIBRARY

FOUNDED BY JAMES LOEB

AESCHYLUS

II

LCL 146

AESCHYLUS

AGAMEMNON
LIBATION-BEARERS
EUMENIDES
FRAGMENTS

WITH AN ENGLISH TRANSLATION BY

HERBERT WEIR SMYTH

APPENDIX AND ADDENDUM BY

HUGH LLOYD-JONES

HARVARD UNIVERSITY PRESS
CAMBRIDGE, MASSACHUSETTS
LONDON, ENGLAND

First published 1926
Reprinted 1930, 1936, 1946, 1952, 1957, 1963, 1971, 1983, 1992, 1995

ISBN 0-674-99161-3

Printed in Great Britain by St Edmundsbury Press Ltd, Bury St Edmunds, Suffolk, on acid-free paper.
Bound by Hunter & Foulis Ltd, Edinburgh, Scotland.

CONTENTS

AGAMEMNON 1

THE LIBATION-BEARERS 153

EUMENIDES 267

FRAGMENTS 373

APPENDIX 523

ADDENDUM: NEW TEXT OF FR. 50 599

INDEX OF PROPER NAMES 604

AGAMEMNON

ΤΑ ΤΟΥ ΔΡΑΜΑΤΟΣ ΠΡΟΣΩΠΑ

ΦΥΛΑΞ
ΧΟΡΟΣ
ΚΛΥΤΑΙΜΗΣΤΡΑ
ΚΗΡΥΞ
ΑΓΑΜΕΜΝΩΝ
ΚΑΣΑΝΔΡΑ
ΑΙΓΙΣΘΟΣ

DRAMATIS PERSONAE

Watchman
Chorus of Argive Elders
Clytaemestra
Herald
Agamemnon
Cassandra
Aegisthus

Scene.—Argos.
Time.—The heroic age.
Date.—458 b.c., at the City Dionysia.

ARGUMENT

When that Helen had fled with Paris to Troyland, her husband Menelaüs and his brother Agamemnon, the sons of Atreus and two-throned Kings of Argos, sought to take vengeance on him who had done outrage to Zeus, the guardian of the rights of hospitality. Before their palace appeared a portent, which the seer Calchas interpreted to them : the two eagles were the Kings themselves and the pregnant hare seized in their talons was the city which held Priam's son and Helen and her wealth. But Artemis, she that loves the wild things of the field, was wroth with the Kings : and when all their host was gathered at Aulis and would sail with its thousand ships, she made adverse winds to blow ; so that the ships rotted and the crews lost heart. Then the seer, albeit in darkling words, spake unto Agamemnon : " If thou wilt appease the goddess and so free the fleet, thou must sacrifice with thine own hand thy daughter Iphigenia." And he did even so, and the Greeks sailed away in their ships. Nine years did they lay siege to Troytown, but they could not take it ; for it was fated that it should not be taken until the tenth year.

Now when King Agamemnon fared forth from Argos, he left at home his Queen, Clytaemestra, Leda's child and Helen's sister (though she had for father Tyndareus, but Helen's was Zeus himself) ; and in her loneliness and because Agamemnon had slain her daughter, she gave ear to the whisperings of another's love, even of Aegisthus, son of that Thyestes who had lain with the wife of his brother Atreus; and for revenge Atreus slew other of Thyestes' sons and gave their father thereof to eat; and when Thyestes learned whereof he had eaten, he cursed his brother's race.

With the coming of the tenth year of the war, Queen Clytaemestra, plotting with Aegisthus against her husband's life, ordered that watch be kept upon the roof of her palace at Argos; for a succession of beacon-fires was to flash the news from Troy when the city should be captured by Agamemnon. For weary months the watchman has been on the look-out—but at last the signal blazes forth in the night. In celebration of the glad event, the Queen has altar-fires kindled throughout the city. The Chorus of Elders will not credit the tidings; nor are their doubts resolved until a herald announces the approach of Agamemnon, whose ship had alone escaped the storm that had raged in the night just passed. Welcomed by his Queen, Agamemnon bespeaks a kindly reception for his captive, Cassandra, Priam's daughter, and on his wife's urgence consents to walk to his palace on costly tapestries. Cassandra seeks in vain to convince the Elders of their master's peril; and, conscious also of her own doom, passes within. Agamemnon's death-shriek is heard; the two corpses are displayed. Clytaemestra exults in her deed and defies the Elders. Aegisthus enters to declare that Agamemnon has been slain in requital for his father's crime. The Elders, on the point of coming to blows with Aegisthus and his body-guard, are restrained by Clytaemestra, but not before they utter the warning that Orestes will return to exact vengeance for the murder of his father.

ΑΓΑΜΕΜΝΩΝ

ΦΥΛΑΞ

Θεοὺς μὲν αἰτῶ τῶνδ᾽ ἀπαλλαγὴν πόνων
φρουρᾶς ἐτείας μῆκος, ἣν[1] κοιμώμενος
στέγαις Ἀτρειδῶν ἄγκαθεν, κυνὸς δίκην,
ἄστρων κάτοιδα νυκτέρων ὁμήγυριν,
καὶ τοὺς φέροντας χεῖμα καὶ θέρος βροτοῖς
λαμπροὺς δυνάστας, ἐμπρέποντας αἰθέρι
[ἀστέρας, ὅταν φθίνωσιν, ἀντολάς τε τῶν].[2]
καὶ νῦν φυλάσσω λαμπάδος τὸ σύμβολον,
αὐγὴν πυρὸς φέρουσαν ἐκ Τροίας φάτιν
ἁλώσιμόν τε βάξιν· ὧδε γὰρ κρατεῖ
γυναικὸς ἀνδρόβουλον ἐλπίζον[3] κέαρ.
εὖτ᾽ ἂν δὲ νυκτίπλαγκτον ἔνδροσόν τ᾽ ἔχω
εὐνὴν ὀνείροις οὐκ ἐπισκοπουμένην
ἐμήν· φόβος γὰρ ἀνθ᾽ ὕπνου παραστατεῖ,
τὸ μὴ βεβαίως βλέφαρα συμβαλεῖν ὕπνῳ·
ὅταν δ᾽ ἀείδειν ἢ μινύρεσθαι δοκῶ,
ὕπνου τόδ᾽ ἀντίμολπον ἐντέμνων[4] ἄκος,
κλαίω τότ᾽ οἴκου τοῦδε συμφορὰν στένων
οὐχ ὡς τὰ πρόσθ᾽ ἄριστα διαπονουμένου.
νῦν δ᾽ εὐτυχὴς γένοιτ᾽ ἀπαλλαγὴ πόνων

[1] δ᾽ ἦν MV, ἦν FV3N.
[2] Bracketed by Pauw.
[3] ἐλπίζων with ο over ω M.
[4] ἐκτέμνων F^1Rom.V3

AGAMEMNON

Watchman

[*Upon the roof of the palace of Agamemnon at Argos*]

Release from this weary task of mine has been my cry unto the gods throughout my long year's watch, wherein, couchant upon the palace roof of the Atreidae, upon my bended arm, like a hound, I have learned to know aright the conclave of the stars of night, yea those radiant potentates conspicuous in the firmament, bringers of winter and summer unto mankind [the constellations, what time they wane and rise].

So now I am still awatch for the signal-flame, the gleaming fire that is to harbinger news from Troy and tidings of its capture. For thus rules my Queen, woman in sanguine heart and man in strength of purpose. And whenever I make here my bed, restless and dank with dew and unvisited by dreams —for instead of sleep fear stands ever by my side, so that I cannot close my eyelids fast in sleep—and whenever I am minded to sing or hum a stave (and thus apply an antidote of song to ward off drowsiness), then it is my tears start forth, as I bewail the fortunes of this our house, not ordered for the best as in days agone. But to-night may there come

εὐαγγέλου φανέντος ὀρφναίου πυρός.
ὦ χαῖρε λαμπτὴρ νυκτός, ἡμερήσιον
φάος πιφαύσκων καὶ χορῶν κατάστασιν
πολλῶν ἐν Ἄργει, τῆσδε συμφορᾶς χάριν.
ἰοὺ ἰού.
Ἀγαμέμνονος γυναικὶ σημαίνω[1] τορῶς
εὐνῆς ἐπαντείλασαν ὡς τάχος δόμοις
ὀλολυγμὸν εὐφημοῦντα τῇδε λαμπάδι
ἐπορθιάζειν,[2] εἴπερ Ἰλίου πόλις
ἑάλωκεν, ὡς ὁ φρυκτὸς ἀγγέλλων[3] πρέπει·
αὐτός τ᾽ ἔγωγε φροίμιον χορεύσομαι.
τὰ δεσποτῶν γὰρ εὖ πεσόντα θήσομαι
τρὶς ἓξ βαλούσης τῆσδέ μοι φρυκτωρίας.
γένοιτο δ᾽ οὖν μολόντος εὐφιλῆ χέρα
ἄνακτος οἴκων τῇδε βαστάσαι χερί.
τὰ δ᾽ ἄλλα σιγῶ· βοῦς ἐπὶ γλώσσῃ μέγας
βέβηκεν· οἶκος δ᾽ αὐτός, εἰ φθογγὴν λάβοι,
σαφέστατ᾽ ἂν λέξειεν· ὡς ἑκὼν ἐγὼ
μαθοῦσιν αὐδῶ κοὐ μαθοῦσι λήθομαι.

ΧΟΡΟΣ

δέκατον μὲν ἔτος τόδ᾽ ἐπεὶ Πριάμου[4]
μέγας ἀντίδικος,
Μενέλαος ἄναξ ἠδ᾽ Ἀγαμέμνων,
διθρόνου Διόθεν καὶ δισκήπτρου

[1] σημαίνω M, σημανῶ VFNV3.
[2] ἐπορθριάζειν MV, ἐπορθιάζειν FNV3.
[3] ἀγγέλων MVF Rom., ἀγγέλλων NV3.
[4] πριάμω MV, πριάμου FNV3.

[1] A proverbial expression (of uncertain origin) for enforced silence. Cp. Frag. 176, "A key stands guard upon my tongue."

happy release from my weary task! May the fire with its glad tidings flash through the gloom!

[*The signal-fire suddenly flashes out*

All hail, thou blaze that showest forth in the night a light as it were of day, thou harbinger of many a choral dance in Argos in thanksgiving for this glad event!

What ho! What ho!

To Agamemnon's Queen I thus cry aloud the signal to rise from her couch and in all haste to uplift in her palace halls a shout of jubilance in welcome of yon fire, if in very truth the city of Ilium is taken, as this beacon doth unmistakably announce. And I will make an overture with a dance upon my own account; for my lord's lucky cast I shall count to mine own score, yon beacon having thrown me treble sixes.

Ah well, may the master of the house come home and may I clasp his welcome hand in mine! For the rest I'm dumb; a great ox stands upon my tongue[1]—yet the house itself, could it but speak, might tell a tale full plain; since, for my part, of mine own choice I have words for such as know, and to those who know not I've lost my memory.

[*He descends by an inner stairway; attendants kindle fires at the altars placed in front of the palace. Enter the chorus of Argive Elders*

CHORUS

This is now the tenth year since Priam's mighty adversary, King Menelaüs, and with him King Agamemnon, the mighty twain of Atreus' sons,

τιμῆς ὀχυρὸν ζεῦγος Ἀτρειδᾶν
στόλον Ἀργείων χιλιοναύτην[1]
τῆσδ' ἀπὸ χώρας
ἦραν, στρατιῶτιν ἀρωγήν,[2]
μέγαν ἐκ θυμοῦ κλάζοντες Ἄρη
τρόπον αἰγυπιῶν, οἵτ' ἐκπατίοις
ἄλγεσι παίδων ὕπατοι λεχέων
στροφοδινοῦνται
πτερύγων ἐρετμοῖσιν ἐρεσσόμενοι,
δεμνιοτήρη
πόνον ὀρταλίχων ὀλέσαντες·
ὕπατος δ' ἀίων ἤ τις Ἀπόλλων
ἢ Πὰν ἢ Ζεὺς οἰωνόθροον
γόον ὀξυβόαν τῶνδε μετοίκων
ὑστερόποινον
πέμπει παραβᾶσιν Ἐρινύν.
οὕτω δ' Ἀτρέως παῖδας ὁ κρείσσων
ἐπ' Ἀλεξάνδρῳ πέμπει ξένιος
Ζεὺς πολυάνορος ἀμφὶ γυναικὸς
πολλὰ παλαίσματα καὶ γυιοβαρῆ
γόνατος κονίαισιν ἐρειδομένου[3]
διακναιομένης τ' ἐν προτελείοις
κάμακος θήσων Δαναοῖσι
Τρωσί θ' ὁμοίως. ἔστι δ' ὅπη νῦν
ἔστι· τελεῖται δ' ἐς τὸ πεπρωμένον·
οὔθ' ὑποκαίων[4] οὔθ' ὑπολείβων
οὔτε δακρύων ἀπύρων ἱερῶν
ὀργὰς ἀτενεῖς παραθέλξει.
ἡμεῖς δ' ἀτῖται σαρκὶ[5] παλαιᾷ

[1] χιλιοναύταν MN (την superscr. m).
[2] ἀρωγὰν M (γὴν superscr. m).
[3] ἐριδομένου M, ἐρειπομένου F[1]N. [4] ὑποκλαίων : Casaubon.
[5] ἀτῖται σαρκὶ corr. from ἀτιτ* σαρκ* M.

joined in honour of throne and sceptre by grace of Zeus, put forth from this land with an armament of a thousand ships by Argives manned, a warrior force to champion their cause.

Loud rang the battle-cry they uttered in their rage, even as eagles scream, that, in lonely grief for their brood, driven by the oarage of their pinions, wheel high over their eyries, for that they have lost their toil of guarding their nurslings' nest.

But some one of the powers supreme—Apollo perchance, or Pan, or Zeus—heareth the shrill wailing scream of the clamorous birds, these sojourners in his realm, and against the transgressors sendeth vengeance at last though late. Even so Zeus, whose power is over all, Zeus lord of host and guest, sendeth against Alexander the sons of Atreus, that for the sake of a woman of many a lord[1] he may inflict struggles full many and wearisome (when the knee is pressed in the dust and the spear is shivered in the onset) on Danaans and on Trojans alike.

The case now standeth where it doth—it moveth to fulfilment at its destined end. Not by offerings burned in secret, not by secret libations, not by tears, shall man soften the stubborn wrath of sacrifices unsanctified.[2]

But we, incapable of service by reason of our aged

[1] Menelaüs, Paris, Deïphobus.

[2] "Unsanctified," literally "fireless," "that will not burn." A veiled reference either to the sacrifice of Iphigenia by Agamemnon and the wrath of Clytaemestra, or to Paris' violation of the laws of hospitality that provoked the anger of Zeus.

τῆς τότ' ἀρωγῆς ὑπολειφθέντες
μίμνομεν ἰσχὺν
ἰσόπαιδα νέμοντες ἐπὶ σκήπτροις.
ὅ τε γὰρ νεαρὸς μυελὸς στέρνων
ἐντὸς ἀνᾴσσων[1]
ἰσόπρεσβυς, Ἄρης δ' οὐκ ἔνι χώρᾳ,
τό θ' ὑπέργηρων[2] φυλλάδος ἤδη
κατακαρφομένης τρίποδας μὲν ὁδοὺς
στείχει, παιδὸς δ' οὐδὲν ἀρείων
ὄναρ ἡμερόφαντον[3] ἀλαίνει.

σὺ δέ, Τυνδάρεω[4]
θύγατερ, βασίλεια Κλυταιμήστρα,[5]
τί χρέος; τί νέον; τί δ' ἐπαισθομένη,
τίνος ἀγγελίας
πειθοῖ[6] περίπεμπτα θυοσκεῖς[7];
πάντων δὲ θεῶν τῶν ἀστυνόμων,
ὑπάτων, χθονίων,
τῶν τ' οὐρανίων τῶν τ' ἀγοραίων,
βωμοὶ δώροισι[8] φλέγονται·
ἄλλη δ' ἄλλοθεν οὐρανομήκης
λαμπὰς ἀνίσχει,
φαρμασσομένη χρίματος ἁγνοῦ
μαλακαῖς ἀδόλοισι παρηγορίαις,
πελάνῳ μυχόθεν βασιλείῳ.
τούτων λέξασ' ὅ τι καὶ δυνατὸν
καὶ θέμις αἰνεῖν,
παιών τε γενοῦ τῆσδε μερίμνης,
ἣ νῦν τοτὲ μὲν κακόφρων τελέθει,
τοτὲ δ' ἐκ θυσιῶν ἀγανὴ[9] φαίνουσ'[10]
ἐλπὶς ἀμύνει φροντίδ' ἄπληστον[11]

[1] ἀνάσσων: Herm.

frame, discarded from that martial mustering of long ago, bide here at home, supporting on our staves a strength like unto a child's. For as the vigour of youth, leaping up within the breast, is like unto that of age, since the war-god is not in his place; so over-age, its leafage already withering, goeth its way on triple feet, and, no better than a child, wandereth, a dream that is dreamed by day.

But, O daughter of Tyndareôs, Queen Clytaemestra, what hath befallen? What tidings hast thou? On what intelligence and convinced by what report is it that thou sendest about thy messengers to enjoin sacrifice? For all the gods our city worships, the gods supreme, the gods below, the gods of the heavens and of the mart, have their altars ablaze with offerings. Now here, now there, the flames rise high as heaven, yielding to the soft and guileless persuasion of hallowed unguent, even the sacrificial oil brought from the inner chambers of the palace. Of all this declare whatsoever thou canst and durst reveal, and be the healer of my soul distraught, which now at one moment bodeth ill, and then again hope, shining with kindly light from the

---

[2] *τίθιπεργήρως* M, *τόθιπεργήρως* VF, *τό θ' ὑπέργηρων* N.
[3] *ἡμερόφατον* M, *ἡμερόφαντον* N.
[4] *τυνδάρεω* (*ω* made from *αο*) *α* and *ου* superscr. M.
[5] *κλυταιμνήστρα* FN. [6] *πυθοῖ* F Rom.
[7] *θυοσκινεῖς*: Turn. [8] *δώροις* M, etc., *δώροισι* N.
[9] *ἀγανὰ*: Karsten. [10] *φαίνεις* M, *φαίνουσ'* FN, *φαίνει* V.
[11] *ἄπλειστον* MN, *ἄπληστον* F.

τῆς θυμοβόρου φρένα λύπης.[1]

[στρ. α.

κύριός εἰμι θροεῖν ὅδιον κράτος αἴσιον ἀνδρῶν
ἐκτελέων· ἔτι γὰρ θεόθεν καταπνεύει[2]
πειθῶ[3] μολπᾶν[4]
ἀλκὰν σύμφυτος αἰών·
ὅπως Ἀχαιῶν
δίθρονον κράτος, Ἑλλάδος ἥβας[5]
ξύμφρονα ταγάν,[6]
πέμπει σὺν δορὶ καὶ χερὶ[7] πράκτορι
θούριος ὄρνις Τευκρίδ' ἐπ' αἶαν,
οἰωνῶν βασιλεὺς βασιλεῦσι νεῶν ὁ κελαινός, ὅ τ' ἐξόπιν ἀργᾶς,[8]
φανέντες ἴκταρ μελάθρων
χερὸς ἐκ δοριπάλτου[9]
παμπρέπτοις[10] ἐν ἕδραισιν,
βοσκόμενοι λαγίναν, ἐρικύμονα[11] φέρματι[12] γένναν,
βλαβέντα λοισθίων δρόμων.
αἴλινον αἴλινον[13] εἰπέ, τὸ δ' εὖ νικάτω.

[ἀντ. α.

κεδνὸς δὲ στρατόμαντις ἰδὼν δύο[14] λήμασι δισσοὺς
Ἀτρεΐδας μαχίμους ἐδάη λαγοδαίτας[15]
πομπούς τ' ἀρχάς·[16]
οὕτω δ' εἶπε τεράζων·

[1] τὴν θυμοφθόρον λύπης φρένα M, τὴν θυμοβόρον λύπης φρένα F: Herm.
[2] καταπνέ*ει M, καταπνεύει VFN.
[3] πειθῶ M[1], πειθὼ M[2].
[4] μολπᾶν M[1], μολπὰν M[2].
[5] ἥβαν: ἥβας Aristoph. *Ran.* 1285.
[6] τὰν γᾶν M, ταγάν VFN.
[7] δορὶ δίκας: δορὶ καὶ χερὶ Aristoph. *Ran.* 1288.
[8] ἀργίας: Blomfield.
[9] δορυπάλτου: Turn.
[10] παμπρέποις (corr. from -πρέπτοις M) F.
[11] ἐρικύματα M, ἐρικύμονα VFN.
[12] φέρβοντο FN.

sacrifice, wards off the cankering care of the sorrow that eateth my heart.

Power is mine to proclaim the augury of triumph given on their way to princely men—since still my age,[1] inspired of the gods, breatheth upon me Persuasion, the strength of song—how that the twin-throned command of the Achaeans, the concordant captains of the youth of Hellas, was sped with avenging spear and arm against the Teucrian land by the inspiriting omen appearing to the kings of the ships—the kingly birds, one black, one white of tail, hard by the palace, on the spear-hand,[2] in a station full conspicuous, devouring a hare with brood unborn checked in the last effort to escape.[3]

Sing the song of woe, the song of woe, but may the good prevail!

Then the goodly seer of the host, marking how that the two warlike sons of Atreus were twain in temper, knew the devourers of the hare for the leaders of the armament, and thus interpreted the portent

[1] *σύμφυτος αἰών*, literally " life that has grown with me," " time of life," here " old age," as the Scholiast takes it. Cp. Mrs. Barbauld, " Life! We've been long together."

[2] The right hand.

[3] The Scholiast, followed by Hermann and some others, takes *λαγίναν γένναν* as a periphrasis for *λαγωόν*, with which *βλαβέντα* agrees (cp. *πᾶσα γέννα . . . δώσων Troad.* 531). With Hartung's *φέρματα*, the meaning is " the brood of a hare, the burthen of her womb, thwarted of their final course." *λοισθίων δρόμων*, on this interpretation, has been thought to mean " their final course " (towards birth) or even their " future racings."

---

[13] *αἴλινον* and ll. 139, 159 M. [14] *δύω* M.
[15] *λογοδαίτας* M. [16] *ἀρχάς* M, *ἀρχούς* FN.

“χρόνῳ μὲν ἀγρεῖ
Πριάμου πόλιν ἅδε κέλευθος,
πάντα δὲ πύργων
κτήνη πρόσθε τὰ[1] δημιοπληθῆ
Μοῖρ’ ἀλαπάξει πρὸς τὸ βίαιον·
οἷον μή τις ἄγα[2] θεόθεν κνεφά-
σῃ προτυπὲν στόμιον μέγα Τροίας
στρατωθέν. οἴκτῳ[3] γὰρ ἐπί-
φθονος Ἄρτεμις ἁγνὰ
πτανοῖσιν κυσὶ πατρὸς
αὐτότοκον πρὸ λόχου μογερὰν πτάκα θυομένοισιν·
στυγεῖ δὲ δεῖπνον αἰετῶν.”
αἴλινον αἴλινον εἰπέ, τὸ δ’ εὖ νικάτω.

[ἐπῳδ.

“τόσον[4] περ εὔφρων, καλά,[5]
δρόσοισι[6] λεπτοῖς[7] μαλερῶν λεόντων[8]
πάντων τ’ ἀγρονόμων φιλομάστοις
θηρῶν ὀβρικάλοισι τερπνά,
τούτων αἰνεῖ[9] ξύμβολα κρᾶναι,
δεξιὰ μέν, κατάμομφα δὲ φάσματα [στρουθῶν].[10]
ἰήιον δὲ καλέω Παιᾶνα,
μή τινας ἀντιπνόους
Δαναοῖς χρονίας ἐχενῇδας
ἀπλοίας τεύξῃ,
σπευδομένα θυσίαν ἑτέραν ἄνομόν τιν’, ἄδαιτον
νεικέων τέκτονα σύμφυτον,
οὐ δεισήνορα. μίμνει γὰρ φοβερὰ παλίνορτος
οἰκονόμος δολία μνάμων μῆνις τεκνόποινος.”
τοιάδε Κάλχας ξὺν μεγάλοις ἀγαθοῖς ἀπέκλαγξεν[11]

1 προσθετὰ M. 2 ἄτα: Herm. 3 οἴκῳ: Scaliger.
4 τόσσων M, τόσον FN. 5 ἁ καλά FN.
6 δρόσοισιν MVF, δρόσοις N.

and spake: "In time they that here issue forth shall seize Priam's town, but before its towered walls all the public store of cattle shall be ravaged perforce by fate. Only may no jealous wrath of Heaven lour down upon the embattled host, the mighty curb forged against Troy, and smite it ere it reach its goal! For, of her pity, holy Artemis is wroth at the winged hounds of her sire that they make sacrifice of a wretched timorous thing, herself and her young ere she hath brought them forth. An abomination unto her is the eagles' feast."

Sing the song of woe, the song of woe, but may the good prevail!

"Although, O Beauteous One, thou art so gracious to the tender whelps of fierce lions, and takest delight in the suckling young of every wild creature that roves the field, vouchsafe that the issue be brought to pass accordant with these signs, portents auspicious yet fraught with ill. And I implore Paean,[1] the healer, that she may not raise adverse gales with long delay to stay the Danaan fleet from putting forth by reason of her urgence of another sacrifice, knowing no law, unmeet for feast, worker of family strife, dissolving wife's reverence for husband. For there abideth wrath—terrible, not to be suppressed, a treacherous warder of the home, ever mindful, a wrath that exacteth vengeance for a child."

Such utterances of doom, derived from auguries

[1] Apollo; who is implored to divert his sister Artemis from accomplishing the evil part of the omen.

---

[7] ἀέλπτοις M, ἀέπτοισι VFN: Wellauer. [8] ὄντων MV.
[9] αἰτεῖ: Gilbert. [10] [ ] Porson. [11] ἀπέκλαιξεν M.

μόρσιμ' ἀπ' ὀρνίθων ὁδίων οἴκοις βασιλείοις·
τοῖς δ' ὁμόφωνον
αἴλινον αἴλινον εἰπέ, τὸ δ' εὖ νικάτω.

Ζεύς, ὅστις ποτ' ἐστίν, εἰ τόδ' αὐ- [στρ. β.
τῷ φίλον κεκλημένῳ,
τοῦτό νιν προσεννέπω.
οὐκ ἔχω προσεικάσαι
πάντ' ἐπισταθμώμενος
πλὴν Διός, εἰ τὸ μάταν[1] ἀπὸ φροντίδος ἄχθος
χρὴ βαλεῖν ἐτητύμως.

οὐδ' ὅστις πάροιθεν ἦν μέγας, [ἀντ. β.
παμμάχῳ θράσει βρύων,
οὐδὲ λέξεται[2] πρὶν ὤν·
ὃς δ' ἔπειτ' ἔφυ, τρια-
κτῆρος οἴχεται τυχών.
Ζῆνα δέ τις προφρόνως ἐπινίκια κλάζων
τεύξεται φρενῶν τὸ πᾶν·

τὸν φρονεῖν βροτοὺς ὁδώ- [στρ. γ.
σαντα, τὸν[3] πάθει μάθος
θέντα κυρίως ἔχειν.
στάζει δ' ἔν θ' ὕπνῳ πρὸ καρδίας
μνησιπήμων πόνος· καὶ παρ' ἄ-
κοντας ἦλθε σωφρονεῖν.
δαιμόνων δέ που χάρις βί-
αιος[4] σέλμα σεμνὸν ἡμένων.

καὶ τόθ' ἡγεμὼν ὁ πρέ- [ἀντ. γ.
σβυς νεῶν Ἀχαιικῶν,
μάντιν οὔτινα ψέγων,

on the march, together with many bodings of good, did Calchas sound forth to the royal house; and in accord therewith

Sing the song of woe, the song of woe, but may the good prevail!

Zeus, whosoe'er he be,—if by this name it well pleaseth him to be invoked, by this name I call to him—as I weigh all things in the balance, I can conjecture none save "Zeus," if in very sooth I needs must cast aside this vain burthen from my heart. He[1] who aforetime was mighty, swelling with insolence for every fray, he shall not even be named as having ever been; and he[2] who arose thereafter, he hath met his overthrower and is past and gone. But whosoe'er, heartily taking thought beforehand, giveth title of victory in triumphant shout to "Zeus," he shall gain wisdom altogether,—Zeus, who leadeth mortals the way of understanding, Zeus, who hath stablished as a fixed ordinance that "wisdom cometh by suffering." But even as trouble, bringing memory of pain, droppeth o'er the mind in sleep, so to men in their despite cometh wisdom. With constraint, methinks, cometh the grace of the powers divine enthroned upon their awful seats.

So then the captain of the Achaean ships, the elder of the twain—holding no seer at fault, bending to

[1] Uranus. [2] Cronus.

---

[1] τόδε μάταν: Pauw. [2] οὐδὲν λέξαι: H. L. Ahrens.
[3] τῷ M: Schütz. [4] βιαίως: Turn.

ἐμπαίοις τύχαισι συμπνέων,
εὖτ' ἀπλοίᾳ κεναγγεῖ βαρύ-
νοντ' Ἀχαιικὸς λεώς,
Χαλκίδος πέραν ἔχων πα-
λιρρόχθοις[1] ἐν Αὐλίδος τόποις·

πνοαὶ δ' ἀπὸ Στρυμόνος μολοῦσαι [στρ. δ.
κακόσχολοι νήστιδες δύσορμοι,
βροτῶν ἄλαι, ναῶν <τε>[2] καὶ
πεισμάτων ἀφειδεῖς,
παλιμμήκη χρόνον τιθεῖσαι
τρίβῳ κατέξαινον ἄν-
θος Ἀργείων· ἐπεὶ δὲ καὶ πικροῦ
χείματος ἄλλο μῆχαρ
βριθύτερον πρόμοισιν
μάντις ἔκλαγξεν[3] προφέρων Ἄρτεμιν, ὥστε χθόνα βάκ-
τροις ἐπικρούσαντας Ἀτρείδας δάκρυ μὴ κατασχεῖν·

ἄναξ δ' ὁ πρέσβυς τότ'[4] εἶπε φωνῶν· [ἀντ. δ.
"βαρεῖα μὲν κὴρ τὸ μὴ πιθέσθαι,[5]
βαρεῖα δ', εἰ τέκνον δαΐ-
ξω, δόμων ἄγαλμα,
μιαίνων παρθενοσφάγοισιν
ῥείθροις[6] πατρῴους χέρας
πέλας βωμοῦ·[7] τί τῶνδ' ἄνευ κακῶν,
πῶς λιπόναυς[8] γένωμαι
ξυμμαχίας ἁμαρτών;
παυσανέμου γὰρ θυσίας παρθενίου θ' αἵματος ὀργᾷ περιόργως ἐπιθυμεῖν θέμις. εὖ γὰρ εἴη."

ἐπεὶ δ' ἀνάγκας ἔδυ λέπαδνον [στρ. ε.
φρενὸς πνέων δυσσεβῆ τροπαίαν

the adverse blasts of fortune, what time the Achaean folk, on the shore over against Chalcis in the region where Aulis' tides surge to and fro, were sore distressed by opposing winds and failing stores; and the breezes that blew from the Strymon, bringing them grievous leisure, hunger, and tribulation of spirit in a cruel port, driving the men distraught, and sparing nor ship nor cable, by doubling the season of their stay, began to wither by wasting the flower of Argos; and when the seer, urging Artemis as cause, proclaimed to the chieftains another remedy, more grievous even than the bitter storm, so that the sons of Atreus smote the ground with their staves and stifled not their tears—

Then the elder king spake and said: "Hard is my fate to refuse obedience, and hard, if I must slay my child, the glory of my home, and at the altar-side stain with streams of a virgin's blood a father's hand. Which of these courses is not fraught with ill? How can I become a deserter to my fleet and fail my allies in arms? For that they should with passionate eagerness crave a sacrifice to lull the winds—even a virgin's blood—stands within their right. May all be for the best."

But when he had donned the yoke of Necessity, with veering of spirit, impious, unholy, unsanctified, from

---

[1] παλιρρόθοις: H. L. Ahrens. [2] <τε> Porson.
[3] ἔκλαγξε: Porson. [4] τόδ': Stanley.
[5] πειθέσθαι M, πείθεσθαι other MSS.: Turn.
[6] ῥεέθροις M, ῥείθροις N. [7] βωμοῦ πέλας: Blomfield.
[8] τί πῶς λιπόναυστε M, πῶς λιπόναυς N.

ἄναγνον ἀνίερον, τόθεν
τὸ παντότολμον φρονεῖν μετέγνω.
βροτοὺς[1] θρασύνει γὰρ αἰσχρόμητις
τάλαινα παρακοπὰ πρωτοπήμων. ἔτλα δ᾽ οὖν
θυτὴρ γενέσθαι θυγατρός,
γυναικοποίνων πολέμων ἀρωγὰν
καὶ προτέλεια ναῶν.

λιτὰς δὲ καὶ κληδόνας πατρῴους [ἀντ. ε.
παρ᾽ οὐδὲν αἰῶ τε[2] παρθένειον[3]
ἔθεντο φιλόμαχοι βραβῆς.
φράσεν δ᾽ ἀόζοις πατὴρ μετ᾽ εὐχὰν
δίκαν χιμαίρας[4] ὕπερθε βωμοῦ
πέπλοισι περιπετῆ παντὶ θυμῷ προνωπῆ
λαβεῖν ἀέρδην, στόματός
τε καλλιπρῴ-
ρου φυλακᾷ[5] κατασχεῖν
φθόγγον ἀραῖον οἴκοις,

βίᾳ χαλινῶν τ᾽ ἀναύδῳ μένει. [στρ. ζ.
κρόκου βαφὰς δ᾽ ἐς πέδον χέουσα
ἔβαλλ᾽ ἕκαστον θυτήρων ἀπ᾽ ὄμματος βέλει φιλοίκτῳ,
πρέπουσά θ᾽ ὡς ἐν γραφαῖς, προσεννέπειν
θέλουσ᾽, ἐπεὶ πολλάκις
πατρὸς κατ᾽ ἀνδρῶνας εὐτραπέζους
ἔμελψεν, ἁγνᾷ[6] δ᾽ ἀταύρωτος αὐδᾷ[6] πατρὸς
φίλου τριτόσπονδον εὔ-
ποτμον παιῶνα[7] φίλως ἐτίμα—

τὰ δ᾽ ἔνθεν οὔτ᾽ εἶδον οὔτ᾽ ἐννέπω· [ἀντ. ζ.
τέχναι δὲ Κάλχαντος οὐκ ἄκραντοι.
Δίκα δὲ τοῖς μὲν παθοῦσιν μαθεῖν

that hour his purpose shifted to resolve that deed of uttermost audacity. For mankind is emboldened by wretched delusion, counsellor of ill, primal source of woe. So then he hardened his heart to sacrifice his daughter that he might prosper a war waged to avenge a woman, and as an offering for the voyaging of a fleet!

Her supplications, her cries of "Father," and her virgin life, the commanders in their eagerness for war reckoned as naught. Her father, after a prayer. bade his ministers lay hold of her as, enwrapped in her robes, she lay fallen forward, and with stout heart to raise her, as it were a kid, high above the altar; and with a guard upon her lovely mouth, the bit's strong and stifling might, to stay a cry that had been a curse on his house.

Then, as she shed to earth her saffron robe, she smote each of her sacrificers with a glance from her eyes beseeching pity, and showing as in a picture, fain to speak; for oft had she sung where men were met at her father's hospitable board, and with her virgin voice had been wont lovingly to do honour to her loved father's prayer for blessing at the third libation[1]—

What next befell, I beheld not, neither do I tell. The art of Calchas failed not of fulfilment. Justice inclineth her scales so that wisdom cometh at

[1] At the end of a banquet, libations were offered (1) to Zeus and Hera, or to the Olympian gods in general, (2) to the Heroes, (3) to Zeus, the Saviour; then came the paean, or song, after which the symposium began.

---

[1] βροτοῖς: Spanheim.
[2] αἰῶνα π.: O. Müller. [3] παρθένιον M, παρθένειον FN.
[4] χειμαίρας MV, χιμαίρας FN. [5] φυλακάν: Blomfield.
[6] ἁγνὰ . . . αὐδὰ M, ἁγνᾷ N, αὐδᾷ FN. [7] αἰῶνα: Hartung.

ἐπιρρέπει· τὸ μέλλον <δ’>[1],
ἐπεὶ γένοιτ’,[2] ἂν κλύοις· προχαιρέτω·[3]
ἴσον δὲ τῷ προστένειν.
τορὸν γὰρ ἥξει σύνορθρον[4] αὐγαῖς.[5]
πέλοιτο δ’ οὖν τἀπὶ τούτοισιν εὖ πρᾶξις,[6] ὡς
θέλει τόδ’ ἄγχιστον Ἀ-
πίας γαίας μονόφρουρον ἕρκος.

ἥκω σεβίζων σόν, Κλυταιμήστρα,[7] κράτος·
δίκη γάρ ἐστι φωτὸς ἀρχηγοῦ τίειν
γυναῖκ’ ἐρημωθέντος ἄρσενος θρόνου.
σὺ δ’ εἴ τι κεδνὸν[8] εἴτε μὴ πεπυσμένη
εὐαγγέλοισιν ἐλπίσιν θυηπολεῖς,
κλύοιμ’ ἂν εὔφρων· οὐδὲ σιγώσῃ φθόνος.

ΚΛΥΤΑΙΜΗΣΤΡΑ

εὐάγγελος μέν, ὥσπερ ἡ παροιμία,
ἕως γένοιτο μητρὸς εὐφρόνης πάρα.
πεύσῃ δὲ χάρμα μεῖζον ἐλπίδος κλύειν·
Πριάμου γὰρ ᾑρήκασιν Ἀργεῖοι πόλιν.

ΧΟΡΟΣ

πῶς φῄς; πέφευγε τοὔπος ἐξ ἀπιστίας.

ΚΛΥΤΑΙΜΗΣΤΡΑ

Τροίαν Ἀχαιῶν οὖσαν· ἦ τορῶς λέγω;

ΧΟΡΟΣ

χαρά μ’ ὑφέρπει δάκρυον ἐκκαλουμένη.

[1] τὸ μέλλον τὸ δὲ προκλύειν M²VF; τὸ μέλλον M¹N: <δ’> Elmsley.
[2] ἐπιγένοιτ’ M.
[3] προχαιρέτω: H. L. Ahrens.
[4] σύνορθον MV, σύναρθρον FN: Wellauer.
[5] αὐταῖς: Herm.
[6] εὔπραξις: Lobeck.

the price of suffering. But what is yet to be, that thou shalt know when it befalleth ; till then, let it be—'tis all one with sorrowing too soon. Clear it will come, together with the light of dawn. However, [*enter Clytaemestra*] as for what shall follow, may the issue be happy, even as is the wish of our sole guardian here, the bulwark of the Apian land, who standeth nearest to our lord.

I am come, Clytaemestra, in obedience to thy royal authority ; for it is meet to do homage to the consort of a sovereign prince when her lord's throne is tenantless. Now whether the tidings thou hast heard be good or ill, and thou dost make sacrifice with hopes that herald gladness, I fain would hear ; yet, if thou wouldst keep silence, I make no complaint.

CLYTAEMESTRA

As herald of gladness, with the proverb, may Morn be born from her mother Night ! Thou shalt hear joyful news surpassing all thy hopes—the Argives have taken Priam's town !

CHORUS

How sayest thou ? The meaning of thy words hath escaped me, so incredible they seemed.

CLYTAEMESTRA

I said that Troy is in the hands of the Achaeans. Is my meaning clear ?

CHORUS

Joy steals over me, giving challenge to my tears.

---

[7] *κλυταιμήστρα* MN, *κλυταιμνήστρα* VF.
[8] *εἴτε κεδνὸν* : Auratus.

ΚΛΥΤΑΙΜΗΣΤΡΑ

εὖ γὰρ φρονοῦντος ὄμμα σοῦ κατηγορεῖ.

ΧΟΡΟΣ

τί γὰρ τὸ[1] πιστόν; ἔστι τῶνδέ σοι τέκμαρ;

ΚΛΥΤΑΙΜΗΣΤΡΑ

ἔστιν· τί δ᾽ οὐχί; μὴ δολώσαντος θεοῦ.

ΧΟΡΟΣ

πότερα δ᾽ ὀνείρων φάσματ᾽ εὐπιθῆ[2] σέβεις;

ΚΛΥΤΑΙΜΗΣΤΡΑ

οὐ δόξαν ἂν λάβοιμι βριζούσης φρενός.

ΧΟΡΟΣ

ἀλλ᾽ ἦ σ᾽ ἐπίανέν τις ἄπτερος φάτις;

ΚΛΥΤΑΙΜΗΣΤΡΑ

παιδὸς νέας ὣς κάρτ᾽ ἐμωμήσω φρένας.

ΧΟΡΟΣ

ποίου χρόνου δὲ καὶ πεπόρθηται πόλις;

ΚΛΥΤΑΙΜΗΣΤΡΑ

τῆς νῦν τεκούσης φῶς τόδ᾽ εὐφρόνης λέγω.

ΧΟΡΟΣ

καὶ τίς τόδ᾽ ἐξίκοιτ᾽ ἂν ἀγγέλων τάχος;

[1] τί γάρ; τὸ: Prien.
[2] εὐπειθῆ: Blomfield.

CLYTAEMESTRA

Aye, for 'tis of a loyal heart that thine eye argues thee.

CHORUS

What then is the proof? Hast thou warranty of this?

CLYTAEMESTRA

I have, indeed; unless some god hath played me false.

CHORUS

Dost thou pay regard to the persuasive visions of dreams?

CLYTAEMESTRA

I would not heed the fancies of a slumbering brain.

CHORUS

But can it be some pleasing rumour that hath fed thy hopes?

CLYTAEMESTRA

Truly thou floutest mine understanding as it were a child's.

CHORUS

But at what time has the city been destroyed?

CLYTAEMESTRA

In the night, I say, that hath but now given birth to yonder sun.

CHORUS

And what messenger could reach here with speed like that?

ΚΛΥΤΑΙΜΗΣΤΡΑ

Ἥφαιστος Ἴδης λαμπρὸν ἐκπέμπων σέλας.
φρυκτὸς δὲ φρυκτὸν δεῦρ᾿ ἀπ᾿ ἀγγάρου[1] πυρὸς
ἔπεμπεν· Ἴδη μὲν πρὸς Ἑρμαῖον[2] λέπας
Λήμνου· μέγαν δὲ πανὸν[3] ἐκ νήσου τρίτον
Ἀθῷον αἶπος Ζηνὸς ἐξεδέξατο,
ὑπερτελής τε, πόντον ὥστε νωτίσαι,
ἰσχὺς πορευτοῦ λαμπάδος πρὸς ἡδονὴν
. . . .[4]
†πεύκη τὸ χρυσοφεγγές, ὥς τις ἥλιος,
σέλας παραγγείλασα Μακίστου σκοπαῖς·[5]
ὁ δ᾿ οὔτι μέλλων οὐδ᾿ ἀφρασμόνως ὕπνῳ
νικώμενος παρῆκεν ἀγγέλου μέρος·
ἑκὰς δὲ φρυκτοῦ φῶς ἐπ᾿ Εὐρίπου ῥοὰς
Μεσσαπίου φύλαξι σημαίνει μολόν.
οἱ δ᾿ ἀντέλαμψαν καὶ παρήγγειλαν πρόσω
γραίας ἐρείκης[6] θωμὸν ἅψαντες πυρί.
σθένουσα λαμπὰς δ᾿ οὐδέπω μαυρουμένη,
ὑπερθοροῦσα πεδίον Ἀσωποῦ,[7] δίκην
φαιδρᾶς σελήνης, πρὸς Κιθαιρῶνος λέπας
ἤγειρεν ἄλλην ἐκδοχὴν πομποῦ πυρός.
φάος δὲ τηλέπομπον οὐκ ἠναίνετο
φρουρὰ πλέον καίουσα τῶν εἰρημένων·
λίμνην δ᾿ ὑπὲρ Γοργῶπιν ἔσκηψεν φάος·
ὄρος τ᾿ ἐπ᾿ Αἰγίπλαγκτον ἐξικνούμενον
ὤτρυνε θεσμὸν μὴ χρονίζεσθαι[8] πυρός.
πέμπουσι δ᾿ ἀνδαίοντες ἀφθόνῳ μένει
φλογὸς μέγαν πώγωνα, καὶ Σαρωνικοῦ
πορθμοῦ κάτοπτον[9] πρῶν᾿ ὑπερβάλλειν πρόσω

[1] ἀγγέλου: Canter from *Et. Mag.*, Photius. [2] ἕρμαιον M.

CLYTAEMESTRA

Hephaestus, from Ida speeding forth his brilliant blaze. Beacon passed beacon on to us by courier-flame: Ida, to the Hermaean scaur in Lemnos; to the mighty blaze upon the island succeeded, third, the summit of Athos sacred unto Zeus; and, soaring high aloft so as to arch the main, the flame, travelling joyously onward in its strength . . . the pine-wood torch, its golden-beamed light, as another sun,[1] passing the message on to the watch-towers of Macistus. He, delaying not nor heedlessly overcome by sleep, neglected not his part as messenger. Far over Euripus' stream came the beacon-light and gave the signal to the sentinels on Messapion. They, kindling a heap of withered heather, lit up their answering blaze and sped the message on. The flame, now gathering strength and in no wise dimmed, like unto a radiant moon o'erleaped the plain of Asopus to Cithaeron's scaur, and roused another relay of missive fire. Nor did the warders there disdain the far-flung light, but made a blaze higher than had been bidden them. Across Gorgopus' water shot the light, reached the mount of Aegiplanctus, and urged the ordinance of fire to make no dallying. Kindling high with unstinted force a mighty beard of flame, they sped it forward that, as it blazed, it o'erpassed even the headland that looks upon the Saronic gulf; until

[1] The Greek text is here corrupt.

---

[3] φανὸν: Casaubon from Athenaeus xv. 700 E, Photius.
[4] Lacuna indicated by Casaubon. [5] σκοπὰς: Turn.
[6] ἐρίκης M^1, ἐρείκης M^2VFN.
[7] παιδίον ὠποῦ MV. [8] χαρίζεσθαι: Casaubon.
[9] κάτοπτρον: Canter.

φλέγουσαν· ἔστ'[1] ἔσκηψεν εὖτ'[1] ἀφίκετο
Ἀραχναῖον αἶπος, ἀστυγείτονας σκοπάς·
κἄπειτ' Ἀτρειδῶν ἐς τόδε σκήπτει στέγος
φάος τόδ' οὐκ ἄπαππον Ἰδαίου πυρός.
[2]τοιοίδε τοί μοι[3] λαμπαδηφόρων νόμοι,
ἄλλος παρ' ἄλλου διαδοχαῖς πληρούμενοι·
νικᾷ δ' ὁ πρῶτος καὶ τελευταῖος δραμών.
τέκμαρ τοιοῦτον σύμβολόν τέ σοι λέγω
ἀνδρὸς παραγγείλαντος ἐκ Τροίας ἐμοί.

ΧΟΡΟΣ

θεοῖς μὲν αὖθις, ὦ γύναι, προσεύξομαι.
λόγους δ' ἀκοῦσαι τούσδε κἀποθαυμάσαι
διηνεκῶς θέλοιμ' ἂν ὡς λέγοις[4] πάλιν.

ΚΛΥΤΑΙΜΗΣΤΡΑ

Τροίαν Ἀχαιοὶ τῇδ' ἔχουσ' ἐν ἡμέρᾳ.
οἶμαι βοὴν ἄμεικτον[5] ἐν πόλει πρέπειν.
ὄξος τ' ἄλειφά τ' ἐγχέας[6] ταὐτῷ κύτει
διχοστατοῦντ' ἄν, οὐ φίλω,[7] προσεννέποις.
καὶ τῶν ἁλόντων καὶ κρατησάντων δίχα
φθογγὰς ἀκούειν ἔστι συμφορᾶς διπλῆς.
οἱ μὲν γὰρ ἀμφὶ σώμασιν πεπτωκότες
ἀνδρῶν κασιγνήτων τε καὶ φυταλμίων
παῖδες γερόντων οὐκέτ' ἐξ ἐλευθέρου
δέρης ἀποιμώζουσι φιλτάτων μόρον·
τοὺς δ' αὖτε νυκτίπλαγκτος ἐκ μάχης πόνος
νήστεις[8] πρὸς ἀρίστοισιν ὧν ἔχει πόλις
τάσσει, πρὸς οὐδὲν ἐν μέρει τεκμήριον,

[1] εἶτ' . . . εἶτ' : Herm.
[2] ll. 312-1067 are missing from M, for 312-348 we have VFN, for 349-1067 FN. [3] τοιοίδ' ἕτοιμοι VN.

it swooped down when it reached the look-out, nigh unto our city, upon the peak of Arachnaeus; and next upon this roof of the Atreidae it leapt, yon fire not undescended from the Idaean flame. Such are the torch-bearers I have arranged—in succession one to the other completing the course; and victor is he who ran both first and last.[1] This is the warrant and the token I give thee, the message of my lord from Troy to me.

CHORUS

Lady, my prayers of thanksgiving to Heaven I will offer anon. But I would fain hear at large and satisfy my wonder at thy tale, so thou wouldst tell it yet again.

CLYTAEMESTRA

Troy is this day in the hands of the Achaeans. Within the town there sounds loud, methinks, a clamour of voices that will not blend. Pour vinegar and oil into the same cruse and thou wilt say that, as foes, they keep asunder; so the cries of vanquished and victors greet the ear, distinct as their fortunes are diverse. Those, flung upon the corpses of their husbands and their brothers, children upon the bodies of their aged sires who gave them life, bewail from lips no longer free the death of their dearest ones, while these—a night of restless toil after battle sets them down famished to break their fast on such fare as the town affords; not billeted in order due,

[1] The light kindled on Mt. Ida is conceived as starting first and finishing last; the light from Mt. Arachnaeus, as starting last and finishing first.

[4] λέγοις FN, λέγεις V. [5] ἄμικτον: Kirchhoff.
[6] ἐκχέας: Canter. [7] φίλως: Stanley.
[8] νῆστις F, νήστισι V, νήστεις N.

ἀλλ᾿ ὡς ἕκαστος ἔσπασεν τύχης πάλον.
ἐν <δ᾿>[1] αἰχμαλώτοις Τρωικοῖς οἰκήμασιν
ναίουσιν ἤδη, τῶν ὑπαιθρίων πάγων
δρόσων τ᾿ ἀπαλλαγέντες,[2] ὡς δ᾿ εὐδαίμονες[3]
ἀφύλακτον εὑδήσουσι πᾶσαν εὐφρόνην.
εἰ δ᾿ εὖ σέβουσι[4] τοὺς πολισσούχους θεοὺς
τοὺς τῆς ἁλούσης γῆς θεῶν θ᾿ ἱδρύματα,
οὔ τἂν ἑλόντες[5] αὖθις ἀνθαλοῖεν[6] ἄν.
ἔρως δὲ μή τις πρότερον ἐμπίπτῃ[7] στρατῷ
πορθεῖν ἃ μὴ χρή, κέρδεσιν νικωμένους.
δεῖ γὰρ πρὸς οἴκους νοστίμου σωτηρίας
κάμψαι διαύλου θάτερον κῶλον πάλιν·
θεοῖς δ᾿ ἀναμπλάκητος εἰ μόλοι στρατός,
ἐγρηγορὸς[8] τὸ πῆμα τῶν ὀλωλότων
γένοιτ᾿ ἄν, εἰ πρόσπαια μὴ τύχοι κακά.
τοιαῦτά τοι γυναικὸς ἐξ ἐμοῦ κλύεις·[9]
τὸ δ᾿ εὖ κρατοίη μὴ διχορρόπως ἰδεῖν.
πολλῶν γὰρ ἐσθλῶν τήνδ᾿[10] ὄνησιν εἱλόμην.

ΧΟΡΟΣ

γύναι, κατ᾿ ἄνδρα σώφρον᾿ εὐφρόνως λέγεις.
ἐγὼ δ᾿ ἀκούσας πιστά σου τεκμήρια
θεοὺς προσειπεῖν εὖ παρασκευάζομαι.
χάρις γὰρ οὐκ ἄτιμος εἴργασται πόνων.

ὦ Ζεῦ βασιλεῦ καὶ νὺξ φιλία
μεγάλων κόσμων κτεάτειρα,
ἥτ᾿ ἐπὶ Τροίας πύργοις ἔβαλες
στεγανὸν δίκτυον, ὡς μήτε μέγαν

1 <δ᾿> Pauw. 2 ἀπαλλαχθέντες V, ἀπαλλαγέντες FN.
3 ὡς δυσδαίμονες: Stanley. 4 εὐσεβοῦσι: Scaliger.
5 οὐκ ἄν γ᾿ ἑλόντες FN, οὐκ ἀνελόντες V: Herm.
6 αὖ (ἂν V) θάνοιεν FN: Auratus.

but as each man hath drawn his lot of chance. And even now they are quartered in the captured Trojan homes, delivered from the frosts and dew of the naked sky, and like happy men will sleep all the night unsentinelled.

Now if they keep them clear of guilt towards the gods of the town—those of the conquered land—and towards their shrines, the captors shall not be made captives in their turn. Only may no mad impulse first assail the soldiery, overmastered by greed, to ravish what they should not! For to win safe passage home they needs must travel back the other length of their double course. But even if, void of such offence towards the gods, our host should reach home, the grievous suffering of the dead might still prove wakeful—so be it fresh mischance do not befall. These are my woman's words; but may the good prevail and that right clearly! For, choosing thus, I have chosen the enjoyment of many a blessing.

Chorus

Lady, like a prudent man thou speakest wisely. And, for my part, now that I have listened to thy certain proofs, I prepare me to address due prayers of thanksgiving to Heaven; for a success hath been achieved that well requites the toil.

Hail, sovereign Zeus, and thou kindly Night, that hast given us great glory for our possession, thou who didst cast thy meshed snare upon the towered walls of Troy, so that nor old nor young could

---

[7] *ἐμπίπτῃ* F[1], *ἐμπίπτει* V, *ἐμπίπτοι* F[2]N.
[8] *ἐγρήγορον*: Porson.
[9] *κλύοις* FN, *κλύεις* V.
[10] *τὴν*: Herm.

μήτ' οὖν νεαρῶν τιν' ὑπερτελέσαι
μέγα δουλείας
  γάγγαμον, ἄτης παναλώτου.
Δία τοι ξένιον μέγαν αἰδοῦμαι
τὸν τάδε πράξαντ' ἐπ' Ἀλεξάνδρῳ
τείνοντα πάλαι τόξον, ὅπως ἂν
μήτε πρὸ καιροῦ μήθ' ὑπὲρ ἄστρων
  βέλος ἠλίθιον σκήψειεν.

Διὸς πλαγὰν ἔχουσιν[1] εἰπεῖν, [στρ. α.
πάρεστιν[2] τοῦτό γ'[3] ἐξιχνεῦσαι.
[ὡς] ἔπραξεν ὡς[4] ἔκρανεν. οὐκ ἔφα τις
θεοὺς βροτῶν ἀξιοῦσθαι μέλειν
ὅσοις ἀθίκτων χάρις
πατοῖθ'· ὁ δ' οὐκ εὐσεβής.
πέφανται δ' ἐκτίνουσ'[5]
ἀτολμήτων ἀρὴ[6]
πνεόντων μεῖζον ἢ δικαίως,
φλεόντων δωμάτων ὑπέρφευ
ὑπὲρ τὸ βέλτιστον. ἔστω δ' ἀπή-
μαντον, ὥστ' ἀπαρκεῖν[7]
εὖ πραπίδων λαχόντα.
οὐ γὰρ ἔστιν ἔπαλξις
πλούτου πρὸς κόρον ἀνδρὶ
λακτίσαντι μέγαν[8] Δίκας
βωμὸν εἰς ἀφάνειαν.

βιᾶται δ' ἁ τάλαινα πειθώ, [ἀντ. α.
προβούλου παῖς[9] ἄφερτος ἄτας.
ἄκος δὲ πᾶν μάταιον. οὐκ ἐκρύφθη,
πρέπει δέ, φῶς αἰνολαμπές, σίνος·
κακοῦ δὲ χαλκοῦ τρόπον

o'erleap the huge enthralling net, all-conquering doom. Great Zeus it is, lord of host and guest, whom I revere—he who hath wrought this, and hath long been bending his bow against Alexander so that his bolt should neither fall short of the mark nor, flying beyond the stars, be launched in vain.

"The stroke of Zeus" they may call it; 'tis his hand that can be traced therein. As he determines, so he acts. It hath been said by some one that the gods deign not to be mindful of mortals who trample underfoot the grace of inviolable sanctities. But that man knew not the fear of God!

Now standeth revealed how ruin is the penalty for reckless crime when men breathe a spirit of pride above just measure for that their mansions teem with abundance o'erpassing their best good. But let there be such portion of wealth as bringeth no distress, so that he who hath a goodly share of sound sense may have a sufficiency therewith. For riches are no bulwark to the man who in wantonness hath spurned from his sight the mighty altar of Righteousness.

No, he is driven on by perverse Temptation, the overmastering child of designing Destruction; and remedy is utterly in vain. His evil is not hidden; it shineth forth, a baleful gleam. Like base metal

---

[1] *ἔχουσαν* F[1]. *ἔχουσ'* F[2] Rom., *ἔχουσιν* N.
[2] *πάρεστι*: Hartung. [3] *τοῦτό γ'* N, *τοῦτ'* F.
[4] *ὡς ἔπραξαν* Rom., *ὡς ἔπραξεν* FN: Herm.
[5] *ἐγγόνους*: Hartung. [6] *ἄρη*: Headlam.
[7] *ἀπαρκεῖν* F, *κἀπαρκεῖν* N. [8] *μεγάλα*: Canter.
[9] *προβουλόπαις*: Hartung.

τρίβῳ τε καὶ[1] προσβολαῖς[2]
μελαμπαγὴς πέλει
δικαιωθείς, ἐπεὶ
διώκει παῖς ποτανὸν[3] ὄρνιν,
πόλει πρόστριμμ' ἄφερτον ἐνθείς.[4]
λιτᾶν δ' ἀκούει μὲν οὔτις θεῶν·
τὸν δ' ἐπίστροφον τῶν[5]
φῶτ' ἄδικον καθαιρεῖ.
οἷος καὶ Πάρις ἐλθὼν
ἐς δόμον τὸν[6] 'Ατρειδᾶν
ᾔσχυνε ξενίαν τράπε-
ζαν κλοπαῖσι[7] γυναικός.

λιποῦσα δ' ἀστοῖσιν ἀσπίστορας [στρ. β.
τε καὶ κλόνους λογχίμους[8]
ναυβάτας <θ'>[9] ὁπλισμούς,
ἄγουσά τ' ἀντίφερνον 'Ιλίῳ φθορὰν
βέβακεν ῥίμφα διὰ πυλᾶν
ἄτλητα τλᾶσα· πολλὰ δ' ἔστενον[10]
τόδ' ἐννέποντες δόμων προφῆται·
"ἰὼ ἰὼ δῶμα δῶμα[11] καὶ πρόμοι,
ἰὼ λέχος καὶ στίβοι φιλάνορες.
πάρεστι σιγὰς ἀτίμους ἀλοιδόρους[12]
ἄλγιστ'[13] ἀφημένων[14] ἰδεῖν.
πόθῳ δ' ὑπερποντίας
φάσμα δόξει δόμων ἀνάσσειν.
εὐμόρφων δὲ κολοσσῶν
ἔχθεται χάρις ἀνδρί·
ὀμμάτων δ' ἐν ἀχηνίαις
ἔρρει πᾶσ' 'Αφροδίτα.

ὀνειρόφαντοι δὲ πενθήμονες [ἀντ. β.
πάρεισι δόξαι φέρου-

beneath the touchstone's rub, when tested he showeth the blackness of his grain (for he is like a child that chaseth a winged bird) and upon his people he bringeth a taint not to be removed. To his prayers all gods are deaf, and the man who is conversant with such deeds, him they destroy in his unrighteousness.

Such was even Paris, who came to the house of the sons of Atreus and did dishonour to his hosts' hospitable board by stealing away a wedded wife.

But she, bequeathing to her people the clang of shield and spear and armament of fleets, and bringing to Ilium destruction in place of dower, with light step she passed through the gates—daring a deed undareable. Then loud wailed the seers of the house crying, "Alas, alas, for the home, the home, and for the princes thereof! Alas for the husband's bed and the impress of her form so dear! Lo, he sits apart in the anguish of his grief, silent, smitten in his honour but upbraiding not. In his yearning for her who sped beyond the sea, a phantom will seem to be lord of the house. The grace of fair-formed statues is hateful to him; and in the hunger of his eyes all loveliness is departed.

In dreams there come to him mournful semblances

---

[1] τε καὶ N, τε F. [2] προβολαῖς: Pearson.
[3] πτανὸν F, πτανόν τιν' N: Schütz.
[4] ἐνθεὶς N, θείς F. [5] τῶνδε: Klausen.
[6] τῶν F, τὸν N. [7] κλοπαῖς F.
[8] κλόνους λογχίμους τε καὶ: H. L. Ahrens.[9] <θ'> Herm.
[10] πολλὰ δ' ἔστενον N, πολὺ δ' ἀνέστενον F.
[11] ἰὼ and δῶμα not repeated F.
[12] σιγᾶς ἄτιμος ἀλοίδορος: Herm.
[13] ἄδιστος: Enger. [14] ἀφεμένων: Dindorf.

σαι χάριν ματαίαν.
μάταν γάρ, εὖτ' ἂν ἐσθλά τις δοκῶν ὁρᾷ,[1]
παραλλάξασα διὰ χερῶν[2]
βέβακεν ὄψις οὐ μεθύστερον
πτεροῖς ὀπαδοῦσ'[3] ὕπνου κελεύθοις."
τὰ μὲν κατ' οἴκους ἐφ' ἑστίας ἄχη
τάδ' ἐστὶ καὶ τῶνδ' ὑπερβατώτερα.
τὸ πᾶν δ' ἀφ' Ἕλλανος[4] αἴας συνορμένοις
πένθει' ἀτλησικάρδιος[5]
δόμων ἑκάστου πρέπει.
πολλὰ γοῦν θιγγάνει πρὸς ἧπαρ·
οὓς μὲν γάρ <τις>[6] ἔπεμψεν
οἶδεν, ἀντὶ δὲ φωτῶν
τεύχη καὶ σποδὸς εἰς ἑκά-
στου δόμους ἀφικνεῖται.

ὁ χρυσαμοιβὸς δ' Ἄρης σωμάτων [στρ. γ.
καὶ ταλαντοῦχος ἐν μάχῃ δορὸς
πυρωθὲν ἐξ Ἰλίου
φίλοισι πέμπει βαρὺ
ψῆγμα δυσδάκρυτον ἀν-
τήνορος σποδοῦ γεμί-
ζων λέβητας εὐθέτους.[7]
στένουσι δ' εὖ λέγοντες ἄνδρα τὸν μὲν ὡς μάχης ἴδρις,
τὸν δ' ἐν φοναῖς καλῶς πεσόντ'—
ἀλλοτρίας διαὶ[8] γυναι-
κός· τάδε σῖγά τις βαΰ-
ζει, φθονερὸν δ' ὑπ' ἄλγος ἕρ-
πει προδίκοις Ἀτρείδαις.
οἱ δ' αὐτοῦ περὶ τεῖχος
θήκας Ἰλιάδος γᾶς

bringing only vain joy; for vainly, whensoever in fancy a man seeth delights, straightway the vision, slipping through his arms, is gone, winging its flight along the paths of sleep." Such are the sorrows at hearth and home, aye and sorrows surpassing these; and at large, in every house of all who sped forth in company from the land of Hellas, is seen grief that passeth bearing. Yea, many are the things that pierce the heart; for whom each sent forth, them he knows; but to the home of each come urns and ashes, not living men.

For Ares bartereth the bodies of men for gold; he holdeth his balance in the contest of the spear; and back from Ilium to their loved ones he sendeth a heavy dust passed through his burning, a dust bewept with plenteous tears, in place of men freighting urns well bestowed with ashes.[1] So they make lament, lauding now this one: "How skilled in battle!" now that one: "Fallen nobly in the carnage,"—"*for another's wife*," some mutter in secret, and grief charged with resentment spreads stealthily against the sons of Atreus, champions in the strife. But there far from home, around the

[1] This passage, in which war is compared to a gold-merchant, is charged with double meanings: ταλαντοῦχος, "balance" and "scales of battle," πυρωθέν of "purified" gold-dust and of the "burnt" bodies of the slain, βαρύ, "heavy" and "grievous," ἀντήνορος, "the price of a man," and "instead of men," λέβητας, "jars" and "funeral urns."

---

[1] ὁρᾶν: Scholefield. [2] χειρῶν F.
[3] ὀπαδοῖς: Dobree. [4] ἑλλάδος: Bamberger.
[5] πένθεια τλησικάρδιος: Headlam.
[6] ⟨τις⟩ Porson. [7] εὐθέτου: Auratus.
[8] διὰ F, γε διὰ N, διαὶ Epimer. Hom. *Anecd. Oxon.* i. 119.

εὔμορφοι κατέχουσιν· ἐχ-
θρὰ δ' ἔχοντας ἔκρυψεν.

βαρεῖα δ' ἀστῶν φάτις ξὺν κότῳ· [ἀντ. γ.
δημοκράντου[1] δ' ἀρᾶς τίνει χρέος.
μένει δ' ἀκοῦσαί τί μου
μέριμνα νυκτηρεφές.
τῶν πολυκτόνων γὰρ οὐκ
ἄσκοποι θεοί. κελαι-
ναὶ δ' Ἐρινύες χρόνῳ
τυχηρὸν ὄντ' ἄνευ δίκας
παλιντυχεῖ[2] τριβᾷ βίου
τιθεῖσ' ἀμαυρόν, ἐν δ' ἀΐ-
στοις τελέθοντος οὔτις ἀλ-
κά· τὸ δ' ὑπερκόπως[3] κλύειν
εὖ βαρύ· βάλλεται γὰρ ὄσ-
σοις Διόθεν κάρανα.[4]
κρίνω δ' ἄφθονον ὄλβον·
μήτ' εἴην πτολιπόρθης
μήτ' οὖν αὐτὸς ἁλοὺς ὑπ' ἄλλων βίον κατίδοιμι.

πυρὸς δ' ὑπ' εὐαγγέλου [ἐπῳδ.
πόλιν διήκει θοὰ
βάξις· εἰ δ' ἐτήτυμος,[5]
τίς οἶδεν, ἤ τι[6] θεῖόν ἐστί πῃ[7] ψύθος.—

τίς ὧδε παιδνὸς ἢ φρενῶν κεκομμένος,
φλογὸς παραγγέλμασιν
νέοις πυρωθέντα καρδίαν ἔπειτ'
ἀλλαγᾷ λόγου καμεῖν;—

[ἐν][8] γυναικὸς αἰχμᾷ πρέπει
πρὸ τοῦ φανέντος χάριν ξυναινέσαι.—

city's walls, those in their beauty's bloom are entombed in Ilian land—the foeman's soil hath covered its conquerors.

Dangerous is a people's voice charged with wrath—it hath the office of a curse of public doom. In anxious fear I wait to hear something shrouded still in gloom; for Heaven is not unmindful of men of blood. In the end the black Spirits of Vengeance bring to obscurity him who hath prospered in unrighteousness and wear down his fortunes by reverse; and once he hath passed among them that are brought to naught, there is no more help for him. Glory in excess is fraught with peril; 'tis the lofty peak that is smitten by heaven's thunderbolt. Prosperity unassailed by envy is my choice. Let me not be a destroyer of cities; no, nor let me be despoiled and live to see my own life in another's power!

(One Elder)

Heralded by a beacon of good tidings a swift report has spread throughout the town. Yet whether it be true, or some deception of the gods, who knows?

(A Second Elder)

Who is so childish or so bereft of sense, once he has let his heart be fired by sudden tidings of a beacon fire, to despond if the story change?

(A Third Elder)

'Tis like a woman's eager nature to yield assent to pleasing news ere yet the truth be clear.

---

[1] δημοκράτου: Porson.
[2] παλιντυχῆ N, παλιντυχῆ F: Scaliger.
[3] ὑπερκότως: Grotius.
[4] κεραυνός: Tucker.
[5] ἐτητύμως: Auratus.
[6] ἤτοι F[1]N, εἴτοι F[2]: Herm.
[7] μή: H. L. Ahrens.
[8] [ἐν] Scaliger.

πιθανὸς ἄγαν ὁ θῆλυς ὅρος ἐπινέμεται
ταχύπορος· ἀλλὰ ταχύμορον
γυναικογήρυτον ὄλλυται κλέος.—

[1]τάχ᾽ εἰσόμεσθα λαμπάδων φαεσφόρων
φρυκτωριῶν τε καὶ πυρὸς παραλλαγάς,
εἴτ᾽ οὖν ἀληθεῖς εἴτ᾽ ὀνειράτων δίκην
τερπνὸν τόδ᾽ ἐλθὸν φῶς ἐφήλωσεν[2] φρένας.
κήρυκ᾽ ἀπ᾽ ἀκτῆς τόνδ᾽ ὁρῶ κατάσκιον
κλάδοις ἐλαίας· μαρτυρεῖ δέ μοι κάσις
πηλοῦ ξύνουρος διψία κόνις τάδε,
ὡς οὔτ᾽ ἄναυδος οὔτε σοι δαίων φλόγα
ὕλης ὀρείας σημανεῖ καπνῷ πυρός,
ἀλλ᾽ ἢ τὸ χαίρειν μᾶλλον ἐκβάξει λέγων—
τὸν ἀντίον δὲ τοῖσδ᾽ ἀποστέργω λόγον·
εὖ γὰρ πρὸς εὖ φανεῖσι προσθήκη πέλοι.—

ὅστις τάδ᾽ ἄλλως τῇδ᾽ ἐπεύχεται πόλει,
αὐτὸς φρενῶν καρποῖτο τὴν ἁμαρτίαν.

ΚΗΡΥΞ

ἰὼ πατρῷον οὖδας Ἀργείας χθονός,
δεκάτου[3] σε φέγγει τῷδ᾽ ἀφικόμην ἔτους,
πολλῶν ῥαγεισῶν ἐλπίδων μιᾶς τυχών.
οὐ γάρ ποτ᾽ ηὔχουν τῇδ᾽ ἐν Ἀργείᾳ χθονὶ
θανὼν μεθέξειν φιλτάτου τάφου μέρος.

[1] ll. 489-500 ascribed to Clyt., 501-502 to the Chorus: Scaliger. [2] ἐφήλωσε: Porson. [3] δεκάτῳ: Wunder.

---

[1] His attire bears evidence of dust and mud. Cp. the description of Sir Walter Blunt, "Stained with the variation of each soil Betwixt that Holmedon and this seat of ours" (*Henry IV.*).

(A Fourth Elder)

Over credulous, a woman's mind has boundaries open to quick encroachment; but quick to perish is rumour by a woman voiced.

(Leader of the Chorus)

We shall know anon about this passing on of flaming lights and beacon signals and fires, whether they perchance be true or whether, dream-like, this light's glad coming hath beguiled our senses. Lo! Yonder, approaching from the shore, I see a herald with boughs of olive overshaded. The thirsty dust, consorting sister of the mire,[1] assures me that neither by dumb show nor by kindling a flame of mountain wood will he give sign with smoke of fire, but in plain words will bid us either to rejoice the more, or else—but God avert the omen of the contrary! To the good that hath appeared may there be addition of good!

(Another Elder)

If there be one who maketh this prayer with other intent toward the State, let him reap himself the fruit of his misguided purpose!

[*Enter a Herald*

Herald

All hail, soil of Argos, land of my fathers! On this happy day in the tenth year I am come to thee. Many a hope hath made shipwreck, one only have I seen fulfilled; for never dared I to dream that here in this land of Argos I should die and have due portion of burial most dear to me. Now blessings

νῦν χαῖρε μὲν χθών, χαῖρε δ' ἡλίου φάος,
ὕπατός τε χώρας Ζεύς, ὁ Πύθιός τ' ἄναξ,
τόξοις ἰάπτων μηκέτ' εἰς ἡμᾶς βέλη·
ἅλις παρὰ Σκάμανδρον ἦσθ'[1] ἀνάρσιος·
νῦν δ' αὖτε σωτὴρ ἴσθι καὶ παιώνιος,[2]
ἄναξ Ἄπολλον. τούς τ' ἀγωνίους θεοὺς
πάντας προσαυδῶ, τόν τ' ἐμὸν τιμάορον
Ἑρμῆν, φίλον κήρυκα, κηρύκων σέβας,
ἥρως τε τοὺς πέμψαντας, εὐμενεῖς πάλιν
στρατὸν δέχεσθαι τὸν λελειμμένον δορός.
ἰὼ μέλαθρα βασιλέων, φίλαι στέγαι,
σεμνοί τε θᾶκοι, δαίμονές τ' ἀντήλιοι,
εἴ που[3] πάλαι, φαιδροῖσι τοισίδ' ὄμμασι
δέξασθε[4] κόσμῳ βασιλέα πολλῷ χρόνῳ.
ἥκει γὰρ ὑμῖν[5] φῶς ἐν εὐφρόνῃ φέρων
καὶ τοῖσδ' ἅπασι κοινὸν Ἀγαμέμνων ἄναξ.
ἀλλ' εὖ νιν ἀσπάσασθε, καὶ γὰρ οὖν πρέπει,
Τροίαν κατασκάψαντα τοῦ δικηφόρου
Διὸς μακέλλῃ, τῇ κατείργασται πέδον.
βωμοὶ δ' ἄιστοι καὶ θεῶν ἱδρύματα,
καὶ σπέρμα πάσης ἐξαπόλλυται χθονός.
τοιόνδε Τροίᾳ περιβαλὼν ζευκτήριον
ἄναξ Ἀτρείδης πρέσβυς εὐδαίμων ἀνὴρ
ἥκει, τίεσθαι δ' ἀξιώτατος βροτῶν
τῶν νῦν· Πάρις γὰρ οὔτε συντελὴς πόλις
ἐξεύχεται τὸ δρᾶμα τοῦ πάθους πλέον.
ὀφλὼν γὰρ ἁρπαγῆς τε καὶ κλοπῆς δίκην
τοῦ ῥυσίου θ' ἥμαρτε καὶ πανώλεθρον

[1] ἦλθες F²N, ἦλθ' F¹: Askew's margin.
[2] καὶ παγώνιος F, κἀπαγώνιος N: Dobree.
[3] ἤπου: Auratus. [4] δέξασθε N, δέξαισθε F.
[5] ὑμῖν N, ἡμῖν F.

on the land, blessings on the light of the sun, and blessed be Zeus, the land's Most High, and Pythc's lord; and may he launch no more his shafts against us. Enough of thine hostility didst thou display by Scamander's banks; but now, in other mood, be thou our preserver and our healer, O lord Apollo. And the gods gathered here, I greet them all; him, too, mine own patron, Hermes, beloved herald, of heralds all revered; and the heroes[1] who sped us forth—I pray that they may receive back in kindliness the remnant of the host that hath escaped the spear. Hail, halls of our Kings, beloved roofs, and ye august seats, and ye divinities that face the sun,[2] if ever in days gone by, give fitting welcome now with gladness in these your eyes unto your King after long lapse of years. For bearing light in darkness to you and to all assembled here alike, he hath returned—Agamemnon, our King. Oh give him goodly greeting, as is meet and right, since he hath uprooted Troy with the mattock of Zeus, the Avenger, wherewith her soil has been uptorn. Demolished are the altars and the shrines of her gods; and the seed of her whole land hath been wasted utterly. Upon the neck of Troy hath he cast a yoke so grievous, and now he hath come home, our King, Atreus' elder son, a man of happy fate, worthy of honour beyond all living men. For neither Paris nor his partner city can vaunt the deed was greater than the suffering. Cast in a suit for rapine and for theft as well, he hath lost the plunder and hath razed in

[1] The heroes are the deified spirits of the ancient kings and other illustrious men. In *Suppl.* 25 they are included under the nether powers (χθόνιοι).

[2] Statues of the gods, in front of the palace, placed to front the east

αὐτόχθονον πατρῷον ἔθρισεν δόμον.
διπλᾶ δ' ἔτεισαν[1] Πριαμίδαι θἀμάρτια.

ΧΟΡΟΣ

κῆρυξ Ἀχαιῶν χαῖρε τῶν ἀπὸ στρατοῦ.

ΚΗΡΥΞ

χαίρω <γε>·[2] τεθνάναι δ' οὐκέτ'[3] ἀντερῶ θεοῖς.

ΧΟΡΟΣ

ἔρως πατρῴας τῆσδε γῆς σ' ἐγύμνασεν;

ΚΗΡΥΞ

ὥστ' ἐνδακρύειν[4] γ' ὄμμασιν χαρᾶς ὕπο.

ΧΟΡΟΣ

τερπνῆς ἄρ' ἦτε[5] τῆσδ' ἐπήβολοι νόσου.

ΚΗΡΥΞ

πῶς δή; διδαχθεὶς τοῦδε δεσπόσω λόγου.

ΧΟΡΟΣ

τῶν ἀντερώντων ἱμέρῳ πεπληγμένοι.[6]

ΚΗΡΥΞ

ποθεῖν ποθοῦντα τήνδε γῆν στρατὸν λέγεις;

[1] ἔτισαν: Kirchhoff.
[2] <γε> Enger.
[3] οὐκέτ' N, οὐκ F.
[4] ἐνδακρύειν F, ἐκδακρύειν N
[5] ἦτε N, ἴστε F.
[6] πεπληγμένος: Tyrwhitt.

utter destruction his father's house and the very place thereof. Twofold the penalty the sons of Priam have paid for their sins.

CHORUS

Joy to thee, Herald from the Achaean host!

HERALD

I do rejoice. I will no longer refuse to die, so it please the gods.

CHORUS

It was yearning for this thy fatherland that troubled thee?

HERALD

Aye, so that my eyes are filled with tears for joy.

CHORUS

It was then a pleasing malady wherewith ye were taken.

HERALD

How so? Resolve me and I shall master what thou sayest.

CHORUS

Ye were smitten with desire for those that returned your love.

HERALD

Meanest thou that our land longed for the longing host?

ΧΟΡΟΣ

ὡς πόλλ' ἀμαυρᾶς ἐκ φρενός <μ'>[1] ἀναστένειν.

ΚΗΡΥΞ

πόθεν τὸ δύσφρον τοῦτ' ἐπῆν θυμῷ στύγος[2];

ΧΟΡΟΣ

πάλαι τὸ σιγᾶν φάρμακον βλάβης ἔχω.

ΚΗΡΥΞ

καὶ πῶς; ἀπόντων κοιράνων[3] ἔτρεις τινάς;

ΧΟΡΟΣ

ὡς νῦν,[4] τὸ σὸν δή, καὶ θανεῖν πολλὴ χάρις.

ΚΗΡΥΞ

εὖ γὰρ πέπρακται. ταῦτα δ' ἐν πολλῷ χρόνῳ
τὰ μέν τις ἂν[5] λέξειεν εὐπετῶς ἔχειν,
τὰ δ' αὖτε κἀπίμομφα. τίς δὲ πλὴν θεῶν
ἅπαντ' ἀπήμων τὸν δι' αἰῶνος χρόνον;
μόχθους γὰρ εἰ λέγοιμι καὶ δυσαυλίας,
σπαρνὰς παρήξεις καὶ κακοστρώτους, τί δ' οὐ
στένοντες, †οὐ λαχόντες† ἤματος μέρος;
τὰ δ' αὖτε χέρσῳ καὶ προσῆν πλέον στύγος·
εὐναὶ γὰρ ἦσαν δηΐων πρὸς τείχεσιν·
ἐξ οὐρανοῦ δὲ κἀπὸ[6] γῆς λειμώνιαι
δρόσοι κατεψάκαζον, ἔμπεδον σίνος
ἐσθημάτων, τιθέντες ἔνθηρον τρίχα.

1 <μ'> Scaliger. 2 ἐπῆν στύγος στρατῷ: Schütz.
3 κοιράνων N, τυράννων F. 4 ὧν νῦν: Scaliger.
5 τις εὖ: Auratus. 6 γὰρ κἀπὸ: Pearson.

CHORUS

So longed that often from a darkly brooding spirit I have sighed.

HERALD

Whence came this gloom of melancholy upon thy spirit?

CHORUS

Long since have I found silence an antidote to harm.

HERALD

How so? Wert thou in fear of any in the absence of our princes?

CHORUS

In such fear that now, in thy own words, even death were great joy.

HERALD

Aye, all's well, well ended. Yet, of what occurred in the long years, one might well say that part fell out happily, and part in turn amiss. But who, save he be a god, is free from suffering all his days? For were I to recount our hardships and our wretched quarters, the scanted space and the sorry berths—what did we not have to complain of . . .[1] Then again, ashore, there was still worse to loathe; for we had to lay us down close to the foeman's walls, and the drizzling from the sky and the dews from the meadows distilled upon us, working constant destruction to our clothes and filling our hair with vermin.

[1] For λαχόντες in l. 557 numerous emendations have been proposed, *e.g.* κλαίοντες, λάσκοντες, χαλῶντες. ἤματος μέρος probably means "as our day's portion."

χειμῶνα δ᾽ εἰ λέγοι[1] τις οἰωνοκτόνον,
οἷον παρεῖχ᾽ ἄφερτον Ἰδαία χιών,
ἢ θάλπος, εὖτε πόντος ἐν μεσημβριναῖς
κοίταις ἀκύμων νηνέμοις εὕδοι πεσών—
τί ταῦτα πενθεῖν δεῖ; παροίχεται πόνος·
παροίχεται δέ, τοῖσι μὲν τεθνηκόσιν
τὸ μήποτ᾽ αὖθις μηδ᾽ ἀναστῆναι μέλειν.
τί τοὺς ἀναλωθέντας ἐν ψήφῳ λέγειν,
τὸν ζῶντα δ᾽ ἀλγεῖν χρὴ τύχης παλιγκότου;
καὶ πολλὰ χαίρειν ξυμφορὰς[2] καταξιῶ.
ἡμῖν δὲ τοῖς λοιποῖσιν Ἀργείων στρατοῦ
νικᾷ τὸ κέρδος, πῆμα δ᾽ οὐκ ἀντιρρέπει·
ὡς κομπάσαι τῷδ᾽ εἰκὸς ἡλίου φάει
ὑπὲρ θαλάσσης καὶ χθονὸς ποτωμένοις·
"Τροίαν ἑλόντες δή ποτ᾽ Ἀργείων στόλος
θεοῖς λάφυρα ταῦτα τοῖς καθ᾽ Ἑλλάδα
δόμοις ἐπασσάλευσαν ἀρχαῖον γάνος."
τοιαῦτα χρὴ κλύοντας εὐλογεῖν πόλιν
καὶ τοὺς στρατηγούς· καὶ χάρις τιμήσεται
Διὸς τόδ᾽ ἐκπράξασα. πάντ᾽ ἔχεις λόγον.

ΧΟΡΟΣ

νικώμενος λόγοισιν οὐκ ἀναίνομαι·
ἀεὶ γὰρ ἥβη[3] τοῖς γέρουσιν εὖ μαθεῖν.
δόμοις δὲ ταῦτα καὶ Κλυταιμήστρᾳ[4] μέλειν
εἰκὸς μάλιστα, σὺν δὲ πλουτίζειν ἐμέ.

ΚΛΥΤΑΙΜΗΣΤΡΑ

ἀνωλόλυξα μὲν πάλαι χαρᾶς ὕπο,
ὅτ᾽ ἦλθ᾽ ὁ πρῶτος νύχιος ἄγγελος πυρός,

[1] λέγει N Rom. [2] ξυμφοραῖς: Blomfield.
[3] ἡβᾷ: Margoliouth. [4] Κλυταιμνήστρᾳ.

And if one were to tell of the wintry cold, past all enduring, when Ida's snow slew the birds; or of the heat, what time upon his waveless noon-day couch, windless the sea sank to sleep—but what need to bewail all this? Our labour's past; past for the dead so that they will never care even to wake to life again. What need for the living to count the number of the slain, what need to repine at fortune's frowns? I hold it fitting that our misfortunes bid us a long farewell. For us, the remnant of the Argive host, the gain hath the advantage and the loss does not bear down the scale; so that, as we speed athwart land and sea, it is meet that we make this boast unto yon light of heaven: "The Argive armament, having taken Troy at last, unto the gods throughout Hellas hath nailed up these spoils to be a glory in their shrines from days of old." Whoso hears the story of these deeds must needs extol the city and the leaders of her host; and the grace of Zeus that brought them to accomplishment shall receive its due meed of gratitude. My tale is told.

Chorus

Thy words have proved me wrong. I deny it not; for the aged have ever youth to learn aright. But these tidings should most have interest for the household and Clytaemestra, and at the same time enrich me. [*Enter Clytaemestra*

Clytaemestra

I raised a shout of triumph in my joy erewhile, when the first flaming messenger arrived by night,

φράζων ἅλωσιν Ἰλίου τ' ἀνάστασιν.
καί τίς μ' ἐνίπτων εἶπε, "φρυκτωρῶν δία
πεισθεῖσα Τροίαν νῦν πεπορθῆσθαι δοκεῖς;
ἦ κάρτα πρὸς γυναικὸς αἴρεσθαι κέαρ."
λόγοις τοιούτοις πλαγκτὸς οὖσ' ἐφαινόμην.
ὅμως δ' ἔθυον, καὶ γυναικείῳ νόμῳ
ὀλολυγμὸν ἄλλος ἄλλοθεν κατὰ πτόλιν
ἔλασκον εὐφημοῦντες ἐν θεῶν ἕδραις
θυηφάγον κοιμῶντες εὐώδη φλόγα.
καὶ νῦν τὰ μάσσω μὲν τί δεῖ σέ μοι[1] λέγειν;
ἄνακτος αὐτοῦ πάντα πεύσομαι λόγον.
ὅπως δ' ἄριστα τὸν ἐμὸν αἰδοῖον πόσιν
σπεύσω πάλιν μολόντα δέξασθαι—τί γὰρ
γυναικὶ τούτου φέγγος ἥδιον δρακεῖν,
ἀπὸ στρατείας ἀνδρὶ σώσαντος θεοῦ
πύλας ἀνοῖξαι;—ταῦτ' ἀπάγγειλον πόσει·
ἥκειν ὅπως τάχιστ' ἐράσμιον πόλει·
γυναῖκα πιστὴν δ' ἐν δόμοις εὕροι μολὼν
οἵανπερ οὖν ἔλειπε, δωμάτων κύνα
ἐσθλὴν ἐκείνῳ, πολεμίαν τοῖς δύσφροσιν,
καὶ τἄλλ' ὁμοίαν πάντα, σημαντήριον
οὐδὲν διαφθείρασαν ἐν μήκει χρόνου.
οὐδ' οἶδα τέρψιν οὐδ' ἐπίψογον φάτιν
ἄλλου πρὸς ἀνδρὸς μᾶλλον ἢ χαλκοῦ βαφάς.

ΚΗΡΥΞ

τοιόσδ' ὁ κόμπος τῆς ἀληθείας γέμων
οὐκ αἰσχρὸς ὡς γυναικὶ γενναίᾳ λακεῖν.

ΧΟΡΟΣ

αὕτη μὲν οὕτως εἶπε μανθάνοντί σοι

telling that Ilium was captured and overthrown. Then there were some who chided me and said: "Art thou so convinced by beacon-fires as to think that Troy has now been sacked? In good sooth 'tis like a woman to be elated in heart." By such taunts I was made to seem as if my wits were wandering. Nevertheless I still held on with my sacrifice, and throughout all the quarters of the city, in woman's wont, they raised a shout of gladsome praise while in the fanes of the gods they lulled to rest the fragrant spice-fed flame.

So now what need for thee to rehearse to me the account at large? From the King himself I shall hear all the tale; but that I may hasten best to welcome my honoured lord on his return—for what joy is sweeter in a woman's eyes than to unbar the gates for her husband when God hath spared him to return from war?—this be my message to my lord: let him come with all speed, his country's fond desire, come to find at home his wife faithful, even as he left her, a watch-dog of his house, loyal to him, a foe to those who wish him ill; yea, for the rest, unchanged in every part; in all this length of time never having broken seal. Of pleasure from other man or voice of scandal I know no more than of dyeing bronze.

[*Exit*

HERALD

Boast like to this, laden to the full with truth, misbeseems not the speech of a noble wife.

CHORUS

Thus hath she spoken for thy schooling, but

---

[1] σ' ἐμοί: Wieseler.

τοροῖσιν ἑρμηνεῦσιν εὐπρεπῶς λόγον.
σὺ δ' εἰπέ, κῆρυξ, Μενέλεων δὲ πεύθομαι,
εἰ νόστιμός τε καὶ[1] σεσωσμένος πάλιν
ἥκει[2] σὺν ὑμῖν, τῆσδε γῆς φίλον κράτος.

ΚΗΡΥΞ

οὐκ ἔσθ' ὅπως λέξαιμι τὰ ψευδῆ καλὰ
ἐς τὸν πολὺν φίλοισι καρποῦσθαι χρόνον.

ΧΟΡΟΣ

[3]πῶς δῆτ' ἂν εἰπὼν κεδνὰ τἀληθῆ τύχοις[4];
σχισθέντα δ' οὐκ εὔκρυπτα γίγνεται τάδε.

ΚΗΡΥΞ

ἀνὴρ[5] ἄφαντος ἐξ Ἀχαιικοῦ στρατοῦ,
αὐτός τε καὶ τὸ πλοῖον. οὐ ψευδῆ λέγω.

ΧΟΡΟΣ

πότερον ἀναχθεὶς ἐμφανῶς ἐξ Ἰλίου,
ἢ χεῖμα, κοινὸν ἄχθος, ἥρπασε στρατοῦ;

ΚΗΡΥΞ

ἔκυρσας ὥστε τοξότης ἄκρος σκοποῦ·
μακρὸν δὲ πῆμα συντόμως ἐφημίσω.

ΧΟΡΟΣ

πότερα γὰρ αὐτοῦ ζῶντος ἢ τεθνηκότος
φάτις πρὸς ἄλλων ναυτίλων ἐκλῄζετο;

[1] γε καὶ: Herm. [2] ἥξει: Karsten.
[3] ll. 622-635 assigned to Clyt. and Herald: Stanley.
[4] τύχῃς: Porson. [5] ἀνὴρ: Herm.

speciously for them that can interpret aright. But, Herald, say—'tis of Menelaüs I would learn—hath he, our land's dear lord, voyaged safe home and hath he returned with you?

HERALD

It were impossible to report false news as fair so that those I love should joy therein for long.

CHORUS

Oh that thou couldst tell tidings true yet good! 'Tis not easy to conceal when true and good are sundered.

HERALD

The prince was swept from the sight of the Achaean host—himself, and his ship likewise. It is no untruth I tell.

CHORUS

Did he put forth in sight of all from Ilium, or did a storm, distressing all in common, snatch him from the fleet?

HERALD

Like master bowman thou hast hit the mark; a long tale of distress hast thou told in brief.

CHORUS

Did the general voice of other voyagers make report of him as alive or dead?

ΚΗΡΥΞ

οὐκ οἶδεν οὐδεὶς ὥστ᾽ ἀπαγγεῖλαι τορῶς,
πλὴν τοῦ τρέφοντος Ἡλίου χθονὸς φύσιν.

ΧΟΡΟΣ

πῶς γὰρ λέγεις χειμῶνα ναυτικῷ στρατῷ
ἐλθεῖν τελευτῆσαί τε δαιμόνων κότῳ;

ΚΗΡΥΞ

εὔφημον ἦμαρ οὐ πρέπει κακαγγέλῳ
γλώσσῃ μιαίνειν· χωρὶς ἡ τιμὴ θεῶν.
ὅταν δ᾽ ἀπευκτὰ πήματ᾽ ἄγγελος πόλει
στυγνῷ προσώπῳ πτωσίμου στρατοῦ φέρῃ,
πόλει μὲν ἕλκος ἓν τὸ δήμιον τυχεῖν,
πολλοὺς δὲ πολλῶν ἐξαγισθέντας δόμων
ἄνδρας διπλῇ μάστιγι, τὴν Ἄρης φιλεῖ,
δίλογχον ἄτην, φοινίαν ξυνωρίδα·
τοιῶνδε μέντοι πημάτων σεσαγμένον[1]
πρέπει λέγειν παιᾶνα τόνδ᾽ Ἐρινύων.
σωτηρίων δὲ πραγμάτων εὐάγγελον
ἥκοντα πρὸς χαίρουσαν εὐεστοῖ πόλιν,
πῶς κεδνὰ τοῖς κακοῖσι συμμείξω,[2] λέγων
χειμῶν᾽ Ἀχαιοῖς[3] οὐκ ἀμήνιτον θεῶν;
ξυνώμοσαν γάρ, ὄντες ἔχθιστοι τὸ πρίν,
πῦρ καὶ θάλασσα, καὶ τὰ πίστ᾽ ἐδειξάτην
φθείροντε τὸν δύστηνον Ἀργείων στρατόν.
ἐν νυκτὶ δυσκύμαντα δ᾽ ὠρώρει κακά.
ναῦς γὰρ πρὸς ἀλλήλαισι[4] Θρῄκιαι πνοαὶ

[1] σεσαγμένων: Schütz.
[2] συμμίξω: Kirchhoff.
[3] Ἀχαιῶν . . . θεοῖς: Blomfield and Dobree.
[4] ἀλλήλῃσι F.

HERALD

None knoweth to give clear report of this—save only the Sun that fostereth life upon the earth.

CHORUS

How then sayest thou rose the storm by Heaven's wrath upon the naval host and passed away ?

HERALD

A day of happy omen it befits not to mar by tale of ill—the honour due to the gods keeps them apart.[1] When a messenger with gloomy countenance reports to a people dire disaster of its army's rout—one common wound inflicted on the State, while from many a home many a victim is devoted to death by the two-handled scourge beloved of Ares, destruction double-armed, a gory pair—when, I say, he is packed with woes of such sort as this, it is meet that he sing the triumph-song of the Avenging Spirits. But when one cometh with glad tidings of deliverance to a city rejoicing in its happiness—how shall I mix fair with foul in telling of the storm that broke upon the Achaeans not unprovoked by Heaven's wrath ? For fire and sea, erstwhile bitterest of foes, swore alliance and for proof thereof destroyed the hapless Argive armament. In the night-time arose the mischief from the cruel surge. Beneath blasts from Thrace ship dashed against ship ; and they, gored

[1] To the Olympian gods belong tales of good, to the Erinyes (l. 645) belong tales of ill. Some interpret the passage to mean that the honour due to the gods is to be kept apart from pollution through the recital of ills.

ἤρεικον·[1] αἱ δὲ κεροτυπούμεναι[2] βίᾳ
χειμῶνι τυφῶ σὺν ζάλῃ τ' ὀμβροκτύπῳ
ᾤχοντ' ἄφαντοι ποιμένος κακοῦ στρόβῳ.
ἐπεὶ δ' ἀνῆλθε λαμπρὸν ἡλίου φάος,
ὁρῶμεν ἀνθοῦν πέλαγος Αἰγαῖον νεκροῖς
ἀνδρῶν Ἀχαιῶν ναυτικοῖς τ' ἐρειπίοις.[3]
ἡμᾶς γε μὲν δὴ ναῦν τ' ἀκήρατον σκάφος
ἤτοι τις ἐξέκλεψεν ἢ 'ξῃτήσατο
θεός τις, οὐκ ἄνθρωπος, οἴακος θιγών.
τύχη δὲ σωτὴρ ναῦν θέλουσ' ἐφέζετο,
ὡς μήτ' ἐν ὅρμῳ κύματος ζάλην ἔχειν
μήτ' ἐξοκεῖλαι πρὸς κραταίλεων χθόνα.
ἔπειτα δ' Ἅιδην πόντιον πεφευγότες,
λευκὸν κατ' ἦμαρ, οὐ πεποιθότες τύχῃ,
ἐβουκολοῦμεν φροντίσιν νέον πάθος,
στρατοῦ καμόντος καὶ κακῶς σποδουμένου.
καὶ νῦν ἐκείνων εἴ τίς ἐστιν ἐμπνέων,
λέγουσιν ἡμᾶς ὡς ὀλωλότας, τί μή;
ἡμεῖς τ' ἐκείνους ταὔτ'[4] ἔχειν δοξάζομεν.
γένοιτο δ' ὡς ἄριστα. Μενέλεων γὰρ οὖν
πρῶτόν τε καὶ μάλιστα προσδόκα μολεῖν.
εἰ γοῦν[5] τις ἀκτὶς ἡλίου νιν ἱστορεῖ
καὶ ζῶντα καὶ βλέποντα, μηχαναῖς Διός,
οὔπω θέλοντος ἐξαναλῶσαι γένος,
ἐλπίς τις αὐτὸν πρὸς δόμους ἥξειν πάλιν.
τοσαῦτ' ἀκούσας ἴσθι τἀληθῆ κλύων.[6]

ΧΟΡΟΣ

τίς ποτ' ὠνόμαζεν ὧδ' [στρ. α.
ἐς τὸ πᾶν ἐτητύμως—

[1] ἤρειπον N. [2] κερωτυπούμεναι: Wasse.

violently by the furious hurricane and rush of pelting rain, were swept out of sight by the whirling gust of an evil shepherd.[1] But when the radiant light of the sun uprose we beheld the Aegean flowering with corpses of Achaean men and wreckage of ships. Ourselves, however, and our ship, its hull unshattered, some power, divine not human, preserved by stealth or intercession, laying hand upon its helm; and Saviour Fortune willed to sit aboard our barque so that it should neither take in the swelling surf at anchorage nor drive upon a rock-bound coast. Then, having escaped death upon the deep, in the clear bright day, scarce crediting our fortune, we brooded in anxious thought over our late mischance, our fleet distressed and sorely buffeted. So now, if any there be of them that still draw the breath of life, they speak of us as lost—and why should they not?—while we imagine like case for them. But may all turn out for the best! For Menelaüs, indeed—first and foremost expect him to return. At least if some beam of the sun discover him alive and well, by the design of Zeus, who is not yet minded utterly to destroy the race, there is some hope that he will come home again. Hearing so much, be assured that it is the truth thou hearest. [*Exit*

Chorus

Who can have given a name so altogether true—

[1] The "evil shepherd" is the storm that drives the ships, like sheep, from their course.

---

[3] ναυτικῶν τ' ἐριπίων: Auratus. [4] ταῦτ': Casaubon.
[5] δ' οὖν: Auratus. [6] κλύειν F²N.

μή τις ὅντιν᾽ οὐχ ὁρῶ-
μεν προνοίαισι[1] τοῦ πεπρωμένου
γλῶσσαν ἐν τύχᾳ νέμων;—
τὰν δορίγαμβρον ἀμφινει-
κῆ θ᾽ Ἑλέναν; ἐπεὶ πρεπόντως
ἑλένας, ἕλανδρος, ἑλέπτολις,
ἐκ τῶν ἁβροτίμων
προκαλυμμάτων ἔπλευσε
ζεφύρου γίγαντος αὔρᾳ,
πολύανδροί τε φεράσπιδες
κυναγοὶ κατ᾽ ἴχνος πλατᾶν[2] ἄφαντον
κελσάντων Σιμόεντος
ἀκτὰς ἐπ᾽[3] ἀεξιφύλλους[4]
δι᾽ ἔριν αἱματόεσσαν.

Ἰλίῳ δὲ κῆδος ὀρθ- [ἀντ. α.
ώνυμον τελεσσίφρων
μῆνις ἤλασεν,[5] τραπέ-
ζας ἀτίμωσιν[6] ὑστέρῳ χρόνῳ
καὶ ξυνεστίου Διὸς
πρασσομένα τὸ νυμφότι-
μον μέλος ἐκφάτως τίοντας,
ὑμέναιον, ὃς τότ᾽ ἐπέρρεπεν
γαμβροῖσιν ἀείδειν.
μεταμανθάνουσα δ᾽ ὕμνον
Πριάμου πόλις γεραιὰ
πολύθρηνον μέγα που στένει
κικλήσκουσα Πάριν τὸν αἰνόλεκτρον,
παμπορθῆ[7] πολύθρηνον
αἰῶνα διαὶ[8] πολιτᾶν[9]
μέλεον αἷμ᾽ ἀνατλᾶσα.

[1] προνοίαις: Pauw.
[2] πλάταν: Heath.

was it some power invisible guiding his tongue aright by forecasting of destiny?—who named that bride of the spear and source of strife with the name of Helen? For, true to her name, a Hell she proved to ships, Hell to men, Hell to city, when stepping forth from her delicate and costly-curtained bower, she sailed the sea before the breath of earth-born Zephyrus. And after her a goodly host of warrior huntsmen followed in pursuit on the oars' vanished track of a quarry that had beached its barque on Simoïs' leafy banks—in a strife to end in blood.

To Ilium, its purpose fulfilling, Wrath brought a marriage rightly named a mourning,[1] exacting in after-time requital for the dishonour done to hospitality and to Zeus, the partaker of the hearth, upon those who with loud voice celebrated the song in honour of the bride, even the bridegroom's kin to whom it fell that day to raise the marriage-hymn. But Priam's city hath learnt, in her old age, an altered strain, and now, I trow, waileth a loud song, even one of plenteous lamentation, calling Paris "evil-wed"; for that she hath borne the burthen of a life fraught with desolation, a life of plenteous lamentation by reason of the wretched slaughter of her sons.

[1] κῆδος has a double sense: "marriage-alliance" and 'sorrow."

---

[3] εἰς N. [4] ἀξιφύλλους F, ἀξιφύλλων Rom.
[5] ἤλασε: Porson. [6] ἀτίμως ἵν' F, ἀτίμως N: Canter.
[7] παμπρόσθη: Seidler. [8] αἰῶν' ἀμφὶ: Emperius.
[9] πολίταν: Auratus.

ἔθρεψεν δὲ λέοντος ἶ- [στρ. β.
νιν[1] δόμοις ἀγάλακτον οὕτως[2] ἀνὴρ φιλόμαστον,
ἐν βιότου προτελείοις
ἅμερον, εὐφιλόπαιδα
καὶ γεραροῖς ἐπίχαρτον.
πολέα δ' ἔσχ' ἐν ἀγκάλαις
νεοτρόφου τέκνου δίκαν,
φαιδρωπὸς ποτὶ χεῖρα σαί-
νων τε γαστρὸς ἀνάγκαις.

χρονισθεὶς δ' ἀπέδειξεν ἦ- [ἀντ. β.
θος[3] τὸ πρὸς τοκέων·[4] χάριν
γὰρ τροφεῦσιν[5] ἀμείβων
μηλοφόνοισιν <ἐν>[6] ἄταις[7]
δαῖτ' ἀκέλευστος ἔτευξεν·
αἵματι δ' οἶκος ἐφύρθη,
ἄμαχον[8] ἄλγος οἰκέταις
μέγα σίνος πολυκτόνον.[9]
ἐκ θεοῦ δ' ἱερεύς τις ἄ-
τας δόμοις προσεθρέφθη.[10]

πάραυτα δ'[11] ἐλθεῖν ἐς Ἰλίου πόλιν [στρ. γ.
λέγοιμ' ἂν φρόνημα μὲν
νηνέμου γαλάνας,
ἀκασκαῖον <δ'>[12] ἄγαλμα πλούτου,
μαλθακὸν ὀμμάτων βέλος,
δηξίθυμον ἔρωτος ἄνθος.
παρακλίνασ'[13] ἐπέκρανεν
δὲ γάμου πικρὰς τελευτάς,
δύσεδρος καὶ δυσόμιλος
συμένα Πριαμίδαισιν,

Even so a man reared in his house a lion's whelp, robbed of its mother's milk yet still desiring the breast. Gentle it was in the prelude of its life, kindly to children, and a delight to the old. Much did it get, held in arms like a nursling child, with its bright eye turned toward his hand, and fawning under compulsion of its belly's need.

But brought to full growth by time it showed forth the nature it had from its parents. Unbidden, in requital for its fostering, it prepared a feast with ruinous slaughter of the flocks; so that the house was defiled with blood, and they that dwelt therein could not control their anguish, and great was the carnage far and wide. A priest of ruin, by ordinance of God, was it reared in the house.

At first, methinks, there came to Ilium the spirit of unruffled calm, a delicate ornament of wealth, a darter of soft glances from the eye, love's flower that stingeth the heart. Then, swerving from her course, she made her marriage end in ruth, sped on to the children of Priam under escort of Zeus, the warder of host and guest, blasting with ruin by her

---

[1] λέοντα σίνιν: Conington. [2] οὗτος F^1 Rom.[2] [3] ἔθος: Conington. [4] τοκήων F. [5] τροφᾶς γὰρ F. [6] <ἐν> Bothe. [7] ἅταισιν N. [8] ἄμαχον δ' F. [9] πολύκτονον: Kirchhoff. [10] προσετράφη: Heath. [11] παραυτὰ δ' οὖν N. [12] <δ'> Porson. [13] παρακλίνουσ' N.

πομπᾷ Διὸς ξενίου,
νυμφόκλαυτος Ἐρινύς.

παλαίφατος δ' ἐν βροτοῖς[1] γέρων λόγος [ἀντ. γ.
τέτυκται, μέγαν τελε-
σθέντα φωτὸς ὄλβον
τεκνοῦσθαι μηδ' ἄπαιδα θνῄσκειν,
ἐκ δ' ἀγαθᾶς τύχας γένει
βλαστάνειν ἀκόρεστον οἰζύν.
δίχα δ' ἄλλων μονόφρων εἰμί. τὸ δυσσεβὲς γὰρ[2] ἔργον
μετὰ μὲν πλείονα τίκτει,
σφετέρᾳ δ' εἰκότα γέννᾳ.
οἴκων δ' ἄρ'[3] εὐθυδίκων
καλλίπαις πότμος αἰεί.

φιλεῖ δὲ τίκτειν Ὕβρις [στρ. δ.
μὲν παλαιὰ νεά-
ζουσαν ἐν κακοῖς βροτῶν
ὕβριν τότ' ἢ τόθ', ὅτε[4] τὸ κύριον μόλῃ
φάος τόκου,[5]
δαίμονά τε τὰν[6] ἄμαχον[7] ἀπόλεμον,
ἀνίερον Θράσος, μελαί-
νας μελάθροισιν[8] Ἄτας,
εἰδομένας[9] τοκεῦσιν.

Δίκα δὲ λάμπει μὲν ἐν [ἀντ. δ.
δυσκάπνοις δώμασιν,
τὸν δ' ἐναίσιμον τίει [βίον].[10]
τὰ χρυσόπαστα δ' ἔδεθλα[11] σὺν πίνῳ χερῶν
παλιντρόποις
ὄμμασι λιποῦσ', ὅσια προσέμολε,[12]

sojourn and her companionship, a fiend whose bridal was fraught with tears.

A venerable utterance proclaimed of old hath been fashioned among mankind : the prosperity of man, when it hath come to full growth, engendereth offspring and dieth not childless, and from his good fortune there springeth up insatiate misery unto his seed.

But I hold my own mind and think apart from other men. It is the deed of iniquity that thereafter begetteth more iniquity and like unto its own breed ; but when a house is righteous, the lot of its children is blessed alway.

But old Arrogance is like to bring forth in evil men, or soon or late, at the fated hour of birth, a young Arrogance and that spirit irresistible, unconquerable, unholy, even Recklessness,—black Curses unto the household, and like are they to their parents.

But Righteousness shineth in smoke-begrimed dwellings and holdeth in esteem him that is virtuous. From gold-bespangled mansions, where men's hands are defiled, she departeth with averted eyes and taketh her way to pure homes ; she worships not the

---

[1] ἐν τοῖς βροτοῖς N.
[2] γὰρ δυσσεβὲς: Pauw.
[3] γὰρ: Auratus.
[4] ὅταν: Klausen.
[5] νεαρὰ φάους κότον: H. L. Ahrens.
[6] τὸν: Herm.
[7] ἄμαχον om. N, but superscr.
[8] μελάθροις F, μελάθροισιν N.
[9] εἰδομέναν: Casaubon.
[10] [βίον] H. L. Ahrens.
[11] ἐσθλὰ: Auratus.
[12] προσέβαλε τοῦ: Herm.

δύναμιν οὐ σέβουσα πλού-
του παράσημον αἴνῳ·
πᾶν δ' ἐπὶ τέρμα νωμᾷ.

ἄγε δή, βασιλεῦ, Τροίας πτολίπορθ'[1]
'Ατρέως γένεθλον,
πῶς σε προσείπω; πῶς σε σεβίζω
μήθ' ὑπεράρας μήθ' ὑποκάμψας
καιρὸν χάριτος;
πολλοὶ δὲ βροτῶν τὸ δοκεῖν εἶναι
προτίουσι δίκην παραβάντες.
τῷ δυσπραγοῦντι δ' ἐπιστενάχειν
πᾶς τις ἕτοιμος· δῆγμα[2] δὲ λύπης
οὐδὲν ἐφ' ἧπαρ προσικνεῖται·
καὶ ξυγχαίρουσιν ὁμοιοπρεπεῖς
ἀγέλαστα πρόσωπα βιαζόμενοι.
ὅστις δ' ἀγαθὸς προβατογνώμων,
οὐκ ἔστι λαθεῖν ὄμματα φωτός,
τὰ δοκοῦντ' εὔφρονος ἐκ διανοίας
ὑδαρεῖ σαίνειν φιλότητι.
σὺ δέ μοι τότε μὲν στέλλων στρατιὰν
'Ελένης ἕνεκ', οὐ γάρ <σ'>[3] ἐπικεύσω,
κάρτ' ἀπομούσως ἦσθα γεγραμμένος,
οὐδ' εὖ πραπίδων οἴακα νέμων
θράσος[4] ἐκ θυσιῶν[5]
ἀνδράσι θνήσκουσι κομίζων.
νῦν δ' οὐκ ἀπ' ἄκρας φρενὸς οὐδ' ἀφίλως
. . . .[6]
εὔφρων[7] πόνος εὖ τελέσασιν.
γνώσῃ δὲ χρόνῳ διαπευθόμενος
τόν τε δικαίως καὶ τὸν ἀκαίρως
πόλιν οἰκουροῦντα πολιτῶν.

power of wealth stamped counterfeit by the praise of men, and she guideth all things to their proper end.

[Enter Agamemnon and Cassandra, in a chariot, with a numerous retinue

All hail, my King, stormer of Troy, offspring of Atreus! How shall I greet thee? How do thee homage, not overshooting or running short of the due measure of courtesy? Many there be of mortal men who put appearance before truth and thereby transgress the right. Every one is prompt to heave a sigh over the unfortunate, albeit no sting of true sorrow reaches to the heart; and in seeming sympathy they join in others' joy, forcing their faces into smiles. But whoso is a discerning shepherd of his flock cannot be deceived by men's eyes which, while they feign loyalty of heart, only fawn upon him with watery[1] affection.

Now in the past, when thou didst marshal the armament in Helen's cause, thou wert depicted in my eyes (for I will not hide it from thee) in most ungracious lineaments, and as not guiding aright the helm of thy mind in seeking through thy sacrifices to bring courage to dying men.

But now, from the depth of my heart and with no lack of love . . . their toil is joy to them that have won success. In course of time thou shalt learn by enquiry who of thy people have been honest, who unfitting, guardians of the State.

[1] The figure is of wine much diluted.

---

[1] πολίπορθ᾽: Blomfield.
[2] δῆγμα N, Stobaeus, *Flor.* 112. 12, δεῖγμα F.
[3] ⟨σ᾽⟩ Musgrave. [4] θάρσος N, θράσος F.
[5] ἑκούσιον: H. L. Ahrens.
[6] Lacuna indicated by Schneidewin. [7] εὔφρων τις N.

ΑΓΑΜΕΜΝΩΝ

πρῶτον μὲν Ἄργος καὶ θεοὺς ἐγχωρίους
δίκη προσειπεῖν, τοὺς ἐμοὶ μεταιτίους
νόστου δικαίων θ' ὧν ἐπραξάμην πόλιν
Πριάμου· δίκας γὰρ οὐκ ἀπὸ γλώσσης θεοὶ
κλύοντες ἀνδροθνῆτας Ἰλίου φθορὰς
ἐς αἱματηρὸν τεῦχος οὐ διχορρόπως
ψήφους ἔθεντο· τῷ δ' ἐναντίῳ κύτει
ἐλπὶς προσῄει χειρὸς οὐ πληρουμένῳ.
καπνῷ δ' ἁλοῦσα νῦν ἔτ' εὔσημος πόλις.
ἄτης θύελλαι ζῶσι· συνθνῄσκουσα δὲ
σποδὸς προπέμπει πίονας πλούτου πνοάς.
τούτων θεοῖσι χρὴ πολύμνηστον χάριν
τίνειν, ἐπείπερ καὶ πάγας ὑπερκότους
ἐφραξάμεσθα[1] καὶ γυναικὸς οὕνεκα
πόλιν διημάθυνεν Ἀργεῖον δάκος,
ἵππου νεοσσός, ἀσπιδηφόρος[2] λεώς,
πήδημ' ὀρούσας ἀμφὶ Πλειάδων δύσιν·
ὑπερθορὼν δὲ πύργον ὠμηστὴς λέων
ἄδην ἔλειξεν αἵματος τυραννικοῦ.
θεοῖς μὲν ἐξέτεινα φροίμιον τόδε·
τὰ δ' ἐς τὸ σὸν φρόνημα, μέμνημαι κλύων,
καὶ φημὶ ταὐτὰ[3] καὶ συνήγορόν μ' ἔχεις.
παύροις γὰρ ἀνδρῶν ἐστι συγγενὲς τόδε,
φίλον τὸν εὐτυχοῦντ' ἄνευ φθόνου σέβειν.
δύσφρων γὰρ ἰὸς καρδίαν προσήμενος
ἄχθος διπλοίζει τῷ πεπαμένῳ[4] νόσον,
τοῖς τ' αὐτὸς αὑτοῦ πήμασιν βαρύνεται
καὶ τὸν θυραῖον ὄλβον εἰσορῶν στένει.

[1] ἐπραξάμεσθα: Francken.
[2] ἀσπιδήστροφος F, ἀσπιδόστροφος N: Blomfield.
[3] ταῦτα: Auratus. [4] πεπαμμένῳ: Porson.

AGAMEMNON

Argos first, as is right and due, I greet, and the gods that dwell therein who have helped me to my safe return and to the justice I exacted from Priam's town. For hearkening to no pleadings by word of mouth,[1] without dissentient voice, they cast into the urn of blood their ballots for the murderous destroying of Ilium; but to the urn of acquittal that no hand filled, Hope alone drew nigh. The smoke still even now declares the city's fall. Destruction's blasts still live, and the embers, as they die, breathe forth rich reek of wealth. For this success it behoves us to render to the gods a return in ever-mindful gratitude, seeing that we have thrown round the city the toils of vengeance, and in a woman's cause it hath been laid low by the fierce Argive beast, brood of the horse,[2] a shield-armed folk, that launched its leap what time the Pleiads waned. Vaulting over its towered walls, the ravening lion lapped his fill of princely blood.

This lengthened prelude to the gods. But, touching thy sentiments—the which I heard and still bear in memory—I both agree and thou hast in me an advocate therein. For few there be among men in whom it is inborn to admire without envy a friend's good fortune. For the venom of malevolence settles upon the heart and doubles the burthen of him afflicted of that plague: he is himself weighed down by his own calamity, and repines at sight of

[1] "Not hearing pleadings from the tongue"—as if the Greeks and Trojans were waging war in words before a human court—but with divine insight of the true merits of the case.

[2] The wooden horse.

εἰδὼς λέγοιμ' ἄν, εὖ γὰρ ἐξεπίσταμαι
ὁμιλίας κάτοπτρον, εἴδωλον σκιᾶς
δοκοῦντας εἶναι κάρτα πρευμενεῖς ἐμοί.
μόνος δ' Ὀδυσσεύς, ὅσπερ οὐχ ἑκὼν ἔπλει,
ζευχθεὶς ἕτοιμος ἦν ἐμοὶ σειραφόρος·
εἴτ' οὖν θανόντος εἴτε καὶ ζῶντος πέρι
λέγω.
τὰ δ' ἄλλα πρὸς πόλιν τε καὶ θεοὺς
κοινοὺς ἀγῶνας θέντες ἐν πανηγύρει
βουλευσόμεσθα. καὶ τὸ μὲν καλῶς ἔχον
ὅπως χρονίζον εὖ μενεῖ βουλευτέον·
ὅτῳ δὲ καὶ δεῖ φαρμάκων παιωνίων,
ἤτοι κέαντες ἢ τεμόντες εὐφρόνως
πειρασόμεσθα πῆμ' ἀποστρέψαι νόσου.[1]
νῦν δ' ἐς μέλαθρα καὶ δόμους ἐφεστίους
ἐλθὼν θεοῖσι πρῶτα δεξιώσομαι,
οἵπερ πρόσω πέμψαντες ἤγαγον πάλιν.
νίκη δ' ἐπείπερ ἕσπετ', ἐμπέδως μένοι.

ΚΛΥΤΑΙΜΗΣΤΡΑ

ἄνδρες πολῖται, πρέσβος Ἀργείων τόδε,
οὐκ αἰσχυνοῦμαι τοὺς φιλάνορας τρόπους
λέξαι πρὸς ὑμᾶς· ἐν χρόνῳ δ' ἀποφθίνει
τὸ τάρβος ἀνθρώποισιν.
οὐκ ἄλλων πάρα
μαθοῦσ', ἐμαυτῆς δύσφορον λέξω βίον
τοσόνδ' ὅσονπερ οὗτος ἦν ὑπ' Ἰλίῳ.

[1] πήματος τρέψαι νόσον: Porson.

another's prosperity. From knowledge—for well am I acquainted with the mirror of companionship—I may call a shadow of a shade those who feigned exceeding loyalty to me.[1] Only Odysseus, even he who sailed against his will, once harnessed, proved my zealous yoke-fellow. This I affirm of him be he alive or dead.

But, for the rest, in what concerns the State and public worship, we shall appoint general assemblies and deliberate in full conclave. Where all goes well, we must take counsel that so it may long endure; but whensoever there is need of healing remedy, we will endeavour to avert the mischief of the malady by kind appliance of cautery or the knife.

And now I will pass to my palace halls and to my household hearth, and first of all pay greeting to the gods. They sped me forth and they have brought me home again. May victory, as it hath attended me, bide ever with me constant to the end!

[*He descends from his chariot; enter Clytaemestra, attended by maid-servants carrying purple tapestries*

Clytaemestra

Burghers of Argos, ye Elders present here, I shall not be ashamed to confess in your presence my fondness for my husband—with time diffidence dies away in man.

Untaught by others, I can tell of my own weary life all the long while this my lord lay beneath

[1] This version takes ὁμιλίας κάτοπτρον to mean that companionship shows the true character of a man's associates. An alternative rendering takes κάτοπτρον in a disparaging sense—the semblance as opposed to reality—and makes κάτοπτρον, εἴδωλον and δοκοῦντας in apposition.

τὸ μὲν γυναῖκα πρῶτον ἄρσενος δίχα
ἧσθαι δόμοις ἔρημον ἔκπαγλον κακόν,
πολλὰς κλύουσαν κληδόνας[1] παλιγκότους·
καὶ τὸν μὲν ἥκειν, τὸν δ' ἐπεσφέρειν κακοῦ
κάκιον ἄλλο πῆμα, λάσκοντας δόμοις.
καὶ τραυμάτων μὲν εἰ τόσων ἐτύγχανεν
ἀνὴρ ὅδ', ὡς πρὸς οἶκον ὠχετεύετο
φάτις, τέτρηται[2] δικτύου πλέον[3] λέγειν.
εἰ δ' ἦν τεθνηκώς, ὡς ἐπλήθυον[4] λόγοι,
τρισώματός τἂν Γηρυὼν ὁ δεύτερος
[πολλὴν ἄνωθεν, τὴν κάτω γὰρ οὐ λέγω,][5]
χθονὸς τρίμοιρον χλαῖναν ἐξηύχει λαβεῖν,[6]
ἅπαξ ἑκάστῳ κατθανὼν μορφώματι.
τοιῶνδ' ἕκατι κληδόνων παλιγκότων
πολλὰς ἄνωθεν ἀρτάνας ἐμῆς δέρης
ἔλυσαν ἄλλοι πρὸς βίαν λελημμένης.
ἐκ τῶνδέ τοι παῖς ἐνθάδ' οὐ παραστατεῖ,
ἐμῶν τε καὶ σῶν κύριος πιστωμάτων,[7]
ὡς χρῆν, Ὀρέστης· μηδὲ θαυμάσῃς τόδε.
τρέφει γὰρ αὐτὸν εὐμενὴς δορύξενος
Στρόφιος ὁ Φωκεύς, ἀμφίλεκτα πήματα
ἐμοὶ προφωνῶν, τόν θ' ὑπ' Ἰλίῳ σέθεν
κίνδυνον, εἴ τε δημόθρους ἀναρχία
βουλὴν καταρρίψειεν, ὥστε σύγγονον
βροτοῖσι τὸν πεσόντα λακτίσαι πλέον.
τοιάδε μέντοι σκῆψις οὐ δόλον φέρει.
ἔμοιγε μὲν δὴ κλαυμάτων ἐπίσσυτοι
πηγαὶ κατεσβήκασιν, οὐδ' ἔνι σταγών.
ἐν ὀψικοίτοις δ' ὄμμασιν βλάβας ἔχω

[1] ἡδονὰς: Auratus.
[2] τέτρωται: H. L. Ahrens. [3] πλέω: Dindorf.
[4] ἐπλήθυνον: Porson. [5] [ ] Schütz.

Ilium's walls. First and foremost, an evil full of terror is it for a wife to sit forlorn at home, severed from her husband, forever hearing malignant rumours manifold, and for one messenger after another to come bearing tidings of disaster, each worse than the last, and cry them to the household. And as for wounds, had this my lord received so many as rumour kept pouring into the house, no net had been pierced so full of holes as he. Or had he died as oft as reports were rife, then in sooth he might have had three bodies—a second Geryon [1]—and have boasted of having taken on him a triple coverture of earth [ample that above—of that below I speak not]—one death for each several shape. By reason of such malignant tales as these, many a time have others had to loose the high-hung halter from my neck, held in its strong grip. 'Tis for this cause, in truth, that our boy, Orestes, stands not here beside me, as he should—he in whom rest the pledges of my love and thine. Nay, think this not strange. For he is in the protecting care of our well-affected ally, Strophius of Phocis, who gave me warning of trouble on two scores—thine own peril beneath Ilium's walls, and then the chance that the people in clamorous revolt might overturn the Council, as it is inborn in men to trample the more upon the fallen. Truly this excuse is not fraught with guile.

As for myself, the welling fountains of my tears are utterly dried up—not a drop remains therein. In night-long vigils mine eyes are sore with weeping

[1] Geryon, a monster (here called "three-bodied," but ordinarily "three-headed") whose oxen were driven away from Spain by Heracles.

---

[6] λαβὼν: Paley. [7] πιστευμάτων: Spanheim.

τὰς ἀμφί σοι κλαίουσα λαμπτηρουχίας
ἀτημελήτους αἰέν. ἐν δ' ὀνείρασιν
λεπταῖς ὕπαὶ κώνωπος ἐξηγειρόμην
ῥιπαῖσι θωΰσσοντος, ἀμφί σοι πάθη
ὁρῶσα πλείω τοῦ ξυνεύδοντος χρόνου.
νῦν ταῦτα πάντα τλᾶσ' ἀπενθήτῳ φρενὶ
λέγοιμ' ἂν ἄνδρα τόνδε τῶν σταθμῶν κύνα,
σωτῆρα ναὸς πρότονον, ὑψηλῆς στέγης
στῦλον[1] ποδήρη, μονογενὲς τέκνον πατρί,
καὶ γῆν φανεῖσαν ναυτίλοις παρ' ἐλπίδα,
κάλλιστον ἦμαρ εἰσιδεῖν ἐκ χείματος,
ὁδοιπόρῳ διψῶντι πηγαῖον ῥέος·
τερπνὸν δὲ τἀναγκαῖον ἐκφυγεῖν ἅπαν.
τοιοῖσδέ τοί νιν[2] ἀξιῶ προσφθέγμασιν.
φθόνος δ' ἀπέστω· πολλὰ γὰρ τὰ πρὶν κακὰ
ἠνειχόμεσθα.
νῦν δέ μοι, φίλον κάρα,
ἔκβαιν' ἀπήνης τῆσδε, μὴ χαμαὶ τιθεὶς
τὸν σὸν πόδ', ὦναξ, Ἰλίου πορθήτορα.
δμῳαί,[3] τί μέλλεθ', αἷς ἐπέσταλται τέλος[4]
πέδον κελεύθου στρωννύναι πετάσμασιν;
εὐθὺς γενέσθω πορφυρόστρωτος πόρος
ἐς δῶμ' ἄελπτον ὡς ἂν ἡγῆται δίκη.
τὰ δ' ἄλλα φροντὶς οὐχ ὕπνῳ νικωμένη
θήσει δικαίως σὺν θεοῖς εἱμαρμένα.

ΑΓΑΜΕΜΝΩΝ

Λήδας γένεθλον, δωμάτων ἐμῶν φύλαξ,
ἀπουσίᾳ μὲν εἶπας εἰκότως ἐμῇ·

[1] στῦλον N, στόλον F.
[2] τοίνυν: Schütz.
[3] δμωαί: Kirchhoff.
[4] τέλος F, τάδε N.

for the beacon-lights set for thee but neglected ever. The faint whirring of the buzzing gnat waked me oft from dreams wherein I beheld more disasters to thee than the time of sleep could have compassed.

But now, having borne all this, my heart freed from its anxiety, I would hail my lord here as the watch-dog of the fold, the saviour forestay of the ship, firm-based pillar of the lofty roof, only-begotten son unto a father, yea land descried by men at sea beyond their hope, dawn most fair to look upon after storm, the gushing rill to wayfarer athirst—sweet is it to escape all stress of need. Such truly are the greetings whereof I deem him worthy. But let envy [1] be far removed, since many were the ills we endured before.

And now, I pray thee, dear my lord, dismount from this thy car, but set not on common earth this foot of thine, my liege, that hath trampled upon Ilium. [*To her attendants*] Why this loitering, women, as whose task I have assigned to strew with tapestries his pathway's floor? Quick! With purple let his path be strewn, that Justice may usher him to a home he ne'er hoped to see. The rest my unslumbering vigilance shall order duly—an it please God—even as is ordained.

AGAMEMNON

Offspring of Leda, guardian of my house, thy speech comports well with my absence; for thou

[1] By her fulsome address Clytaemestra invites, while seeming to deprecate, the envy of the gods.

μακρὰν γὰρ ἐξέτεινας· ἀλλ᾽ ἐναισίμως
αἰνεῖν, παρ᾽ ἄλλων χρὴ τόδ᾽ ἔρχεσθαι γέρας·
καὶ τἄλλα μὴ γυναικὸς ἐν τρόποις ἐμὲ
ἅβρυνε, μηδὲ βαρβάρου φωτὸς δίκην
χαμαιπετὲς βόαμα[1] προσχάνῃς ἐμοί,
μηδ᾽ εἵμασι στρώσασ᾽ ἐπίφθονον πόρον
τίθει· θεούς τοι τοῖσδε τιμαλφεῖν χρεών·
ἐν ποικίλοις δὲ θνητὸν ὄντα κάλλεσιν
βαίνειν ἐμοὶ μὲν οὐδαμῶς ἄνευ φόβου.
λέγω κατ᾽ ἄνδρα, μὴ θεόν, σέβειν ἐμέ.
χωρὶς ποδοψήστρων τε καὶ τῶν ποικίλων
κληδὼν ἀυτεῖ· καὶ τὸ μὴ κακῶς φρονεῖν
θεοῦ μέγιστον δῶρον. ὀλβίσαι δὲ χρὴ
βίον τελευτήσαντ᾽ ἐν εὐεστοῖ φίλῃ.
εἰ πάντα δ᾽ ὣς πράσσοιμ᾽ ἄν, εὐθαρσὴς[2] ἐγώ.

ΚΛΥΤΑΙΜΗΣΤΡΑ

καὶ μὴν τόδ᾽ εἰπὲ μὴ παρὰ γνώμην ἐμοί.

ΑΓΑΜΕΜΝΩΝ

γνώμην μὲν ἴσθι μὴ διαφθεροῦντ᾽ ἐμέ.

ΚΛΥΤΑΙΜΗΣΤΡΑ

ηὔξω θεοῖς δείσας ἂν ὧδ᾽ ἔρδειν τάδε.

ΑΓΑΜΕΜΝΩΝ

εἴπερ τις, εἰδώς γ᾽ εὖ τόδ᾽ ἐξεῖπον τέλος.

[1] βόημα F²N. [2] πράσσοιμ᾽ ἄνευ θάρσους N.

hast drawn it out to ample length. But becoming praise—this meed should of right proceed from other lips. For the rest, pamper me not after woman's wise, nor, like some barbarian,[1] grovel to me with wide-mouthed acclaim; and draw not down envy upon my path by strewing it with tapestries. 'Tis the gods we must honour thus; but for a mortal to tread upon broidered fineries is, to my judgment, not without ground for dread. I bid thee revere me not as a god, but as a man. Foot mats and broideries sound diverse in the voice of Rumour; to think no folly is Heaven's best gift. Only when man's life comes to its end in prosperity dare we pronounce him happy; and if in all things so I might act as now, I have good confidence.

CLYTAEMESTRA

Nay now, speak not thus to flout my purpose.

AGAMEMNON

Purpose! Be assured I shall not weaken mine.

CLYTAEMESTRA

Thou must in fear have vowed to Heaven thus to act.

AGAMEMNON

With full knowledge I pronounced this my final 'ord, if ever man did.

[1] Some take this to mean: "Nor, as if I were a barbaric chieftain, grovel to me."

ΚΛΥΤΑΙΜΗΣΤΡΑ

τί δ' ἂν δοκεῖ[1] σοι Πρίαμος, εἰ τάδ' ἤνυσεν;

ΑΓΑΜΕΜΝΩΝ

ἐν ποικίλοις ἂν κάρτα μοι βῆναι δοκεῖ.[2]

ΚΛΥΤΑΙΜΗΣΤΡΑ

μή νυν τὸν ἀνθρώπειον αἰδεσθῇς[3] ψόγον.

ΑΓΑΜΕΜΝΩΝ

φήμη γε μέντοι δημόθρους μέγα σθένει.

ΚΛΥΤΑΙΜΗΣΤΡΑ

ὁ δ' ἀφθόνητός γ' οὐκ ἐπίζηλος πέλει.

ΑΓΑΜΕΜΝΩΝ

οὔτοι γυναικός ἐστιν ἱμείρειν μάχης.

ΚΛΥΤΑΙΜΗΣΤΡΑ

τοῖς δ' ὀλβίοις γε καὶ τὸ νικᾶσθαι πρέπει.

ΑΓΑΜΕΜΝΩΝ

ἦ καὶ σὺ νίκην τήνδε δήριος τίεις;

ΚΛΥΤΑΙΜΗΣΤΡΑ

πιθοῦ· κράτος μέντοι πάρες γ' ἑκὼν ἐμοί.

[1] δοκῇ: Stanley. [2] δοκῇ F^1, δοκεῖ (?) F^2. [3] αἰδεσθεὶς F.

CLYTAEMESTRA

What, think'st thou, had Priam done, had he achieved thy triumph?

AGAMEMNON

He would have set foot upon the broideries, I do verily believe.

CLYTAEMESTRA

Then be not thou swayed by fear of men's cavillings.

AGAMEMNON

And yet a people's voice is a mighty power.

CLYTAEMESTRA

True, yet he who is unenvied is unenviable.

AGAMEMNON

Surely 'tis not woman's part to be fond of contest.

CLYTAEMESTRA

Aye, but it beseems the happy victor even to yield the victory.

AGAMEMNON

What? is this the kind of victory in strife that *thou* dost prize?

CLYTAEMESTRA

Oh yield! Yet of thy free accord consent to leave the victory with me.

ΑΓΑΜΕΜΝΩΝ

ἀλλ' εἰ δοκεῖ σοι ταῦθ', ὑπαί τις ἀρβύλας
λύοι τάχος, πρόδουλον ἔμβασιν ποδός.
καὶ τοῖσδέ μ' ἐμβαίνονθ' ἁλουργέσιν θεῶν
μή τις πρόσωθεν ὄμματος βάλοι φθόνος.
πολλὴ γὰρ αἰδὼς δωματοφθορεῖν[1] ποσὶν
φθείροντα πλοῦτον ἀργυρωνήτους θ' ὑφάς.
τούτων μὲν οὕτω· τὴν ξένην δὲ πρευμενῶς
τήνδ' ἐσκόμιζε· τὸν κρατοῦντα μαλθακῶς
θεὸς πρόσωθεν εὐμενῶς προσδέρκεται.
ἑκὼν γὰρ οὐδεὶς δουλίῳ χρῆται ζυγῷ.
αὕτη[2] δὲ πολλῶν χρημάτων ἐξαίρετον
ἄνθος, στρατοῦ δώρημ', ἐμοὶ ξυνέσπετο.
ἐπεὶ δ' ἀκούειν σοῦ κατέστραμμαι τάδε,
εἶμ' ἐς δόμων μέλαθρα πορφύρας πατῶν.

ΚΛΥΤΑΙΜΗΣΤΡΑ

ἔστιν θάλασσα, τίς δέ νιν κατασβέσει;
τρέφουσα πολλῆς πορφύρας ἰσάργυρον[3]
κηκῖδα παγκαίνιστον, εἱμάτων βαφάς.
οἶκος δ' ὑπάρχει τῶνδε σὺν θεοῖς ἅλις[4]
ἔχειν· πένεσθαι δ' οὐκ ἐπίσταται δόμος.
πολλῶν πατησμὸν δ' εἱμάτων[5] ἂν ηὐξάμην,[6]
δόμοισι προυνεχθέντος ἐν χρηστηρίοις,
ψυχῆς κόμιστρα τῆσδε μηχανωμένῃ.[7]
ῥίζης γὰρ οὔσης φυλλὰς ἵκετ' ἐς δόμους,
σκιὰν ὑπερτείνασα σειρίου κυνός.
καὶ σοῦ μολόντος δωματῖτιν ἑστίαν,
θάλπος μὲν ἐν χειμῶνι σημαίνεις μολόν·[8]

[1] σωματοφθορεῖν: Schütz.
[2] αὐτή: Auratus.
[3] εἰς ἄργυρον: Salmasius.
[4] ἄναξ: Karsten.

Agamemnon

Well, if thou wilt have thy way, quick, let some one loose my sandals, which, slave-like, serve the treading of my foot! As I tread upon these purple vestments may I not be smitten from afar by any glance of Heaven's jealous eye. Sore shame it is for my foot to mar the substance of the house by making waste of wealth and costly woven work.

Thus much for this. Yon stranger damsel do thou receive into the house with kindness. God from afar looks graciously upon a gentle master; for of free choice no one takes upon him the yoke of slavery. But she, the choicest flower of rich treasure, has followed in my train, my army's gift.

Since I have been overborne to hearken to thee in this, I will tread upon a purple pathway as I pass to my palace halls.

Clytaemestra

There is the sea (and who shall drain it dry?) producing stain of plenteous purple, costly as silver and ever fresh, wherewith to dye our vestments; and of these our house, thanks be to Heaven, hath ample store; it knows no penury. Vestments enow I would have devoted to be trampled underfoot had it been so enjoined me in the seat of oracles when I was devising the ransom of thy life. For if the root still lives, leafage comes again to the house and spreads its over-reaching shade against the scorching dog-star; so, now that thou hast come to hearth and home, thou showest that warmth hath

---

[5] δειμάτων: Canter. [6] εὐξάμην: Weil.
[7] μηχανωμένης: Abresch. [8] μολών: H. Voss.

ὅταν δὲ τεύχῃ Ζεὺς ἀπ'[1] ὄμφακος πικρᾶς
οἶνον, τότ' ἤδη ψῦχος ἐν δόμοις πέλει,
ἀνδρὸς τελείου δῶμ' ἐπιστρωφωμένου.[2]
Ζεῦ, Ζεῦ τέλειε, τὰς ἐμὰς εὐχὰς τέλει·
μέλοι[3] δέ τοι σοὶ τῶνπερ ἂν μέλλῃς τελεῖν.

ΧΟΡΟΣ

τίπτε μοι τόδ' ἐμπέδως [στρ. α.
δεῖμα[4] προστατήριον
καρδίας τερασκόπου ποτᾶται,
μαντιπολεῖ δ' ἀκέλευστος ἄμισθος ἀοιδά,
οὐδ' ἀποπτύσαι[5] δίκαν
δυσκρίτων ὀνειράτων
θάρσος εὐπειθὲς[6] ἵζει[7]
φρενὸς φίλον θρόνον; χρόνος δ' ἐπὶ[8]
πρυμνησίων ξυνεμβολαῖς[9]
ψαμμί' ἀκτᾶς παρή-
μησεν,[10] εὖθ' ὑπ' Ἴλιον
ὦρτο ναυβάτας στρατός.

πεύθομαι δ' ἀπ' ὀμμάτων [ἀντ. α.
νόστον, αὐτόμαρτυς ὤν·
τὸν δ' ἄνευ λύρας ὅμως[11] ὑμνῳδεῖ
θρῆνον Ἐρινύος[12] αὐτοδίδακτος ἔσωθεν
θυμός, οὐ τὸ πᾶν ἔχων
ἐλπίδος φίλον θράσος.
σπλάγχνα δ' οὔτοι ματᾴζει
πρὸς ἐνδίκοις φρεσὶν τελεσφόροις
δίναις κυκώμενον[13] κέαρ.

[1] τ' ἀπ' FN : Auratus.
[2] ἐπιστρεφωμένου F, ἐπιστροφωμένου N : Vict.
[3] μέλῃ (superscr. οι) δέ σοι F. [4] δεῖμα N, δεῖγμα F.
[5] ἀποπτύσαι N, ἀποπτύσας F.

come in winter-time; aye, and when Zeus maketh wine from the bitter grape,[1] then forthwith there is coolness in the house when its rightful lord ranges through his halls. [*As Agamemnon enters the palace*] O Zeus, Zeus, thou who fulfillest, fulfil my prayers! Thine be the care of that thou meanest to fulfil!

[*Exit*

CHORUS

Why ever thus persistently doth this terror hover at the portals of my prophetic soul? Why doth my song, unbidden and unfeed, chant strains of augury? Why doth assuring confidence not sit on my bosom's throne and spurn away the terror like an uninterpretable dream? But Time hath collected the sands of the shore upon the cables cast thereon when the ship-borne armament had sped forth for Ilium.[2]

Of their coming home I am assured by mine own eyes and need no other witness. Yet still my soul within me, self-inspired, intoneth the lyreless dirge of the Avenging Spirit, and cannot wholly win its wonted confidence of hope. Not for naught is my bosom disquieted as my heart throbs against my justly boding breast in eddying tides that presage

[1] That is, when the summer heat is ripening the grapes.

[2] The sense of the Greek passage (of which no entirely satisfactory emendation has been offered) is that so much time has passed since the fleet, under Agamemnon's command, was detained at Aulis by the wrath of Artemis, that Calchas' prophecy of evil, if true, would have been fulfilled long ago.

[6] εὐπιθὲς: Jacob. [7] ἵξει N, ἴξει F: Scaliger.
[8] δ' ἐπεὶ F, δ' ἐπὶ N: E. A. J. Ahrens.
[9] ξυνεμβόλοις: J. G. Schneider.
[10] ψαμμίας ἀκάτας N (ἀκάτα F) παρήβησεν F (– βησ' N): Verrall.
[11] ὅπως: Auratus.
[12] ἐριννὺς: Porson. [13] κυκλούμενον: Headlam.

εὔχομαι δ' ἐξ[1] ἐμᾶς[2]
ἐλπίδος ψύθη[3] πεσεῖν
ἐς τὸ μὴ τελεσφόρον.

μάλα γέ τοι[4] τὸ μεγάλας[5] ὑγιείας [στρ. β.
ἀκόρεστον τέρμα· νόσος γὰρ <ἀεὶ>[6]
γείτων ὁμότοιχος ἐρείδει.
καὶ πότμος εὐθυπορῶν
ἀνδρὸς ἔπαισεν <ἄφνω
δυστυχίας πρὸς>[7] ἄφαντον ἕρμα.
καὶ πρὸ μέν τι[8] χρημάτων
κτησίων ὄκνος βαλὼν
σφενδόνας ἀπ' εὐμέτρου,
οὐκ ἔδυ πρόπας δόμος
πημονᾶς[9] γέμων ἄγαν,
οὐδ' ἐπόντισε σκάφος.
πολλά τοι δόσις ἐκ[10] Διὸς ἀμ-
φιλαφής τε καὶ ἐξ ἀλόκων ἐπετειᾶν
νῆστιν ὤλεσεν νόσον.

τὸ δ' ἐπὶ γᾶν πεσὸν[11] ἅπαξ θανάσιμον [ἀντ. β.
προπάροιθ'[12] ἀνδρὸς μέλαν αἷμα τίς ἂν
πάλιν ἀγκαλέσαιτ' ἐπαείδων;
οὐδὲ τὸν ὀρθοδαῆ
τῶν φθιμένων ἀνάγειν
Ζεὺς ἀπέπαυσεν[13] ἐπ' εὐλαβείᾳ[14];
εἰ δὲ μὴ τεταγμένα
μοῖρα μοῖραν ἐκ θεῶν

[1] δ' ἀπ' N, δ' ἐξ F. [2] ἐμᾶς τοι N, ἐμᾶς F.
[3] ψύδη: Stephanus. [4] γάρ τοι F, γέ τοι δὴ N.
[5] τᾶς πολλᾶς: τὸ μεγάλας Paley.

fulfilment. But I pray that my expectation may fall out false and come not to fulfilment.

Of a truth lusty health resteth not content within its due bounds; for disease ever presseth close against it, its neighbour with a common wall.[1] So human fortune, when holding onward in straight course, of a sudden striketh upon a hidden reef of calamity. And yet, if with well-measured cast, caution heave overboard a portion of the gathered wealth, the whole house, with woe overladen, doth not founder nor doth it engulf the hull.[2] Verily a rich and bounteous gift from Zeus, even from the furrows that furnish forth yearly, stayeth the plague of famine.

But man's blood, once it hath first fallen by murder to earth in darkling tide—who by magic spell shall call it back? Even him[3] who possessed the skill to raise from the dead — did not Zeus make an end of him as warning? And were it not that one fate ordained of the gods doth restrain

[1] Abounding health, ignoring its limitations, is separated from disease only by a slight dividing line. The suppressed thought is that remedies, if applied betimes, may save the body.

[2] The house of Agamemnon, full of calamity, is likened to an overloaded ship, which will founder if some part of its freight is not jettisoned. By confusion of the symbol and the thing signified, *δόμος* is boldly said to "sink its hull."

[3] Aesculapius, who was blasted by the thunderbolt of Zeus for this offence.

---

[6] <*ἀεὶ*> Blomfield. [7] < > H. L. Ahrens.
[8] *τὸ μὲν πρὸ*: Enger. [9] *πημονὰς*: Vict.
[10] *ἐκ* om. N. [11] *πεσόνθ'*: Auratus. [12] *πρόπαρ* F.
[13] *αὔτ' ἔπαυσ'*: Hartung. [14] *αὐλαβεία* F, *ἀβλαβείᾳ γε* N.

εἶργε μὴ πλέον φέρειν,
προφθάσασα καρδία
γλῶσσαν ἂν τάδ' ἐξέχει.
νῦν δ' ὑπὸ σκότῳ βρέμει
θυμαλγής τε καὶ οὐδὲν ἐπελ-
πομένα[1] ποτὲ καίριον ἐκτολυπεύσειν
ζωπυρουμένας φρενός.

ΚΛΥΤΑΙΜΗΣΤΡΑ

εἴσω κομίζου καὶ σύ, Κασάνδραν λέγω,
ἐπεί σ' ἔθηκε Ζεὺς ἀμηνίτως δόμοις
κοινωνὸν εἶναι χερνίβων, πολλῶν μέτα
δούλων σταθεῖσαν κτησίου βωμοῦ πέλας·
ἔκβαιν' ἀπήνης τῆσδε, μηδ' ὑπερφρόνει.
καὶ παῖδα γάρ τοί φασιν 'Αλκμήνης ποτὲ
πραθέντα τλῆναι δουλίας μάζης τυχεῖν.[2]
εἰ δ' οὖν ἀνάγκη τῆσδ' ἐπιρρέποι[3] τύχης,
ἀρχαιοπλούτων δεσποτῶν πολλὴ χάρις.
οἳ δ' οὔποτ' ἐλπίσαντες ἤμησαν καλῶς,
ὠμοί τε δούλοις πάντα καὶ παρὰ στάθμην.
ἔχεις παρ' ἡμῶν οἷάπερ νομίζεται.

ΧΟΡΟΣ

σοί τοι λέγουσα παύεται σαφῆ λόγον.
ἐντός δ' ἂν οὖσα μορσίμων ἀγρευμάτων
πείθοι' ἄν, εἰ πείθοι'· ἀπειθοίης δ' ἴσως.

[1] θυμαλγής . . . ἐπ. om. N.
[2] δουλείας μ. βία F, καὶ ζυγῶν θιγεῖν βίᾳ N: Enger.
[3] ἐπιρρέπει N.

---

[1] The further expression of their forebodings is checked by the desperate hope that since divine forces sometimes clash, the evil destiny of Agamemnon may yet be averted by a superior fate, which they dimly apprehend will ordain

another fate from winning the advantage, my heart would outstrip my tongue and pour forth its bodings [1]; but, as it is, it muttereth only in the dark, distressed and hopeless ever to unravel aught to timely purpose when my soul's aflame. [*Enter Clytaemestra*

CLYTAEMESTRA

Get thee within, thou too, Cassandra [2]; since in no unkindness hath Zeus appointed thee a partaker in the holy water of a house where thou mayest take thy stand, with many another slave, at the altar of the god who guards its wealth. Dismount thee from the car and be not over-proud; for even Alcmene's son,[3] men say, in days of old endured to be sold and eat the bread of slavery. But if such fortune should perforce fall to the lot of any, there is good cause for thankfulness in having masters of ancient wealth; for they who, beyond their hope, have reaped a rich harvest of possessions, are cruel to their slaves in every way, even exceeding due measure. Thou hast from us such usage as custom warranteth.

CHORUS

It is to thee she hath been speaking and clearly. Since thou art in the toils of destiny, belike thou wilt obey, if thou art so inclined; but belike thou wilt not.

his deliverance from the consequences of his shedding the blood of Iphigenia.

[2] I have retained the ordinary form of the name in Greek and English.

[3] Heracles, because of his murder of Iphitus, was sold as a slave to Omphale, queen of Lydia.

ΚΛΥΤΑΙΜΗΣΤΡΑ

ἀλλ' εἴπερ ἐστὶ μὴ χελιδόνος δίκην
ἀγνῶτα φωνὴν βάρβαρον κεκτημένη,
ἔσω φρενῶν λέγουσα πείθω νιν λόγῳ.

ΧΟΡΟΣ

ἕπου. τὰ λῷστα τῶν παρεστώτων λέγει.
πιθοῦ[1] λιποῦσα τόνδ' ἁμαξήρη θρόνον.

ΚΛΥΤΑΙΜΗΣΤΡΑ

οὔτοι θυραίᾳ[2] τῇδ'[3] ἐμοὶ σχολὴ πάρα
τρίβειν· τὰ μὲν γὰρ ἑστίας μεσομφάλου
ἕστηκεν ἤδη μῆλα πρὸς σφαγὰς πάρος[4],
ὡς οὔποτ' ἐλπίσασι τήνδ' ἕξειν χάριν.
σὺ δ' εἴ τι δράσεις τῶνδε, μὴ σχολὴν τίθει.
εἰ δ' ἀξυνήμων οὖσα μὴ δέχῃ λόγον,
σὺ δ' ἀντὶ φωνῆς φράζε καρβάνῳ χερί.

ΧΟΡΟΣ

ἑρμηνέως ἔοικεν ἡ ξένη τοροῦ
δεῖσθαι· τρόπος δὲ θηρὸς ὡς νεαιρέτου.

ΚΛΥΤΑΙΜΗΣΤΡΑ

ἦ μαίνεταί γε καὶ κακῶν κλύει φρενῶν,
ἥτις λιποῦσα μὲν πόλιν νεαίρετον
ἥκει, χαλινὸν δ' οὐκ ἐπίσταται φέρειν,[5]
πρὶν αἱματηρὸν ἐξαφρίζεσθαι μένος.
οὐ μὴν[6] πλέω ῥίψασ' ἀτιμασθήσομαι.

[1] πεῖθου: Blomfield. [2] θυραίαν: Casaubon.
[3] τήνδ': Musgrave. [4] πυρὸς: Musgrave.
[5] M is extant for ll. 1068-1158. [6] μὴ M[1], μὴν M[2].

Clytaemestra

Well, if her speech be not strange and outlandish, even as a swallow's, I must speak within the compass of her wits and move her to comply.

Chorus

Go with her. Of what is thine to choose she giveth thee the best choice. Do as she bids thee and quit thy seat in the car.

Clytaemestra

I have no leisure—mark me that—to dally with this woman here outside; for already the victims stand by the central hearth awaiting the sacrifice—a joy we never expected to be ours. As for thee, if thou wilt take any part therein, make no delay. But if, failing to understand, thou dost not catch my meaning, then, instead of speech, make sign with thy barbarian hand.

Chorus

'Tis an interpreter and a plain one that the stranger seems to need. She bears herself like a wild creature newly captured.

Clytaemestra

Nay, mad she is and hearkens to her wild mood, since she hath come hither from a city newly captured, and knoweth not how to brook the curb until she hath foamed away her fretfulness in blood. No! I will waste no more words upon her to be insulted thus. [*Exit*

ΧΟΡΟΣ

ἐγὼ δ', ἐποικτίρω[1] γάρ, οὐ θυμώσομαι.
ἴθ', ὦ τάλαινα, τόνδ' ἐρημώσασ' ὄχον,
εἴκουσ'[2] ἀνάγκῃ τῇδε καίνισον ζυγόν.

ΚΑΣΑΝΔΡΑ

ὀτοτοτοῖ πόποι δᾶ.[3] [στρ. α.
ὦπολλον ὦπολλον.[4]

ΧΟΡΟΣ

τί ταῦτ' ἀνωτότυξας ἀμφὶ Λοξίου;
οὐ γὰρ τοιοῦτος ὥστε θρηνητοῦ τυχεῖν.

ΚΑΣΑΝΔΡΑ

ὀτοτοτοῖ πόποι δᾶ. [ἀντ. α.
ὦπολλον ὦπολλον.

ΧΟΡΟΣ

ἡ δ' αὖτε δυσφημοῦσα τὸν θεὸν καλεῖ
οὐδὲν προσήκοντ' ἐν γόοις παραστατεῖν.

ΚΑΣΑΝΔΡΑ

Ἄπολλον Ἄπολλον [στρ. β.
ἀγυιᾶτ', ἀπόλλων ἐμός.
ἀπώλεσας γὰρ οὐ μόλις τὸ δεύτερον.

ΧΟΡΟΣ

χρήσειν ἔοικεν ἀμφὶ τῶν αὑτῆς[5] κακῶν.
μένει τὸ θεῖον δουλίᾳ περ ἐν[6] φρενί.

[1] ἐποικτείρω: Kirchhoff. [2] ἑκοῦσ': Rob. (Sophianus).
[3] ll. 1072, 1077 ὀτοτοτοτοῖ M.
[4] ll. 1073, 1077 ὤπολλον ὤπολλον M, ἄπολλον FN (ῶ over voc. N).
[5] αὐτῆς M. [6] παρ' ἐν M, παρὲν F, παρὸν N: Schütz.

CHORUS

But I will not be angry, since I pity her. Prithee, unhappy one, leave the car; yield to necessity and take upon thee this novel yoke.

CASSANDRA

Woe, woe, woe! O Apollo, O Apollo!

CHORUS

Wherefore thy cry of "woe" in Loxias' name? No god is he that hath to do with those who wail.

CASSANDRA

Woe, woe, woe! O Apollo, O Apollo!

CHORUS

Once more with ill-omened words she crieth upon the god whom it beseems not to be present at times of lamentation.

CASSANDRA

Apollo, Apollo! God of the Ways,[1] my destroyer! For thou hast destroyed me—and utterly—this second time.[2]

CHORUS

Methinks she is about to prophesy touching her own miseries. The gift divine still abides even in the soul of one enslaved.

[1] Cassandra sees an image of Apollo, the protector on journeys, close to the door leading to the street (ἀγυιά).

[2] Ἀπόλλων is here derived from ἀπόλλυμι, "destroy"—*nomen omen*. The god had "destroyed" her the first time in making vain his gift of prophecy (1209 ff.); whereby she became the object of derision in Troy.

ΚΑΣΑΝΔΡΑ

Ἄπολλον Ἄπολλον [ἀντ. β.
ἀγυιᾶτ', ἀπόλλων ἐμός.
ἆ ποῖ ποτ' ἤγαγές με; πρὸς ποίαν στέγην;

ΧΟΡΟΣ

πρὸς τὴν Ἀτρειδῶν· εἰ σὺ μὴ τόδ' ἐννοεῖς,
ἐγὼ λέγω σοι· καὶ τάδ' οὐκ ἐρεῖς ψύθη.

ΚΑΣΑΝΔΡΑ

[1]μισόθεον μὲν οὖν, πολλὰ συνίστορα[2] [στρ. γ.
αὐτόφονα κακὰ καρατόμα,[3]
ἀνδροσφαγεῖον[4] καὶ πεδορραντήριον.[5]

ΧΟΡΟΣ

ἔοικεν εὔρις ἡ ξένη κυνὸς δίκην
εἶναι, ματεύει[6] δ' ὧν ἀνευρήσει[7] φόνον.

ΚΑΣΑΝΔΡΑ

μαρτυρίοισι[8] γὰρ τοῖσδ' ἐπιπείθομαι·[9] [ἀντ. γ.
κλαιόμενα τάδε βρέφη σφαγάς,
ὀπτάς τε σάρκας πρὸς πατρὸς βεβρωμένας.

ΧΟΡΟΣ

τὸ μὲν[10] κλέος σοῦ μαντικὸν πεπυσμένοι
ἦμεν·[11] προφήτας δ' οὔτινας ματεύομεν.[12]

[1] ἆ ἆ prefixed in M, om. FN. [2] ξυνίστορα M.
[3] καρτάναι M, κἀρτάναι F, κἀρτάνας N: Kayser.
[4] ἀνδρὸς σφάγιον: Dobree (ἀνδροσφάγιον Casaub., σφάγειον Turn.).
[5] πέδον ῥαντηριον M²FN.

CASSANDRA

Apollo, Apollo! God of the Ways, my destroyer! Ah, what way is this that thou hast brought me! To what a house!

CHORUS

To that of Atreus' sons. If thou dost not perceive this, I'll tell it thee. And thou shalt not say 'tis untrue.

CASSANDRA

Nay, nay, rather to a house of Heaven loathed, a house that knoweth many a horrible butchery of kin, a human shambles and a floor swimming with blood.

CHORUS

Methinks the stranger is keen-scented as a hound; she is on the trail where she will discover blood.

CASSANDRA

Aye, here is the evidence wherein I put my trust! Behold yon babes bewailing their own butchery and their roasted flesh eaten by their sire!

CHORUS

Thy fame to read the future had reached our ears; but of prophets we are not in quest.

---

[6] *μαντεύει* M, *ματεύει* FN. [7] *ἂν εὑρήσῃ* M: Porson.
[8] *μαρτυρίοις*: Pauw. [9] *τοῖσδε πεπείθομαι*: Abresch.
[10] *'ἤμην* M (*ἦμεν* superscr.), *ἦμεν ἤγουν ἐσμέν* FNV3: Headlam.
[11] *ἡμὲν* M, *ἦμεν* FNV3. [12] *μαστεύομεν*: Schütz.

ΚΑΣΑΝΔΡΑ

ἰὼ πόποι, τί ποτε μήδεται; [στρ. δ.
τί τόδε νέον ἄχος μέγα
μέγ' ἐν δόμοισι τοῖσδε μήδεται κακὸν
ἄφερτον φίλοισιν, δυσίατον; ἀλκὰ δ'
ἑκὰς ἀποστατεῖ.

ΧΟΡΟΣ

τούτων ἄιδρίς εἰμι τῶν μαντευμάτων.
ἐκεῖνα δ' ἔγνων· πᾶσα γὰρ πόλις βοᾷ.

ΚΑΣΑΝΔΡΑ

ἰὼ τάλαινα, τόδε γὰρ τελεῖς, [ἀντ. δ.
τὸν ὁμοδέμνιον πόσιν
λουτροῖσι φαιδρύνασα—πῶς φράσω τέλος;
τάχος γὰρ τόδ' ἔσται· προτείνει δὲ χεὶρ ἐκ
χερὸς ὀρέγματα.[1]

ΧΟΡΟΣ

οὔπω ξυνῆκα· νῦν γὰρ ἐξ αἰνιγμάτων
ἐπαργέμοισι θεσφάτοις ἀμηχανῶ.

ΚΑΣΑΝΔΡΑ

ἒ ἔ, παπαῖ παπαῖ, τί τόδε φαίνεται; [στρ. ε.
ἦ δίκτυόν τι [γ'][2] Ἅιδου[3];
ἀλλ' ἄρκυς ἡ ξύνευνος, ἡ ξυναιτία
φόνου. στάσις δ' ἀκόρετος[4] γένει
κατολολυξάτω θύματος λευσίμου.

[1] ὀρεγόμενα M^1, ὀρεγομένα M^2, ὀρεγμένα FNV3: Herm. from Schol.
[2] [γ'] Dindorf. [3] ἀΐδου: Schütz. [4] ἀκόρεστος: Bothe.

CASSANDRA

O God, what can it be she purposeth[1]? What is this strange woe she purposeth here within, what monstrous, monstrous horror, beyond love's enduring, beyond all remedy? And help[2] stands far away!

CHORUS

These prophesyings pass my comprehension; but those I understood—the whole city rings with them.

CASSANDRA

Ah, fell woman, so thou wilt do this deed? Thy husband, the partner of thy bed, when thou hast cheered him with the bath, wilt thou—how shall I tell the end? Aye, soon it will be done. Now this hand, now that, she stretches forth!

CHORUS

Not yet do I comprehend; for now, after riddles, I am bewildered by dark oracles.

CASSANDRA

Ha! Ha! What apparition's this? Is it a net of death? Nay, she is a snare that shares his bed, that shares the guilt of murder. Let the fatal pack, insatiable against the race, raise a shout of jubilance over a victim accursed[3]!

[1] A play on the name Κλυταιμήστρα (μήδομαι).
[2] Menelaüs (cp. l. 674) or Orestes.
[3] Literally "fit for stoning."

ΧΟΡΟΣ

ποίαν Ἐρινὺν τήνδε δώμασιν κέλῃ
ἐπορθιάζειν; οὔ με φαιδρύνει λόγος.
ἐπὶ δὲ καρδίαν ἔδραμε κροκοβαφὴς
σταγών, ἅτε καιρία[1] πτώσιμος
ξυνανύτει βίου δύντος αὐγαῖς·
ταχεῖα δ' ἄτα πέλει.

ΚΑΣΑΝΔΡΑ

ἆ ἆ, ἰδοὺ ἰδού· ἄπεχε τῆς βοὸς [ἀντ. ε.
τὸν ταῦρον· ἐν πέπλοισι
μελαγκέρῳ[2] λαβοῦσα μηχανήματι
τύπτει· πίτνει δ' <ἐν>[3] ἐνύδρῳ τεύχει.
δολοφόνου λέβητος τύχαν σοι λέγω.

ΧΟΡΟΣ

οὐ κομπάσαιμ' ἂν θεσφάτων γνώμων ἄκρος
εἶναι, κακῷ δέ τῳ προσεικάζω τάδε.
ἀπὸ δὲ θεσφάτων τίς[4] ἀγαθὰ φάτις
βροτοῖς τέλλεται[5]; κακῶν γὰρ διαὶ[6]
πολυεπεῖς τέχναι θεσπιῳδὸν
φόβον φέρουσιν[7] μαθεῖν.

ΚΑΣΑΝΔΡΑ

ἰὼ ἰὼ ταλαίνας κακόποτμοι τύχαι· [στρ. ζ.
τὸ γὰρ ἐμὸν θροῶ πάθος ἐπεγχύδαν.[8]
ποῖ δή με δεῦρο τὴν τάλαιναν ἤγαγες;
οὐδέν ποτ' εἰ μὴ ξυνθανουμένην. τί γάρ;

[1] καὶ δορία M, καὶ δωρία FV3, δωρίᾱ N: Dindorf.

[2] μελάγκέρων with ν changed to ι, and ν superscr. M, μελάγκερων FNV3.

[3] <ἐν> Schütz.

Chorus

What Spirit of Vengeance is this thou dost bid raise high its voice o'er this house? Thy utterance cheers me not. Back to my heart surge the drops of my pallid blood, even as when they drip from a mortal wound, ebbing away as life's beams sink low; and death cometh speedily.

Cassandra

Ha, ha, see there, see there! Keep the bull from his mate! She hath caught him in the robe and gores him with the crafty device of her black horn! He falls in a vessel of water! It is of doom wrought by guile in a murderous bath that I am telling thee.

Chorus

I cannot vaunt myself a keen judge of prophecies; but these, methinks, spell some evil. But from prophecies what word of good ever comes to mortals? Through terms of evil their wordy arts bring men to know fear chanted in prophetic strains.

Cassandra

Alas, alas, the sorrow of my ill-starred doom! For 'tis mine own affliction, crowning the cup, that I bewail. Ah, to what end didst thou bring me hither, unhappy that I am? For naught save to die—and not alone. What else?

---

[4] τις M, τίς FV3. [5] στέλλεται: Emperius.
[6] διὰ M, δὴ αἱ FNV3: Herm. [7] φέρουσι M.
[8] ἐπεγχέασα M, ἐπαγχέασα FNV3: Headlam.

ΧΟΡΟΣ

φρενομανής τις εἶ θεοφόρητος, ἀμφὶ δ' αὐτᾶς θροεῖς
νόμον ἄνομον, οἷά[1] τις ξουθὰ
ἀκόρετος[2] βοᾶς,[3] φεῦ, ταλαίναις[4] φρεσὶν
Ἴτυν Ἴτυν στένουσ' ἀμφιθαλῆ κακοῖς
ἀηδὼν βίον.

ΚΑΣΑΝΔΡΑ

ἰὼ ἰὼ λιγείας μόρον ἀηδόνος·[5] [ἀντ. ζ.
περέβαλον[6] γάρ οἱ πτεροφόρον δέμας
θεοὶ γλυκύν τ' αἰῶνα[7] κλαυμάτων ἄτερ·
ἐμοὶ δὲ μίμνει σχισμὸς ἀμφήκει δορί.

ΧΟΡΟΣ

πόθεν ἐπισσύτους θεοφόρους [τ'][8] ἔχεις
ματαίους δύας,
τὰ δ' ἐπίφοβα[9] δυσφάτῳ κλαγγᾷ
μελοτυπεῖς ὁμοῦ τ' ὀρθίοις ἐν νόμοις;
πόθεν ὅρους ἔχεις θεσπεσίας ὁδοῦ
κακορρήμονας;

ΚΑΣΑΝΔΡΑ

ἰὼ γάμοι γάμοι Πάριδος ὀλέθριοι φίλων. [στρ. η.
ἰὼ Σκαμάνδρου πάτριον ποτόν.
τότε μὲν ἀμφὶ σὰς ἀιόνας τάλαιν'
ἠνυτόμαν τροφαῖς·[10]
νῦν δ' ἀμφὶ Κωκυτόν τε κἀχερουσίους
ὄχθας[11] ἔοικα θεσπιῳδήσειν τάχα.

[1] οἵα M. [2] ἀκόρεστος: Aldina. [3] βοαῖς M.
[4] φεῦ ταλαίναις M, φιλοίκτοις ταλαίναις FV3, φιλοίκτοισι N.

CHORUS

Frenzied in soul thou art, by some god possessed, and dost wail in wild strains thine own fate, like some brown nightingale that never ceases making lament (ah me!), and in the misery of her heart moans *Itys*, *Itys*, throughout all her days abounding in sorrow.

CASSANDRA

Ah, fate of the tuneful nightingale! The gods clothed her in winged form and gave to her a sweet life without tears.[1] But for me waiteth destruction by the two-edged sword.

CHORUS

Whence come these vain pangs of prophecy that assail thee? And wherefore dost thou mould to melody these terrors with dismal cries blent with piercing strains? Whence knowest thou the bounds of the path of thine ill-boding prophecy?

CASSANDRA

Ah, bridal, bridal of Paris, fraught with ruin to his kin! Ah me, Scamander, my native stream! Upon thy banks in byegone days, unhappy maid, was I nurtured with fostering care; now by Cocytus and the banks of Acheron, methinks, I soon must chant my prophecies.

[1] The wailing (l. 1144) of the bird is unconscious (Schol.).

---

[5] *ἀηδόνος μόρον*: Herm.
[6] *περεβάλοντο* M, *περιβαλόντες* FNV3: Herm.
[7] *ἀγῶνα* MFNV3, *αἰῶνα* M *γρ.* [8] [*τ'*] Herm.
[9] *ἐπίφοβα* M^1, *ἐπὶ φόβῳ* $M^2F^2N^2V3^2$.
[10] M ends, ll. 1160-1673 in FNV3. [11] *ὄχθους*: Casaubon.

ΧΟΡΟΣ

τί τόδε τορὸν ἄγαν ἔπος ἐφημίσω;
νεόγονος ἂν ἀίων[1] μάθοι.
πέπληγμαι δ' ὑπαὶ[2] δάκει[3] φοινίῳ
δυσαλγεῖ[4] τύχᾳ μινυρὰ [κακὰ][5] θρεομένας·
θραυματ'[6] ἐμοὶ κλύειν.

ΚΑΣΑΝΔΡΑ

ἰὼ πόνοι πόνοι πόλεος ὀλομένας[7] τὸ πᾶν. [ἀντ. η.
ἰὼ πρόπυργοι θυσίαι πατρὸς
πολυκανεῖς βοτῶν ποιονόμων· ἄκος δ'
οὐδὲν ἐπήρκεσαν
τὸ μὴ πόλιν μὲν ὥσπερ οὖν ἔχει[8] παθεῖν.
ἐγὼ δὲ θερμόνους τάχ' ἐν πέδῳ[9] βαλῶ.

ΧΟΡΟΣ

ἑπόμενα προτέροισι[10] τάδ' ἐφημίσω.
καί τίς σε κακοφρονῶν[11] τίθη-
σι δαίμων ὑπερβαρὴς ἐμπίτνων
μελίζειν πάθη γοερὰ θανατοφόρα.
τέρμα δ' ἀμηχανῶ.

ΚΑΣΑΝΔΡΑ

καὶ μὴν ὁ χρησμὸς οὐκέτ' ἐκ καλυμμάτων
ἔσται δεδορκὼς νεογάμου νύμφης[12] δίκην·
λαμπρὸς δ' ἔοικεν ἡλίου πρὸς ἀντολὰς
πνέων ἐσᾴξειν,[13] ὥστε κύματος δίκην
κλύζειν[14] πρὸς αὐγὰς τοῦδε πήματος πολὺ
μεῖζον· φρενώσω δ' οὐκέτ' ἐξ αἰνιγμάτων.

[1] νεόγονος ἀνθρώπων: Karsten.
[2] ὑπαὶ N, ὑπὸ FV3.
[3] δήγματι: Herm.

Chorus

What words are these thou utterest, words all too plain? A new-born child hearing them could understand. I am smitten with a deadly pain, the while, by reason of thy cruel fortune, thou criest aloud thy piteous plaint that breaks my heart to hear.

Cassandra

O travail, travail of my city utterly destroyed! Alas, the sacrifices my father offered, the many pasturing kine slain to save its towers! Yet they availed naught to save the city from suffering even as it hath; and I, my soul on fire, must soon fall to the ground.

Chorus

Thy present speech chimes with thy former strain. Surely some spirit malign, falling upon thee with heavy swoop, moveth thee to chant thy piteous woes fraught with death. But the end I am helpless to discover.

Cassandra

Lo now, no more shall my prophecy peer forth from behind a veil like a new-wedded bride; but 'tis like to rush upon me clear as a fresh wind blowing against the sun's uprising so as to dash against its rays, like a wave, a woe mightier far than mine. No more by riddles will I instruct you. And do ye bear

---

[4] δυσαγγεῖ: Canter. [5] [κακὰ] Schütz.
[6] θραύματ' FV3, θαύματ' N.
[7] ὀλωμένας FV3, ὀλουμένας N: Casaubon.
[8] ἔχει N, ἔχειν FV3. [9] ἐμπέδῳ: Casaubon.
[10] προτέροις: Pauw. [11] κακοφρονεῖν: Schütz.
[12] νύμφας F, νύμφης NV3.
[13] ἐς ἧξειν: Bothe. [14] κλύειν: Auratus.

καὶ μαρτυρεῖτε συνδρόμως ἴχνος κακῶν
ῥινηλατούσῃ τῶν πάλαι πεπραγμένων.
τὴν γὰρ στέγην τήνδ᾽ οὔποτ᾽ ἐκλείπει χορὸς
ξύμφθογγος[1] οὐκ εὔφωνος· οὐ γὰρ εὖ λέγει.
καὶ μὴν πεπωκώς γ᾽, ὡς θρασύνεσθαι πλέον,
βρότειον αἷμα κῶμος ἐν δόμοις μένει,
δύσπεμπτος ἔξω, συγγόνων Ἐρινύων.[2]
ὑμνοῦσι δ᾽ ὕμνον δώμασιν προσήμεναι
πρώταρχον[3] ἄτην· ἐν μέρει δ᾽ ἀπέπτυσαν
εὐνὰς ἀδελφοῦ τῷ πατοῦντι δυσμενεῖς.
ἥμαρτον, ἢ θηρῶ[4] τι τοξότης τις ὥς;
ἢ ψευδόμαντίς εἰμι θυροκόπος φλέδων;
ἐκμαρτύρησον προυμόσας τό μ᾽ εἰδέναι
λόγῳ παλαιὰς τῶνδ᾽ ἁμαρτίας δόμων.

ΧΟΡΟΣ

καὶ πῶς ἂν ὅρκος, πῆγμα[5] γενναίως παγέν,
παιώνιον γένοιτο; θαυμάζω δέ σου,
πόντου πέραν τραφεῖσαν ἀλλόθρουν πόλιν
κυρεῖν λέγουσαν, ὥσπερ εἰ παρεστάτεις.

ΚΑΣΑΝΔΡΑ

μάντις μ᾽ Ἀπόλλων τῷδ᾽ ἐπέστησεν τέλει.

ΧΟΡΟΣ

1204 μῶν καὶ θεός περ ἱμέρῳ πεπληγμένος;

ΚΑΣΑΝΔΡΑ

1203 προτοῦ μὲν αἰδὼς ἦν ἐμοὶ λέγειν τάδε.[6]

[1] ξύμφθογγος N, σύμ φογγος F, ξύμφογγος V3.
[2] ἐριννύων : Blomfield.
[3] πρώταρχον N, πρώταρχος FV3.
[4] τηρῶ : Canter. [5] πῆμα : Auratus.

me witness, as, coursing close behind, I scent the track of crimes wrought in days of yore. For from this roof doth never depart a choir chanting in unison, but unmelodious; for it telleth not of good. And lo, having quaffed human blood, to be the more emboldened, a revel-rout of kindred Furies haunteth the house, hard to be driven forth. Lodged within its halls they chant their chant, the primal sin; and, each in turn, they spurn with loathing a brother's bed, for that they are bitter with wroth against him that defiled it.[1] Have I missed the mark, or, like true archer, do I strike my quarry? Or am I prophet of lies, a babbler from door to door? Bear witness upon thine oath that I do know the deeds of sin, ancient in story, of this house.

CHORUS

How could an oath, a pledge albeit plighted in honour, work aught of cure? Yet I marvel at thee that, though bred beyond the sea, thou dost speak sooth of a foreign city, even as if thou hadst been present there.

CASSANDRA

It was the seer Apollo who appointed me to this office.

CHORUS

Can it be that he, a god, was smitten with desire?

CASSANDRA

Ere now I was ashamed to speak of this.

[1] Thyestes' corruption of Aërope, wife of his brother Atreus.

[6] ll. 1203, 1204 transposed by Herm.

ΧΟΡΟΣ

ἁβρύνεται γὰρ πᾶς τις εὖ πράσσων πλέον.

ΚΑΣΑΝΔΡΑ

ἀλλ' ἦν παλαιστὴς κάρτ' ἐμοὶ πνέων χάριν.

ΧΟΡΟΣ

ἦ καὶ τέκνων εἰς ἔργον ἠλθέτην νόμῳ;

ΚΑΣΑΝΔΡΑ

ξυναινέσασα Λοξίαν ἐψευσάμην.

ΧΟΡΟΣ

ἤδη τέχναισιν ἐνθέοις ᾑρημένη;

ΚΑΣΑΝΔΡΑ

ἤδη πολίταις πάντ' ἐθέσπιζον πάθη.

ΧΟΡΟΣ

πῶς δῆτ' ἄνατος[1] ἦσθα Λοξίου κότῳ;

ΚΑΣΑΝΔΡΑ

ἔπειθον οὐδέν' οὐδέν,[2] ὡς τάδ' ἤμπλακον.

ΧΟΡΟΣ

ἡμῖν γε μὲν δὴ πιστὰ θεσπίζειν δοκεῖς.

[1] ἄνακτος: Canter. [2] οὐδὲν οὐδὲν: Canter.

CHORUS

Aye, in prosperity we all grow over nice.

CASSANDRA

Oh, but he struggled to win me, breathing ardent love for me.

CHORUS

Came ye in due course to wedlock's rite?

CASSANDRA

I promised consent to Loxias but broke my word.

CHORUS

Wert thou already possessed by the art inspired of the god?

CASSANDRA

Already I prophesied to my countrymen all their disasters.

CHORUS

How came it then that thou wert unscathed by Loxias' wrath?

CASSANDRA

Ever since that fault I could persuade no one of aught.

CHORUS

And yet to us at least the prophecies thou utterest seem true enough.

ΚΑΣΑΝΔΡΑ

ἰοὺ ἰού, ὢ ὢ κακά.
ὑπ᾽ αὖ με δεινὸς ὀρθομαντείας πόνος
στροβεῖ ταράσσων φροιμίοις <δυσφροιμίοις>.[1]
ὁρᾶτε τούσδε τοὺς δόμοις ἐφημένους
νέους, ὀνείρων προσφερεῖς μορφώμασιν;
παῖδες θανόντες ὡσπερεὶ πρὸς τῶν φίλων,
χεῖρας κρεῶν πλήθοντες οἰκείας βορᾶς,
σὺν ἐντέροις τε σπλάγχν᾽, ἐποίκτιστον γέμος,
πρέπουσ᾽ ἔχοντες, ὧν πατὴρ ἐγεύσατο.
ἐκ τῶνδε ποινὰς φημὶ βουλεύειν τινὰ
λέοντ᾽ ἄναλκιν ἐν λέχει στρωφώμενον
οἰκουρόν, οἴμοι, τῷ μολόντι δεσπότῃ
ἐμῷ· φέρειν γὰρ χρὴ τὸ δούλιον ζυγόν·
νεῶν τ᾽ ἄπαρχος Ἰλίου τ᾽ ἀναστάτης
οὐκ οἶδεν οἷα γλῶσσα μισητῆς κυνὸς
λείξασα κἀκτείνασα φαιδρὸν οὖς,[2] δίκην
Ἄτης λαθραίου, τεύξεται κακῇ τύχῃ.
τοιάδε[3] τόλμα·[4] θῆλυς ἄρσενος φονεὺς
ἔστιν. τί νιν καλοῦσα δυσφιλὲς δάκος
τύχοιμ᾽ ἄν; ἀμφίσβαιναν, ἢ Σκύλλαν τινὰ
οἰκοῦσαν ἐν πέτραισι, ναυτίλων βλάβην,
θύουσαν Ἅιδου μητέρ᾽ ἄσπονδόν τ᾽ Ἄρη[5]
φίλοις πνέουσαν; ὡς δ᾽ ἐπωλολύξατο
ἡ παντότολμος, ὥσπερ ἐν μάχης τροπῇ,
δοκεῖ δὲ χαίρειν νοστίμῳ σωτηρίᾳ.
καὶ τῶνδ᾽ ὅμοιον εἴ τι μὴ πείθω· τί γάρ;

[1] φροιμίοις ἐφημένους FV3N[1] (-μένοις N[2]): ἐφημ. del. Butler, δυσφρ. add. Herm.

[2] λέξασα καὶ κτείνασα φαιδρόνους: λείξασα Tyrwhitt, κἀκτείνασα Canter, φαιδρὸν οὖς H. L. Ahrens.

[3] τοιαῦτα N. [4] τολμᾶ FV3, τολμᾷ N: H. L. Ahrens.

[5] ἀρὰν: Ἄρη Franz, Ἄρην Anonymus.

Cassandra

Ha, ha! Oh, oh, the agony! Once more the dreadful throes of true prophecy whirl and distract me with their ill-boding onset. Mark ye those yonder—sitting before the house—young creatures like unto phantoms of dreams? Children, they seem, slaughtered by their own kindred, their hands full of the meat of their own flesh; clear to my sight are they, holding their vitals and their inward parts (piteous burthen!), whereof their father tasted. 'Tis for this cause I tell you that vengeance is plotted by a dastard lion wallowing in his couch, keeping ward of the house (ah me!) against my master's coming home—aye, my master, for I needs must bear the yoke of slavery. The commander of the fleet and the overthrower of Ilium little knows what deeds shall be brought to evil accomplishment by the hateful hound, whose tongue licked his hand, who stretched forth her ears in gladness, like treacherous Ate. Such boldness hath she—a woman to slay a man. What odious monster shall I fitly call her? An amphisbaena[1]? Or a Scylla, tenanting the rocks, a pest of mariners, a raging, devilish dam, breathing relentless war against her lord? And how the all-daring woman raised a shout of triumph, like as when the battle turns, the while she feigned to joy at his safe return! And yet, 'tis all one, whether or not I win belief. What matters

[1] Amphisbaena, a fabulous snake "moving both ways," backwards and forwards. Tennyson's "an amphisbaena, each end a sting," reproduces Pliny's description.

τὸ μέλλον ἥξει. καὶ σύ μ' ἐν τάχει[1] παρὼν
ἄγαν γ' ἀληθόμαντιν οἰκτίρας[2] ἐρεῖς.

ΧΟΡΟΣ

τὴν μὲν Θυέστου δαῖτα παιδείων[3] κρεῶν
ξυνῆκα καὶ πέφρικα, καὶ φόβος μ' ἔχει
κλύοντ' ἀληθῶς οὐδὲν ἐξῃκασμένα.
τὰ δ' ἄλλ' ἀκούσας ἐκ δρόμου πεσὼν τρέχω.

ΚΑΣΑΝΔΡΑ

Ἀγαμέμνονός σέ φημ' ἐπόψεσθαι μόρον.

ΧΟΡΟΣ

εὔφημον, ὦ τάλαινα, κοίμησον στόμα.

ΚΑΣΑΝΔΡΑ

ἀλλ' οὔτι παιὼν τῷδ' ἐπιστατεῖ λόγῳ.

ΧΟΡΟΣ

οὔκ, εἴπερ ἔσται[4] γ'· ἀλλὰ μὴ γένοιτό πως.

ΚΑΣΑΝΔΡΑ

σὺ μὲν κατεύχῃ, τοῖς δ' ἀποκτείνειν μέλει.

ΧΟΡΟΣ

τίνος πρὸς ἀνδρὸς τοῦτ' ἄγος[5] πορσύνεται;

ΚΑΣΑΝΔΡΑ

ἦ κάρτα τἄρ' ἂν παρεκόπης[6] χρησμῶν ἐμῶν.

[1] μὴν τάχει: Auratus.
[2] οἰκτείρας: Kirchhoff.
[3] παιδίων: Schütz.
[4] εἰ παρέσται: Schütz.
[5] ἄχος: Auratus.

it? What is to come, will come. Soon thou, present here thyself, shalt of thy pity pronounce me all too true a prophetess.

CHORUS

Thyestes' banquet on his children's flesh I understood and I tremble. Terror possesses me as I hear the truth, naught fashioned out of falsehood to resemble truth. But at the rest I heard I am thrown off the track.

CASSANDRA

I say thou shalt look upon Agamemnon dead.

CHORUS

To words propitious, hapless maiden, lull thy speech.

CASSANDRA

Nay, over what I tell no healing god presides.

CHORUS

No, if it is to be; but God forbid!

CASSANDRA

Thou dost but pray; their business is to slay.

CHORUS

What man is he that contrived this wickedness?

CASSANDRA

Surely thou must have missed the meaning of my prophecies.

---

[6] *κάρτ' ἄρ' ἂν παρεσκόπεις* F[1], *παρεσκόπῃς* F[2]N: *κάρτα τἄρα* (*κάρτα τἄρ' ἂν* Sidgwick) *παρεκόπης* Hartung.

ΧΟΡΟΣ

τοῦ γὰρ τελοῦντος οὐ ξυνῆκα μηχανήν.

ΚΑΣΑΝΔΡΑ

καὶ μὴν ἄγαν γ᾽ Ἕλλην᾽ ἐπίσταμαι φάτιν.

ΧΟΡΟΣ

καὶ γὰρ τὰ πυθόκραντα· δυσμαθῆ[1] δ᾽ ὅμως.

ΚΑΣΑΝΔΡΑ

παπαῖ, οἷον τὸ πῦρ· ἐπέρχεται δέ μοι.
ὀτοτοῖ, Λύκει᾽ Ἄπολλον, οἳ ἐγὼ ἐγώ.
αὕτη δίπους[2] λέαινα συγκοιμωμένη
λύκῳ, λέοντος εὐγενοῦς ἀπουσίᾳ,
κτενεῖ με τὴν τάλαιναν· ὡς δὲ φάρμακον
τεύχουσα κἀμοῦ μισθὸν ἐνθήσειν[3] κότῳ
ἐπεύχεται, θήγουσα φωτὶ φάσγανον
ἐμῆς ἀγωγῆς ἀντιτείσασθαι[4] φόνον.
τί δῆτ᾽ ἐμαυτῆς καταγέλωτ᾽ ἔχω τάδε,
καὶ σκῆπτρα καὶ μαντεῖα περὶ δέρῃ στέφη;
σὲ μὲν πρὸ μοίρας τῆς ἐμῆς διαφθερῶ.
ἴτ᾽ ἐς φθόρον· πεσόντα γ᾽ ὧδ᾽[5] ἀμείβομαι.[6]
ἄλλην τιν᾽ ἄτης[7] ἀντ᾽ ἐμοῦ πλουτίζετε.
ἰδοὺ δ᾽ Ἀπόλλων αὐτὸς ἐκδύων ἐμὲ
χρηστηρίαν ἐσθῆτ᾽, ἐποπτεύσας[8] δέ με
κἀν τοῖσδε κόσμοις καταγελωμένην μέγα[9]
φίλων ὑπ᾽ ἐχθρῶν οὐ διχορρόπως, μάτην—

[1] δυσπαθῆ FV3, δυσμαθῆ N. [2] δίπλους: Vict.
[3] ἐνθήσει FN[1], ἐνθήσειν N[2].
[4] ἀντιτίσασθαι: Headlam.
[5] πεσόντ᾽ · ἀγαθῷ δ᾽: Blomfield.
[6] ἀμείβομαι F[1], ἀμείψομαι F[2]NV3.

CHORUS

Aye, since I do not understand the scheme of him who is to do the deed.

CASSANDRA

And yet all too well I know the speech of Hellas.

CHORUS

So too do the Pythian oracles; yet they are hard to understand.

CASSANDRA

Oh, oh! What fire! It comes upon me! Woe, woe! Lycean Apollo! Ah me, ah me! This two-footed lioness, who couches with a wolf in the absence of the noble lion, will slay me, wretched that I am. Brewing as it were a drug, she vows that with her wrath she will mix requital for me too, while she whets her sword against her lord, to take murderous vengeance for my bringing hither. Why then do I bear these mockeries of myself, this wand, these prophetic chaplets on my neck? [*Breaking her wand, she throws it and the other insignia of her prophetic office upon the ground, and tramples them under foot.*] Thee at least I will destroy before I die myself. To destruction with you! And fallen there, thus do I avenge myself on you. Enrich with doom some other in my stead. Lo, Apollo's self is stripping me of my prophetic garb—he that looked on me mocked to bitter scorn, even in this bravery, by friends turned foes, with one accord, without cause—

---

[7] ἄτην: Stanley. [8] ἐπώπτευσας N.
[9] μέτα: Herm.

καλουμένη δὲ φοιτὰς ὡς ἀγύρτρια
πτωχὸς τάλαινα λιμοθνὴς ἠνεσχόμην—
καὶ νῦν ὁ μάντις μάντιν ἐκπράξας ἐμὲ
ἀπήγαγ᾽ ἐς τοιάσδε θανασίμους τύχας.
βωμοῦ πατρῴου δ᾽ ἀντ᾽ ἐπίξηνον[1] μένει,
θερμῷ κοπείσης φοινίῳ προσφάγματι.
οὐ μὴν ἄτιμοί γ᾽ ἐκ θεῶν τεθνήξομεν.
ἥξει γὰρ ἡμῶν ἄλλος αὖ τιμάορος,
μητροκτόνον φίτυμα, ποινάτωρ πατρός·
φυγὰς δ᾽ ἀλήτης τῆσδε γῆς ἀπόξενος
κάτεισιν, ἄτας τάσδε θριγκώσων φίλοις·
ὀμώμοται γὰρ ὅρκος ἐκ θεῶν μέγας,[2]
ἄξειν[3] νιν ὑπτίασμα κειμένου πατρός.
τί δῆτ᾽ ἐγὼ κάτοικτος[4] ὧδ᾽ ἀναστένω;
ἐπεὶ τὸ πρῶτον εἶδον[5] Ἰλίου πόλιν
πράξασαν ὡς ἔπραξεν, οἳ δ᾽ εἷλον πόλιν
οὕτως ἀπαλλάσσουσιν ἐν θεῶν κρίσει,
ἰοῦσα πράξω· τλήσομαι τὸ κατθανεῖν.
1284 Ἅιδου πύλας δὲ τάσδ᾽ ἐγὼ[6] προσεννέπω·
ἐπεύχομαι δὲ καιρίας πληγῆς τυχεῖν,
ὡς ἀσφάδαστος, αἱμάτων εὐθνησίμων
ἀπορρυέντων, ὄμμα συμβάλω τόδε.

ΧΟΡΟΣ

ὦ πολλὰ μὲν τάλαινα, πολλὰ δ᾽ αὖ σοφὴ
γύναι, μακρὰν ἔτεινας. εἰ δ᾽ ἐτητύμως
μόρον τὸν αὐτῆς οἶσθα, πῶς θεηλάτου
βοὸς δίκην πρὸς βωμὸν εὐτόλμως πατεῖς;

[1] ἀντεπίξηνον: Schütz.
[2] l. 1284 after 1290: transposed by Herm.
[3] ἄξειν F, ἄξει NV3. [4] κάτοικος: Scaliger.
[5] εἶχον: Musgrave.

but, like some vagrant mountebank, called "beggar," "wretch," "starveling," I bore it all—. And now the prophet, having undone me, his prophetess, hath brought me to this deadly pass. In place of my father's altar a block awaits me, butchered by the hot stroke of bloody sacrifice. Yet, unavenged of Heaven, shall we not die; for there shall come in turn another, our avenger, a scion of the race, to slay his mother and exact requital for his sire; an exile, a wanderer, strangered from this land, he shall return to put the coping-stone upon these infatuate iniquities of his house. For a mighty oath hath been sworn of the gods that his slain father's outstretched corpse shall bring him home. Why then thus raise my voice in piteous lament? Since at the first I saw the city of Ilium meet the fate it hath, while her captors, by Heaven's sentence, are come to such an end, I will go in and meet my fate. I will dare to die. This portal I greet as the gates of Death. And I pray that, dealt a mortal stroke, without a struggle, my life-blood ebbing away in easy death, I may close these eyes.

CHORUS

O woman, pitiable exceedingly and exceeding wise, long hath been thy speech. But if, in very truth, thou hast knowledge of thine own death, how canst thou step with calm courage to the altar like an ox destined of God to the sacrifice?

---

[6] *τὰς λέγω*: Auratus. [7] *δ' αὖ* N, *δὲ* FV3.

ΚΑΣΑΝΔΡΑ

οὐκ ἔστ' ἄλυξις, οὔ, ξένοι, χρόνον[1] πλέω.[2]

ΧΟΡΟΣ

ὁ δ' ὕστατός γε τοῦ χρόνου πρεσβεύεται.

ΚΑΣΑΝΔΡΑ

ἥκει τόδ' ἦμαρ· σμικρὰ κερδανῶ φυγῇ.

ΧΟΡΟΣ

ἀλλ' ἴσθι τλήμων οὖσ' ἀπ' εὐτόλμου φρενός.

ΚΑΣΑΝΔΡΑ

οὐδεὶς ἀκούει ταῦτα τῶν εὐδαιμόνων.

ΧΟΡΟΣ

ἀλλ' εὐκλεῶς τοι κατθανεῖν χάρις βροτῷ.

ΚΑΣΑΝΔΡΑ

ἰὼ πάτερ σοῦ σῶν[3] τε γενναίων τέκνων.

ΧΟΡΟΣ

τί δ' ἐστὶ χρῆμα; τίς σ' ἀποστρέφει φόβος;

ΚΑΣΑΝΔΡΑ

φεῦ φεῦ.

ΧΟΡΟΣ

τί τοῦτ' ἔφευξας; εἴ τι μὴ φρενῶν στύγος.

[1] χρόνῳ: Herm. [2] πλέω FV3, πλέῳ N.
[3] τῶν: Auratus.

CASSANDRA

There is no escape; no, my friends, there is none any more.[1]

CHORUS

Yet he that is last has the advantage in respect of time.

CASSANDRA

The day is come ; flight would profit me but little.

CHORUS

Well, be assured, thou bravest suffering with a courageous spirit.

CASSANDRA

None who is happy is commended thus.

CHORUS

Yet surely to die nobly is a boon for mortals.

CASSANDRA

Alas for thee, my father and for thy noble children!

[*She starts back in horror*

CHORUS

What aileth thee ? What terror turns thee back ?

CASSANDRA

Faugh, faugh !

CHORUS

Why criest thou " faugh " ? Unless perchance there be some horror in thy soul.

[1] Auratus read χρόνου πλέων : "more than that of time," "save for time."

ΚΑΣΑΝΔΡΑ

φόνον[1] δόμοι πνέουσιν αἱματοσταγῆ.

ΧΟΡΟΣ

καὶ πῶς; τόδ᾽ ὄζει θυμάτων ἐφεστίων.

ΚΑΣΑΝΔΡΑ

ὅμοιος ἀτμὸς ὥσπερ ἐκ τάφου πρέπει.

ΧΟΡΟΣ

οὐ Σύριον ἀγλάισμα δώμασιν λέγεις.

ΚΑΣΑΝΔΡΑ

ἀλλ᾽ εἶμι κἀν δόμοισι κωκύσουσ᾽ ἐμὴν
᾽Αγαμέμνονός τε μοῖραν. ἀρκείτω βίος.
ἰὼ ξένοι,
οὔτοι δυσοίζω θάμνον ὡς ὄρνις φόβῳ
ἄλλως·[2] θανούσῃ μαρτυρεῖτέ μοι τόδε,
ὅταν γυνὴ γυναικὸς ἀντ᾽ ἐμοῦ θάνῃ,
ἀνήρ τε δυσδάμαρτος ἀντ᾽ ἀνδρὸς πέσῃ.
ἐπιξενοῦμαι ταῦτα δ᾽ ὡς θανουμένη.

ΧΟΡΟΣ

ὦ τλῆμον, οἰκτίρω[3] σε θεσφάτου μόρου.

ΚΑΣΑΝΔΡΑ

ἅπαξ ἔτ᾽ εἰπεῖν ῥῆσιν ἢ[4] θρῆνον θέλω
ἐμὸν τὸν αὐτῆς. ἡλίῳ δ᾽ ἐπεύχομαι

[1] *φόνον* N[2], *φόβον* FV3N[1].
[2] *ἀλλ᾽ ὡς*: Herm.
[3] *οἰκτείρω*: Kirchhoff.
[4] *ἢ*: *οὐ* Herm. (cp. *v.l.* *Eum.* 426).

CASSANDRA

The house reeks with blood-dripping slaughter.

CHORUS

What wouldst thou ? 'Tis but the savour of victims at the hearth.

CASSANDRA

'Tis like a breath from a charnel-house.

CHORUS

Not of proud Syrian incense for the house dost thou speak.

CASSANDRA

Nay, I will go to bewail also within the palace mine own and Agamemnon's fate. Enough of life ! Alas, my friends, not with vain terror do I shrink, as bird that misdoubteth bush. After I am dead, do ye bear witness for me of this—when for me, a woman, another woman shall be slain, and for an ill-wedded man another man shall fall. I claim this boon from you now that my hour is come.

CHORUS

Poor woman, I pity thee for thy death foretold.

CASSANDRA

Yet once more I am fain to speak, but not mine own dirge. I pray unto the sun, in presence of his

πρὸς ὕστατον φῶς †τοῖς ἐμοῖς τιμαόροις
ἐχθροῖς φονεῦσι τοῖς ἐμοῖς τίνειν ὁμοῦ,†
δούλης θανούσης, εὐμαροῦς χειρώματος.
ἰὼ βρότεια πράγματ᾽· εὐτυχοῦντα μὲν
σκιά τις ἂν τρέψειεν·[1] εἰ δὲ δυστυχῇ,
βολαῖς ὑγρώσσων σπόγγος ὤλεσεν γραφήν.
καὶ ταῦτ᾽ ἐκείνων μᾶλλον οἰκτίρω[2] πολύ.

ΧΟΡΟΣ

τὸ μὲν εὖ πράσσειν[3] ἀκόρεστον ἔφυ
πᾶσι βροτοῖσιν·[4] δακτυλοδείκτων δ᾽
οὔτις ἀπειπὼν εἴργει μελάθρων,
μηκέτ᾽ ἐσέλθῃς,[5] τάδε φωνῶν.
καὶ τῷδε πόλιν μὲν ἑλεῖν ἔδοσαν
μάκαρες Πριάμου·
θεοτίμητος δ᾽ οἴκαδ᾽ ἱκάνει.
νῦν δ᾽ εἰ προτέρων αἷμ᾽ ἀποτείσῃ[6]
καὶ τοῖσι θανοῦσι θανὼν ἄλλων
ποινὰς θανάτων ἐπικράνῃ,[7]
τίς ἂν <ἐξ>εύξαιτο[8] βροτῶν ἀσινεῖ
δαίμονι φῦναι τάδ᾽ ἀκούων;

ΑΓΑΜΕΜΝΩΝ

ὤμοι, πέπληγμαι καιρίαν πληγὴν ἔσω.

1 ἀντρέψειεν: Porson. 2 οἰκτείρω: Kirchhoff.
3 πράττειν: Porson. 4 βροτοῖς: Pauw.
5 μηκέτι δ᾽ εἰσέλθῃς: Herm.
6 ἀποτίσει: -τίσῃ Sidgwick, -τείσει Kirchhoff.
7 ἐπικρανεῖ: Sidgwick. 8 εὔξαιτο: Schneidewin.

latest light, that mine enemies[1] may at the same time pay to my avengers a bloody penalty for slaughtering a slave, an easy prey. Alas for human fortune! When prosperous, a mere shadow can overturn it;[2] if calamitous, the dash of a wet sponge blots out the drawing. And this last I deem far more pitiable than that. [*Enters the palace*

Chorus

'Tis the nature of all human kind to be unsatisfied with prosperity. From stately halls none barreth it with warning voice that uttereth the words "Enter no more." So unto our prince the Blessed Ones have granted to capture Priam's town; and, honoured of Heaven, he returns to his home. Yet if he now must pay the penalty for the blood shed by others before him, and by dying for the dead he is to bring to pass retribution of other deaths,[3] what mortal man, on hearing this, can boast that he was born with scatheless destiny?

[*A shriek is heard from within*

Agamemnon

Ay me! I am smitten deep with a mortal blow!

[1] Of this corrupt passage no emendation yet made commends itself irresistibly. The translation is based on the reading ἐχθροὺς φόνευσιν τοὺς ἐμούς, where φόνευσιν is due to Bothe, the rest to J. Pearson.

[2] Some editors, altering the passage to σκιᾷ τις ἂν πρέψειεν, "one may liken it to a shadow," understand "shadow" either literally or as a "sketch."

[3] If Agamemnon is now to pay the price for his father's killing of Thyestes' children, and by his own death is to atone for his slaying of Iphigenia, and is thus to bring about requital consisting in yet other deaths (Clytaemestra and Aegisthus).

ΧΟΡΟΣ

σῖγα· τίς πληγὴν ἀυτεῖ καιρίως οὐτασμένος;

ΑΓΑΜΕΜΝΩΝ

ὤμοι μάλ' αὖθις, δευτέραν πεπληγμένος.

ΧΟΡΟΣ

τοὔργον εἰργάσθαι δοκεῖ μοι βασιλέως οἰμώγμασιν.
ἀλλὰ κοινωσώμεθ' ἤν πως[1] ἀσφαλῆ βουλεύματα.
1. ἐγὼ μὲν ὑμῖν τὴν ἐμὴν γνώμην λέγω,
πρὸς δῶμα δεῦρ' ἀστοῖσι κηρύσσειν βοήν.—
2. ἐμοὶ δ' ὅπως τάχιστά γ' ἐμπεσεῖν δοκεῖ
καὶ πρᾶγμ' ἐλέγχειν σὺν νεορρύτῳ ξίφει.—
3. κἀγὼ τοιούτου γνώματος κοινωνὸς ὢν
ψηφίζομαί τι δρᾶν· τὸ μὴ μέλλειν δ' ἀκμή.—
4. ὁρᾶν πάρεστι· φροιμιάζονται γὰρ ὡς
τυραννίδος σημεῖα πράσσοντες πόλει.—
5. χρονίζομεν γάρ. οἱ δὲ τῆς μελλοῦς[2] κλέος
πέδοι[3] πατοῦντες οὐ καθεύδουσιν χερί.—
6. οὐκ οἶδα βουλῆς ἧστινος τυχὼν λέγω.
τοῦ δρῶντός ἐστι καὶ τὸ βουλεῦσαι πέρι.—
7. κἀγὼ τοιοῦτός εἰμ', ἐπεὶ δυσμηχανῶ
λόγοισι τὸν θανόντ' ἀνιστάναι πάλιν.—
8. ἦ καὶ βίον τείνοντες[4] ὧδ' ὑπείξομεν
δόμων καταισχυντῆρσι τοῖσδ' ἡγουμένοις;—
9. ἀλλ' οὐκ ἀνεκτόν, ἀλλὰ κατθανεῖν κρατεῖ·[5]
πεπαιτέρα γὰρ μοῖρα τῆς τυραννίδος.—

[1] ἄν πως: Weil.
[2] τῆς μελλοῦς Trypho Περὶ τρόπων (iii. 196 Spengel), τῆς μελλούσης FV3, μελλούσης N. [3] πέδον: Herm.
[4] κτείνοντες: Canter. [5] κράτει: Casaubon.

CHORUS

Silence! Who is this that crieth out, wounded by a mortal blow?

AGAMEMNON

And once again, ay me! I am smitten by a second blow.

CHORUS

The deed is done, methinks—to judge by the groans of the King. But come, let us take counsel together if there be haply some safe plan of action.

[*The members of the Chorus deliver their opinions on the course to be taken*

1. I tell you my advice: summon the townsfolk to bring rescue hither to the palace.

2. To my thinking we must burst in amain and charge them with the deed while the sword is still dripping in their hands.

3. And I am for taking part in some such plan, and vote for action of some sort. 'Tis no time to keep on dallying.

4. It is plain. Their opening act marks a plan to set up a tyranny in the State.

5. Aye, because we are wasting time, while they, spurning to earth that lauded name, Delay, allow their hands no slumber.

6. I know not what plan I could hit on to propose. 'Tis the doer's part likewise to do the planning.

7. I too am of this mind, for I know no way how by mere words to bring the dead back to life.

8. What! To prolong our lives shall we thus submit to the rule of those defilers of the house?

9. No, it is not to be endured. No, death were better, for that were a milder lot than tyranny.

10. ἦ γὰρ τεκμηρίοισιν ἐξ οἰμωγμάτων
μαντευσόμεσθα τἀνδρὸς ὡς ὀλωλότος;—
11. σάφ᾽ εἰδότας χρὴ τῶνδε θυμοῦσθαι[1] πέρι·
τὸ γὰρ τοπάζειν τοῦ σάφ᾽ εἰδέναι δίχα.—
12. ταύτην ἐπαινεῖν πάντοθεν πληθύνομαι,
τρανῶς Ἀτρείδην εἰδέναι κυροῦνθ᾽ ὅπως.

ΚΛΥΤΑΙΜΗΣΤΡΑ

πολλῶν πάροιθεν καιρίως εἰρημένων
τἀναντί᾽ εἰπεῖν οὐκ ἐπαισχυνθήσομαι.
πῶς γάρ τις ἐχθροῖς ἐχθρὰ πορσύνων, φίλοις
δοκοῦσιν εἶναι, πημονῆς[2] ἀρκύστατ᾽ ἂν[3]
φράξειεν, ὕψος κρεῖσσον ἐκπηδήματος;
ἐμοὶ δ᾽ ἀγὼν ὅδ᾽ οὐκ ἀφρόντιστος πάλαι
νείκης[4] παλαιᾶς ἦλθε, σὺν χρόνῳ γε μήν·
ἕστηκα δ᾽ ἔνθ᾽ ἔπαισ᾽[5] ἐπ᾽ ἐξειργασμένοις.
οὕτω δ᾽ ἔπραξα, καὶ τάδ᾽ οὐκ ἀρνήσομαι·
ὡς μήτε φεύγειν μήτ᾽ ἀμύνεσθαι[6] μόρον,
ἄπειρον ἀμφίβληστρον, ὥσπερ ἰχθύων,
περιστιχίζω,[7] πλοῦτον εἵματος κακόν.
παίω δέ νιν δίς· κἀν δυοῖν οἰμωγμάτοιν[8]
μεθῆκεν αὑτοῦ[9] κῶλα· καὶ πεπτωκότι
τρίτην ἐπενδίδωμι, τοῦ κατὰ χθονὸς
Διὸς[10] νεκρῶν σωτῆρος εὐκταίαν χάριν.
οὕτω τὸν αὑτοῦ[11] θυμὸν ὁρμαίνει πεσών·
κἀκφυσιῶν ὀξεῖαν αἵματος σφαγὴν
βάλλει μ᾽ ἐρεμνῇ ψακάδι φοινίας δρόσου,

[1] μυθοῦσθαι: E. A. J. Ahrens.
[2] πημονὴν: Auratus. [3] ἀρκύστατον: Elmsley.
[4] νίκης: Heath. [5] ἔπεσ᾽ F. [6] ἀμύνασθαι: Vict.
[7] περιστιχίζω N, περιστιχίζων V3, -στοιχίζων F.
[8] οἰμώγμασιν: Elmsley. [9] αὐτοῦ: I. Voss.
[10] ἅιδου: Enger. [11] αὐτοῦ: Schütz.

10. And shall we, upon the evidence of mere groans, divine that our lord is dead?

11. We should be sure of the facts ere we indulge our wrath. For surmise differs from assurance.

12. I am supported on all sides to approve this course—that we have clear assurance how it stands with Atreus' son.

[*The bodies of Agamemnon and Cassandra are disclosed; the Queen stands by their side*

CLYTAEMESTRA

Much have I said before to serve my need and I shall feel no shame to contradict it now. For how else could one, devising hate against a hated foe who bears the semblance of a friend, fence the snares of ruin too high to be o'erleaped? This is the crisis of an ancient feud, pondered by me of old, and it has come—howbeit long delayed. I stand where I dealt the blow; my purpose is achieved. Thus have I wrought the deed—deny it I will not. Round him, like as to catch a haul of fish, I cast a net impassable—a fatal wealth of robe—so that he should neither escape nor ward off doom. Twice I smote him, and with two groans his limbs relaxed. Once he had fallen, I dealt him yet a third stroke to grace my prayer to the infernal Zeus, the saviour of the dead. Fallen thus, he gasped away his life, and as he breathed forth quick spurts of blood, he smote me with dark drops of ensanguined dew;

χαίρουσαν οὐδὲν ἧσσον ἢ διοσδότῳ
γάνει[1] σπορητὸς κάλυκος ἐν λοχεύμασιν.
ὡς ὧδ᾽ ἐχόντων, πρέσβος Ἀργείων τόδε,
χαίροιτ᾽ ἄν, εἰ χαίροιτ᾽, ἐγὼ δ᾽ ἐπεύχομαι.
εἰ δ᾽ ἦν πρεπόντων ὥστ᾽ ἐπισπένδειν νεκρῷ,
τῷδ᾽[2] ἂν δικαίως ἦν, ὑπερδίκως μὲν οὖν.
τοσῶνδε κρατῆρ᾽ ἐν δόμοις κακῶν ὅδε
πλήσας ἀραίων αὐτὸς ἐκπίνει μολών.

ΧΟΡΟΣ

θαυμάζομέν σου γλῶσσαν, ὡς θρασύστομος,
ἥτις τοιόνδ᾽ ἐπ᾽ ἀνδρὶ κομπάζεις λόγον.

ΚΛΥΤΑΙΜΗΣΤΡΑ

πειρᾶσθέ μου γυναικὸς ὡς ἀφράσμονος·
ἐγὼ δ᾽ ἀτρέστῳ καρδίᾳ πρὸς εἰδότας
λέγω· σὺ δ᾽ αἰνεῖν εἴτε με ψέγειν θέλεις
ὅμοιον. οὗτός ἐστιν Ἀγαμέμνων, ἐμὸς
πόσις, νεκρὸς δέ, τῆσδε δεξιᾶς χερὸς
ἔργον, δικαίας τέκτονος. τάδ᾽ ὧδ᾽ ἔχει.

ΧΟΡΟΣ

τί κακόν, ὦ γύναι, χθονοτρεφὲς ἐδανὸν
ἢ ποτὸν πασαμένα ῥυτᾶς[3] ἐξ ἁλὸς ὅρμενον[4]
τόδ᾽ ἐπέθου θύος, δημοθρόους τ᾽ ἀράς;
ἀπέδικες ἀπέταμες·[5] ἀπόπολις[6] δ᾽ ἔσῃ
μῖσος ὄβριμον[7] ἀστοῖς.

[1] διὸς νότῳ γᾶν εἰ: Porson. [2] τάδ᾽: Tyrwhitt.
[3] ῥυσᾶς and ῥύσας: Stanley
[4] ὀρώμενον FV3, ὁρώμενον N: Abresch.
[5] ἀπέταμες F^1N^2, ἀπέτεμες N^1F^2.
[6] ἄπολις: Seidler. [7] ὄμβριμον: Blomfield.

while I rejoiced no less than the sown earth is gladdened in heaven's refreshing rain at the birth-time of the flower buds.

Since then the case stands thus, ye Argive ancients, rejoice ye, if ye would rejoice ; as for me, I glory in the deed. And had it been a fitting act to pour libations on the corpse, over him this had been done justly, aye more than justly. With so many accursed ills hath he filled the mixing-bowl in his own house, and now he hath come home and himself drained it to the dregs.

Chorus

We marvel at thy tongue, how bold-mouthed thou art, that over thy husband thou canst utter such a vaunting speech.

Clytaemestra

Ye are proving me as if I were a witless woman. But my heart quails not, and I say to you who know it well—and whether ye are minded to praise or to blame me, 'tis all one—here is Agamemnon, my husband, done to death, the work of this right hand, a workman true. So stands the case.

Chorus

Woman, what poisonous herb nourished by the earth hast thou tasted, what potion drawn from the flowing sea, that thou hast taken upon thyself this maddened rage and execration of the public voice ? Thou hast cast him off ; thou hast cut him off ; and out from the land shalt thou be cast, a burthen of hatred unto thy people.

ΚΛΥΤΑΙΜΗΣΤΡΑ

νῦν μὲν δικάζεις ἐκ πόλεως φυγὴν ἐμοὶ
καὶ μῖσος ἀστῶν δημόθρους τ᾽ ἔχειν ἀράς,
οὐδὲν τότ᾽ ἀνδρὶ τῷδ᾽[1] ἐναντίον φέρων·
ὃς οὐ προτιμῶν, ὡσπερεὶ βοτοῦ μόρον,
μήλων φλεόντων εὐπόκοις νομεύμασιν,
ἔθυσεν αὑτοῦ[2] παῖδα, φιλτάτην ἐμοὶ
ὠδῖν᾽, ἐπῳδὸν Θρῃκίων ἀημάτων.[3]
οὐ τοῦτον ἐκ γῆς τῆσδε χρῆν[4] σ᾽ ἀνδρηλατεῖν,
μιασμάτων ἄποιν᾽; ἐπήκοος δ᾽ ἐμῶν
ἔργων δικαστὴς τραχὺς εἶ. λέγω δέ σοι
τοιαῦτ᾽ ἀπειλεῖν, ὡς παρεσκευασμένης
ἐκ τῶν ὁμοίων χειρὶ νικήσαντ᾽ ἐμοῦ
ἄρχειν· ἐὰν δὲ τοὔμπαλιν κραίνῃ θεός,
γνώσῃ διδαχθεὶς ὀψὲ γοῦν τὸ σωφρονεῖν.

ΧΟΡΟΣ

μεγαλόμητις εἶ, περίφρονα δ᾽ ἔλακες.
ὥσπερ οὖν φονολιβεῖ τύχᾳ φρὴν ἐπιμαίνεται,
λίπος ἐπ᾽ ὀμμάτων αἵματος εὖ πρέπει·
ἀτίετον[5] ἔτι σὲ χρὴ στερομέναν φίλων
τύμμα τύμματι[6] τεῖσαι.[7]

ΚΛΥΤΑΙΜΗΣΤΡΑ

καὶ τήνδ᾽ ἀκούεις ὁρκίων ἐμῶν θέμιν·
μὰ τὴν τέλειον τῆς ἐμῆς παιδὸς Δίκην,
Ἄτην Ἐρινύν[8] θ᾽, αἷσι τόνδ᾽ ἔσφαξ᾽ ἐγώ,

[1] τόδ᾽: I. Voss. [2] αὐτοῦ: Vict.
[3] θρηκίων τὲ (τε N) λημμάτων: Canter.
[4] χρή: Porson. [5] ἀτίετον N, ἀντίετον FV3.
[6] τύμμα τύμμα: I. Voss.
[7] τίσαι: Kirchhoff. [8] ἐριννύν: Blomfield.

CLYTAEMESTRA

'Tis *now* that thou wouldst doom me to exile from the land, to the hatred of my people and the execration of the public voice ; though *then* thou hadst naught to urge against him that lieth here. And yet *he*, recking no more than if it had been a beast that perished—though sheep were plenty in his fleecy folds—he sacrificed his own child, even her I bore with dearest travail, to charm the blasts of Thrace. Is it not *he* whom thou shouldst have banished from this land in requital for his polluting deed? No! When thou arraignest what *I* have done, thou art a stern judge. Well, I warn thee: menace me thus on the understanding that I am prepared, conditions equal, to let thee lord it over me if thou shalt vanquish me by force. But if God shall bring the contrary to pass, thou shalt learn discretion though taught the lesson late.

CHORUS

Haughty of spirit art thou and overweening is thy speech. Even as thy mind is maddened by thy deed of blood, upon thy visage a stain of blood showeth full plain to behold. Reft of all honour, forsaken of thy friends, thou shalt hereafter atone for stroke with stroke.

CLYTAEMESTRA

This too thou hearest, this the righteous sanction of my oath: By Justice, exacted for my child, by Ate, by the Avenging Spirit, unto whom I sacrificed

οὔ μοι φόβου μέλαθρον ἐλπὶς ἐμπατεῖ,
ἕως ἂν αἴθῃ πῦρ ἐφ' ἑστίας ἐμῆς[1]
Αἴγισθος, ὡς τὸ πρόσθεν εὖ φρονῶν ἐμοί.
οὗτος γὰρ ἡμῖν ἀσπὶς οὐ σμικρὰ[2] θράσους.
κεῖται γυναικὸς τῆσδε λυμαντήριος,
Χρυσηίδων μείλιγμα τῶν ὑπ' Ἰλίῳ·
ἥ τ' αἰχμάλωτος ἥδε καὶ τερασκόπος
καὶ κοινόλεκτρος τοῦδε, θεσφατηλόγος
πιστὴ ξύνευνος, ναυτίλων δὲ σελμάτων
ἰσοτριβής.[3] ἄτιμα δ' οὐκ ἐπραξάτην.
ὁ μὲν γὰρ οὕτως, ἡ δέ τοι κύκνου δίκην
τὸν ὕστατον μέλψασα θανάσιμον γόον
κεῖται, φιλήτωρ[4] τοῦδ'· ἐμοὶ δ' ἐπήγαγεν
εὐνῆς παροψώνημα[5] τῆς ἐμῆς χλιδῆς.

ΧΟΡΟΣ

φεῦ, τίς ἂν ἐν τάχει, μὴ περιώδυνος, [στρ. α.
μηδὲ δεμνιοτήρης,
μόλοι τὸν αἰεὶ φέρουσ' ἐν ἡμῖν
Μοῖρ' ἀτέλευτον ὕπνον, δαμέντος
φύλακος εὐμενεστάτου καὶ
πολλὰ τλάντος γυναικὸς διαί·
πρὸς γυναικὸς δ' ἀπέφθισεν βίον.

ἰὼ <ἰὼ>[6] παράνους[7] Ἑλένα [ἐφυμν. α.
μία τὰς πολλάς, τὰς πάνυ πολλὰς
ψυχὰς ὀλέσασ' ὑπὸ Τροίᾳ.
νῦν [δὲ][8] τέλεαν[9] πολύμναστον ἐπηνθίσω
δι' αἷμ' ἄνιπτον. ἦ τις[10] ἦν τότ' ἐν δόμοις
ἔρις ἐρίδματος ἀνδρὸς οἰζύς.

[1] ἐμὰς: Porson (ἐμᾶς Scaliger). [2] μικρὰ: Blomfield.
[3] ἰσοτριβὴς Rom., ἰστοτριβὴς FV3N: Pauw.

yon man, hope doth not tread for me the halls of fear, so long as the fire upon my hearth is kindled by Aegisthus, loyal in heart to me as in days gone by. For he is no slight shield of confidence to me. Here lies the man that did me wrong, minion of each Chryseïs at Ilium; and here she lies, his captive, and auguress, and concubine, his oracular faithful bedfellow, yet equally familiar with the seamen's benches. The pair has met no undeserved fate. For he lies thus; while she, who, like a swan, hath sung her last lament in death, lies here, his beloved; but to *me* she has brought for my bed an added relish of delight.

CHORUS

Alas! Ah that some fate, free from excess of suffering, nor yet with lingering bed of pain, might come full soon and bring to us everlasting and endless sleep, now that our most gracious guardian hath been laid low, who in a woman's cause had much endured and by a woman's hand hath lost his life.

O infatuate Helen, who didst of thyself alone work the destruction of these many lives, these lives exceeding many, beneath the walls of Troy. Now thou hast bedecked thyself with thy final crown, that shall long last in memory, by reason of blood not to be washed away. Verily in those days there dwelt in the house a spirit of strife, an affliction that hath subdued its lord.

---

[4] φιλήτωρ F. [5] παροψώνημα: Casaubon.
[6] ⟨ἰώ⟩ Blomfield. [7] παρανόμους: Herm
[8] [δὲ] Wilam. [9] τέλειαν: Wilam. [10] ἥτις: Schütz.

ΚΛΥΤΑΙΜΗΣΤΡΑ

μηδὲν θανάτου μοῖραν ἐπεύχου [anap
τοῖσδε βαρυνθείς·
μηδ' εἰς Ἑλένην κότον ἐκτρέψῃς,[1]
ὡς ἀνδρολέτειρ', ὡς μία πολλῶν
ἀνδρῶν ψυχὰς Δαναῶν ὀλέσασ'[2]
  ἀξύστατον ἄλγος ἔπραξεν.

ΧΟΡΟΣ

δαῖμον, ὃς ἐμπίτνεις[3] δώμασι καὶ διφυί- [ἀντ. α.
οισι[4] Τανταλίδαισιν,
κράτος ‹τ'›[5] ἰσόψυχον ἐκ γυναικῶν
καρδιόδηκτον[6] ἐμοὶ κρατύνεις.
ἐπὶ δὲ σώματος δίκαν μοι
κόρακος ἐχθροῦ σταθεῖσ'[7] ἐκνόμως[8]
1474 ὕμνον ὑμνεῖν ἐπεύχεται. . .[9]

1455 ‹ἰὼ ‹ἰὼ› παράνους Ἑλένα [ἐφυμν. α.
μία τὰς πολλάς, τὰς πάνυ πολλὰς
  ψυχὰς ὀλέσασ' ὑπὸ Τροίᾳ.
νῦν [δὲ] τέλεαν πολύμναστον ἐπηνθίσω
δι' αἷμ' ἄνιπτον. ἦ τις ἦν τότ' ἐν δόμοις
1461 ἔρις ἐρίδματος ἀνδρὸς οἰζύς.›

ΚΛΥΤΑΙΜΗΣΤΡΑ

νῦν δ' ὤρθωσας στόματος γνώμην, [anap.
τὸν τριπάχυντον[10]
δαίμονα γέννης τῆσδε κικλήσκων.

[1] ἐκτρέχης F.
[2] ὄλεσαν FV3.
[3] ἐμπίπτεις: Canter.
[4] διφυεῖσι: Herm.
[5] ‹τ'› Herm.
[6] καρδία δηκτὸν: Abresch

CLYTAEMESTRA

Burthen not thyself with thoughts such as these, nor invoke upon thyself the fate of death. Nor yet turn thy wrath upon Helen, and deem her a slayer of men, as if she alone had destroyed many a Danaan life and had wrought anguish past all cure.

CHORUS

O thou Fiend that fallest upon this house and Tantalus' twain descendants,[1] thou that by the hands of women dost wield a sway matching their temper, a sway bitter to my soul! Perched o'er his body like a hateful raven, in hoarse notes she chanteth her song of triumph.

O infatuate Helen who didst of thyself alone work the destruction of these many lives, these lives exceeding many, beneath the walls of Troy. Now thou hast bedecked thyself with thy final crown, that shall long last in memory by reason of blood not to be washed away. Verily in those days there dwelt in the house a spirit of strife, an affliction that hath subdued its lord.

CLYTAEMESTRA

Now thou hast set aright the judgment of thy lips in that thou namest the thrice-gorged Fiend of

[1] Agamemnon and Menelaüs.

---

[7] *σταθεὶς*: Stanley. [8] *ἐκνόμως* N, *ἐννόμως* FV3.
[9] *δόμοις* suppl. Butler, *νεκρῷ* Enger. After l. 1474, ll. 1455-1461 repeated as refrain by Burney.
[10] *τριπάχυιον*: Bamberger.

ἐκ τοῦ γὰρ ἔρως αἱματολοιχὸς
νείρᾳ[1] τρέφεται, πρὶν καταλῆξαι
  τὸ παλαιὸν ἄχος, νέος ἰχώρ.

ΧΟΡΟΣ

ἦ μέγαν οἰκονόμον[2] [στρ. β.
δαίμονα καὶ βαρύμηνιν αἰνεῖς,
φεῦ φεῦ, κακὸν αἶνον ἀτη-
ρᾶς τύχας ἀκορέστου·
ἰὴ ἰή, διαὶ Διὸς
παναιτίου πανεργέτα·[3]
τί γὰρ βροτοῖς ἄνευ Διὸς τελεῖται;
τί τῶνδ᾽ οὐ θεόκραντόν ἐστιν;

ἰὼ ἰὼ βασιλεῦ βασιλεῦ, [ἐφυμν. β.
πῶς σε δακρύσω;
  φρενὸς ἐκ φιλίας τί ποτ᾽ εἴπω;
κεῖσαι δ᾽ ἀράχνης ἐν ὑφάσματι τῷδ᾽
ἀσεβεῖ θανάτῳ βίον ἐκπνέων.
ὤμοι μοι κοίταν τάνδ᾽ ἀνελεύθερον
δολίῳ μόρῳ δαμεὶς <δάμαρτος>[4]
ἐκ χερὸς ἀμφιτόμῳ βελέμνῳ.

ΚΛΥΤΑΙΜΗΣΤΡΑ

αὐχεῖς εἶναι τόδε τοὔργον ἐμόν; [anap.
μηδ᾽ ἐπιλεχθῇς
Ἀγαμεμνονίαν εἶναί μ᾽ ἄλοχον.
φανταζόμενος δὲ γυναικὶ νεκροῦ
τοῦδ᾽ ὁ παλαιὸς δριμὺς ἀλάστωρ
Ἀτρέως χαλεποῦ θοινατῆρος
τόνδ᾽ ἀπέτεισεν,[5]
  τέλεον νεαροῖς ἐπιθύσας.

this race. For from him it cometh that the lust for lapping blood is fostered in the maw; ere ever the ancient wound is healed, fresh blood is spilled.

Chorus

Verily of a mighty Fiend thou tellest, haunting the house, and heavy in his wrath (alas, alas!)—an evil tale of baneful fate insatiate; woe, woe, by will of Zeus, author of all, worker of all! For what is brought to pass for mortal men save by will of Zeus? What herein is not wrought of Heaven?

Alas, alas, my King, my King, how shall I bewail thee? How voice my heartfelt love for thee? To lie in this spider's web, breathing forth thy life in impious death! Ah me, to lie on this ignoble bed, struck down in treacherous death wrought by a weapon of double edge wielded by the hand of thine own wife!

Clytaemestra

Dost thou affirm this deed is mine? Nay, imagine not that I am Agamemnon's spouse. Taking the semblance of the wife of yon corpse, the ancient bitter evil genius of Atreus, that grim banqueter, hath offered him in payment, sacrificing a full-grown victim in vengeance for those slain babes.

---

[1] *νείρει*: Wellauer (*νείρῃ* Casaubon).

[2] *οἴκοις τοῖσδε*: Schneider.

[3] *πανεργέτα* N, *πανεργέταν* FV3.

[4] <*δάμαρτος*> Enger.

[5] *ἀπέτισεν*: Kirchhoff.

ΧΟΡΟΣ

ὡς μὲν ἀναίτιος εἶ [ἀντ. β.
τοῦδε φόνου τίς ὁ μαρτυρήσων;
πῶς πῶς[1]; πατρόθεν δὲ συλλή-
πτωρ γένοιτ' ἂν ἀλάστωρ.
βιάζεται δ' ὁμοσπόροις
ἐπιρροαῖσιν αἱμάτων
μέλας Ἄρης, ὅποι δίκαν[2] προβαίνων[3]
πάχνᾳ κουροβόρῳ παρέξει.

ἰὼ ἰὼ βασιλεῦ βασιλεῦ, [ἐφυμν. β.
πῶς σε δακρύσω;
  φρενὸς ἐκ φιλίας τί ποτ' εἴπω;
κεῖσαι δ' ἀράχνης ἐν ὑφάσματι τῷδ'
  ἀσεβεῖ θανάτῳ βίον ἐκπνέων.
ὤμοι μοι κοίταν τάνδ' ἀνελεύθερον
δολίῳ μόρῳ δαμεὶς <δάμαρτος>
ἐκ χερὸς ἀμφιτόμῳ βελέμνῳ.

ΚΛΥΤΑΙΜΗΣΤΡΑ

[οὔτ' ἀνελεύθερον οἶμαι θάνατον [anap.
τῷδε γενέσθαι.][4]
οὐδὲ γὰρ οὗτος δολίαν ἄτην
οἴκοισιν ἔθηκ';
ἀλλ' ἐμὸν ἐκ τοῦδ' ἔρνος ἀερθέν,
τὴν πολυκλαύτην[5] Ἰφιγενείαν,
ἄξια δράσας[6] ἄξια πάσχων
μηδὲν ἐν Ἅιδου μεγαλαυχείτω,
ξιφοδηλήτῳ
  θανάτῳ τείσας[7] ἅπερ ἦρξεν.

[1] πῶ, πῶ: Auratus.

CHORUS

That thou art guiltless of this murder—who will bear thee witness? Nay, nay! And yet the evil genius of his sire might well be thine abettor. By force 'mid streams of kindred blood black Havoc presseth on to where he shall grant vengeance for the gore of children served for meat.

Alas, alas, my King, my King, how shall I bewail thee? How voice my heartfelt love for thee? To lie in this spider's web, breathing forth thy life in impious death! Ah me, to lie on this ignoble bed, struck down in treacherous death wrought by a weapon of double edge wielded by the hand of thine own wife!

CLYTAEMESTRA

[Neither do I think he met an ignoble death.] And did he not then himself by treachery bring ruin on his house? Yet, as he hath suffered—worthy meed of worthy deed—for what he did unto my sweet flower, shoot sprung from him, the sore-wept Iphigenia, let him make no high vaunt in the halls of Hades, since with death dealt him by the sword he hath paid for what he first began.

---

[2] ὅποι δὲ καί: Scholefield (δίκην Butler).
[3] προσβαίνων: Canter.
[4] ll. 1521-22 bracketed by Seidler.
[5] πολύκλαυτόν τ': Porson.
[6] ἀνάξια δράσας: Herm. [7] τίσας: Kirchhoff.

ΧΟΡΟΣ

ἀμηχανῶ φροντίδος στερηθεὶς [στρ. γ.
εὐπάλαμον[1] μέριμναν
ὅπα τράπωμαι, πίτνοντος οἴκου.
δέδοικα δ' ὄμβρου κτύπον δομοσφαλῆ
τὸν αἱματηρόν· ψακὰς[2] δὲ λήγει.
δίκην[3] δ' ἐπ' ἄλλο πρᾶγμα θηγάνει[4] βλάβης
πρὸς ἄλλαις θηγάναισι[5] μοῖρα.

ἰὼ γᾶ γᾶ, εἴθ' ἔμ' ἐδέξω, [ἐφυμν. γ.
πρὶν τόνδ' ἐπιδεῖν ἀργυροτοίχου
  δροίτης[6] κατέχοντα χάμευναν.[7]
τίς ὁ θάψων νιν; τίς ὁ θρηνήσων;
ἦ σὺ τόδ' ἔρξαι τλήσῃ, κτείνασ'
ἄνδρα τὸν αὑτῆς ἀποκωκῦσαι
ψυχῇ τ' ἄχαριν[8] χάριν ἀντ' ἔργων
  μεγάλων ἀδίκως ἐπικρᾶναι;
τίς δ' ἐπιτύμβιον αἶνον[9] ἐπ' ἀνδρὶ θείῳ
σὺν δακρύοις ἰάπτων
ἀληθείᾳ φρενῶν πονήσει;

ΚΛΥΤΑΙΜΗΣΤΡΑ

οὐ σὲ προσήκει τὸ μέλημ' ἀλέγειν[10] [anap.
τοῦτο· πρὸς ἡμῶν
κάππεσε, κάτθανε, καὶ καταθάψομεν,
οὐχ ὑπὸ κλαυθμῶν τῶν ἐξ οἴκων,
ἀλλ' Ἰφιγένειά νιν[11] ἀσπασίως
θυγάτηρ, ὡς χρή,
πατέρ' ἀντιάσασα πρὸς ὠκύπορον
πόρθμευμ' ἀχέων
  περὶ χεῖρε[12] βαλοῦσα φιλήσει.[13]

CHORUS

Bereft of any ready expedient of thought, I am bewildered whither to turn now that the house is tottering. I fear the beating storm of bloody rain that shakes the house; no longer doth it descend in drops. Yet on other whetstones Destiny is whetting justice for another deed of bale.

O Earth, Earth, would thou hadst taken me to thyself ere ever I had lived to see this my liege the tenant of the lowly bed of a silver-sided laver! Who shall bury him? Who shall lament him? Wilt thou harden thy heart to do this—thou who hast slain thine own husband—to make lament for him and crown thy unholy work with a graceless grace to his spirit in atonement for thy monstrous deeds? And who, as with tears he utters his praise over the hero's grave, shall sorrow in sincerity of heart?

CLYTAEMESTRA

To care for that office is no concern of *thine*. By *our* hands down he fell, down to death, and down below shall we bury him—but not with wailings from his household. No! Iphigenia, his daughter, as is due, shall meet her father lovingly at the swift-flowing ford of sorrows, and shall fling her arms around him and kiss him.

---

[1] εὐπάλαμνον: Porson. [2] ψεκὰς: Blomfield.
[3] δίκη FV3[2]N[2], δίκα V3[1], δίκᾳ N[1]: Auratus.
[4] θήγει: Herm. [5] θηγάναις: Pauw.
[6] δροίτας: Kirchhoff. [7] χαμεύναν: Solmsen.
[8] ψυχὴν ἄχαριν: E. A. J. Ahrens.
[9] ἐπιτύμβιος αἶνος: I. Voss.
[10] μέλημα λέγειν: Karsten. [11] Ἰφιγένειαν ἵν': Auratus.
[12] χεῖρα: Porson. [13] φιλήσῃ (-η): Abresch.

ΧΟΡΟΣ

ὄνειδος ἥκει τόδ᾽ ἀντ᾽ ὀνείδους. [ἀντ. γ.
δύσμαχα δ᾽ ἔστι κρῖναι.
φέρει φέροντ᾽, ἐκτίνει δ᾽ ὁ καίνων.
μίμνει δὲ μίμνοντος ἐν θρόνῳ[1] Διὸς
παθεῖν τὸν ἔρξαντα· θέσμιον γάρ.
τίς ἂν γονὰν ἀραῖον[2] ἐκβάλοι δόμων;
κεκόλληται γένος πρὸς ἄτᾳ.[3]

<ἰὼ γᾶ γᾶ, εἴθ᾽ ἔμ᾽ ἐδέξω, [ἐφυμν. γ.
πρὶν τόνδ᾽ ἐπιδεῖν ἀργυροτοίχου
δροίτης κατέχοντα χάμευναν.
τίς ὁ θάψων νιν; τίς ὁ θρηνήσων;
ἦ σὺ τόδ᾽ ἔρξαι τλήσῃ, κτείνασ᾽
ἄνδρα τὸν αὑτῆς ἀποκωκῦσαι
ψυχῇ τ᾽ ἄχαριν χάριν ἀντ᾽ ἔργων
μεγάλων ἀδίκως ἐπικρᾶναι;
τίς δ᾽ ἐπιτύμβιον αἶνον ἐπ᾽ ἀνδρὶ θείῳ
σὺν δακρύοις ἰάπτων
ἀληθείᾳ φρενῶν πονήσει;>

ΚΛΥΤΑΙΜΗΣΤΡΑ

ἐς τόνδ᾽ ἐνέβης[4] ξὺν[5] ἀληθείᾳ [anap.
χρησμόν. ἐγὼ δ᾽ οὖν
ἐθέλω δαίμονι τῷ Πλεισθενιδῶν
ὅρκους θεμένη τάδε μὲν στέργειν,
δύστλητά περ ὄνθ᾽· ὃ δὲ λοιπόν, ἰόντ᾽
ἐκ τῶνδε δόμων ἄλλην γενεὰν
τρίβειν θανάτοις αὐθένταισι·

[1] χρόνῳ: Schütz (cp. *Eum.* 18). [2] ῥᾶον: Herm.
[3] προσάψαι: Blomfield. After l. 1566 Burney repeats ll. 1537-50. [4] ἐνέβη: Canter. [5] σὺν FV3, ξὺν N.

Chorus

Reproach thus meeteth reproach in turn—hard is the struggle to decide. The spoiler is spoiled, the slayer payeth penalty. Yet, while Zeus abideth on his throne, it abideth that to him who doeth it shall be done—for it is an ordinance. Who can cast from out the house the seed of the curse? The race is fast-bound in calamity.

O Earth, Earth, would thou hadst taken me to thyself ere ever I had lived to see this my liege the tenant of the lowly bed of a silver-sided laver! Who shall bury him? Who shall lament him? Wilt thou harden thy heart to do this—thou who hast slain thine own husband—to make lament for him and crown thy unholy work with a graceless grace to his spirit in atonement for thy monstrous deeds? And who, as with tears he utters his praise over the hero's grave, shall sorrow in sincerity of heart?

Clytaemestra

Upon this divine deliverance hast thou rightly touched. As for me, however, I am willing to make a sworn compact with the Fiend of the house of Pleisthenes [1] that I will be content with what is done, hard to endure though it be; and that henceforth he shall leave this habitation and bring tribulation upon some other race by murder of kin. A small

[1] The Pleisthenidae, here apparently a synonym of Atreidae, take their name from Pleisthenes, of whom Porphyry in his *Questions* says that he was the son of Atreus and the real father of Agamemnon and Menelaüs; and that, as he died young, without having achieved any distinction, his sons were brought up by their grandfather and hence called *Atreidae*.

κτεάνων τε μέρος
βαιὸν ἐχούσῃ πᾶν ἀπόχρη μοι
μανίας μελάθρων
ἀλληλοφόνους ἀφελούσῃ.[1]

ΑΙΓΙΣΘΟΣ

ὦ φέγγος εὖφρον ἡμέρας δικηφόρου.
φαίην ἂν ἤδη νῦν βροτῶν τιμαόρους
θεοὺς ἄνωθεν γῆς ἐποπτεύειν ἄχη,
ἰδὼν ὑφαντοῖς ἐν πέπλοις Ἐρινύων
τὸν ἄνδρα τόνδε κείμενον φίλως ἐμοί,
χερὸς πατρῴας ἐκτίνοντα μηχανάς.
Ἀτρεὺς γὰρ ἄρχων τῆσδε γῆς, τούτου πατήρ,
πατέρα Θυέστην τὸν ἐμόν, ὡς τορῶς φράσαι,
αὑτοῦ δ'[2] ἀδελφόν, ἀμφίλεκτος ὢν κράτει,
ἠνδρηλάτησεν ἐκ πόλεώς τε καὶ δόμων.
καὶ προστρόπαιος ἑστίας μολὼν πάλιν
τλήμων Θυέστης μοῖραν ηὕρετ'[3] ἀσφαλῆ,
τὸ μὴ θανὼν πατρῷον αἱμάξαι πέδον,
αὐτός[4]· ξένια δὲ τοῦδε δύσθεος πατὴρ
Ἀτρεύς, προθύμως μᾶλλον ἢ φίλως, πατρὶ
τὠμῷ, κρεουργὸν ἦμαρ εὐθύμως ἄγειν
δοκῶν, παρέσχε δαῖτα παιδείων κρεῶν.
τὰ μὲν ποδήρη καὶ χερῶν ἄκρους κτένας
ἔθρυπτ', ἄνωθεν . . . .
. . . .
. . . . . ἀνδρακὰς καθήμενος.[5]
ἄσημα δ' αὐτῶν αὐτίκ' ἀγνοίᾳ λαβὼν
ἔσθει βορὰν ἄσωτον, ὡς ὁρᾷς, γένει.

[1] ll. 1574-76 μοι δ' ἀλληλοφόνους μανίας μελάθρων: [δ'] Canter, transp. Erfurdt. [2] αὐτοῦ τ': Elmsley.

part of the wealth fully suffices me, if I may but rid these halls of the frenzy of mutual murder.

[*Enter Aegisthus with armed retainers*

Aegisthus

Hail gracious light of the day of retribution! At last the hour is come when I can say that the gods who avenge mortal men look down from on high upon the crimes of earth—now that, to my joy, I behold this man lying here in a robe spun by the Avenging Spirits and making full payment for the deeds contrived in craft by his father's hand.

For Atreus, lord of this land, this man's father, challenged in his sovereignty, drove forth, from city and from home, Thyestes, who (to speak it clearly) was my father and his own brother. And when that he had come back as a suppliant to his hearth, unhappy Thyestes secured such safety for his lot as not himself to suffer death and stain with his blood his native soil. But Atreus, the godless father of this slain man, with welcome more hearty than kind, on the pretence that he was celebrating with good cheer a festive day with offering of meat, served up to my father as entertainment a banquet of his own children's flesh. The toes and fingers he broke off . . . sitting apart.[1] And when all unwittingly my father had forthwith taken portions thereof that he could not distinguish, he ate a meal which, as thou seest, hath proved fatal to his race. Anon,

[1] The sense of the lacuna may have been: "and *over them* he placed the other parts. This dish my father, *sitting apart*, received as his share."

---

[3] εὕρετ᾽: Dindorf. [4] αὐτοῦ: Blomfield.
[5] Lacuna indicated by Herm., Wilam.

κἄπειτ' ἐπιγνοὺς ἔργον οὐ καταίσιον
ᾤμωξεν, ἀμπίπτει[1] δ' ἀπὸ σφαγὴν[2] ἐρῶν,
μόρον δ' ἄφερτον Πελοπίδαις ἐπεύχεται,
λάκτισμα δείπνου ξυνδίκως τιθεὶς ἀρᾷ,
οὕτως ὀλέσθαι[3] πᾶν τὸ Πλεισθένους γένος.
ἐκ τῶνδέ σοι πεσόντα τόνδ' ἰδεῖν πάρα.
κἀγὼ δίκαιος τοῦδε τοῦ φόνου ῥαφεύς.
τρίτον γὰρ ὄντα μ' ἐπὶ δυσαθλίῳ[4] πατρὶ
συνεξελαύνει τυτθὸν ὄντ' ἐν σπαργάνοις·
τραφέντα δ' αὖθις ἡ δίκη κατήγαγεν.
καὶ τοῦδε τἀνδρὸς ἡψάμην θυραῖος ὤν,
πᾶσαν συνάψας μηχανὴν δυσβουλίας.
οὕτω καλὸν δὴ καὶ τὸ κατθανεῖν ἐμοί,
ἰδόντα[5] τοῦτον τῆς δίκης ἐν ἕρκεσιν.

ΧΟΡΟΣ

Αἴγισθ', ὑβρίζειν ἐν κακοῖσιν οὐ σέβω.
σὺ δ' ἄνδρα τόνδε φῂς[6] ἑκὼν κατακτανεῖν,
μόνος δ' ἔποικτον τόνδε βουλεῦσαι φόνον·
οὔ φημ' ἀλύξειν ἐν δίκῃ τὸ σὸν κάρα
δημορριφεῖς, σάφ' ἴσθι, λευσίμους ἀράς.

ΑΙΓΙΣΘΟΣ

σὺ ταῦτα φωνεῖς νερτέρᾳ προσήμενος
κώπῃ, κρατούντων τῶν ἐπὶ ζυγῷ δορός;
γνώσῃ γέρων ὢν ὡς διδάσκεσθαι βαρὺ
τῷ τηλικούτῳ, σωφρονεῖν εἰρημένον.
δεσμὸς[7] δὲ καὶ τὸ γῆρας αἵ τε νήστιδες
δύαι διδάσκειν ἐξοχώταται φρενῶν

[1] ἀν-πίπτει: Canter. [2] σφαγῆς: Auratus.
[3] ὀλέσθαι Tzetzes, *An. Ox.* iii. 378, ὀλέσθη mss.
[4] δέκ' ἀθλίῳ: Schömann.

discovering his unhallowed deed, he uttered a great cry, reeled back, vomiting forth the slaughtered flesh, and invoked a doom intolerable upon the line of Pelops, spurning the banquet board to aid his curse—" thus perish all the race of Pleisthenes!" For this cause it is that thou beholdest this man fallen here. I am he who planned this murder and with justice. For together with my hapless father he drove me out, me his third child, as yet a babe in swaddling-clothes. But grown to manhood, justice has brought me back again. Exile though I was, I laid my hand upon my enemy, compassing every device of cunning to his ruin. So even death were sweet to me now that I behold him in the toils of justice.

Chorus

Aegisthus, insult amid distress I hold dishonourable. Thou sayest that of thine own intent thou slewest this man and didst alone plot this piteous murder. I tell thee in the hour of justice thou thyself—be sure of that—shalt not escape the people's curses and death by stoning at their hand.

Aegisthus

Speakest thou thus, thou that sittest at the lower oar when those upon the higher thwart control the ship?[1] Old as thou art, thou shalt learn how bitter it is at thy years to be schooled when prudence is the lesson bidden thee. Bonds and the pangs of hunger are far the best mediciners of wisdom for the

[1] In a bireme, the rowers on the lower tier were called θαλαμῖται; those on the upper tier, ζευγῖται.

[5] ἰδόντι N. [6] τόνδ' ἔφης: Pauw.
[7] δεσμὸς N, δεσμὸν FV3.

ἰατρομάντεις. οὐχ ὁρᾷς ὁρῶν τάδε;
πρὸς κέντρα μὴ λάκτιζε, μὴ παίσας[1] μογῇς.

ΧΟΡΟΣ

γύναι, σὺ τοὺς ἥκοντας ἐκ μάχης μένων[2]
οἰκουρὸς εὐνὴν ἀνδρὸς αἰσχύνων[3] ἅμα
ἀνδρὶ στρατηγῷ τόνδ' ἐβούλευσας μόρον;

ΑΙΓΙΣΘΟΣ

καὶ ταῦτα τἄπη κλαυμάτων ἀρχηγενῆ.
'Ορφεῖ δὲ γλῶσσαν τὴν ἐναντίαν ἔχεις.
ὁ μὲν γὰρ ἦγε πάντ' ἀπὸ φθογγῆς χαρᾷ,
σὺ δ' ἐξορίνας νηπίοις[4] ὑλάγμασιν
ἄξῃ· κρατηθεὶς δ' ἡμερώτερος φανῇ.

ΧΟΡΟΣ

ὡς δὴ σύ μοι τύραννος 'Αργείων ἔσῃ,
ὃς οὐκ, ἐπειδὴ τῷδ' ἐβούλευσας[5] μόρον,
δρᾶσαι τόδ' ἔργον οὐκ ἔτλης αὐτοκτόνως.

ΑΙΓΙΣΘΟΣ

τὸ γὰρ δολῶσαι πρὸς γυναικὸς ἦν σαφῶς·
ἐγὼ δ' ὕποπτος ἐχθρὸς ἦ[6] παλαιγενής.
ἐκ τῶν δὲ τοῦδε[7] χρημάτων πειράσομαι
ἄρχειν πολιτῶν· τὸν δὲ μὴ πειθάνορα
ζεύξω βαρείαις οὔτι μοι[8] σειραφόρον
κριθῶντα πῶλον· ἀλλ' ὁ δυσφιλὴς σκότῳ[9]
λιμὸς ξύνοικος μαλθακόν σφ' ἐπόψεται.

[1] παίσας Herm. from schol. Pind. *Pyth.* ii. 173, πήσας MSS.
[2] μάχης νέον: Wieseler.
[3] αἰσχύνουσ': Keck.
[4] ἠπίοις: Jacob.
[5] τῷδε βουλεύσας FV3.
[6] ἦ: Porson.
[7] τῶνδε: Jacob.
[8] οὔτι μὴ: Pauw.
[9] κότῳ: Scaliger.

instruction even of old age. Hast eyes and lackest understanding? Kick not against the pricks lest thou strike to thy hurt.

CHORUS

Woman that thou art! Skulking at home and biding the return of the men from war, the while thou wast defiling a hero's bed, didst *thou* contrive this death against a warrior chief?

AEGISTHUS

These words of thine likewise shall prove a source of tears. The tongue of Orpheus is quite the opposite of thine. He haled all things by the rapture of his voice; but thou, who hast stirred our wrath by thy silly yelping, shalt be haled off thyself. Thou'lt show thyself the tamer when put down by force.

CHORUS

As if forsooth thou shouldst ever be my master here in Argos, thou who didst contrive our King's death, and then hadst not the courage to do this deed of murder with thine own hand!

AEGISTHUS

Because to ensnare him was clearly the woman's part; I was suspect as his enemy of old. However, with his gold I shall endeavour to control the people; and whosoever is unruly, him I'll yoke with a heavy collar—and in sooth he shall be no high-fed trace-colt[1]! No! Loathsome hunger that houseth with darkness shall see him gentle.

[1] The trace-horse bore no collar, and was harnessed by the side of the pair under the yoke.

ΧΟΡΟΣ

τί δὴ τὸν ἄνδρα τόνδ' ἀπὸ ψυχῆς κακῆς
οὐκ αὐτὸς ἠνάριζες, ἀλλά νιν γυνὴ[1]
χώρας μίασμα καὶ θεῶν ἐγχωρίων
ἔκτειν'; Ὀρέστης ἆρά που βλέπει φάος,
ὅπως κατελθὼν δεῦρο πρευμενεῖ τύχῃ
ἀμφοῖν γένηται τοῖνδε παγκρατὴς φονεύς;

ΑΙΓΙΣΘΟΣ

ἀλλ' ἐπεὶ δοκεῖς τάδ' ἔρδειν καὶ λέγειν, γνώσῃ τάχα—
εἶα δή, φίλοι λοχῖται, τοὔργον οὐχ ἑκὰς τόδε.[2]

ΧΟΡΟΣ

εἶα δή, ξίφος πρόκωπον πᾶς τις εὐτρεπιζέτω.

ΑΙΓΙΣΘΟΣ

ἀλλὰ κἀγὼ μὴν πρόκωπος οὐκ ἀναίνομαι θανεῖν.

ΧΟΡΟΣ

δεχομένοις λέγεις θανεῖν σε· τὴν τύχην δ' αἱρούμεθα.[3]

ΚΛΥΤΑΙΜΗΣΤΡΑ

μηδαμῶς, ὦ φίλτατ' ἀνδρῶν, ἄλλα δράσωμεν[4] κακά.
ἀλλὰ καὶ τάδ' ἐξαμῆσαι πολλά, δύστηνον θέρος.[5]
πημονῆς δ' ἅλις γ' ὑπάρχει·[6] μηδὲν αἱματώμεθα.[7]

[1] σὺν γυνὴ: Spanheim.
[2] Given to the Chorus in MSS., to Aegisthus by Stanley.
[3] ἐρούμεθα: Auratus.

Chorus

Why then, in the baseness of thy soul, didst thou not kill him thyself, but leave his slaying to a woman, pest of her country and her country's gods? Oh, doth Orestes haply still behold the light, that, with favouring fortune, he may come home and be the slayer of this pair with victory complete?

Aegisthus

Oh well, since thou art minded thus to act and speak, thou shalt be taught a lesson soon. What ho! My trusty men-at-arms, your work lies close to hand.

Chorus

What ho! Let every one make ready his sword with hand on hilt.

Aegisthus

My hand too is laid on hilt and I shrink not from death.

Chorus

"Death for thyself," thou sayest. We hail the omen. We welcome fortune's test.

Clytaemestra

Nay, my beloved, let us work no further ills. Even these are many to reap, a wretched harvest. Of woe we have enough; let us have no bloodshed.

---

[4] δράσομεν: Vict.
[5] ὁ ἔρως: Schütz.
[6] ὕπαρχε: Scaliger.
[7] ἡματώμεθα: Stanley.

στείχετ᾽ αἰδοῖοι γέροντες[1] πρὸς δόμους, πεπρωμένοις[2] [τούσδε][3]
πρὶν παθεῖν εἴξαντες[4] ὥρᾳ· χρῆν[5] τάδ᾽ ὡς ἐπράξαμεν.[6]
εἰ δέ τοι μόχθων γένοιτο τῶνδ᾽ ἅλις, δεχοίμεθ᾽[7] ἄν,
δαίμονος χηλῇ βαρείᾳ δυστυχῶς πεπληγμένοι.
ὧδ᾽ ἔχει λόγος γυναικός, εἴ τις ἀξιοῖ μαθεῖν.

ΑΙΓΙΣΘΟΣ

ἀλλὰ τούσδ᾽ ἐμοὶ[8] ματαίαν γλῶσσαν ὧδ᾽ ἀπανθίσαι
κἀκβαλεῖν ἔπη τοιαῦτα δαίμονος[9] πειρωμένους,
σώφρονος γνώμης θ᾽[10] ἁμαρτεῖν τὸν[11] κρατοῦντά <θ᾽ ὑβρίσαι>.[12]

ΧΟΡΟΣ

οὐκ ἂν Ἀργείων τόδ᾽ εἴη, φῶτα προσσαίνειν κακόν.

ΑΙΓΙΣΘΟΣ

ἀλλ᾽ ἐγώ σ᾽ ἐν ὑστέραισιν ἡμέραις μέτειμ᾽ ἔτι.

ΧΟΡΟΣ

οὔκ, ἐὰν δαίμων Ὀρέστην δεῦρ᾽ ἀπευθύνῃ μολεῖν.

ΑΙΓΙΣΘΟΣ

οἶδ᾽ ἐγὼ φεύγοντας ἄνδρας ἐλπίδας σιτουμένους.

ΧΟΡΟΣ

πρᾶσσε, πιαίνου, μιαίνων τὴν δίκην, ἐπεὶ πάρα.

1 στείχετε δ᾽ οἱ γέροντες: H. L. Ahrens.
2 πεπρωμένους: Madvig. 3 [τούσδε] Auratus.
4 ἔρξαντες F, ἔρξαντα NV3: Madvig.
5 καιρὸν χρῆν: Headlam (ὥραν Housman).
6 ἐπραξάμην: Vict. 7 γ᾽ ἐχοίμεθ᾽: Martin.

Venerable Elders, betake ye to your homes, and yield betimes to destiny before ye come to harm. What we did had to be done. But should this trouble prove enough, we will accept it, sore smitten as we are by the heavy hand of fate. Such is a woman's counsel, if any deign to give it heed.

AEGISTHUS

But to think that these men should let their wanton tongues thus blossom into speech against me and cast about such gibes, putting their fortune to the test! To reject wise counsel and insult their master!

CHORUS

It would not be like men of Argos to cringe before a knave.

AEGISTHUS

Ha! I'll visit thee with vengeance yet in days to come.

CHORUS

Not if fate shall guide Orestes to return home.

AEGISTHUS

Of myself I know that exiles feed on hope.

CHORUS

Keep on, grow thee fat, polluting justice, since thou canst.

---

[8] τούσδε μοι: I. Voss. [9] δαίμονας: Casaubon.
[10] γνώμης δ': Stanley.
[11] ἁμαρτῆτον FN (om. V3): Casaubon.
[12] <θ' ὑβρίσαι> Blomfield.

ΑΙΓΙΣΘΟΣ

ἴσθι μοι δώσων ἄποινα τῆσδε μωρίας χάριν.

ΧΟΡΟΣ

κόμπασον θαρσῶν,[1] ἀλέκτωρ ὥστε[2] θηλείας πέλας.

ΚΛΥΤΑΙΜΗΣΤΡΑ

μὴ προτιμήσῃς ματαίων τῶνδ' ὑλαγμάτων· <ἐγὼ>[3]
καὶ σὺ θήσομεν κρατοῦντε τῶνδε δωμάτων <καλῶς>.[4]

[1] θαρρῶν: Porson.
[2] ὥσπερ: Scaliger.
[3] <ἐγὼ> Canter.
[4] <καλῶς> Auratus.

AEGISTHUS

Know that thou shalt make me atonement for thy insolent folly.

CHORUS

Brag in thy bravery like a cock beside his hen.

CLYTAEMESTRA

Care not for their idle yelpings. I and thou will be masters of this house and order it aright.

[*Exeunt omnes*

THE LIBATION-BEARERS

ΤΑ ΤΟΥ ΔΡΑΜΑΤΟΣ ΠΡΟΣΩΠΑ

ΟΡΕΣΤΗΣ
ΧΟΡΟΣ
ΗΛΕΚΤΡΑ
ΟΙΚΕΤΗΣ
ΚΛΥΤΑΙΜΗΣΤΡΑ
ΠΥΛΑΔΗΣ
ΤΡΟΦΟΣ
ΑΙΓΙΣΘΟΣ

DRAMATIS PERSONAE

Orestēs
Chorus of Slave-women
Electra
A Servant
Clytaemēstra
Pyladês
Nurse
Aegisthus

Scene.—Argos.
Time.—The heroic age.
Date.—458 B.C., at the City Dionysia.

ARGUMENT

Now when she had slain Agamemnon, Queen Clytaemestra with her lover Aegisthus ruled in the land of Argos. But the spirit of her murdered lord was wroth and sent a baleful vision to distress her soul in sleep. She dreamed that she gave birth to a serpent and that she suckled it, as if it had been a babe; but together with the mother's milk the noxious thing drew clotted blood from out her breast. With a scream of horror she awoke, and when the seers of the house had interpreted the portent as a sign of the anger of the nether powers, she bade Electra, her daughter, and her serving-women bear libations to the tomb of Agamemnon, if haply she might placate his angry spirit.

Now Princess Electra dwelt in the palace, but was treated no better than a slave; but, before that Agamemnon was slain, her brother, Prince Orestes, had been sent to abide with his uncle Strophius in a far country, even in Phocis. There he had grown to youthful manhood, and on the selfsame day that his mother sought to avert the evil omen of her dream, accompanied by his cousin Pylades, he came to Argos seeking vengeance for his father's murder.

On the tomb of Agamemnon he places a lock of his hair, and when Electra discovers it, she is confident that it must be an offering to the dead made by none other than her brother. She has been recognized by him by reason of her mourning garb; but not until she has had further proof, by signs and tokens, will she be convinced that it is he in very truth.

Orestes makes known that he has been divinely commissioned to his purpose of vengeance. Lord Apollo himself has commanded him thereto with threats that, if he disobey, he shall be visited with assaults of the Erinyes of his father—banned from the habitations of men and the altars of the gods, he shall perish blasted in mind and body.

Grouped about the grave of their father, brother and sister, aided by the friendly Chorus, implore his ghostly assistance to their just cause. Orestes and Pylades, disguised as Phocian travellers, are given hospitable welcome by Clytaemestra, to whom it is reported that her son is dead. The Queen sends as messenger Orestes' old nurse to summon Aegisthus from outside accompanied by his bodyguard. The Chorus persuades her to alter the message and bid him come unattended. His death is quickly followed by that of Clytaemestra, whose appeals for mercy are rejected by her son. Orestes, displaying the bloody robe in which his father had been entangled when struck down, proclaims the justice of his deed. But his wits begin to wander; the Erinyes of his mother, unseen by the others, appear before his disordered vision; he rushes from the scene.

ΧΟΗΦΟΡΟΙ

ΟΡΕΣΤΗΣ

[1]<Ἑρμῆ χθόνιε, πατρῷ' ἐποπτεύων κράτη,
σωτὴρ γενοῦ μοι ξύμμαχός τ' αἰτουμένῳ·
ἥκω γὰρ ἐς γῆν τήνδε καὶ κατέρχομαι.
τύμβου δ' ἐπ' ὄχθῳ τῷδε κηρύσσω πατρὶ
κλύειν, ἀκοῦσαι. . . . . .
. . . .
. . . πλόκαμον Ἰνάχῳ θρεπτήριον.
τὸν δεύτερον δὲ τόνδε πενθητήριον
. . . .
οὐ γὰρ παρὼν ᾤμωξα σόν, πάτερ, μόρον
οὐδ' ἐξέτεινα χεῖρ' ἐπ' ἐκφορᾷ[2] νεκροῦ.>
. . . .
[3]τί χρῆμα λεύσσω; τίς ποθ' ἥδ' ὁμήγυρις
στείχει γυναικῶν φάρεσιν μελαγχίμοις

[1] ll. 1-9 supplied: 1-5 by Canter from Aristoph. *Ranae* 1126-1128, 1172, 1173; 6-7 by Stanley from schol. Pind. *Pyth.* iv. 145; 8-9 by Dindorf from schol. Eur. *Alc.* 768.
[2] ἐκφορᾶ: Vat. 909.
[3] Here begin M and its copy Guelferbytanus 88. The MS. readings cited are those of M except when Guelf. is mentioned (G).

---

[1] Hermes is invoked (1) as a god of the lower world, because he is the "conductor of souls" and herald between

THE LIBATION-BEARERS

[Scene: The tomb of Agamemnon. Enter Orestes and Pylades]

ORESTES

Hermes of the nether world, thou who dost guard the powers that are thy sire's,[1] prove thyself my saviour and ally, I beseech thee, now that I am come to this land and am returning home from exile. On this mounded grave I cry unto my father to hearken, to give ear. . . .

[Lo, I bring] a lock to Inachus [2] in requital for my nurture; and here, a second, in token of my grief.

For I was not present, father, to bewail thy death, nor did I stretch forth my hand for thy corpse to be borne out to burial.

What is it I behold? What may be this throng of women that wends its way hither marked by their

the celestial and infernal gods (l. 124), and can thus convey Orestes' appeal to the rulers of the dead and to the spirit of his father; (2) as administrator of the powers committed to him by his father, Zeus the Saviour. Some prefer to take πατρῷ' not as πατρῷα but as πατρῷε, *i.e.* "god of my fathers."

[2] Orestes offers a lock of his hair to do honour to Inachus, the river-god of Argos, because rivers were worshipped as givers of life.

πρέπουσα; ποίᾳ ξυμφορᾷ προσεικάσω;
πότερα δόμοισι πῆμα προσκυρεῖ νέον;
ἢ πατρὶ τὠμῷ τάσδ' ἐπεικάσας τύχω
χοὰς φερούσας νερτέροις μειλίγματα[1];
οὐδέν ποτ' ἄλλο· καὶ γὰρ Ἠλέκτραν δοκῶ
στείχειν ἀδελφὴν τὴν ἐμὴν πένθει λυγρῷ
πρέπουσαν. ὦ Ζεῦ, δός με τείσασθαι[2] μόρον
πατρός, γενοῦ δὲ σύμμαχος θέλων ἐμοί.
Πυλάδη, σταθῶμεν ἐκποδών,[3] ὡς ἂν σαφῶς
μάθω γυναικῶν ἥτις ἥδε προστροπή.

ΧΟΡΟΣ

ἰαλτὸς ἐκ δόμων ἔβαν[4] [στρ. α.
χοὰς προπομπὸς ὀξύχειρι σὺν κτύπῳ.[5]
πρέπει παρηὶς φοινίοις ἀμυγμοῖς[6]
ὄνυχος ἄλοκι νεοτόμῳ·
δι' αἰῶνος δ' ἰυγμοῖσι[7] βόσκεται κέαρ.
λινοφθόροι δ' ὑφασμάτων
λακίδες ἔφλαδον ὑπ' ἄλγεσιν,[8]
προστέρνῳ στολμῷ[9]
πέπλων ἀγελάστοις
ξυμφοραῖς πεπληγμένων.

τορὸς δὲ[10] Φοῖβος ὀρθόθριξ [ἀντ. α.
δόμων ὀνειρόμαντις, ἐξ ὕπνου κότον

[1] μειλίγμασιν: Casaubon.
[2] τίσασθαι: Kirchhoff.
[3] ἐκποδῶν: Stanley.
[4] ἐ . . . (ἔβην? M), ἔβη G: Dindorf (ἔβην Rob.).
[5] συγκυ·ωι corrected to συνκύπτωι: Arnaldus.
[6] φοινισσαμυγμοῖς: Stanley.
[7] διοιγμοῖσι: Canter.
[8] ἄλγεσι: *Et. Gen.* 403. 47.
[9] πρόσστελνοι (with ρ over λ m) στολμοί: Blass.
[10] γὰρ: Lachmann.

sable weeds? To what that hath befallen am I to refer it? Is it some new sorrow that cometh upon the house? Or am I right in my surmise that it is in honour of my sire that they bear these libations to appease the powers below? It can be only for this cause; for, methinks, it is indeed mine own sister Electra who advances yonder, conspicuous among the rest by her bitter mourning. Oh grant me, Zeus, to avenge my father's death, and of thy grace lend me thine aid!

Pylades, let us stand apart, that I may learn of a surety what this band of suppliant women may import. [*Exit Orestes and Pylades*

[*Enter Electra with women carrying libations*

CHORUS

Sent forth from the palace I am come to convey libations to the accompaniment of blows dealt swift and sharp by my hands. My cheek is marked with bloody gashes where my nails have cut fresh furrows—and yet throughout all my life my heart is fed with lamentation. To the tune of grievous blows the rendings sounded loud as they made havoc of my vesture of woven linen where my bosom is covered[1] by a robe smitten by reason of fortunes stranger to all mirth.

For with thrilling voice that set each hair on end, the inspiring power who divines for the house in

[1] στολμῷ goes closely with πέπλων, "enfolding robe."

πνέων, ἀωρόνυκτον ἀμβόαμα
μυχόθεν ἔλακε[1] περὶ φόβῳ,
γυναικείοισιν[2] ἐν δώμασιν βαρὺς πίτνων.[3]
κριταί <τε>[4] τῶνδ' ὀνειράτων
θεόθεν ἔλακον[5] ὑπέγγυοι
μέμφεσθαι τοὺς γᾶς
νέρθεν περιθύμως
τοῖς κτανοῦσί τ' ἐγκοτεῖν.

τοιάνδε χάριν[6] ἀχάριτον ἀπότροπον κακῶν, [στρ. β.
ἰὼ γαῖα μαῖα,
μωμένα μ' ἰάλλει[7]
δύσθεος γυνά. φοβοῦ-
μαι δ' ἔπος τόδ' ἐκβαλεῖν.[8]
τί γὰρ λύτρον[9] πεσόντος αἵματος πέδοι[10];
ἰὼ πάνοιζυς ἑστία,
ἰὼ κατασκαφαὶ δόμων.
ἀνήλιοι βροτοστυγεῖς
δνόφοι καλύπτουσι δόμους
δεσποτῶν[11] θανάτοισι.

σέβας δ' ἄμαχον ἀδάματον[12] ἀπόλεμον τὸ πρὶν [ἀντ. β.
δι' ὤτων φρενός[13] τε
δαμίας περαῖνον
νῦν ἀφίσταται. φοβεῖ-
ται δέ τις. τὸ δ' εὐτυχεῖν,
τόδ' ἐν βροτοῖς[14] θεός τε καὶ θεοῦ πλέον.
ῥοπὴ δ' ἐπισκοπεῖ δίκας[15]
ταχεῖα τοὺς[16] μὲν ἐν φάει,

[1] ἔλαχε, κε over χε m.
[2] γυναικίοισιν: Vict.
[3] πιτνῶν: Blomfield.
[4] <τε> Porson.
[5] ἔλαχον: Turn.
[6] ἄχαριν: Elmsley.
[7] μιλλεῖ: Stanley.
[8] ἐκβάλλειν: Stanley.

dreams, with breath of wrath in sleep, at dead of night uttered a cry for terror from the inmost chamber, falling heavily upon the women's bower.[1] And the readers of dreams like these, interpreting Heaven's will under pledge, declared that those beneath the earth complain in bitter anger and are wroth against their slayers.

Purposing such a graceless grace to ward off ill (O mother Earth!), she sendeth me forth, godless woman that she is. But I am afraid to utter the words she bade me speak. For what redemption is there for blood once fallen on the earth? Ah, hearth of utter grief! Ah, house laid low in ruin! Darkness, unillumined of the sun and loathed of men, enshrouds the house now that its lord hath been done to death.

The awe of majesty that of yore none might withstand, none resist, none quell, that pierced the public ear and heart, is now cast off. But fear men feel. For Success—this, in men's eyes, is God and more than God. But the balanced scale of Justice keepeth watch: swift it descendeth on some who

[1] The language of the passage is accommodated to a double purpose: (1) to indicate an oracular deliverance on the part of the inspired prophetess at Delphi, and (2) to show the alarming nature of Clytaemestra's dream; while certain limiting expressions (as ἀωρόνυκτον, ὕπνου) show the points of difference. "Phoebus" is used for a prophetic "possession," which assails Clytaemestra as a nightmare (cp. βαρὺς πίτνων); so that her vision is itself called an ὀνειρόμαντις.

---

[9] λυγρὸν: Canter. [10] πέδῳ: Dindorf.
[11] δεσποτῶμ: Aldina. [12] ἀδάμαντον: Herm.
[13] φρένες: Vict. [14] ἐμβροτοῖσι: Vict.
[15] δίκαν: Turn. (ῥοπὴ τῆς δίκης Schol.). [16] τοῖς: Turn.

τὰ δ' ἐν μεταιχμίῳ σκότου
μένει χρονίζοντας[1] ἄχη [βρύει],[2]
τοὺς δ' ἄκραντος ἔχει νύξ.

δι' αἵματ' ἐκποθένθ'[3] ὑπὸ χθονὸς τροφοῦ [στρ. γ.
τίτας φόνος πέπηγεν οὐ διαρρύδαν.[4]
διαλγὴς <δ'>[5] ἄτα[6] διαφέρει
τὸν αἴτιον παναρκέτας νόσου βρύειν.[7]

θιγόντι[8] δ' οὔτι νυμφικῶν ἑδωλίων [ἀντ. γ.
ἄκος, πόροι τε πάντες ἐκ μιᾶς ὁδοῦ
<προ>βαίνοντες[9] τὸν χερομυσῆ[10]
φόνον καθαίροντες ἴθυσαν[11] μάταν.[12]

ἐμοὶ δ'—ἀνάγκαν γὰρ ἀμφίπτολιν [ἐπῳδ.
θεοὶ προσήνεγκαν· (ἐκ γὰρ οἴκων
πατρῴων δούλιόν <μ'>[13] ἐσᾶγον αἶσαν)—
δίκαια καὶ μὴ δίκαια ἀρχὰς πρέπον
βίᾳ φρενῶν αἰνέσαι
πικρὸν[14] στύγος κρατούσῃ.
δακρύω δ' ὑφ' εἱμάτων
ματαίοισι δεσποτᾶν
τύχαις, κρυφαίοις πένθεσιν παχνουμένη.[15]

ΗΛΕΚΤΡΑ

δμωαὶ γυναῖκες, δωμάτων εὐθήμονες,
ἐπεὶ πάρεστε τῆσδε προστροπῆς ἐμοὶ
πομποί, γένεσθε τῶνδε σύμβουλοι πέρι·
τί φῶ χέουσα[16] τάσδε κηδείους χοάς;

[1] χρονίζοντ': Dindorf. [2] [βρύει] Herm.
[3] ἔκποθεν: Schütz. [4] διαρρυδᾶν: Lobeck.
[5] <δ'> Schütz. [6] ἄτη: Schütz.
[7] After l. 70, l. 65 repeated: del. Heath.

still stand in the light; sometimes sorrows await them that tarry in the twilight of life's close; and some are enshrouded by ineffectual night.

Because of blood drunk to her fill by fostering earth, the vengeful gore lieth clotted and will not dissolve away. Calamity, racking his soul, distracts the guilty man so that he is steeped in misery utter and complete.

But for him that violateth a bridal bower there is no cure; so, albeit all streams flow in one current to cleanse the blood from a polluted hand, they speed their course to no avail.

For me—since the gods laid constraining doom about my city (for from my father's house they led me to the fate of slavery)—it beseemeth, against my will, to conquer my bitter hate and submit to the behests—or just or unjust—of my masters. Yet 'neath my veil, my heart chilled by secret grief, I bewail the foul undoing of my lord.

Electra

Ye handmaidens, who duly order the household's cares, since ye are present here to attend me in this rite of supplication, give me your advice touching this. While I pour these offerings of sorrow, what

---

[8] οἴγοντι: Stephanus. [9] βάίνοντες: Bamberger.
[10] χαιρομυσῆ: Porson. [11] ἰοῦσαν: Musgrave.
[12] ἄτην with α over η: μάτην Scaliger: μάταν Heath.
[13] <μ'> Conington.
[14] ll. 78-80 δίκαια πρέποντ' ἀρχὰς (ἀπ' ἀρχᾶς Schol.) βίου βίᾳ φερομένων αἰνέσαι πικρῶν (πικρὸν Schol.): βίᾳ φρενῶν H. L. Ahrens, πρέπον βίᾳ Wilam. [15] παχνουμένην: Turn.
[16] τύφω (οἶμαι τύμβῳ m) δὲ χέουσα: τί φῶ H. L. Ahrens, [δὲ] Turn.

πῶς εὔφρον'[1] εἴπω, πῶς κατεύξομαι πατρί;
πότερα λέγουσα παρὰ φίλης φίλῳ φέρειν
γυναικὸς ἀνδρί, τῆς ἐμῆς μητρὸς πάρα;
τῶνδ' οὐ πάρεστι θάρσος, οὐδ' ἔχω τί φῶ,
χέουσα τόνδε πέλανον ἐν τύμβῳ πατρός.
ἢ τοῦτο φάσκω τοὔπος, ὡς νόμος βροτοῖς,
ἔσθλ'[2] ἀντιδοῦναι τοῖσι πέμπουσιν[3] τάδε
στέφη, δόσιν γε[4] τῶν κακῶν ἐπαξίαν;
ἢ σῖγ' ἀτίμως, ὥσπερ οὖν ἀπώλετο
πατήρ, τάδ' ἐκχέασα,[5] γάποτον χύσιν,
στείχω καθάρμαθ' ὥς τις ἐκπέμψας πάλιν
δικοῦσα τεῦχος ἀστρόφοισιν ὄμμασιν;
τῆσδ' ἐστὲ βουλῆς, ὦ φίλαι, μεταίτιαι·
κοινὸν γὰρ ἔχθος ἐν δόμοις νομίζομεν.
μὴ κεύθετ' ἔνδον καρδίας φόβῳ τινός.
τὸ μόρσιμον γὰρ τόν τ' ἐλεύθερον μένει
καὶ τὸν πρὸς ἄλλης δεσποτούμενον χερός.
λέγοις ἄν, εἴ τι τῶνδ' ἔχοις ὑπέρτερον.

ΧΟΡΟΣ

αἰδουμένη σοι βωμὸν ὣς τύμβον πατρὸς
λέξω, κελεύεις γάρ, τὸν ἐκ φρενὸς λόγον.

ΗΛΕΚΤΡΑ

λέγοις ἄν, ὥσπερ ᾐδέσω τάφον πατρός.

[1] εὔφρων M, εὔφρον' m.
[2] ἔστ': Bamberger.
[3] πέμπουσι: Vict.
[4] τε: Stanley.
[5] ἐγχέουσα: Dindorf.

am I to say? How shall I find gracious words, how voice the prayer unto my father? Shall I say that I bring these offerings to a loved husband from a loving wife—from her that is mine own mother? For that I have not the assurance; nor know I what words to say as I pour this draught upon my father's tomb. Or shall I speak the speech that men are wont to use: "that to those who send these funeral honours may he make return with good"—a gift forsooth to match their evil[1]?

Or, in silence and dishonour, even as my father perished, shall I pour them out for the earth to drink, and then retrace my steps, like as one who carries forth refuse from a rite, hurling the vessel from me with averted eyes?

Herein, my friends, be ye my fellow-counsellors; for common is the hate we cherish within the house. Hide not your counsel in your hearts through fear of any. For the fated hour awaits alike the free and him made bondsman by another's might. If thou hast a better course to urge, oh speak!

CHORUS

In reverence for thy father's tomb, like as it were an altar, I will voice my inmost thoughts, since thou commandest me.

ELECTRA

Speak, even as thou hast reverence for my father's grave.

[1] "Their evil" is unexpectedly substituted for "their good." The question is ironical, since it was natural for a Greek to return evil for evil (cp. 123).

ΧΟΡΟΣ

φθέγγου χέουσα κεδνὰ[1] τοῖσιν εὔφροσιν.

ΗΛΕΚΤΡΑ

τίνας δὲ τούτους τῶν φίλων προσεννέπω;

ΧΟΡΟΣ

πρῶτον μὲν αὑτὴν χὤστις Αἴγισθον στυγεῖ.

ΗΛΕΚΤΡΑ

ἐμοί τε καὶ σοί τἄρ' ἐπεύξομαι τάδε;

ΧΟΡΟΣ

αὐτὴ σὺ ταῦτα μανθάνουσ' ἤδη φράσαι.

ΗΛΕΚΤΡΑ

τίν' οὖν ἔτ' ἄλλον τῇδε προστιθῶ στάσει;

ΧΟΡΟΣ

μέμνησ' Ὀρέστου, κεἰ θυραῖός ἐσθ' ὅμως.

ΗΛΕΚΤΡΑ

εὖ τοῦτο, κἀφρένωσας οὐχ ἥκιστά με.

ΧΟΡΟΣ

τοῖς αἰτίοις νῦν τοῦ φόνου μεμνημένη—

ΗΛΕΚΤΡΑ

τί φῶ; δίδασκ' ἄπειρον ἐξηγουμένη.

[1] σεμνὰ: Hartung.

CHORUS

The while thou pourest, utter words fraught with good to loyal hearts.

ELECTRA

And to whom of those near to me am I to give this name?

CHORUS

To thyself first—then to all who hate Aegisthus.

ELECTRA

For myself then and for thee as well shall I make this prayer?

CHORUS

It is for thee, using thy judgment, forthwith to consider that thyself.

ELECTRA

Who else then is there that I am to add to our company?

CHORUS

Forget not Orestes, though he be still from home.

ELECTRA

Well said! Most excellently hast thou admonished me

CHORUS

For the guilty murderers now, with mindful thought—

ELECTRA

What shall I pray? Instruct my inexperience, prescribe the form.

ΧΟΡΟΣ

ἐλθεῖν τιν' αὐτοῖς δαίμον' ἢ βροτῶν τινα—

ΗΛΕΚΤΡΑ

πότερα δικαστὴν ἢ δικηφόρον λέγεις[1];

ΧΟΡΟΣ

ἁπλῶς τι φράζουσ', ὅστις ἀνταποκτενεῖ.

ΗΛΕΚΤΡΑ

καὶ ταῦτά μοὐστὶν εὐσεβῆ θεῶν πάρα;

ΧΟΡΟΣ

πῶς δ' οὐ τὸν ἐχθρὸν ἀνταμείβεσθαι κακοῖς;

ΗΛΕΚΤΡΑ

124 κῆρυξ μέγιστε[2] τῶν ἄνω τε καὶ κάτω,[3]
124a ⟨ἄρηξον,⟩[4] Ἑρμῆ χθόνιε, κηρύξας ἐμοὶ
τοὺς γῆς ἔνερθε δαίμονας κλύειν ἐμὰς
εὐχάς, πατρῴων δωμάτων[5] ἐπισκόπους,
καὶ Γαῖαν αὐτήν, ἣ τὰ πάντα τίκτεται,
θρέψασά τ' αὖθις τῶνδε κῦμα λαμβάνει·
κἀγὼ χέουσα τάσδε χέρνιβας βροτοῖς
λέγω καλοῦσα πατέρ', "ἐποίκτιρόν[6] τ' ἐμὲ
φίλον τ' Ὀρέστην· πῶς ἀνάξομεν δόμοις;
πεπραμένοι[7] γὰρ νῦν γέ πως ἀλώμεθα
πρὸς τῆς τεκούσης, ἄνδρα δ' ἀντηλλάξατο
Αἴγισθον, ὅσπερ σοῦ φόνου μεταίτιος.

[1] λέγω: Weil. [2] μεγίστη: Stanley.
[3] Transferred from after l. 164 by Herm.
[4] ⟨ἄρηξον⟩ Klausen. [5] δ' ὀμμάτων: Stanley.
[6] ἐποίκτειρον: Kirchhoff. [7] πεπραγμένοι: Casaubon.

CHORUS

That upon them there may come some one or god or mortal—

ELECTRA

As judge or as avenger, meanest thou?

CHORUS

Say in plain speech "one who shall take life for life."

ELECTRA

And is this a righteous thing for me to ask of Heaven?

CHORUS

Righteous? How not? To requite an enemy evil for evil!

ELECTRA

Herald supreme between the world above and world below, O nether Hermes, come to my aid and summon me the spirits beneath the earth to attend my prayers, spirits that keep watch o'er my father's house, aye, and Earth herself, that bringeth all things to birth, and having nurtured them receiveth their increase in turn. And I the while, as I pour these lustral offerings to the dead, invoke my father and thus voice my prayer: "Have compassion both on me and on dear Orestes! How shall we be lords in our estate? For now we are vagrants, as it were, bartered away by her that bare us, by her who in exchange hath bought Aegisthus as her mate, even him who was her partner in thy murder. As

κἀγὼ μὲν ἀντίδουλος· ἐκ δὲ χρημάτων
φεύγων[1] Ὀρέστης ἐστίν, οἱ δ' ὑπερκόπως
ἐν τοῖσι σοῖς πόνοισι[2] χλίουσιν μέγα.[3]
ἐλθεῖν δ' Ὀρέστην δεῦρο σὺν τύχῃ τινὶ
κατεύχομαί σοι, καὶ σὺ κλῦθί μου, πάτερ·
αὐτῇ τέ μοι δὸς σωφρονεστέραν[4] πολὺ
μητρὸς γενέσθαι χεῖρά τ' εὐσεβεστέραν.
ἡμῖν μὲν εὐχὰς τάσδε, τοῖς δ' ἐναντίοις
λέγω φανῆναί σου, πάτερ, τιμάορον,
καὶ τοὺς κτανόντας ἀντικατθανεῖν δίκῃ.[5]
ταῦτ' ἐν μέσῳ τίθημι τῆς καλῆς[6] ἀρᾶς,
κείνοις λέγουσα τήνδε τὴν κακὴν ἀράν·
ἡμῖν δὲ πομπὸς ἴσθι τῶν ἐσθλῶν ἄνω,
σὺν θεοῖσι καὶ Γῇ καὶ Δίκῃ νικηφόρῳ."
τοιαῖσδ' ἐπ' εὐχαῖς τάσδ' ἐπισπένδω χοάς.
ὑμᾶς δὲ κωκυτοῖς ἐπανθίζειν νόμος,
παιᾶνα τοῦ θανόντος ἐξαυδωμένας.

ΧΟΡΟΣ

ἵετε δάκρυ καναχὲς ὀλόμενον
ὀλομένῳ δεσπότᾳ
πρὸς ἔρυμα τόδε κακῶν, κεδνῶν τ'
ἀπότροπον ἄγος[7] ἀπεύχετον
κεχυμένων χοᾶν. κλύε δέ μοι, κλύε, σέβας ὦ[8] δέσποτ', ἐξ ἀμαυρᾶς φρενός.

[1] φεύγειν: Rob. [2] πόνοισιν: Rob.
[3] μέτα: Rob. [4] σωφρονεστέρα M: -αν m.
[5] δίκην: Scaliger. [6] κακῆς: Schütz.
[7] ἄλγος M, ἄγος Schol.: Vict. [8] σεβάσω: Turn.

for me, I am no better than a slave, Orestes is an outcast from his substance, while they in insolence of pride wanton bravely in the winnings of thy toil. Yet may Orestes come home—and with happy fortune! This is my prayer to thee, and do thou hearken unto me, my father. For myself, oh grant that I may prove in heart more chaste, far more, than my mother and in hand more innocent.

These invocations on our behalf; but for our foes I implore that there appear one who will avenge thee, father, and that thy slayers may be slain in just retribution. ('Tis thus I interrupt my prayer for good, for them uttering this prayer for evil.) But to us be thou a bringer of blessings to the upper world by favour of the gods and Earth and Justice crowned with victory." [*She pours out the libations*

Such are my prayers, and over them I pour out these libations. 'Tis your due service to crown them with flowers of lamentation, raising your voices in a chant for the dead.

Chorus

Pour forth your tears, plashing as they fall for our fallen lord, to accompany this protection against evil—this means to avert from the good the loathed pollution of outpoured libations.[1] Hearken unto me, oh hearken, my august lord, with thy gloom-enshrouded spirit.[2]

[1] An alternative rendering is: . . . "fallen lord, on this barrier against ill and good (*i.e.* the *tomb*), to avert the cursed pollution, now that the libations have been poured out."

[2] Or ἀμαυρᾶς may mean "feeble," "helpless," to contrast the spirit of the dead with that of the living. But cp. 323.

ὀτοτοτοτοτοτοτοτοῖ,
ἴτω τις[1] δορυ-
σθενὴς ἀνήρ, ἀναλυτὴρ δόμων,
Σκυθικά τ'[2] ἐν χεροῖν παλίντον'
ἐν ἔργῳ βέλη 'πιπάλλων Ἄρης
σχέδιά τ' αὐτόκωπα νωμῶν ξίφη.[3]

ΗΛΕΚΤΡΑ

ἔχει μὲν ἤδη γαπότους[4] χοὰς πατήρ·
νέου δὲ μύθου τοῦδε κοινωνήσατε.

ΧΟΡΟΣ

λέγοις ἄν· ὀρχεῖται[5] δὲ καρδία φόβῳ.

ΗΛΕΚΤΡΑ

ὁρῶ τομαῖον τόνδε βόστρυχον τάφῳ.

ΧΟΡΟΣ

τίνος ποτ' ἀνδρός, ἢ βαθυζώνου κόρης;

ΗΛΕΚΤΡΑ

εὐξύμβολον τόδ' ἐστὶ παντὶ δοξάσαι.

ΧΟΡΟΣ

πῶς οὖν; παλαιὰ παρὰ νεωτέρας μάθω.

ΗΛΕΚΤΡΑ

οὐκ ἔστιν ὅστις πλὴν ἐμοῦ κείραιτό νιν.[6]

[1] ἰὼ τίς: Bothe. [2] σκυθιτατ' with ης over ι: Rob.
[3] βέλη: Pauw from Schol.

Woe, woe, woe! Oh for a man mighty with the spear to deliver the house, a very god of war, brandishing in the fray the Scythian rebounding bow and wielding in close combat his hilted brand!

[*As they conclude, Electra discovers the lock of Orestes' hair*

ELECTRA

My father hath by now received the libations, which the earth hath quaffed. But here is startling news! Share it with me.

CHORUS

Speak on—and yet my heart is dancing with fear.

ELECTRA

I see here a lock, a shorn offering for the tomb.

CHORUS

Whose can it be—some man's or some deep-girdled maid's?

ELECTRA

That is easy to conjecture—anyone may guess.

CHORUS

How then? Let my age be lessoned by thy youth.

ELECTRA

There is no one who could have shorn it save—myself.

---

[4] ἀπό, του: γαπότους Turn. After l. 164 M has l. 124.

[5] ἀνορχεῖται: Turn.

[6] κείρετό νειν (with νιν over νειν m): Turn.

ΧΟΡΟΣ

ἐχθροὶ γὰρ οἷς προσῆκε πενθῆσαι τριχί.

ΗΛΕΚΤΡΑ

καὶ μὴν ὅδ' ἐστὶ κάρτ' ἰδεῖν ὁμόπτερος—

ΧΟΡΟΣ

ποίαις ἐθείραις; τοῦτο γὰρ θέλω μαθεῖν.

ΗΛΕΚΤΡΑ

αὐτοῖσιν ἡμῖν κάρτα προσφερὴς ἰδεῖν.

ΧΟΡΟΣ

μῶν οὖν Ὀρέστου κρύβδα δῶρον ἦν[1] τόδε;

ΗΛΕΚΤΡΑ

μάλιστ' ἐκείνου βοστρύχοις προσείδεται.

ΧΟΡΟΣ

καὶ πῶς ἐκεῖνος δεῦρ' ἐτόλμησεν μολεῖν;

ΗΛΕΚΤΡΑ

ἔπεμψε χαίτην[2] κουρίμην χάριν πατρός.

ΧΟΡΟΣ

οὐχ ἧσσον εὐδάκρυτά μοι λέγεις τάδε,
εἰ τῆσδε χώρας μήποτε ψαύσει[3] ποδί.

[1] ἦ: Scholefield. [2] ἔπεμψεν καὶ τὴν: Vict.
[3] ψαύδει with η over ε m: Turn.

CHORUS

Aye, for foes are they whom it had beseemed to make such mournful offering of their hair.

ELECTRA

And further, to look upon, 'tis very like—

CHORUS

Whose locks? This I fain would know.

ELECTRA

Our own—yes, very like, to look upon.

CHORUS

Can it then be that Orestes offered it in secret here?

ELECTRA

'Tis *his* curling locks that it most resembles.

CHORUS

But how did *he* venture to come hither?

ELECTRA

He hath but *sent* this shorn lock to do honour to his sire.

CHORUS

In thy words lies still greater cause for tears, if he shall never more set foot upon this land.

ΗΛΕΚΤΡΑ

κἀμοὶ προσέστη καρδίας κλυδώνιον
χολῆς, ἐπαίσθην[1] δ' ὡς διανταίῳ βέλει·
ἐξ ὀμμάτων δὲ δίψιοι πίπτουσί μοι
σταγόνες ἄφρακτοι δυσχίμου πλημμυρίδος,
πλόκαμον ἰδούσῃ τόνδε· πῶς γὰρ ἐλπίσω
ἀστῶν τιν' ἄλλον τῆσδε δεσπόζειν φόβης;
ἀλλ' οὐδὲ μήν νιν ἡ κτανοῦσ' ἐκείρατο,
ἐμὴ δὲ μήτηρ, οὐδαμῶς ἐπώνυμον
φρόνημα παισὶ δύσθεον πεπαμένη.
ἐγὼ δ' ὅπως μὲν ἄντικρυς τάδ' αἰνέσω,
εἶναι τόδ' ἀγλάισμά μοι τοῦ φιλτάτου
βροτῶν 'Ορέστου—σαίνομαι δ' ὑπ' ἐλπίδος.
φεῦ.
εἴθ' εἶχε φωνὴν εὔφρον' ἀγγέλου δίκην,
ὅπως δίφροντις οὖσα μὴ 'κινυσσόμην,[2]
ἀλλ' εὖ 'σαφήνει[3] τόνδ' ἀποπτύσαι πλόκον,
εἴπερ γ' ἀπ' ἐχθροῦ κρατὸς ἦν τετμημένος·
ἢ ξυγγενὴς ὢν εἶχε συμπενθεῖν ἐμοὶ
ἄγαλμα τύμβου τοῦδε καὶ τιμὴν πατρός.
ἀλλ' εἰδότας μὲν τοὺς θεοὺς καλούμεθα,
οἵοισιν ἐν χειμῶσι ναυτίλων δίκην[4]
στροβούμεθ'· εἰ δὲ χρὴ τυχεῖν σωτηρίας,
σμικροῦ γένοιτ' ἂν σπέρματος μέγας πυθμήν.
καὶ μὴν στίβοι γε, δεύτερον τεκμήριον,
ποδῶν[5] ὅμοιοι τοῖς τ' ἐμοῖσιν ἐμφερεῖς—
καὶ γὰρ δύ' ἐστὸν τώδε περιγραφὰ ποδοῖν,
αὐτοῦ τ' ἐκείνου καὶ συνεμπόρου τινός.
πτέρναι τενόντων θ' ὑπογραφαὶ μετρούμεναι
εἰς ταὐτὸ συμβαίνουσι τοῖς ἐμοῖς στίβοις.
πάρεστι δ' ὠδὶς καὶ φρενῶν καταφθορά.

ELECTRA

Over my heart, too, there sweeps a surge of bitterness, and I am smitten as if a sword had stabbed me through and through. From my eyes thirsty drops of a stormy flood fall unchecked at sight of this tress. For how can I expect to find that someone else, some townsman, owns this lock? Nor yet in truth did she shear it from her head—she the murderess, my own mother, who towards her children hath taken to herself a godless spirit ill-according with the name of mother. But, for my part, how am I to assent to this outright—that it adorned the head of him who is dearest to me in all the world, Orestes? Ah no! hope but flatters me.

Ah me! If only, like a messenger, it had a kindly voice so that I were not tossed by my distracted thoughts—but would plainly bid me spurn away this tress, had it been severed from a hated head; or, if it claimed kin to me, would share my grief, an adornment to this tomb and a tribute to my sire.

But Heaven, which I invoke, knoweth by what storms we are tossed like men upon the sea. Yet, if it is our fate to win safety, from a little seed may spring a mighty stock.

And lo! why here are tracks—a second proof—tracks of feet, matching each other—and like unto my own! Yes, for here are two sorts of footprints, his own and some companion's. The heels and markings of the tendons agree in their proportions with mine own tracks. I am in torment, my brain is in a whirl! [*Enter Orestes*

[1] ἐπαίθην: Canter. [2] μήκηννυσσόμην: Turn.
[3] σαφηνῆ: Paley. [4] δίκῃ: Aldina.
[5] ποδῶν δ': Turn.

ΟΡΕΣΤΗΣ

εὔχου τὰ λοιπά, τοῖς θεοῖς τελεσφόρους
εὐχὰς ἐπαγγέλλουσα, τυγχάνειν καλῶς.

ΗΛΕΚΤΡΑ

ἐπεὶ τί νῦν ἕκατι δαιμόνων κυρῶ;

ΟΡΕΣΤΗΣ

εἰς ὄψιν ἥκεις ὧνπερ ἐξηύχου[1] πάλαι.

ΗΛΕΚΤΡΑ

καὶ τίνα σύνοισθά μοι καλουμένῃ βροτῶν;

ΟΡΕΣΤΗΣ

σύνοιδ' Ὀρέστην πολλά σ' ἐκπαγλουμένην.[2]

ΗΛΕΚΤΡΑ

καὶ πρὸς τί δῆτα τυγχάνω κατευγμάτων;

ΟΡΕΣΤΗΣ

ὅδ' εἰμί· μὴ μάτευ'[3] ἐμοῦ μᾶλλον φίλον.

ΗΛΕΚΤΡΑ

ἀλλ' ἦ δόλον τιν', ὦ ξέν', ἀμφί μοι πλέκεις;

ΟΡΕΣΤΗΣ

αὐτὸς καθ' αὑτοῦ τἄρα[4] μηχανορραφῶ.

[1] ἐξηύκου: Rob.
[2] ἐκπαγλουμένης: Rob.
[3] μάστευ' M, μάτευ' G.
[4] ταρρα: Dindorf.

ORESTES

Make acknowledgment to Heaven that thy prayers have been fulfilled, and pray that for the future success attend thee.

ELECTRA

How so? Wherein have I now obtained success by Heaven's grace?

ORESTES

Thou hast come to the sight of that for which thou hast prayed for long.

ELECTRA

And whom of men dost thou know I was invoking?

ORESTES

I know that for Orestes thou art much empassioned.

ELECTRA

And wherein then have I found answer to my prayers?

ORESTES

Here am I. Seek for no nearer friend than me.

ELECTRA

Nay, surely, sir, 'tis some snare that thou art weaving about me?

ORESTES

'Tis then against myself that I am devising plots.

ΗΛΕΚΤΡΑ

ἀλλ᾽ ἐν κακοῖσι τοῖς ἐμοῖς γελᾶν θέλεις.

ΟΡΕΣΤΗΣ

κἀν τοῖς ἐμοῖς[1] ἄρ᾽, εἴπερ ἔν γε τοῖσι σοῖς.

ΗΛΕΚΤΡΑ

ὡς ὄντ᾽ Ὀρέστην τάδε σ᾽ ἐγὼ προσεννέπω[2];

ΟΡΕΣΤΗΣ

αὐτὸν μὲν οὖν[3] ὁρῶσα δυσμαθεῖς ἐμέ·
κουρὰν δ᾽ ἰδοῦσα τήνδε κηδείου τριχὸς
ἰχνοσκοποῦσά τ᾽ ἐν στίβοισι τοῖς ἐμοῖς
ἀνεπτερώθης κἀδόκεις ὁρᾶν ἐμέ.[4]
σκέψαι τομῇ[5] προσθεῖσα βόστρυχον τριχὸς
σαυτῆς ἀδελφοῦ σύμμετρον[6] τὠμῷ[7] κάρᾳ.[8]
ἰδοῦ δ᾽ ὕφασμα τοῦτο, σῆς ἔργον χερός,
σπάθης τε πληγὰς ἠδὲ[9] θήρειον[10] γραφήν.
ἔνδον γενοῦ, χαρᾷ δὲ μὴ ᾽κπλαγῇς[11] φρένας·
τοὺς φιλτάτους γὰρ οἶδα νῷν ὄντας πικρούς.

ΗΛΕΚΤΡΑ

ὦ φίλτατον μέλημα δώμασιν πατρός,
δακρυτὸς ἐλπὶς σπέρματος σωτηρίου,
ἀλκῇ πεποιθὼς δῶμ᾽ ἀνακτήσῃ πατρός.
ὦ τερπνὸν ὄμμα τέσσαρας μοίρας ἔχον
ἐμοί· προσαυδᾶν δ᾽ ἔστ᾽ ἀναγκαίως ἔχον

[1] ἐμοῖσιν: Turn. [2] ἐγώ σε προυννέπω: Arnaldus. [3] μὲν νῦν: Turn. [4] l. 228, transf. Rob. [5] σκέψαι το μὴ: Turn. [6] συμμέτρου: Pauw. [7] τῷ σῷ: Dindorf.

ELECTRA

Nay, thou art fain to mock at my distress.

ORESTES

At mine own then also, if indeed at thine.

ELECTRA

Am I then to address thee as in truth Orestes?

ORESTES

Nay, though thou seest in me his very self, thou art but slow to learn. Yet at sight of this shorn tress of mourning and when thou wast scanning the footprints of my tracks, thy thought took wings and thou didst deem it was I thou didst behold. Put to the spot whence it was shorn the lock of hair —thine own brother's—and mark how it agrees with that of my head. And see this piece of weaving, thy handiwork, the batten strokes and the beasts in the design. Control thyself! Be not distraught for joy! For our nearest kin, I know, are bitter foes to us twain.

ELECTRA

O best beloved darling of thy father's house, its hope of saving seed, longed for with tears, trust in thy prowess and thou shalt win again thy father's house. O thou fond presence that hath for me four parts of love: for father I needs must call

---

[8] ll. 230-229 transf. Bothe. [9] εἰς δὲ: Turn.
[10] θηρίον: Bamberger. [11] μὴκπλαγιῇ: Turn.

πατέρα τε, καὶ τὸ μητρὸς ἐς σέ μοι ῥέπει
στέργηθρον· ἡ δὲ πανδίκως ἐχθαίρεται·
καὶ τῆς τυθείσης νηλεῶς ὁμοσπόρου·
πιστὸς δ' ἀδελφὸς ἦσθ', ἐμοὶ σέβας φέρων
μόνος· Κράτος τε καὶ Δίκη σὺν τῷ τρίτῳ
πάντων μεγίστῳ Ζηνὶ συγγένοιτό σοι.[1]

ΟΡΕΣΤΗΣ

Ζεῦ Ζεῦ, θεωρὸς τῶνδε πραγμάτων[2] γενοῦ·
ἰδοῦ δὲ γένναν[3] εὖνιν αἰετοῦ πατρός,
θανόντος ἐν πλεκταῖσι καὶ σπειράμασιν[4]
δεινῆς ἐχίδνης. τοὺς δ' ἀπωρφανισμένους
νῆστις πιέζει λιμός· οὐ γὰρ ἐντελεῖς[5]
θήραν πατρῴαν[6] προσφέρειν σκηνήμασιν.
οὕτω δὲ κἀμὲ τήνδε τ', Ἠλέκτραν λέγω,[7]
ἰδεῖν πάρεστί σοι, πατροστερῆ γόνον,
ἄμφω φυγὴν ἔχοντε τὴν αὐτὴν δόμων.
καὶ τοῦ θυτῆρος καί σε τιμῶντος μέγα
πατρὸς νεοσσοὺς τούσδ' ἀποφθείρας πόθεν
ἕξεις ὁμοίας χειρὸς εὔθοινον[8] γέρας;
οὔτ' αἰετοῦ γένεθλ' ἀποφθείρας, πάλιν
πέμπειν ἔχοις ἂν σήματ' εὐπιθῆ[9] βροτοῖς·
οὔτ' ἀρχικός σοι πᾶς ὅδ' αὐανθεὶς πυθμὴν
βωμοῖς ἀρήξει βουθύτοις ἐν ἤμασιν.[10]
κόμιζ', ἀπὸ σμικροῦ δ' ἂν ἄρειας[11] μέγαν
δόμον, δοκοῦντα κάρτα νῦν πεπτωκέναι.

[1] μοι: Stanley. [2] πρηγμάτων: Rob.
[3] γένναν ιν: Turn. [4] σπιράμασιν M, σπειράμασιν G.
[5] ἐντελής: Pauw.
[6] θῆρα πατρῶα (-ώα m): Rob. from Schol.
[7] ἐγώ: Aldina.
[8] εὔθυνον M (οι over υ m), εὔθοινον G.

thee, and to thee falls the love I should bear my mother—she whom I most rightly hate—and the love I bore my sister, victim of a pitiless sacrifice; and as brother thou hast been my trust, winning reverence even for me, thou only. May Might and Justice, with Zeus the third,[1] supreme over all, lend thee their aid!

ORESTES

O Zeus, O Zeus, look upon our cause! Behold the orphaned brood of an eagle sire that perished in the meshes—aye in the coils—of a fell viper. Utterly orphaned are they, gripped by hunger's famine; for they are not grown to full strength to bring their father's quarry to the nest. So thou mayest behold even me and poor Electra here—children bereft of their father, outcasts both alike from our home. If thou destroyest these nestlings of a sire who made sacrifice and paid high worship unto thee, from what like hand wilt thou receive the homage of rich feasts? Destroy the offspring of the eagle and thou canst not henceforth send tokens wherein mankind will trust; nor, if this royal stock wither utterly away, will it serve thy altars on days of sacrifice of oxen. Oh foster it, and thou canst raise a house from low estate to great, though now it seemeth utterly o'erthrown.

[1] Zeus "the third," because *three* is the mystical effectual number. Zeus "the third" is Zeus "the Saviour" in *Suppl.* 25, *Eum.* 759; cp. *Agam.* 1387.

---

[9] εὐπειθῆ M (ι over ει m). [10] ἐνήμασιν: Turn. [11] δαναρίας: Turn.

ΧΟΡΟΣ

ὦ παῖδες, ὦ σωτῆρες ἑστίας πατρός,
σιγᾶθ', ὅπως μὴ πεύσεταί τις, ὦ τέκνα,
γλώσσης χάριν δὲ πάντ' ἀπαγγείλῃ τάδε
πρὸς τοὺς κρατοῦντας· οὓς ἴδοιμ' ἐγώ ποτε
θανόντας ἐν κηκῖδι πισσήρει φλογός.

ΟΡΕΣΤΗΣ

οὔτοι[1] προδώσει Λοξίου μεγασθενὴς
χρησμὸς κελεύων τόνδε κίνδυνον περᾶν,
κἀξορθιάζων[2] πολλὰ καὶ δυσχειμέρους
ἄτας ὑφ' ἧπαρ θερμὸν ἐξαυδώμενος,
εἰ μὴ μέτειμι τοῦ πατρὸς τοὺς αἰτίους·
τρόπον τὸν αὐτὸν ἀνταποκτεῖναι λέγων,
ἀποχρημάτοισι ζημίαις ταυρούμενον·
αὐτὸν δ' ἔφασκε τῇ φίλῃ ψυχῇ τάδε
τείσειν[3] μ' ἔχοντα πολλὰ δυστερπῆ κακά.
τὰ μὲν γὰρ ἐκ γῆς δυσφρόνων μηνίματα[4]
βροτοῖς πιφαύσκων εἶπε, τὰς δ' αἰνῶν νόσους,[5]
σαρκῶν ἐπαμβατῆρας ἀγρίαις γνάθοις
λειχῆνας[6] ἐξέσθοντας ἀρχαίαν φύσιν·
λευκὰς δὲ κόρσας τῇδ' ἐπαντέλλειν[7] νόσῳ·
ἄλλας τ' ἐφώνει[8] προσβολὰς Ἐρινύων
ἐκ τῶν πατρῴων αἱμάτων τελουμένας·
τὸ γὰρ σκοτεινὸν τῶν ἐνερτέρων βέλος
ἐκ προστροπαίων ἐν γένει πεπτωκότων,

[1] οὔτι: Turn.
[2] κἀξοθριάζων: Turn.
[3] τίσειν: Kirchhoff.
[4] μειλίγματα: Lobeck.
[5] δὲ νωνόσσους M¹ (νῶν νόσους M²): Herm.
[6] λιχῆνας: Blomfield.
[7] ἐπαντέλλει: Rob. (-ειν *Et. Mag.* 530. 51).
[8] τε φωνεῖ: Auratus.

Chorus

O children, O saviours of your father's hearth, speak not so loud, dear children, lest someone overhear and for mere talk's sake report all this to our masters—may I some day behold them dead amidst the pitchy ooze of flame!

Orestes

Of a surety the mighty oracle of Loxias will not abandon me, charging me to brave this peril to the end, and, with loud utterance, proclaiming afflictions chilling my warm heart's blood, if I avenge not my father on the guilty; bidding me, infuriated by the loss of my possessions,[1] slay them in requital even as they slew. And with mine own life, he declared, I should else pay the debt myself by many grievous sufferings. For he spake revealing to mankind the wrath of malignant powers from underneath the earth, and telling of plagues: leprous ulcers that mount with fierce fangs on the flesh, eating away its primal nature; and how, upon this disease, a white down[2] should sprout forth. And of other assaults of the Avenging Spirits he spake, destined to be brought to pass from a father's blood; for the darkling bolt of the infernal powers, who are stirred by slain victims of kindred race calling for venge-

[1] Tucker interprets this passage to mean "fiercely stern with penalties not to be paid with money," that is, penalties demanding the death of the guilty, who may not offer money to satisfy the claims of vengeance; and thus an allusion to "wer-gild," known in Homeric times.

[2] The down upon the sore, not the temples turned white (cp. Leviticus xiii. 3).

καὶ λύσσα καὶ μάταιος ἐκ νυκτῶν φόβος
ὁρῶντα λαμπρὸν ἐν σκότῳ νωμῶντ᾽ ὀφρὺν[1]
κινεῖ, ταράσσει, καὶ διώκεσθαι πόλεως
χαλκηλάτῳ πλάστιγγι λυμανθὲν δέμας.
καὶ τοῖς τοιούτοις οὔτε κρατῆρος[2] μέρος
εἶναι μετασχεῖν, οὐ φιλοσπόνδου λιβός,
βωμῶν τ᾽ ἀπείργειν οὐχ ὁρωμένην πατρὸς
μῆνιν· δέχεσθαι <δ᾽>[3] οὔτε συλλύειν τινά.
πάντων δ᾽ ἄτιμον κἄφιλον θνῄσκειν χρόνῳ
κακῶς ταριχευθέντα παμφθάρτῳ μόρῳ.
τοιοῖσδε χρησμοῖς ἆρα[4] χρὴ πεποιθέναι;
κεἰ μὴ πέποιθα, τοὔργον ἔστ᾽ ἐργαστέον.
πολλοὶ γὰρ εἰς ἓν συμπίτνουσιν[5] ἵμεροι,
θεοῦ τ᾽ ἐφετμαὶ καὶ πατρὸς πένθος μέγα,
καὶ πρὸς πιέζει[6] χρημάτων ἀχηνία,
τὸ μὴ πολίτας εὐκλεεστάτους βροτῶν,
Τροίας ἀναστατῆρας εὐδόξῳ φρενί,
δυοῖν γυναικοῖν ὧδ᾽ ὑπηκόους πέλειν.
θήλεια γὰρ φρήν· εἰ δὲ μή, τάχ᾽ εἴσεται.

ΧΟΡΟΣ

ἀλλ᾽ ὦ μεγάλαι Μοῖραι,[7] Διόθεν
τῇδε τελευτᾶν,
ᾗ τὸ δίκαιον μεταβαίνει.
ἀντὶ μὲν ἐχθρᾶς γλώσσης ἐχθρὰ
γλῶσσα τελείσθω· τοὐφειλόμενον
πράσσουσα Δίκη[8] μέγ᾽ ἀυτεῖ·[9]
ἀντὶ δὲ πληγῆς φονίας φονίαν
πληγὴν τινέτω. δράσαντι παθεῖν,
τριγέρων μῦθος τάδε φωνεῖ.

[1] Transposed from after l. 284: Herm. [2] κρατερός: Rob.
[3] Erasure before οὔτε: <δ᾽> Herm. [4] ἄρα: Stanley.

ance, and both madness and groundless terrors out of the night torment and harass the man, who seeth clearly, though he moveth his eyebrows in the dark;[1] so that, his body marred by the brazen scourge, he be even chased in exile from his country. For an offender such as this 'tis not allowed—so the god declared—to have part either in the festal bowl or in the genial draught; his father's wrath, albeit unseen, bars him from the altar; no one receives him or lodges with him; and at last, unhonoured of all, unfriended, he perishes, shrivelled pitifully by a death that wastes him utterly away.

In oracles such as these must I not put my trust? Nay, even if I trust them not, the deed must still be done. For many impulses conspire to one conclusion: besides the god's behest, my keen grief for my father, and withal the pinch of poverty—that my countrymen, the most renowned of mankind, who overthrew Troy with gallant spirit, should not thus be at beck and call of a brace of women; for woman he is at heart; or, if he is not, he shall soon put it to the test.

CHORUS

Ye mighty Fates, through the power of Zeus vouchsafe fulfilment thus even as Justice now turneth! "For word of hate let word of hate be said," crieth Justice aloud as she exacteth the debt, "and for murderous stroke let murderous stroke be paid." "To him that doeth, it shall be done by," so saith a precept thrice-aged.

[1] He cannot sleep through terror of the Erinyes of his murdered kin whom he has not avenged.

---

[5] συμπίτνουσιν M, συμπίπτουσιν m. [6] προσπιέζει: Abresch.
[7] μοῖρε with αι over ε. [8] δίκην M, δίκη mG.
[9] μέγαυτι M, μέγ' ἀϋτεῖ mG.

ΟΡΕΣΤΗΣ

ὦ πάτερ αἰνόπατερ, τί σοι [στρ. α.
φάμενος ἢ τί ῥέξας
τύχοιμ' ἂν ἕκαθεν[1] οὐρίσας,
ἔνθα σ' ἔχουσιν εὐναί,
σκότῳ φάος ἀντίμοι-
ρον[2]; χάριτες δ' ὁμοίως
κέκληνται γόος εὐκλεὴς
προσθοδόμοις Ἀτρείδαις.

ΧΟΡΟΣ

τέκνον, φρόνημα τοῦ [στρ. β.
θανόντος οὐ δαμάζει
πυρὸς [ἡ][3] μαλερὰ γνάθος,
φαίνει δ' ὕστερον ὀργάς·
ὀτοτύζεται δ' ὁ θνῄσκων,
ἀναφαίνεται δ' ὁ βλάπτων.
πατέρων τε καὶ τεκόντων
γόος ἔνδικος ματεύει
τὸ πᾶν ἀμφιλαφὴς ταραχθείς.

ΗΛΕΚΤΡΑ

κλῦθί νυν,[4] ὦ πάτερ, ἐν μέρει [ἀντ. α.
πολυδάκρυτα πένθη.
δίπαις τοί σ'[5] ἐπιτύμβιος[6]
θρῆνος ἀναστενάζει.[7]
τάφος δ' ἱκέτας δέδεκται
φυγάδας θ' ὁμοίως.
τί τῶνδ' εὖ, τί δ' ἄτερ κακῶν;
οὐκ ἀτρίακτος ἄτα;

ORESTES

O father, unhappy father, by what word or deed of mine can I succeed in wafting from afar to thee, where thy resting-place holds thee, a light to oppose thy darkness? Yet a funeral lament in honour of the Atreidae who erst possessed the house is none the less a joyous service.

CHORUS

My child, the consciousness of the dead is not quelled by fire's ravening jaw; but he bewrayeth thereafter what stirreth him. The slain man hath his dirge, the guilty man is revealed. Lament for fathers and for parents that hath just cause, when raised full loud and strong, maketh search on every hand.

ELECTRA

Hear then, O father, as in turn we mourn with plenteous tears. Lo, 'tis thy children twain that bewail thee in a dirge o'er thy tomb. As suppliants and as exiles likewise have they sought harbourage at thy sepulchre. What is there here of good, what free from ill? Is it not hopeless to wrestle against doom?

---

[1] καθεν with ἕ over κ m.
[2] ἰσοτίμοιρον: Erfurdt.
[3] [ἡ] Porson.
[4] νῦν: Canter.
[5] τοῖς: Schütz.
[6] ἐπιτυμβιδίοις: Herm.
[7] ἀναστενάξει M, ἀναστενάζει G.

ΧΟΡΟΣ

ἀλλ' ἔτ' ἂν ἐκ τῶνδε θεὸς χρῄζων [anap.
θείη[1] κελάδους εὐφθογγοτέρους·
ἀντὶ δὲ θρήνων ἐπιτυμβιδίων
παιὰν[2] μελάθροις ἐν βασιλείοις
νεοκρᾶτα φίλον κομίσειεν.[3]

ΟΡΕΣΤΗΣ

εἰ γὰρ ὑπ' Ἰλίῳ [στρ. γ.
πρός τινος Λυκίων, πάτερ,
δορίτμητος κατηναρίσθης·[4]
λιπὼν ἂν εὔκλειαν ἐν δόμοισι
τέκνων τ' ἐν κελεύθοις[5]
ἐπιστρεπτὸν αἰῶ[6]
κτίσας[7] πολύχωστον ἂν εἶχες
τάφον διαποντίου γᾶς[8]
δώμασιν εὐφόρητον,

ΧΟΡΟΣ

φίλος φίλοισι τοῖς [ἀντ. β.
ἐκεῖ καλῶς θανοῦσιν
κατὰ χθονὸς ἐμπρέπων
σεμνότιμος ἀνάκτωρ,
πρόπολός τε τῶν μεγίστων
χθονίων ἐκεῖ τυράννων·
βασιλεὺς γὰρ ἦσθ',[9] ὄφρ' ἔζης,
μόριμον λάχος πιπλάντων[10]
χεροῖν πεισίβροτόν[11] τε βάκτρον.

[1] θήη: Turn. [2] παίων: Jacob. [3] κομίζει: Porson.
[4] κατεναρίσθης: Porson. [5] τε κελεύθοις: Wellauer.
[6] αἰῶνα: H. L. Ahrens. [7] κτίσσας: Rob.

CHORUS

Yet, Heaven, if so it please, may still turn our utterance to sounds of more joyful tone. In place of dirges o'er a tomb, a song of triumph within the royal halls shall welcome back a reunited friend.[1]

ORESTES

Ah, would that 'neath Ilium's walls, my father, thou hadst been slain, gashed by some Lycian spear! Then hadst thou left fair renown for thy children in their halls, and in their going forth hadst made their life admired of men, and in a land beyond the sea thou hadst found a tomb heaped high with earth—no heavy burthen for thy house to bear—

CHORUS

—Welcomed there below by thy comrades who nobly fell, a ruler of august majesty conspicuous beneath the earth, and minister of the mightiest, the deities who there in the nether world hold rule.[2] For in thy life thou wast a king of them who by their power allot the doom of death[3] and wield the staff that all obey.

[1] νεοκρᾶτα, lit. "newly-mixed." As friendship, when begun, was pledged by a loving-cup, so Orestes, after his long absence, is to be welcomed as a new friend.

[2] Pluto and Proserpine.

[3] He was a king of those princes who have the right to apportion life or death to their subjects.

---

[8] διαποντιουτας: Turn.

[9] ἦν with σ over ν: Abresch.

[10] πιμπλάντων: Heath.

[11] πισίμβροτὸν (πεισίμβροτὸν Aldina): Pauw.

ΗΛΕΚΤΡΑ

μηδ' ὑπὸ Τρωίας [ἀντ. γ.
τείχεσι[1] φθίμενος, πάτερ,
μετ' ἄλλῳ[2] δουρικμῆτι[3] λαῷ
παρὰ Σκαμάνδρου πόρον τεθάφθαι.[4]
πάρος δ' οἱ κτανόντες
νιν οὕτως[5] δαμῆναι
<φίλοις>[6], θανατηφόρον αἶσαν
πρόσω[7] τινὰ πυνθάνεσθαι
τῶνδε πόνων ἄπειρον.

ΧΟΡΟΣ

ταῦτα μέν, ὦ παῖ, κρείσσονα χρυσοῦ, [anap.
μεγάλης δὲ τύχης καὶ ὑπερβορέου
μείζονα φωνεῖς· δύνασαι[8] γάρ.
ἀλλὰ διπλῆς γὰρ τῆσδε μαράγνης[9]
δοῦπος ἱκνεῖται· τῶν μὲν ἀρωγοὶ
κατὰ γῆς ἤδη, τῶν δὲ κρατούντων
χέρες οὐχ ὅσιαι στυγερῶν τούτων·
παισὶ δὲ μᾶλλον γεγένηται.

ΟΡΕΣΤΗΣ[10]

τοῦτο διαμπερὲς οὖς[11] [στρ. δ.
ἵκεθ' ἅπερ τι[12] βέλος.
Ζεῦ Ζεῦ, κάτωθεν ἀμπέμπων

[1] τείχεσσι: Heath.
[2] ἄλλων: Stanley.
[3] δορικμῆτι: Blomfield.
[4] τέθαψαι: Tafel.
[5] οὕτω: Porson.
[6] <φίλοις> Conington.
[7] πρόσσω: Herm.
[8] φωνεῖ· ὁ δυνᾶσαι: Herm.
[9] μαράγμης: Rob.
[10] In the absence of person-signs in M from l. 380 to l. 585 (except l. 479, ascribed to Electra), the distribution of the parts is conjectural.
[11] ὡς: Schütz.
[12] τε: Schütz.

ELECTRA

Nay, not even 'neath the walls of Troy, father, would I have had thee fall and have thy grave beside Scamander's stream among the other folk that perished by the spear. Would rather that his murderers had been slain by their own kin, even as they slew thee, so that some one in a far-off land, knowing naught of these our present troubles, should learn their doom of death.

CHORUS

Therein, my child, is thy wish for better than gold, for what surpasseth great good fortune, yea even that of the supremely blest;[1] since to wish is easy. But now—since the thud of this double scourge[2] reacheth home—our cause hath already its champions beneath the earth, while the hands of the other side, though they have the mastery—those wretches—are hands unholy. 'Tis the children that have gained the day!

ORESTES

This hath pierced the earth and reached thine ear,[3] as it were an arrow. O Zeus, O Zeus, who

[1] The Hyperboreans, a fabulous people dwelling "beyond the North wind," were imagined to live longer and in greater felicity than other mortals.

[2] The "thud of the double scourge" refers to the appeal to the dead, lashing him to vengeance, to the beating of the head and breast, and to the stamping on the ground, which, like the invocation of the dead, were intended to arouse the nether powers. The scourge is "double" (cp. *Agam.* 647) because the participants in the scene are the two children (l. 334) and the Chorus.

[3] The ear of Agamemnon.

ὑστερόποινον ἄταν[1]
βροτῶν τλάμονι[2] καὶ πανούργῳ
χειρί—τοκεῦσι δ' ὅμως τελεῖται.

ΧΟΡΟΣ

ἐφυμνῆσαι γένοιτό μοι πυκά- [στρ. ε.
εντ'[3] ὀλολυγμὸν ἀνδρὸς
θεινομένου, γυναικός τ'
ὀλλυμένας· τί γὰρ κεύθω φρενὸς οἷον[4] ἔμπας
ποτᾶται; πάροιθεν δὲ πρῴρας
δριμὺς ἄηται κραδίας[5]
θυμὸς ἔγκοτον στύγος.

ΗΛΕΚΤΡΑ

καὶ πότ' ἂν ἀμφιθαλὴς [ἀντ. δ.
Ζεὺς ἐπὶ χεῖρα βάλοι,
φεῦ φεῦ, κάρανα δαΐξας;
πιστὰ γένοιτο χώρᾳ.
δίκαν δ' ἐξ ἀδίκων ἀπαιτῶ.
κλῦτε δὲ Γᾶ χθονίων τε τιμαί.[6]

ΧΟΡΟΣ

ἀλλὰ νόμος[7] μὲν φονίας σταγόνας
χυμένας ἐς πέδον ἄλλο προσαιτεῖν
αἷμα. βοᾷ γὰρ λοιγὸς Ἐρινὺν[8]
παρὰ τῶν πρότερον[9] φθιμένων ἄτην
ἑτέραν ἐπάγουσαν ἐπ' ἄτῃ.

[1] ἄτην with α over η m (and so in l. 403).
[2] τλήμονι: Herm. [3] πευκήεντ': Dindorf.
[4] θεῖον: Herm. [5] καρδίας: Herm.
[6] ταχθονίων τετιμαι (with ἐν over μαι m): H. L. Ahrens.

dost send up from the world below upon the reckless and wicked deeds wrought by the hands of men their retribution long-deferred—and nevertheless it shall be accomplished for a father's sake.[1]

CHORUS

May it be mine to raise a lusty shout in triumph over the man when he is stabbed and over the woman as she perishes! Wherefore should I strive to keep hidden what nevertheless hovers before my soul? Full against my heart's prow wrath bloweth keen in rancorous hate.

ELECTRA

And when will mighty Zeus bring down his hand upon them—ah me!—and cleave their heads asunder? Let the land have pledges thereof! After injustice 'tis justice I demand as of my right. Hearken, O Earth, and ye honoured powers below!

CHORUS

Nay, it is the eternal rule that drops of blood spilt upon the ground demand yet other blood. Murder crieth aloud on the Spirit of Vengeance, which from those slain before bringeth one ruin in another's train.

[1] He thus justifies his (unvoiced) prayer, "slay my mother."

---

[7] ἀλλ' ἄνομος: Turn.
[8] λοιγὸν ἐρινὺς: Schütz. [9] προτέρων: Portus.

ΟΡΕΣΤΗΣ

πόποι[1] δὴ νερτέρων τυραννίδες, [στρ. ζ.
ἴδετε πολυκρατεῖς Ἀραὶ φθινομένων,[2]
ἴδεσθ' Ἀτρειδᾶν τὰ λοίπ' ἀμηχάνως
ἔχοντα καὶ δωμάτων
ἄτιμα. πᾷ τις τράποιτ' ἄν,[3] ὦ Ζεῦ;

ΧΟΡΟΣ

πέπαλται[4] δαὖτέ μοι φίλον κέαρ [ἀντ. ε.
τόνδε κλύουσαν οἶκτον
καὶ τότε μὲν δύσελπις,
σπλάγχνα δέ μοι[5] κελαινοῦ-
ται πρὸς ἔπος κλυούσᾳ.
ὅταν δ' αὖτ' ἐπ' ἀλκῆς ἐπάρῃ <μ'
ἐλπίς>, ἀπέστασεν ἄχος
προσφανεῖσά[6] μοι καλῶς.

ΗΛΕΚΤΡΑ

τί δ' ἂν φάντες[7] τύχοιμεν ἢ[8] τάπερ [ἀντ. ζ.
πάθομεν ἄχεα[9] πρός γε τῶν τεκομένων;
πάρεστι σαίνειν, τὰ δ' οὔτι θέλγεται.
λύκος γὰρ ὥστ' ὠμόφρων
ἄσαντος ἐκ ματρός ἐστι θυμός.

ΧΟΡΟΣ

ἔκοψα κομμὸν Ἄριον[10] ἔν τε[11] Κισσίας[12] [στρ. η.
νόμοις ἰηλεμιστρίας,[13]

[1] ποῖ ποῖ: Bamberger.
[2] φθειμένων (ι over ει m): H. L. Ahrens.
[3] πετιστραποιταν corr. m.
[4] πεπάλατε (αι over ε m): Turn. [5] μου: Schütz.
[6] ll. 415-17 ἐπαλκὲς θραρέαπέστασεν ἄχος πρὸς τὸ φανεῖσθαι: ἐπ' ἀλκῆς ἐπάρῃ Paley, <μ'> Conington, <ἐλπίς> Blomfield, προσφανεῖσα Bamberger. [7] πάντες: Bothe.

ORESTES

Alas, ye sovereign powers of the world below, behold, ye puissant Curses of the slain, behold the remnants of the line of Atreus in their helpless plight, from house and home cast out in dishonour. Which way can we turn, O Zeus?

CHORUS

But again my heart throbs as I hear this piteous plaint. Anon I am reft of hope and my reins are darkened at the words I hear; but when again hope uplifts and strengthens me, it puts away my distress, dawning brightly upon me.

ELECTRA

To what could we more fittingly appeal than to those very miseries we have endured—even from her who gave us birth? Fawn upon us she may, yet they are past all soothing; for, like a wolf of savage heart, our temper from our mother is implacable.

CHORUS

Upon my breast I did beat[1] an Arian[2] dirge, even after the wont of a Cissian[3] wailing-woman. With

[1] At the time of Agamemnon's murder, when the women wailed with the extravagance of professional Asiatic mourners. Here they repeat those signs of mourning.

[2] Aria was a district of Persia. For "Eranians" (Old-Persian *Ariya*) the Greeks used Ἄριοι; at least Herodotus says this was an ancient name of the Medes.

[3] Cissia formed part of Susiana.

[8] ἂν ἢ: Herm. [9] ἄχθεα: Schwenk.
[10] ἄρειον: Herm. [11] εἴτε Bothe.
[12] κισσίαις: Rob. [13] νόμοισιλεμιστρίας: Herm.

ἀπριγδόπληκτα πολυπλάνητα[1] δ' ἦν[2] ἰδεῖν
ἐπασσυτεροτριβῆ τὰ χερὸς ὀρέγματα
ἄνωθεν ἀνέκαθεν, κτύπῳ δ' ἐπερρόθει[3]
κροτητὸν ἀμὸν καὶ πανάθλιον κάρα.

ΗΛΕΚΤΡΑ

ἰὼ [ἰὼ][4] δαΐα [στρ. θ.
πάντολμε μᾶτερ,[5] δαΐαις ἐν ἐκφοραῖς
ἄνευ πολιτᾶν ἄνακτ',
ἄνευ δὲ πενθημάτων
ἔτλας[6] ἀνοίμωκτον ἄνδρα θάψαι.

ΟΡΕΣΤΗΣ

τὸ πᾶν ἀτίμως ἔλεξας, οἴμοι. [στρ. ι.
πατρὸς δ' ἀτίμωσιν ἆρα[7] τείσει[8]
ἕκατι μὲν δαιμόνων,
ἕκατι δ' ἁμᾶν χερῶν;
ἔπειτ' ἐγὼ νοσφίσας ὀλοίμαν.[9]

ΧΟΡΟΣ

ἐμασχαλίσθη[10] δέ γ', ὡς τόδ' εἰδῇς.[11] [ἀντ. ι.
ἔπρασσε δ', ἅπερ[12] νιν ὧδε θάπτει,
μόρον κτίσαι[13] μωμένα
ἄφερτον[14] αἰῶνι σῷ.
κλύεις[15] πατρῴους δύας ἀτίμους.[16]

[1] ἄπριγκτοι πλ·κτὰ πολυπάλαγκτα: Blomfield.
[2] δὴν: Rob. [3] ἐπιρροθεῖ: Stanley. [4] [ ] Wellauer.
[5] μῆτερ: Schütz. [6] ἔτλης: Dindorf.
[7] ἀρὰ: Heath. [8] τίσει: Kirchhoff.
[9] ἐλοίμαν: Turn. [10] ἐμασχαλίσθης: Rob.
[11] δὲ τωστοστεἰδης: δέ γε Herm.; ὡς εἰδῇς Canter; τόδ' Pauw.
[12] ἅπερ: Portus.

clenched blows rained thick and fast one might have seen my outstretched hands, now on this side now on that, descending from above—from far above—till my battered and wretched head resounded with the strokes.

ELECTRA

Out upon thee, cruel, all-daring mother! In cruel burial, a king unattended by his people, unattended by lamentation, thou didst find the heart to bury thy husband unbewailed.

ORESTES

Ah me, thy words spell utter dishonour. Yet by God's help, and by help of mine own hands, shall she not make atonement for the dishonour done my sire? Let me but take her life, then let me die!

CHORUS

Aye, and he was foully mangled,[1] I would have thee know. And even as she thus buried him, she wrought with the design to make the manner of his murder a burthen on thy life, past all power to bear. Thou hearest the story of the ignominious outrage done to thy father.

[1] An allusion to the savage custom by which the extremities of the murdered man were cut off, then hung about his neck and tied together under the arm-pits (μασχάλαι). At least one object of this "arm-pitting" was to disable the spirit of the dead from taking vengeance on the murderer.

[13] κτεῖ·αι with ν in erasure: Stanley.
[14] ἄφερκτον: Rob. [15] κλύει: Turn.
[16] δυσατίμους: Stanley.

ΗΛΕΚΤΡΑ

λέγεις πατρῷον μόρον· ἐγὼ δ᾽ ἀπεστάτουν [ἀντ. η.
ἄτιμος, οὐδὲν ἀξία·
μυχῷ[1] δ᾽ ἄφερκτος πολυσινοῦς[2] κυνὸς δίκαν
ἑτοιμότερα γέλωτος ἀνέφερον λίβη,
χέουσα[3] πολύδακρυν γόον κεκρυμμένα.
τοιαῦτ᾽ ἀκούων ἐν φρεσὶν[4] γράφου <⏑ –>.[5]

ΧΟΡΟΣ

δι᾽ ὤτων δὲ συν- [ἀντ. θ.
τέτραινε μῦθον ἡσύχῳ φρενῶν[6] βάσει.
τὰ μὲν γὰρ οὕτως ἔχει,
τὰ δ᾽ αὐτὸς ὄργα[7] μαθεῖν.
πρέπει δ᾽ ἀκάμπτῳ μένει καθήκειν.

ΟΡΕΣΤΗΣ

σέ τοι λέγω, ξυγγενοῦ, πάτερ, φίλοις.[8] [στρ. κ.

ΗΛΕΚΤΡΑ

ἐγὼ δ᾽ ἐπιφθέγγομαι κεκλαυμένα.

ΧΟΡΟΣ

στάσις δὲ πάγκοινος ἅδ᾽ ἐπιρροθεῖ·
ἄκουσον ἐς φάος μολών,
ξὺν δὲ γενοῦ πρὸς ἐχθρούς.

ΟΡΕΣΤΗΣ

Ἄρης Ἄρει ξυμβαλεῖ,[9] Δίκᾳ Δίκα. [ἀντ. κ.

[1] μυχοῦ: Stanley.
[2] πολυσίνους M (with final ς erased): Blomfield.
[3] χέρουσα M^1, χαίρουσα M^2: Dobree. [4] φρεσσὶν: Rob.

Electra

My father was murdered even as thou tellest. But I, the while, despised, accounted as a thing of naught, was kept aloof; kennelled, as I had been a vicious cur, in my chamber, I gave free vent to my streaming tears—that came more readily than laughter—as in my concealment I poured forth my lament in plenteous weeping. Hear my tale and grave it on thy heart.

Chorus

Aye, let it sink deep into thine ears, but keep withal a quiet steadfastness of soul. Thus far the case stands thus; but what's to follow do thou of thyself be eager to resolve. Thou must enter the lists with wrath inflexible.

Orestes

Father, on thee I call; side with thine own!

Electra

And I, all tears, join my voice to his.

Chorus

And all our company blend our voices in echoing the prayer. Hearken! Come to the light! Side with us against the foe!

Orestes

War-god shall encounter War-god, Right shall encounter Right.

---

[5] An iambus has been lost somewhere in the line.
[6] φρονῶν: Turn.
[7] ὀργᾷ: Scaliger.
[8] φίλοισι: Porson.
[9] ξυμβάλλει: Pauw.

ΗΛΕΚΤΡΑ

ἰὼ θεοί, κραίνετ' ἐνδίκως <δίκας>.[1]

ΧΟΡΟΣ

τρόμος μ' ὑφέρπει κλύουσαν εὐγμάτων.
τὸ μόρσιμον μένει πάλαι,
εὐχομένοις δ' ἂν ἔλθοι.

ὦ[2] πόνος ἐγγενὴς [στρ. λ.
καὶ παράμουσος Ἄτας[3]
αἱματόεσσα πλαγά.
ἰὼ δύστον' ἄφερτα κήδη·
ἰὼ δυσκατάπαυστον ἄλγος.

δώμασιν ἔμμοτον [ἀντ. λ.
τῶνδ' ἄκος,[4] οὐδ' ἀπ' ἄλλων
ἔκτοθεν, ἀλλ' ἀπ' αὐτῶν,
δι' ὠμὰν ἔριν αἱματηράν.[5]
θεῶν <τῶν>[6] κατὰ γᾶς ὅδ' ὕμνος.

ἀλλὰ κλύοντες, μάκαρες χθόνιοι, [anap.
τῆσδε κατευχῆς πέμπετ' ἀρωγὴν
  παισὶν προφρόνως ἐπὶ νίκῃ.[7]

ΟΡΕΣΤΗΣ

πάτερ, τρόποισιν οὐ τυραννικοῖς θανών,
αἰτουμένῳ[8] μοι δὸς κράτος τῶν σῶν δόμων.

ΗΛΕΚΤΡΑ

κἀγώ, πάτερ, τοιάνδε[9] σου χρείαν ἔχω,
φυγεῖν μέγαν προσθεῖσαν Αἰγίσθῳ <φθόρον>.[10]

ELECTRA

O ye gods, decide aright the plea of right!

CHORUS

A shudder steals o'er me as I hear these prayers. Doom hath long been waiting, but, in answer to them that pray, come it will.

Ah, trouble inbred in the race and bloody stroke of Ruin grating harsh discord! Ah, sorrows lamentable and grievous! Ah, the staunchless pain!

The house hath a cure to heal these woes—a cure not from without, from others' hand—but from itself, by savage strife of blood. To the gods beneath the earth this hymn is sung.

O ye blest powers below, give ear to this our supplication, and of your ready will send forth to the children your succour unto victory!

ORESTES

O father, who perished by an unroyal death, grant, as answer to my prayer, the lordship o'er thy halls!

ELECTRA

And I too, father, have like request of thee—to escape when I have wrought great destruction upon Aegisthus.

---

[1] <δίκας> Herm.
[2] ἰὼ: Herm.
[3] ἄτης: Herm.
[4] ἑκὰς: Schütz.
[5] αιωμαναιρειν: δι' ὠμὰν Klausen; ἔριν Herm.
[6] <τῶν> Herm.
[7] νίκην: Portus.
[8] αἰτούμενός: Turn.
[9] τοιάδε: Turn.
[10] <φθόρον> Herm.

ΟΡΕΣΤΗΣ

οὕτω γὰρ ἄν σοι δαῖτες ἔννομοι βροτῶν
κτιζοίατ'· εἰ δὲ μή, παρ' εὐδείπνοις ἔσῃ
ἄτιμος ἐμπύροισι[1] κνισωτοῖς χθονός.

ΗΛΕΚΤΡΑ

κἀγὼ χοάς σοι τῆς ἐμῆς παγκληρίας
οἴσω πατρῴων ἐκ δόμων γαμηλίους·
πάντων δὲ πρῶτον τόνδε πρεσβεύσω τάφον.

ΟΡΕΣΤΗΣ

ὦ Γαῖ', ἄνες μοι πατέρ'[2] ἐποπτεῦσαι μάχην.

ΗΛΕΚΤΡΑ

ὦ Περσέφασσα, δὸς δ' ἔτ'[3] εὔμορφον κράτος.

ΟΡΕΣΤΗΣ

μέμνησο λουτρῶν οἷς ἐνοσφίσθης, πάτερ.

ΗΛΕΚΤΡΑ

μέμνησο δ' ἀμφίβληστρον ὡς[4] ἐκαίνισαν.

ΟΡΕΣΤΗΣ

πέδαις δ' ἀχαλκεύτοις ἐθηρεύθης, πάτερ.

ΗΛΕΚΤΡΑ

αἰσχρῶς τε βουλευτοῖσιν ἐν καλύμμασιν.

[1] ἐν πυροῖσι: Auratus. [2] πάτερ: Rob.
[3] δέ τ': Paley. [4] ᾧ σ': Blomfield.

ORESTES

Aye, for then the wonted funeral feasts of men would be stablished to thy honour; but otherwise, at the rich and savoury banquet of burnt offerings made to earth, thou shalt be portionless of honour.

ELECTRA

And I, likewise, of the fulness of my inheritance will from my father's house at my bridal offer libations unto thee; and before all else I will hold this thy tomb in chiefest honour.

ORESTES

O Earth, send up my father to watch my battle!

ELECTRA

O Persephassa, grant us even yet glorious victory!

ORESTES

Father, remember the bath, wherewith thou wast robbed of life.

ELECTRA

And remember how they devised a strange casting-net for thee.

ORESTES

Thou wast caught, my father, in gyves forged by no smith's hand.

ELECTRA

And in a wrapping shamefully devised.

ΟΡΕΣΤΗΣ

ἆρ' ἐξεγείρῃ τοῖσδ' ὀνείδεσιν,[1] πάτερ;

ΗΛΕΚΤΡΑ

ἆρ' ὀρθὸν αἴρεις φίλτατον τὸ σὸν κάρα;

ΟΡΕΣΤΗΣ

ἤτοι δίκην ἴαλλε σύμμαχον φίλοις,
ἢ τὰς ὁμοίας ἀντίδος λαβὰς[2] λαβεῖν,
εἴπερ κρατηθείς γ' ἀντινικῆσαι θέλεις.

ΗΛΕΚΤΡΑ

καὶ τῆσδ' ἄκουσον λοισθίου βοῆς, πάτερ,
ἰδὼν νεοσσοὺς τούσδ' ἐφημένους τάφῳ·
οἴκτιρε[3] θῆλυν ἄρσενός θ' ὁμοῦ γόνον,
καὶ μὴ 'ξαλείψῃς σπέρμα Πελοπιδῶν τόδε·
οὕτω γὰρ οὐ τέθνηκας οὐδέ περ θανών·
παῖδες γὰρ ἀνδρὶ κληδόνες σωτήριοι
θανόντι· φελλοὶ δ' ὣς ἄγουσι δίκτυον,
τὸν ἐκ βυθοῦ κλωστῆρα σῴζοντες λίνου.[4]
ἄκου', ὑπὲρ σοῦ τοιάδ' ἔστ' ὀδύρματα.
αὐτὸς δὲ σῴζῃ τόνδε τιμήσας λόγον.

ΧΟΡΟΣ

καὶ μὴν ἀμεμφῆ τόνδ' ἐτείνατον[5] λόγον,
τίμημα τύμβου τῆς ἀνοιμώκτου τύχης.

[1] ὀνείδεσσιν: Rob.
[2] βλάβας: Canter.
[3] οἴκτειρε: Kirchhoff.
[4] λίνου M, λίνον m.
[5] ἀμόμφητον δε τινατὸν: ἀμεμφῆ τόνδ' Canter; ἐτείνατον Herm.

ORESTES

Father, art thou not roused by such taunts as these?

ELECTRA

Dost not uplift that dearest head of thine?

ORESTES

Either send Justice to battle for those dear to thee, or grant us in turn to get like grip[1] of them, if indeed after defeat thou wouldst in turn win victory.

ELECTRA

So hearken, father, to this my last appeal as thou beholdest these fledglings crouching at thy tomb. Have compassion on thy offspring, on the woman and at the same time on the male, and let not this seed of Pelops' line be blotted out; for then, in spite of death, thou art not dead. For children are voices of salvation to a man, though he be dead; like corks, they buoy up the net, saving the flaxen cord from out the deep. Hearken! For thine own sake we make this plaint. Show honour to this our plea and thou dost save thyself.

CHORUS

In truth, to your content have ye drawn out this your plea in showing honour to this unlamented tomb. For the rest, since thy heart

[1] Orestes prays that, as Clytaemestra and Aegisthus had "got grip" of Agamemnon by deception, so he may "get like grip" of them and kill them.

τὰ δ' ἄλλ', ἐπειδὴ δρᾶν κατώρθωσαι φρενί,
ἔρδοις ἂν ἤδη δαίμονος πειρώμενος.

ΟΡΕΣΤΗΣ

ἔσται· πυθέσθαι δ' οὐδέν ἐστ' ἔξω δρόμου,
πόθεν χοὰς ἔπεμψεν, ἐκ τίνος λόγου
μεθύστερον τιμῶσ' ἀνήκεστον πάθος;
θανόντι[1] δ' οὐ φρονοῦντι δειλαία χάρις
ἐπέμπετ'· οὐκ ἔχοιμ' ἂν εἰκάσαι τόδε.[2]
τὰ δῶρα μείω[3] δ' ἐστὶ τῆς ἁμαρτίας.
τὰ πάντα γάρ τις ἐκχέας ἀνθ' αἵματος
ἑνός, μάτην ὁ μόχθος· ὧδ' ἔχει λόγος.
θέλοντι δ', εἴπερ οἶσθ', ἐμοὶ φράσον τάδε.

ΧΟΡΟΣ

οἶδ', ὦ τέκνον, παρῆ[4] γάρ· ἔκ τ' ὀνειράτων
καὶ νυκτιπλάγκτων δειμάτων πεπαλμένη
χοὰς ἔπεμψε τάσδε δύσθεος γυνή.

ΟΡΕΣΤΗΣ

ἦ καὶ πέπυσθε τοὔναρ, ὥστ' ὀρθῶς φράσαι;

ΧΟΡΟΣ

τεκεῖν δράκοντ' ἔδοξεν, ὡς αὐτὴ λέγει.

ΟΡΕΣΤΗΣ

καὶ ποῖ τελευτᾷ καὶ καρανοῦται λόγος;

ΧΟΡΟΣ

ἐν σπαργάνοισι παιδὸς ὁρμίσαι δίκην.

[1] θανοῦντι: Abresch. [2] τάδε changed to τόδε.
[3] μέσω: Turn. [4] πάρει (ει in erasure): Porson.

is rightly set on action, put thy fortune to the proof and get thee to thy work forthwith.

ORESTES

It shall be so. But it is in no wise amiss to enquire how, from what motive, she came to send libations, seeking too late to make requital for a deed past remedy. To the unconscious dead they were a sorry boon to send; their import I cannot guess. The gifts are too paltry for the offence. For, though a man pour out his all in atonement for one deed of blood, it is labour lost; so runs the saw. If indeed thou knowest, resolve me; I am fain to learn.

CHORUS

I know, my child, for I was there. It was because she was shaken of heart by reason of dreams and wandering terrors of the night, that she sent these offerings, godless woman that she is.

ORESTES

And have ye learnt the nature of the dream so as to tell it aright?

CHORUS

She dreamed she gave birth to a serpent—such is her own account.

ORESTES

And where ends the tale and what its consummation?

CHORUS

That she laid it to rest, as it were a child, in swaddling bands.

ΟΡΕΣΤΗΣ

τίνος[1] βορᾶς χρῄζοντα, νεογενὲς[2] δάκος;

ΧΟΡΟΣ

αὐτὴ προσέσχε μαζὸν ἐν τὠνείρατι.[3]

ΟΡΕΣΤΗΣ

καὶ πῶς ἄτρωτον οὖθαρ ἦν[4] ὑπὸ στύγους[5];

ΧΟΡΟΣ

ὥστ' ἐν γάλακτι θρόμβον αἵματος σπάσαι.

ΟΡΕΣΤΗΣ

οὔτοι μάταιον· ἀνδρὸς ὄψανον πέλει.

ΧΟΡΟΣ

ἡ δ' ἐξ ὕπνου κέκλαγγεν[6] ἐπτοημένη.
πολλοὶ δ' ἀνῆθον,[7] ἐκτυφλωθέντες σκότῳ,
λαμπτῆρες ἐν δόμοισι δεσποίνης χάριν·
πέμπει τ' ἔπειτα τάσδε κηδείους χοάς,
ἄκος τομαῖον ἐλπίσασα πημάτων.

ΟΡΕΣΤΗΣ

ἀλλ' εὔχομαι γῇ τῇδε καὶ πατρὸς τάφῳ
τοὔνειρον εἶναι τοῦτ' ἐμοὶ τελεσφόρον.
κρίνω δέ τοί νιν ὥστε συγκόλλως[8] ἔχειν.

[1] τινὸς: Wellauer. [2] νεορενὲς: Turn.
[3] τ' ὀνείρατι: Porson.
[4] οὐχαρην (changed to -ριν): Pauw. [5] ὑποστύγος: Schütz.

ORESTES

What food did it crave, the new-born, noxious thing?

CHORUS

She herself in her dream offered it her breast.

ORESTES

Surely her nipple was not unwounded by the loathsome beast?

CHORUS

No; with the milk it drew in clotted blood.

ORESTES

Sooth, 'tis not meaningless—the vision means a man!

CHORUS

Then from out her sleep she raised a shriek and awoke appalled; and many a lamp, which had been blinded in the darkness, flared up within the house to cheer our mistress. Thereupon she sent these libations for the dead, in hope that they might prove an effectual cure for her distress.

ORESTES

Nay, then, I pray to this earth and to my father's grave that this dream come to its fulfilment in me. As I interpret, it fits at every point. For if the

---

[6] κέκλαγεν: H. L. Ahrens. [7] ἀνῆλθον: Valckenaer.
[8] συσκόλως (with a second λ superscribed): Vict.

εἰ γὰρ τὸν αὐτὸν χῶρον ἐκλιπὼν[1] ἐμοὶ
οὔφις ἐμοῖσι[2] σπαργάνοις ὡπλίζετο,[3]
καὶ μαστὸν[4] ἀμφέχασκ' ἐμὸν θρεπτήριον,
θρόμβῳ δ' ἔμειξεν[5] αἵματος φίλον γάλα,
ἡ δ' ἀμφὶ τάρβει τῷδ'[6] ἐπῴμωξεν πάθει,
δεῖ τοί νιν, ὡς ἔθρεψεν ἔκπαγλον τέρας,
θανεῖν βιαίως· ἐκδρακοντωθεὶς δ' ἐγὼ
κτείνω νιν, ὡς τοὔνειρον ἐννέπει τόδε.

ΧΟΡΟΣ

τερασκόπον δὴ[7] τῶνδέ σ' αἱροῦμαι πέρι.
γένοιτο δ' οὕτως. τἄλλα δ' ἐξηγοῦ φίλοις,
τοὺς μέν[8] τι ποιεῖν, τοὺς δὲ μή τι δρᾶν λέγων.

ΟΡΕΣΤΗΣ

ἁπλοῦς ὁ μῦθος· τήνδε μὲν στείχειν[9] ἔσω,
αἰνῶ δὲ κρύπτειν τάσδε συνθήκας ἐμάς,
ὡς ἂν δόλῳ κτείναντες[10] ἄνδρα τίμιον
δόλοισι[11] καὶ ληφθῶσιν ἐν ταὐτῷ βρόχῳ
θανόντες, ᾗ καὶ Λοξίας ἐφήμισεν,
ἄναξ Ἀπόλλων, μάντις ἀψευδὴς τὸ πρίν.
ξένῳ γὰρ εἰκώς, παντελῆ σαγὴν ἔχων,
ἥξω σὺν ἀνδρὶ τῷδ' ἐφ' ἑρκείους[12] πύλας
Πυλάδῃ, ξένος τε καὶ δορύξενος δόμων.
ἄμφω δὲ φωνὴν ἥσομεν[13] Παρνησσίδα,
γλώσσης ἀυτὴν Φωκίδος μιμουμένω.
καὶ δὴ θυρωρῶν οὔτις ἂν φαιδρᾷ φρενὶ
δέξαιτ',[14] ἐπειδὴ δαιμονᾷ δόμος κακοῖς·

[1] ἐκλείπων corrected from ἐκλείπει: Blomfield.
[2] οὐφεῖς επᾶσα: Porson.
[3] σπαργανηπλείζετο: Vict.
[4] μασθὸν: Blomfield.
[5] ἔμιξον: Kirchhoff.
[6] ἀμφιταρβίτωδ': Porson.
[7] δὲ: Kirchhoff.

snake quitted the same place as I; if it was furnished with my swaddling bands; if it sought to open its mouth to take the breast that nourished me, and with clotted blood mixed the sweet milk, while she for terror shrieked at this: then surely, as she hath nourished a portentous thing of horror, so die she must—by violence. For I, turned serpent, am her slayer, as this dream declares.

CHORUS

I choose thy reading of this prodigy. So be it! For the rest, give thy friends their parts. Bid some what to do, others what to leave undone.

ORESTES

'Tis simple telling. My sister must go within, and I charge her to keep concealed this covenant with me, to the intent that, as by craft they slew a man of high estate, so by craft likewise they may be caught and perish in the self-same snare; even as Loxias decreed, lord Apollo, the seer who hath never ere this proved false.

In the guise of an alien, thereto full-equipped, I shall come to the outer gate—and with me Pylades, whom ye see here, as guest and ally of the house. Both of us will speak the speech of Parnassus, imitating the utterance of a Phocian tongue. And in case no one of the keepers of the door will give us hearty welcome, on the plea that the house is

---

[8] τοὺς δ' ἐν: Stanley. [9] στίχειν: Porson.
[10] κτείναντας: Rob. [11] δόλῳ τε: Hartung.
[12] ἐφερκίους: Turn. [13] οἴσομεν: Turn.
[14] λέξαιτ': Turn.

μενοῦμεν οὕτως ὥστ' ἐπεικάζειν τινὰ
δόμους[1] παραστείχοντα[2] καὶ τάδ' ἐννέπειν·
"τί δὴ πύλαισι[3] τὸν ἱκέτην ἀπείργεται
Αἴγισθος, εἴπερ οἶδεν ἔνδημος παρών;"
εἰ δ' οὖν ἀμείψω βαλὸν ἑρκείων[4] πυλῶν
κἀκεῖνον ἐν θρόνοισιν εὑρήσω πατρός,
ἢ καὶ μολὼν ἔπειτά μοι κατὰ στόμα
ἀρεῖ,[5] σάφ' ἴσθι, καὶ κατ' ὀφθαλμοὺς βαλεῖ,[6]
πρὶν αὐτὸν εἰπεῖν "ποδαπὸς ὁ ξένος;" νεκρὸν
θήσω, ποδώκει περιβαλὼν χαλκεύματι.
φόνου δ' Ἐρινὺς οὐχ ὑπεσπανισμένη
ἄκρατον αἷμα πίεται τρίτην πόσιν.
νῦν[7] οὖν σὺ μὲν φύλασσε τἀν οἴκῳ καλῶς,
ὅπως ἂν ἀρτίκολλα συμβαίνῃ τάδε·
ὑμῖν δ' ἐπαινῶ γλῶσσαν εὔφημον φέρειν,
σιγᾶν θ' ὅπου δεῖ καὶ λέγειν τὰ καίρια.
τὰ δ' ἄλλα τούτῳ δεῦρ' ἐποπτεῦσαι λέγω,
ξιφηφόρους ἀγῶνας ὀρθώσαντί μοι.

ΧΟΡΟΣ

πολλὰ μὲν γᾶ[8] τρέφει [στρ. α.
δεινὰ [καὶ][9] δειμάτων ἄχη,
πόντιαί τ' ἀγκάλαι κνωδάλων
ἀνταίων βρύουσι·[10]
πλάθουσι [βλαστοῦσι][11] καὶ πεδαίχμιοι
λαμπάδες πεδάοροι,[12]

---

[1] δόμοις: Boissonade. [2] παραστίχοντα: Vict.
[3] πύλῃσι: Blomfield.
[4] βαλῶν changed to βαλὸν; ἕρκειον changed to ἑρκίον: Stanley. [5] ἐρεῖ: Bamberger.
[6] βαλεῖν: Rob. [7] σὺν' with ν' erased: Blomfield.
[8] μὲν γὰρ: Schütz. [9] [ ] Heath.

visited of Heaven with trouble, then we shall so wait that any who passeth by the house will make surmise and say: "Why then does Aegisthus have his door shut upon his suppliant, if indeed he is at home and knows?"

But if once I shall pass the outermost threshold of the gate and shall find that man sitting on my father's throne, or if thereafter coming face to face with me he shall—mark well!—lift and cast down his eyes ere ever he can say "Of what land is the stranger?" with my swift sword I'll spit him and lay him dead. The Avenging Spirit that hath no stint of gore shall for her third and crowning draught quaff blood unmixed!

Now do thou, Electra, keep strict watch of what passes within the house, that so our plans may fit together well. You [*addressing the Chorus*] had best keep a discreet tongue—to be silent when there is need and to speak only what occasion bids. For the rest, I call on Him[1] to cast his glance hither and direct for me aright the conflict of the sword.

[*Exeunt Orestes, Pylades, and Electra*

CHORUS

Full many are the horrors, dread and appalling, bred of earth, and the arms of the deep teem with hateful monsters. Likewise 'twixt heaven and earth there draw nigh lights[2] hung aloft in the air; and

[1] Apollo, his champion (ll. 269, 558), whose statue stood before the palace (cp. *Agam.* 513). [2] Meteors.

---

[10] βροτοῖσι: Herm. [11] [ ] Knick.
[12] πεδάμαροι m: Stanley.

πτανά τε καὶ πεδοβά-
μονα κἀνεμοέντ' ἂν[1]
αἰγίδων φράσαι κότον.

ἀλλ' ὑπέρτολμον ἀν- [ἀντ. α.
δρὸς φρόνημα τίς λέγοι
καὶ γυναικῶν φρεσὶν[2] τλαμόνων[3] [καὶ][4]
παντόλμους ἔρωτας
ἄταισι συννόμους βροτῶν;
ξυζύγους δ' ὁμαυλίας
θηλυκρατὴς ἀπέρω-
τος ἔρως παρανικᾷ
κνωδάλων τε καὶ βροτῶν.

ἴστω δ', ὅστις οὐχ ὑπόπτερος [στρ. β.
φροντίσιν, δαεὶς
τὰν ἁ παιδολυ-
μὰς τάλαινα Θεστιὰς μήσατο
πυρδαῆτιν[5] πρόνοιαν,
καταίθουσα[6] παιδὸς δαφοινὸν
δαλὸν ἥλικ', ἐπεὶ μολὼν
ματρόθεν κελάδησε,
ξύμμετρόν τε διαὶ[7] βίου
μοιρόκραντον[8] ἐς ἆμαρ.[9]

ἄλλαν[10] δεῖ τιν'[11] ἐν λόγοις στυγεῖν [ἀντ. β.
φοινίαν κόραν,[12]
ἅτ' ἐχθρῶν ὕπαὶ
φῶτ' ἀπώλεσεν[13] φίλον Κρητικοῖς

[1] κἀνεμοέντων: Blomfield.
[2] φρεσσὶν: Aldina.
[3] τλημόνων: Dindorf.
[4] [ ] Klausen.
[5] πυρδαῆ τινα: Herm.

winged things and things that walk the earth can also tell of the stormy wrath of whirlwinds.

But of man's spirit overbold who can tell and of the reckless passions of women hardened of soul, comates with the woes of mortals? Inordinate passion, overmastering the female, gains fatal victory over the wedded unions of brutes and men alike.

If any there be who is not light-minded in his understanding, let him know this, when he hath learned of the device of a lighted brand, planned by Thestius' heartless daughter,[1] who wrought the ruin of her own child, when that she consumed the charred brand, which was to be like-aged with him from the hour when he came forth from his mother's womb and cried aloud, and which kept pace with him throughout his life unto the day foredoomed of fate.

And there is in legend another dame,[2] meet theme for abomination, a maiden of blood, who wrought destruction on one dear to her at the bidding of his foes, when, lured by Minos' gift, the

[1] When Meleager, the child of Althaea, who was daughter of Thestius, king of Aetolia, and wife to Oeneus of Calydon, was a week old, the Fates appeared to the mother and declared that he would die when the brand on the hearth was consumed. Whereupon Althaea took the brand and put it in a chest; but when Meleager, grown to youthful manhood, slew her brothers, she threw it into the fire, and her son died suddenly.

[2] Nisus was besieged in his town of Megara by Minos, king of Crete. Nisus' daughter Scylla, being in love with Minos, cut from the head of her father the purple hair on which his life depended, so that he was slain by the Cretans.

[6] κ' αἰθοῦσα M, κ' αἴθουσα m: Canter. [7] διὰ: Canter.
[8] μοιρόκραντος (ν over ς) δ': Canter. [9] ἦμαρ: Dindorf.
[10] ἄλλα: Portus. [11] δή τιν': Turn.
[12] φοινίαν σκύλλαν: Merkel. [13] ἀπόλεσεν: Rob.

χρυσοκμήτοισιν[1] ὅρμοις
πιθήσασα[2] δώροισι[3] Μίνω,
Νῖσον ἀθανάτας τριχὸς
νοσφίσασ' ἀπροβούλως
πνέονθ' ἁ κυνόφρων ὕπνῳ.
κιγχάνει[4] δέ μιν Ἑρμῆς.

ἐπεὶ δ' ἐπεμνασάμαν[5] ἀμειλίχων [στρ. γ.
πόνων, ὁ καιρὸς[6] δὲ δυσφιλὲς γαμή-
λευμ' ἀπεύχετον δόμοις
γυναικοβούλους τε μήτιδας φρενῶν
ἐπ' ἀνδρὶ τευχεσφόρῳ,
ἐπ' ἀνδρὶ δᾴοις[7] ἐπεικότως σέβαι.[8]
τίω[9] δ' ἀθέρμαντον ἑστίαν δόμων
γυναικείαν ‹τ'›[10] ἄτολμον αἰχμάν.[11]

κακῶν δὲ πρεσβεύεται τὸ Λήμνιον [ἀντ. γ.
λόγῳ· γοᾶται δὲ δὴ πάθος[12] κατά-
πτυστον· ᾔκασεν δέ τις
τὸ δεινὸν αὖ Λημνίοισι πήμασιν.
θεοστυγήτῳ δ' ἄχει
βροτῶν ἀτιμωθὲν οἴχεται γένος.
σέβει γὰρ οὔτις τὸ δυσφιλὲς θεοῖς.
τί τῶνδ' οὐκ ἐνδίκως ἀγείρω;

τὸ δ' ἄγχι πλευμόνων ξίφος [στρ. δ.
διανταίαν ὀξυπευκὲς οὐτᾷ[13]
διαὶ Δίκας. τὸ μὴ θέμις γὰρ οὖν[14]

[1] χρυσεοδμήτοισιν: Herm. [2] πειθήσασα: Abresch.
[3] δόροισι: Aldina. [4] κι·χάνει with γ erased.
[5] ἐπεμνήσαμεν, with ά over ή m: -ησάμην Heath, -ασάμαν Dindorf.

retan necklace forged of gold, she reft Nisus f his immortal hair, as he drew his breath in unspecting sleep—dog-hearted that she was. And im Hermes[1] overtook.

But since I have called to mind tales of pitiless fflictions, it is the fitting time to tell of a marriage oid of love, an abomination to the house, and the lots devised by a wife's cunning against her warrior rd, against her lord with reason by his foes revered. ut I hold in honour a hearth and home stranger to assion's fires and in woman a spirit that shrinks om audacious deeds.

Of crimes indeed the Lemnian[2] holdeth first place story; long hath it been told with groans as a alamity abominable: each new horror men liken to emnian troubles; and by reason of that woeful eed, abhorred of the gods, the race hath disappeared, ast out in infamy from among mankind. For no nan holdeth in reverence that which merits Heaven's ate. Is there one of these gathered tales that I do ot justly cite?

But the keen and bitter sword is nigh the breast nd driveth home its blow at the bidding of Justice. 'or verily the unrighteousness of him who hath un-

[1] Hermes, the conductor to Hades of the souls of the dead.

[2] The women of Lemnos, jealous of Thracian slaves, illed their husbands, so that when the Argonauts visited he island they found no men.

---

[6] ἀκαίρως: Weil (formerly). But here, as in ll. 628, 632, o one of the many suggestions has altogether freed the assage from its almost desperate obscurity.

[7] δηΐοις: Herm. [8] ἐπικότῳ σέβας: H. L. Ahrens.

[9] τίων: Stanley. [10] ⟨τ'⟩ Herm.

[11] αἰχμᾶν changed to αἰχμάν. [12] ποθει with ι over ει.

[13] σοῦται: Herm. [14] οὐ: Wilam.

λὰξ πέδοι[1] πατούμενον, τὸ πᾶν Διὸς
σέβας παρεκβάντος[2] οὐ θεμιστῶς.[3]

Δίκας[4] δ' ἐρείδεται πυθμήν· [ἀντ. δ
προχαλκεύει[5] δ' Αἶσα φασγανουργός·
τέκνον δ' ἐπεισφέρει δόμοισιν[6]
αἱμάτων[7] παλαιτέρων τίνειν[8] μύσος
χρόνῳ κλυτὰ[9] βυσσόφρων Ἐρινύς.

ΟΡΕΣΤΗΣ

παῖ παῖ, θύρας ἄκουσον ἑρκείας κτύπον.
τίς ἔνδον, ὦ παῖ, παῖ, μάλ' αὖθις, ἐν δόμοις;
τρίτον τόδ' ἐκπέραμα δωμάτων καλῶ,
εἴπερ φιλόξεν' ἐστὶν Αἰγίσθου διαί.

ΟΙΚΕΤΗΣ

εἶεν, ἀκούω· ποδαπὸς ὁ ξένος; πόθεν;

ΟΡΕΣΤΗΣ

ἄγγελλε τοῖσι κυρίοισι δωμάτων,
πρὸς οὕσπερ ἥκω καὶ φέρω καινοὺς λόγους.
τάχυνε δ', ὡς καὶ νυκτὸς ἅρμ' ἐπείγεται
σκοτεινόν, ὥρα[10] δ' ἐμπόρους καθιέναι[11]
ἄγκυραν ἐν δόμοισι πανδόκοις ξένων.
ἐξελθέτω τις δωμάτων τελεσφόρος
γυνὴ τόπαρχος,[12] ἄνδρα δ'[13] εὐπρεπέστερον·

[1] πέδον: Herm. [2] παρεκβάντες: Stanley.
[3] ἀθεμίστως with ἀ changed to ου: Dindorf.
[4] δίκης with α over η m. [5] προσχαλκεύει: Jacob.
[6] διμασε (σ in erasure): δόμοισι Pauw, -ιν Herm.
[7] δωμάτων: Stephanus. [8] τείνει: Lachmann.
[9] κλυτή: Dindorf.

righteously transgressed the sovereign majesty of Zeus lieth on the ground trampled under foot.[1]

The anvil of Justice is planted firm. Destiny fashioneth her arms and forgeth her sword betimes; and the famed and deep-brooding Spirit of Vengeance is bringing the son into the house, to requite at last the pollution of blood shed of old.

[*Enter, with attendants, Orestes and Pylades before the palace*

ORESTES

Porter! Porter! Hear my knocking at the outer door! Who's within, porter, porter, I say once more, who's at home? Again for the third time I call for some one to come forth from the house, if by Aegisthus' will it offers welcome to strangers.

SERVANT

Yes, yes, I hear. Of what land is the stranger, and whence?

ORESTES

Announce me to the masters of the house; for it is even to them I come as bearer of tidings. And make haste, since the car of Night is speeding on with darkness, and it is time for wayfarers to drop anchor in some house of common entertainment. Bid some one come forth who hath authority over the house, the mistress that hath charge—yet the

[1] The translation is based on the reading παρεκβάντος (Stanley); but this and all other alterations do not remove the difficulties of the original.

---

10 ὥρα (ὧραι m): Rob. 11 μεθιέναι: Dindorf.
12 ταπαρχος with ὁ over the first α m, τόπαρχος G. 13 τ': Turn.

αἰδὼς γὰρ ἐν λεχθεῖσιν οὐκ ἐπαργέμους
λόγους τίθησιν· εἶπε θαρσήσας ἀνὴρ
πρὸς ἄνδρα κἀσήμηνεν ἐμφανὲς τέκμαρ.

ΚΛΥΤΑΙΜΗΣΤΡΑ

ξένοι, λέγοιτ' ἂν εἴ τι δεῖ· πάρεστι γὰρ
ὁποῖάπερ δόμοισι τοῖσδ' ἐπεικότα,
καὶ θερμὰ λουτρὰ καὶ πόνων θελκτηρία[1]
στρωμνή, δικαίων τ' ὀμμάτων παρουσία.
εἰ δ' ἄλλο πρᾶξαι δεῖ τι βουλιώτερον,
ἀνδρῶν τόδ' ἐστὶν ἔργον, οἷς κοινώσομεν.

ΟΡΕΣΤΗΣ

ξένος μέν εἰμι Δαυλιεὺς ἐκ Φωκέων·
στείχοντα δ' αὐτόφορτον οἰκείᾳ[2] σαγῇ
εἰς Ἄργος, ὥσπερ δεῦρ' ἀπεζύγην πόδα,[3]
ἀγνὼς πρὸς ἀγνῶτ' εἶπε συμβαλὼν ἀνήρ,
ἐξιστορήσας καὶ σαφηνίσας ὁδόν,
Στροφίος ὁ Φωκεύς· πεύθομαι γὰρ ἐν λόγῳ
"ἐπείπερ ἄλλως, ὦ ξέν', εἰς Ἄργος κίεις,
πρὸς τοὺς τεκόντας πανδίκως μεμνημένος
τεθνεῶτ' Ὀρέστην εἰπέ, μηδαμῶς λάθῃ.
εἴτ' οὖν κομίζειν δόξα νικήσει φίλων,
εἴτ' οὖν μέτοικον, εἰς τὸ πᾶν ἀεὶ ξένον,
θάπτειν, ἐφετμὰς τάσδε πόρθμευσον πάλιν.
νῦν γὰρ λέβητος χαλκέου πλευρώματα
σποδὸν κέκευθεν ἀνδρὸς εὖ κεκλαυμένου."
τοσαῦτ' ἀκούσας εἶπον. εἰ δὲ τυγχάνω

[1] θελκτήρια: Wakefield.
[2] οἰκίαι: Turn.
[3] πόδας: Dindorf.

master were seemlier ; for then no delicacy in speaking makes words obscure : man speaks to man with boldness and sets forth his meaning without reserve.

[*The Servant withdraws. Clytaemestra appears at the door with a maid-servant in attendance*

CLYTAEMESTRA

Strangers, ye have only to declare your need ; for we have all that befits this house—warm baths, beds to charm away fatigue, and the presence of courteous eyes. But if, apart from this, there is matter requiring graver counsel, that is the concern of men, and with them we will communicate.

ORESTES

I am a stranger, a Daulian of the Phocians. As I was on my way, carrying my pack, on business of my own, to Argos—even as I have ended here my journey [1]—a man, a stranger to me as I to him, fell in with me, and enquired my way and told me his, Strophius, a Phocian (for as we talked I learned his name) and said to me, " Since, in any case, stranger, thou art bound for Argos, bear in mind my message most sacredly and say to his parents ' Orestes is dead '—and let it no wise escape thee. Whether his friends decide to bring him home or to bury him in the land of his sojourn, an alien utterly forevermore, convey their bidding back to me. Meantime a bronze urn encloses the ashes of a man bewept right well." Thus much I tell thee as

[1] Literally " I have been unyoked," his feet being his horses.

τοῖς κυρίοισι καὶ προσήκουσιν λέγων
οὐκ οἶδα, τὸν τεκόντα δ' εἰκὸς εἰδέναι.

ΚΛΥΤΑΙΜΗΣΤΡΑ

οἳ 'γώ,[1] κατ' ἄκρας εἶπας[2] ὡς πορθούμεθα.
ὦ δυσπάλαιστε τῶνδε δωμάτων 'Αρά,
ὡς πόλλ' ἐπωπᾷς, κἀκποδὼν εὖ κείμενα
τόξοις πρόσωθεν εὐσκόποις χειρουμένη,
φίλων ἀποψιλοῖς με τὴν παναθλίαν.
καὶ νῦν 'Ορέστης—ἦν γὰρ εὐβούλως ἔχων,
ἔξω κομίζων[3] ὀλεθρίου πηλοῦ πόδα,—
νῦν δ' ἥπερ[4] ἐν δόμοισι βακχείας[5] καλῆς
ἰατρὸς ἐλπὶς ἦν, προδοῦσαν ἔγγραφε.[6]

ΟΡΕΣΤΗΣ

ἐγὼ μὲν οὖν[7] ξένοισιν ὧδ' εὐδαίμοσιν
κεδνῶν ἕκατι πραγμάτων ἂν ἤθελον
γνωστὸς γενέσθαι καὶ ξενωθῆναι· τί γὰρ
ξένου ξένοισίν ἐστιν εὐμενέστερον;
πρὸς δυσσεβείας <δ'>[8] ἦν ἐμοὶ τόδ' ἐν φρεσίν,
τοιόνδε πρᾶγμα μὴ καρανῶσαι φίλοις,
καταινέσαντα καὶ κατεξενωμένον.

ΚΛΥΤΑΙΜΗΣΤΡΑ

οὔτοι κυρήσεις μεῖον ἀξίως σέθεν,

[1] οἶ εγὼ: Canter. [2] ἐνπᾶσ (-σ' m): Bamberger.
[3] νομίζων: Rob. (Schol.). [4] δήπερ: Turn.
[5] βακχίας: Turn. [6] παροῦσαν ἐγγράφει: H. L. Ahrens.
[7] ὢν with οὖν superscribed by m. [8] <δ'> Portus.

---

[1] Clytaemestra's outward meaning is that, with her son alive and far from the blood-stained house, she had hoped

I heard it. Whether by any chance I speak to those with whom the question rests and whose concern it is, I know not; but his parent should know the fact.

Clytaemestra

Ah me! Thy tale spells our utter undoing. O Curse that hauntest this house—so hard to wrestle down — how far thy vision reaches! Even what was well bestowed out of harm's way, thou bringest down with thy well-aimed shafts from afar, and strippest me of those I love, all unhappy that I am. And now Orestes—for well-counselling was he in keeping his foot out of the slough of destruction—but now, the hope that once was within the house to medicine its fair revelry, do thou record it as abandoning us.[1]

Orestes

For myself, I am sure, with hosts so prosperous, I had rather been made known and welcomed by reason of good tidings. For where is good-will greater than from guest to host? Yet to my thought it had been a breach of sacred duty not to fulfil for friends a charge like this when I was bound by promise and by hospitality pledged to me.

Clytaemestra

Nay, rest assured, thou shalt receive no less

that there has been an end of the carousing of the Curses (cp. *Agam.* 1188). That hope is gone—they still hold their "fair revelry," as she ironically calls it. Her inner emotion is joy that the hope of Electra is crushed—the hope that her brother would return and end the unseemly revelry. Reading παροῦσαν (so M) ἐγγράφῃ the meaning is "thou dost inscribe it 'present' in thy list."

οὐδ' ἧσσον ἂν γένοιο δώμασιν φίλος.
ἄλλος δ' ὁμοίως ἦλθεν ἂν τάδ' ἀγγελῶν.
ἀλλ' ἔσθ' ὁ καιρὸς ἡμερεύοντας ξένους
μακρᾶς κελεύθου τυγχάνειν τὰ πρόσφορα.
ἄγ' αὐτὸν εἰς ἀνδρῶνας εὐξένους δόμων,
ὀπισθόπους τε[1] τούσδε καὶ ξυνέμπορον·[2]
κἀκεῖ κυρούντων δώμασιν τὰ πρόσφορα.
αἰνῶ δὲ πράσσειν ὡς ὑπευθύνῳ[3] τάδε.
ἡμεῖς δὲ ταῦτα τοῖς κρατοῦσι δωμάτων
κοινώσομέν[4] τε κοὐ σπανίζοντες φίλων
βουλευσόμεσθα[5] τῆσδε συμφορᾶς πέρι.

ΧΟΡΟΣ

εἶέν, φίλιαι δμωίδες[6] οἴκων,
πότε δὴ στομάτων
  δείξομεν ἰσχὺν ἐπ' Ὀρέστῃ;
ὦ πότνια χθὼν καὶ πότνι' ἀκτὴ
χώματος, ἣ νῦν ἐπὶ ναυάρχῳ
σώματι κεῖσαι τῷ βασιλείῳ,
νῦν ἐπάκουσον, νῦν ἐπάρηξον·
νῦν γὰρ ἀκμάζει Πειθὼ δολίαν[7]
ξυγκαταβῆναι, χθόνιον δ' Ἑρμῆν[8]
καὶ τὸν νύχιον τοῖσδ' ἐφοδεῦσαι
  ξιφοδηλήτοισιν ἀγῶσιν.

ἔοικεν ἁνὴρ[9] ὁ ξένος τεύχειν κακόν·
τροφὸν δ' Ὀρέστου τήνδ' ὁρῶ κεκλαυμένην.
ποῖ δὴ πατεῖς, Κίλισσα, δωμάτων πύλας,
λύπη δ' ἄμισθός ἐστί σοι ξυνέμπορος;

[1] δὲ: Bamberger.
[2] ξυνεμπόρους: Herm.
[3] ἐπευθύνῳ: Turn.
[4] κοινώσωμεν M, -σομεν G.
[5] βουλευόμεθα: Stephanus.
[6] δμωιίδες M, δμωίδες G.

guerdon than is thy desert nor be the less welcome to this house — another would equally have borne thy message. But it is the hour when strangers who have been travelling on a long day's journey should have their proper entertainment. [*To an attendant*] Conduct him to the chambers where the men are hospitably lodged, him and his attendants here and fellow-traveller; and let them there be tended as beseems our house. I charge thee do this as thou shalt be held to strict account. Meantime we will impart this matter to the master of the house, and—since we are in no lack of friends—will take counsel touching this event. [*All withdraw except the Chorus*

CHORUS

Ah, loyal handmaidens of the house, how long shall it be before we show forth what power lies in our lips to do Orestes service?

O hallowed earth, and hallowed high-raised barrow that liest now upon the royal form of the commander of the fleet, now hearken, now lend me aid! Now is the hour for Persuasion with her guile to enter the lists with him, and for Hermes of the nether world—even he that worketh in stealth—to direct this encounter of the deadly sword. [*Enter Orestes' Nurse*

Our stranger, methinks, is working mischief; for yonder I see Orestes' nurse all in tears. Cilissa[1]! whither away? How comes it that thou art thus setting foot in the palace-gate, with grief for thy unhired companion?

[1] Slaves were commonly named from their native country.

[7] δολία: Pauw. [8] ἑρμῆα: Turn. [9] ἀνὴρ: Porson.

ΤΡΟΦΟΣ

Αἴγισθον ἡ κρατοῦσα τοῖς ξένοις[1] καλεῖν
ὅπως τάχιστ᾽ ἄνωγεν, ὡς σαφέστερον
ἀνὴρ ἀπ᾽ ἀνδρὸς τὴν νεάγγελτον φάτιν
ἐλθὼν πύθηται τήνδε, πρὸς μὲν οἰκέτας
θετοσκυθρωπῶν[2] ἐντὸς ὀμμάτων γέλων
κεύθουσ᾽ ἐπ᾽ ἔργοις διαπεπραγμένοις καλῶς
κείνῃ, δόμοις δὲ τοῖσδε παγκάκως ἔχειν,
φήμης ὕφ᾽[3] ἧς ἤγγειλαν οἱ ξένοι τορῶς.
ἦ δὴ κλύων ἐκεῖνος[4] εὐφρανεῖ νόον,
εὖτ᾽ ἂν πύθηται μῦθον. ὦ τάλαιν᾽ ἐγώ·
ὥς μοι τὰ μὲν παλαιὰ συγκεκραμένα
ἄλγη δύσοιστα τοῖσδ᾽ ἐν Ἀτρέως δόμοις
τυχόντ᾽ ἐμὴν ἤλγυνεν ἐν στέρνοις φρένα.
ἀλλ᾽ οὔτι πω τοιόνδε πῆμ᾽ ἀνεσχόμην·
τὰ μὲν γὰρ ἄλλα τλημόνως ἤντλουν κακά·
φίλον δ᾽ Ὀρέστην, τῆς ἐμῆς ψυχῆς τριβήν,
ὃν ἐξέθρεψα μητρόθεν δεδεγμένη,—
κἀκ[5] νυκτιπλάγκτων ὀρθίων κελευμάτων
καὶ πολλὰ καὶ μοχθήρ᾽ ἀνωφέλητ᾽ ἐμοὶ
τλάσῃ·—τὸ μὴ φρονοῦν γὰρ ὡσπερεὶ βοτὸν
τρέφειν ἀνάγκη, πῶς γὰρ οὔ; τρόπῳ φρενός·
οὐ γάρ τι φωνεῖ παῖς ἔτ᾽ ὢν ἐν σπαργάνοις,
εἰ[6] λιμός, ἢ δίψη τις, ἢ λιψουρία
ἔχει· νέα δὲ νηδὺς αὐτάρκης τέκνων.
τούτων πρόμαντις οὖσα, πολλὰ δ᾽, οἴομαι,
ψευσθεῖσα παιδὸς σπαργάνων φαιδρύντρια,
γναφεὺς τροφεύς[7] τε ταὐτὸν εἰχέτην τέλος.
ἐγὼ διπλᾶς δὲ τάσδε χειρωναξίας
ἔχουσ᾽ Ὀρέστην ἐξεδεξάμην πατρί·[8]
τεθνηκότος δὲ νῦν τάλαινα πεύθομαι.

NURSE

My mistress bids me summon Aegisthus for the strangers with all speed, that he may come and learn more clearly, as man from man, these tidings that have just arrived. Before the servants, indeed, behind eyes that made sham gloom she hid her laughter over what hath befallen happily for her—but for this house, the news so plainly told by the strangers spells utter ruin. He, I warrant, on hearing it, will rejoice in heart when he hears the story. Miserable woman that I am! How the old troubles of every sort, so hard to bear, that befell in this house of Atreus, have ever made my heart to ache within my breast! But never yet have I endured a blow like this; for all the other troubles I bore patiently; but my beloved Orestes, on whom I spent my soul, whom I took from his mother at his birth and nursed, and the many and troublesome tasks—fruitless for all my enduring them—when his loud and urgent cries broke my rest. For the senseless thing one must nurse like a dumb beast—of course one must—by following its humour. For while it is still a babe in swaddling clothes, it has no speech at all—whether it be that hunger moves it, or thirst belike, or call of need—children's young inwards work their own relief. These needs I would forecast; yet many a time, I trow, mistaken, having to wash the child's linen—laundress and nurse had the same office. 'Twas I who, with these two handicrafts, received Orestes at his father's hands. And now, unhappy that I am, I hear that

[1] τοὺς ξένους: Pauw. [2] θέτο σκυθρωπὸν: Conington.
[3] ὑφ': Sidgwick. [4] ἐκεῖνον: Rob. [5] καὶ: Portus.
[6] ᾗ: Stanley. [7] στροφεύς: Rob. [8] πατρὸς m.

στείχω[1] δ' ἐπ' ἄνδρα τῶνδε[2] λυμαντήριον
οἴκων, θέλων δὲ τόνδε πεύσεται λόγον.

ΧΟΡΟΣ

πῶς οὖν κελεύει νιν μολεῖν ἐσταλμένον;

ΤΡΟΦΟΣ

ἦ[3] πῶς; λέγ' αὖθις, ὡς μάθω σαφέστερον.

ΧΟΡΟΣ

εἰ[4] ξὺν λοχίταις εἴτε καὶ μονοστιβῆ.

ΤΡΟΦΟΣ

ἄγειν κελεύει δορυφόρους ὀπάονας.

ΧΟΡΟΣ

μή νυν σὺ ταῦτ' ἄγγελλε[5] δεσπότου στύγει·
ἀλλ' αὐτὸν ἐλθεῖν, ὡς ἀδειμάντως κλύῃ,
ἄνωχθ' ὅσον τάχιστα γηθούσῃ[6] φρενί.
ἐν ἀγγέλῳ γὰρ κυπτὸς ὀρθοῦται λόγος.[7]

ΤΡΟΦΟΣ

ἀλλ' ἦ φρονεῖς εὖ τοῖσι νῦν ἠγγελμένοις;

ΧΟΡΟΣ

ἀλλ' εἰ τροπαίαν Ζεὺς κακῶν θήσει ποτέ.

[1] στείχων: Aldina. [2] τῶνδε . . . λόγων: Blomfield. [3] ᾖ: Wellauer. [4] ᾗ: Turn. [5] ἄγγελε: Rob.
[6] τάχιστ' ἀγαθούσῃ: Pauw (γαθούσῃ Turn.).
[7] κρυπτὸς: Blomfield from *v.l.* Schol. B on Hom. O 207; ὀρθούσῃ φρενὶ: Musgrave from Eustathius and Schol. B on Hom. O 207. In both cases the line is quoted as from Euripides.

he is dead. But I am on my way to fetch the man who wrought the ruin of the house, and glad enough will he be to hear these tidings.

CHORUS

How then arrayed does she bid him come?

NURSE

How—arrayed? Say it again that I may catch thy meaning better.

CHORUS

With his guards or, maybe, unattended.

NURSE

She bids him come with his retinue of spearmen.

CHORUS

Nay, do not thou give this message to our hated master; but with all speed and with a cheerful heart bid him come himself, alone, that he may be told without alarm. For in the mouth of a messenger a crooked message is made straight.[1]

NURSE

What! Art thou glad of heart at the present news?

CHORUS

Why not, if Zeus at last may cause our ill wind to change?

[1] A proverbial saying, meant for the Nurse, and not for Aegisthus: "In passing through the mouth of its bearer a message may be changed as he pleases."

ΤΡΟΦΟΣ

καὶ πῶς; Ὀρέστης ἐλπὶς οἴχεται δόμων.

ΧΟΡΟΣ

ὔπω· κακός γε μάντις ἂν γνοίη τάδε.

ΤΡΟΦΟΣ

τί φής; ἔχεις τι τῶν λελεγμένων δίχα;

ΧΟΡΟΣ

ἄγγελλ'[1] ἰοῦσα, πρᾶσσε τἀπεσταλμένα.
μέλει[2] θεοῖσιν ὧνπερ ἂν μέλῃ[2] πέρι.

ΤΡΟΦΟΣ

ἀλλ' εἶμι καὶ σοῖς ταῦτα πείσομαι λόγοις.
γένοιτο δ' ὡς ἄριστα σὺν θεῶν δόσει.

ΧΟΡΟΣ

νῦν παραιτουμένᾳ μοι,[3] πάτερ [στρ. α.
Ζεῦ θεῶν Ὀλυμπίων,
δὸς τύχας τυχεῖν δόμου[4] κυρίως
τὰ σώφρον' εὖ[5] μαιομένοις ἰδεῖν.
διὰ δίκας[6] πᾶν ἔπος
ἔλακον· <ὦ> Ζεῦ, σύ[7] νιν φυλάσσοις.

ἒ ἔ, πρὸ δὲ δὴ 'χθρῶν [ἐφ. α.
τὸν ἔσωθεν μελάθρων, Ζεῦ,[8]
θές, ἐπεί νιν[9] μέγαν ἄρας,[10]
δίδυμα καὶ τριπλᾶ
παλίμποινα θέλων ἀμείψει.

NURSE

Nay, how can that be? Orestes, the hope of the house, is gone.

CHORUS

Not yet; he were a poor prophet that would interpret thus.

NURSE

What sayest thou? Dost know aught beyond what has been told?

CHORUS

Go, give thy message! Do what is bidden thee! The gods have care for that whereof they care.

NURSE

Well, I will go and do thy bidding. With the gods' blessing may all turn out for the best! [*Exit*

CHORUS

Now at my supplication, O Zeus, father of the Olympian gods, grant that the fortunes of the house be firmly established, so that they who rightly desire the rule of order may behold it. In justice hath my every word been uttered. O Zeus, do thou safeguard it!

O Zeus, set him that is within the palace before his foes; since, if thou exaltest him, gladly will he pay thee with recompense twofold and threefold.

---

[1] *ἄγγελ'*: Rob. [2] *μέλλει . . . μέλλῃ*: Aldina. [3] *παραιτουμέν' ἐμοί*: *-μένῃ* (*-μένᾳ* Herm.) *μοι* Turn. [4] *δέ μου*: Bothe. [5] *σωφροσυνεν*: Herm. [6] *διαδικᾶσαι*: Pauw. [7] *ζεῦ σὺ δὲ*: Herm. [8] *τῶν ἔσω μ. ὦ ζεῦ*: Seidler. [9] *μιν*: Seidler. [10] *ἀίρας* M (*ι* in erasure).

ἴσθι δ' ἀνδρὸς φίλου πῶλον εὖ- [ἀντ. α.
νιν ζυγέντ' ἐν ἅρμασιν[1]
πημάτων. <σὺ δ'>[2] ἐν δρόμῳ προστιθεὶς
μέτρον κτίσον[3] σῳζόμενον ῥυθμὸν
τοῦτ' ἰδεῖν διὰ πέδον[4]
ἀνομένων βημάτων ὄρεγμα;

οἵ τ' ἔσω[5] δωμάτων [στρ. β.
πλουτογαθῆ[6] μυχὸν νομίζετε,
κλῦτε,[7] σύμφρονες[8] θεοί·
[ἄγετε][9] τῶν πάλαι πεπραγμένων
λύσασθ' αἷμα προσφάτοις[10] δίκαις.
γέρων φόνος μηκέτ' ἐν δόμοις τέκοι.

τὸ δὲ[11] καλῶς κτίμενον[12] ὦ μέγα ναίων [ἐφ. β.
στόμιον, εὖ δὸς ἀνιδεῖν δόμον ἀνδρός,
καί νιν ἐλευθερίας <φῶς>
λαμπρὸν[13] ἰδεῖν φιλίοις
ὄμμασιν <ἐκ>[14] δνοφερᾶς καλύπτρας.

ξυλλάβοι δ' ἐνδίκως [ἀντ. β.
παῖς ὁ Μαίας, ἐπεὶ φορώτατος[15]
πρᾶξιν οὐρίαν θέλων.[16]
[πολλὰ δ' ἄλλα φανεῖ χρηίζων κρυπτά].[17]
ἄσκοπον δ' ἔπος λέγων
νύκτα πρό τ' ὀμμάτων σκότον φέρει,
καθ' ἡμέραν δ' οὐδὲν ἐμφανέστερος.

[1] ἅρματι: Herm.
[2] <σὺ δὲ> O. Müller.
[3] τίς ἂν: κτίσον Schoemann.
[4] δάπεδον: Blomfield.
[5] ἔσωθε: Herm.
[6] πλουταγαθῆ: Turn.
[7] κλύετε: Dindorf.
[8] σώφρονες M, corr. m.
[9] [ ] Schütz.
[10] προφάτοις M, σ superscr. m.
[11] τάδε (or τῶδε) altered to τόδε: Rob.
[12] κταμενων M, κτάμενον m: Bamberger.

Bethink thee that the orphaned colt of one dear unto thee is harnessed to the chariot of distress. And do thou, setting bounds to his running, grant that we may see him keeping a steady pace over this course, in the straining stride of a gallop winning to the goal![1]

And ye who within the house inhabit the inner chamber that exulteth in its wealth, hear me, ye gods, that feel with us! By fresh award redeem the blood of deeds done of old. May aged Murder cease to beget offspring in the house!

And thou, that tenantest the mighty, fair-builded cavern,[2] grant that the house of the man may lift up its eyes again in joy, and that with glad eyes from out its veil of gloom it may behold freedom's radiant light!

May Maia's son,[3] as rightfully he ought, lend aid, for none can better waft a deed on a favouring course, when so he will;[4] but by his mysterious utterance he bringeth darkness o'er men's eyes by night, and by day he is no whit clearer.

[1] That is, let him bide his time by guarding against haste.

[2] The inner sanctuary of Apollo at Delphi was a narrow cave or vault in which, over a cleft, stood a tripod covered by a slab on which the prophetess sat (Athenaeus, 701 c, Strabo, ix. 641).

[3] Hermes, the patron of guile and god of eloquence.

[4] The bracketed line 815 reads "And many another hidden thing he will make plain, if he desires."

---

[13] ἐλευθερίως λαμπρῶς: Dindorf.

[14] ὄμμασι: ὄμμασιν <ἐκ> Herm. [15] ἐπιφορώτατος: Emperius.

[16] θέλεν M, ω superscr. m. [17] [ ] Heimsoeth.

καὶ τότ᾽ ἤδη[1] κλυτὸν[2] [στρ. γ.
δωμάτων λυτήριον,
θῆλυν οὐριοστάταν οὐδ᾽[3]
ὀξύκρεκτον[4] γοα-
τᾶν[5] νόμον θήσομεν·[6] "πλεῖ[7] τάδ᾽[8] εὖ·
ἐμὸν ἐμὸν κέρδος αὔξεται[9] τόδ᾽· ἄ-
τα δ᾽ ἀποστατεῖ φίλων."

σὺ δὲ θαρσῶν, ὅταν ἥκῃ μέρος ἔργων, [ἐφ. γ.
ἐπαΰσας Πατρὸς αὐδὰν
θροούσᾳ [πρὸς σὲ] Τέκνον [πατρὸς αὐδὰν][10]
[καὶ] πέραιν᾽[11] ἀνεπίμομφον[12] ἄταν.

Περσέως τ᾽ ἐν φρεσὶν[13] [ἀντ. γ.
καρδίαν ἀνασχεθών,[14]
τοῖς θ᾽[15] ὑπὸ χθονὸς φίλοισιν,
τοῖς τ᾽ ἄνωθεν πρόπρασ-
σε[16] χάριν[17] ὀργᾶς λυγρᾶς,[18] ἔνδοθεν
φόνιον[19] ἄταν τιθείς, τὸν αἴτιον δ᾽
ἐξαπολλύων[20] μόρον.

ΑΙΓΙΣΘΟΣ

ἥκω μὲν οὐκ ἄκλητος, ἀλλ᾽ ὑπάγγελος·
νέαν φάτιν δὲ πεύθομαι λέγειν τινὰς
ξένους μολόντας οὐδαμῶς ἐφίμερον,
μόρον δ᾽ Ὀρέστου. καὶ τόδ᾽ ἀμφέρειν δόμοις
γένοιτ᾽ ἂν ἄχθος δειματοσταγὲς[21] φόνῳ
τῷ πρόσθεν ἑλκαίνουσι καὶ δεδηγμένοις.[22]
πῶς ταῦτ᾽ ἀληθῆ καὶ βλέποντα δοξάσω;

[1] τότε δὴ: Blomfield. [2] πλοῦτον: Bamberger.
[3] ὁμοῦ (ὁμο in erasure): Blomfield. [4] κρεκτὸν: Kirchhoff.
[5] γοήτων: Blaydes. [6] μεθήσομεν: Herm.
[7] πόλει: Kirchhoff. [8] τὰ δ᾽: Blomfield. [9] ἀέξεται M².

And then at last with loud voice shall we sing a song of the deliverance of the house, the song that women raise when the wind sits fair, and not the shrill strain of them that mourn—" The ship goes well. To me, to me, this increaseth unto gain, and calamity holdeth aloof from those I love."

But do thou, with good courage, when the part of action comes, cry aloud the name " Father " when she exclaims " Son," and despatch the baneful but offenceless deed.

Uplift Perseus' spirit within thy breast, and for those dear to thee below the earth, and for those above, exact satisfaction for their dire wrath, working bloody ruin within the house and utterly destroying the guilty cause of death.[1]

[*Enter Aegisthus*

AEGISTHUS

I have come not unasked but summoned by a messenger. 'Tis startling tidings that, as I hear, are told by certain strangers who have come, tidings far from welcome—that Orestes is dead. To lay this too upon the house would prove a fearful burthen when it is still festering and galled by the wound inflicted by a former murder. How can I deem this tale is the living truth ? Or is it but a panic-stricken

[1] Of verses 819-837 only the general sense is clear.

---

[10] *πατρὸς ἔργῳ θροούσᾳ πρὸς σὲ τέκνον πατρὸς αὐδὰν*: Seidler.
[11] *καὶ περαίνων*: Auratus. [12] *ἐπίμομφον*: Schütz.
[13] *φρεσσὶν*: Aldina. [14] *σχέθων*: Grotefend.
[15] *τοῖσδ'*: Rob. [16] *προπράσσων*: Herm.
[17] *χάριτος*: Emperius. [18] *λυπρᾶς*: Blomfield.
[19] *φοινίαν*: Newman. [20] *ἐξαπολλὺς*: Heimsoeth.
[21] *δειματοστάγ' ἐς*: Vict.
[22] *ἐλκαίνοντι καὶ δεδηγμένῳ*: Bamberger.

ἢ πρὸς γυναικῶν δειματούμενοι λόγοι
πεδάρσιοι θρῴσκουσι, θνῄσκοντες μάτην;
τί τῶνδ᾽ ἂν εἴποις ὥστε δηλῶσαι φρενί;

ΧΟΡΟΣ

ἠκούσαμεν μέν, πυνθάνου δὲ τῶν ξένων
ἔσω παρελθών. οὐδὲν ἀγγέλων σθένος
ὡς αὐτὸν[1] αὐτῶν[2] ἄνδρα πεύθεσθαι πάρα.[3]

ΑΙΓΙΣΘΟΣ

ἰδεῖν ἐλέγξαι τ᾽ αὖ[4] θέλω τὸν ἄγγελον,
εἴτ᾽ αὐτὸς ἦν θνῄσκοντος[5] ἐγγύθεν παρών,
εἴτ᾽ ἐξ ἀμαυρᾶς κληδόνος λέγει μαθών.
οὔτοι φρέν᾽ ἂν[6] κλέψειεν[7] ὠμματωμένην.

ΧΟΡΟΣ

Ζεῦ Ζεῦ, τί λέγω, πόθεν ἄρξωμαι
τάδ᾽ ἐπευχομένη κἀπιθεάζουσ᾽,[8]
ὑπὸ δ᾽ εὐνοίας
πῶς ἴσον εἰποῦσ᾽ ἀνύσωμαι;
νῦν γὰρ μέλλουσι μιανθεῖσαι
πειραὶ κοπάνων ἀνδροδαΐκτων
ἢ πάνυ θήσειν Ἀγαμεμνονίων
οἴκων ὄλεθρον διὰ παντός,
ἢ πῦρ καὶ φῶς ἐπ᾽ ἐλευθερίᾳ
δαίων ἀρχάς τε πολισσονόμους
πατέρων <θ᾽> ἕξει[9] μέγαν ὄλβον.
τοιάνδε πάλην μόνος ὢν ἔφεδρος
δισσοῖς μέλλει θεῖος[10] Ὀρέστης
ἅψειν. εἴη δ᾽ ἐπὶ νίκῃ.

[1] αὐτὸς: Canter. [2] αὐτὸν: Turn.
[3] πέρι: Portus. [4] αὖ in erasure m, εὖ (?) M.

report spread by women that leaps aloft to die away in nothingness? What canst thou tell me hereof to make it plain of comprehension?

CHORUS

We heard the tale, 'tis true—but pass within and make enquiry of the strangers. The sureness of a messenger's report is naught compared with one's own enquiry of the man himself.

AEGISTHUS

I wish to see the messenger and put him to the proof again—whether he himself was present at the death or but repeats from vague report what he has heard. No! Be sure he cannot cheat a mind that's open-eyed. [*Exit*

CHORUS

O Zeus, O Zeus, what am I to say? Wherewith shall I begin this my prayer and appeal to the gods? How, in my loyal zeal, can I succeed in finding words to match the need? Now is the moment when either the blood-stained edges of the blades that lay men low are utterly forevermore to destroy the house of Agamemnon, or else, kindling a flaming light in freedom's cause, Orestes shall win both the sway over his realm and the rich possessions of his fathers. In such a bout our gallant Orestes, with none to second him, is now to cope with two. And may it be to triumph!

[*A shriek is heard from within*

---

[5] ἠ***κοτος M, ἦεν θνῄσκοντος m and margin: Turn.

[6] φρένα: Elmsley. [7] κλέψειαν: Stephanus.

[8] καἰπιθοάζουσα (οα in erasure): Schütz.

[9] ἕξει πατέρων: Weil. [10] θείοις: Turn.

ΑΙΓΙΣΘΟΣ

ἒ ἔ, ὀτοτοτοῖ.

ΧΟΡΟΣ

ἔα ἔα μάλα·
πῶς ἔχει; πῶς κέκρανται δόμοις;
ἀποσταθῶμεν[1] πράγματος τελουμένου,
ὅπως δοκῶμεν τῶνδ᾽ ἀναίτιαι κακῶν
εἶναι· μάχης γὰρ δὴ κεκύρωται τέλος.

ΟΙΚΕΤΗΣ

οἴμοι, πανοίμοι[2] δεσπότου πεπληγμένου·[3]
οἴμοι μάλ᾽ αὖθις ἐν τρίτοις προσφθέγμασιν.
Αἴγισθος οὐκέτ᾽ ἔστιν. ἀλλ᾽ ἀνοίξατε
ὅπως τάχιστα, καὶ γυναικείους πύλας
μοχλοῖς χαλᾶτε· καὶ μάλ᾽ ἡβῶντος δὲ δεῖ,
οὐχ ὡς δ᾽ ἀρῆξαι διαπεπραγμένῳ·[4] τί γάρ;
ἰοὺ ἰού.
κωφοῖς ἀυτῶ καὶ καθεύδουσιν μάτην
ἄκραντα βάζω;[5] ποῖ Κλυταιμήστρα; τί δρᾷ;
ἔοικε νῦν αὐτῆς ἐπὶ ξυροῦ πέλας
αὐχὴν πεσεῖσθαι πρὸς δίκην[6] πεπληγμένος.

ΚΛΥΤΑΙΜΗΣΤΡΑ

τί δ᾽ ἐστὶ χρῆμα; τίνα βοὴν ἵστης δόμοις;

ΟΙΚΕΤΗΣ

τὸν ζῶντα καίνειν τοὺς τεθνηκότας λέγω.

[1] ἀποσταθῶμὲν M, ἄπο, σταθῶ μὲν m: Rob.
[2] πὰν· οἴμοι: Porson. [3] τελουμένου: Schütz.
[4] διαπεπραγμένων: Turn. [5] βάζω;: Tucker.
[6] προσδίκη* M, πρὸς δίκην G.

AEGISTHUS (*within*)

Oh! Oh! Woe is me!

CHORUS

Ha! Ha! I say! How goes it? How has it been determined for the house? Let us stand aloof while the affair is still unsettled in order that we may be accounted blameless in this evil business. For the issue of the fighting has now been decided.

[*The Chorus withdraws to the side of the scene; thereupon a servant of Aegisthus rushes in*

SERVANT

Woe's me, oh utter woe! My master's slain! Woe's me! yet again, for the third time, I cry. Aegisthus is no more! Come, open with all speed! Unbar the women's door! And a right strong arm it needs—but not to help him who's already slain—what good in that? Ho! ho! Am I shouting to the deaf and wasting my voice in vain on folk asleep? Where's Clytaemestra gone? What is she doing? Her own neck, nigh the razor's edge, is now fair to fall beneath the stroke.

[*Clytaemestra hurries in unattended*

CLYTAEMESTRA

What's this? What cry for help art thou raising in the house?

SERVANT

The dead are killing the living, I say.[1]

[1] The Greek admits either meaning: "the dead are killing the living man" or "the living man is killing the dead."

ΚΛΥΤΑΙΜΗΣΤΡΑ

οἲ 'γώ.[1] ξυνῆκα τοὔπος ἐξ αἰνιγμάτων.
δόλοις ὀλούμεθ', ὥσπερ οὖν ἐκτείναμεν.
δοίη τις ἀνδροκμῆτα πέλεκυν ὡς τάχος·
εἰδῶμεν εἰ[2] νικῶμεν, ἢ νικώμεθα·
ἐνταῦθα γὰρ δὴ τοῦδ' ἀφικόμην κακοῦ.

ΟΡΕΣΤΗΣ

σὲ καὶ ματεύω· τῷδε δ' ἀρκούντως ἔχει.

ΚΛΥΤΑΙΜΗΣΤΡΑ

οἲ 'γώ. τέθνηκας, φίλτατ' Αἰγίσθου βία.

ΟΡΕΣΤΗΣ

φιλεῖς τὸν ἄνδρα; τοιγὰρ ἐν ταὐτῷ τάφῳ
κείσῃ· θανόντα δ' οὔτι μὴ προδῷς ποτε.

ΚΛΥΤΑΙΜΗΣΤΡΑ

ἐπίσχες, ὦ παῖ, τόνδε δ' αἴδεσαι,[3] τέκνον,
μαστόν, πρὸς ᾧ σὺ[4] πολλὰ δὴ βρίζων ἅμα
οὔλοισιν ἐξήμελξας εὐτραφὲς γάλα.

ΟΡΕΣΤΗΣ

Πυλάδη, τί δράσω; μητέρ' αἰδεσθῶ κτανεῖν;

ΠΥΛΑΔΗΣ

ποῦ δὴ[5] τὰ λοιπὰ Λοξίου μαντεύματα

[1] οἲ ἐγώ (and so ll. 893, 928). [2] ἤ: Turn.
[3] δήσεται: Sophianus. [4] ὠκὺ: ᾧ σὺ Rob
[5] δαί: Auratus.

CLYTAEMESTRA

Oh me! I catch the meaning of the riddle. By guile we are to perish even as we slew. Someone give me a battle-axe, and quick! Let us know if we are victors or vanquished; for even to this have I come in this evil business.

[*Exit Servant. The door is opened and the corpse of Aegisthus is discovered. Near by stands Orestes, and at a distance Pylades*

ORESTES

Thou art the very one I seek. He yonder—he has had enough.

CLYTAEMESTRA

Oh me! Dead, valiant Aegisthus, my beloved!

ORESTES

Thou lovest the man? Then in the same grave shalt thou lie; and never shalt thou abandon him in death.

CLYTAEMESTRA

Hold, my son! Have pity, child, upon this breast at which full oft, sleeping the while, with toothless gums thou didst suck the milk that nourished thee.

ORESTES

Pylades, what shall I do? Shall I for pity spare my mother?

PYLADES

What then becomes henceforth of Loxias' oracles,

τὰ πυθόχρηστα, πιστὰ δ' εὐορκώματα;
ἅπαντας ἐχθροὺς τῶν θεῶν ἡγοῦ πλέον.

ΟΡΕΣΤΗΣ

κρίνω σὲ νικᾶν, καὶ παραινεῖς μοι καλῶς.
ἕπου, πρὸς αὐτὸν τόνδε σὲ σφάξαι θέλω.
καὶ ζῶντα γάρ νιν κρείσσον'[1] ἡγήσω πατρός·
τούτῳ θανοῦσα ξυγκάθευδ', ἐπεὶ φιλεῖς
τὸν ἄνδρα τοῦτον, ὃν δ' ἐχρῆν φιλεῖν στυγεῖς.

ΚΛΥΤΑΙΜΗΣΤΡΑ

ἐγώ σ' ἔθρεψα, σὺν[2] δὲ γηράναι θέλω.

ΟΡΕΣΤΗΣ

πατροκτονοῦσα γὰρ ξυνοικήσεις ἐμοί;

ΚΛΥΤΑΙΜΗΣΤΡΑ

ἡ Μοῖρα τούτων, ὦ τέκνον, παραιτία.

ΟΡΕΣΤΗΣ

καὶ τόνδε τοίνυν Μοῖρ' ἐπόρσυνεν[3] μόρον.

ΚΛΥΤΑΙΜΗΣΤΡΑ

οὐδὲν σεβίζῃ γενεθλίους ἀράς, τέκνον;

ΟΡΕΣΤΗΣ

τεκοῦσα γάρ μ' ἔρριψας ἐς τὸ δυστυχές.

[1] κρέσσων' altered to κρέσσον' : Turn.
[2] νῦν : Auratus. [3] ἐπώρσυνεν : Turn.

declared at Pytho, and of our covenant pledged on oath? Count all men thy enemies rather than the gods.

ORESTES

I judge thee victor; thou counsellest me well. [*To Clytaemestra*] Come, this way! By his very side I mean to kill thee. And since, while he lived, thou heldest him better than my father, sleep with him in death, since he is the man thou lovest, but hadst hate for him whom thou wast bound to love.

CLYTAEMESTRA

'Twas I who nourished thee, and with thee I would grow old.

ORESTES

What! Slay my father and then make thy home with me?

CLYTAEMESTRA

Fate, my child, must share the blame for this.

ORESTES

Then it is Fate that hath worked this thy death likewise.

CLYTAEMESTRA

Hast thou no awe of a parent's curse, my son?

ORESTES

Thou gavest me birth and yet didst cast me out to misery.

ΚΛΥΤΑΙΜΗΣΤΡΑ

οὔτοι σ᾽ ἀπέρριψ᾽ εἰς δόμους δορυξένους.

ΟΡΕΣΤΗΣ

αἰκῶς[1] ἐπράθην ὢν ἐλευθέρου πατρός.

ΚΛΥΤΑΙΜΗΣΤΡΑ

ποῦ δῆθ᾽ ὁ τῖμος, ὅντιν᾽ ἀντεδεξάμην;

ΟΡΕΣΤΗΣ

αἰσχύνομαί σοι[2] τοῦτ᾽ ὀνειδίσαι σαφῶς.

ΚΛΥΤΑΙΜΗΣΤΡΑ

μὴ ἀλλ᾽ εἴφ᾽ ὁμοίως καὶ πατρὸς τοῦ σοῦ μάτας.

ΟΡΕΣΤΗΣ

μὴ ᾽λεγχε τὸν πονοῦντ᾽ ἔσω καθημένη.

ΚΛΥΤΑΙΜΗΣΤΡΑ

ἄλγος γυναιξὶν ἀνδρὸς εἴργεσθαι, τέκνον.

ΟΡΕΣΤΗΣ

τρέφει δέ γ᾽ ἀνδρὸς μόχθος ἡμένας ἔσω.

ΚΛΥΤΑΙΜΗΣΤΡΑ

κτενεῖν ἔοικας, ὦ τέκνον, τὴν μητέρα.

[1] διχῶς: Bothe. [2] σου: Canter.

CLYTAEMESTRA

Nay, surely I cast thee not out in sending thee to the house of an ally.

ORESTES

Vilely was I sold, son though I was of a freeborn sire.

CLYTAEMESTRA

Where then is any price I got for thee?

ORESTES

Shame forbids that I should reproach thee with that outright.

CLYTAEMESTRA

Nay, but fail not to proclaim likewise the follies of that father of thine.

ORESTES

Accuse him not who toiled whilst thou wert sitting idle at home.

CLYTAEMESTRA

'Tis a cruel thing, my child, for women to be deprived of a husband.

ORESTES

Aye, but it is the husband's toil that supports them the while they sit at home.

CLYTAEMESTRA

Thou art resolved, it seems, my child, to slay thy mother.

ΟΡΕΣΤΗΣ

σύ τοι σεαυτήν, οὐκ ἐγώ, κατακτενεῖς.

ΚΛΥΤΑΙΜΗΣΤΡΑ

ὅρα, φύλαξαι μητρὸς ἐγκότους κύνας.

ΟΡΕΣΤΗΣ

τὰς τοῦ πατρὸς δὲ πῶς φύγω, παρεὶς τάδε;

ΚΛΥΤΑΙΜΗΣΤΡΑ

ἔοικα θρηνεῖν ζῶσα πρὸς τύμβον μάτην.

ΟΡΕΣΤΗΣ

πατρὸς γὰρ αἶσα τόνδε σοὐρίζει[1] μόρον.

ΚΛΥΤΑΙΜΗΣΤΡΑ

οἲ 'γὼ τεκοῦσα τόνδ' ὄφιν ἐθρεψάμην.

ΟΡΕΣΤΗΣ

ἦ κάρτα μάντις οὐξ ὀνειράτων φόβος.
ἔκανες[2] ὃν οὐ χρῆν, καὶ τὸ μὴ χρεὼν πάθε.

ΧΟΡΟΣ

στένω μὲν οὖν καὶ τῶνδε συμφορὰν διπλῆν.

[1] πορίζει altered to σ' ὁρίζει: Elmsley. [2] κάνεσγ': Pauw.

---

[1] "To wail to a tomb" was a proverbial expression according to the Scholiast, who cites the saying, "'tis the same thing to cry to a tomb as to a fool." Here, though in strictness ζῶσα is added only to point the contrast with τύμβον—the sentient being with the senseless thing—it also defines the application of τύμβον to Orestes; and its in-

ORESTES

'Tis thou who wilt slay thyself, not I.

CLYTAEMESTRA

Take heed, beware the wrathful sleuth-hounds that avenge a mother.

ORESTES

But my father's—how shall I escape them, if I leave this deed undone?

CLYTAEMESTRA

Methinks, still living, I wail before a tomb[1] in vain.

ORESTES

Aye, for 'tis my father's fate that marks out this doom for thee.

CLYTAEMESTRA

Ah me, this is the serpent that I bare and suckled!

ORESTES

Aye, a prophet in sooth was the terror from thy dream. Thou slewest whom thou shouldst not; so suffer what should not be.

[*He forces Clytaemestra within; Pylades follows*

CHORUS

I have sorrow indeed even for these in their two-

sertion serves to *suggest* that Clytaemestra means that, though living, she is bewailing her own death.

ἐπεὶ δὲ πολλῶν αἱμάτων ἐπήκρισε
τλήμων Ὀρέστης, τοῦθ᾽ ὅμως αἱρούμεθα,
ὀφθαλμὸν οἴκων μὴ πανώλεθρον πεσεῖν.

ἔμολε μὲν δίκα Πριαμίδαις χρόνῳ, [στρ. α.
βαρύδικος[1] ποινά·
ἔμολε δ᾽ ἐς δόμον τὸν Ἀγαμέμνονος
διπλοῦς λέων, διπλοῦς Ἄρης.
ἔλασε[2] δ᾽ ἐς τὸ πᾶν
ὁ πυθόχρηστος[3] φυγὰς
θεόθεν εὖ φραδαῖσιν[4] ὡρμημένος.

ἐπολολύξατ᾽ ὦ δεσποσύνων δόμων [ἐφυμν. α.
ἀναφυγᾶς[5] κακῶν καὶ κτεάνων τριβᾶς[6]
ὑπαὶ[7] δυοῖν μιαστόροιν,[8]
δυσοίμου τύχας.

ἔμολε δ᾽ ᾧ μέλει κρυπταδίου μάχας [ἀντ. α.
δολιόφρων ποινά·
ἔθιγε δ᾽ ἐν[9] μάχᾳ χερὸς ἐτήτυμος
Διὸς κόρα—Δίκαν δέ νιν
προσαγορεύομεν βροτοὶ τυχόντες καλῶς—
ὀλέθριον πνέουσ᾽ ἐν ἐχθροῖς κότον.

<ἐπολολύξατ᾽ ὦ δεσποσύνων δόμων [ἐφυμν. α.
ἀναφυγᾶς κακῶν καὶ κτεάνων τριβᾶς
ὑπαὶ δυοῖν μιαστόροιν,
δυσοίμου τύχας.>[10]

τάπερ ὁ Λοξίας ὁ Παρνασσίας[11] [στρ. β.

[1] καρύδικος: Vict. [2] ἔλακε: Pauw.
[3] πυθοχρήστας, with η over α m: Butler.
[4] εὐφραδαῖσιν: Herm.

fold downfall. Yet, since sore-tried Orestes hath mounted the crest of many a deed of blood, we would rather have it thus—that the eye of the house should not perish utterly.

As unto Priam and his sons justice came at last in crushing retribution, so unto Agamemnon's house came a twofold lion, twofold slaughter.[1] Unto the uttermost hath the exile, the suppliant of Pytho's god, fulfilled his course, urged justly on by counsels from above.

Oh raise a shout of triumph over the escape of our master's house from its misery and the wasting of its wealth by a polluted pair, its grievous fortune!

And he hath come whose part is the crafty vengeance of stealthy attack; and in the battle his hand was guided by her who is in very truth daughter of Zeus, breathing wrath to the death upon her foes. Justice we mortals call her name, hitting well the mark.[2]

Oh raise a shout of triumph over the escape of our master's house from its misery and the wasting of its wealth by a polluted pair, its grievous fortune!

The commands loud proclaimed by Loxias, tenant

[1] As a "twofold" lion (Clytaemestra and Aegisthus) has ravaged the house, so there has been a twofold slaughter by its defenders. There is no reference to Orestes and Pylades or to Agamemnon and Cassandra.

[2] Δί-κα is here derived from Δι(ὸς) κ(όρ)α, "daughter of Zeus."

---

[5] ἀναφυγὰς: Stanley. [6] τριβὰς: Stanley.
[7] ὑπὸ: Herm. [8] δοιοῖν μιαιστόροιν M (δυοῖν G).
[9] δὲ: δ' ἐν Abresch. [10] G. C. Schneider repeats ll. 942-5.
[11] παρνάσσιος: Paley.

μέγαν ἔχων μυχὸν χθονὸς ἐπωρθιά-
ξεν[1] ἀδόλως δόλοις[2]
βλάβαν[3] ἐγχρονισθεῖσαν[4] ἐποίχεται.
†κρατεῖταί πως τὸ θεῖον παρὰ τὸ μὴ
ὑπουργεῖν κακοῖς†.
ἄξια[5] δ' οὐρανοῦχον ἀρχὰν σέβειν.

πάρα τε φῶς ἰδεῖν [ἐφυμν. β.
μέγα[6] τ' ἀφῃρέθην ψάλιον οἰκέων.[7]
ἄναγε μὰν[8] δόμοι[9]· πολὺν ἄγαν χρόνον
χαμαιπετεῖς ἔκεισθ'[10] ἀεί.[11]

τάχα δὲ παντελὴς χρόνος ἀμείψεται [ἀντ. β.
πρόθυρα δωμάτων, ὅταν ἀφ' ἑστίας
πᾶν ἐλαθῇ[12] μύσος
καθαρμοῖσιν[13] ἀτᾶν ἐλατηρίοις.[14]
τύχαι δ' εὐπροσωποκοῖται[15] τὸ πᾶν
ἰδεῖν [ἀκοῦσαι][16] πρευμενεῖς[17]
μετοίκοις δόμων[18] πεσοῦνται πάλιν.

πάρα τε φῶς ἰδεῖν [ἐφυμν. β.
962 <μέγα τ' ἀφῃρέθην ψάλιον οἰκέων.
963 ἄναγε μὰν δόμοι· πολὺν ἄγαν χρόνον
964 χαμαιπετεῖς ἔκεισθ' ἀεί.>[19]

ΟΡΕΣΤΗΣ

Ἴδεσθε χώρας τὴν διπλῆν τυραννίδα
πατροκτόνους τε δωμάτων πορθήτορας.

1 ἐπ' ὄχθει ἄξεν: Meineke. 2 δολίας: Schütz.
3 βλαπτομέναν: H. L. Ahrens.
4 ἐν χρόνοις θεῖσαν: Bothe from χρονισθεῖσαν Herm.
5 ἄξιον: Herm.
6 μέγαν: Stanley. 7 οἴκων: Sidgwick.
8 αναγεμὰν M, ἄναγε μὰν m. 9 δόμοις: Herm.

of Parnassus' mighty cavern shrine, with guileless guile assail the mischief now become inveterate. May the word of God prevail that so I serve not the wicked![1] It is right to reverence the rule of Heaven.

Lo, the light hath come, and I am freed from the cruel curb that restrained the household. Arise, ye halls! Too long a while have ye lain prostrate on the ground.

But soon shall all-accomplishing Time pass the portals of the house when from the hearth all pollution shall be driven by cleansing rites that drive out calamity. The dice of fortune shall change as they fall and lie with faces full fair to behold, well-disposed to those who sojourn in the house.

Lo, the light hath come, and I am freed from the cruel curb that restrained the household. Arise ye halls! Too long a while have ye lain prostrate on the ground.

[*Orestes with the branch and wreath of a suppliant is disclosed standing by the bodies. With him are Pylades and attendants who display the robe of Agamemnon*

ORESTES

Behold this pair, oppressors of the land, who slew my sire and made plunder of my house! Majestic

[1] The translation is based on Hermann's text: *κρατείτω δ' ἔπος τὸ θεῖον τὸ μή μ' | ὑπουργεῖν κακοῖς.*

---

10 *χαμαιπετεῖσε κεῖσθ'*: Schwenk. 11 *αἰεὶ*: Aldina.
12 *μῦσος πᾶν ἐλάσει* M, with *η* over *ει* m: *ἐλαθῇ* Kayser; transposed by Bamberger.
13 *καθαρμοῖς*: Herm. 14 *ἅπαν ἐλατήριον*: Schütz.
15 *τύχα δ' εὐπροσώπω* (with *ι* over final *ω*) *κοῖται*: Franz.
16 [ ] Herm. 17 *θρεομένοις*: Paley.
18 *μετοικοδόμων*: Schütz. 19 G. C. Schneider repeats 962-4.

σεμνοὶ μὲν ἦσαν ἐν θρόνοις τόθ' ἥμενοι,
φίλοι δὲ καὶ[1] νῦν, ὡς ἐπεικάσαι πάθη
πάρεστιν, ὅρκος τ' ἐμμένει πιστώμασι.
ξυνώμοσαν μὲν θάνατον ἀθλίῳ[2] πατρὶ
καὶ ξυνθανεῖσθαι· καὶ τάδ' εὐόρκως ἔχει.
  ἴδεσθε δ' αὖτε, τῶνδ' ἐπήκοοι κακῶν,
τὸ μηχάνημα, δεσμὸν ἀθλίῳ πατρί,
πέδας τε χειροῖν καὶ ποδοῖν ξυνωρίδα.
ἐκτείνατ' αὐτὸ[3] καὶ κύκλῳ παρασταδὸν
στέγαστρον ἀνδρὸς δείξαθ', ὡς ἴδῃ πατήρ,
οὐχ οὑμός, ἀλλ' ὁ πάντ' ἐποπτεύων τάδε
Ἥλιος, ἄναγνα μητρὸς ἔργα τῆς ἐμῆς,
ὡς ἂν παρῇ μοι μάρτυς ἐν δίκῃ ποτέ,
ὡς τόνδ' ἐγὼ μετῆλθον ἐνδίκως μόρον
τὸν μητρός· Αἰγίσθου γὰρ οὐ λέγω[4] μόρον·
ἔχει γὰρ αἰσχυντῆρος, ὡς νόμος,[5] δίκην·
  ἥτις δ' ἐπ' ἀνδρὶ τοῦτ' ἐμήσατο στύγος,
ἐξ οὗ[6] τέκνων ἤνεγχ' ὑπὸ[7] ζώνην βάρος,
φίλον τέως, νῦν δ' ἐχθρόν, ὡς φαίνει, κακόν,
τί σοι δοκεῖ; μύραινά γ' εἴτ'[8] ἔχιδν' ἔφυ
σήπειν θιγοῦσ' ἂν[9] ἄλλον οὐ δεδηγμένον
τόλμης ἕκατι κἀκδίκου[10] φρονήματος.
  τί νιν προσείπω, κἂν τύχω μάλ' εὐστομῶν;
ἄγρευμα θηρός, ἢ νεκροῦ ποδένδυτον
δροίτης κατασκήνωμα; δίκτυον μὲν οὖν,

[1] τε καὶ: Abresch. [2] ἀθλίως: Portus.
[3] αὐτὸν: Auratus.
[4] ψέγω: Turn. λέγω from Schol. [5] νόμου: Portus.
[6] ἐκ σοῦ: Rob. [7] ην ἔχῃ ὑπὸ: Vict.
[8] τ' ἤτ' with γ over the first τ m: Herm.
[9] θίγουσαν: θίγουσ' ἂν Rob., θιγοῦσ' ἂν Blomfield.
[10] κἀνδίκου: H. L. Ahrens.

they were once what time they sat upon their thrones, and loving even now, as one may judge by what hath befallen them; and their oath holds true to their pledges. Together they swore a league of death against my unhappy father, and together they swore to die; and well have they kept their oath.

But now again behold, ye who hearken to this disastrous cause, the device for binding fast my unhappy father, wherewith his hands were manacled, his feet were fettered. Spread it out! Stand round in a throng, and display it—a covering for a man!—that the Father (not mine, but he that surveyeth all things in this world, the Sun) may behold the impious work of my own mother; and so in the day of judgment may be present as my witness that with just cause I pursued this death, even my mother's; for of Aegisthus' death I speak not; for he hath suffered the adulterer's punishment as the law allows.

But she who devised this abhorrent deed against her husband, whose children she had conceived, a burthen beneath her zone, a burthen sometime dear, but now, as the event shows, of deadly hate—what thinkest thou of her? Had she been born sea-snake or viper, methinks her very touch without her bite had made some other to rot, if shamelessness and wickedness of spirit could do it.

[*He takes up again the bloody robe*

What name shall I give it, be I never so fair-spoken? A trap for a wild beast? Or a covering for a corpse in his bier,[1] wrapt round his feet? No, rather 'tis a net—a hunting-net, you might call it,

[1] δροίτης κατασκήνωμα also means "curtain of a bath."

ἄρκυν τ' ἂν[1] εἴποις καὶ ποδιστῆρας πέπλους.
τοιοῦτον ἂν[2] κτήσαιτο φηλήτης[3] ἀνήρ,
ξένων ἀπαιόλημα κἀργυροστερῆ
βίον νομίζων,[4] τῷδέ τ' ἂν δολώματι
πολλοὺς ἀναιρῶν πολλὰ θερμαίνοι φρένα.[5]
τοιάδ' ἐμοὶ ξύνοικος ἐν δόμοισι μὴ
γένοιτ'· ὀλοίμην πρόσθεν[6] ἐκ θεῶν ἄπαις.

ΧΟΡΟΣ

αἰαῖ[7] <αἰαῖ> μελέων ἔργων·
στυγερῷ θανάτῳ διεπράχθης.
ἒ ἔ,
μίμνοντι δὲ καὶ πάθος ἀνθεῖ.

ΟΡΕΣΤΗΣ

ἔδρασεν ἢ οὐκ ἔδρασε[8]; μαρτυρεῖ δέ μοι
φᾶρος τόδ', ὡς ἔβαψεν Αἰγίσθου ξίφος.
φόνου δὲ κηκὶς ξὺν χρόνῳ ξυμβάλλεται,
πολλὰς βαφὰς φθείρουσα τοῦ ποικίλματος
νῦν αὐτὸν αἰνῶ, νῦν ἀποιμώζω παρών,
πατροκτόνον θ' ὕφασμα προσφωνῶν τόδε.
ἀλγῶ μὲν ἔργα καὶ πάθος γένος τε πᾶν,
ἄζηλα νίκης τῆσδ' ἔχων μιάσματα.

ΧΟΡΟΣ

οὔτις μερόπων ἀσινὴς[9] βίοτον
διὰ παντὸς[10] ἀπήμον'[11] ἀμείψει.[12]
ἒ ἔ,[13]
μόχθος[14] δ' ὁ μὲν αὐτίχ', ὁ δ' ἥξει.[15]

[1] δ' ἂν: Herm.
[2] τοιοῦτο μὰν: Turn.
[3] φιλήτης: Scaliger.
[4] νομίζω: Turn.
[5] φρενὶ: Lobeck.
[6] πρόσθ': Turn.

or robes to entangle a man's feet. This were the sort of thing a highwayman might get, who tricks strangers and plies a robber's trade; and with this cunning snare he might slay many a man and gladden his heart thereby.

May such a woman not dwell with me in my house! Ere that God grant I perish childless!

CHORUS

Alack, alack, woeful work! Wretched was the death that ended thee. Alas! alas! And for him that surviveth suffering also is blossoming

ORESTES

Did she the deed or not? Nay, my witness is this vesture, dyed by Aegisthus' sword. 'Tis of blood this stain, that aideth time to spoil the many tinctures of broidered stuff.

Now at last do I speak his praises; now at last I am present to make lament for him, as I address this web that wrought my father's death; howbeit I grieve for deed and punishment and for the whole race—my victory is a pollution unenviable.

CHORUS

No mortal wight shall scatheless pass his life free from all suffering unto the end. Alas! Alas! One tribulation cometh to-day, another the morrow.

---

[7] *αἶ αἶ*: Bothe, Dindorf. [8] *ἔδρασεν*: Turn.
[9] *ἀσινεῖ* altered to *ἀσινῆ*: Herwerden.
[10] *πάντ'*: Heath. [11] *ἄτιμος*: Weil.
[12] *ἀμείψεται*: Erfurdt. [13] *ἐς*: *ἒ ἔ* Klausen.
[14] *μόχθο** M, the rest supplied by m (*σ δ' ὁ μὲν αὐτίχ' ὅδ' ἧξε*).
[15] *ἥξει* Turn.

ΟΡΕΣΤΗΣ

ἀλλ', ὡς ἂν εἰδῆτ', οὐ γὰρ[1] οἶδ' ὅπῃ τελεῖ,
ὥσπερ ξὺν ἵπποις ἡνιοστροφῶ[2] δρόμου
ἐξωτέρω· φέρουσι γὰρ νικώμενον
φρένες δύσαρκτοι· πρὸς δὲ καρδίᾳ φόβος
ᾄδειν ἕτοιμος ἠδ' ὑπορχεῖσθαι κότῳ.
ἕως δ' ἔτ'[3] ἔμφρων εἰμί, κηρύσσω φίλοις
κτανεῖν τέ φημι μητέρ' οὐκ ἄνευ δίκης,
πατροκτόνον μίασμα καὶ θεῶν στύγος.
καὶ φίλτρα τόλμης τῆσδε πλειστηρίζομαι
τὸν πυθόμαντιν Λοξίαν, χρήσαντ' ἐμοὶ
πράξαντι μὲν ταῦτ' ἐκτὸς αἰτίας κακῆς
εἶναι, παρέντα δ'—οὐκ ἐρῶ τὴν ζημίαν·
τόξῳ γὰρ οὔτις πημάτων ἐφίξεται.[4]
καὶ νῦν ὁρᾶτέ μ', ὡς παρεσκευασμένος
ξὺν τῷδε θαλλῷ καὶ στέφει προσίξομαι
μεσόμφαλόν θ' ἵδρυμα, Λοξίου πέδον,
πυρός τε φέγγος ἄφθιτον κεκλημένον,
φεύγων τόδ' αἷμα κοινόν· οὐδ' ἐφ' ἑστίαν[5]
ἄλλην τραπέσθαι Λοξίας ἐφίετο.
καὶ μαρτυρεῖν μὲν ὡς[6] ἐπορσύνθη κακὰ
τάδ' ἐν χρόνῳ μοι πάντας Ἀργείους λέγω·
ἐγὼ δ' ἀλήτης τῆσδε γῆς ἀπόξενος,
ζῶν καὶ τεθνηκὼς τάσδε κληδόνας λιπών.

ΧΟΡΟΣ

ἀλλ' εὖ γ' ἔπραξας,[7] μηδ' ἐπιζευχθῇς[8] στόμα

[1] ἀλλοσᾶν εἰ δὴ τούτ' ἄρ: ἀλλ' ὡς ἂν Blomfield, εἰδῆτ' Martin, Emperius, οὐ γὰρ Erfurdt.
[2] ἡνιοστρόφου: Stanley. [3] ἕως δέ τ' supplied by m: Rob.
[4] προσίξεται: Schütz from Schol. [5] ἐφέστιον: Turn.

ORESTES

But—since I would have you know—for I know not how 'twill end—methinks I am a charioteer driving my team far outside the course; for my wits, hard to govern, whirl me away o'ermastered, and at my heart fear is fain to sing and dance to a tune of wrath. But while I still keep my senses, I proclaim to those who hold me dear and declare that not without justice did I slay my mother, polluted murderess of my father, and a thing loathed of Heaven.

And as for the promptings that gave me courage for this deed, I offer as my chiefest surety Loxias, Pytho's prophet, who declared that, if I did this thing, I should stand clear of evil charge, but if I forebore—I will not name the penalty; for no bow-shot could reach such height of woe.

And now behold me, how, armed with this branch and wreath, I go as suppliant to earth's central seat, Loxias' demesne, and to the bright fire famed "imperishable,[1]" an exile for this deed of kindred bloodshed; to no other hearth did Loxias bid me turn. And as to the manner how this evil deed was wrought, I charge all men of Argos in time to come to bear me witness. I go forth a wanderer, strangered from this land, leaving behind, in life or death, this report of me.

CHORUS

Nay, thou hast done well. Therefore yoke not

[1] In the Delphic shrine there was an undying fire.

---

[6] μοι μενέλεως: μὲν ὡς Blomfield, who put l. 1041 after l. 1039, reversing the order in M.

[7] τε πράξας: Tyrwhitt. [8] ἐπιζευχθῇ: Heath.

φήμῃ πονηρᾷ[1] μηδ' ἐπιγλωσσῶ κακά,
ἐλευθερώσας πᾶσαν Ἀργείων[2] πόλιν,
δυοῖν δρακόντοιν εὐπετῶς τεμὼν κάρα.

ΟΡΕΣΤΗΣ

ἆ, ἆ.
δμωαὶ γυναῖκες, αἵδε Γοργόνων δίκην
φαιοχίτωνες καὶ πεπλεκτανημέναι
πυκνοῖς δράκουσιν· οὐκέτ' ἂν μείναιμ'[3] ἐγώ.

ΧΟΡΟΣ

τίνες σε δόξαι, φίλτατ' ἀνθρώπων πατρί,
στροβοῦσιν; ἴσχε, μὴ φόβου νικῶ[4] πολύ.

ΟΡΕΣΤΗΣ

οὐκ εἰσὶ δόξαι τῶνδε πημάτων ἐμοί·
σαφῶς γὰρ αἵδε μητρὸς ἔγκοτοι κύνες.

ΧΟΡΟΣ

ποταίνιον γὰρ αἷμά σοι χεροῖν ἔτι·
ἐκ τῶνδέ τοι ταραγμὸς ἐς φρένας πίτνει.

ΟΡΕΣΤΗΣ

ἄναξ Ἄπολλον, αἵδε πληθύουσι[5] δή,
κἀξ ὀμμάτων στάζουσιν αἷμα δυσφιλές.

ΧΟΡΟΣ

εἷς σοὶ[6] καθαρμός· Λοξίας[7] δὲ προσθιγὼν
ἐλεύθερόν σε τῶνδε πημάτων κτίσει.

[1] φῆμαι πονηραὶ: Heath.

[2] ἀργείην M, ἀργείων G.

thy tongue to ill-omened speech nor let thy lips give vent to evil bodings, since thou hast freed the whole realm of Argos by lopping off with happy stroke the heads of two serpents.

ORESTES

Ah, ah! Ye handmaidens, see them yonder—like Gorgons, stoled in sable garb, entwined with swarming snakes! I can no longer stay.

CHORUS

What fancies disturb thee, thou dearest of sons unto thy sire? Hold, be not greatly overborne by fear.

ORESTES

To me these are no fancied troubles. For in very truth yonder are the wrathful sleuth-hounds that avenge my mother.

CHORUS

'Tis that the blood is still fresh upon thy hands—this is the cause of the disorder that assails thy wits.

ORESTES

O lord Apollo, lo! now they come in troops, and from their eyes they drip loathsome blood!

CHORUS

One way there is to cleanse thee—Loxias' touch will set thee free from this affliction.

---

[3] *οὐκ ἔτ' ἀμμείνοιμ'*: Tzetzes, *An. Ox.* iii. 359 (reading *δεινοῖς δρακ. κτλ.*).

[4] *φοβοῦ νικῶν*: Porson.

[5] *πληθύουσαι*: Turn.

[6] *εἴσω* altered to *εἰσσ' ὁ*: Erfurdt.

[7] *λοξίου*: Auratus.

ΟΡΕΣΤΗΣ

ὑμεῖς μὲν οὐχ ὁρᾶτε τάσδ᾽, ἐγὼ δ᾽ ὁρῶ·
ἐλαύνομαι δὲ κοὐκέτ᾽ ἂν μείναιμ᾽[1] ἐνώ.

ΧΟΡΟΣ

ἀλλ᾽ εὐτυχοίης, καί σ᾽ ἐποπτεύων πρόφρων
θεὸς φυλάσσοι καιρίοισι συμφοραῖς.

ὅδε τοι μελάθροις τοῖς βασιλείοις
τρίτος αὖ χειμὼν
  πνεύσας[2] γονίας ἐτελέσθη.
παιδοβόροι[3] μὲν πρῶτον ὑπῆρξαν
μόχθοι τάλανές [τε Θυέστου]·[4]
δεύτερον ἀνδρὸς βασίλεια πάθη·
λουτροδάικτος δ᾽ ὤλετ᾽ Ἀχαιῶν
πολέμαρχος ἀνήρ·
νῦν δ᾽ αὖ τρίτος ἦλθέ ποθεν σωτήρ,
ἢ μόρον εἴπω;
ποῖ δῆτα κρανεῖ, ποῖ καταλήξει
  μετακοιμισθὲν μένος ἄτης;

[1] κοὐκ ἔτ᾽ ἀμμείναιμ᾽: Rob.
[2] τρεούσᾱς: Scaliger.
[3] παιδόμοροι: Auratus.
[4] [ ] Herm.

ORESTES

Ye see them not, but I see them. I am pursued. I can no longer stay. [*Rushes out*

CHORUS

Then blessings go with thee; and may God watch kindly o'er thee and guard thee with favouring fortune!

Lo! Now again, for the third time, hath the tempest of the race burst upon the royal house and run its course. First, at the beginning, came the cruel woes of children slain for food; next, the fate of a man, a king, when, murdered in a bath, perished the war-lord of the Achaeans. And now, once again, hath come somewhence, a third, a deliverer—or shall I say a doom? Oh when will it work its accomplishment, when will the fury of calamity, lulled to rest, find an end and cease?

EUMENIDES

ΤΑ ΤΟΥ ΔΡΑΜΑΤΟΣ ΠΡΟΣΩΠΑ

ΠΥΘΙΑΣ ΠΡΟΦΗΤΙΣ
ΑΠΟΛΛΩΝ
ΟΡΕΣΤΗΣ
ΚΛΥΤΑΙΜΗΣΤΡΑΣ ΕΙΔΩΛΟΝ
ΧΟΡΟΣ ΕΥΜΕΝΙΔΩΝ
ΑΘΗΝΑ
ΠΡΟΠΟΜΠΟΙ

DRAMATIS PERSONAE

The Pythian Prophētess
Apollō
Orestēs
Shade of Clytaemēstra
Chorus of Furies
Athēna
Escort

Scene.—(1) The temple of Apollo at Delphi;
(2) Athena's temple at Athens.
Time.—The heroic age.
Date.—458 b.c., at the City Dionysia.

ARGUMENT

The priestess of Apollo discovers Orestes as a suppliant in the inner shrine of the god at Delphi, and fronting him the Erinyes of his mother, a band of fearsome creatures who, wearied with the pursuit of the fugitive, have fallen on sleep. Under promise of his support, Apollo bids Orestes flee to Athens, where he shall submit his case to judgment and be released from his sufferings. The ghost of Clytaemestra rises to upbraid the sleeping Erinyes because of their neglect, whereby she is dishonoured among the other dead. Awakened by her taunts, they revile Apollo for that he has given sanctuary to a polluted man whom they rightly pursue by reason of their office—to take vengeance on all who shed kindred blood.

The scene shifts to Athens, whither his pursuers have tracked their prey. Orestes, clasping the ancient image of Pallas, implores her protection on the plea that the blood upon his hands has long since been washed away by sacred rites and that his presence has worked harm to none who have given him shelter. The Erinyes chant a hymn to bind the soul of their victim with its maddening spell. In answer to Orestes' call, the goddess appears and with the consent of the Erinyes undertakes to judge the case, not by herself alone but with the assistance of a chosen number of her best citizens who are to constitute the jury.

The trial opens with Apollo present as advocate of his suppliant and as representative of Zeus, whose commands he has merely to set forth in all his oracles. Orestes, he declares, slew his mother by his express behest. The accused confesses to the deed but urges in his defence that in killing her husband Clytaemestra killed his father and that his accusers should justly have taken vengeance upon her. On their rejecting this argument on the ground that the murderess was not blood-kin to him she murdered, Orestes denies blood-kinship with his mother; in which contention he is supported by Apollo, who asserts that the father alone is the proper parent of the child, the mother being only the nurse of the implanted seed.

Athena announces that the court, the first to try a case of homicide, is now established by her for all time to come. The jury cast their ballots; and the goddess, declaring that it is her duty to pronounce final judgment on the case, makes known that her vote is to count for Orestes, who is to win if the ballots are equally divided. Proclaimed victor by the tie, Orestes quits the scene; his antagonists threaten to bring ruin on the land that has denied the justice of their cause. It is the part of Athena by promises of enduring honours to assuage their anger; and now no longer Spirits of Wrath but Spirits of Blessing, they are escorted in solemn procession to their sanctuary beneath the Hill of Ares.

ΕΥΜΕΝΙΔΕΣ

ΠΥΘΙΑΣ

Πρῶτον μὲν εὐχῇ τῇδε πρεσβεύω θεῶν
τὴν πρωτόμαντιν Γαῖαν· ἐκ δὲ τῆς Θέμιν,
ἣ δὴ τὸ μητρὸς δευτέρα τόδ᾽ ἕζετο
μαντεῖον, ὡς λόγος τις· ἐν δὲ τῷ τρίτῳ
λάχει, θελούσης, οὐδὲ πρὸς βίαν τινός,
Τιτανὶς ἄλλη παῖς Χθονὸς καθέζετο,
Φοίβη· δίδωσι δ᾽ ἣ γενέθλιον δόσιν
Φοίβῳ· τὸ Φοίβης δ᾽ ὄνομ᾽ ἔχει παρώνυμον.
λιπὼν δὲ λίμνην Δηλίαν τε χοιράδα,
κέλσας ἐπ᾽ ἀκτὰς ναυπόρους τὰς Παλλάδος,
ἐς τήνδε γαῖαν ἦλθε Παρνησοῦ θ᾽[1] ἕδρας.
πέμπουσι δ᾽ αὐτὸν καὶ σεβίζουσιν μέγα
κελευθοποιοὶ παῖδες Ἡφαίστου, χθόνα
ἀνήμερον τιθέντες ἡμερωμένην.
μολόντα δ᾽ αὐτὸν κάρτα τιμαλφεῖ λεώς,
Δελφός τε χώρας τῆσδε πρυμνήτης ἄναξ.
τέχνης δέ νιν Ζεὺς ἔνθεον κτίσας φρένα
ἵζει τέταρτον τοῖσδε[2] μάντιν ἐν θρόνοις·[3]
Διὸς προφήτης δ᾽ ἐστὶ Λοξίας πατρός.
τούτους ἐν εὐχαῖς φροιμιάζομαι θεούς.

[1] παρ∗νησοῦσθ᾽: Rob. [2] τόνδε: I. Voss.
[3] χρόνοις: Turn. (cp. *Ag.* 1563).

EUMENIDES

Prophetess

First, in this my prayer, I give the place of chiefest honour among the gods to the first prophet, Earth; and after her to Themis; for she, as is told, took second this oracular seat of her mother. And third in succession, with Themis' consent and by constraint of none, another Titan, Phoebe, child of Earth, took here her seat. She bestowed it, as birth-gift, upon Phoebus, who has his name from Phoebe. He, quitting the mere[1] and ridge of Delos, landed on Pallas' ship-frequented shores, and came to this region and the dwelling places on Parnassus. With mighty reverence was he given escort by Hephaestus' children,[2] who fashion highways, taming the wildness of the untamed land. And on his coming, high worship was paid him by the folk and by Delphus, helmsman and sovereign of this land. With the prophet's art Zeus inspired his soul, and stablished him upon this throne as fourth and present seer; but it is of Zeus, his sire, that Loxias is spokesman.

These are the gods I place in the forefront of my

[1] A circular lake in the island of Apollo's birth.

[2] The Athenians, because Erichthonius, who was identified with Erechtheus, was the son of Hephaestus, who first fashioned axes.

Παλλὰς προναία δ' ἐν λόγοις πρεσβεύεται·
σέβω δὲ νύμφας, ἔνθα Κωρυκὶς πέτρα
κοίλη, φίλορνις, δαιμόνων ἀναστροφή·[1]
Βρόμιος ἔχει τὸν χῶρον, οὐδ' ἀμνημονῶ,
ἐξ οὗτε Βάκχαις ἐστρατήγησεν θεός,
λαγὼ δίκην Πενθεῖ καταρράψας μόρον·
Πλειστοῦ[2] τε πηγὰς καὶ Ποσειδῶνος κράτος
καλοῦσα καὶ τέλειον ὕψιστον Δία,
ἔπειτα μάντις ἐς θρόνους καθιζάνω.
καὶ νῦν τυχεῖν με τῶν πρὶν εἰσόδων μακρῷ
ἄριστα δοῖεν· κεἰ παρ' Ἑλλήνων τινές,
ἴτων πάλῳ λαχόντες, ὡς νομίζεται.
μαντεύομαι γὰρ ὡς ἂν ἡγῆται θεός.

ἦ δεινὰ λέξαι, δεινὰ δ' ὀφθαλμοῖς δρακεῖν,
πάλιν μ' ἔπεμψεν ἐκ δόμων τῶν Λοξίου,
ὡς μήτε σωκεῖν μήτε μ' ἀκταίνειν βάσιν.[3]
τρέχω δὲ χερσίν, οὐ ποδωκείᾳ[4] σκελῶν·
δείσασα γὰρ γραῦς οὐδέν, ἀντίπαις μὲν οὖν.
ἐγὼ μὲν ἕρπω πρὸς πολυστεφῆ μυχόν·
ὁρῶ δ' ἐπ' ὀμφαλῷ μὲν ἄνδρα θεομυσῆ[5]
ἕδραν ἔχοντα[6] προστρόπαιον, αἵματι
στάζοντα χεῖρας καὶ νεοσπαδὲς[7] ξίφος

[1] ἀναστροφά M, -φή Schol., -φαί FV3N.
[2] πλείστους: Turn.
[3] στάσιν M γρ., βάσιν m.
[4] ὀύπω δοκία M, οὐ ποδωκίᾳ m¹N, οὐ ποδωκείᾳ FV3.
[5] θεομυσῆι M, -μισῆ FV3N.
[6] ἔχοντι M, ἔχοντα FV3N.
[7] νεοσπαθὲς FV3N.

---

[1] The shrine of Pallas "before the temple," close to Delphi on the main road leading to the sanctuary of Apollo.

[2] The Corycian cave, sacred to the Nymphs and Pan, has been identified with a grotto on the great plateau above Delphi.

prayer. And Pallas of the Precinct[1] hath likewise honour in my words, and I revere the Nymphs, who dwell where is the Corycian[2] caverned rock, delight of birds and haunt of powers divine. Bromius hath held the region (him I forget not) ever since the time when, a god indeed, he headed the Bacchic host and contrived for Pentheus death as of a hunted hare. The waters of Pleistus, too, I invoke, and Poseidon's might, and Zeus the Fulfiller, Most High; thereafter I take my seat as prophetess upon my throne. And may they grant that now fairest fortune may be mine, far beyond my ingoings aforetime. And if there be any here from among the Hellenes, let them enter, in turn, by lot, as is the wont. For as the god doth lead, so do I prophesy.

[*She enters the temple and after a brief interval returns terror-stricken*

Horrible! Horrors to relate, horrors for my eyes to behold, have sent me back from the house of Loxias; so that I have no strength left in me nor can I go upright. I run with the aid of my hands, not with any nimbleness of limb; for an aged woman, overcome with fright, is a thing of naught—nay rather, she is but as a child.

I was on my way to the inner shrine, enriched with many a wreath, when, on the centre-stone,[3] I beheld a man defiled before Heaven occupying the seat of suppliants. His hands were dripping gore; he held a sword just drawn and a lofty olive-

[3] ὀμφαλός "navel" was the name given by the Delphians to a white stone (in Aeschylus' time placed in the inmost sanctuary of Apollo), which they regarded as marking the exact centre of the earth. Near the great altar of Apollo the French excavators of Delphi discovered a navel-stone. ὀμφαλός is sometimes used of Delphi itself.

ἔχοντ᾽ ἐλαίας θ᾽ ὑψιγέννητον κλάδον,
λήνει[1] μεγίστῳ σωφρόνως ἐστεμμένον,
ἀργῆτι μαλλῷ· τῇδε γὰρ τρανῶς ἐρῶ.
πρόσθεν δὲ τἀνδρὸς τοῦδε θαυμαστὸς λόχος[2]
εὕδει γυναικῶν ἐν θρόνοισιν ἥμενος.
οὔτοι γυναῖκας, ἀλλὰ Γοργόνας λέγω,
οὐδ᾽ αὖτε Γοργείοισιν εἰκάσω τύποις.
εἶδόν ποτ᾽ ἤδη Φινέως γεγραμμένας
δεῖπνον φερούσας· ἄπτεροί γε μὴν ἰδεῖν
αὗται, μέλαιναι δ᾽ ἐς τὸ πᾶν βδελύκτροποι·
ῥέγκουσι δ᾽ οὐ πλατοῖσι[3] φυσιάμασιν·
ἐκ δ᾽ ὀμμάτων λείβουσι δυσφιλῆ λίβα·[4]
καὶ κόσμος οὔτε πρὸς θεῶν ἀγάλματα
φέρειν δίκαιος οὔτ᾽ ἐς ἀνθρώπων στέγας.
τὸ φῦλον οὐκ ὄπωπα τῆσδ᾽ ὁμιλίας
οὐδ᾽ ἥτις αἶα τοῦτ᾽ ἐπεύχεται γένος
τρέφουσ᾽ ἀνατεὶ μὴ μεταστένειν πόνον.[5]
τἀντεῦθεν ἤδη τῶνδε δεσπότῃ δόμων
αὐτῷ μελέσθω Λοξίᾳ μεγασθενεῖ.
ἰατρόμαντις δ᾽ ἐστὶ καὶ τερασκόπος
καὶ τοῖσιν ἄλλοις δωμάτων καθάρσιος.

ΑΠΟΛΛΩΝ

οὔτοι προδώσω· διὰ τέλους δέ σοι φύλαξ
ἐγγὺς παρεστὼς καὶ πρόσω δ᾽ ἀποστατῶν
ἐχθροῖσι τοῖς σοῖς οὐ γενήσομαι πέπων.
καὶ νῦν ἁλούσας τάσδε τὰς μάργους ὁρᾷς·

1 λίνει FV3N.
2 λέχος M, λόχος FV3N. 3 πλαστοῖσι : Elmsley.
4 δία M, βίαν FV3N: Burges.
5 πόνων : Arnaldus.

1 The Harpies.

branch reverently crowned with a tuft of wool exceeding large—white was the fleece; for as to this I can speak clearly.

Before this man there sat asleep on thrones a wondrous throng of women. No! women they were surely not, Gorgons I rather call them. Nor yet can I liken them to forms of Gorgons either. Once ere this I saw some pictured creatures[1] carrying off the feast of Phineus—but these are wingless, sable, and altogether detestable. Their snorting nostrils blow forth fearsome blasts, and from their eyes oozes a loathly rheum. Their garb, too, was such as is unfit to bring before the statues of the gods or into the abodes of men. The tribe which owns this company I have never seen; nor do I know what region boasts to rear unscathed this brood and not repent its pains.

But for the outcome, let that be now the care of the lord of this house, even Loxias himself, the puissant, for he is a revealer of healing remedies, a reader of portents, and for others he purgeth their habitations. [*Exit*

[*The interior of the temple is disclosed. Enter, from the inner sanctuary, Apollo, who takes his stand beside Orestes at the centre-stone. Near the suppliant are the Furies asleep. Hermes in the background*

APOLLO

No! I will not abandon thee. Thy guardian to the end, close by thy side, or even far removed, I will not show me gentle to thine enemies. So now thou see'st these maddened women overcome;

ὕπνῳ πεσοῦσαι δ᾽ αἱ κατάπτυστοι κόραι,
γραῖαι παλαιαὶ παῖδες, αἷς οὐ μείγνυται
θεῶν τις οὐδ᾽ ἄνθρωπος οὐδὲ θήρ ποτε.
κακῶν δ᾽ ἕκατι κἀγένοντ᾽, ἐπεὶ κακὸν
σκότον νέμονται Τάρταρόν θ᾽ ὑπὸ χθονός,
μισήματ᾽ ἀνδρῶν καὶ θεῶν Ὀλυμπίων.
ὅμως δὲ φεῦγε μηδὲ μαλθακὸς γένῃ.
ἐλῶσι γάρ σε καὶ δι᾽ ἠπείρου μακρᾶς
βιβῶντ ἀν᾽[1] αἰεὶ τὴν πλανοστιβῆ χθόνα
ὑπέρ τε πόντον[2] καὶ περιρρύτας πόλεις.
καὶ μὴ πρόκαμνε τόνδε βουκολούμενος
πόνον· μολὼν δὲ Παλλάδος ποτὶ πτόλιν
ἵζου παλαιὸν ἄγκαθεν λαβὼν βρέτας.
κἀκεῖ δικαστὰς τῶνδε καὶ θελκτηρίους
μύθους ἔχοντες μηχανὰς εὑρήσομεν,
ὥστ᾽ ἐς τὸ πᾶν σε τῶνδ᾽ ἀπαλλάξαι πόνων·
καὶ γὰρ κτανεῖν σ᾽ ἔπεισα μητρῷον δέμας.

ΟΡΕΣΤΗΣ

ἄναξ Ἄπολλον, οἶσθα μὲν τὸ μὴ ᾽δικεῖν·
ἐπεὶ δ᾽ ἐπίστᾳ, καὶ τὸ μὴ ᾽μελεῖν μάθε.
σθένος δὲ ποιεῖν εὖ φερέγγυον τὸ σόν.

ΑΠΟΛΛΩΝ

μέμνησο, μὴ φόβος σε νικάτω φρένας.
σὺ δ᾽, αὐτάδελφον αἷμα καὶ κοινοῦ πατρός,
Ἑρμῆ, φύλασσε· κάρτα δ᾽ ὢν ἐπώνυμος
πομπαῖος ἴσθι, τόνδε ποιμαίνων ἐμὸν

[1] βεβῶντ᾽ ἂν M, βεβόντ᾽ ἂν FN: βιβῶντ᾽ Stephanus, ἀν᾽ Herm.
[2] πόντου: Turn.

fallen on sleep are these loathsome maidens—beldames, aged children, with whom nor any god nor man nor beast consorteth ever. For evil's sake were they even born, since they inhabit the evil gloom of Tartarus beneath the earth—creatures loathed of men and of Olympian gods. Nevertheless, do thou fly on and grow not faint of heart. For as thou ever tread'st the travelled earth, they will chase thee even over the wide continent and beyond the main and the cities girdled by the sea. And grow not weary ere thy course be run by brooding on this thy toil; but when thou art come to Pallas' burgh, sit thee down and clasp in thine arms her ancient image. And there, with judges of thy cause and speech of persuasive charm, we shall discover means to release thee utterly from thy distress; for it was at my behest that thou didst take thy mother's life.

Orestes

Lord Apollo, thou knowest not to be unrighteous; and, since thou knowest, learn also not to be unheedful. For thy *power* of doing good hath ample warranty.

Apollo

Remember, let not fear overmaster thy soul. And do thou, Hermes, my very own brother and blood of my sire, keep watch over him. True to thy name, be thou his "Conductor,[1]" as a shepherd

[1] Hermes is the guide of the living on their journeys; as he is also the conductor of the souls of the dead to the nether world.

ἱκέτην—σέβει τοι Ζεὺς τόδ᾽ ἐκνόμων σέβας—
ὁρμώμενον βροτοῖσιν εὐπόμπῳ τύχῃ.

ΚΛΥΤΑΙΜΗΣΤΡΑΣ ΕΙΔΩΛΟΝ

εὕδοιτ᾽ ἄν, ὠή, καὶ καθευδουσῶν τί δεῖ;
ἐγὼ δ᾽ ὑφ᾽ ὑμῶν ὧδ᾽ ἀπητιμασμένη
ἄλλοισιν ἐν νεκροῖσιν, ὧν[1] μὲν ἔκτανον
ὄνειδος ἐν φθιτοῖσιν οὐκ ἐκλείπεται,
αἰσχρῶς δ᾽ ἀλῶμαι· προυννέπω δ᾽ ὑμῖν ὅτι
ἔχω μεγίστην αἰτίαν κείνων ὕπο·
παθοῦσα δ᾽ οὕτω δεινὰ πρὸς τῶν φιλτάτων,
οὐδεὶς ὑπέρ μου δαιμόνων μηνίεται,
κατασφαγείσης πρὸς χερῶν μητροκτόνων.
ὁρᾶτε[2] πληγὰς τάσδε καρδίας ὅθεν.[3]
εὕδουσα γὰρ φρὴν ὄμμασιν λαμπρύνεται,
ἐν ἡμέρᾳ δὲ μοῖρ᾽ ἀπρόσκοπος[4] βροτῶν.
ἦ πολλὰ μὲν δὴ τῶν ἐμῶν ἐλείξατε,
χοάς τ᾽ ἀοίνους, νηφάλια[5] μειλίγματα,
καὶ νυκτίσεμνα[6] δεῖπν᾽ ἐπ᾽ ἐσχάρᾳ πυρὸς
ἔθυον, ὥραν οὐδενὸς κοινὴν θεῶν.
καὶ πάντα ταῦτα λὰξ ὁρῶ πατούμενα.
ὁ δ᾽ ἐξαλύξας οἴχεται νεβροῦ δίκην,
καὶ ταῦτα κούφως ἐκ μέσων ἀρκυστάτων[7]
ὤρουσεν ὑμῖν ἐγκατιλλώψας[8] μέγα.
ἀκούσαθ᾽ ὡς ἔλεξα τῆς ἐμῆς περὶ
ψυχῆς, φρονήσατ᾽, ὦ κατὰ χθονὸς θεαί.
ὄναρ γὰρ ὑμᾶς νῦν Κλυταιμήστρα[9] καλῶ.

[1] ὡς: Tyrwhitt. [2] ὅρα δὲ: Paley.
[3] καρδία (altered to καρδίαι) σέθεν M: Herm.
[4] μοῖρα πρόσκοπος: Turn. [5] νιφάλια: Rob.
[6] νυκτὸ (changed to νυκτὶ) σεμνὰ M: Turn.
[7] ἀρκυσμάτων: Turn.

guiding this my suppliant—of a truth Zeus holdeth in reverence this revered right of outcasts—sped forth to men with prospering guidance.

[*Exit. Orestes departs escorted by Hermes. The Ghost of Clytaemestra appears*

GHOST OF CLYTAEMESTRA

Sleep on! Aha! Yet what need is there of sleepers? 'Tis due to you that I am thus dishonoured among the other dead; because of my deeds of blood the dead never cease reviling me, and I wander in disgrace. I declare to you that they bring against me charge most grievous. And yet, howbeit I have suffered thus cruelly from my nearest kin, no power divine is wroth in my behalf, slaughtered as I have been by the hands of mine own son. Mark ye these gashes in my heart, whence they come! For the mind asleep hath clear vision, but in the daytime the fate of mortal men cannot be foreseen.

In sooth ye have lapped up full many an offering of mine—wineless libations, a sober appeasement, and banquets in the solemn night have I often sacrificed upon a hearth of fire at an hour unshared by any god. All this I see trampled under foot. But he has escaped away from you, and is gone, even as a fawn; aye, and has lightly bounded away from out the midmost of your snare, mocking at you with derisive leers. Hear me! Since I plead for my very life, awake to consciousness, ye goddesses of the nether world! 'Tis in a dream I, Clytaemestra, now invoke you.

---

[8] ἐκκατιλλώψας: Turn.

[9] κλυταιμνήστρα M (and here only).

ΧΟΡΟΣ

(μυγμός.)

ΚΛΥΤΑΙΜΗΣΤΡΑΣ ΕΙΔΩΛΟΝ

μύζοιτ' ἄν, ἀνὴρ δ' οἴχεται φεύγων πρόσω·
φίλοι γάρ εἰσιν οὐκ ἐμοῖς προσεικότες.[1]

ΧΟΡΟΣ

(μυγμός.)

ΚΛΥΤΑΙΜΗΣΤΡΑΣ ΕΙΔΩΛΟΝ

ἄγαν ὑπνώσσεις κοὐ κατοικτίζεις πάθος·
φονεὺς δ' Ὀρέστης τῆσδε μητρὸς οἴχεται.

ΧΟΡΟΣ

(ὠγμός.)[2]

ΚΛΥΤΑΙΜΗΣΤΡΑΣ ΕΙΔΩΛΟΝ

ᾤζεις, ὑπνώσσεις· οὐκ ἀναστήσῃ τάχος;
τί σοι πέπρωται[3] πρᾶγμα πλὴν τεύχειν κακά;

ΧΟΡΟΣ

(ὠγμός.)[2]

ΚΛΥΤΑΙΜΗΣΤΡΑΣ ΕΙΔΩΛΟΝ

ὕπνος πόνος τε κύριοι συνωμόται
δεινῆς δρακαίνης ἐξεκήραναν μένος.

ΧΟΡΟΣ

(μυγμὸς διπλοῦς ὀξύς.)
λαβὲ λαβὲ λαβὲ λαβέ, φράζου.

ΚΛΥΤΑΙΜΗΣΤΡΑΣ ΕΙΔΩΛΟΝ

ὄναρ διώκεις θῆρα, κλαγγαίνεις δ' ἅπερ
κύων μέριμναν οὔποτ' ἐκλείπων[4] πόνου.

[*The Chorus begins to move uneasily, uttering a whining sound*]

Whine, if ye will! But the man is gone, fled far away. For he hath friends not like to mine!

[*The Chorus continues to whine*]

Too heavy art thou with sleep and hast no pity for my misery. Orestes, the murderer of his mother here, is gone!

[*The Chorus begins to moan*]

Thou moanest, slumberest. Wilt thou not arise at once? What task hath been allotted thee save to work ill?

[*The Chorus continues to moan*]

Slumber and travail, fit conspirators, have destroyed the might of the dreaded dragoness.

CHORUS

[*with whining redoubled and intensified*]

Seize him! seize him! seize him! seize him! Mark him!

GHOST OF CLYTAEMESTRA

'Tis but in a dream thou art hunting thy game, and art whimpering like a hound that never leaves off its keenness for the chase. What *work* hast

---

[1] φίλοις . . . προσίκτορες: Weil.
[2] μωγμός: Rob. ὠγμός.
[3] πέπρακται: Stanley.
[4] ἐκλιπὼν: Blomfield.

τί δρᾷς; ἀνίστω, μή σε νικάτω πόνος,
μηδ' ἀγνοήσῃς πῆμα μαλθαχθεῖσ' ὕπνῳ.
ἄλγησον ἦπαρ ἐνδίκοις ὀνείδεσιν·[1]
τοῖς σώφροσιν γὰρ ἀντίκεντρα γίγνεται.[2]
σὺ δ'[3] αἱματηρὸν πνεῦμ' ἐπουρίσασα τῷ,
ἀτμῷ κατισχναίνουσα,[4] νηδύος πυρί,
ἕπου, μάραινε δευτέροις διώγμασιν.

ΧΟΡΟΣ

ἔγειρ', ἔγειρε καὶ σὺ τήνδ', ἐγὼ δὲ σέ.
εὕδεις; ἀνίστω, κἀπολακτίσασ' ὕπνον,
ἰδώμεθ'[5] εἴ τι τοῦδε φροιμίου ματᾷ.

ἰοὺ ἰοὺ πύπαξ. ἐπάθομεν, φίλαι,— [στρ. α.
ἦ πολλὰ δὴ παθοῦσα καὶ μάτην ἐγώ,—
ἐπάθομεν πάθος δυσαχές, ὦ πόποι,
ἄφερτον κακόν·
ἐξ ἀρκύων πέπτωκεν οἴχεταί θ' ὁ[6] θήρ.—
ὕπνῳ κρατηθεῖσ' ἄγραν ὤλεσα.

ἰὼ παῖ Διός, ἐπίκλοπος πέλῃ,— [ἀντ. α.
νέος δὲ γραίας δαίμονας καθιππάσω,—
τὸν ἱκέταν σέβων, ἄθεον ἄνδρα καὶ
τοκεῦσιν πικρόν·
τὸν μητραλοίαν δ' ἐξέκλεψας ὢν θεός.—
τί τῶνδ' ἐρεῖ τις δικαίως ἔχειν;

[1] ὀνείδεσσιν M, ὀνείδεσιν FV3N. [2] γίνεται: Porson.
[3] οὐδ': σὺ δ' Pearson (Stanley).
[4] κατισχαίνουσα: Rob.
[5] εἰδώμεθ': Turn. [6] δ' ὁ: Abresch.

[1] The utterances of the Furies, as they rouse themselves to action, will be only a prelude to the fuller expression of their wrath. It is uncertain whether the first and second

thou afoot? Arise! Let not fatigue overmaster thee, nor let slumber so soften thee as to forget my wrong. Sting thy heart with merited reproaches; for to the right-minded reproach serveth as a spur. Waft thou upon him thy bloody breath, shrivel him with the fiery vapour from thy vitals, on after him, wither him with fresh pursuit!

[*The Ghost of Clytaemestra disappears; the Furies, roused by their leader, awake one after the other*

CHORUS

Awake! Waken thou her, as I waken thee. Still asleep? Arise, spurn slumber from thee, and let us see whether in this prelude [1] there be aught in vain.

Oh, oh! Ugh! Friends, we have suffered.

Sooth I have suffered sore indeed and all in vain.

We have suffered grievous wrong, alack! an intolerable hurt; our quarry hath slipped from out our toils, and is gone.

Overcome by sleep I have lost my prey.

Shame! Thou son of Zeus, thou art given to theft,

And thou, a youth, hast ridden down aged divinities,

By showing respect unto thy suppliant, a godless man and cruel to a parent; god though thou art, thou hast stolen away him that slew his mother.

What is there herein that any shall call just?

strophic groups were sung by single voices or by semichoruses.

ἐμοὶ δ' ὄνειδος ἐξ ὀνειράτων μολὸν [στρ. β.
ἔτυψεν δίκαν διφρηλάτου
μεσολαβεῖ κέντρῳ
ὑπὸ φρένας, ὑπὸ λοβόν.—
πάρεστι μαστίκτορος δαΐου δαμίου
βαρὺ τὸ περίβαρυ κρύος ἔχειν.

τοιαῦτα δρῶσιν οἱ νεώτεροι θεοί, [ἀντ. β.
κρατοῦντες τὸ πᾶν δίκας πλέον
φονολιβῆ[1] θρόνον
περὶ πόδα, περὶ κάρα.—
πάρεστι γᾶς ὀμφαλὸν προσδρακεῖν αἱμάτων
βλοσυρὸν ἀρόμενον[2] ἄγος ἔχειν.

ἐφεστίῳ δὲ μάντις ὢν[3] μιάσματι [στρ. γ.
μυχὸν[4] ἐχράνατ'[5] αὐτόσσυτος, αὐτόκλητος,
παρὰ νόμον[6] θεῶν βρότεα μὲν τίων,
παλαιγενεῖς δὲ μοίρας φθίσας.

κἀμοί γε[7] λυπρός, καὶ τὸν οὐκ ἐκλύσεται, [ἀντ. γ.
ὑπό τε γᾶν φυγὼν[8] οὔ ποτ' ἐλευθεροῦται.
ποτιτρόπαιος ὢν δ'[9] ἕτερον ἐν κάρᾳ
μιάστορ' ἐκ γένους[10] πάσεται.[11]

ΑΠΟΛΛΩΝ

ἔξω, κελεύω, τῶνδε δωμάτων τάχος
χωρεῖτ', ἀπαλλάσσεσθε μαντικῶν μυχῶν,
μὴ καὶ λαβοῦσα πτηνὸν ἀργηστὴν ὄφιν,

[1] φονολειβῆ: Arnaldus.
[2] αἱρούμενον with υ partly deleted M, αἱρόμενον FV3N: Abresch.
[3] μάντι σῷ: Schütz.
[4] μυκὸν M, σὸν οἶκον FV3N: Rob.
[5] ἔχρανά τ' M, ἐχράνατ' F, ἐχθράνατ' V3N.

Reproach, coming to me in a dream, smote me like a charioteer with goad grasped tight, under my heart, under my vitals.
'Tis mine to feel the cruel, the exceedingly cruel smart of the doomster's direful scourge.

Such are the doings of the younger gods, who rule, altogether beyond the right, a throne dripping blood, about its foot, about its head.
'Tis mine to see the centre-stone of the earth defiled with a terrible pollution of blood.

Seer though he is, at his own bidding, at his own urgence, he hath stained his sanctuary with pollution at its hearth; transgressing the ordinance of the gods, he hath held mortal things in honour and set at naught the apportionments of eld.

To me too he bringeth distress, but *him* he shall not deliver; though he fly beneath the earth, never is he set free. Stained with the guilt of murder, he shall get upon his head another avenger of his kin.[1]

APOLLO

[*Enters from the inner sanctuary*]

Avaunt, I charge ye! Get ye gone forthwith from out this house, quit my prophetic sanctuary, lest ye may be even smitten by a winged glistering

[1] As Agamemnon was slain by Clytaemestra and Clytaemestra by Orestes, so Orestes shall be slain by one of his own race. μιάστωρ is properly "polluter."

---

[6] παρανόμων M[1] (-νόμον M[2]), παρὰ νόμων FV3N, παρὰ νόμον Par. 2886.
[7] τε: Casaubon. [8] φεύγων: Porson.
[9] δ' ὢν: Porson. [10] ἐκείνου: Weil.
[11] παύσεται corrected to πάσεται M, πάσσεται FV3N.

χρυσηλάτου θώμιγγος ἐξορμώμενον,
ἀνῇς ὑπ' ἄλγους μέλαν' ἀπ' ἀνθρώπων ἀφρόν,
ἐμοῦσα θρόμβους οὓς ἀφείλκυσας φόνου.
οὔτοι δόμοισι τοῖσδε χρίμπτεσθαι πρέπει·
ἀλλ' οὗ[1] καρανιστῆρες[2] ὀφθαλμωρύχοι
δίκαι σφαγαί τε σπέρματός τ' ἀποφθορᾷ[3]
παίδων κακοῦται χλοῦνις, ἠδ' ἀκρωνία,
λευσμός[4] τε, καὶ μύζουσιν οἰκτισμὸν πολὺν
ὑπὸ ῥάχιν[5] παγέντες. ἆρ' ἀκούετε
οἵας ἑορτῆς ἔστ' ἀπόπτυστοι θεοῖς
στέργηθρ' ἔχουσαι; πᾶς δ' ὑφηγεῖται τρόπος
μορφῆς. λέοντος ἄντρον αἱματορρόφου
οἰκεῖν τοιαύτας εἰκός, οὐ χρηστηρίοις
ἐν τοῖσδε πλησίοισι[6] τρίβεσθαι μύσος.
χωρεῖτ' ἄνευ βοτῆρος αἰπολούμεναι.
ποίμνης τοιαύτης δ' οὔτις εὐφιλὴς θεῶν.

ΧΟΡΟΣ

ἄναξ Ἄπολλον, ἀντάκουσον ἐν μέρει.
αὐτὸς σὺ τούτων οὐ μεταίτιος πέλῃ,
ἀλλ' εἷς[7] τὸ πᾶν ἔπραξας ὢν[8] παναίτιος.

ΑΠΟΛΛΩΝ

πῶς δή; τοσοῦτο μῆκος ἔκτεινον λόγου.

ΧΟΡΟΣ

ἔχρησας ὥστε τὸν ξένον μητροκτονεῖν.

[1] οὐ: Turn.
[2] καρανηστῆρες M, ῠ over first η in FV3N: Stanley.
[3] ἀποφθοραὶ: Musgrave. [4] λευσμὸν: Casaubon.
[5] ὑπορράχιν MSS. (ὸ altered to ο M): Aldina.
[6] πλησίοις M, πλησίοισι FV3N.
[7] εἰς: Canter. [8] ὡς: Wakefield.

snake[1] shot forth from a bow-string wrought of gold, and disgorge in agony the black spume ye have sucked from men, vomiting the clotted gore ye have drained. This is, in sooth, no house meet for your approach; no, your place is where there are sentences to beheading, gouging out of eyes, and cutting of throats; where, by destruction of the seed, the manhood of youth is ruined; where men are mutilated, stoned to death, and where, impaled beneath their spine, they make moaning long and piteous. D'ye hear what sort of feast ye love that makes you detestible to the gods? The whole fashion of your form doth set it forth. Creatures such as ye should inhabit the den of some blood-lapping lion, and not inflict pollution on all near you in this oracular shrine. Begone, ye herd without a shepherd! Such flock is loved by no one of the gods.

CHORUS

Lord Apollo, hearken in turn to our reply. Thou thyself art no mere abettor of this deed; 'tis thy sole doing, and upon thee falls all the guilt.

APOLLO

How mean ye? Extend thy speech so far.

CHORUS

By thy behest thou didst prompt the stranger to slay his mother.

[1] The arrow sped from Apollo's gold-wrought string is called a "winged glistering snake" because it stings like a serpent's bite. There is also a latent word-play: ὄφις "snake" suggests ἰός "snake's poison" which also means "arrow."

ΑΠΟΛΛΩΝ

ἔχρησα ποινὰς τοῦ πατρὸς πρᾶξαι.[1] τί μήν[2];

ΧΟΡΟΣ

κἄπειθ' ὑπέστης αἵματος δέκτωρ[3] νέου.

ΑΠΟΛΛΩΝ

καὶ προστραπέσθαι τούσδ' ἐπέστελλον δόμους.

ΧΟΡΟΣ

καὶ τὰς προπομποὺς δῆτα τάσδε λοιδορεῖς;

ΑΠΟΛΛΩΝ

οὐ γὰρ δόμοισι τοῖσδε πρόσφορον μολεῖν.

ΧΟΡΟΣ

ἀλλ' ἔστιν ἡμῖν τοῦτο προστεταγμένον.

ΑΠΟΛΛΩΝ

τίς ἥδε τιμή; κόμπασον γέρας καλόν.

ΧΟΡΟΣ

τοὺς μητραλοίας ἐκ δόμων ἐλαύνομεν.

ΑΠΟΛΛΩΝ

τί γὰρ[4] γυναικὸς ἥτις ἄνδρα νοσφίσῃ;

[1] πέμψαι: Bigot's ms. (Paris. 2786?).

Apollo

By my behest I prompted him to exact vengeance for his sire. What then?

Chorus

And thereafter thou didst engage thyself to give sanctuary to the red-handed murderer.

Apollo

And I bade him turn for expiation to this house.

Chorus

And then forsooth dost thou revile us who sped him on his way hither?

Apollo

Aye, for it was unmeet that ye approach this my house.

Chorus

But to us this part hath been assigned.

Apollo

What is this office of thine? Vaunt thy glorious prerogative!

Chorus

We chase from their homes those who slay their mothers.

Apollo

But how then with a wife who kills her husband?

---

[2] τί μήν MV3N, τί μή F. [3] δ' ἕκτωρ MFV3N, δέκτωρ m.
[4] τίς γὰρ M¹FV3N, τί γάρ M².

ΧΟΡΟΣ

οὐκ ἂν γένοιθ' ὅμαιμος αὐθέντης φόνος.

ΑΠΟΛΛΩΝ

ἦ κάρτ' ἄτιμα καὶ παρ' οὐδὲν εἰργάσω[1]
Ἥρας τελείας καὶ Διὸς πιστώματα.
Κύπρις δ' ἄτιμος τῷδ' ἀπέρριπται λόγῳ,
ὅθεν βροτοῖσι γίγνεται[2] τὰ φίλτατα.
εὐνὴ γὰρ ἀνδρὶ καὶ γυναικὶ μόρσιμος[3]
ὅρκου 'στὶ μείζων τῇ δίκῃ φρουρουμένη.
εἰ[4] τοῖσιν οὖν κτείνουσιν ἀλλήλους χαλᾷς
τὸ μὴ τίνεσθαι[5] μηδ' ἐποπτεύειν κότῳ,
οὔ φημ' Ὀρέστην σ'[6] ἐνδίκως ἀνδρηλατεῖν.
τὰ μὲν γὰρ οἶδα κάρτα σ' ἐνθυμουμένην,
τὰ δ' ἐμφανῶς πράσσουσαν ἡσυχαιτέραν.
δίκας δὲ Παλλὰς[7] τῶνδ' ἐποπτεύσει θεά.

ΧΟΡΟΣ

τὸν ἄνδρ' ἐκεῖνον οὔ τι μὴ λίπω[8] ποτέ.

ΑΠΟΛΛΩΝ

σὺ δ' οὖν δίωκε καὶ πόνον πλείω[9] τίθου.

ΧΟΡΟΣ

τιμὰς σὺ μὴ σύντεμνε τὰς ἐμὰς λόγῳ.

1 ἠρκέσω: Wordsworth.
2 γίνεται: Porson. 3 μόρσιμοι MF^{1}V3^1, μόρσιμος F^{2}V3^{2}N.
4 ἡ: Canter. 5 γενέσθαι: Meineke.
6 γ' M, om. FN: σ' Rob. 7 δ' ἐπάλλας: Sophianus.
8 λείπω: Porson.
9 πλέον: Auratus πλέω, Dindorf πλείω.

CHORUS

That would not be murder of the self-same blood and kin.

APOLLO

In good sooth thou heapest dishonour and contempt upon the pledges of Hera, the Fulfiller, and of Zeus.[1] Cypris too is cast aside dishonoured by this plea of thine, and from her mankind derive their nearest and their dearest joys. For marriage appointed by fate 'twixt man and woman is mightier than an oath and Justice is its guardian. If then, should one slay the other, thou art so lenient as not to punish or to visit them with wrath, then I pronounce thy pursuit of Orestes to have no justice in it. For the one cause, I perceive thou takest it sore to heart, whereas, in the other, thou art manifestly more remiss in act. But the goddess Pallas will review the pleadings in this case.

CHORUS

That man I will never, never quit!

APOLLO

Pursue him then and get thee more trouble for thyself.

CHORUS

Seek not to curtail my privileges by thy words.

[1] In connection with marriage, Hera was *τελεία*, as Zeus was *τέλειος*; and the adjective applies also to him here. The ancients derived *τέλειος* (of marriage) from *τέλος* meaning "rite," "consummation." Inasmuch as *τέλος* often has the sense "supreme authority," "full power," some modern scholars hold that Hera *τελεία* is Hera the Queen, Hera the Wife.

ΑΠΟΛΛΩΝ

οὐδ' ἂν δεχοίμην ὥστ' ἔχειν τιμὰς σέθεν.

ΧΟΡΟΣ

μέγας γὰρ ἔμπας πὰρ Διὸς θρόνοις λέγῃ.
ἐγὼ δ', ἄγει[1] γὰρ αἷμα μητρῷον,[2] δίκας
μέτειμι τόνδε φῶτα κἀκκυνηγετῶ.[3]

ΑΠΟΛΛΩΝ

ἐγὼ δ' ἀρήξω τὸν ἱκέτην τε ῥύσομαι·
δεινὴ γὰρ ἐν βροτοῖσι κἀν θεοῖς[4] πέλει
τοῦ προστροπαίου μῆνις, εἰ προδῶ σφ' ἑκών.

ΟΡΕΣΤΗΣ

ἄνασσ' Ἀθάνα, Λοξίου κελεύμασιν[5]
ἥκω, δέχου δὲ πρευμενῶς ἀλάστορα,
οὐ προστρόπαιον οὐδ' ἀφοίβαντον χέρα,
ἀλλ' ἀμβλὺς ἤδη προστετριμμένος[6] τε πρὸς
ἄλλοισιν οἴκοις καὶ πορεύμασιν[7] βροτῶν.
ὅμοια χέρσον καὶ θάλασσαν ἐκπερῶν,
σῴζων ἐφετμὰς Λοξίου χρηστηρίους,
πρόσειμι δῶμα καὶ βρέτας τὸ σόν, θεά.
αὐτοῦ φυλάσσων ἀναμένω τέλος δίκης.

[1] ἄγειν M, ἄγει FN.
[2] μητρώων M, μητρῷον FV3N.
[3] κἀκκυνηγέτης MF: Erfurdt.
[4] θεοῖσι M, θεοῖς FV3N.
[5] κελεύσμασιν MF, κελεύμασιν N.
[6] ἀμβλὺν . . . προστετριμμένον: Prien.
[7] πορεύμασι: Porson.

APOLLO

I would not take them as a gift, thy privileges.

CHORUS

No, for in any case thou art accounted great by the throne of Zeus. But as for me—since a mother's blood leads me, I will pursue my suit against this man and even now am on his track.

[*Exeunt*

APOLLO

And I will succour and rescue my suppliant! For appalling in heaven and on earth is the wrath of him who seeketh purification, should I of mine own intent abandon him. [*Enters the Sanctuary*

[*The scene changes to Athens, before the temple of Athena. Enter Hermes with Orestes, who embraces the ancient image of the goddess*

ORESTES

Queen Athena, at Loxias' bidding I am come; and do thou of thy grace receive an accursed wretch, no suppliant for purification, or uncleansed of hand, but with my guilt's edge already blunted and worn away at other habitations and in the travelled paths of men. Holding my course over land and sea alike, obedient to the behests of Loxias' oracle, I now approach thy house and thine image, O goddess. Here will I keep my post and abide the issue of my trial.

[*The Furies enter dispersedly, hunting Orestes' trail by scent*

ΧΟΡΟΣ

εἶέν· τόδ' ἐστὶ τἀνδρὸς ἐκφανὲς τέκμαρ.
ἕπου δὲ μηνυτῆρος ἀφθέγκτου φραδαῖς.
τετραυματισμένον γὰρ ὡς κύων νεβρὸν[1]
πρὸς αἷμα καὶ σταλαγμὸν ἐκματεύομεν.[2]
πολλοῖς δὲ μόχθοις ἀνδροκμῆσι φυσιᾷ
σπλάγχνον· χθονὸς γὰρ πᾶς πεποίμανται τόπος,
ὑπέρ τε πόντον ἀπτέροις ποτήμασιν[3]
ἦλθον διώκουσ', οὐδὲν ὑστέρα νεώς.
καὶ νῦν ὅδ' ἐνθάδ' ἐστί που καταπτακών.
ὀσμὴ βροτείων αἱμάτων με προσγελᾷ.

ὅρα ὅρα μάλ' αὖ,
λεύσσετε[4] πάντα,[5] μὴ
λάθῃ φύγδα[6] βὰς
[ὁ][7] ματροφόνος ἀτίτας.
ὁ δ' αὖτέ γ' [οὖν][7] ἀλκὰν ἔχων
περὶ βρέτει πλεχθεὶς θεᾶς ἀμβρότου
ὑπόδικος θέλει γενέσθαι χρεῶν.[8]
τὸ δ' οὐ πάρεστιν· αἷμα μητρῷον χαμαὶ
δυσαγκόμιστον, παπαῖ,
τὸ διερὸν πέδοι χύμενον[9] οἴχεται.
ἀλλ' ἀντιδοῦναι δεῖ σ' ἀπὸ ζῶντος ῥοφεῖν
ἐρυθρὸν ἐκ μελέων πέλανον· ἀπὸ δὲ σοῦ[10]
φεροίμαν βοσκὰν[11] πώματος δυσπότου·
καὶ ζῶντά σ' ἰσχνάνασ'[12] ἀπάξομαι κάτω,
ἀντίποιν' ὡς[13] τίνῃς[14] ματροφόνου[15] δύας.

[1] νεκρὸν : Vict.
[2] ἐκμαστεύομεν : Dindorf. [3] πωτήμασι(ν) : Dindorf.
[4] λεύσσε erasure τον M, λεύσσετον N, λεῦσσε τὸν FV3 : Wilam.
[5] πάντα M^1FV3N, πάνται M^2.
[6] φυγάδα M^1, φύγδα M^2 [7] [ ] Herm.
[8] χερῶν : χρεῶν Schol. (χρεωστεῖ), Scaliger.

Chorus

Aha! Here is the trail of the man, and plain! Follow the evidence of a voiceless informant. For as a hound a wounded fawn, so do we track him by the drops of blood. My heart pants at my sore and wearying toil; for I have ranged over every region of the earth, and in wingless flight I came in pursuit of him over the sea, swift as a swift ship. So now, somewhere hereabout he must be crouching. The smell of human blood makes me laugh for joy.

Look! Look again! Scan every spot lest unawares the slayer of his mother escape by secret flight and pay not his debt!

Aye, here he is again! In shelter, his arms twined round the image of the immortal goddess, he is fain to submit to trial for his debt![1]

But that may not be. A mother's blood upon the earth is past recovery; alack, the flowing stream once spilled upon the ground is lost and gone!

Nay, thou art bound in requital to suffer that I suck the ruddy clouts of gore from thy living limbs. May I feed myself on thee—a gruesome draught!

I'll waste thy strength and hale thee living to the world below that thou mayest pay recompense for thy murdered mother's agony.

[1] The reading χερῶν seems to mean "deed of violence."

---

[9] πέδωι κεχυμένον: Porson. [10] δὲ σοῦ M, δέ σου N.
[11] βοσκὰν φεροίμαν M: Wellauer.
[12] ἰχνάνασ' M, ἰσχάνασ' FV3N: Turn.
[13] ἀντιποίνους: Schütz.
[14] τείνῃς with ει over η M, τίνῃς FV3, ἵνα τίνῃς N.
[15] μητροφόνας: Casaubon.

ὄψει δὲ κεἴ τις[1] ἄλλος[2] ἤλιτεν βροτῶν
ἢ θεὸν ἢ ξένον
τιν'[3] ἀσεβῶν† ἢ τοκέας φίλους,
ἔχονθ' ἕκαστον τῆς δίκης ἐπάξια.
μέγας γὰρ Ἅιδης ἐστὶν εὔθυνος βροτῶν
ἔνερθε χθονός,
δελτογράφῳ δὲ πάντ' ἐπωπᾷ φρενί.

ΟΡΕΣΤΗΣ

ἐγὼ διδαχθεὶς ἐν κακοῖς ἐπίσταμαι
πολλοὺς καθαρμούς, καὶ λέγειν ὅπου δίκη
σιγᾶν θ' ὁμοίως· ἐν δὲ τῷδε πράγματι
φωνεῖν ἐτάχθην πρὸς σοφοῦ διδασκάλου.
βρίζει γὰρ αἷμα καὶ μαραίνεται χερός,
μητροκτόνον μίασμα δ' ἔκπλυτον πέλει·
ποταίνιον γὰρ ὂν πρὸς ἑστίᾳ θεοῦ
Φοίβου καθαρμοῖς ἠλάθη χοιροκτόνοις.
πολὺς δέ μοι γένοιτ' ἂν ἐξ ἀρχῆς λόγος,
ὅσοις προσῆλθον ἀβλαβεῖ ξυνουσίᾳ.
[χρόνος καθαιρεῖ πάντα γηράσκων ὁμοῦ.][4]
καὶ νῦν ἀφ' ἁγνοῦ στόματος εὐφήμως καλῶ
χώρας ἄνασσαν τῆσδ' Ἀθηναίαν ἐμοὶ
μολεῖν ἀρωγόν· κτήσεται δ' ἄνευ δορὸς
αὐτόν τε καὶ γῆν καὶ τὸν Ἀργεῖον λεὼν
πιστὸν δικαίως ἐς τὸ πᾶν τε σύμμαχον.
ἀλλ' εἴτε χώρας ἐν τόποις Λιβυστικοῖς,
Τρίτωνος ἀμφὶ χεῦμα γενεθλίου πόρου,
τίθησιν ὀρθὸν ἢ κατηρεφῆ πόδα,

[1] δ' ἐκεῖ τίς: Schütz.
[2] ἄλλον: Heath.
[3] τίν': Porson.
[4] [ ] Musgrave: διδάσκων with γε superscr. F, γε διδάσκων NV3.

And thou shalt see whoever else of mankind hath sinned the sin of irreverence against god or stranger or his parents dear, having each his meed of justice.

For the Lord of Death is mighty in holding mortals to account beneath the earth; and he surveyeth all things with his recording mind.

ORESTES

Schooled by misery, I have knowledge of many ordinances of purification and I know where speech is proper and silence likewise; and in this present case hath speech been ordered me by a wise teacher. For the blood upon my hand is slumbering now and fading—the pollution wrought by my mother's slaying is washed away; for while yet fresh it was expelled at the hearth of a god, even Phoebus, by purification of slaughtered swine. It were a long tale to tell from the beginning of all I visited and harmed not by my dwelling with them. [Aging time wears away all things that age the while.]

So now with pure lips I piously invoke Athena, this country's queen, to come to my aid. Without effort of her spear, shall she win myself, my land and the Argive folk as staunch and true allies forevermore. But whether in some region of the Libyan land, about the waters of Triton, her natal stream, she be in action or at rest,[1] aiding those

[1] Literally, "she places her foot upright or covered over." The poet may have in mind statues of the goddess: ὀρθὸν referring to upright posture, κατηρεφῆ to her long garment falling over her foot when she was represented as sitting.

φίλοις ἀρήγουσ᾽, εἴτε Φλεγραίαν πλάκα
θρασὺς ταγοῦχος ὣς ἀνὴρ ἐπισκοπεῖ,
ἔλθοι—κλύει δὲ καὶ πρόσωθεν ὢν θεός—
ὅπως γένοιτο τῶνδ᾽ ἐμοὶ λυτήριος.

ΧΟΡΟΣ

οὔτοι σ᾽[1] Ἀπόλλων οὐδ᾽ Ἀθηναίας σθένος
ῥύσαιτ᾽ ἂν ὥστε μὴ οὐ παρημελημένον
ἔρρειν, τὸ χαίρειν μὴ μαθόνθ᾽ ὅπου φρενῶν,
ἀναίματον βόσκημα δαιμόνων, σκιάν.[2]
οὐδ᾽ ἀντιφωνεῖς, ἀλλ᾽ ἀποπτύεις λόγους,
ἐμοὶ τραφείς τε καὶ καθιερωμένος;[3]
καὶ ζῶν με δαίσεις οὐδὲ πρὸς βωμῷ σφαγείς·
ὕμνον δ᾽ ἀκούσῃ τόνδε δέσμιον σέθεν.

ἄγε δὴ καὶ χορὸν ἅψωμεν, ἐπεὶ
μοῦσαν στυγερὰν
ἀποφαίνεσθαι δεδόκηκεν,
λέξαι τε λάχη τὰ κατ᾽ ἀνθρώπους
ὡς ἐπινωμᾷ στάσις ἁμά.[4]
εὐθυδίκαιοι δ᾽[5] οἰόμεθ᾽ εἶναι·[6]
τὸν μὲν καθαρὰς χεῖρας προνέμοντ᾽[7]
οὔτις ἐφέρπει μῆνις ἀφ᾽ ἡμῶν,[8]
ἀσινὴς δ᾽ αἰῶνα διοιχνεῖ·
ὅστις δ᾽ ἀλιτὼν[9] ὥσπερ ὅδ᾽ ἀνὴρ[10]
χεῖρας φονίας ἐπικρύπτει,
μάρτυρες ὀρθαὶ τοῖσι θανοῦσιν
παραγιγνόμεναι[11] πράκτορες αἵματος
αὐτῷ τελέως ἐφάνημεν.

1 οὔτις σ᾽ M¹FV3N, οὔτοι σ᾽ M²Fγρ.
2 σκιά: Heath. 3 ; Herm. 4 ἅμα: Canter.
5 εὐθυδίκαι θ᾽ (δ᾽ F, τ᾽ N) οἰδ᾽ (οἶδ᾽ FV3N): Herm.

whom she loves; or whether, like a bold marshal, she be surveying the Phlegraean[1] plain, oh may she come—for goddess that she is, she hears even from afar—to prove my deliverer from distress!

CHORUS

Nay, be sure, not Apollo nor Athena's might can save thee from perishing, spurned and neglected, knowing not where in thy soul is joy—a bloodless victim of the powers below, a shadow of thyself.

What! Dost thou not even answer, but scornest my words, thou victim fatted and consecrate to me? At no altar shalt thou be slain, but, living, shalt thou be my feast; and thou shalt now hearken to our song to bind thee with its spell.

Come now, let us also link the dance, since we are resolved to display our drear minstrelsy and to declare our office, how our company directeth the affairs of men. Just and upright do we claim to be. Whoso holdeth out hands undefiled, no wrath from us assaileth him, and unscathed he passeth all his days; but whoso committeth sin as this man hath, and hideth his blood-stained hands, as upright witnesses for the slain do we present ourselves, and as avengers of bloodshed do we appear against him to the end.

[1] The scene of the battle of the Gods and Giants, in which Athena slew Enceladus.

---

[6] *οἰμεθ' εἶναι* (*οἶμαι θεῖναι* FV3N): H. L. Ahrens.
[7] *τοὺς . . . προνέμοντας* (*προσνέμοντας* M): Herm.
[8] *ἀφ' ἡμῶν μῆνις ἐφέρπει*: Porson.
[9] *ἀλιτρῶν*: Auratus. [10] *ἀνὴρ*: Porson.
[11] *παραγινόμεναι*: Porson.

μᾶτερ ἅ μ' ἔτικτες, ὦ μᾶτερ [στρ. α.
Νύξ, ἀλαοῖσι[1] καὶ[2] δεδορκόσιν
ποινάν, κλῦθ'. ὁ Λατοῦς γὰρ ἶ-
νίς μ' ἄτιμον τίθησιν
τόνδ' ἀφαιρούμενος
πτῶκα,[3] ματρῷον ἅ-
γνισμα κύριον φόνου.

ἐπὶ δὲ τῷ τεθυμένῳ [ἐφυμν. α.
τόδε μέλος, παρακοπά,
παραφορὰ[4] φρενοδαλής,[5]
ὕμνος ἐξ Ἐρινύων,
δέσμιος φρενῶν, ἀφόρ-
μικτος, αὑονὰ βροτοῖς.

τοῦτο γὰρ λάχος διανταία [ἀντ. α.
Μοῖρ' ἐπέκλωσεν ἐμπέδως ἔχειν,
θνατῶν[6] τοῖσιν αὐτουργίαι
ξυμπέσωσιν[7] μάταιοι,
τοῖς ὁμαρτεῖν, ὄφρ' ἂν
γᾶν ὑπέλθῃ· θανὼν δ'
οὐκ ἄγαν ἐλεύθερος.

ἐπὶ δὲ τῷ τεθυμένῳ [ἐφυμν. α.
τόδε μέλος, παρακοπά,
παραφορὰ φρενοδαλής,[8]
ὕμνος[9] ἐξ Ἐρινύων,
δέσμιος φρενῶν, ἀφόρ-
μικτος, αὑονὰ βροτοῖς.

γιγνομέναισι λάχη τάδ' ἐφ' ἁμὶν[10] ἐκράνθη· [στρ. β.
ἀθανάτων δ' ἀπέχειν χέρας, οὐδέ τις ἐστί
συνδαίτωρ[11] μετάκοινος·

O mother Night, mother who didst bear me to be a retribution unto the dead and the living, hearken unto me! For Leto's son would bring me to dishonour by wresting from my grasp yon cowering wretch, fit offering to expiate a mother's blood.

O'er our victim consecrate, this is our song—fraught with madness, fraught with frenzy, crazing the brain, the Furies' hymn, spell to bind the soul, untuned to the lyre, withering the life of mortal man.

For this is the office that ever-determining Fate, when it span the thread of our life, assigned unto us to hold unalterably: that upon those of mortals on whom have come wanton murdering of kinsfolk, upon them we should attend until such time as they pass beneath the earth; and after death they have no large liberty.

O'er our victim consecrate, this is our song—fraught with madness, fraught with frenzy, crazing the brain, the Furies' hymn, spell to bind the soul, untuned to the lyre, withering the life of mortal man.

At our birth this office was ratified unto us; but the Deathless Ones may not lay hand upon us, nor doth any of them share our feasts in common

---

[1] *ἀλαοῖσιν* M, *ἀλαοῖς* FV3N: Paley. [2] *καὶ* om. N.
[3] *πτάκα* altered to *πτᾶκα* (*πτᾶκα* FV3N): Sophianus.
[4] *παραφ ορὰ* M, *παράφρονα* FV3N.
[5] *φρενοδα . . ς* altered to -*λὶς* and then to -*λῆς* (margin -*δαής*).
[6] *θανάτων*: Canter. [7] *αὐτουργίαις ξύμπασ ωσιν*: Turn.
[8] *παράφρονα φρενόδαλης* M; cp. l. 330. [9] *ὕμνοις* M.
[10] *ἀμῖν*: Porson. [11] *συνδάτωρ*: Turn.

παλλεύκων δὲ πέπλων ἀπόμοιρος[1] ἄκληρος ἐτύχθην
—⏑ —, —⏑ —.[2]

δωμάτων[3] γὰρ εἱλόμαν [ἐφυμν. β.
ἀνατροπάς, ὅταν Ἄρης
τιθασὸς[4] ὢν φίλον[5] ἕλῃ.
ἐπὶ τὸν ὧδ' ἱέμεναι[6]
κρατερὸν ὄνθ' ὅμως[7] ἀμαυ-
ροῦμεν[8] ὑφ'[9] αἵματος νέου.

[ἀντ. β.
σπεύδομεν αἵδ'[10] ἀφελεῖν τινὰ τάσδε[11] μερίμνας,
θεῶν δ' ἀτέλειαν ἐμαῖς μελέταις[12] ἐπικραίνειν,
μηδ' εἰς[13] ἄγκρισιν ἐλθεῖν·
Ζεὺς[14] δ'[15] αἱμοσταγὲς[16] ἀξιόμισον ἔθνος τόδε λέσχας
ἃς ἀπηξιώσατο.

[17]<δωμάτων γὰρ εἱλόμαν [ἐφυμν. β.
ἀνατροπάς, ὅταν Ἄρης
τιθασὸς ὢν φίλον ἕλῃ.
ἐπὶ τὸν ὧδ' ἱέμεναι
κρατερὸν ὄνθ' ὅμως ἀμαυ-
ροῦμεν ὑφ' αἵματος νέου.>

δόξαι τ' ἀνδρῶν καὶ μάλ' ὑπ' αἰθέρι σεμναὶ [στρ. γ.
τακόμεναι κατὰ γᾶν μινύθουσιν ἄτιμοι
ἁμετέραις ἐφόδοις μελανείμοσιν, ὀρχη-
σμοῖς τ' ἐπιφθόνοις[18] ποδός.

μάλα γὰρ οὖν ἁλομένα [ἐφυμν. γ.
ἀνέκαθεν[19] βαρυπεσῆ
καταφέρω ποδὸς ἀκμάν,

[1] ἄμοιρος: O. Müller. [2] lacuna Schroeder.
[3] δομάτων MF, δωμάτων N.
[4] πίθασ(σ)ος MFV3N, τιθασὸς Paris. 2886.

with us; and in festal robes of pure white I have nor lot nor portion. . . .

For I have made mine own the overthrow of houses, whensoever strife nurtured in the home layeth low one near and dear. Even so, speeding after this man, for all his strength nevertheless we waste him away because of a fresh deed of blood.

Lo, eager are we to wrest from another this charge and to bring it to pass that the gods have no authority over concerns of mine, so that it shall not even come before them for trial; for Zeus hath deemed unworthy of his converse this our hateful and blood-streaming band.

For I have made mine own the overthrow of houses, whensoever strife nurtured in the home layeth low one near and dear. Even so, speeding after this man, for all his strength nevertheless we waste him away because of a fresh deed of blood.

And the proud thoughts of men, that flaunt themselves full high under the heavens, they waste away and dwindle in dishonour 'neath the earth at our sable-stoled assault and the vengeful rhythm of our feet.

For assuredly with a mighty leap from aloft do I bring down the heavy-falling force of my foot,

---

[5] *φίλος*: Turn. [6] *ὦ διόμεναι*: E. A. J. Ahrens.
[7] *ὁμοίως*: Arnaldus. [8] *μαυροῦμεν*: Burges.
[9] *ὑφ'* M, *ἐφ'* FV3N.
[10] *σπευδόμενα* (changed to *σπευδόμεναι*) *δ'* M: Doederlein.
[11] *τᾶσδε* M, *τάσδε* Aldina. [12] *ἐμαῖσι λιταῖς*: H. Voss.
[13] *ἐς*: Pauw. [14] *ζεῦ* M¹FN, *ζεὺς* m.
[15] *γὰρ*: Linwood. [16] *αἱματοσταγὲς*: Bothe.
[17] ll. 355-359 repeated G. C. Schneider.
[18] *ἐπιφόνοις*: Heath. [19] *ἄγκαθεν*: Pearson.

σφαλερὰ ⟨καὶ⟩[1] τανυδρόμοις
κῶλα, δύσφορον ἄταν.

πίπτων δ' οὐκ οἶδεν τόδ' ὑπ' ἄφρονι λύμᾳ· [ἀντ. γ.
τοῖον [γὰρ][2] ἐπὶ κνέφας ἀνδρὶ μύσος πεπόταται,
καὶ δνοφεράν τιν' ἀχλὺν κατὰ δώματος αὐδᾶ-
ται πολύστονος φάτις.

[3]⟨μάλα γὰρ οὖν ἁλομένα [ἐφυμν. γ.
ἀνέκαθεν βαρυπεσῆ
καταφέρω ποδὸς ἀκμάν,
σφαλερὰ καὶ τανυδρόμοις
κῶλα, δύσφορον ἄταν.⟩

μένει γάρ. εὐμήχανοί [στρ. δ.
τε[4] καὶ τέλειοι, κακῶν
τε μνήμονες σεμναὶ
καὶ δυσπαρήγοροι βροτοῖς,
ἄτιμ' ἀτίετα[5] διόμεναι
λάχη θεῶν διχοστατοῦντ' ἀνηλίῳ
λάμπᾳ, δυσοδοπαίπαλα
δερκομένοισι καὶ δυσομμάτοις ὁμῶς.

τίς οὖν τάδ' οὐχ ἅζεταί[6] [ἀντ. δ.
τε καὶ δέδοικεν[7] βροτῶν,
ἐμοῦ κλύων θεσμὸν
τὸν μοιρόκραντον ἐκ θεῶν
δοθέντα τέλεον; ἔτι[8] δέ μοι
⟨μένει⟩[9] γέρας παλαιόν, οὐδ' ἀτιμίας
κύρω,[10] καίπερ ὑπὸ χθόνα
τάξιν ἔχουσα καὶ δυσήλιον κνέφας.

[1] ⟨καὶ⟩ Schoemann.   [2] [ ] Heath.

limbs that trip even swift runners—downfall unendurable.

But, as he falleth, he knoweth it not by reason of his insensate folly. In so dark a cloud doth pollution hover over the man: and rumour, fraught with many a woe proclaimeth that a mist-like gloom hangeth over against his house.

For assuredly with a mighty leap from aloft do I bring down the heavy-falling force of my foot, limbs that trip even swift runners—downfall unendurable.

For it abideth. Skilled to contrive, powerful to execute are we, mindful of evil wrought, awful and inexorable to mankind, pursuing our appointed office dishonoured, despised, separated from the gods by a light not of the sun—an office that maketh rough the path of the living and the dead alike.

Who then of mortal men doth not hold this in holy awe and dread, when he heareth from my lips the ordinance ratified unto me by Fate under grant made by the gods for its perfect fulfilment? Mine ancient prerogative still abideth, nor do I meet with dishonour, albeit my appointed place is beneath the earth and in sunless gloom.

[*Enter Athena, wearing the aegis*

---

[3] ll. 372-376 repeated G. C. Schneider.

[4] δὲ: Wakefield. [5] ἀτίεται M, ἀτίετον FV3N: Canter.

[6] οὐχάζεταί: Turn. [7] δέδοικε: Schütz.

[8] ἔπι: Herm. [9] <μένει> Herm. [10] κυρῶ: Herm.

ΑΘΗΝΑ

πρόσωθεν ἐξήκουσα κληδόνος βοὴν
ἀπὸ Σκαμάνδρου γῆν καταφθατουμένη,[1]
ἣν δῆτ' Ἀχαιῶν ἄκτορές τε καὶ πρόμοι,
τῶν αἰχμαλώτων χρημάτων λάχος μέγα,
ἔνειμαν αὐτόπρεμνον εἰς τὸ πᾶν ἐμοί,
ἐξαίρετον δώρημα Θησέως τόκοις·
ἔνθεν διώκουσ' ἦλθον ἄτρυτον πόδα,
πτερῶν ἄτερ ῥοιβδοῦσα κόλπον αἰγίδος.
[πώλοις ἀκμαίοις τόνδ' ἐπιζεύξασ' ὄχον][2]
καινὴν[3] δ' ὁρῶσα τήνδ' ὁμιλίαν χθονὸς
ταρβῶ μὲν οὐδέν, θαῦμα δ' ὄμμασιν πάρα.
τίνες ποτ' ἐστέ; πᾶσι δ' ἐς κοινὸν λέγω·
βρέτας τε τοὐμὸν τῷδ' ἐφημένῳ ξένῳ,
ὑμᾶς θ' ὁμοίας οὐδενὶ σπαρτῶν γένει,
οὔτ' ἐν θεαῖσι πρὸς θεῶν ὁρωμένας[4]
οὔτ' οὖν βροτείοις ἐμφερεῖς μορφώμασιν.
λέγειν δ' ἄμομφον[5] ὄντα τοὺς πέλας κακῶς
πρόσω δικαίων ἠδ'[6] ἀποστατεῖ θέμις.

ΧΟΡΟΣ

πεύσῃ τὰ πάντα συντόμως, Διὸς κόρη.
ἡμεῖς γάρ ἐσμεν Νυκτὸς αἰανῆ[7] τέκνα.
Ἀραὶ[8] δ' ἐν οἴκοις γῆς ὑπαὶ κεκλήμεθα.

ΑΘΗΝΑ

γένος μὲν οἶδα κληδόνας τ' ἐπωνύμους.

[1] τὴν καταφθατουμένην : Stanley.
[2] [ ] Wilam.
[3] καὶ νῦν : Canter.
[4] ὁρωμέναις : Stanley.
[5] ἄμορφον : Rob.
[6] ἠδ' F, ἤδ' MN.
[7] αἰανῆ M, αἰανῆς FV3N, Tzet. on Lycophr. 406.
[8] ἀρὰ M, ἀραὶ FV3N.

Athena

From afar I heard the call of a summons, even from the Scamander, the while I was taking possession of the land, which the leaders and chieftains of the Achaeans assuredly assigned to me, as a goodly portion of the spoil their spears had won, to be mine utterly and forever, a choice gift unto Theseus' sons.[1] Thence have I come, speeding onward my unwearied foot, whirring, instead of wings, the folds of my aegis.[2] As I behold this unfamiliar concourse of visitants to my land, fear indeed I feel not but astonishment is upon my eyes. Who in the world be ye? I address you all in common—both yon stranger kneeling at mine image, and you, who are like to no race of creatures born, neither beheld of gods among goddesses, nor yet having resemblance to shapes of human kind. But to speak ill of one's neighbour who is innocent of offence, is far from just, and Right standeth aloof.

Chorus

Daughter of Zeus, thou shalt hear all in brief. Night's dread children are we. " Curses " are we named in our habitations beneath the earth.

Athena

Your lineage I now know and the names whereby ye are called.

[1] Athena confirms as ancient her possession of the district of Sigeum, which had been won from the Mityleneans by the Athenians early in the sixth century.

[2] Line 405 " yoking to this my car my steeds of prime " contradicts the statement in the preceding verse, and may have been interpolated for a later representation of the play when Athena appeared on a chariot (Paley, Wilam.).

ΧΟΡΟΣ

τιμάς γε μὲν δὴ τὰς ἐμὰς πεύσῃ τάχα.

ΑΘΗΝΑ

μάθοιμ᾽ ἄν, εἰ λέγοι τις ἐμφανῆ λόγον.

ΧΟΡΟΣ

βροτοκτονοῦντας ἐκ δόμων ἐλαύνομεν.

ΑΘΗΝΑ

καὶ τῷ κτανόντι ποῦ τὸ[1] τέρμα τῆς φυγῆς[2];

ΧΟΡΟΣ

ὅπου τὸ χαίρειν μηδαμοῦ νομίζεται.

ΑΘΗΝΑ

ἦ καὶ τοιαύτας τῷδ᾽ ἐπιρροιζεῖς[3] φυγάς;

ΧΟΡΟΣ

φονεὺς γὰρ εἶναι μητρὸς ἠξιώσατο.

ΑΘΗΝΑ

ἄλλαις ἀνάγκαις,[4] ἤ τινος[5] τρέων κότον;

ΧΟΡΟΣ

ποῦ γὰρ τοσοῦτο κέντρον ὡς μητροκτονεῖν;

[1] τοῦτο: Arnaldus. [2] τῆς σφαγῆς: Scaliger.
[3] ἐπιρροιζεῖν M[1]FV3N, ἐπιρροιζεῖ M[2]: Scaliger.
[4] ἄλλης ἀνάγκης: Bothe.
[5] οὔτινος M, Schol. on 465, ἤ τινος FV3N.

CHORUS

My office, however, thou shalt learn anon.

ATHENA

I shall understand, if plainly told.

CHORUS

We drive slayers of men from out their homes.

ATHENA

And where is the bourne of the slayer in his flight?

CHORUS

Where joy is absent and unknown.[1]

ATHENA

Would'st thou indeed hound him with thy screeching to such flight?

CHORUS

Aye, for he held it his duty to be his mother's murderer.

ATHENA

Because of other constraint or through fear of someone's wrath?

CHORUS

Where is there a spur so keen as to compel to murder of a mother?

[1] Literally "where joy (or the word *joy*) is nowhere in use."

ΑΘΗΝΑ

δυοῖν παρόντοιν[1] ἥμισυς λόγου[2] πάρα.

ΧΟΡΟΣ

ἀλλ' ὅρκον οὐ δέξαιτ' ἄν, οὐ δοῦναι θέλοι.[3]

ΑΘΗΝΑ

κλύειν δίκαιος[4] μᾶλλον ἢ πρᾶξαι θέλεις.

ΧΟΡΟΣ

πῶς δή; δίδαξον· τῶν σοφῶν γὰρ οὐ πένῃ.

ΑΘΗΝΑ

ὅρκοις τὰ μὴ δίκαια μὴ νικᾶν λέγω.

ΧΟΡΟΣ

ἀλλ' ἐξέλεγχε, κρῖνε δ' εὐθεῖαν δίκην.

ΑΘΗΝΑ

ἦ κἀπ' ἐμοὶ τρέποιτ' ἂν αἰτίας τέλος;

ΧΟΡΟΣ

πῶς δ' οὔ; σέβουσαί γ' ἀξίαν κἀπ' ἀξίων.[5]

ΑΘΗΝΑ

τί πρὸς τάδ' εἰπεῖν, ὦ ξέν', ἐν μέρει θέλεις;
λέξας δὲ χώραν καὶ γένος καὶ ξυμφορὰς

[1] παρόντοιν M, παρόντων FV3N.
[2] λόγου M, λόγος FV3N.
[3] θέλει: Schütz.

ATHENA

Two parties are here present; half only of the case is heard.

CHORUS

But the oath—he will neither take nor is fain to give.

ATHENA

Thou art fain to be just in name rather than in deed.

CHORUS

How so? Instruct me. For in subtleties thou art not poor.

ATHENA

I say that oaths must not win victory for injustice.

CHORUS

Well then, question him and pronounce righteous judgment.

ATHENA

Is it unto *me* that ye would in very truth commit the decision of the charge?

CHORUS

How not?—in reverence for thy worth and worthy birth.

ATHENA

Stranger, what wilt thou in turn say in reply to this? First, tell me thy country, thy lineage,

---

[4] δικαίους with ου in erasure and ω over ου M, δικαίως FV3N: Dindorf. [5] ἀξίαν τ' ἐπαξίων: Arnaldus.

τὰς σάς, ἔπειτα τόνδ' ἀμυναθοῦ[1] ψόγον·
εἴπερ πεποιθὼς τῇ δίκῃ βρέτας τόδε
ἧσαι φυλάσσων ἑστίας ἁμῆς πέλας
σεμνὸς προσίκτωρ ἐν τρόποις Ἰξίονος.
τούτοις ἀμείβου πᾶσιν εὐμαθές τί μοι.

ΟΡΕΣΤΗΣ

ἄνασσ' Ἀθάνα, πρῶτον ἐκ τῶν ὑστάτων
τῶν σῶν ἐπῶν μέλημ' ἀφαιρήσω μέγα.
οὐκ εἰμὶ προστρόπαιος, οὐδ' ἔχων[2] μύσος
πρὸς χειρὶ τἠμῇ τὸ σὸν ἐφεζόμην[3] βρέτας.
τεκμήριον δὲ τῶνδέ σοι λέξω μέγα.
ἄφθογγον εἶναι τὸν παλαμναῖον νόμος,
ἔστ' ἂν πρὸς ἀνδρὸς αἵματος καθαρσίου
σφαγαὶ καθαιμάξωσι νεοθήλου βοτοῦ.[4]
πάλαι πρὸς ἄλλοις ταῦτ' ἀφιερώμεθα
οἴκοισι, καὶ βοτοῖσι καὶ ῥυτοῖς πόροις.
ταύτην μὲν οὕτω φροντίδ' ἐκποδὼν λέγω.
γένος δὲ τοὐμὸν ὡς ἔχει πεύσῃ τάχα.
Ἀργεῖός εἰμι, πατέρα δ' ἱστορεῖς καλῶς,
Ἀγαμέμνον', ἀνδρῶν ναυβατῶν ἁρμόστορα,
ξὺν ᾧ σὺ Τροίαν ἄπολιν Ἰλίου πόλιν
ἔθηκας. ἔφθιθ' οὗτος[5] οὐ καλῶς, μολὼν
εἰς οἶκον· ἀλλά νιν κελαινόφρων ἐμὴ
μήτηρ κατέκτα, ποικίλοις ἀγρεύμασιν
κρύψασ', ἃ λουτρῶν[6] ἐξεμαρτύρει φόνον.
κἀγὼ κατελθών, τὸν πρὸ τοῦ φεύγων χρόνον,
ἔκτεινα τὴν τεκοῦσαν, οὐκ ἀρνήσομαι,

[1] ἀμυνάθου: Dindorf.
[2] ἔχει: Wieseler.
[3] ἐφεζομένη: Wieseler.
[4] καθαιμάξουσιν οθηλοῦ βοτοῦ M (ὀθνείου βροτοῦ FV3N): Turn.
[5] οὕτως M, οὗτος FV3N.
[6] κρύψασα λουτρῶν: Musgrave.

and thy fortunes ; thereafter, defend thee against this charge—if indeed it so be that, in reliance on the justice of thy cause, thou art seated here, clinging to mine image hard by my hearth, a sacred suppliant after the fashion of Ixion.[1] To all this make me some plain answer.

ORESTES

Queen Athena, first of all I will remove a great misgiving that lies hidden in thy last utterance. A suppliant in need of purification I am not ; nor with pollution on my hands did I fall at the feet of thine image. And of this I will offer thee weighty proof. It is the law that he who is defiled by shedding blood shall be debarred all speech until the blood of a suckling victim shall have besprinkled him by the ministrations of one empowered to purify from murder. Long since, at other houses, have I been thus purified both by victims and flowing streams.

This cause for thy anxiety I thus dispel. As to my lineage, thou shalt hear forthwith. I am an Argive ; my father—and fittingly dost thou make enquiry concerning him—was Agamemnon, he who marshalled the sea-host, in concert with whom thou didst make Ilium, city of Troyland, to be no city. Upon his returning home, he perished by no honourable death ; nay, he was slain by my black-hearted mother, who enfolded him in a crafty snare that still remains to witness his murder in the bath. And I, when that I came back home—an exile I had been beforetime—I slew her that gave me birth

[1] Ixion, king of the Lapiths, murdered the father of his bride, and was given purification by Zeus after having been denied by the other gods. Cp. 718.

ἀντικτόνοις ποιναῖσι φιλτάτου πατρός.
καὶ τῶνδε κοινῇ Λοξίας ἐπαίτιος,
ἄλγη προφωνῶν ἀντίκεντρα καρδίᾳ,
εἰ μή τι τῶνδ' ἔρξαιμι τοὺς ἐπαιτίους.
σὺ δ'[1] εἰ δικαίως εἴτε μὴ κρῖνον δίκην·
πράξας γὰρ ἐν σοὶ πανταχῇ τάδ' αἰνέσω.

ΑΘΗΝΑ

τὸ πρᾶγμα μεῖζον, εἴ τις οἴεται τόδε
βροτὸς δικάζειν· οὐδὲ μὴν ἐμοὶ θέμις
φόνου[2] διαιρεῖν ὀξυμηνίτου δίκας·
ἄλλως τε καὶ σὺ μὲν κατηρτυκὼς ἐμοῖς[3]
ἱκέτης προσῆλθες καθαρὸς ἀβλαβὴς δόμοις·
οὕτως[4] δ' ἄμομφον ὄντα σ' αἰδοῦμαι[5] πόλει.
αὗται δ' ἔχουσι μοῖραν οὐκ εὐπέμπελον,
καὶ μὴ τυχοῦσαι πράγματος νικηφόρου,
χώρᾳ μεταῦθις[6] ἰὸς ἐκ φρονημάτων
πέδοι πεσὼν[7] ἄφερτος αἰανὴς νόσος.
τοιαῦτα μὲν τάδ' ἐστίν· ἀμφότερα, μένειν
πέμπειν τε[8] δυσπήμαντ'[9] ἀμηχάνως ἐμοί.
ἐπεὶ δὲ πρᾶγμα δεῦρ' ἐπέσκηψεν τόδε,
φόνων δικαστὰς ὁρκίους αἱρουμένη[10]
θεσμὸν τὸν εἰς ἅπαντ' ἐγὼ θήσω χρόνον.
ὑμεῖς δὲ μαρτύριά τε καὶ τεκμήρια
καλεῖσθ', ἀρωγὰ τῆς δίκης ὁρκώματα·
κρίνασα δ' ἀστῶν τῶν ἐμῶν τὰ βέλτατα

[1] σύ τ': Pearson. [2] φόνους: Rob.
[3] ὅμως: Pauw. [4] ὅμως: Wilam.
[5] αἰροῦμαι: Herm.
[6] χῶραι μετ' αὖθις: Wellauer.
[7] πέδω: Dindorf. [8] δὲ: Abresch.
[9] δυσπήματ': Scaliger.

—disavow it I will not—in vengeance to requite the murder of my sire I most dearly loved. And for this deed Loxias, in common with me, is answerable, who, to spur my purpose, threatened me with cruel woes should I fail to do this deed upon the guilty. Whether my deed was wrought in righteousness or not, do thou pronounce judgment; for howsoever I fare at thy ruling, I shall rest content.

ATHENA

The affair is too grave, if any mortal thinks to pass judgment thereon; nay, it is not lawful even for me to decide on cases of murder that demands swift wrath; above all since thou, by rites fully performed, hast come a suppliant purified and harmless to my house; and so I have respect unto thee as void of offence to my city. Yet these women have an office that does not permit them lightly to be dismissed; and if they fail to gain the victory in their cause, the venom from their resentment will fall upon the ground and become hereafter an intolerable and perpetual pestilence to afflict the land.

So then stands the case: either course—to suffer them to stay, to drive them forth—is fraught with disaster and perplexity to me. But since this cause hath devolved on me, I will appoint judges of homicide bound by oath and stablish a tribunal, a tribunal to endure for all time. Do ye call your witnesses and adduce your proofs, sworn evidence to support your cause; and I will return when I have singled out the best of my burghers, that

[10] ὁρκίων αἱρουμένους: Casaubon.

ἥξω, διαιρεῖν τοῦτο πρᾶγμ' ἐτητύμως.
ὅρκον[1] πορόντας[2] μηδὲν ἔκδικον φρυσεῖν.[3]

ΧΟΡΟΣ

νῦν καταστροφαὶ νέων [στρ. α.
θεσμίων, εἰ κρατή-
σει δίκα <τε>[4] καὶ βλάβα
τοῦδε ματροκτόνου.
πάντας ἤδη τόδ' ἔργον εὐχερεί-
ᾳ[5] συναρμόσει βροτούς·
πολλὰ δ' ἔτυμα παιδότρωτα
πάθεα προσμένει τοκεῦ-
σιν μεταῦθις ἐν χρόνῳ.

οὐδὲ[6] γὰρ βροτοσκόπων [ἀντ. α.
μαινάδων τῶνδ' ἐφέρ-
ψει κότος τις ἐργμάτων—
πάντ' ἐφήσω μόρον.
πεύσεται δ' ἄλλος ἄλλοθεν, προφωνῶν τὰ τῶν πέλας κακά,
λῆξιν ὑπόδοσίν[7] τε μόχθων·
ἄκεά[8] τ' οὐ βέβαια[9] τλά-
μων [δέ[10] τις[11]] μάταν παρηγορεῖ.

μηδέ τις κικλησκέτω [στρ. β.
ξυμφορᾷ τετυμμένος,
τοῦτ' ἔπος θροούμενος,
ὦ[12] δίκα,
ὦ[12] θρόνοι τ' Ἐρινύων.
ταῦτά τις τάχ' ἂν πατὴρ
ἢ τεκοῦσα νεοπαθὴς
οἶκτον οἰκτίσαιτ', ἐπει-
δὴ πίτνει δόμος δίκας.

they may decide this issue in accordance with the truth, having bound themselves by oath to pronounce no judgment contrary to justice. [*Exit*

CHORUS

Now is the end of all things wrought by new ordinances, if the wrongful cause of this slayer of his mother is to triumph. Straightway will his deed reconcile all men to licence; and many woeful wounds, dealt in very truth by children, are in store for parents in time yet to come.

For from us, the Furious Ones that keep watch upon mortals, shall no wrath for such misdeeds draw nigh—I will let loose death in every form. And as he anticipates his neighbour's evil plight, one man shall ask of another when tribulation is to end or to decrease; and the poor wretch offereth the vain consolation of remedies that bring no certain cure.

Nor let anyone henceforth, when he hath been smitten by calamity, make appeal and cry aloud "O Justice!" "O enthroned Spirits of Vengeance!" Peradventure some father, or mother, newly stricken, may thus make piteous lament, now that the house of Justice is falling.

---

[1] ὅρκων M[1], ὅρκον M[2]FV3N. [2] περῶντας: Herm.
[3] ἔκδικον φρεσὶν M, ἔνδικον φρενὶ FV3N: Markland. In FV3N 489 stands after 485.
[4] < > Heath. [5] εὐχερίᾳ M, εὐχαρίᾳ FV3N: Turn.
[6] οὔτε: Elmsley. [7] ὑπόδοσιν M (-δησιν F, -δυσιν V3N).
[8] ἄκετ' M, ἄκεστα FV3N: Schütz.
[9] οὐ βέβαια MV3N, ἀβέβαια F.
[10] [δέ] Schwenk. [11] [τις] Pauw. [12] ἰὼ: Pauw.

ἔσθ᾿ ὅπου τὸ δεινὸν εὖ, [ἀντ. β.
καὶ φρενῶν ἐπίσκοπον
δεῖ μένειν[1] καθήμενον.
ξυμφέρει
σωφρονεῖν ὑπὸ στένει.
τίς δὲ μηδὲν ἐν δέει[2]
καρδίαν <ἂν>[3] ἀνατρέφων
ἢ πόλις βροτός θ᾿ ὁμοί-
ως ἔτ᾿ ἂν σέβοι δίκαν;

μήτ᾿ ἀνάρχετον[4] βίον [στρ. γ.
μήτε δεσποτούμενον
αἰνέσῃς.
παντὶ[5] μέσῳ τὸ κράτος
θεὸς ὤπασεν, ἄλλ᾿[6]
ἄλλᾳ[7] δ᾿[8] ἐφορεύει.
ξύμμετρον δ᾿ ἔπος λέγω,
δυσσεβίας[9] μὲν ὕβρις
τέκος ὡς ἐτύμως·
ἐκ δ᾿ ὑγιεί-
ας φρενῶν ὁ πάμφιλος[10]
καὶ πολύευκτος ὄλβος.

ἐς τὸ πᾶν δέ σοι λέγω, [ἀντ. γ.
βωμὸν αἴδεσαι Δίκας·
μηδέ νιν
κέρδος ἰδὼν ἀθέῳ
ποδὶ λὰξ ἀτίσῃς·
ποινὰ γὰρ ἐπέσται.
κύριον μένει τέλος.
πρὸς τάδε τις τοκέων
σέβας εὖ προτίων
καὶ ξενοτί-

Times there are when fear is well and should abide enthroned as guardian of the heart. It profiteth to learn wisdom with groaning. But who that traineth not his heart in fear, be it State or be it man, is like in the future to reverence justice as heretofore?

Approve thou not a life ungoverned nor one subjected to a tyrant's sway. To moderation in every form God giveth the victory, but his other dispensations he directeth in varying wise. I give utterance to a timely truth: arrogance is in very sooth the child of impiety; but from health of soul cometh happiness, dear unto all and oft besought in prayer.

And as for the whole matter I say unto thee: reverence the altar of Righteousness, and spurn it not to dishonour with godless foot because thine eyes look to worldly profit; for punishment will come upon thee. The appointed issue abideth. Wherefore let a man duly put in front place of honour the piety he oweth to his parents, and have

---

[1] δειμαίνει: Anon. in the copy of the Aldina in Camb. Univ. Lib. (Dobree, *Adversaria* on l. 519).
[2] ἐν φάει: Auratus.
[3] < > Lachmann.
[4] ἄναρκτον M, ἀνάρκητον FV3, ἀνάρκετον N: Wieseler.
[5] ἅπαντι: Pauw.
[6] ἄλλα: Wellauer.
[7] ἄλλα M (Schol. ἄλλως), ἄλλᾳ G.
[8] δι' M, δ' FV3N.
[9] δυσσεβείας MFV3, -βίας N.
[10] πᾶσι φίλος: Herm.

μους δόμων[1] ἐπιστροφὰς
αἰδόμενός τις ἔστω.

ἑκὼν δ'[2] ἀνάγκας ἄτερ δίκαιος ὢν [στρ. δ.
οὐκ ἄνολβος ἔσται·
πανώλεθρος <δ'>[3] οὔποτ' ἂν γένοιτο.
τὸν ἀντίτολμον δέ φαμι παρβάταν[4]
ἄγοντα[5] πολλὰ παντόφυρτ' ἄνευ δίκας[6]
βιαίως ξὺν χρόνῳ καθήσειν
λαῖφος, ὅταν λάβῃ πόνος
θραυομένας κεραίας.

καλεῖ δ' ἀκούοντας οὐδὲν <ἐν>[7] μέσᾳ [ἀντ. δ
δυσπαλεῖ τε[8] δίνᾳ·
γελᾷ δὲ δαίμων ἐπ' ἀνδρὶ θερμῷ,[9]
τὸν οὔποτ' αὐχοῦντ' ἰδὼν ἀμαχάνοις
δύαις λαπαδνὸν[10] οὐδ' ὑπερθέοντ' ἄκραν·
δι' αἰῶνος δὲ τὸν πρὶν ὄλβον
ἕρματι προσβαλὼν δίκας
ὤλετ' ἄκλαυτος,[11] αἶστος.[12]

ΑΘΗΝΑ

κήρυσσε, κῆρυξ, καὶ στρατὸν κατειργαθοῦ,[13]
ἤ τ'[14] οὖν διάτορος[15] Τυρσηνικὴ

[1] δωμάτων: Hartung.
[2] ἐκ τῶνδ': Wieseler.
[3] < > Pauw.
[4] περαιβάδαν M, περβάδαν FV3N: Herm., later preferring παραιβάταν.
[5] τὰ: ἄγοντα O. Müller (τὰ πολ. παντ. ἄγοντα Pauw).
[6] δίκης M, δίκας FV3N.
[7] < > Abresch.
[8] δυσπαλεῖται: Turn.
[9] θερμοεργῷ MF, θερμῷ N.
[10] λέπαδνον: Musgrave.
[11] ἄκλαυστος: Dindorf.
[12] ἄιστος: Hartung (αἴστος Porson).
[13] κατεργάθου: Porson.
[14] ἐιτ' M, ἤ τ' m, εἴτ' FN.

respect unto the stranger he welcometh within his gates.

Whoso of his own free will and without constraint is righteous, he shall not fail of happiness; utterly cut off he shall never be. But whoso transgresseth in daring defiance, and is laden with rich store that he hath heaped up unjustly, I say that he shall perforce, in due season, strike his sail when the tempest of trouble breaketh upon him as the yard-arm is splintered.

He calleth upon them who hear him not, and he struggleth to no purpose amid the whirling waters. Heaven laughs at the reckless wight as it beholds him, who boasted himself that this should never be, now helpless by reason of his irremediable distress and unable to surmount the cresting wave. He wrecks on the reef of Justice the prosperity that had been his throughout all his days, and he perishes unwept, unseen.

[*Enter, in procession, Athena, a Herald, the Jury of Areopagites, a crowd of Citizens. Orestes removes to the place appointed for the accused. Apollo appears after Athena's first speech*

ATHENA

Herald, give the signal and restrain the crowd; and let the piercing Tyrrhene[1] trumpet, filled

[1] The Etruscans were regarded as the inventors of the trumpet.

---

15 διάκτορος FV3N (with space after it in FV3: αἰθέρος Emperius). For οὖν Askew read οὐρανοῦ.

σάλπιγξ, βροτείου πνεύματος πληρουμένη,
ὑπέρτονον γήρυμα φαινέτω στρατῷ.
πληρουμένου γὰρ τοῦδε βουλευτηρίου
σιγᾶν ἀρήγει καὶ μαθεῖν θεσμοὺς ἐμοὺς
πόλιν τε πᾶσαν εἰς τὸν αἰανῆ χρόνον
καὶ τούσδ'[1] ὅπως ἂν εὖ καταγνωσθῇ δίκη.[2]

ΧΟΡΟΣ

ἄναξ Ἄπολλον, ὧν ἔχεις αὐτὸς κράτει.
τί τοῦδε σοὶ μέτεστι πράγματος λέγε.

ΑΠΟΛΛΩΝ

καὶ μαρτυρήσων ἦλθον—ἔστι γὰρ νόμῳ[3]
ἱκέτης ὅδ' ἀνὴρ[4] καὶ δόμων ἐφέστιος[5]
ἐμῶν, φόνου δὲ τοῦδ' ἐγὼ καθάρσιος—
καὶ ξυνδικήσων αὐτός· αἰτίαν δ' ἔχω
τῆς τοῦδε μητρὸς τοῦ φόνου.[6] σὺ δ' εἴσαγε
ὅπως <τ'>[7] ἐπίστᾳ τήνδε κύρωσον δίκην.

ΑΘΗΝΑ

[8]ὑμῶν ὁ μῦθος, εἰσάγω δὲ τὴν δίκην·
ὁ γὰρ διώκων πρότερος ἐξ ἀρχῆς λέγων
γένοιτ' ἂν ὀρθῶς πράγματος διδάσκαλος.

ΧΟΡΟΣ

πολλαὶ μέν ἐσμεν, λέξομεν δὲ συντόμως.
ἔπος δ' ἀμείβου πρὸς ἔπος ἐν μέρει τιθείς·
τὴν μητέρ' εἰπὲ πρῶτον εἰ κατέκτονας.

[1] τόνδ' M, τῶνδ' Schol. M, FV3N: Weil.
[2] δίκη M, δίκῃ FV3N.
[3] γὰρ δόμων (δήμων M[1]): Erfurdt, Burges.

with human breath, send forth its shrill blare to the folk! For while this council-hall is filling, it is well that silence be maintained and that my ordinances be learned both by the whole city for time everlasting and by these appellants, that their case may be decided on its just merits.

[*Enter Apollo*

CHORUS

Lord Apollo, do thou rule thine own domain. Declare what part hast thou in this affair.

APOLLO

I have come both to bear witness—for the accused yonder was in due form a suppliant and an inmate of my sanctuary, and it is I who purged him of the blood he shed—and myself to be his advocate. I am answerable for his slaying of his mother. (*To Athena*) Do thou bring in the case, and, in accordance with thy wisdom, conduct it to final decision.

ATHENA

(*To the Furies*) 'Tis for you to speak—I am but bringing in the case; the plaintiff at the commencement, speaking first, shall rightly inform us of the issue.

CHORUS

We are many, but our speech shall be brief. (*To Orestes*) Do thou make answer to our questions, one by one. First, say—didst thou slay thy mother?

---

[4] ἀνὴρ: Porson. [5] ἐφέστιως with ο over ω M, ἐφεστίων FV3N, ἐφέστιος GAug. (Aug. contains 576-1047).
[6] τοῦδε φόνου: Turn. [7] < > Herm.
[8] ll. 582-644 wanting in FV3N.

ΟΡΕΣΤΗΣ

ἔκτεινα· τούτου δ᾽ οὔτις ἄρνησις πέλει.

ΧΟΡΟΣ

ἓν μὲν τόδ᾽ ἤδη τῶν τριῶν παλαισμάτων.

ΟΡΕΣΤΗΣ

οὐ κειμένῳ πω τόνδε κομπάζεις λόγον.

ΧΟΡΟΣ

εἰπεῖν γε μέντοι δεῖ σ᾽ ὅπως κατέκτανες.

ΟΡΕΣΤΗΣ

λέγω· ξιφουλκῷ χειρὶ πρὸς δέρην τεμών.

ΧΟΡΟΣ

πρὸς τοῦ δ᾽ ἐπείσθης καὶ τίνος βουλεύμασιν;

ΟΡΕΣΤΗΣ

τοῖς τοῦδε θεσφάτοισι· μαρτυρεῖ δέ μοι.

ΧΟΡΟΣ

ὁ μάντις ἐξηγεῖτό σοι μητροκτονεῖν;

ΟΡΕΣΤΗΣ

καὶ δεῦρό γ᾽ ἀεὶ τὴν τύχην οὐ μέμφομαι.

ΧΟΡΟΣ

ἀλλ᾽ εἴ σε μάρψει ψῆφος, ἄλλ᾽ ἐρεῖς τάχα.

ORESTES

I slew her. Of this I make no denial.

CHORUS

Of the three falls [1] this is already ours.

ORESTES

Thou makest this boast though thy foe is not yet down.

CHORUS

Thou must, however, state the manner of thy slaying.

ORESTES

I answer: with drawn sword in hand I stabbed her in the throat.

CHORUS

By whom persuaded and on whose advice?

ORESTES

By this god's divine injunction; he is my witness.

CHORUS

The seer instructed thee to kill thy mother?

ORESTES

Aye, and to this very hour, I blame not my fortune.

CHORUS

But let the verdict get thee in its grip and thou'lt soon tell another tale.

[1] Wrestling-matches were decided by three falls.

ΟΡΕΣΤΗΣ

πέποιθ'. ἀρωγὰς δ' ἐκ τάφου πέμψει[1] πατήρ.

ΧΟΡΟΣ

νεκροῖσί νυν[2] πέπισθι[3] μητέρα κτανών.

ΟΡΕΣΤΗΣ

δυοῖν γὰρ εἶχε προσβολὰς μιασμάτοιν.[4]

ΧΟΡΟΣ

πῶς δή; δίδαξον τοὺς δικάζοντας τάδε.

ΟΡΕΣΤΗΣ

ἀνδροκτονοῦσα πατέρ' ἐμὸν κατέκτανεν.

ΧΟΡΟΣ

τοιγὰρ σὺ μὲν ζῇς, ἡ δ' ἐλευθέρα φόνῳ.[5]

ΟΡΕΣΤΗΣ

τί δ' οὐκ ἐκείνην ζῶσαν ἤλαυνες φυγῇ;

ΧΟΡΟΣ

οὐκ ἦν ὅμαιμος φωτὸς ὃν κατέκτανεν.

ΟΡΕΣΤΗΣ

ἐγὼ δὲ μητρὸς τῆς ἐμῆς ἐν αἵματι;

[1] πέμπει: Scaliger from Schol. [2] νῦν: Schütz.
[3] πέπεισθι: Veitch. [4] μιασμάτων: Elmsley.
[5] φόνου: Schütz.

ORESTES

I have good confidence. My father will send succour from his grave.

CHORUS

In the dead put then thy confidence, thou slayer of thy mother!

ORESTES

I do, for she was attainted by a twofold defilement.

CHORUS

How so, I pray? Instruct the judges as to this.

ORESTES

She murdered her husband and therewith slew my father.

CHORUS

Therefore, though thou livest, she is quit—by her death.[1]

ORESTES

But why, while she still lived, didst thou not pursue her into banishment?

CHORUS

She was not of one blood with the man she slew.

ORESTES

But am I blood-kin to my own mother?

[1] She is freed from blood-guiltiness because her blood has been shed.

ΧΟΡΟΣ

πῶς γάρ σ' ἔθρεψ' ἂν[1] ἐντός, ὦ μιαιφόνε,
ζώνης; ἀπεύχῃ μητρὸς αἷμα φίλτατον;

ΟΡΕΣΤΗΣ

ἤδη σὺ μαρτύρησον· ἐξηγοῦ δέ μοι,
Ἄπολλον, εἴ σφε σὺν δίκῃ κατέκτανον.
δρᾶσαι γὰρ ὥσπερ ἐστὶν οὐκ ἀρνούμεθα.
ἀλλ' εἰ δίκαιον[2] εἴτε μὴ τῇ σῇ φρενὶ
δοκεῖ τόδ' αἷμα, κρῖνον, ὡς τούτοις φράσω.

ΑΠΟΛΛΩΝ

λέξω πρὸς ὑμᾶς τόνδ' Ἀθηναίας μέγαν
θεσμὸν δικαίως,—μάντις ὢν δ' οὐ[3] ψεύσομαι.
οὐπώποτ' εἶπον μαντικοῖσιν ἐν θρόνοις,
οὐκ ἀνδρός, οὐ γυναικός, οὐ πόλεως πέρι,
ὃ μὴ κελεύσαι[4] Ζεὺς Ὀλυμπίων πατήρ.
τὸ μὲν δίκαιον τοῦθ' ὅσον σθένει μαθεῖν,
βουλῇ[5] πιφαύσκω δ' ὔμμ' ἐπισπέσθαι πατρός·
ὅρκος γὰρ οὔτι Ζηνὸς ἰσχύει πλέον.

ΧΟΡΟΣ

Ζεύς, ὡς λέγεις σύ, τόνδε χρησμὸν ὤπασε,
φράζειν Ὀρέστῃ τῷδε,[6] τὸν[7] πατρὸς φόνον
πράξαντα μητρὸς μηδαμοῦ τιμὰς νέμειν;

[1] ἔθρεψεν: Blass.
[2] δικαίως: Auratus. [3] δ' ὢν: Canter.
[4] κελεύσει: Herm. [5] βουλὴ with ι added M.
[6] τῷ M^1, τῷδε M^2. [7] τοῦ M^1, τὸν M^2.

---

[1] The oath taken by the judges (489) may pronounce Orestes guilty as to the fact; but as his deed was done at the command of Zeus, whose representative is his son, Zeus therefore assumes all moral responsibility.

Chorus

How else, thou blood-stained man, had she nourished thee beneath her zone? Dost disown that nearest bond, a mother's blood?

Orestes

Do thou now, Apollo, give thy testimony; and, I pray thee, expound the law, whether I was justified in slaying her. For to have done the deed, as done it is, I deny it not. But whether this deed of blood seemeth to thy understanding to have been wrought in righteousness or in unrighteousness, do thou decide that I may inform the court.

Apollo

Unto you, this high tribunal created by Athena, I will speak as justice bids,—seer that I am, I cannot utter untruth. Never yet, on my oracular throne, have I spoken aught touching man or woman or commonwealth, but what hath been commanded by Zeus, the father of the Olympians.

Mark how potent is this plea of justice; and I charge you to yield obedience to the Father's will; for an oath hath not greater authority than Zeus.[1]

Chorus

Zeus—on thy saying—gave thee this oracular command: to declare to Orestes here that he avenge the slaying of his father, but of the honour due his mother take no account at all?

ΑΠΟΛΛΩΝ

οὐ γάρ τι ταὐτὸν ἄνδρα γενναῖον θανεῖν
διοσδότοις σκήπτροισι τιμαλφούμενον,
καὶ ταῦτα πρὸς γυναικός, οὔ τι θουρίοις
τόξοις ἑκηβόλοισιν, ὥστ' Ἀμαζόνος,
ἀλλ' ὡς ἀκούσῃ, Παλλὰς οἵ τ' ἐφήμενοι
ψήφῳ διαιρεῖν τοῦδε πράγματος πέρι.
ἀπὸ στρατείας[1] γάρ νιν[2] ἠμποληκότα
†τὰ πλεῖστ' ἄμεινον[3] εὔφροσιν δεδεγμένη,[4]
δροίτῃ[5] περῶντι λουτρὰ κἀπὶ τέρματι
φᾶρος περεσκήνωσεν[6]†, ἐν δ' ἀτέρμονι
κόπτει πεδήσασ' ἄνδρα δαιδάλῳ πέπλῳ.
ἀνδρὸς μὲν ὑμῖν οὗτος εἴρηται μόρος
τοῦ παντοσέμνου, τοῦ στρατηλάτου νεῶν.
ταύτην τοιαύτην εἶπον, ὡς δηχθῇ[7] λεώς,
ὅσπερ τέτακται τήνδε κυρῶσαι δίκην.

ΧΟΡΟΣ

πατρὸς προτιμᾷ Ζεὺς μόρον τῷ σῷ λόγῳ·
αὐτὸς δ' ἔδησε[8] πατέρα πρεσβύτην Κρόνον.
πῶς ταῦτα τούτοις οὐκ ἐναντίως λέγεις;
ὑμᾶς δ' ἀκούειν ταῦτ' ἐγὼ μαρτύρομαι.

ΑΠΟΛΛΩΝ

ὦ παντομισῆ κνώδαλα, στύγη θεῶν,
[9]πέδας μὲν ἂν λύσειεν, ἔστι τοῦδ' ἄκος

[1] στρατείας M¹, στρατιᾶς M². [2] μιν: Porson.
[3] ἀμείνον' M (*i.e.* ἄμεινον and ἀμείνον').
[4] After l. 632 one or more verses may have been lost.
[5] δροίτῃ MG, δροίτη Schol. M, Aug. Paris. 2886.
[6] περέσκήνωσεν MG, παρεσκήνωσεν Aug. M marg. but περ- in explanation. [7] δειχθῇ altered to δηχθῇ M.
[8] ἔδεισε altered to ἔδησε M. [9] ll. 645-1047 in FV3N.

APOLLO

Aye, for it was in no wise the same thing—the murder of a high-born *man*, invested with the sceptre of god-given sway, and murder wrought, too, by a woman's hand, not with gallant weapons, arrows sped from afar, it might be, by an Amazon, but in the manner as thou shalt hear, Pallas, and ye who here hold session to decide by vote upon this present cause.

On his returning from the war, wherein, in the judgment of his well-affected subjects, he had for the most part won success beyond expectation,[1] she gave him welcome; then, as he was stepping from the bath, on its very edge, she curtained the laver with a tented cloak, enveloped her husband in a broidered robe's inextricable maze, and hewed him down.

Such was the manner of his taking off, as I have told it you—a hero, all-majestic, commander of the fleet. As for that woman, I have described her thus to whet the indignation of the folk to whom it hath been appointed to decide this cause.

CHORUS

A father's death, according to thy plea, is held by Zeus as of more account; yet he himself cast into bonds his aged father Cronus. How does not this act belie thy argument? I call upon you (*turning to the judges*) to give heed to this.

APOLLO

Oh, monsters utterly loathed and detested of the gods! Bonds Zeus might undo; from them

[1] Literally "trafficked better"—"better" either "than his foes, the Trojans"; or "beyond expectation" (since he was guilty of the death of his daughter); or possibly, without any implicit comparative force, simply "well."

καὶ κάρτα πολλὴ μηχανὴ λυτήριος·
ἀνδρὸς δ' ἐπειδὰν αἷμ' ἀνασπάσῃ κόνις
ἅπαξ θανόντος, οὔτις ἔστ' ἀνάστασις.
τούτων ἐπῳδὰς οὐκ ἐποίησεν[1] πατὴρ
οὑμός, τὰ δ' ἄλλα πάντ' ἄνω τε[2] καὶ κάτω
στρέφων τίθησιν οὐδὲν ἀσθμαίνων[3] μένει.

ΧΟΡΟΣ

πῶς γὰρ τὸ φεύγειν τοῦδ' ὑπερδικεῖς ὅρα·
τὸ μητρὸς αἷμ' ὅμαιμον ἐκχέας πέδοι[4]
ἔπειτ' ἐν Ἄργει δώματ' οἰκήσει πατρός;
ποίοισι βωμοῖς χρώμενος τοῖς δημίοις;
ποία δὲ χέρνιψ φρατέρων προσδέξεται;[5]

ΑΠΟΛΛΩΝ

καὶ τοῦτο λέξω, καὶ μάθ' ὡς ὀρθῶς ἐρῶ.
οὐκ ἔστι μήτηρ ἡ κεκλημένου[6] τέκνου
τοκεύς, τροφὸς δὲ κύματος νεοσπόρου.
τίκτει δ' ὁ θρῴσκων,[7] ἡ δ' ἅπερ ξένῳ ξένη
ἔσωσεν ἔρνος, οἷσι μὴ βλάψῃ θεός.
τεκμήριον δὲ τοῦδέ σοι δείξω λόγου.
πατὴρ μὲν ἂν γένοιτ' ἄνευ μητρός· πέλας
μάρτυς πάρεστι παῖς Ὀλυμπίου Διός,

1 ἐποίησε MGAug., ἐποίησεν FV3N.
2 ἄνω τε FV3NAug., ἄνω MG.
3 οὐδ' ἐν ἀσθμαίνω M, οὐδὲν ἀσθμαίνων FV3N.
4 πέδῳ: Dindorf.
5 προσδέξαιτε M, προσδέξεται FV3NAug.
6 κεκλημένου M, κεκλημένη FV3N.
7 θρώσκων: Weckline.

1 Kinsfolk, actual or fictitious, were united in *phratriai*, with common worship, offerings, and festivals.

2 This notion appears in Egypt (Diodorus Siculus i. 80,

there is a remedy, and full many a means of their undoing. But when the dust hath drained the blood of man, once he is slain, there is no return to life. For this my Father hath provided no remedial spells, though all things else he reverseth and disposeth at his will; nor doth his exercise of might cost him a breath.

CHORUS

Mark now the meaning of thy plea for his acquittal! Shall he who has spilled upon the ground his mother's kindred blood, shall he thereafter inhabit his father's house in Argos? To what altars of common worship shall he have access? What brotherhood[1] will admit him to its lustral rite?

APOLLO

This, too, I will set forth, and mark how rightful shall be my answer. The mother of what is called her child is not its parent, but only the nurse of the newly implanted germ.[2] The begetter is the parent, whereas she, as a stranger for a stranger, doth but preserve the sprout, except God shall blight its birth. And I will offer thee a sure proof of what I say: fatherhood there may be, when mother there is none. Here at hand is a witness, the child of Olympian Zeus—and not so much as

whose source was Hecataeus, an older contemporary of Aeschylus) and in various Greek authors later than Aeschylus, *e.g.* Euripides, *Orestes* 552, Frag. 1064, the Pythagoreans cited by Stobaeus (Hense ii. 72). The passage in the play has been invoked as evidence that the Athenians of the fifth century B.C. were upholding, some the ancient mode of tracing descent from the mother (the argument of the Erinyes); others, the patrilinear theory advocated by Apollo.

οὐδ' ἐν σκότοισι νηδύος τεθραμμένη,
ἀλλ' οἷον ἔρνος οὔτις ἂν τέκοι θεός.
ἐγὼ δέ, Παλλάς, τἄλλα θ' ὡς ἐπίσταμαι,
τὸ σὸν πόλισμα καὶ στρατὸν τεύξω μέγαν,
καὶ τόνδ' ἔπεμψα σῶν δόμων ἐφέστιον,
ὅπως γένοιτο πιστὸς εἰς τὸ πᾶν χρόνου
καὶ τόνδ' ἐπικτήσαιο σύμμαχον, θεά,
καὶ τοὺς ἔπειτα, καὶ τάδ' αἰανῶς μένοι
στέργειν τὰ πιστὰ[1] τῶνδε τοὺς ἐπισπόρους.

ΑΘΗΝΑ

ἤδη κελεύω τούσδ'[2] ἀπὸ γνώμης φέρειν
ψῆφον δικαίαν, ὡς ἅλις λελεγμένων;

ΧΟΡΟΣ

ἡμῖν μὲν ἤδη πᾶν τετόξευται βέλος.
μένω δ' ἀκοῦσαι πῶς ἀγὼν κριθήσεται.

ΑΘΗΝΑ

τί γάρ; πρὸς ὑμῶν πῶς τιθεῖσ' ἄμομφος ὦ;

ΑΠΟΛΛΩΝ[3]

ἠκούσαθ' ὧν ἠκούσατ', ἐν δὲ καρδίᾳ
ψῆφον φέροντες ὅρκον αἰδεῖσθε,[4] ξένοι.

ΑΘΗΝΑ

κλύοιτ' ἂν ἤδη θεσμόν, Ἀττικὸς λεώς,
πρώτας δίκας κρίνοντες αἵματος χυτοῦ.

[1] τ' ἄπιστα M, τὰ πιστὰ FV3N. [2] τάσδ' F²N.
[3] ΧΟΡΟΣ: Karsten. [4] αἰδεῖσθαι with ε over αι M.

nursed in the darkness of the womb, but such a scion as no goddess could bring forth.

But for my part, O Pallas, as in all things else, as I well know how, will I exalt thy city and thy people, so with this man; for I have sent him as suppliant to thy sanctuary that he might prove faithful for all time to come, and that thou, O Goddess, mightest win him as a new ally, him and his after-race, and it abide everlastingly that the posterity of this people maintain their plighted bond.

ATHENA

Am I to assume that enough has been said, and shall I charge the judges now to cast their honest ballots in accordance with their true judgment?

CHORUS

For our part, our every bolt is already shot. But I remain to hear the issue of the trial.

ATHENA

Why should ye not? As for you (*to Apollo and Orestes*), how shall I so dispose as to escape censure at your hands?

APOLLO

Ye have heard what ye have heard; and as ye cast your ballots, let your hearts, my friends, hold sacred the oath ye have sworn.

ATHENA

Hear now my ordinance, ye men of Attica, who pronounce judgment at the first trial ever held for

ἔσται δὲ καὶ τὸ λοιπὸν Αἰγέως[1] στρατῷ
αἰεὶ δικαστῶν[2] τοῦτο βουλευτήριον.
πάγον δ' Ἄρειον τόνδ', Ἀμαζόνων ἕδραν
σκηνάς θ', ὅτ' ἦλθον Θησέως κατὰ φθόνον
στρατηλατοῦσαι, καὶ πόλιν νεόπτολιν
τήνδ' ὑψίπυργον ἀντεπύργωσαν τότε,
Ἄρει δ' ἔθυον, ἔνθεν ἔστ' ἐπώνυμος
πέτρα, πάγος τ' Ἄρειος· ἐν δὲ τῷ σέβας
ἀστῶν φόβος τε ξυγγενὴς τὸ μὴ ἀδικεῖν
σχήσει τό τ'[3] ἦμαρ καὶ κατ' εὐφρόνην ὁμῶς,[4]
αὐτῶν πολιτῶν μὴ 'πιχραινόντων[5] νόμους
κακαῖς ἐπιρροαῖσι· βορβόρῳ δ' ὕδωρ
λαμπρὸν μιαίνων οὔποθ' εὑρήσεις ποτόν.
τὸ μήτ' ἄναρχον μήτε[6] δεσποτούμενον
ἀστοῖς περιστέλλουσι βουλεύω σέβειν,[7]
καὶ μὴ τὸ δεινὸν πᾶν πόλεως ἔξω βαλεῖν.
τίς γὰρ δεδοικὼς μηδὲν ἔνδικος βροτῶν;
τοιόνδε τοι ταρβοῦντες ἐνδίκως σέβας
ἔρυμά τε χώρας καὶ πόλεως σωτήριον
ἔχοιτ' ἄν, οἷον οὔτις ἀνθρώπων ἔχει,
οὔτ' ἐν Σκύθησιν οὔτε Πέλοπος ἐν τόποις.
κερδῶν ἄθικτον τοῦτο βουλευτήριον,
αἰδοῖον, ὀξύθυμον, εὑδόντων ὕπερ
ἐγρηγορὸς φρούρημα γῆς καθίσταμαι.
ταύτην μὲν ἐξέτειν' ἐμοῖς παραίνεσιν
ἀστοῖσιν εἰς τὸ λοιπόν· ὀρθοῦσθαι δὲ χρὴ

[1] αἰγέῳ M. αἰγέως FV3N.
[2] δ' ἐκάστων M, δ' ἑκάστω FV3, δ' ἑκάστῳ N: Canter.
[3] τόδ': Grotius. [4] ὅμως: Turn.
[5] 'πικαινόντων: Wakefield. [6] μηδὲ MFV3N, μήτε G.
[7] σέθεν M, σέβειν M marg., FN.

[1] The Amazons, as "daughters of Ares," invaded Attica to take vengeance on Theseus either, as one story reports,

bloodshed. Henceforth, even as now, this court of judges shall abide unto the people of Aegeus forevermore. And this Hill of Ares, whereon the Amazons had their seat and pitched their tents, what time they came, embattled, in resentment against Theseus, and in those days built up this new citadel with lofty towers to rival his, and sacrificed to Ares; whence the rock takes its name from him, even the Hill of Ares[1]—upon this hill, I say, Reverence, indwelling in my burghers, and her kinsman Fear, shall withhold them from doing wrong by day and night alike, so be it they do not themselves pollute the laws with evil influences; stain clear water with mud and thou shalt never find sweet drink.

Neither anarchy nor tyranny—this I counsel my burghers to maintain and hold in reverence, nor quite to banish fear from out the city. For who among mortal men is righteous that hath no fear of aught? Stand then in just awe of such majesty and ye shall possess a bulwark to safeguard your country and your government, such as none of mankind hath either among the Scythians or in Pelops' realm. This tribunal I do now establish, inviolable by lust of gain, august, quick to avenge, a guardian of the land, vigilant in defence of them that sleep.

I have thus dwelt at length in exhortation to my people for time yet to be; but ye must needs now

because he had carried off Antiope, their queen: or because he did not enclose the hill within the confines of his newly-founded city, which included the Acropolis. Aeschylus apparently rejects the legend whereby the Hill of Ares had its name from the fact that Ares was here tried for the murder of Halirrothius, a son of Poseidon, and acquitted by a tie vote of the gods, his judges.

καὶ ψῆφον αἴρειν καὶ διαγνῶναι δίκην
αἰδουμένους[1] τὸν ὅρκον. εἴρηται λόγος.

ΧΟΡΟΣ

καὶ μὴν βαρεῖαν τήνδ᾽ ὁμιλίαν χθονὸς
ξύμβουλός εἰμι μηδαμῶς ἀτιμάσαι.

ΑΠΟΛΛΩΝ

κἄγωγε[2] χρησμοὺς τοὺς ἐμούς τε καὶ Διὸς
ταρβεῖν κελεύω μηδ᾽ ἀκαρπώτους κτίσαι.

ΧΟΡΟΣ

ἀλλ᾽ αἱματηρὰ πράγματ᾽ οὐ λαχὼν σέβεις,
μαντεῖα δ᾽ οὐκέθ᾽ ἁγνὰ μαντεύσῃ νέμων.[3]

ΑΠΟΛΛΩΝ

ἦ καὶ πατήρ τι σφάλλεται βουλευμάτων
πρωτοκτόνοισι προστροπαῖς Ἰξίονος;

ΧΟΡΟΣ

λέγεις· ἐγὼ δὲ μὴ τυχοῦσα τῆς δίκης
βαρεῖα χώρᾳ τῇδ᾽ ὁμιλήσω πάλιν.

ΑΠΟΛΛΩΝ

ἀλλ᾽ ἔν τε τοῖς νέοισι καὶ παλαιτέροις
θεοῖς ἄτιμος εἶ σύ· νικήσω δ᾽ ἐγώ.

[1] αἰδουμένοις MGAug. Paris. 2886, αἰρουμένοις N: Canter.
[2] κἀγώ (κἀγὼ M) τε: Porson (κἀγώγε Rob.).
[3] μένων: Herm.

rise, take each his ballot, and decide the cause under the sacred obligation of your oath. I have done.

[*The Judges rise from their seats and cast their ballots one by one during the following altercation*

CHORUS

And hark ye! I counsel ye in no wise to dishonour us, whose visitation can oppress your land.

APOLLO

And for my part, I charge ye to stand in fear of the oracles, not mine alone—for they are also from Zeus—and not to render them fruitless.

CHORUS

Nay, thou hast respect for deeds of blood that exceed thy office. The oracles thou dispensest shall no more be oracles undefiled.

APOLLO

And was then the Father in aught mistaken in his purposes, when Ixion, he who first shed blood, made suppliance unto him for purification?

CHORUS

Thou art for argument! But if I fail to win the cause, I will visit this land hereafter as a burdensome guest.

APOLLO

Nay, among the younger and the elder deities alike, thou hast no honour. I shall gain the victory.

ΧΟΡΟΣ

τοιαῦτ' ἔδρασας καὶ Φέρητος ἐν δόμοις·
Μοίρας ἔπεισας ἀφθίτους θεῖναι βροτούς.

ΑΠΟΛΛΩΝ

οὔκουν[1] δίκαιον τὸν σέβοντ' εὐεργετεῖν,
ἄλλως τε πάντως χὤτε δεόμενος τύχοι;

ΧΟΡΟΣ

σύ τοι παλαιὰς διανομὰς[2] καταφθίσας
οἴνῳ παρηπάτησας ἀρχαίας θεάς.

ΑΠΟΛΛΩΝ

σύ τοι τάχ' οὐκ ἔχουσα τῆς δίκης τέλος
ἐμῇ τὸν ἰὸν οὐδὲν ἐχθροῖσιν[3] βαρύν.

ΧΟΡΟΣ

ἐπεὶ καθιππάζῃ με πρεσβῦτιν νέος,
δίκης γενέσθαι τῆσδ' ἐπήκοος μένω,
ὡς ἀμφίβουλος[4] οὖσα θυμοῦσθαι πόλει.

ΑΘΗΝΑ

ἐμὸν τόδ' ἔργον, λοισθίαν κρῖναι δίκην·
ψῆφον δ' Ὀρέστῃ τήνδ' ἐγὼ προσθήσομαι.

[1] οὐκοῦν: Aldina.
[2] δαίμονας: Schol. Eur. *Alc.* 12.
[3] ἐχθροῖσι MFAug., ἐχθροῖσιν V3N.
[4] ἀμφίβολος MV3N, ἀμφίβουλος F.

---

[1] In atonement for having shed blood (according to one legend, that of the dragon at Delphi, according to another, that of the Cyclopes), Apollo was compelled by Zeus to serve as a thrall in the house of Admetus, son of Pheres.

Chorus

Such was thy style of action also in the house of Pheres, when thou didst move the Fates to make mortals free from death.[1]

Apollo

Is it not then right to befriend a votary, above all in his hour of need?

Chorus

Thou it was in truth who didst beguile with wine those ancient goddesses and thus abolish the dispensations of eld.

Apollo

But thou, cast in thy suit, anon shalt spew thy venom—no whit an ill to thy enemies.

[*The balloting is now ended*

Chorus

Since thou, a youth, would'st override mine age, I wait to hear the verdict in the case, for that I am still in doubt whether or not to be wroth against the town.

Athena

My office it is now to give final judgment; and this, my vote, I shall add to Orestes' side. For

[1] An ancient story, adopted by Aeschylus, reported that, when the time came for Admetus to die, Apollo, in gratitude for the kindness shown him by the prince, plied the Fates with wine (l. 728) and thus secured their consent that Admetus should be released from death on condition that some one should voluntarily choose to die in his stead, Euripides, in his *Alcestis*, tells how, when both the father and the mother of Admetus refused to give up to him the remnant of their days, his wife Alcestis died for him.

μήτηρ γὰρ οὔτις ἐστὶν ἥ μ' ἐγείνατο,
τὸ δ' ἄρσεν αἰνῶ πάντα, πλὴν γάμου τυχεῖν,
ἅπαντι θυμῷ, κάρτα δ' εἰμὶ τοῦ πατρός.
οὕτω γυναικὸς οὐ προτιμήσω μόρον
ἄνδρα κτανούσης δωμάτων ἐπίσκοπον.
νικᾷ δ' Ὀρέστης, κἂν ἰσόψηφος κριθῇ.
ἐκβάλλεθ' ὡς τάχιστα τευχέων πάλους,
ὅσοις δικαστῶν τοῦτ' ἐπέσταλται τέλος.

ΟΡΕΣΤΗΣ

ὦ Φοῖβ' Ἄπολλον, πῶς ἀγὼν κριθήσεται;

ΧΟΡΟΣ

ὦ Νὺξ μέλαινα μῆτερ, ἆρ' ὁρᾷς τάδε;

ΟΡΕΣΤΗΣ[1]

νῦν ἀγχόνης μοι τέρματ', ἢ φάος βλέπειν.

ΧΟΡΟΣ

ἡμῖν γὰρ ἔρρειν, ἢ πρόσω τιμὰς νέμειν.

ΑΠΟΛΛΩΝ[2]

πεμπάζετ' ὀρθῶς ἐκβολὰς ψήφων, ξένοι,
τὸ μὴ 'δικεῖν σέβοντες ἐν διαιρέσει.
γνώμης δ' ἀπούσης πῆμα γίγνεται[3] μέγα,
βαλοῦσά τ' οἶκον ψῆφος ὤρθωσεν μία.

ΑΘΗΝΑ

ἀνὴρ ὅδ'[4] ἐκπέφευγεν αἵματος δίκην·
ἴσον γάρ ἐστι τἀρίθμημα τῶν πάλων.

[1] ll. 745-7 ETM, 748 παράγραφος: Abresch.
[2] <ΑΠ>: Vict. [3] γίνεται: Porson. [4] ὅ γ' M, ὅδ' FV3N.

mother have I none that gave me birth, and in all things, save wedlock, I am for the male with all my soul, and am entirely on the father's side. Wherefore I shall not hold of greater account the death of a wife, who slew her lord, the lawful master of the house. Orestes, even with equal ballots, wins.

Quick! Cast forth the ballots from the urns, ye of the jury to whom this office hath been assigned

[*The ballots are turned out and separated*

ORESTES

O Phoebus Apollo! How will the verdict go?

CHORUS

O Night, our Mother dark, seest thou this?

ORESTES

The end has come—either I am to live or perish by the noose.

CHORUS

Aye, and ruin for us, or henceforth to maintain our honours.

APOLLO

Count fairly, my friends, the ballots now cast forth; and as ye make division pay due heed to do no wrong. Error of judgment is the source of much distress, and the cast of a single ballot hath restored the welfare of a house.

[*The ballots are shown to Athena*

ATHENA

This man stands acquitted on the charge of murder. The numbers of the casts are equal.

[*Apollo disappears*

ΟΡΕΣΤΗΣ

ὦ Παλλάς, ὦ σώσασα τοὺς ἐμοὺς δόμους.
γαίας[1] πατρῴας ἐστερημένον σύ τοι
κατῴκισάς με· καί τις Ἑλλήνων ἐρεῖ,
"Ἀργεῖος ἀνὴρ[2] αὖθις ἔν τε χρήμασιν
οἰκεῖ πατρῴοις, Παλλάδος καὶ Λοξίου
ἕκατι, καὶ τοῦ πάντα κραίνοντος τρίτου
σωτῆρος," ὃς πατρῷον αἰδεσθεὶς μόρον
σῴζει[3] με, μητρὸς τάσδε συνδίκους ὁρῶν.
ἐγὼ δὲ χώρᾳ τῇδε καὶ τῷ σῷ στρατῷ
τὸ λοιπὸν εἰς ἅπαντα πλειστήρη χρόνον
ὁρκωμοτήσας νῦν ἄπειμι πρὸς δόμους,
μήτοι τιν' ἄνδρα δεῦρο πρυμνήτην χθονὸς
ἐλθόντ' ἐποίσειν εὖ κεκασμένον δόρυ.
αὐτοὶ γὰρ ἡμεῖς ὄντες ἐν τάφοις τότε
τοῖς τἀμὰ παρβαίνουσι νῦν ὁρκώματα
ἀμηχάνοισι[4] πράξομεν δυσπραξίαις,
ὁδοὺς ἀθύμους καὶ παρόρνιθας πόρους
τιθέντες, ὡς αὐτοῖσι μεταμέλῃ πόνος·
ὀρθουμένων δέ, καὶ πόλιν τὴν Παλλάδος
τιμῶσιν αἰεὶ[5] τήνδε συμμάχῳ δορί,
αὐτοῖσιν ἡμεῖς ἐσμεν εὐμενέστεροι.
καὶ χαῖρε, καὶ σὺ καὶ πολισσοῦχος λεώς·
πάλαισμ' ἄφυκτον τοῖς ἐναντίοις ἔχοις,
σωτήριόν τε καὶ δορὸς νικηφόρον.

ΧΟΡΟΣ

[6]ἰὼ θεοὶ νεώτεροι, παλαιοὺς νόμους [στρ. α.
καθιππάσασθε κἀκ χερῶν εἵλεσθέ μου.

[1] καὶ γῆς: Dindorf. [2] ἀνήρ: Wakefield.
[3] σώζει: Kirchhoff (cp. l. 241).
[4] ἀμηχάνοις M, ἀμηχάνοισι FV3N.
[5] ἀεὶ M, αἰεὶ FV3N. [6] ll. 778-807 wanting in FV3N.

ORESTES

O Pallas, O Saviour of my house! I was bereft of fatherland, and it is thou who hast given me a home therein again. And it shall be said in Hellas: "The man is an Argive once more, and dwells in his father's heritage by grace of Pallas and of Loxias and of that third God, the all-ordaining one, the Saviour"—even he who hath had respect unto my father's death, and preserveth me, seeing that my mother's cause has advocates such as these.

And now I depart unto my home, first unto this thy land and folk[1] having pledged mine oath for the future, even to the fulness of all time to come, that verily no chieftain of my country shall come hither to bear against them the embattled spear. For I myself, then in my grave, will bring it to pass by baffling ill-success, even by visiting their marches with discouragement and their ways with evil omens, that they who violate my present oath shall repent them of their enterprise. But while the straight course is preserved and they hold in everlasting honour this city of Pallas with their confederate spears, I shall be the more graciously disposed unto them.

And so farewell—thou and thy people that guard thy city. May thy struggle with thy foes let none escape and may it bring thee safety and victory in war! [*Exit*

CHORUS

Shame! Ye younger gods, ye have ridden down the ancient laws and have wrested them from my

[1] The passage points to the league between Athens and Argos, formed after Cimon was ostracized (461 B.C.) and the treaty with Sparta denounced.

ἐγὼ δ' ἄτιμος ἁ τάλαινα βαρύκοτος
ἐν γᾷ τᾷδε, φεῦ,
ἰὸν ἰὸν ἀντιπενθῆ[1]
μεθεῖσα καρδίας, σταλαγμὸν χθονὶ
ἄφορον·[2] ἐκ δὲ τοῦ
λειχὴν[3] ἄφυλλος, ἄτεκνος,
ἰὼ δίκα, πέδον ἐπισύμενος[4]
βροτοφθόρους κηλῖδας ἐν χώρᾳ βαλεῖ.[5]
στενάζω·[6] τί ῥέξω;
γελῶμαι[7] πολίταις.
δύσοισθ' ἄπαθον.[8]
ἰὼ μεγάλα τοι κόραι δυστυχεῖς
Νυκτὸς ἀτιμοπενθεῖς.

ΑΘΗΝΑ

ἐμοὶ πίθεσθε[9] μὴ βαρυστόνως φέρειν.
οὐ γὰρ νενίκησθ', ἀλλ' ἰσόψηφος δίκη
ἐξῆλθ' ἀληθῶς, οὐκ ἀτιμίᾳ σέθεν·
ἀλλ' ἐκ Διὸς γὰρ λαμπρὰ μαρτύρια παρῆν,
αὐτός θ'[10] ὁ χρήσας[11] αὐτὸς ἦν ὁ μαρτυρῶν,
ὡς ταῦτ' Ὀρέστην δρῶντα μὴ βλάβας ἔχειν.
ὑμεῖς δὲ μὴ θυμοῦσθε μηδὲ τῇδε γῇ
βαρὺν κότον σκήψητε,[12] μηδ' ἀκαρπίαν
τεύξητ', ἀφεῖσαι †δαιμόνων[13] σταλάγματα,
βρωτῆρας αἰχμὰς σπερμάτων ἀνημέρους.
ἐγὼ γὰρ ὑμῖν πανδίκως ὑπίσχομαι
ἕδρας τε καὶ κευθμῶνας ἐνδίκου χθονὸς

[1] ἀντιπενθῆ M, -παθῆ antistr. MFN.
[2] χθονιαφόρον: Turn. [3] λιχὴν: Bothe.
[4] ἐπισύμενος M, ἐπεσσύμενος antistr. MFN.
[5] βαλεῖν: Turn. [6] στενάζω M, -άζω antistr. MN.
[7] γένωμαι: Tyrwhitt.
[8] δύσοιστα πολίταις ἔπαθον: Herm.

grasp![1] And I, bereft of honour, unhappy that I am, in my grievous wrath, upon this land (and woe unto it!) discharge from my heart venom in requital for my grief, aye venom, in drops its soil shall not endure. And from it a canker, blasting leaf, blasting child (ah! just return!), speeding over the land shall cast upon the ground infection ruinous to human kind. I groan aloud. What shall I do? I am mocked by the people. Intolerable are the wrongs I have suffered. Ah, cruel indeed the wrongs of the woeful daughters of Night, bereft of honour and distressed!

Athena

Let me prevail with you not to bear it with sore lament. For ye have not been vanquished. Nay, the trial resulted fairly in ballots equally divided without disgrace to thee; but from Zeus was offered testimony clear, and he that himself uttered the oracle himself bare witness that Orestes should not suffer harm for his deed. And be ye no longer indignant, launch not your grievous wrath upon this land, nor visit it with unfruitfulness by discharging drops whose wasting influence will devour the seed. For I do promise you most sacredly that ye shall occupy a cavernous seat in a righteous land,

[1] To avoid the collision of metaphors, Abresch assumed the loss of a line in which some qualification of Orestes would have been named as object of the second verb Verrall thought the object was designedly omitted to indicate the passion of the Erinyes.

---

[9] *πείθεσθε*: Turn. [10] *δ'* M[1]. [11] *ὀ∗θήσας* M: Turn.
[12] ll. 800-1 *ὑμεῖς δέ τε τῇδε γῇ βαρὺν κότον σκήψησθε μὴ θυμοῦσθε* M: Weil formerly (*σκήψητε* Elmsley).
[13] *πλευμόνων* Wakefield.

λιπαροθρόνοισιν ἡμένας ἐπ' ἐσχάραις
ἕξειν ὑπ' ἀστῶν τῶνδε τιμαλφουμένας.

ΧΟΡΟΣ

ἰὼ θεοὶ νεώτεροι, παλαιοὺς νόμους [ἀντ. α.
καθιππάσασθε κἀκ χερῶν εἵλεσθέ μου.
ἐγὼ δ' ἄτιμος ἁ τάλαινα βαρύκοτος
ἐν γᾷ τᾷδε, φεῦ,
ἰὸν ἰὸν ἀντιπενθῆ
μεθεῖσα καρδίας, σταλαγμὸν χθονὶ
ἄφορον· ἐκ δὲ τοῦ
λειχὴν ἄφυλλος, ἄτεκνος,
ἰὼ δίκα, πέδον ἐπισύμενος
βροτοφθόρους κηλῖδας ἐν χώρᾳ βαλεῖ.
στενάζω· τί ῥέξω;
γελῶμαι πολίταις·
δύσοισθ' ἅπαθον.
ἰὼ μεγάλα τοι κόραι δυστυχεῖς
Νυκτὸς ἀτιμοπενθεῖς.

ΑΘΗΝΑ

οὐκ ἔστ' ἄτιμοι, μηδ' ὑπερθύμως ἄγαν
θεαὶ βροτῶν κτίσητε[1] δύσκηλον χθόνα.
κἀγὼ πέποιθα Ζηνί, καὶ τί δεῖ λέγειν;
καὶ κλῇδας οἶδα δώματος[2] μόνη θεῶν,
ἐν ᾧ κεραυνός ἐστιν ἐσφραγισμένος·
ἀλλ' οὐδὲν αὐτοῦ δεῖ· σὺ δ' εὐπιθὴς[3] ἐμοὶ
γλώσσης ματαίας μὴ 'κβάλῃς ἔπη χθονί,[4]
καρπὸν φέροντα πάντα μὴ πράσσειν καλῶς.
κοίμα κελαινοῦ κύματος πικρὸν μένος
ὡς σεμνότιμος καὶ ξυνοικήτωρ ἐμοί·

where by your hearths ye shall sit on radiant thrones, worshipped with honour by my burghers here.

CHORUS

Shame! Ye younger gods, ye have ridden down the ancient laws and have wrested them from my grasp! And I, bereft of honour, unhappy that I am, in my grievous wrath, upon this land (and woe unto it!) discharge from my heart venom in requital for my grief, aye venom, in drops its soil shall not endure. And from it a canker, blasting leaf, blasting child (ah! just return!), speeding over the land shall cast upon the ground infection ruinous to human kind. I groan aloud. What shall I do? I am mocked by the people. Intolerable are the wrongs I have suffered. Ah, cruel indeed the wrongs of the woeful daughters of Night, bereft of honour and distressed!

ATHENA

Bereft of honour ye are not; wherefore, goddesses though ye be, do not in excess of wrath blight past all cure a land of mortal men. I, too, rely on Zeus—what need to speak of that?—and know, I alone of the gods, the keys of the armoury wherein his thunderbolt is sealed. Yet thereof there is no need. But yield thee to my persuasion, and let not a froward tongue utter threats against the land that all things bearing fruit shall fail to prosper. Lull to rest the black billow's bitter rage, since thou shalt receive proud honours and shalt dwell with me.

[1] στήσητε: Linwood. [2] δωμάτων: Casaubon.
[3] εὐπειθὴς: Herm. [4] ἐπὶ χθόνα: Burges.

πολλῆς δὲ χώρας τῆσδ' ἔτ'[1] ἀκροθίνια
θύη πρὸ παίδων καὶ γαμηλίου τέλους
ἔχουσ' ἐς αἰεὶ τόνδ' ἐπαινέσεις λόγον.

ΧΟΡΟΣ

ἐμὲ παθεῖν τάδε, φεῦ, [στρ. β.
ἐμὲ παλαιόφρονα κατά τε[2] γᾶς[3] οἰκεῖν,
φεῦ, ἀτίετον[4] μύσος.
πνέω τοι μένος ἅπαντά τε κότον.
οἶ οἶ δᾶ, φεῦ.
τίς μ' ὑποδύεται,[5] <τίς>[6] ὀδύνα πλευράς[7];
θυμὸν ἄιε, μᾶτερ
Νύξ· ἀπὸ γάρ με τι-
μᾶν[8] δαναιᾶν[9] θεῶν
δυσπάλαμοι παρ' οὐδὲν ἦραν δόλοι.[10]

ΑΘΗΝΑ

ὀργὰς ξυνοίσω σοι· γεραιτέρα γὰρ εἶ.
καὶ τῷ μὲν <εἶ> σὺ[11] κάρτ' ἐμοῦ σοφωτέρα·
φρονεῖν δὲ κἀμοὶ Ζεὺς ἔδωκεν οὐ κακῶς.
ὑμεῖς δ' ἐς ἀλλόφυλον ἐλθοῦσαι χθόνα
γῆς τῆσδ' ἐρασθήσεσθε· προυννέπω τάδε.
οὑπιρρέων γὰρ τιμιώτερος χρόνος
ἔσται πολίταις τοῖσδε. καὶ σὺ τιμίαν
ἕδραν ἔχουσα πρὸς δόμοις Ἐρεχθέως
τεύξῃ παρ' ἀνδρῶν καὶ γυναικείων στόλων,
ὅσων[12] παρ' ἄλλων οὔποτ' ἂν σχέθοις βροτῶν.

[1] τῆσδέ τ': Herm.
[2] κατά τε M antistr., κατὰ MFV3N.
[3] γᾶν (and in l. 871): Herm.
[4] ἀτίετον φεῦ: Weil.
[5] ὑποδύεται M antistr., ὑπόδεται str.
[6] < > Herm.
[7] πλευρὰς (-ᾶς N) ὀδύνα: Herm.

And when the first fruits of this broad land are thine henceforth forevermore—offerings in behalf of children and of marriage rite—thou shalt then commend my counsel.

CHORUS

I to be treated thus, oh shame! I, sage in ancient wisdom, to dwell beneath the earth a thing dishonoured (oh shame!) and detested! My spirit pants with fury and utter rage. Oh, oh, the shame of it! What anguish steals into my breast! O mother Night, give ear to the cry of my passion! The gods, holding me a thing of naught, have reft me of mine immemorial honours by their resistless craft.

ATHENA

I will bear with thy wrathful mood since thou art mine elder. And in that respect thou hast no doubt wisdom greater than I; yet Zeus hath granted to me, too, no mean understanding. But as for you, if ye depart to a land inhabited of other tribes of men, ye shall come to love this land—I forewarn you that. For time, in his on-flowing course, shall bring yet greater honours to this my people. And thou, enthroned in dignity nigh unto Erechtheus' house, shalt obtain, from trains of men and women, more honours than thou could'st ever win from all the world beside. Upon this realm,

---

[8] *τιμῶν* M, with ·*α*· over *ῶ* m, *τιμᾶν* FV3N.

[9] *δαμαί·ων* with ·*αν*· over *ων* M (*δαμίαν* in l. 879), *δαμέαν* FV3N: L. Dindorf.

[10] *δόλω* M (*οι* over *ω* m) FV3, *δόλῳ* N.

[11] *καίτοι μὲν σὺ* M, *καίτοι γε μὴν σὺ* FV3N: *καὶ τῷ μὲν* Wakefield, <*εἶ*> Abresch.

[12] *ὅσην*: Pauw (and *ὅσον*)

σὺ δ' ἐν τόποισι τοῖς ἐμοῖσι μὴ βάλῃς
μήθ' αἱματηρὰς θηγάνας, σπλάγχνων βλάβας
νέων, ἀοίνοις[1] ἐμμανεῖς θυμώμασιν,
μήτ',[2] ἐξελοῦσ' ὡς καρδίαν ἀλεκτόρων,
ἐν τοῖς ἐμοῖς[3] ἀστοῖσιν ἱδρύσῃς Ἄρη[4]
ἐμφύλιόν τε καὶ πρὸς ἀλλήλους θρασύν.
θυραῖος ἔστω πόλεμος, οὐ μόλις παρών,
ἐν ᾧ τις ἔσται[5] δεινὸς εὐκλείας ἔρως·
ἐνοικίου δ' ὄρνιθος οὐ λέγω μάχην
τοιαῦθ' ἑλέσθαι σοι πάρεστιν ἐξ ἐμοῦ,
εὖ δρῶσαν, εὖ πάσχουσαν, εὖ τιμωμένην
χώρας μετασχεῖν τῆσδε θεοφιλεστάτης.

ΧΟΡΟΣ

ἐμὲ παθεῖν τάδε, φεῦ, [ἀντ. β
ἐμὲ παλαιόφρονα κατά τε γᾶς οἰκεῖν,
φεῦ, ἀτίετον μύσος.
πνέω τοι μένος ἅπαντά τε κότον.
οἶ οἶ δᾶ, φεῦ.
τίς μ' ὑποδύεται, τίς ὀδύνα πλευράς;
θυμὸν ἄιε, μᾶτερ
Νύξ· ἀπὸ γάρ με τι-
μᾶν δαναιᾶν θεῶν
δυσπάλαμοι παρ' οὐδὲν ἦραν δόλοι.

ΑΘΗΝΑ

οὔτοι καμοῦμαί σοι λέγουσα τἀγαθά,
ὡς μήποτ' εἴπῃς πρὸς νεωτέρας ἐμοῦ
θεὸς παλαιὰ καὶ πολισσούχων βροτῶν
ἄτιμος ἔρρειν τοῦδ' ἀπόξενος πέδου.
ἀλλ' εἰ μὲν ἁγνόν ἐστί σοι Πειθοῦς σέβας,

my realm, do thou cast no keen incentives to bloodshed, injurious to young hearts, maddening them with a fury not of wine ; nor yet, plucking as it were the heart out of fighting-cocks, implant in my people the spirit of intestine war in mutual recklessness. Let their warring be with foreign foes—and without stint for him in whom there shall live a strong passion for renown ; but of birds' battling within the home I will have naught.

Such blessings from my hand are thine to choose —bestowing good, receiving good, in goodly honour, to have a portion in this most god-beloved land.

Chorus

I to be treated thus, oh shame ! I, sage in ancient wisdom, to dwell beneath the earth a thing dishonoured (oh shame !) and detested ! My spirit pants with fury and utter rage. Oh, oh, the shame of it ! What anguish steals into my breast ! O mother Night, give ear to the cry of my passion. The gods, holding me a thing of naught, have reft me of mine immemorial honours by their resistless craft.

Athena

Nay, I will not weary of telling of my boons to thee, that thou mayst never say that thou, an ancient goddess, wast by me, a younger goddess, and by the mortal guardians of my city, dishonoured and strangered, cast from out this land. No ! But if thou holdest sacred the majesty of Suasion,

[1] *ἀοίνους* : Rob. [2] *μηδ'* : Dindorf. [3] *ἐμοῖσιν* M, *ἐμοῖς* FV3N.
[4] *ἱδρύσῃ κάρα* (*κάρῃ*? M[1]) : Stephanus.
[5] *τίς ἐστι* with *α* over *ι* M, *τίς ἔσται* FV3N.

γλώσσης ἐμῆς μείλιγμα καὶ θελκτήριον,
σὺ δ' οὖν μένοις ἄν· εἰ δὲ μὴ θέλεις μένειν,
οὔ τἂν[1] δικαίως τῇδ' ἐπιρρέποις πόλει
μῆνίν τιν' ἢ κότον τιν' ἢ βλάβην στρατῷ.
ἔξεστι γάρ σοι τῆσδε γαμόρῳ[2] χθονὸς
εἶναι δικαίως ἐς τὸ πᾶν τιμωμένῃ.

ΧΟΡΟΣ

ἄνασσ' Ἀθάνα, τίνα με φὴς ἔχειν ἕδραν;

ΑΘΗΝΑ

πάσης ἀπήμον' οἰζύος· δέχου δὲ σύ.

ΧΟΡΟΣ

καὶ δὴ δέδεγμαι· τίς δέ μοι τιμὴ μένει;

ΑΘΗΝΑ

ὡς μή τιν' οἶκον εὐθενεῖν[3] ἄνευ σέθεν.

ΧΟΡΟΣ

σὺ τοῦτο πράξεις, ὥστε με σθένειν τόσον;

ΑΘΗΝΑ

τῷ γὰρ σέβοντι συμφορὰς ὀρθώσομεν.

ΧΟΡΟΣ

καί μοι πρόπαντος[4] ἐγγύην θήσῃ χρόνου;

[1] οὔτ' ἂν: Wellauer. [2] τῇδε (and τῆδε) γ' ἀμοίρου: Dobree.
[3] εὐσθενεῖν: Scaliger. [4] προπαντὸς: Abresch.

the soothing appeasement and spell of my tongue—then thou wilt, perchance, abide. But if thou art minded not to abide, then surely it were unjust for thee to bring down upon this city any manner of wrath or rage or harm unto its folk. For it lieth with thee to hold an owner's portion in this land justly enjoying full meed of honour.

CHORUS

Queen Athena, what manner of abode is it thou sayest is to be mine?

ATHENA

One free from all pain and annoy. And do thou accept it.

CHORUS

Say that I have accepted it, what honour is in store for me?

ATHENA

That without thee no house shall thrive.

CHORUS

Wilt thou gain for me the possession of such power?

ATHENA

Aye, for we will prosper the fortunes of our votaries.

CHORUS

And wilt thou give me a pledge for all time to come?

ΑΘΗΝΑ

ἔξεστι[1] γάρ μοι μὴ λέγειν ἃ μὴ τελῶ.

ΧΟΡΟΣ

θέλξειν μ' ἔοικας καὶ μεθίσταμαι κότου.

ΑΘΗΝΑ

τοιγὰρ κατὰ χθόν' οὖσ' ἐπικτήσῃ φίλους.

ΧΟΡΟΣ

τί οὖν μ' ἄνωγας τῇδ' ἐφυμνῆσαι χθονί;

ΑΘΗΝΑ

ὁποῖα νίκης μὴ κακῆς ἐπίσκοπα,
καὶ ταῦτα γῆθεν ἔκ τε ποντίας δρόσου
ἐξ οὐρανοῦ τε· κἀνέμων ἀήματα
εὐηλίως πνέοντ' ἐπιστείχειν χθόνα·
καρπόν τε γαίας καὶ βοτῶν[2] ἐπίρρυτον
ἀστοῖσιν εὐθενοῦντα[3] μὴ κάμνειν χρόνῳ,
καὶ τῶν βροτείων σπερμάτων σωτηρίαν.
τῶν εὐσεβούντων[4] δ' ἐκφορωτέρα πέλοις.
στέργω γάρ, ἀνδρὸς φιτυποίμενος[5] δίκην,
τὸ τῶν δικαίων τῶνδ' ἀπένθητον γένος.
  τοιαῦτα σοὔστι.[6] τῶν ἀρειφάτων δ' ἐγὼ
πρεπτῶν ἀγώνων οὐκ ἀνέξομαι τὸ μὴ οὐ
τήνδ' ἀστύνικον ἐν βροτοῖς τιμᾶν πόλιν.

[1] ἔξεστιν MN, ἔξεστι FV3.
[2] βροτῶν: Stanley.
[3] εὐθενοῦντας (*i.e.* -τα) M, εὐστενοῦντα FV3N^1 (εὐσθενοῦντα N^2).
[4] δυσσεβούντων: Headlam.

ATHENA

Yea, for I need not say what I shall not fulfil.

CHORUS

Methinks thou wilt win me by thy spells; my anger departs from me.

ATHENA

Abide then in the land and thou shalt gain thee other friends.

CHORUS

What blessings dost thou then bid me invoke upon this land?

ATHENA

Such blessings as have regard to no evil victory. I implore blessings from the earth and from the waters of the deep and from the heavens; and that the breathing gales may pass o'er the land in radiant sunshine, that the increase of the earth and grazing beasts, teeming with overflowing plenty, may not fail my citizens in after time, and that the seed of man may ever be kept safe. May it be godly men whose increase thou prosperest the more; for, like him that careth for the growing plant, I cherish the stock of these just men (*pointing to the audience*) that bring no blight of sorrow.

Such boons are thine to give; and for my part, I will not suffer this city to be unhonoured among men, this city victorious in the glorious contests of deadly war.

---

[5] φῖτυ ποιμένος M, φιτυποιμένος FV3N: Lobeck.
[6] σόυστι M, σοῦστὶ N: Porson.

ΧΟΡΟΣ

δέξομαι Παλλάδος ξυνοικίαν, [στρ. α.
οὐδ' ἀτιμάσω πόλιν,
τὰν καὶ Ζεὺς ὁ παγκρατὴς Ἄρης τε
φρούριον θεῶν νέμει,
ῥυσίβωμον Ἑλλάνων ἄγαλμα δαιμόνων·
ᾇτ' ἐγὼ κατεύχομαι
θεσπίσασα πρευμενῶς
ἐπισσύτους βίου τύχας ὀνησίμους
γαίας ἐξαμβρῦσαι[1]
φαιδρὸν ἁλίου σέλας.

ΑΘΗΝΑ

τάδ' ἐγὼ προφρόνως τοῖσδε πολίταις
πράσσω, μεγάλας καὶ δυσαρέστους
δαίμονας αὐτοῦ κατανασσαμένη.
πάντα γὰρ αὗται τὰ κατ' ἀνθρώπους
ἔλαχον διέπειν.
ὁ δὲ μὴ κύρσας βαρεῶν[2] τούτων
οὐκ οἶδεν ὅθεν πληγαὶ βιότου.
τὰ γὰρ ἐκ προτέρων ἀπλακήματά[3] νιν
πρὸς τάσδ' ἀπάγει, σιγῶν <δ'>[4] ὄλεθρος
καὶ μέγα φωνοῦντ'
ἐχθραῖς ὀργαῖς ἀμαθύνει.

ΧΟΡΟΣ

δενδροπήμων δὲ μὴ πνέοι βλάβα, [ἀντ. α.
τὰν ἐμὰν χάριν λέγω·
φλογμός τ'[5] ὀμματοστερὴς φυτῶν, τὸ
μὴ περᾶν ὅρον τόπων,
μηδ' ἄκαρπος αἰανὴς ἐφερπέτω νόσος,

Chorus

I will accept a home wherein to dwell with Pallas, and I will not visit with dishonour a city which she, with Zeus, the omnipotent, and Ares, holds as a fortress of the gods, the bright ornament that guards the altars of the gods of Hellas. For her I make my prayer, with propitious auguries, that the radiant splendour of the sun may cause to burgeon from the earth, in bounteous plenty, blessings that give happiness to life.

Athena

In loving zeal towards these my burghers I act thus, installing here among them divinities powerful and hard to please. For to their office it hath fallen to hold dominion over all things mortal. Yet he who hath not found them grievous, he knoweth not whence come the blows of life. For it is the sins of his fathers that hale him before them, and, for all his loud boasting, Destruction, in silence and dread wrath, levelleth him to the dust.

Chorus

May no hurtful wind blow to the destruction of the trees—'tis thus I declare my grace—and may no scorching heat, blasting the budding plants, pass the borders of its proper clime; may no deadly blight draw nigh to kill the fruit; may the earth

---

[1] *ἐξαμβρόσαι* M, *ἐξαμυρόσαι* FV3N : Pauw.

[2] *βαρέων* : H. L. Ahrens.

[3] *ἀμπλακήματά* M, *ἁμαρτήματα* without *νιν* FV3N : Pauw.

[4] < > Musgrave.

[5] *φλοιγμὸς* M, *φλογμὸς* FV3, *φλογμός τ'* N.

μῆλά τ' εὐθενοῦντα[1] γᾶ[2]
ξὺν διπλοῖσιν[3] ἐμβρύοις
τρέφοι χρόνῳ τεταγμένῳ· γόνος <δ' ἀεὶ>[4]
πλουτόχθων ἑρμαίαν
δαιμόνων δόσιν τίοι.

ΑΘΗΝΑ

ἦ τάδ' ἀκούετε, πόλεως φρούριον,
οἷ' ἐπικραίνει[5]; μέγα γὰρ δύναται
πότνι' Ἐρινὺς παρά τ' ἀθανάτοις
τοῖς θ' ὑπὸ γαῖαν, περί τ' ἀνθρώπων
φανερῶς τελέως διαπράσσουσιν,
τοῖς μὲν ἀοιδάς, τοῖς δ' αὖ δακρύων[6]
  βίον ἀμβλωπὸν παρέχουσαι.

ΧΟΡΟΣ

ἀνδροκμῆτας δ' ἀώρ- [σαρ. β.
ους ἀπεννέπω τύχας,
νεανίδων τ' ἐπηράτων
ἀνδροτυχεῖς βιότους
δότε, κύρι'[7] ἔχοντες,
θεαί τ' ὦ[8] Μοῖραι
ματροκασιγνῆται,
δαίμονες ὀρθονόμοι,
παντὶ δόμῳ μετάκοινοι,[9]
παντὶ χρόνῳ δ' ἐπιβριθεῖς
ἐνδίκοις ὁμιλίαις,
πάντᾳ[10] τιμιώταται θεῶν.

[1] εὐθενοῦντ' M, εὐθηνοῦντ' FV3N.
[2] ἄγαν : Dobree.
[3] διπλοῖς M, διπλοῖσιν FV3N.
[4] < > Musgrave.
[5] ἐπικραίνει M^1FV3N, -κρανεῖ M^2.

foster the teeming flocks with twin increase at the appointed time; and ever may the rich produce of the earth pay the gods' gift of lucky gain.[1]

ATHENA

Do ye hear, ye warders of my city, what blessings they would bring to pass? For mighty is the potency of the revered Erinyes both with the deathless high gods and with the powers of the world below; and in their dealings with mankind, visibly, perfectly, they work their will, unto some giving song, unto others a life bedimmed by tears.

CHORUS

And I ban deadly and untimely fate for men. O ye that have the rightful power, grant that lovely maidens may live each to find her mate; and grant it, O ye Fates divine, our sisters by one mother, ye divinities whose award is just, who have a common part in every home, and whose righteous visitations are grievous at every season, O ye most honoured everywhere among the gods!

[1] Because the god's gifts of precious metals (the Athenians have especially silver in mind) must be found, as it were, by luck; and Hermes is the god of lucky finds. ἕρμαιον is an "unexpected find."

---

[6] κρύων MFV3, δακρύων N.
[7] κύρι' M (υ in erasure). κύριες FV3N.
[8] θεαὶ τῶν: Herm.
[9] μέγα κοινοι M, μεγάκοινοι FV3N: Turn.
[10] πάντα MF, πάντων N: Canter.

ΑΘΗΝΑ

τάδε τοι χώρᾳ τήμῇ προφρόνως
ἐπικραινομένων
γάνυμαι· στέργω δ' ὄμματα Πειθοῦς,
ὅτι μοι γλῶσσαν καὶ στόμ' ἐπωπᾷ
πρὸς τάσδ' ἀγρίως ἀπανηναμένας·
ἀλλ' ἐκράτησε Ζεὺς ἀγοραῖος·
νικᾷ δ' ἀγαθῶν
ἔρις ἡμετέρα διὰ παντός.

ΧΟΡΟΣ

τὰν δ' ἄπληστον κακῶν [ἀντ. β.
μήποτ' ἐν πόλει στάσιν
τᾷδ' ἐπεύχομαι βρέμειν.
μηδὲ πιοῦσα κόνις
μέλαν αἷμα πολιτᾶν
δι' ὀργὰν ποινᾶς[1]
ἀντιφόνους ἄτας
ἁρπαλίσαι πόλεως.
χάρματα δ' ἀντιδιδοῖεν
κοινοφιλεῖ[2] διανοίᾳ,
καὶ στυγεῖν μιᾷ φρενί·
πολλῶν γὰρ τόδ' ἐν βροτοῖς ἄκος.

ΑΘΗΝΑ

ἆρα[3] φρονοῦσιν γλώσσης ἀγαθῆς
ὁδὸν εὑρίσκειν;[4]
ἐκ τῶν φοβερῶν τῶνδε προσώπων
μέγα κέρδος ὁρῶ τοῖσδε πολίταις·

[1] ποινάς M, ποινᾶς FV3N.
[2] κοινοφελεῖ M^1, κοινωφελεῖ M^2FV3N: Herm.

ATHENA

It gladdens me that with loving zeal they promise to confirm these blessings for my land; and I am grateful to Suasion that her glance kept ever watch o'er my tongue and lips when I encountered their fierce refusal. But Zeus, he that sways men's tongues,[1] hath triumphed. Victorious is our rivalry in doing good forevermore.

CHORUS

May faction, insatiate of ill, ne'er raise her loud voice within this city—this I pray; and may the dust not drink the black blood of its people and through passion work ruinous slaughtering for vengeance to the destruction of the State.[2] Rather may they return joy for joy in a spirit of common love, and may they hate with one accord; for therein lieth the cure of many an evil in the world.

ATHENA

Are they then not minded to find out the path of a propitious tongue? From these appalling visages I foresee great profit in store for these my

[1] Zeus presides over the assemblies of citizens and directs the speech of public men.

[2] The expression of the thought "take reprisals in a civil war," is overloaded and the grammatical relation of the words is involved. More exactly: "seize greedily (as a wild beast seizes his prey) upon calamities—of vengeance—to the State, calamities in which blood is shed in requital for blood."

---

[3] ἄρα M, ἀρὰ m, ἆρα FV3N.

[4] εὑρίσκει; Pauw (; Herm.).

τάσδε γὰρ εὔφρονας[1] εὔφρονες αἰεὶ[2]
μέγα τιμῶντες καὶ γῆν καὶ πόλιν
ὀρθοδίκαιον
πρέψετε πάντως[3] διάγοντες.

ΧΟΡΟΣ [στρ. γ.

<χαίρετε>[4] χαίρετ' ἐν αἰσιμίαισι[5] πλούτου.
χαίρετ' ἀστικὸς λεώς,
ἴκταρ ἥμενοι Διός,
παρθένου[6] φίλας φίλοι
σωφρονοῦντες ἐν χρόνῳ.
Παλλάδος δ' ὑπὸ πτεροῖς
ὄντας ἅζεται πατήρ.

ΑΘΗΝΑ

χαίρετε χὐμεῖς· προτέραν δ' ἐμὲ[7] χρὴ
στείχειν θαλάμους ἀποδείξουσαν
πρὸς φῶς ἱερὸν τῶνδε προπομπῶν.[8]
ἴτε καὶ σφαγίων τῶνδ' ὑπὸ σεμνῶν
κατὰ γῆς σύμεναι τὸ μὲν ἀτηρὸν[9]
χώρας κατέχειν, τὸ δὲ κερδαλέον
πέμπειν πόλεως ἐπὶ νίκῃ.
ὑμεῖς[10] δ' ἡγεῖσθε, πολισσοῦχοι
παῖδες Κραναοῦ, ταῖσδε μετοίκοις.[11]
εἴη δ' ἀγαθῶν
ἀγαθὴ διάνοια πολίταις.

[1] εὐφράνας M, εὐφρόνας FV3N: Turn.
[2] ἀεὶ M, αἰεὶ FV3N.
[3] πάντες MFN, πάντως V3.
[4] < >: Turn.
[5] ἐναισιμίαις MFV3, ἐναισιμίαισι N.
[6] παρθένους MF, -οις V3N: Rob.
[7] δέ με: Wakefield.
[8] πρόπομπον: Bentley.
[9] ἀτήριον: Bentley.
[10] ἡμεῖς?: Turn.
[11] μέτοικοι: Turn.

burghers. If kindly, even as they are kindly, ye pay them high worship evermore, ye shall surely be pre-eminent, guiding your land and your city in the straight path of righteousness.

CHORUS

Fare ye well, fare ye well, amid the wealth vouchsafed by fate. Fare ye well, ye folk of the city, ye that are seated nigh unto Zeus, ye beloved of the beloved Maiden, learning at last the way of wisdom. Nestling beneath the wings of Pallas, the Father holdeth ye in reverence.

ATHENA

Fare ye well likewise. But I needs must lead the way to make known your dwellings by the sacred light of these, your escorts.[1] Do ye now depart, and sped beneath the earth with these solemn sacrifices, restrain whate'er is to our country's bane, but whate'er may profit her, send forth to win her victory! Ye children of Cranaüs[2] that hold this city, lead on their way these new dwellers therein. And may the citizens cherish good will in requital for the good done unto them!

[1] The Chorus is now to be solemnly conducted to the cave beneath the Hill of Ares, the seat of the worship of the Venerable Ones (Σεμναί, l. 1041), with whom the poet here identifies the Erinyes, the Angry Ones, the Avenging Spirits. The identification seems also to include the Eumenides, the Kindly Ones, who were worshipped at Sicyon, at Argos, and in Attica at Phlya and Colonus (see Sophocles' *Oedipus Coloneus*). The procession is formed by Athena (at its head), the Chorus, the Areopagites, torch-bearers, the women who guard the Palladium, and various others. In the rear came the Athenian public.

[2] Cranaüs was the mythical founder of the "rocky city" (κραναός "rocky"), a favourite name of Athens.

ΧΟΡΟΣ

χαίρετε, χαίρετε δ' αὖθις, ἐπανδιπλάζω,[1] [ἀντ. γ.
πάντες οἱ κατὰ πτόλιν,
δαίμονές τε καὶ βροτοί,
Παλλάδος πόλιν νέμον-
τες· μετοικίαν δ' ἐμὴν
εὖ σέβοντες[2] οὔτι μέμ-
ψεσθε συμφορὰς βίου.

ΑΘΗΝΑ

αἰνῶ τε[3] μύθους τῶνδε τῶν κατευγμάτων
πέμψω τε φέγγει λαμπάδων σελασφόρων
εἰς τοὺς ἔνερθε καὶ κατὰ[4] χθονὸς τόπους
ξὺν προσπόλοισιν, αἵτε φρουροῦσιν βρέτας
τοὐμὸν δικαίως. ὄμμα γὰρ πάσης χθονὸς
Θησῇδος[5] ἐξίκοιτ' ἂν εὐκλεὴς λόχος
παίδων, γυναικῶν, καὶ στόλος πρεσβυτίδων.
φοινικοβάπτοις ἐνδυτοῖς ἐσθήμασι
τιμᾶτε,[6] καὶ τὸ φέγγος ὁρμάσθω πυρός,
ὅπως ἂν εὔφρων ἥδ' ὁμιλία χθονὸς
τὸ λοιπὸν εὐάνδροισι συμφοραῖς πρέπῃ.

ΠΡΟΠΟΜΠΟΙ[7]

βᾶτε δόμῳ,[8] μεγάλαι φιλότιμοι [στρ. α.
Νυκτὸς παῖδες ἄπαιδες, ὑπ' εὔφρονι[9] πομπᾷ,
εὐφαμεῖτε δέ, χωρῖται,[10]

γᾶς ὑπὸ κεύθεσιν ὠγυγίοισιν, [ἀντ. α.
[καὶ][11] τιμαῖς καὶ θυσίαις περίσεπτα τυχοῦσαι,[12]
εὐφαμεῖτε δὲ πανδαμεί.[13]

[1] ἐπιδιπλοΐζω: Sidgwick. [2] εὐσεβοῦντες: Turn.
[3] δὲ: Herm. [4] κάτω: Blass. [5] θησηΐδος M: Wakefield.
[6] τιμᾶται with ε over αι M, τιμᾶτε FV3N.

Chorus

Fare ye well, fare ye well again, I repeat, all ye in the city, gods and mortals both, who inhabit Pallas' burgh. Reverence duly my sojourn among you and ye shall not have cause to blame in aught your lot in life.

Athena

I approve the words of your invocation, and will escort you by the light of gleaming torches to your nether home beneath the earth, attended by the ministrants who in duty bound keep watch over mine image ; for the very eye of the whole land of Theseus shall come forth, a glorious train, maidens and matrons, and a throng of ancient dames.

Apparel them honourably in festal robes of scarlet, and let the torches' flare move on, that the kindly disposition of this company of visitants to our land may henceforth make its presence manifest in blessings that bring prosperity unto its sons.

Chorus of the Processional Escort

Pass on your way to your abode, O ye mighty children of Night, children, yet aged, lovers of honour, under kindly escort—

Hush! Good words, ye dwellers in the land!

Under the primeval caverns of the earth, portioned with the high honour of worship and oblation—

Hush ! Good words, all ye folk !

---

[7] *προπομποί* Schol. M, Schol. F ; and N.
[8] *βᾶτ'* (*βάτ* M) *ἐν δόμῳ*: Wellauer.
[9] *εὐθύφρονι*: L. Dindorf. [10] *χωρεῖτε*: Herm. [11] [ ] Herm.
[12] *περισέπται τύχαι τε* M, *περισέπτᾳ τύχᾳ τε* FN (*-τα τύχα τε* V3): Herm. [13] *πανδιμί* M, *πανδημεί* FV3N.

ἵλαοι δὲ καὶ σύμφρονες[1] γᾷ [στρ. β.
δεῦρ' ἴτε, Σεμναί, <ξὺν>[2] πυριδάπτῳ
λαμπάδι τερπόμεναι καθ' ὁδόν.[3]
ὀλολύξατε νῦν ἐπὶ μολπαῖς.

σπονδαὶ δ' ἐς τὸ πᾶν ἐκ μετοίκων[4] [ἀντ. β.
Παλλάδος ἀστοῖς. Ζεὺς[5] <ὁ> πανόπτας[6]
οὕτω Μοῖρά τε συγκατέβα.
ὀλολύξατε νῦν ἐπὶ μολπαῖς.

[1] εὐθύφρονες: Wilam.
[2] < > Herm.
[3] ὁδὸν δ': Boissonade.
[4] πᾶν ἔνδαιδες (ἔνδαδες FV3N) οἴκων: Wilam.
[5] ἀστοῖσι ζεὺς: Musgrave.
[6] παντόπτας: Aldina.

Gracious and propitious to the land, come hither, ye Venerable Goddesses, attended by the flame-fed torch, rejoicing as ye go.

Raise a glad shout in echo to our song!

Peace endureth for future time between the citizens of Pallas' burgh and them that have come to dwell therein. Zeus, the all-seeing, and Fate have lent their aid unto this end.

Raise a glad shout in echo to our song!

[*Exeunt omnes*

FRAGMENTS

SELECTED FRAGMENTS

This selection includes those fragments of which at least one entire verse, or two connected half-verses, is preserved. The numbers in parentheses, unless otherwise designated, are those of the second edition of Nauck's *Tragicorum Graecorum fragmenta* (1889). Fragments not included in Nauck's collection are numbered according to the arrangement adopted in "Unlisted Fragments of Aeschylus," *American Journal of Philology*, xli. (1920) 101-114. Unidentified fragments assigned to Aeschylus by modern scholars are indicated either by "Anon.," followed by the numbers of Nauck's Ἀδέσποτα, or by the numbers of Weckléin's edition, or by both.

THE PLAYS OF AESCHYLUS

Seventy-three of the under-mentioned titles appear in the list of the dramas that is found in the Medicean manuscript.

Ἀγαμέμνων.
Ἀθάμας.
Αἰγύπτιοι.[3]
Αἰτναῖαι (γνήσιοι).[4]
5 Αἰτναῖαι (νόθοι).[4]
Ἀλκμήνη.[1, 3]
Ἀμυμώνη.
Ἀργεῖοι or Ἀργεῖαι.
Ἀργὼ ἢ Κωπαστής.[5]
10 Ἀταλάντη.[2]
Βάκχαι.
Βασσάραι.
Γλαῦκος πόντιος.[6]
Γλαῦκος Ποτνιεύς.[6]
15 Δαναΐδες.
Δικτυουλκοί.[3]
Διονύσου τροφοί (οἱ Τροφοί).[3, 5]
Ἐλευσίνιοι.
Ἐπίγονοι.
20 Ἑπτὰ ἐπὶ Θήβας.
Εὐμενίδες.

[1] Not mentioned in the *Κατάλογος τῶν Αἰσχύλου δραμάτων*.
[2] No identified fragment is extant.
[3] No identified fragment forming an entire verse is extant.
[4] The two plays of this name are not to be distinguished in the extant fragments.
[5] Alternative titles are due to Alexandrian scholars whose explanatory designations sought to avoid confusion between dramas of the same name. Where such alternative titles occur, that denoting the Chorus is presumably older than that denoting a principal personage or the subject matter of the play.
[6] The descriptive epithet added after a title may be due to Alexandrian scholars, who sought thereby to distinguish dramas of the same name.

Ἠδωνοί.
Ἡλιάδες.
Ἡρακλεῖδαι.
25 Θαλαμοποιοί.
Θεωροὶ ἢ Ἰσθμιασταί.[5]
Θρῇσσαι.
Ἱέρειαι.[1]
Ἱκέτιδες.
30 Ἰξίων.
Ἰφιγένεια.
Κάβειροι.
Καλλιστώ.[3]
Κᾶρες ἢ Εὐρώπη.[5]
35 Κερκυών.[3]
Κήρυκες.
Κίρκη.[3]
Κρῆσσαι.
[Κύκνος.][1]
40 Λάϊος.[3]
Λέων.
Λήμνιοι or Λήμνιαι.[2]
Λυκοῦργος.
Μέμνων.
45 Μυρμιδόνες.
Μυσοί.
Νεανίσκοι.
Νεμέα.[3]
Νηρεΐδες.
50 Νιόβη.
Ξάντριαι.
Οἰδίπους.
Ὅπλων κρίσις.
Ὀστολόγοι.
55 Παλαμήδης.[1]
Πενθεύς.
Περραιβίδες.
Πέρσαι.
Πηνελόπη.
60 Πολυδέκτης.[2]
Προμηθεὺς δεσμώτης.[6]
Προμηθεὺς λυόμενος.[6]
Προμηθεὺς πυρκαεύς.[1, 6]
Προμηθεὺς πυρφόρος.[6]
65 Προπομποί.[3]
Πρωτεύς.
Σαλαμίνιαι.

[1] Not mentioned in the Κατάλογος τῶν Αἰσχύλου δραμάτων.
[2] No identified fragment is extant.
[3] No identified fragment forming an entire verse is extant.
[5] Alternative titles are due to Alexandrian scholars whose explanatory designations, sought to avoid confusion between dramas of the same name. Where such alternative titles occur, that denoting the Chorus is presumably older than that denoting a principal personage or the subject matter of the play.
[6] The descriptive epithet added after a title may be due to Alexandrian scholars, who sought thereby to distinguish dramas of the same name.

Σεμέλη ἢ Ὑδροφόροι.[3, 5]
Σίσυφος δραπέτης.[4, 6]
Σίσυφος πετροκυλιστής.[4, 6]
Σφίγξ.
Τήλεφος.
Τοξότιδες.
Ὑψιπύλη.[3]
Φιλοκτήτης.
Φινεύς.[1]
Φορκίδες.
Φρύγες ἢ Ἕκτορος λύτρα.[5]
Φρύγιοι.[2]
Χοηφόροι.
Ψυχαγωγοί.
Ψυχοστασία.[3]
Ὠρείθυια.[1]

Satyric plays attested: Κερκυών, Κήρυκες, Κίρκη, Λέων, Λυκουργός, Προμηθεὺς (πυρκαεύς), Πρωτεύς, Σφίγξ. Possibly satyric are: Ἀμυμώνη, Γλαῦκος πόντιος, Καλλιστώ, Κάβειροι, Ξάντριαι, Σίσυφος δραπέτης, Φορκίδες.

Tetralogies attested:

1. (472 B.C.) Φινεύς, Πέρσαι, Γλαῦκος (Ποτνιεύς), Προμηθεὺς (πυρκαεύς).
2. (467 B.C.) Λάϊος, Οἰδίπους, Ἑπτὰ ἐπὶ Θήβας, Σφίγξ.
3. Λυκούργεια: Ἠδωνοί, Βασσάραι, Νεανίσκοι, Λυκοῦργος.
4. Ὀρέστεια (458 B.C.): Ἀγαμέμνων, Χοηφόροι, Εὐμενίδες, Πρωτεύς.

[1] Not mentioned in the Κατάλογος τῶν Αἰσχύλου δραμάτων.

[2] No identified fragment is extant. Φρύγιοι is probably the same play as Φρύγες.

[3] No identified fragment forming an entire verse is extant.

[4] The two plays are not to be distinguished in the extant fragments.

[5] Alternative titles are due to Alexandrian scholars whose explanatory designations sought to avoid confusion between dramas of the same name. Where such alternative titles occur, that denoting the Chorus is presumably older than that denoting a principal personage or the subject matter of the play.

[6] The descriptive epithet added after a title may be due to Alexandrian scholars, who sought thereby to distinguish dramas of the same name.

By reason of the myth or of other indication of connexion between their several members, the following groups may be assumed with some probability. (The order within the group is often uncertain.)

Ἱκέτιδες, Αἰγύπτιοι, Δαναΐδες, Ἀμυμώνη (satyric).
Ψυχαγωγοί, Ὀστολόγοι, Πηνελόπη, Κίρκη (satyric).
Προμηθεὺς δεσμώτης, Προμηθεὺς λυόμενος, Προμηθεὺς πυρφόρος.
Ὅπλων κρίσις, Θρῇσσαι, Σαλαμίνιαι.
Μυρμιδόνες, Νηρεΐδες, Φρύγες ἢ Ἕκτορος λύτρα.
Ἀργώ, Λήμνιοι (Λήμνιαι ?), Ὑψιπύλη, Κάβειροι (satyric ?).
Ἐλευσίνιοι, Ἀργεῖοι (Ἀργεῖαι ?), Ἐπίγονοι.
Δικτυουλκοί, Πολυδέκτης, Φορκίδες.
Μέμνων, Ψυχοστασία.
Περραιβίδες, Ἰξίων.
Μυσοί, Τήλεφος.

Theban legends of Dionysus seem to have formed the subject of no less than five plays: Σεμέλη ἢ Ὑδροφόροι, Διονύσου τροφοί (or Τροφοί), Βάκχαι, Ξάντριαι, Πενθεύς. The Argument to Euripides' Βάκχαι asserts that the story of that drama had been handled in Πενθεύς.

To reduce the number of these Dionysus-plays to the compass of a trilogy or tetralogy, various expedients have been proposed:

1. To seek other connexions for Διονύσου τροφοί and assume a tetralogy consisting of Σεμέλη ἢ Ὑδροφόροι, Βάκχαι, Πενθεύς, Ξάντριαι (satyric).

2. To regard Βάκχαι as an alternative name for

Πενθεύς, or for Ξάντριαι (not satyric), or even for Βασσάραι.

3. To make Βάκχαι the title of the group Σεμέλη ἢ Ὑδροφόροι, Πενθεύς, Ξάντριαι.

4. To make Πενθεύς the name of the trilogy Σεμέλη ἢ Ὑδροφόροι, Βάκχαι, Ξάντριαι.

ΑΘΑΜΑΣ

Athamas, a hero localized in Boeotia and Thessaly, was the son of Aeolus according to the genealogy commonly adopted in antiquity. By his divine wife Nephele he had two children, Phrixus and Helle; by his second wife Ino, daughter of Cadmus, he had two sons, Learchus and Melicertes. Apollodorus, *Library*, iii. 4. 3 (cp. i. 9. 2) narrates that Zeus entrusted the newly-born Dionysus to Hermes, who conveyed him to Ino and Athamas, and persuaded them to rear the babe as a girl. In consequence of madness brought upon them by Hera in her indignation, Athamas hunted his elder son as a deer and killed him; Ino threw Melicertes into a boiling cauldron, and then, carrying it, together with the dead body of the child, leaped into the sea. The Argument to the first Isthmian Ode of Pindar reports a different version: that the corpse of Learchus was thrown into the cauldron by Ino, who then, having become mad, plunged into the sea. The Isthmian games were instituted by Sisyphus in honour of Melicertes.

1 (1)

τὸν μὲν τρίπους ἐδέξατ' οἰκεῖος λέβης
αἰεὶ φυλάσσων τὴν ὑπὲρ πυρὸς στάσιν·

Athenaeus, *Deipnosophists*, ii. 6. p. 37 F; cp. vii. 100. p. 316 B.

The one was cast into the three-legged cauldron of the house, that ever kept its place above the fire.

2 (2)

χαλκέοισιν ἐξαυστῆρσιν ἐξαιρούμενοι[1]

Etymologicum Florentinum 116 (Miller); cp. *Etymologicum Magnum* 346. 56.

[1] ἐξαυστῆρες χειρούμενοι: Dindorf.

Taking out with bronze flesh-hooks

AITNAIAI

A Sicilian maiden named Thaleia or Aetna, having been embraced by Zeus, in fear of Hera's wrath prayed that the earth might open and swallow her up. Her prayer was granted, but when the time of her delivery was at hand, the earth opened again and twin boys came forth, who were called Palīci, because they had "come back" (ἀπὸ τοῦ πάλιν ἱκέσθαι) from the earth. The Palici were worshipped (originally with human sacrifices) in the neighbourhood of Mount Aetna (Macrobius, *Saturnalia*, v. 19. 17; cp. Servius on Virgil, *Aeneid*, ix. 584).

"Having arrived in Sicily, as Hiero was then (476 B.C.) founding the city of Aetna, Aeschylus exhibited his *Aetnae* as an augury of a prosperous life for those who were uniting in the settlement of the city" (*Life of Aeschylus*).

The play is named Αἰτναῖαι, *The Women of Aetna*, in the Medicean Catalogue, and so apparently in Frag. 9 and Frag. 10 (Nauck). The title has the form Αἶτναι in the *Life* and in Nauck's 7 and 8;

Αἴτνα in Nauck's 11, *Aetna* in Macrobius. Alexandrian scholars thought to distinguish a genuine from a spurious play of this name. See p. 375.

3 (6)

Α. τί δῆτ' ἐπ' αὐτοῖς ὄνομα θήσονται βροτοί;
Β. σεμνοὺς Παλικοὺς Ζεὺς ἐφίεται[1] καλεῖν.
Α. ἦ καὶ Παλικῶν εὐλόγως μενεῖ[2] φάτις;
Β. πάλιν γὰρ ἥξουσ' ἐκ σκότου[3] τόδ' εἰς φάος.

Macrobius, *Saturnalia* v. 19. 24.

[1] ΕΦΥΤΑΙ P^1, ΕΦΥΕΤΑΙ P^2: Stanley.
[2] μένει edd. before Schneidewin.
[3] ΗΚΟΥΣΕΚΣΤΟΥΣ P: ἥξουσ' Burges, ἐκ σκότου Hermann.

A. What name, then, shall mortals put upon them?

B. Zeus commandeth that they be called the holy Palici.

A. And shall the name "Palici" abide as rightly given?

B. Aye, for they shall "come back" from darkness to this light.

Ll. 3-4 form the motto of Bridges' *Palicio*.

ΑΜΥΜΩΝΗ

"But the land of Argos being waterless, since Poseidon had dried up even the springs because of his anger at Inachus for testifying that it belonged to Hera, Danaüs sent his daughters to draw water. One of them, Amymone, as she was searching for water, threw a dart at a deer and hit a sleeping satyr. He, starting up, desired to force her; but Poseidon appearing on the scene, the satyr fled, and

Amymone lay with Poseidon, and he revealed to her the springs at Lerna " (Apollodorus, *Library*, ii. 1. 4). The play was probably satyric.

4 (13)

σοὶ μὲν γαμεῖσθαι μόρσιμον, γαμεῖν δ' ἐμοί.[1]

Ammonius, *On Words of like Form but different Meaning* 37 (Valckenaer), Bachmann, *Anecdota Graeca*, ii. 375. 8.

[1] δὲ μή Ammonius, δ' ἐμοί Bachm. *Anecd.*

It is thy fate to be my wife; mine to be thy husband.

5 (14)

κἄγωγε τὰς σὰς βακκάρεις τε καὶ μύρα

Athenaeus, *Deipnosophists* xv. 41. p. 690 c.

And for my part I [wish] thy nards and balsam too

ΑΡΓΕΙΟΙ

In the Medicean Catalogue and the *Etymologicum Magnum* (see under Fragment 7) the play bears the title 'Αργεῖοι, *The Men of Argos*. In the authors citing Fragment 6 and Nauck's 18 (Hesychius, *Lexicon* 1. 257) the name is 'Αργεῖαι, which suggests that the Chorus was formed of the mothers of the Argive commanders who fell in the attack on Thebes described in the extant play of Aeschylus. According to Welcker, the 'Ελευσίνιοι anticipated the first, the 'Αργεῖοι the second, part of Euripides' *Suppliants*. M. Schmidt in *Philologus*, xvi. (1860) 161, conjectured that the drama was entitled 'Αργεία from the daughter of Adrastus who married Polynices, and who, in Statius' *Thebaïd*, was joined by Antigone in burying her father.

Fragment 155 has been assigned to this play.

6 (16)

καὶ παλτὰ κἀγκυλητὰ καὶ χλῆδον βελῶν[1]

Harpocration, *Glossary of the Ten Attic Orators* 306. 11.

[1] βαλών: M. Schmidt.

Both darts and looped javelins and heaped missiles

7 (17)

†Καπανεύς μοι[1] καταλείπεται
λοιποῖς[2] ἃ κεραυνὸς[3] ἄρθρων[4]
ἐνηλυσίων[5] ἀπέλιπεν†

Etymologicum Magnum 341. 5, *Lexicon Sabbaïticum* 21.

[1] μου *Et. Mag.*, μοι *Lex. Sab.*

[2] λοιποῖς *Et. Mag.*, λοιπὸν *Lex. Sab.*

[3] ἀκέραυνος: Welcker (cp. *Et. Mag.* ἐνηλύσια λέγεται εἰς ἃ κεραυνὸς εἰσβέβηκεν).

[4] ἀρόρων: M. Schmidt.

[5] ἐπηλυσίων: Stanley.

Capaneus is left me with the remains of his lightning-smitten limbs that the thunderbolt had left behind (?)

From a lament, probably by the Chorus, on the Argive chieftains who fell in the first attack on Thebes; or possibly by Evadne over the body of her husband Capaneus, of whose destruction, by the lightning of Zeus, Eteocles is confident in *Seven against Thebes* 444. In Euripides' *Suppliants* the bodies of the other Argive champions were burned on a single funeral pyre, that of Capaneus was burned apart as a consecrated corpse; and upon his pyre his wife threw herself.

ΑΡΓΩ

In the Medicean Catalogue the play is entitled Ἀργὼ ἡ κωπαστής (so M); in the Aldine edition, Ἀργὼ ἢ κωπευστής. Referring the sub-title to the rowers of the Argo, Welcker proposed κωπευσταί; Hippenstiel, *De Graecorum tragicorum principum fabularum nominibus*, κωπασταί. Hartung, approved by Dieterich, read κωμασταί "revellers."

See Fragments 164, 221.

8 (20)

ποῦ δ' ἐστὶν Ἀργοῦς ἱερὸν αὐδᾶεν[1] ξυλόν;

Philo of Alexandria, *On the Virtuous being also Free* 20. 143 (Cohn and Reiter vi. 41).

[1] αὔδασον edd., δαπεν with ο over ν in M, αὔδασαι G, αὔδασε other MSS.: Cobet.

Where is Argo's sacred speaking beam?

Apollodorus, *Library* i. 9. 16: "and at the prow (of the Argo) Athena fitted a speaking timber from the oak of Dodona."

ΒΑΚΧΑΙ

See p. 378. Fragment 215 has been referred to the *Bacchae*.

9 (22)

τό τοι[1] κακὸν ποδῶκες ἔρχεται βροτοῖς
καὶ τἀμπλάκημα[2] τῷ περῶντι τὴν θέμιν.

Stobaeus, *Anthology* i. 3. 26 (Wachsmuth i. 57), Theophilus, *To Autolycus* 2. 37. p. 178. The verses are ascribed to the Βάκχαι only in the margin of the Farnesianus of Stobaeus (αἰσχύλου κάκχῶν).

[1] τό τοι P, τὸ Theoph. (without τοι), τῶ τοι F.

[2] καὶ τ' ἀμπλάκημα F, καὶ τ' ἀπλάκημα (with μ over π by the first hand) P.

Truly upon mortals cometh swift of foot their evil and his offence upon him that trespasseth against Right.

ΒΑΣΣΑΡΑΙ

Eratosthenes, *Legends of the Constellations*, 24. p. 140 (Robert), says of Orpheus that he paid no honour to Dionysus, but considered Helios to be the greatest of the gods and addressed him as Apollo; that, by making haste during the night, he reached at dawn the summit of Mt. Pangaeus, and waited there that he might see the rising of the sun; and that Dionysus, in his wrath, sent against him the Bassarides (as Aeschylus tells the story), who tore him to pieces and scattered his members, which were collected and buried by the Muses in Leibethra. To the same effect, Scholiast Germanicus, 84. 11.

The name Βασσάραι was given to Thracian (and to Phrygian and Lydian) bacchanals, who wore fox-skin caps and long embroidered cloaks, pictured in Miss Harrison's *Prolegomena to the Study of Greek Religion*, 458. The word βασσάρα (possibly of Phrygian origin, but carried elsewhere) means "fox." Cp. Fragment 29.

The play is entitled Βασσαρίδες in the Scholiast on Aristophanes, *Thesmophoriazusae* 135, and on Nicander, *Theriaca* 288.

To the *Bassarae* have been assigned Fragments 187, 215.

10 (23)

ὁ ταῦρος δ' ἔοικεν κυρίξειν[1] ἐνόρχαν[2]
†φθάσαντος δ' ἐπ' ἔργοις προπηδήσεταί νιν[3]†

Hephaestion, *Handbook of Metres* 13. p. 43 (Consbruch) and Choeroboscus, *Commentary* p. 84. 3.

[1] κηρύξειν A, κυρίζειν I, κερίζειν Choer.

[2] τιν' ἀρχόν: Stadtmüller.

[3] L. 2, if it belongs with l. 1 in this frag. of choral song, must be remade to yield a normal construction and an intelligible sense. Wecklein proposed ἄσαντος δ' ἐναργῶς κτλ., Blaydes φθάσαντος ἐνεργῶς . . . τις, Stadtmüller φθάσας δ' ἐς λεωργοὺς . . . νῦν ("and he will now get the start in leaping forth upon the knaves").

The bull was like to butt the goat with his horns. . . .

Dionysus is the bull, the goat is Lycurgus, the king of the Edonians, who refused to adopt the worship of the god.

11 (24)

κάρφει[1] παλαιῷ κἀπιβωμίῳ ψόλῳ

Scholiast on Nicander, *Theriaca* 288.

[1] σκάρφει KPR, κάρφει V.

Old chips and sooty ashes on the altar

12 (25 A)

Παγγαίου γὰρ ἀργυρήλατον
πρῶν' ἀστραπῆς[1] <πίμπλησι>[2] πευκᾶεν σέλας.

Scholiast (cod. Vaticanus Graecus 909) on Euripides, *Rhesus* 922.

[1] πρῶνες τὸ τῆς: Mekler.
[2] < > Mekler.

For his gleaming torch doth flood with flashing light Pangaeus' headland, silver-seamed.

Probably from the Messenger's report to Dionysus concerning Orpheus' ascent of the mountain to behold the rising sun.

ΓΛΑΥΚΟΣ ΠΟΝΤΙΟΣ [1]

Pausanias, *Description of Greece* ix. 22. 7: "At Anthedon by the sea is what is called 'Glaucus' Leap.' That Glaucus was a fisherman, who, because he had eaten of a grass, was changed into a daimon of the sea and foretells men the future, is believed by people in general, and especially do seafaring men every year tell stories about his prophetic art. Pindar and Aeschylus learned from the Anthedonians concerning him, but whereas the former did not have much to do with the legends in his poems, the latter worked them into a play." Plutarch, in his *Life of Cicero* 2, reports that there still existed in his time a short poem in tetrameters on Glaucus of the Sea written by the orator in his youth.

In Fragments 17-19 Glaucus describes his wanderings by sea. To the play, which was probably satyric, have been ascribed Fragments 203, 230, 231.

[1] See appendix, p. 529.

13 (26)

[ἀνθρωποειδὲς θηρίον ὕδατι συζῶν]

Phrynichus in Bekker, *Anecdota Graeca* 5. 21, Photius, *Lexicon* 140. 22 (Reitzenstein). The line is a metrical attempt by a grammarian interpreting a verse of Aeschylus, which Nauck would restore as ἀνθρωπόμορφον κῆτος ὕδατι σύννομον, an improvement on Dindorf's ἀνθρωπόμορφον κῆτος ἐξ ἁλὸς φανέν.

[A creature, like unto a man, living in the water]

14 (27)

δαῦλος[1] δ' ὑπήνη καὶ γενειάδος[2] πυθμήν

Etymologicum Magnum 250. 4, Eustathius on *Iliad* 274. 24; cp. Pausanias, *Description of Greece* x. 4. 7.

[1] δαῦλος MSS., δαυλός Herodian according to Arcadius, *Accent* 53. 7.

[2] πολιάδος *Etymologicum Florentinum* 82 (Miller), *i.e.* παρηΐδος; cp. Euripides, *Ion* 1460.

Shaggy his moustache and his beard's base

15 (28)

ὁ τὴν ἀείζων ἄφθιτον πόαν φαγών

Bekker, *Anecdota Graeca* 347. 24, Photius, *Lexicon* 36. 12 (Reitzenstein).

He that ate the ever-living, imperishable grass

Ovid, *Metamorphoses* xiii. 930, relates that Glaucus was moved to eat of a certain grass because a fish that he had caught, on touching the same, regained life and sprang into the sea. The effect produced by the magic herb (according to the legend adopted by Nicander, *Ther.*, Frag. 2) was that Glaucus became a god and leaped into the sea.

16 (29)

καὶ γεύομαί πως τῆς ἀειζώου πόας.

Bekker, *Anecdota Graeca* 347. 29, Photius, *Lexicon* 36. 16 (Reitzenstein).

And I taste, methinks, the ever-living grass.

17 (30)

Εὐβοΐδα καμπὴν[1] ἀμφὶ Κηναίου Διὸς
ἀκτήν, κατ' αὐτὸν τύμβον ἀθλίου Λίχα

Strabo, *Geography* x. 1. 9. p. 447.

[1] καμπὴν most MSS., καμπτὴν Bkl.

The bend at Euboïs about the headland of Cenaean Zeus, close to the tomb of wretched Lichas

Strabo says that Euboïs was a city that had been engulfed by an earthquake. The Cenaean promontory is situated at the end of the peninsula at the N.W. extremity of Euboea. Near by is a mountain (about 2800 feet high), on the top of which Zeus Cenaeus was worshipped. From the promontory, Lichas, the herald of Heracles, was hurled into the sea by his master because he had been the bearer of the poisoned robe sent by Deïaneira. Cp. Sophocles, *Women of Trachis* 237, 750.

18 (31)

κἄπειτ' Ἀθήνας Διάδας[1] παρεκπερῶν[2]

Life of Aratus, Westermann's *Lives of the Greeks* 53. 26, from Petavius, *Uranologia* 269 A (Paris, 1637).

[1] δαΐδας: Valckenaer. [2] παρ' ἐκ περσῶν: Scaliger.

And thereafter going out past Diad Athens

From Dion, a city on the promontory of Cenaeum, a settlement of Athenians was called Athenae Diades.

19 (32)

καλοῖσι λουτροῖς ἐκλελουμένος[1] δέμας
εἰς ὑψίκρημνον Ἱμέραν [δ'][2] ἀφικόμην.

Scholiast on Pindar, *Pythian* 1. 79 (152).

[1] ἐκλέλουμαι: Heyne. [2] [ ] Heyne.

Having washed my body in fair baths, I came to steep-banked Himeras.

ΓΛΑΥΚΟΣ ΠΟΤΝΙΕΥΣ

Potniae was a city in Boeotia where Glaucus, the son of Sisyphus and Merope, kept mares that he had accustomed to feed on human flesh in order to make them charge against the enemy with greater eagerness and speed. When this food failed, they devoured their master at the funeral games in honour of Pelias (Asclepiades, *On the Subjects of Tragedy* in Probus on Virgil, *Georgics* iii. 267). According to the Scholiast on Euripides, *Orestes* 318, the horses had eaten a (poisonous) grass, whereby they became mad and tore Glaucus asunder. Strabo, *Geography* x. 409, omits any mention of the cause of madness, which other writers attribute, now to the water of a sacred spring near Potniae, now to the anger of Aphrodite (because Glaucus prevented his mares from mating in order to increase their speed), now to their human food.

In Fragment 20 the Chorus utter their good wishes on Glaucus' departure for the games. In 21, 22, 23 the Messenger describes the contest, in which the title-hero was hurled from his chariot in the collision caused by the madness of the mares.

The *Glaucus of Potniae* was produced in 472 B.C. as the third member of the tetralogy Φινεύς, Πέρσαι, Γλαῦκος (Ποτνιεύς according to a later Argument), Προμηθεύς (probably πυρκαεύς).

See Fragments 88, 181, 184, 205.

20 (36)

εὐοδίαν μὲν πρῶτον[1] ἀπὸ στόματος χέομεν.

Scholiast on Aristophanes, *Frogs* 1528.

[1] πρῶτον Ven., πρῶτα other MSS.

"A prosperous journey!" is the first wish we pour forth from our lips.

21 (37)

ἀγὼν γὰρ ἄνδρας οὐ μένει λελειμμένους.

Scholiast on Plato, p. 904 B 36 (Baiter-Orelli).

Not for laggards doth a contest wait.

22 (38)

ἐφ' ἅρματος[1] γὰρ ἅρμα[2] καὶ νεκρῷν νεκροί[3],
ἵπποι δ' ἐφ' ἵπποις ἦσαν ἐμπεφυρμένοι[4].

Scholiast on Euripides, *Women of Phoenicia* 1194.

[1] ἅρματι C. [2] ἅρματα M.

[3] νεκρῶν νεκροὶ ACM, νεκρῷ νεκρὸς BI, and Aristophanes, *Frogs* 1403, citing l. 1 (from this play Schol. Rav.).

[4] ἐμπεφυγμένοι C, ἐκπεφυγμένοι ABIM[1], ἐκπεφυμένοι M[2]: Valckenaer.

For chariot on chariot, corpse upon corpse, horse on horse, had been heaped in confusion.

23 (39)

εἷλκον <δ'>[1] ἄνω λυσσηδόν,[2] ὥστε διπλόοι
λύκοι νεβρὸν φέρουσιν ἀμφὶ μασχάλαις.

Scholiasts BLTV on *Il.* N 198; cp. Eustathius on *Il.* 927. 39.

[1] < > Hermann, who referred the Frag. to this play.
[2] λυκηδόν: Naber.

In their fury they dragged him aloft, even as two wolves bear off a fawn by its shoulders.

ΔΑΝΑΪΔΕΣ [1]

When marriage with their cousins, the sons of Aegyptus, had been forced upon the daughters of Danaüs, their father commanded each to kill her husband during the marriage-night. Hypermestra alone, swayed by the charm of love, disobeyed (cp. *Prometheus Bound* 865). Of her, Horace, *Od.* iii. 11. 33 ff., says

> una de multis face nuptiali
> digna periurum fuit in parentem
> splendide mendax et in omne virgo
> 　　nobilis aevum.

To *The Danaïds* have been assigned Fragments 162, 163, 177, 206, 208, 231, 234, 238.

24 (43)

κἄπειτα δ' εἶσι[2] λαμπρὸν ἡλίου φάος
ἕως[3] ἐγείρω[4] πρευμενεῖς[5] τοὺς νυμφίους
νόμοισι θέντων[6] σὺν κόροις τε καὶ κόραις.

[1] See appendix, p. 595.
[2] κἄπειτ' ἄνεισι Toup, κἄπειτα δ' εὖτε Wilam.
[3] Ἠώς τ' Heath, τέως δ' Süvern, ἐγὼ δ' Bothe.
[4] ἐγείρει Heath, ἐπεγερεῖ Herwerden, ἐγείρῃ Wilam.
[5] πρευμενὴς Heath (cp. MSS. *Pers.* 685), πρευμενῶς Herwerden.
[6] νόμοισι(ν) θέλγων Heyne, τέρπων Oberdick, ὕμνων Herwerden, θείοις Blaydes, νόμοις ἀοιδῶν Heath, γάμους ἰδόντων Hartung, ὕμνους τιθέντων Wecklein.

The fragment refers to the custom that, on the morning after the marriage, newly-wed couples were wakened by song (cp. Theocritus, *Idyll* xviii. 56). If the speaker was a servant (who was not privy to the intended murder), the verses may belong to a prologue, which was followed by the appearance of the Chorus of Danaïds; but, so far as we know, the "wakening" was sung by friends of the bride and bridegroom, presumably the same as had, on the previous evening, sung the hymenaeus. If, as seems more probable, the speaker is Danaüs, he is describing what occurred either on the evening of the wedding or on the morning thereafter, before the discovery of the murder, and the lines form part of his defence before the court that tried him for his participation in the killing of his sons-in-law (Scholiast on Euripides, *Orestes* 872). The difficulty of interpretation is largely concerned with the application of the last five words of the text.

1. σὺν κόροις τε καὶ κόραις is the stereotyped form of a wish that the marriage may be fruitful in children. These words were said to brides by the singers of the wedding-song according to the Scholiast on Pindar and Hesychius, *Lexicon* s.v. κουριζόμενοι. Hermann holds to the MS. reading:

"And then the radiant light of the sun is setting, while I call them forth, *saying* 'let them make their bridegrooms graciously disposed, as is the custom, with boys and girls.'"

On this interpretation, Danaüs describes how, after the brides had departed to their new home, he addressed their companions; but the situation is not clear, the meaning of ἐγείρω is strained, and the explanation of νόμοισι peculiar. Toup's ἄνεισι transfers the scene to the morning, as does Wilamowitz' εὖτε . . . ἐγείρῃ ("and when Dawn shall rouse the radiant light of the sun"); but the latter scholar can find in the following words no more definite idea than that certain persons are enjoined to make the young husbands (or the newly-wedded couples) friendly "with boys and girls."

2. σὺν κόροις τε καὶ κόραις means the companions of the speaker, who, with him, awaken the sleepers. So Welcker, reading ἄνεισι and θέλγων:

"And thereafter uprises the radiant light of the sun, while I, in company with youths and maidens, awaken the bridegrooms graciously disposed."

θέλγων is ironical; as is *πρευμενεῖς*, since Danaüs had married his daughters to suitors whom they, and he, detested, and whose murder he had planned.

The situation is moving: when the waking-song was sung, the husbands—all save Lynceus, who was married to Hypermestra—were sleeping the sleep of death. But the scene, because reported, is less dramatic than that in Euripides' *Phaëthon*, in which play (Frag. 781) Merops appears with a chorus of maidens who sing the nuptial song in honour of Phaëthon at the very moment when Phaëthon's corpse is being carried into the chamber of Clymene, the wife of Merops. In *Wilhelm Tell* the music of a wedding-procession is heard while Gessler is in the agonies of death.

25 (44)

ἐρᾷ μὲν ἁγνὸς οὐρανὸς τρῶσαι χθόνα,
ἔρως δὲ γαῖαν λαμβάνει γάμου τυχεῖν,
ὄμβρος δ' ἀπ' εὐνασθέντος[1] οὐρανοῦ πεσὼν
ἔκυσε γαῖαν· ἡ δὲ τίκτεται βροτοῖς
μήλων τε βοσκὰς καὶ βίον Δημήτριον·
δενδρῶτις ὥρα[2] δ' ἐκ νοτίζοντος γάμου
τέλειός ἐστι. τῶνδ' ἐγὼ παραίτιος.

Athenaeus, *Deipnosophists* xiii. 73. p. 600 B; Eustathius, on *Iliad* 978. 25 (omitting ll. 6-7), misled by the reference to Aeschylus of Alexandria in Athen. 599 E, ascribed ll. 1-5 to that poet.

[1] εὐνάεντος Athen. A, with ο over the second ε in C, εὐνάοντος with ε over the first ο in E, εὐνάοντος Eust.: Lobeck.

[2] δένδρων τις ὥρα: Hermann.

The holy heaven yearns to wound the earth, and yearning layeth hold on the earth to join in wedlock; the rain, fallen from the amorous heaven, impregnates the earth, and it bringeth forth for mankind the food of flocks and herds and Demeter's gifts; and from that moist marriage-rite the woods put on their bloom. Of all these things I am the cause.

These lines—the Bridal of Heaven and Earth, imitated by Euripides, Fragment 898—were spoken, says Athenaeus, by Aphrodite herself; and probably in defence of Hypermestra at her trial for disobedience to her father's command. Cp. Lucretius i. 250 (*imbres*) *pater aether in gremium matris terrai praecipitavit*, and Virgil, *Georg.* ii. 235.

ΕΛΕΥΣΙΝΙΟΙ

Plutarch, in his *Life of Theseus* 29, states that Theseus, in conjunction with Adrastus, effected the recovery of the bodies of the Argives slain before Thebes (in the expedition against that city undertaken by the seven champions); that Aeschylus made the recovery the result of persuasion on the part of Theseus, whereas Euripides, in his *Suppliants*, ascribed it to a victory over the Argives; and that Theseus appeared in Aeschylus' play, and out of kindness to Adrastus caused the leaders to be buried at Eleusis, the soldiery at Eleutherae, where their tombs were still shown in his day.

To *The Men of Eleusis* have been assigned Fragments 178, 199, 200, 214, 215, 241.

25 A (54 A)

ὤργα τὸ πρᾶγμα, διεμύδαιν' ἤδη νέκυς.

Didymus, *Commentary on Demosthenes*' *Philippic* xii (xiii) in Berliner Papyrus 9780 (*Berliner Klassikertexte* i. (1904) 66).

The matter pressed, rotting already was the corpse.

ΕΠΙΓΟΝΟΙ

Ten years after the unsuccessful attack on Thebes described in *The Seven against Thebes*, the sons of the fallen chieftains, called the *After-Born*, avenged the death of their fathers in a second expedition, which resulted in the capture of the city. At the end of Euripides' *Suppliants* (l. 1213) Athena prophesies the success of the sons in the war that formed the theme of the Aeschylean drama. The legend of the victorious issue of the second expedition is known to the *Iliad*, in which (Δ 406) Sthenelus, the son of Capaneus, boasts the superiority of the sons over their fathers. But the tradition that the seven champions had each a son (named in Apollodorus, *Library* iii. 7. 2) who joined in the war, is apparently later than Homer. In *The Seven against Thebes*, Aeschylus made both Eteocles and Polynices die childless; but Pindar knew of Thersander, the son of Polynices and successor to his claim to the throne; and late writers report that Laodamas was the son of Eteocles.

Fragments 176, 247, 248 have been referred to *The Epigoni*.

26 (55)

λοιβὰς Διὸς μὲν πρῶτον ὡραίου γάμου
Ἥρας τε . . . . . .
τὴν δευτέραν δὲ[1] κρᾶσιν ἥρωσιν νέμω
. . . .
τρίτον Διὸς σωτῆρος εὐκταίαν λίβα.

Scholiast on Pindar, *Isthmian* 6. 10 (7).

[1] τε: Schütz.

First, libations to Zeus and Hera for timely marriage

The second cup of mixed wine I serve out to the Heroes

Third, a libation for blessing to Zeus, the Saviour.

ΗΔΩΝΟΙ

Apollodorus, *Library* iii. 5. 1, gives the following version of the legend of Lycurgus and his rejection of the god Dionysus :

" And afterwards he (Dionysus) arrived at Cybela in Phrygia, and there, having been purified by Rhea, and learning the rites of initiation, he received from her the costume, and hastened through Thrace [against the Indians]. But Lycurgus, king of the Edonians, who dwell beside the river Strymon, was the first to insult and expel him. And Dionysus took refuge in the sea with Thetis, the daughter of Nereus, and the Bacchanals were taken captive and the multitude of the satyrs that followed him. But afterwards the Bacchanals were suddenly released, and Dionysus brought madness upon Lycurgus. And he, in his frenzy, struck with an axe and killed his son Dryas, imagining that he was lopping off the branch of a vine ; and when he had cut off his son's extremities, he came to his senses. But since the land remained barren, the god made known by an oracle that it would bear fruit if Lycurgus were put to death. On hearing this, the Edonians took him to Mt. Pangaeus, and bound him ; and there, by the will of Dionysus, he died, destroyed by horses."

Fragment 27 refers to the arrival of Dionysus and his worshippers, 28 to the house of Lycurgus ; to whom, or to one of his attendants, belong the satirical descriptions of the god in 29-32.

To *The Edonians* have been ascribed Fragments 173, 188, 193, 201, 202.

27 (57)

σεμνὰ Κοτυτοῦς ὄργι'[1] ἔχοντες

. . . . . .

ὁ μὲν ἐν χερσὶν βόμβυκας[2] ἔχων,
τόρνου κάματον,
δακτυλόδικτον[3] πίμπλησι μέλος,
μανίας ἐπαρωγὸν ὁμοκλάν.
ὁ δὲ χαλκοδέτοις[4] κοτύλαις ὀτοβεῖ[5]

. . . . . .

. . ψαλμὸς δ' ἀλαλάζει·
ταυρόφθογγοι δ' ὑπομυκῶνταί[6]
ποθεν ἐξ ἀφανοῦς φοβεροὶ[7] μῖμοι,
τυπάνου[8] δ' εἰκὼν[9] ὥσθ' ὑπογαίου[10]
βροντῆς φέρεται βαρυταρβής.

Strabo, *Geography* x. 3. 16. p. 470 (l. 6 Athenaeus, *Deipnosophists* xi. 57. p. 479 B, Scholiasts BT on *Iliad* Ψ 34).

[1] σεμνὰ Κότυς (κόπτουσ' Dh, κόπτους C) ὄρια (ὄρεια Dh) δ' ὄργαν' ἔχοντες (ἔχοντας Dhinop): Nauck.
[2] βομβῆκας Bkoxy.
[3] δακτυλόδεικτον: Pauw.
[4] χαλκοδέτοις Athen., Schol. *Il.*, χαλκοθέοις Strabo's MSS. (except χαλκοθέτοις E).
[5] ὀτοβεῖ Ch, ὀττόβει D, ἠχεῖ Schol. *Il.*
[6] ὑπομηκῶνται Bkno.
[7] φοβεροὶ E, φομέριοι B²Ck, φοβέριοι Dhilnox.
[8] τυμπάνου: Kramer.
[9] εἰχὼν B²Llx, ἠχὼ kno.
[10] ὑπογείου Bk, ὑπογέου CDhims.

Practising the holy rites of Cotyto. . . . One, holding in his hands the pipe, the labour of the lathe, blows forth his fingered tune, even the sound that wakes to frenzy. Another, with brass-bound cymbals, raises a clang . . . the twang shrills ; and unseen, unknown, bull-voiced mimes in answer bellow fearfully, while the timbrel's echo, like that of subterranean thunder, rolls along inspiring a mighty terror.

From the parodus of the play. In ll. 2-11 the Chorus of Edonians describes what Milton calls "the barbarous dissonance of Bacchus and his revellers." Cotys, Cotyto, or Cotytto, was a Thracian goddess, akin to Rhea-Cybele, whose worship became popular at Athens. Her rites resembled those of the Phrygian Sabazius, whose ritual was similar to that of Bacchus. The Orphic ceremonies had their origin among the Thracians.

28 (58)

ἐνθουσιᾷ δὴ δῶμα, βακχεύει στέγη.

Pseudo-Longinus, *On the Sublime* 15. 6.

Lo, the house is frenzied with the god, the roof revels, Bacchant-like.

29 (59)

ὅστις[1] χιτῶνας βασσάρας τε Λυδίας[1]
ἔχει ποδήρεις

Etymologicum Florentinum 62 (Miller), *Lexicon Sabbaïticum* 5.

[1] ὅτις and Λυδείας *Lex. Sab.*

One who wears Lydian tunics and fox-skin cloaks reaching to the feet

Dionysus is described as wearing Lydian garments, which were famous for their luxuriousness.

30 (60)

τίς ποτ' ἔσθ' ὁ μουσόμαντις ἄλαλος[1] †ἀβρατεὺς[2] ὃν σθένει†[3]

Scholiast on Aristophanes, *Birds* 276, Suidas, *Lexicon* s.v. μουσόμαντις.

Aristophanes has τίς ποτ' ἔσθ' ὁ μουσόμαντις ἄτοπος ὄρνις ἀβροβάτης (MSS. ὀρειβάτης): 'who in the world is this poet-prophet, extraordinary, dainty-stepping bird?'

[1] ἄλαλος RΓ[3] Suid., ἄλλος V, ἄλλο Ven. 475.
[2] ἀβρατεὺς R Suid., ἀκρατοῦς V, ἀβρατά Γ[3].
[3] ὃν σθένει om. Suid.

Who in the world is this poet-prophet, speechless . . .

Bothe read ἀβρός, ἀσθενής "dainty, weakling"; Hermann ἀμαλὸς ἀβροβάτης σθένει "soft, a dainty stepper in his strength."

31 (61)

ποδαπὸς ὁ γύννις; τίς πάτρα; τίς ἡ στολή;

Scholiast on Aristophanes, *Thesmophoriazusae* 135.

Whence hails this woman-man? What's his country? What's his attire?

32 (62)

μακροσκελὴς μέν· ἆρα[1] μὴ χλούνης τις ἦν[2];

Scholiast B on *Iliad* I 539; cp. Eustathius on *Iliad* 772. 53.

[1] ἄρα: Hermann. [2] ᾖ: Hermann.

Long-legged indeed! Was he not a χλούνης?

The sense of χλούνης is here obscure. In *Iliad* I 539 the word was explained by the ancients as meaning "entire" (not castrated) or "couching in the grass"; elsewhere, as "rascal," "thief," or "clothes-stealer." Hermann thought it was a designation of a locust. See Wilamowitz, *Aischylos: Interpretationen* p. 217.

ΗΛΙΑΔΕΣ

The Daughters of Helios dealt with the legend of Phaëthon, whose rashness in driving the chariot of the Sun, his father, caused the parching of the earth, and thereby his punishment at the hands of Zeus, whose thunderbolt hurled him into the river Eridanus. In pity for the unceasing grief of Phaëthon's sisters, Zeus turned them into poplars, from which, it was believed, their tears oozed forth and became amber, the stone of light; a poetic fancy due to the association of ἤλεκτρον "amber" with ἠλέκτωρ "the beaming sun."

The form assumed by the myth in Aeschylus is unknown; but it is certain that Euripides in his *Phaëthon* differed widely from the older poet. Aeschylus was in part dependent on Hesiod for the story; but whereas Hesiod knew of seven daughters of Helios, Aeschylus recognized only three—Lampetië, Aegle, and Phaëthousa—children of the Sun-god and Rhode. Furthermore he transferred to Iberia the scene of the fall of Phaëthon.

Fragments **172**, 177, 185 have been ascribed to the play.

33 (69)

ἔνθ'
ἐπὶ δυσμαῖσι τεοῦ[1]
πατρὸς Ἡφαιστοτυκὲς[2]
δέπας, ἐν τῷ διαβάλλει
πολὺν οἰδματόεντα περίδρομον[3] πόρον συθεὶς[4]

[1] δυσμαῖς ισου: Hermann. [2] ἡφαιστοτευχὲς: Hermann.
[3] φέρει δρόμον: Sidgwick. [4] οὔθεις: M. Schmidt.

μελανίππου προφυγὼν
ἱερᾶς νυκτὸς ἀμολγόν.

Athenaeus, *Deipnosophists* xi. 38. p. 469 F.

Where, in the west, is the bowl wrought by Hephaestus, the bowl of thy sire, speeding wherein he crosseth the mighty, swelling stream that girdleth earth, fleeing the gloom of holy night of sable steeds.

To explain the rising of the sun in the east after it had set in the west, Greek fancy invented the myth that the Sun-god possessed a golden bowl, in which he, together with his steeds, was carried during the night across the ocean to the place of his rising. When Heracles was journeying to Erythea to capture the oxen of Geryon (Frag. 37), Helios lent his bowl to the hero; who, in Gerhard's *Auserlesene griechische Vasenbilder*, pl. 109, is pictured sitting therein. In the Veda and in Germanic and Lettic myths the sun appears in the form of a golden bowl.

34 (70)

Ζεύς ἐστιν αἰθήρ, Ζεὺς δὲ γῆ, Ζεὺς δ' οὐρανός,
Ζεύς τοι τὰ πάντα χὤτι τῶνδ' ὑπέρτερον.

Clement of Alexandria, *Miscellanies* v. 14. p. 718; cp. Philodemus, *On Piety* 22.

Zeus is air, Zeus is earth, Zeus is heaven, yea, Zeus is all things and whatsoever transcendeth them.

35 (71)

Ἀδριαναί τε γυναῖκες τρόπον ἕξουσι γόων.

Bekker, *Anecdota Graeca* 346. 10.

And Adria's daughters shall learn a (new) way of mourning.

Phaëthon was hurled into the Eridanus, which Aeschylus, according to Pliny, *Nat. Hist.* xxxvii. 31, placed in Iberia and identified with the Rhone, a river confused with the Po, on the banks of which was the city of Adria. Polybius, *History* ii. 16 and Plutarch, *On the Delay of Divine Vengeance* 12. p. 557, report that the inhabitants along the Eridanus wore black in mourning for Phaëthon. Knaack, *Quaestiones Phaëthonteae* 18, refers " the way of mourning " to the tears of amber from the poplars into which the maidens had been transformed.

36 (72)

ὤρουσε[1] κρήνης ἀφθονεστέρα λιβάς.

Etymologicum Genuinum (cod. Vaticanus Graecus 1818) s.v. ἀφθονέστατον; cp. Athenaeus, *Deipnosophists* x. 24. p. 424 D, Eustathius on *Iliad* 746. 45, *Lexicon Sabbaïticum* 2.

[1] ὅρα σε: Reitzenstein.

Gushed from the spring a more abundant stream.

ΗΡΑΚΛΕΙΔΑΙ[1]

Of the personages, action, and scene of *The Children of Heracles* nothing is known. It is, however, probable that Aeschylus in part anticipated Euripides, who, in his same-named play, represented Athens as the refuge of the fugitives from the persecution of Eurystheus, the willingness of Macaria, the daughter of Heracles, to sacrifice her life as the price of victory over the Argive invaders of Attica, and the triumph of the children under the leadership of the aged Iolaüs, the nephew of Heracles.

The play is entitled Ἡρακλεῖδαι, except in the Catalogue in the Medicean MS., which has Ἡρακλείδης.

37 (74)

ἐκεῖθεν
ὅρμενος ὀρθόκερως βοῦς ἤλασ' ἀπ' ἐσχάτων

[1] See appendix, p. 586.

γαίας, ὠκεανὸν περάσας ἐν δέπᾳ χρυσηλάτῳ,
βοτῆράς τ' ἀδίκους κατέκτα δεσπότην τε τρίπτυχον
τρία δόρη πάλλοντα χερσίν·
τρία δὲ λαιαῖς σάκη προτείνων τρεῖς τ' ἐπισ-
σείων λόφους
ἔστειχεν ἴσος Ἄρει βίαν.

Scholiast on Aristeides (cod. Marcianus 423).

The MS. has ἐκεῖθεν ὅρμενος ὀρθοκέρως βοῦς ἤλασεν . . . γαίης . . . ἐν διπλῆ . . . ἀδίκους κτεῖναι δεσποτῶν τε τριύτατον· τρία . . . χεροῖν· τρία διὰ τῆς σακου προτείνων τρεῖς δέ τις ειπλοφουσ-εστειχισοσαρη βίαν. The restorations are due to Wilamowitz, except l. 4 κατέκτα, τρίπτυχον, l. 5 χερσίν Weil, l. 6 τρία δὲ λαιαῖς, l. 7 ἔστειχεν Wecklein.

Starting thence, when that he had crossed the ocean in a golden bowl, he drave the straight-horned kine from the uttermost parts of the earth, slew the evil herdsmen and their triple-bodied master, who wielded three spears in his (right) hands ; in his left, extending three shields, and shaking his three crests, he advanced like unto Ares in his might.

A description of the tenth labour of Heracles—to fetch the kine of Geryon from the island of Erythea, near the ocean, now Cadiz. Geryon had the body of three men grown together and joined in one at the waist, but parted in three from the flanks and thighs (Apollodorus, *Library* ii. 5. 10). Cp. *Agam.* 870. For the golden bowl see under Fragment 33.

38 (75)

οὐ γάρ τι μεῖζον ἄλλο τοῦδε πείσομαι[1].

Stobaeus, *Anthology* iv. 54. 2 (Hense v. 1113).

[1] πήσομαι MA.

For I shall not suffer any evil greater than this.

ΘΑΛΑΜΟΠΟΙΟΙ

A play of this name is unknown to the Catalogue in the Medicean MS., and is mentioned only by Pollux, citing Fragment 39. Some suppose that it is an alternative title of the Αἰγύπτιοι, and that the name is derived from the carpenters who constructed the bridal chambers in which the Danaïds killed their husbands. Hartung proposed to read Θαλαμηπόλοι "attendants on the bridal chambers." Welcker rejected connexion with the Danaïd-myth and made the play precede the Ἰφιγένεια and Ἱέρειαι.

To the play have been referred Fragments 162, 163, 178, 189, 206, 238.

39 (78)

ἀλλ' <εἶ'>[1] ὁ μέν τις Λέσβιον φατνώματι[2]
κῦμ' ἐν τριγώνοις ἐκπεραινέτω[3] ῥυθμοῖς.

Pollux, *Vocabulary* 7. 122.

[1] < > Nauck. [2] φάτνωμά τί: Pauw.
[3] ἐμπεραινέτω: Jungermann.

Come! Let some one work out in the ceiling a Lesbian moulding in triangular rhythms.

A ceiling-compartment was formed, at its lower part, by "ladders" (κλιμακίδες) laid across the "main beams" (σελίδες). Below the former, in the present case, ran a moulding with swelling above and hollow below (a *cyma reversa*) and ornamented with a leaf-and-tongue pattern that approximates a triangle. The Lesbian cyma appears in the Tholos at Epidaurus.

ΘΕΩΡΟΙ ἢ ΙΣΘΜΙΑΣΤΑΙ[1]

The original title was probably Θεωροί, *The Spectators*; to which was added that defining the scene: *The Spectators at the Isthmian games.*

40 (79)

καὶ μὴν παλαιῶν τῶνδέ σοι σκωπευμάτων

Athenaeus, *Deipnosophists* xiv. 27. p. 629 F.

And further these old σκωπεύματα

Athenaeus defines the form of the σκώψ-dance as a figure in which people are represented as looking at an object (ἀποσκοπούντων) by making an arch over their brows. He has, however, here confused σκώψ with σκοπός, which Hesychius, *Lexicon* 4. 216, describes as a dance in which the dancers shaded their eyes (cp. ὑπόσκοπον χέρα, Aeschylus, Frag. 339 Nauck). The screech-owl dance (σκώψ) got its name, says Athenaeus ix. 45. p. 391 A, from the variety of motion displayed by the bird.

[1] For a new Fragment cf. appendix pp. 541 ff.

ΘΡΗΙΣΣΑΙ

The play derives its title from Thracian women, captives of Ajax, who formed the Chorus and had a like function with the sailors from Salamis in Sophocles' *Ajax*: to support with their sympathy the hero who had suffered the ignominy of defeat at the hands of Odysseus in the contest for the arms of Achilles, and after his suicide to bewail his death. Though captives, they even dared to protest against the inhumanity of Menelaüs, who would refuse burial to the body of their master. In Sophocles' play, Ajax killed himself on the stage and in solitude; in Aeschylus, his suicide was reported by a messenger, an eye-witness of the deed.

See Fragments 159, 194, 264.

41 (83)

ἔκαμπτε, τόξον ὥς τις ἐντείνων, ξίφος,
τοῦ χρωτὸς ἐνδιδόντος οὐδαμοῦ σφαγῇ,
πρὶν δὴ παροῦσα δαιμόνων ἔδειξέ τις

Scholiast on Sophocles, *Ajax* 833: φησὶν δὲ περὶ αὐτοῦ (τοῦ Αἴαντος) Αἰσχύλος ὅτι καὶ τὸ ξίφος ἐκάμπτετο, οὐδαμῇ ἐνδιδόντος τοῦ χρωτὸς τῇ σφαγῇ, τόξον ὥς τις ἐντείνων, πρὶν δή τις, φησί, παροῦσα δαίμων ἔδειξεν αὐτῷ κατὰ ποῖον μέρος δεῖ χρήσασθαι τῇ σφαγῇ. L. 1 restored by Hermann, l. 2 (as l. 1) by Hartung, l. 3 by Sidgwick. The vital part was τὰ περὶ (or κατὰ) τὴν μασχάλην according to the Scholiast on Sophocles and to Scholiasts TV on Ξ 404 (cp. Eustathius on *Iliad* 995. 1); the collar-bone or the side according to the Scholiast on Lycophron, *Alexandra* 455 (cp. *Ajax* 834). Wecklein reads ἔκαμπτε for Hermann's ἔκαμψε, and πρὶν δὴ παρών τις δαιμόνων <τὸ καίριον> ἔδειξεν αὐτῷ μασχάλης.

Back he bent his sword, as when a man bends a bow, for that his body offered no place to murderous death, until at last some goddess appeared and showed him [the vital spot].

The passage has reference to the legend that the body of Ajax, when a babe, having been wrapped by Heracles in his lion-skin, became invulnerable except at the spot where Heracles' quiver prevented the hide from touching it. According to Homer, Ajax was vulnerable, hence the legend was probably derived by Aeschylus from a Cyclic poet; and is certainly due to the desire to make Ajax equally invulnerable with Achilles. The sword with which Ajax slew himself had been given him by Hector.

ΙΕΡΕΙΑΙ

The Priestesses was made by Welcker the third member of a trilogy, whose preceding parts were the Θαλαμοποιοί and the Ἰφιγένεια. By others it has been associated with the Μυσοί and Τήλεφος, or with the Τήλεφος and Ἰφιγένεια. See Fragment 214.

42 (86)

στέλλειν ὅπως τάχιστα· ταῦτα γὰρ πατὴρ
Ζεὺς ἐγκαθίει[1] Λοξίᾳ θεσπίσματα.

Macrobius, *Saturnalia* v. 22. 13, Scholiast on Sophocles, *Oedipus Coloneus* 793.

[1] ἐγκαθιεῖ Schol. Soph., omitting θεσπίσματα.

Send with all speed; for these are the oracles that Father Zeus doth entrust unto Loxias.

43 (87)

εὐφαμεῖτε· μελισσονόμοι δόμον Ἀρτέμιδος πέλας
οἴγειν.

Aristophanes, *Frogs* 1274, with Scholiast.

Hold your peace! The bee-keepers are at hand to open the house of Artemis.

From Ἰφιγένεια according to Vater.

The Scholiast on Pindar, *Pythian* 4. 104 (60) says that "μέλισσαι is a term used primarily of the priestesses of Demeter, and by a misuse of language applied to all priestesses because of the purity of the animal." Coins of the Ephesian Artemis as early as the sixth century, and a Vatican statue of the same goddess, show the bee as an emblem.

ΙΞΙΩΝ

Ixion was famous in Greek tradition as the first man to shed kindred blood (Pindar, *Pythian* 2. 31, cp. *Eumenides* 718), and as the first to receive purification from the crime of murder. His father's name is variously reported, usually as Phlegyas, but Aeschylus made him the son of Antion. His mother was Perimela, the daughter of Amythaon. Under promise of rich wedding-gifts to Eïoneus (or Deïoneus), the father of Dia, he married her, and by her had a son, Peirithoüs. On his refusal to make over to his father-in-law the wedding-gifts due to him, Eïoneus took Ixion's horses as a pledge of payment; whereupon Ixion, pretending that he would submit himself to his good pleasure, sent for Eïoneus and caused him to fall into a fiery pit. For this offence he could obtain purification from neither man nor any god, until Zeus, showing himself a "gracious avenger" (Frag. 92 N.), took compassion on his suppliant, cleansed him of bloodshed, and even raised him to Olympus. There Ixion conceived a mad passion for the Queen of Heaven, and having besought her to yield to his desires, Zeus fashioned a cloud in the semblance of Hera. Ixion lay with the cloud, and from this union sprang the centaurs. In punishment for this impious crime, Zeus bound him to a wheel on which he whirls in an eternity of torment. To the above effect, in the main, Diodorus of Sicily, *Historical Library* iv. 69. 3.

The play probably followed the *Perrhaebides*, which took its name from the Chorus of women of Perrhaebia in Thessaly, which district, or the city of Gyrton in the same, Ixion had subjected to his rule. The theme of the first play may have been the deception and murder of Eïoneus; that of the *Ixion*, the purification of the murderer. The third member of the trilogy is unknown.

Fragment 182 has been referred to the *Ixion*.

44 (90)

βίου πονηροῦ θάνατος εὐκλεέστερος.

Stobaeus, *Anthology* iv. 53. 15 (Hense v. 1101), *Munich Anthology* 134 (cod. Augustanus-Monacensis 429).

Death hath a fairer fame than a life of toil.

Cp. Fragment 229 and Euripides, *Women of Troy* 637. πονηρός, lit. "laborious," may not yet have acquired the meaning "bad," "evil."

45 (91)

τὸν δ' ἡμίοπον [καὶ τὸν ἐλάσσονα][1]
ταχέως ὁ μέγας καταπίνει.

Athenaeus, *Deipnosophists* iv. 79. p. 182 c.

[1] [ ] Bothe.

But anon the long flute swallows up the half-holed.

Ixion's lesser offence—the murder of his father-in-law—is obscured by the enormity of his crime against Hera and against Zeus.

ἡμίοποι αὐλοί were the same as those used by boys (παιδικοί) and had higher tones than the τέλειοι. They were half as long as (perhaps) the ὑπερτέλειοι, which had the lowest pitch, and may have had no more than four holes. See Howard, *Harvard Studies in Classical Philology* iv. (1898).

ΙΦΙΓΕΝΕΙΑ

The theme of the play was probably the sacrifice of Iphigenia at Aulis, to which place she was brought by her mother at the instance of Agamemnon, who alleged his intention of betrothing his daughter to Achilles. The subject may thus have anticipated Sophocles' *Iphigenia* and Euripides' *Iphigenia at Aulis*

See Fragments 43, 130, 214.

46 (94)

οὔτοι γυναιξὶ <δεῖ>[1] κυδάζεσθαι· τί γάρ;

Scholiast on Sophocles, *Ajax* 722.

[1] < > Elmsley.

Surely it befits not to be reviled by women. How should it?

ΚΑΒΕΙΡΟΙ[1]

This drama, which has its name from the Chorus, is the earliest literary witness to the Cabiri, more often called the Great Gods in Samothrace and Lemnos, the most ancient and famous seats of their worship in the Aegean. Originally pre-Hellenic chthonian divinities, whose primal home was Phrygia, Phoenicia, or among the Pelasgians of Greece, their cult gradually accommodated itself to the religion of the peoples with which it came into contact; until, in the historical period, the Cabiri appear as daimones who foster vegetative life and protect seafaring folk, and whose Mysteries in course of time spread over the greater part of the Greek world.

Athenaeus, *Deipnosophists* x. 33. p. 428 F, declares that it was Aeschylus, not Euripides (in the *Alcestis*), who first introduced drunken people to the sight of the spectators of "tragedy"; and that this evil eminence was displayed in his *Cabiri*, in which play he represented Jason and his companions as drunk. Fragment 48 would seem to refer to the hospitable reception of the Argonauts by the Cabiri, who furnished them with an abundance of wine upon their landing at Lemnos, the first stopping-place of the Argo on its eastward voyage. The introduction of a drunken orgy has caused many scholars to regard the play as satyric rather than tragic. Whether pure tragedy may thus relax its gravity is a question that has been raised also in connexion with the Ὀστολόγοι of Aeschylus and the Σύνδειπνοι of Sophocles.

[1] Inscriptions and manuscripts vary between Κάβειροι and Κάβιροι.

The Scholiast on Pindar, *Pythian* 4. 303 (171), states that the names of the heroes of the Argonautic expedition were set forth in the Κάβειροι, as also in the Λήμνιαι of Sophocles.

Fragment 164 has been referred to this play.

47 (95)

ὄρνιθα δ' οὐ ποιῶ σε τῆς ἐμῆς ὁδοῦ.

Athenaeus, *Deipnosophists* ix. 15. p. 373 D.

But I take thee not as an omen of my journey.

48 (96)

μήτε κρωσσοὺς
μήτ' οἰνηροὺς μήθ' ὑδατηρούς[1]
λείπειν[2] ἀφνεοῖσι δόμοισιν.

Pollux, *Vocabulary* 10. 23 ; cp. Antiattacistes in Bekker, *Anecdota Graeca* 115. 3.

[1] ὑδρηροὺς Antiatt. [2] λιπεῖν : Blomfield.

Jars neither of wine nor of water shall fail in the houses of the rich.

Or λείπειν may be used imperatively.

49 (97)

ὄξους σπανίζειν δῶμα ‹μὲν ποιήσομεν›[1].

Plutarch, *Table Talk* ii. 1. 7. p. 632 F.

[1] ‹ › Stanley.

We shall make the house to be scant of vinegar.

The Cabiri jestingly threaten to produce so excellent, or so abundant, a vintage that either the Argonauts will drink so much that no wine will be kept to make vinegar; or that vinegar shall be poured out from the casks to give place to wine. If ὄξους means " ordinary wine," the meaning is that it will have to be thrown away for the better quality.

ΚΑΡΕΣ ἢ ΕΥΡΩΠΗ [1]

Europe, the protagonist in the drama bearing her name as an alternative title, in Fragment 50 tells of her carrying-off by the bull, of the three sons she bore to Zeus (Minos, Rhadamanthys, and Sarpedon), and of her anxiety as to the fate of her youngest, Sarpedon, whose warlike spirit had incited him to leave his home for Troy in order to render assistance to the city now attacked by the Achaeans.

The scene was Lycia, whither Europe had come from Crete together with her son. That the Chorus consisted of Carians, though Sarpedon was Prince of Lycia, may be due to the fact that (as Strabo, *Geography* xiv. 5. p. 675, informs us) the poets often included the Lycians among the Carians, who were the most famous of all the races in south-western Asia Minor. The confusion had the advantage of enabling the poet to reproduce the lamentations over the dead for which the Carians were celebrated.

Popular tradition was inconsistent as to the name of Sarpedon's mother. Aeschylus followed the Hesiodic version in preference to that of Homer, who calls her Laodamia. Nor was he disturbed by the Homeric genealogy, by which Sarpedon was made the grandson of Bellerophon on the mother's side. In the poet's time no one had yet sought, as did the mythographers later, to remove the difficulty, either by assuming two Sarpedons (one the son of Laodamia, the other the son of Europe) or by the notion that there was one Sarpedon, who had been permitted by his father Zeus to live through three generations.

[1] See appendix, p. 599.

The drama probably dealt with the reception of the news of the hero's death at the hands of Patroclus and with the arrival of his body in Lycia, borne thither by Sleep and Death (cp. Π 682). All other Homeric warriors who fell before Troy were buried in the Troad; Sarpedon alone had burial in his own land.

To this play have been ascribed Fragments **175, 231.**

50 (99)

ταύρῳ τε λειμὼν[1] ξένια πάμβοτος[2] παρῆν.
τοιόνδ' ἐμὲ[3] Ζεὺς κλέμμα πρεσβύτου πατρὸς
αὐτοῦ μένων ἄμοχθον[4] ἤνυσεν[5] λαβεῖν.
τί[6] οὖν τὰ πολλὰ κεῖνα; διὰ παύρων[7] λέγω·
γυνὴ θεῷ[8] μειχθεῖσα παρθένου σέβας
ἤμειψα,[9] παίδων δ' ἐζύγην[10] ξυνωνίᾳ.[11]
καὶ τρὶς[12] γοναῖσι[13] τοὺς γυναικείους πόνους
ἐκαρτέρησ'.[14] ἄρουρα δ' οὐκ[15] ἐμέμψατο
τὸ μὴ 'ξενεγκεῖν σπέρμα γενναίου πατρός.[16]
ἐκ τῶν μεγίστων δ' ἠρξάμην φυτευμάτων[17]
Μίνω τεκοῦσα . . . .
. . .[18] ‹δεύτερον δ' ἐγεινάμην›[19]

[1] ΛΙΜΩ. [2] ΠΑΜΠΟΔΟΣ.
[3] ΤΟΙΟΝΤΕΜΕΝ (ἐμὲ Schenkl).
[4] ἄμοχθος Wilam. [5] ΗΝΟΣΟΝ: Blass.
[6] ΤΕΙ: Wilam. [7] ΠΑΥΡΩ.
[8] ΘΕΟΥ. [9] ΕΜΕΙΨΑ. [10] ΕΣΥΓΗ.
[11] ΞΥΝΑΓΩΝΕΙ. [12] ΤΡΙΑ: Blass, Bücheler.
[13] ΓΩΝΕΙΣ. [14] ΕΚΑΡΤΕΡΗΣΑ.
[15] ΑΡΟΥΡΑΣ ΚΑΙ ΟΥΚ: Wecklein.
[16] ΓΕΝΑΙ ΠΑΤΡΟΣ. [17] ΕΡΞΑΜΗΝ ΦΥΔΕΥΜΑΤΩΝ.
[18] Lacuna, of some length, indicated by Bücheler.
[19] ‹ › Blass.

Ῥαδάμανθυν, ὅσπερ ἄφθιτος[1] παίδων ἐμῶν·
ἀλλ᾽ οὐκ ἐν αὐγαῖς[2] ταῖς ἐμαῖς ζόη σφ᾽ ἔχει[3],
τὸ μὴ παρόν[4] τε τέρψιν οὐκ ἔχει φίλοις[5]·
τρίτον δέ, τοῦ νῦν φροντίσιν[6] χειμάζομαι[7],
Σαρπηδόν᾽.[8] αἰχμὴ δ᾽ ἐξ Ἄρεως[9] καθίκετο.
κλέος[10] γὰρ ἥκειν[11] Ἑλλάδος λωτίσματα[12]
πάσης, ὑπερφέροντας[13] ἀλκίμῳ σθένει[14],
αὐχεῖν[15] δὲ Τρώων[16] ἄστυ πορθήσειν βίᾳ[17].
πρὸς οὗ δέδοικα[18] μή τι[19] μαργαίνων[20] δόρι[21]
ὑπέρτατον[22] δράσῃ τε καὶ πάθῃ κακόν.
λεπτὴ γὰρ ἐλπὶς ἥδ᾽ ἐπὶ ξύρου τ᾽ ἔβη[23]
μὴ πάντα παιδὸς[24] ἐκχέαι[25] πρὸς αἵματι[26].

Weil, *Un papyrus inédit de la bibliothèque de M. Ambroise Firmin-Didot* (1879); cp. Weil, *Revue de philologie* nouv. Sér. iv. (1880) 10-13, 145-150.

The papyrus is relatively late and exceedingly corrupt. The verses are without word-division. The restorations are Weil's except where otherwise stated.

1 ΡΑΔΑΜΑΝΘΟΝΩΣΠΕΡΑΦΘΙΔΟΣ.
2 ΑΛΛΑΚΕΜΑΓΑΙΣ: Gomperz, Kock.
3 ΖΟΑΣ ΕΧΕΙΝ.
4 ΠΑΡΩΝ.
5 ΦΙΛΟΥΣ.
6 ΦΡΟΝΤΙΖΕΙΝ.
7 ΧΕΙΜΑΖΕΤΑΙ: Bücheler.
8 ΣΑΛΦΗΔΟΝ.
9 ΑΙΑΧΜΗΣ ΔΕΞ ΑΡΕΟΣ.
10 ΚΔΕΟ ?
11 ΗΚΕΙΕΝ.
12 ΛΟΤΙΣΛΟΤΙΣΜΑΤΟΣ.
13 ΥΠΕΡΠΕΡΩΝΤΕΣ: Wilam.
14 ΑΛΚΙΜΟΥ ΣΤΕΝΗΣ: Gomperz, Bergk.
15 ΑΥΧΕΙ: Wilam.
16 ΤΡΩΑΝ.
17 ΠΑΡΘΗΣΗ ΒΙΟΝ.
18 ΔΕΔΩΚΑ.
19 ΤΕΙ.
20 ΜΑΡΓΑΙΑ (with Ν over Ι).
21 ΔΟΡΕΙ: Wecklein.
22 ΑΣΤΥ ΠΕΡΒΑΡΤΟΝ: Herwerden.
23 ΙΗΔΗΕΠΙΞΥΡΗΜΕΝΗΙ: Wilam.
24 ΠΑΙΣΑΣ: Bücheler.
25 ΕΚΧΕΩ.
26 ΑΙΜΑΤΕΙ.

And a lush meadow gave friendly welcome to the bull. In such wise, biding where he was,[1] did Zeus succeed in his unlaboured theft of me from my aged sire.[2] Why the whole tale? In few words I recount it all. A mortal woman, united to a god I lost the holiness of maidenhood, but I was joined in wedlock with him who owned his children equally with me.[3] Thrice in childbirth did I endure the pangs of womankind, and the field wherein he sowed complained not to bring forth the seed of a noble sire. First of these mighty implantings that I bare was Minos. . . .[4] Second, I brought forth Rhadamanthys,[5] he who of my sons is free from death; yet, though he lives, mine eyes behold him not—and to them that love, the absent bring no delight. Third was he for whom I am now sore distressed in heart, even Sarpedon; for Ares' warlike spirit hath laid hold of him. For it is famed abroad that the choicest flower of all Hellas has come, preëminent in valorous strength, and makes loud boast

[1] Since Europe declares that Zeus remained "where he was" (namely in Crete), she implies that her carrying-off had been effected by the bull as the agent of the god, and not (as in the ordinary version of the legend) by the god himself transformed into the animal.

[2] Phoenix.

[3] Since she bore no less than three children to Zeus, her relation to the god is conceived as that of formal marriage founded on his desire for offspring. *ξυνωνία παίδων*, lit. joint-ownership of children. Cp. *κοινὰν τεκέων τύχαν*, Euripides, *Ion* 1101.

[4] In the lacuna were described the deeds, honours, and death of Minos; but Minos, since Rhadamanthys alone is called immortal, was probably not made the judge of the dead.

[5] Rhadamanthys had been translated either to the Elysian Field (δ 563) or to the Islands of the Blest (Pindar, *Olympian* 2. 73).

that it will perforce destroy the city of the Trojans. It is for my son I fear, lest, raging with his lance, he may do and suffer[1] some surpassing ill. For slight is this my hope—and it standeth on the razor's edge—that by the bloody death of my child I may not lose my all.

[1] The desire to employ the favourite antithesis of δρᾶν and πάσχειν is responsible for the condensed phrase, in which the emphasis rests on πάθῃ (I fear lest, as he may work some evil upon his foes, so he may suffer some evil at their hands).

51 (100)

ἀλλ' Ἄρης φιλεῖ
ἀεὶ τὰ λῷστα πάντ' ἀπανθίζειν[1] στρατοῦ.

Stobaeus, *Anthology* iv. 10. 24 (Hense iv. 333).

[1] πάντα τἀνθρώπων: Kidd.

But Ares ever loves to pluck all the fairest flower of an armed host.

ΚΕΡΚΥΩΝ

A satyric play dealing with the story of Cercyon, son of Poseidon and king of Eleusis, who forced all passers-by to wrestle with him. Bacchylides 17. 26 says that Theseus " closed his wrestling-school."

52 (102)

ἀμφωτίδες τοι τοῖς ἐνωτίοις πέλας

Pollux, *Vocabulary* 10. 175.

Ear-coverings close to his ear-rings

ἀμφωτίδες were worn to protect the ears of wrestlers.

ΚΗΡΥΚΕΣ

The Heralds or *The Messengers* was a satyric play on an unknown subject; possibly connected with Heracles.

See Fragments 168, 170, 171, 178.

53 (109)

κατὰ τῆς σισύρνης τῆς λεοντείας ‹δορᾶς›[1]

Pollux, *Vocabulary* 10. 186.

[1] λεοντέας: λεοντείας δορᾶς Toup from Hesychius' λεόντειος δορά.

Down over the skin-coat of lion's hide

ΚΡΗΣΣΑΙ

The seer Polyidus of Corinth discovered the dead body of Glaucus, the lost son of Minos, and restored it to life by his skill in interpreting Apollo's oracle that had been made known to the father. The power to bring the child back alive—so the god declared—was to be given him who could find the most appropriate object to be compared to Minos' marvellous cow, which each day became in turn white, red, and black (cp. Frag. 54). The legend of Polyidus was the theme of Sophocles' *Seers*.

To *The Women of Crete* have been ascribed Fragments 165, 173.

54 (116)

λευκοῖς τε γὰρ μόροισι καὶ μελαγχίμοις
καὶ μιλτοπρέπτοις[1] βρίθεται ταὐτοῦ χρόνου[2].

Athenaeus, *Deipnosophists* ii. 36. p. 51 D; cp. Eustathius on *Iliad* 1254. 25.

[1] μιλτοπρέποις Athen. CE, μιλτοπρέπτοις Eust.
[2] χροιᾶ Eust.

For at the same season [the branch] is weighed down by mulberries, white and black and red.

ΛΕΩΝ

The Lion was a satyric play of unknown subject. The title may be derived from the Nemean lion overcome by Heracles.

55 (123)

ὁδοιπόρων[1] δήλημα, χωρίτης δράκων

Stephen of Byzantium, *Lexicon* 699. 13.

[1] ὁδοιπορῶν: Salmasius.

The bane of wayfarers, the serpent that haunts the place

ΛΥΚΟΥΡΓΟΣ

The satyric play of the Lycurgean trilogy.

56 (124)

κἀκ τῶνδ' ἔπινε βρῦτον ἰσχνανθὲν[1] χρόνῳ
κἀσεμνοκόμπει[2] τοῦτ' ἐν ἀνδρείᾳ στέγῃ†.

Athenaeus, *Deipnosophists* x. 67. p. 447 c.

[1] ἰσχναίνω: Blaydes.
[2] καὶ σεμνοκοπτει A: Lobeck and Dindorf.

And after this he drank beer thinned by age, and made thereof loud boast in the banquet-hall (?).

ΜΕΜΝΩΝ

According to the story in the *Aethiopis* of the Cyclic poet Arctinus of Miletus, as summarized by Proclus in his *Chrestomathy* 458, Achilles is informed by his mother Thetis that Memnon, the son of Eos, clad in full armour fashioned by Hephaestus, has come to the aid of the Trojans. Antilochus, the son of Nestor, is slain in battle by the Ethiopian prince, who in turn is slain by Achilles, whose mother begs of Zeus the boon of immortality for her son. Achilles routs the Trojans, bursts into the city, is killed by Paris and Apollo ; his body is borne to the ships by Ajax, while Odysseus keeps the Trojans at bay. Thetis, attended by the Muses and her sister Nereïds, arrives on the scene, bewails her son, whose body she takes from the funeral pyre and carries to the island of Leuce.

The trilogy consisted of *The* Μέμνων, *Ψυχοστασία, The Weighing of Souls* (the order is disputed), and a third play unknown, but probably dealing with the death of Achilles. In the *Ψυχοστασία* Zeus was represented as holding aloft the balance, in the scales of which were the souls of Achilles and Memnon, while beneath each stood Thetis and Eos, praying each for the life of her son. Comparing the passage in the *Iliad* (X 210), in which Zeus weighs the fates of Achilles and Hector, Plutarch (*How a Young Man ought to hear Poems* 2. p. 17 A) says that Aeschylus accommodated a whole play to this fable.

Fragments 155, 161, 181, 183 have been referred to the *Memnon*.

57 (127)

καὶ μὴν πελάζει καὶ καταψύχει, πνοὴ
ἄρκειος[1] ὡς ναύτῃσιν ἀσκευοις, μολών.

Eustathius on *Iliad* 1156. 18, Bekker, *Anecdota Graeca* 445. 18 (καὶ . . . ἄρκιος); cp. Hesychius, *Lexicon*: ἀσκεύοις· ψιλοῖς, ἀπαρασκεύοις (Αἰσχύλος Ἀγαμέμνονι: Μέμνονι Bergk; Hermann would insert ἀσκεύοις in a verse after *Agam.* 1324).

[1] ἄρκιος: Lobeck.

And lo, he draws near and his advance fills us with chilling fear, like a blast from the North that falls on sailors unprepared.

58 (128)

χαλκὸν ἀθέριστον[1] ἀσπίδος <τ'>[2] ὑπερτενῆ

Bekker, *Anecdota Graeca* 353. 11 (Αἰσχύλος Ἀγαμέμνονι: Μέμνονι Wellauer), Photius, *Lexicon* 42. 16 (Reitzenstein).

[1] ἀθέριτον *An. Gr.*, ἀθέρητον Phot.: Blomfield.
[2] < > M. Schmidt.

Bronze, unshorn (?) and stretched over the shield

Restoration and translation are wholly uncertain. The ancients were hopelessly confused between the words ἀθηρής, ἀθειρής, ἀτειρής, ἀτηρής, ἀθέρητος, ἀθέριτος. Possibly the bronze of a shield may be said to be "unshorn," "unconquered," since a weapon "shears off" what it strikes (cp. Euripides, *Suppliants* 716). Tovey, *Journal of Philology* v. (1878) 221, proposed to read, after *Seven against Thebes* 559, χαλκὸν ἀθέριστον· ἀσπίδος δ' ὑπερτενὴς | ἔξωθεν κτλ. Blomfield would put the verse after *Agam.* 897.

ΜΥΡΜΙΔΟΝΕΣ[1]

The Achilles-trilogy, the "tragic Iliad," consisting of the Μυρμιδόνες, Νηρεΐδες, Φρύγες ἢ Ἕκτορος λύτρα, dramatized (so far as this was appropriate by visible action or reported description) the chief

[1] See appendix, pp. 582, 590.

events of the Homeric story of the death of Patroclus, the slaying of Hector, and Priam's ransom of the body of his son.

See Fragments 155, 240, 263, 266.

59 (131)

τάδε μὲν λεύσσεις, φαίδιμ' Ἀχιλλεῦ,
δοριλυμάντους Δαναῶν μόχθους,
οὓς <προπεπωκὼς>[1] εἴσω κλισίας
<θάσσεις>;[2]

Harpocration, *Glossary of the Ten Attic Orators* 259. 11, explaining προπεπωκώς as having the meaning of προδεδωκώς; l. 1 Aristophanes, *Frogs* 992 with Scholiast.

[1] < > Heath. [2] < > Hermann.

Beholdest thou this, glorious Achilles, beholdest thou the distress wrought by the destructive lance upon the Danaans, whom thou hast betrayed, yet sittest idle within thy tent?

From the parodus of the Chorus of Myrmidons.

60 (132)

Φθιῶτ' Ἀχιλλεῦ,[1] τί ποτ', ἀνδροδάϊκτον ἀκούων
ἰὴ κόπον,[2] οὐ πελάθεις ἐπ' ἀρωγάν;

Aristophanes, *Frogs* 1264 with Scholiast.

[1] ἀχιλεῦ inferior MSS. [2] ἰήκοπον: Heath.

Lord of Phthia, Achilles! Why, oh why, when thou hearest the man-slaying
(Ah woe!) buffetings of war, dost thou not draw nigh to our rescue?

By the repetition of l. 2 in *Frogs* 1266, 1271, 1275, 1277, after other high-sounding dactylic measures, Euripides is here seeking (*inter alia*) to ridicule Aeschylus for his iteration of the refrain and his strange use of interjections. In the present instance κόπον yields an intelligible sense with ἀνδροδάϊκτον; in the other cases the word (and the entire verse) has no connexion with what precedes, being solely designed to mark the obscurity of Aeschylus' choral lyrics.

A later Scholiast on *Frogs* 1264 and on *Prom.* 441 ascribes the two verses to envoys, whose pleadings that Achilles enter the battle were received with inflexible silence.

61 (134)

ἐπάνδετος[1] δὲ ξουθὸς ἱππαλεκτρυὼν
στάζει, χυθέντων[2] φαρμάκων πολὺς πόνος.

Scholiast Venetus on Aristophanes, *Peace* 1177; l. 1 Scholiast Ravennas on *Frogs* 932.

[1] ἀπὸ δ' αὖτε Schol. *Peace*, ἐπὶ δ' αἰετὸς Schol. *Frogs*: Headlam. [2] κηρόθεν τῶν or κηροθέντων V: Blaydes.

The buff horse-cock fastened thereon, the laborious work of outpoured paints, is dripping.

When the Trojans set fire to a ship of the Greeks (in O 717 Hector attempts to burn that of Protesilaüs), the heat caused the melting of the paint of the figure (or picture) of a horse-cock, the emblem of the vessel. A horse-cock is pictured in Harrison and MacColl, *Greek Vase-Paintings* pl. viii.

62 (138)

Ἀντίλοχ', ἀποίμωξόν με τοῦ τεθνηκότος
τὸν ζῶντα μᾶλλον· τἀμὰ γὰρ διοίχεται.

Aristophanes, *Women in Parliament* 392 with Scholiast. The Scholiast ends the quotation with μᾶλλον, but, since Gataker, the following words are also generally ascribed to Aeschylus.

Antilochus, bewail me, the living, rather than him, the dead; for I have lost my all.

63 (139)

ὧδ'[1] ἐστὶ μύθων τῶν Λιβυστικῶν[2] κλέος[3],
πληγέντ' ἀτράκτῳ τοξικῷ τὸν αἰετὸν
εἰπεῖν ἰδόντα μηχανὴν[4] πτερώματος·
τάδ' οὐχ ὑπ' ἄλλων, ἀλλὰ τοῖς αὑτῶν πτεροῖς
ἁλισκόμεσθα.[5]

Scholiast on Aristophanes, *Birds* 807, 808, Suidas, *Lexicon* s.v. ταυτὶ μὲν ; l. 1 Pseudo-Diogenianus, *Proverbs* (*Paroemiographi Graeci* i. 180) ; ll. 4-5 *Birds* 808 and often in late writers : Dionysius of Halicarnassus, *On the Power of the Style of Demosthenes* 7, Philo of Alexandria, *On the Incorruptibility of the World* 14. 49 (Cohn and Reiter vi. 88), Galen, *On the Opinions of Hippocrates and Plato* iv (vol. v. 395), Aristeides, *On Rhetoric* 15 (ii. 17), Athenaeus, *Deipnosophists* xi. 86. p. 494 B, Eustathius on *Iliad* 632. 35.

[1] ὧδ' Pseudo-Diogen., ὡς δὲ Schol. Aristoph., ὅδ' Suid.
[2] Λιβυκῶν τὸ Pseudo-Diogen.
[3] λόγος Schol. Aristoph., Suid.
[4] τὴν μηχανὴν τοῦ Suid.
[5] ἁλισκόμεθα in most citations.

Even so is the Libyan fable famed abroad : the eagle, pierced by the bow-sped shaft, looked at the feathered device, and said, " Thus, not by others, but by means of our own plumage, are we slain."

Achilles has lost his friend Patroclus, who, by his consent and clad in his armour, fought to rescue the Greeks only to lose his life.

Compare Waller's " To a Lady singing a Song of his own Composing " :

That eagle's fate and mine are one,
Which, on the shaft that made him die,
Espy'd a feather of his own,
Wherewith he wont to soar so high.

64 (135)

σέβας δὲ μηρῶν ἁγνὸν[1] οὐκ ἐπῃδέσω[2],
ὦ δυσχάριστε τῶν πυκνῶν[3] φιλημάτων.

Athenaeus, *Deipnosophists* xiii. 79. p. 602 E, cp. Plutarch, *On Love* 5. p. 751 C; l. 2 Plutarch, *How to know a Flatterer from a Friend*, 19. 61 A.

[1] ἅγιον Athen. A: Canter. [2] οὐ κατῃδέσω Plut.
[3] πικρῶν Plut. 751 C, πυκνῶν 61 A.

No reverence hadst thou for the unsullied holiness of thy limbs, oh thou most ungrateful for my many kisses!

Fragments 64-66 are from the address of Achilles in the presence of the corpse of Patroclus, who had been slain by Hector (Π 821) and lay with his lower limbs uncovered. Achilles here mournfully urges against him the reproach that, in his forbidden advance against the Trojans, he had been heedless of the affection of his friend.

65 (136)

μηρῶν τε τῶν σῶν[1] εὐσεβὴς ὁμιλία[2]

[Lucian], *The Loves* 54.

[1] om. Ω.
[2] ὁμιλία Ω; after ὁμιλία, καλλίω ΩΓ, καλλίων TV (*i.e.* κλαίων), deleted by Winckelmann, Dobree.

And the chaste nearness of thy limbs

The Fragment was ascribed to Aeschylus by Porson.

66 (137)

καὶ μήν, φιλῶ γάρ, ἀβδέλυκτ' ἐμοὶ τάδε.

Bekker, *Anecdota Graeca* 321. 22, Suidas, *Lexicon* s.v. ἀβδέλυκτα, etc.

And yet—for that I love him—they are not repulsive to my sight.

ΜΥΣΟΙ

According to the common version of the legend, Telephus, son of Heracles and Auge, daughter of Aleüs of Tegea, being ignorant of his parents, was directed by an oracle to seek for them in Mysia, of which country Teuthras was ruler. Aristotle (*Poetics* 1460 a 32), however, referring to the fault that improbable incidents are sometimes set forth *within* a play (whereas they ought, if possible, to be external, as part of the fable) alludes to Telephus as having come speechless all the way from Tegea to Mysia, a taboo explicable only if he had incurred blood-guiltiness (cp. *Eumenides* 448). Telephus had, in fact, killed his maternal uncles.

Fragment 208 has been referred to *The Mysians.*

67 (143)

ἰὼ Κάϊκε Μύσιαί τ' ἐπιρροαί

Strabo, *Geography* xiii. 1. 70. p. 616 (wrongly ascribing the verse to the prologue of *The Myrmidons*, an error corrected by Pauw), Macrobius, *Saturnalia* v. 20. 16.

Hail, Caïcus and ye streams of Mysia!

68 (144)

ποταμοῦ Καΐκου χαῖρε πρῶτος ὀργεών,
εὐχαῖς δὲ σῴζοις[1] δεσπότας παιωνίαις.

Photius, *Lexicon* 344. 19, Suidas, *Lexicon* s.v. ὀργεῶνες.

[1] σῴζοις Phot., σώσεις Suid.

Hail, thou first priest of Caïcus' stream, by thy healing prayers mayest thou preserve thy lords!

69 (145 A)

εἶδον καλπάζοντας ἐν αἰχμαῖς.

Photius, *Lexicon* 113. 15 (Reitzenstein).

I saw them trotting (?) amid the spears.

ΝΕΑΝΙΣΚΟΙ

The Youths, the third play of the Lycurgus-trilogy, apparently has its name from the Edonians who celebrated the worship of Dionysus that had gained admission into the kingdom of Lycurgus despite the opposition of that prince.

See Fragments 179, 187, 193, 210, 256.

70 (146)

αὔρας[1] ὑποσκίοισιν[2] ἐν ψυκτηρίοις[3]

Athenaeus, *Deipnosophists* xi. 109. p. 503 c.

[1] σαύρας: Valckenaer.
[2] ὑποσκίοισιν C, ὑπηκόοισιν A.
[3] ψυκτηρίοις E, ψυκτηρίοισι C.

Breezes in cool, shady places

71 (149 A)

πρὸς δ' ἐπὶ τοῖς ἀμφιλαφῆ πήματ' ἔχων ἀθανάτων

Photius, *Lexicon* 102. 13 (Reitzenstein).

Besides, in addition to these, having the plenteous woes of the immortals

ΝΗΡΕΪΔΕΣ

Thetis, accompanied by her sister Nereïds, comes from the depths of the sea to enquire the cause of the lamentations of her son (cp. Σ 53 ff.). She finds Achilles by the dead body of Patroclus and promises to procure from Hephaestus new armour that he may take vengeance on Hector, who has been exulting over the death of Patroclus. The play probably contained a description of Achilles' new armour, his reconciliation with Agamemnon, and his combat with Hector, whose corpse was dragged in at the close.

See Fragments 158, 189.

72 (150)

δελφινοφόρον[1] πεδίον πόντου
διαμειψάμεναι

Scholiast on Euripides, *Women of Phoenicia* 209.

[1] δελφινόφορον M, δελφίνορον BCT, δελφίνηρον Pal. 343: Barnes.

Having crossed the plain of the sea, that bears dolphins

73 (153)

λεπτὸς δὲ σινδὼν ἀμφιβαλλέσθω χροΐ.

Herodianus Technicus, *Excerpts* 22. 31 (Hilgard).

Let fine linen be cast about his body.

74 (151)

ἐναροκτάντας δὲ φθογγ . . . κότος ὑψοῦ
τέλος ἀθανάτων ἀπολείψει

Hesychius, *Lexicon* s.v. ἐναροφόρος, states that ancient commentators compared χ 412: "for it is unholy to boast over slain men," and gives the meaning of the much mangled words as follows: ὁ δὲ ἐναροκτάντας θάνατός (θάνατον corr. Heinsius) μοι (μὴ corr. Musurus) ἐπικαυχώμενος τὸ ἐκ τῶν θεῶν τέλος ὑψοῦ ἀπολείψει (ἀπολέψει corr. Musurus), τὰ τῶν ἀθανάτων ὕψη, καὶ ἐπὶ τοὺς ἐχθροὺς ἥξει. Sidgwick read ἐναροκτάντας δὲ Φόνος κόμποις | ἔγκοτος ὑψοῦ | τέλος κτλ. "Death, the spoiler and slayer, angry at boastings, will quit the company of the immortals on high" (?).

75 (152)

κάμακος δ' ἱεὶς[1] [κάμακος][2] γλωχῖνα δίκρουν[3]

Scholiast on Pindar, *Nemean* 6. 85 (53).

[1] εἶσι: Heimsoeth. [2] [ ] Hermann.
[3] διπλάσιον: Hermann.

Hurling the shaft with forked point

NIOBH [1]

The place and progress of the action of this famous drama cannot be determined with certainty. Apart from the title-heroine, the only person known to participate in the action is Tantalus, the father of Niobe—himself, like his daughter, destroyed because of evil pride engendered by great good fortune. Niobe, according to Homer (*Ω*602 ff.), had vaunted herself a more prolific mother than Leto, whose two children, Apollo and Artemis, therefore slew her seven sons and seven daughters. From Fragment 81 it has been inferred that the scene remained Thebes throughout the play. Since it is expressly reported that Sophocles in his *Niobe* made the mother return to her native Lydia after the destruction of her

[1] See appendix, p. 556.

children in Thebes, it is likely that this transference of the place of action from Thebes to Lydia was not anticipated by Aeschylus.—The older poet gives no hint as to the reason for the calamity visited by Zeus upon Amphion, Niobe's husband and his own son.

Sources other than the text inform us that Aeschylus gave Niobe fourteen children, a number adopted by Euripides and Aristophanes ; whereas, apart from other variations in the tradition, Homer states that they were twelve, Hesiod twenty, equally divided as to sex.—Until the third part of the play Niobe sat speechless upon the tomb of her dead offspring, apparently the most celebrated instance of the dramatic device of silence often employed by Aeschylus, and for which he is ridiculed by Euripides in Aristophanes, *Frogs* 911.

It has been disputed whether the title refers only to the one play *Niobe*, or whether, like *Prometheus*, it was both a collective designation of an entire trilogy and also the name of a single drama ; in any case, as to the dramas presented at the same time we have no information. Welcker sought to establish the group Τροφοί (distinct from *Διονύσου τροφοί*), Νιόβη, Προπομποί. R. J. Walker finds a trilogy in Καλλιστώ, Αταλάντη, Νιόβη on the ground that all the persons thus named suffered metamorphosis, and that Artemis was prominent in each member of the group. From Aristotle (*Poetics* 18. 1456 a 16) it would seem that Aeschylus did not, like some playwrights, deal with the whole story of Niobe. There is no indication whether or not Aeschylus adopted the legend that Niobe was turned into stone.

Fragments 197, 227, 240 have been ascribed to the *Niobe*.

76 (155)

Ἴστρος τοιαύτας παρθένους[1] ἐξεύχεται[2]
τρέφειν ὅ θ' ἁγνὸς Φᾶσις[3].

Choeroboscus (41. 10) on Hephaestion's *Handbook of Metres* 7 (Consbruch 3. 15).

[1] οἶστρος τοιαύτης παρθένου Heph. inferior MSS.

[2] l. 1 is often cited by itself, generally with λοχεύεται, sometimes with μαιεύεται or μνηστεύεται.

[3] ἐξεύχεται . . . Φᾶσις only in Choeroboscus.

Maidens such as these Ister and pure Phasis claim to breed.

77 (156)

. . . θεὸς μὲν αἰτίαν φύει βροτοῖς
ὅταν κακῶσαι δῶμα παμπήδην θέλῃ.

Plato, *Republic* ii. 380 A, whence Eusebius, *Preparation for the Gospel* xiii. 3. 643 C; without mention of the poet's name: Plutarch, *How a Young Man ought to hear Poems* 2. 17 B, *On Common Conceptions against the Stoics* 14. 1065 E.

God planteth in mortal men the cause of sin whensoever he wills utterly to destroy a house.

78 (157)

ἐφημένη[1]
τάφον τέκνοις ἐπῴζε[2] τοῖς τεθνηκόσιν.

Hesychius, *Lexicon* s.v. ἐπώζειν (he took the passage to mean that Niobe sat over her dead children as a hen sits on her eggs—an interpretation still current).

[1] ἐφιμένη: Musurus. [2] ἔπωζε: Nauck.

Seated on their tomb she made lament over her dead children.

79 (158)

σπείρω δ' ἄρουραν δώδεχ' ἡμερῶν ὁδόν,
Βερέκυντα χῶρον, ἔνθ' Ἀδραστείας ἕδος
Ἴδη[1] τε μυκηθμοῖσι καὶ βρυχήμασιν
πρέπουσι[2] μήλων, πᾶν δ' ὀρεχθεύει[3] πέδον.

Strabo, *Geography* xii. 7. 18. p. 580; σπείρω . . . χῶρον Plutarch, *On Banishment* 10. 603 A, *That a Philosopher ought chiefly to converse with Great Men* 3. 778 B.

[1] ἴδης: Casaubon.
[2] βρέμουσι: H. L. Ahrens.
[3] ὀρεχθεῖ ux, ἐρέχθει Cglrvw, ἐρέχθεον Dhi: Headlam.

I sow a field twelve days' journey wide, even the Berecynthian land, where Adrastea's seat and Ida resound with lowing oxen and bleating sheep, and the whole plain roars.

Spoken by Tantalus. The words of Fragment 80 have regard to the overthrow of his house and followed close upon those of Fragment 79.

80 (159)

οὑμὸς δὲ πότμος[1] οὐρανῷ κυρῶν ἄνω
ἔραζε πίπτει καί με προσφωνεῖ τάδε·
" γίγνωσκε τἀνθρώπεια μὴ σέβειν ἄγαν."

Plutarch, *On Banishment* 10. 603 A.

[1] θυμὸς δέ ποθ' ἁμὸς: Porson.

My fate, that dwelt aloft in Heaven, now falleth to earth and saith to me " Learn not to esteem human things overmuch."

81 (160)

καὶ δόμους Ἀμφίονος
καταιθαλώσω πυρφόροισιν αἰετοῖς.

Aristophanes, *Birds* 1247-1248.

And to ashes will I burn the house of Amphion by my fire-bearing eagles.

The eagle is *Iovis armiger, minister fulminis.* Amphion's death was variously explained, but apparently this is the only place where it is ascribed to Zeus. κατηθάλωσε "burned to ashes" is a probable conjecture of E. A. J. Ahrens.

82 (161)

μόνος θεῶν γὰρ[1] Θάνατος οὐ δώρων ἐρᾷ,
οὐδ'[2] ἄν τι θύων οὐδ'[2] ἐπισπένδων ἄνοις[3],
οὐδ' ἔστι βωμὸς[4] οὐδὲ παιωνίζεται·
μόνου δὲ Πειθὼ δαιμόνων ἀποστατεῖ.

Stobaeus, *Anthology* iv. 51. 1 (Hense v. 1066) in cod. Sambuci ; ll. 1-3 Scholiasts AB on *Iliad* I 158 (cp. Eustathius on *Iliad* 744. 3) ; l. 1 Aristophanes, *Frogs* 1392, Scholiast on Sophocles, *Electra* 139, and on Euripides, *Alcestis* 55, Suidas, *Lexicon* s.v. θανατῶν, μόνος θεῶν, πάγκοινος.

[1] γὰρ θεῶν Schol. Soph. Eur., θεῶν γε Suid. s.v. πάγκοινος, γὰρ om. Suid. s.v. μόνος θεῶν, Eust.
[2] οὔτ' . . . οὔτ' Stob., οὐδ' . . . οὐδ' Schol. *Il.*, Eust.
[3] ναοῖς Stob., λάβοις Schol. *Il.*, Eust. : Dobree.
[4] οὐ βωμός ἐστιν Stob., οὐδ' ἔστι βωμὸς Schol. *Il.*, Eust.

For, alone of gods, Death loves not gifts ; no, not by sacrifice, nor by libation, canst thou aught avail with him ; he hath no altar nor hath he hymn of praise ; from him, alone of gods, Persuasion stands aloof.

83 (162)

οἱ θεῶν ἀγχίσποροι
οἱ Ζηνὸς ἐγγύς, ὧν κατ' Ἰδαῖον πάγον[1]
Διὸς πατρῴου βωμός ἐστ' ἐν αἰθέρι,
κοὔπω σφιν ἐξίτηλον αἷμα δαιμόνων.

Plato, *Republic* iii. 391 E; cp. Strabo, *Geography* xii. 8. 21. p. 580.

[1] ὧν κατ' Ἰδαῖον πάγον Plato, οἷς ἐν Ἰδαίῳ πάγῳ Strabo.

The kindred of the gods, men near to Zeus, whose is the altar of Zeus, their sire, high in clear air on Ida's hill, and in their veins not yet hath ceased to flow the blood divine.

Spoken by Niobe, says Strabo.

ΞΑΝΤΡΙΑΙ

The subject of this play is the rejection of the newly instituted worship of Dionysus either by Pentheus or by the daughters of Minyas. The Scholiast on *Eumenides* 24 states that the death of Pentheus took place, in the Ξάντριαι, on Mt. Cithaeron; and Philostratus (*Images* 3. 18) describes a picture in which the mother and aunts of Pentheus rend asunder (ξαίνουσι) the body of the unbelieving prince. On the other hand, Aelian (*Historical Miscellanies* 3. 42, cp. Ovid, *Metamorphoses* 14. 32 ff.) relates that Leucippe, Arsippe, and Alcithoë, the daughters of Minyas, out of love for their husbands, held themselves aloof from the orgiastic rites of Dionysus and attended to their weaving (in which case Ξάντριαι might yield the meaning "Wool-Carders") and to punish their obstinacy, the god brought madness upon the sisters, so that they tore to pieces the son of Leucippe; in consequence of which deed of blood they were pursued by the Maenads.—Hera appeared in the play in the guise of a priestess begging alms (Fragment 84); and Bacchic frenzy was incorporated as Lyssa (Fragment 85). By some the drama is regarded as satyric.

See Fragments 184, 197, 210.

84 (168)

ὀρεσσιγόνοισι
νύμφαις κρηνιάσιν κυδραῖσι θεαῖσιν ἀγείρω
Ἰνάχου Ἀργείου ποταμοῦ παισὶν βιοδώροις.

Scholiast on Aristophanes, *Frogs* 1344, Diogenes, *Letters* 34. 2; l. 3 Plato, *Republic* ii. 381 D.

νύμφαι ὀρεσιγόνιαι (ὀρεσιγόνιοι V) θεαῖσιν ἀγείρω Ἰνάχου Ἀργείου ὑπὸ ποταμοῦ κτλ. Schol. Aristoph.; (Ἥραν) νύμφαις κρήναισιν κυδραῖς ἀγείρουσαν Ἰνάχου Ἀργείαις . . . βιοδώροις Diog.: ὀρεσσιγόνοισι νύμφαις κρηνιάσιν Meineke, κυδραῖσι Dindorf.

For the nymphs of the springs, the glorious goddesses mountain-born, I beg a dole, even for the life-giving children of Inachus, the Argive river.

85 (169)

ἐκ ποδῶν δ' ἄνω
ὑπέρχεται σπαραγμὸς εἰς ἄκρον κάρα,
κέντημα Λύσσης,[1] σκορπίου βέλος λέγω.

Photius, *Lexicon* 326. 22, Suidas, *Lexicon* s.v. ὀκτώπουν.

[1] γλώσσης: Lobeck.

From the feet up to the crown of the head steals a spasm, the stab of Frenzy, aye, the scorpion's sting.

Spoken by Lyssa.

86 (171)

κάμακες πεύκης οἱ πυρίφλεκτοι

Pollux, *Vocabulary* 10. 117.

Shafts of a pine tree ablaze with fire.

87 (170)

ἃς οὔτε πέμφιξ ἡλίου προσδέρκεται
οὔτ' ἀστερωπὸν ὄμμα[1] *Λητῴας κόρης.*

Galen, *Commentary on Hippocrates' Epidemics* **vi, vol.** xvli. 1. 880.

[1] ἀστέρων στόμα : Bentley.

[Women] upon whom looketh neither the sun's flashing ray nor the starry eye of Leto's child.

Possibly from a description of the Maenads, whose appearance is represented as equally strange with that of the daughters of Phorcys, upon whom "neither doth the sun with his beams look down, nor ever the nightly moon" (*Prom.* 796). Hecate, a moon-goddess, is here identified with Artemis.

ΟΙΔΙΠΟΥΣ

The second play of the *Oedipodea* : Λάϊος, Οἰδίπους, Ἑπτὰ ἐπὶ Θήβας, Σφίγξ. Of the Λάϊος no certain remains are attested.

See Fragments 164, 186, 201, 214, 229.

88 (173)

ἐπῆμεν[1] τῆς ὁδοῦ τροχήλατον
σχιστῆς κελεύθου τρίοδον, ἔνθα συμβολὰς
τριῶν κελεύθων[2] Ποτνιάδων ἠμείβομεν.

Scholiast on Sophocles, *Oedipus Tyrannus* 733.

[1] ἐπείημεν (ἐπηειμεν G): Brunck. [2] κέλευθον: Brunck.

We were coming on our journey to the place from which three highways part in branching roads, where we crossed the junction of the triple roads at Potniae.

Οἰδίπους Valckenaer, Γλαῦκος Ποτνιεύς Hermann.

ΟΠΛΩΝ ΚΡΙΣΙΣ

The Award of the Arms, the first play of the Ajax-trilogy, dealt with the contest between Ajax and Odysseus for the arms of Achilles after that hero's death. From Fragment 90 it appears that each of the chieftains set forth his pretensions and indulged in detraction of his rival. According to a verse of the *Odyssey* (λ 547, rejected by Aristarchus) the Trojans were the judges; according to the *Aethiopis* of Arctinus the award was made by Trojan captives; according to Lesches' *Little Iliad* the decision in favour of Odysseus resulted from the fact that a Trojan, overheard by Achaean scouts under the walls of the city, pronounced that warrior more redoubtable than Ajax. The constitution of the Chorus is uncertain. Fragment 89 is cited as addressed to Thetis by some one who called upon the Nereïds to make the award. Welcker held that Trojan captives formed the choral group.

Fragment 189 has been referred to the play.

89 (174)

δέσποινα πεντήκοντα Νηρῄδων κορᾶν

Scholiast on Aristophanes, *Acharnians* 883.

Queen of Nereus' fifty daughters

90 (175)

ἀλλ' Ἀντικλείας ἆσσον ἦλθε Σίσυφος,
τῆς σῆς λέγω τοι μητρός, ἥ σ' ἐγείνατο.

Scholiast on Sophocles, *Ajax* 190.

But Sisyphus drew nigh unto Anticleia—aye, unto thy mother, I say, who bare thee.

Ajax calls Odysseus a bastard of Sisyphus, the crafty knave.

91 (177)

τί γὰρ καλὸν ζῆν ᾧ βίος[1] λύπας φέρει;

Stobaeus, *Anthology* iv. 53. 24 (Hense v. 1104).

[1] ζῆν βίον ὃς : Nauck.

For wherein is life sweet to him who suffers grief?

Spoken by Ajax.

92 (176)

ἁπλᾶ γάρ ἐστι τῆς ἀληθείας ἔπη.

Stobaeus, *Anthology* 3. 11. 4 (Hense iii. 431).

For simple are the words of truth.

93 (178 A)

καὶ διὰ πνευμάτων θερμὸν ἄησιν ὕπνον.

Photius, *Lexicon* 39. 7 (Reitzenstein).

And through his lungs he breathes fevered sleep.

ΟΣΤΟΛΟΓΟΙ

The Bone-Gatherers was a tragedy, if, as seems not improbable, the Chorus consisted of the relatives of the suitors of Penelope who came to exact vengeance from Odysseus for the slaughter of their kin and to collect their bones after their bodies had been burned on the funeral pyre (cp. ω 417). On this supposition, Fragments 94 and 95 were spoken by Odysseus standing by the corpses of the suitors and recounting the insults he had received at their hands.

A counter interpretation, regarding the play as satyric, derives the title from the hungry beggars in the palace at Ithaca, who collected the bones hurled at them by the suitors (cp. υ 299, σ 394).

94 (179)

Εὐρύμαχος οὗτος ἄλλος[1] οὐδὲν ἥσσονας[2]
ὕβριζ᾽ ὑβρισμοὺς οὐκ ἐναισίους[3] ἐμοί·
ἦν μὲν γὰρ αὐτῷ σκοπὸς[4] ἀεὶ τοὐμὸν[5] κάρα,
τοῦ δ᾽ ἀγκυλητοῖς κοσσάβοις[6] ἐπίσκοπος[7]
†ἐκτεμὼν[8] ἡβῶσα χεὶρ ἐφίετο.

Athenaeus, *Deipnosophists* xv. 5. p. 667 c.

[1] οὐκ ἄλλος A : Hermann. [2] ἧσσον A : Musurus.
[3] αἰνεσίους A : Porson, Coray. [4] κότταβος : Dobree.
[5] τοῦ μὲν A : Petit. [6] ἀγκυλητοῦ κοσσάβιός : Dobree.
[7] ἐστιν σκοπὸς A : Kaibel.
[8] Headlam conj. ὡς ἐκτομῶν "as of javelins" : οὗ ἐκτενῶς Schweighäuser.

Eurymachus here, another, brought no less unseemly outrage upon me; for he continually made my head his mark, and at it, with bent-armed casts, his vigorous hand kept aiming true.

The poet has in mind that form of the cottabus-game (κότταβος or κόσσαβος) in which each of the players so bent his arm and turned his wrist as to aim the wine left in the bottom of his cup at the head of a small bronze figure (μάνης) placed in a saucer (πλάστιγξ).

95 (180)

ὅδ᾽ ἐστὶν ὅς ποτ᾽ ἀμφ᾽ ἐμοὶ βέλος
γελωτοποιόν, τὴν κάκοσμον οὐράνην,
ἔρριψεν οὐδ᾽ ἥμαρτε· περὶ δ᾽ ἐμῷ κάρᾳ
πληγεῖσ᾽ ἐναυάγησεν ὀστρακουμένη,
χωρὶς μυρηρῶν[1] τευχέων πνέουσ᾽ ἐμοί.

Athenaeus, *Deipnosophists* i. 30. p. 17 c; cp. Eustathius on *Odyssey* 1828. 28; τὴν κάκοσμον . . . κάρᾳ Sophocles, Frag. 565.

Ascribed to Aeschylus by Athenaeus, to this play by Welcker.

[1] μυραρῶν C.

There is the man who once hurled at me (nor did he miss his aim) a missile that caused them all to laugh, even the ill-smelling chamber-pot; crashed about my head, it was shivered into shards, breathing upon me an odour unlike that of unguent-jars.

ΠΑΛΑΜΗΔΗΣ

Palamedes, son of Nauplius, was the human, as Prometheus was the divine, inventor or discoverer of arts and sciences useful to man; and to both were ascribed the introduction of the alphabet, number, and the skill to know the periods of the stars. Later epic and the tragic drama were especially concerned with the manner of his death at Troy. According to the legend probably preferred by the tragedians, his violent end was due to the ancient enmity of Odysseus, whose feigned madness to escape participation in the Trojan war had been detected by the ingenuity of Palamedes. One account had him drowned by Odysseus and Diomedes; another had him lured into a well in search of treasure and then crushed with stones. More famous was the story that Odysseus, in concert with Agamemnon (to whom Palamedes, as leader of the peace party, was opposed) concocted a plot to show that their adversary purposed to betray the Greeks: gold was hidden in his tent, likewise a letter purporting to be written to him by Priam, on the discovery of which by the people he was stoned to death by Odysseus and Diomedes.

Nauplius, failing to obtain justice from the murderers of his son, took vengeance on the Greek commanders by raising deceptive fire-signals on the Capherean cliffs in Euboea at the time of their homeward voyage.

Fragment 252 has been referred to this play.

96 (182)

καὶ ταξιάρχους χἀκατοντάρχους[1] στρατῷ
ἔταξα, σῖτον δ' εἰδέναι διώρισα,
ἄριστα, δεῖπνα, δόρπα θ'[2] αἱρεῖσθαι τρίτα[3].

Athenaeus, *Deipnosophists* i. 19. p. 11 D; σῖτον . . . τρίτα Eustathius on *Odyssey* 1791. 42; l. 3 often in later writers.

[1] ταξιάρχας καὶ στρατάρχας καὶ ἑκατοντάρχας: Porson (-ους for -ας Wilam.). [2] δ' Athen.

[3] τρία Schol. on *Iliad* in Cramer, *Anecdota Graeca Parisiensia* iii. 7. 15, Eustathius on *Iliad* 1358. 4, on *Odyssey* 1432. 5, 1791. 42.

Both commanders of regiments[1] and centurions did I appoint for the host, and I determined their knowledge of different foods,[2] and for them to take breakfast, dinner, and supper third.

Spoken by Palamedes (Athenaeus).

[1] At Athens ταξίαρχοι commanded the troops raised from each of the tribes.

[2] It is uncertain whether the mention of food refers to soldiers' rations or has regard to a distinct invention on the part of Palamedes. Possibly εἰδέναι is corrupt.

97 (181)

τίνος κατέκτας ἕνεκα παῖδ' ἐμὸν βλάβης;

Scholiast A on *Iliad* Δ 319.

By reason of what injury hast thou slain my son?

Nauplius reproaches Odysseus for the death of his son.

ΠΕΝΘΕΥΣ

The *Pentheus* anticipated Euripides' *Bacchae*, in which play Dionysus, angered at the refusal of Pentheus, ruler of Thebes, to recognize his godhead, inspired with frenzy the prince's mother Agave and her sisters. In their madness the women tore Pentheus to pieces, and Agave bore his head in triumph in the delusion that it was that of a lion. See *Eumenides* 26, and cp. Fragment 197.

98 (183)

μηδ' αἵματος πέμφιγα πρὸς πέδῳ βάλῃς.

Galen, *Commentary on Hippocrates' Epidemics* vi, vol. xvii. 1. 880.

Nor do thou cast a drop of blood upon the ground.

ΠΕΡΡΑΙΒΙΔΕΣ

The Women of Perrhaebia belongs with the *Ixion* (see p. 410). Compare Fragments 182, 192, 222.

99 (184)

ποῦ μοι τὰ πολλὰ δῶρα κἀκροθίνια;
ποῦ χρυσότευκτα κἀργυρᾶ σκυφώματα;

Athenaeus, *Deipnosophists* xi. 99. p. 499 A, Eustathius on *Odyssey* 1775. 22.

Where are my many promised gifts and spoils of war? Where are my gold and silver cups?

Eïoneus here, as in Frag. 100, demands the bridal-gifts promised him by Ixion.

100 (185)

ἀργυρηλάτοις
κέρασι χρυσᾶ στόμια προσβεβλημένοις

Athenaeus, *Deipnosophists* xi. 51. p. 476 c, Eustathius on *Iliad* 917. 63.

With silver-mounted drinking-horns, fitted with golden mouthpieces

101 (186)

τέθνηκεν οἰκτρῶς[1] *χρημάτων ἀπαιόλῃ.*

Eustathius on *Iliad* 352. 34, Favorinus, *Lexicon* s.v. ἀπαιόλῃ.

[1] *αἰσχρὸς* Eust., *αἰσχρῶς* Fav.: F. W. Schmidt.

He has perished piteously, defrauded of his own.

ΠΗΝΕΛΟΠΗ

102 (187)

ἐγὼ γένος μέν εἰμι Κρὴς ἀρχέστατον.

Etymologicum Genuinum s.v. ἀοιδοιέστατον; cp. *Etymologicum Magnum* 31. 6.

I am a Cretan of most ancient lineage.

Odysseus, on the occasion of his first conversation with Penelope after his return, fabricates the tale that he is a Cretan, the grandson of Minos (τ 180). In ξ 199 he tells Eumaeus that he is a Cretan, the son of Castor.

ΠΡΟΜΗΘΕΙΣ

The Medicean Catalogue of Aeschylus' plays names three entitled Προμηθεύς (δεσμώτης, λυόμενος, πυρφόρος); a fourth, Προμηθεὺς πυρκαεύς (Pollux, *Vocabulary* 9. 156, 10. 64) was probably the satyric drama of the trilogy Φινεύς, Πέρσαι, Γλαῦκος (πόντιος) produced in 472 B.C. From the Scholiast on *Prom.* 511 it is to be inferred that the Λυόμενος followed the Δεσμώτης. The theme and place of the Πυρφόρος are still disputed: (1) it is another name for the Πυρκαεύς; (2) it preceded the Δεσμώτης in the trilogy and dealt with the Titan's theft of fire—in this sense, it is the *Fire-Bringer* or *Fire-Giver*; (3) as the *Fire-Bearer*, it followed the Λυόμενος, and described the inauguration of the Προμήθεια, the Athenian festival at which torch-races were held in honour of the Titan, now become the god of the potter-guild. Some, who follow Canter in identifying the Πυρφόρος with the Πυρκαεύς, maintain that it was the satyric drama, and dealt with the Attic worship of the god. A satyr-play in the Prometheus-trilogy is unknown.

The extract from the *Literary History*, appended to the *Life* of the poet in the Medicean and many other manuscripts, says that "some of Aeschylus' plays, as those entitled *Prometheus* (οἱ Προμηθεῖς), dealt only with gods." The singular Προμηθεύς may at times be a collective title; but it generally indicates a particular play whose more exact designation was unknown or neglected. Late writers sometimes cite, as from the Δεσμώτης, passages not appearing in that play: these should, if possible, be located among the other dramas of the group rather than forced into the text of the extant tragedy.

103 (188)

πολλοῖς γάρ ἐστι κέρδος ἡ σιγὴ βροτῶν[1].

Scholiast on Aristeides, *In Defence of the Four Statesmen*, vol. iii. 501. 17 (ἐν Προμηθεῖ δεσμώτῃ).

[1] βροτῶν in Dindorf's edition, βροτοῖς in Frommel's.

For silence is gain to many of mankind.

Cp. *Agam.* 548, Frag. 118.

ΠΡΟΜΗΘΕΥΣ ΛΥΟΜΕΝΟΣ

Fragments 104, 105, 106 are from the parodus of the Chorus of Titans, now released from Tartarus by the clemency of Zeus. To them Prometheus describes his tortures (Frag. 107) and his benefits to man (Frag. 108). In his search for the golden apples of the Hesperides, Heracles, having come to the Caucasus, where Prometheus is confined, receives from him directions concerning his course through the land of the peoples in the farthest north (Frag. 109–111) and the perils to be encountered on his homeward march after slaying Geryon in the farthest west (Frag. 112, cp. 37). Frag. 113–114 refer to Heracles' shooting of the eagle that fed on the vitals of the Titan.

See Fragments 204, 208, 209, 230, 261.

104 (190)

ἥκομεν . . .
τοὺς σοὺς ἄθλους τούσδε, Προμηθεῦ,
δεσμοῦ τε πάθος τόδ' ἐποψόμενοι[1].

Arrian, *Voyage in the Euxine* 99. 22, Anonymous in Müller, *Fragmenta Historicorum Graecorum* v. 184.

[1] ἐσοψόμενοι Arrian.

We have come to look upon these thy ordeals, Prometheus, and the affliction of thy bonds.

105 (192)

φοινικόπεδόν τ' ἐρυθρᾶς ἱερὸν
χεῦμα θαλάσσης
†χαλκοκέραυνόν τε παρ' Ὠκεανῷ
λίμνην[1] παντοτρόφον Αἰθιόπων,
ἵν' ὁ παντόπτης[2] Ἥλιος αἰεὶ
χρῶτ' ἀθάνατον κάματόν θ' ἵππων
θερμαῖς ὕδατος
μαλακοῦ προχοαῖς [τ'][3] ἀναπαύει.

Strabo, *Geography* i. 2. 27. p. 33.

[1] λίμναν: Dindorf.

[2] παντεπόπτας: παντόπτας Tyrwhitt, παντόπτης Dindorf.

[3] [ ] Editors.

[Leaving] the Erythraean Sea's sacred stream red of floor, and the mere by Oceanus, the mere of the Aethiopians . . that giveth nourishment unto all, where the all-seeing Sun doth ever, in warm outpourings of soft water, refresh his undying body and his wearied steeds.

Cited by Strabo as proof that the ancient Greeks designated as Aethiopia all the southern countries toward the ocean. In l. 3 χαλκοκέραυνον is credited with the meaning "flashing like bronze." But κεραυνός is not used for στεροπή (χαλκοστέροπον Weil, χαλκομάραυγον Hermann; but neither satisfies).

106 (191)

τῇ[1] μὲν δίδυμον χθονὸς Εὐρώπης
μέγαν ἠδ'[2] Ἀσίας τέρμονα Φᾶσιν[3]

Arrian, *Voyage in the Euxine* 99. 22, Anonymous in Müller, *Fragmenta Historicorum Graecorum* v. 184.

[1] πῇ: Editors. [2] ἠ δ' Arr., τῇ δ' Anon.
[3] Φᾶσιν ποταμόν Anon.

Here Phasis, the mighty common boundary of the land of Europe and Asia

107 (193)

Titánum suboles, sócia nostri sánguinis,
generáta Caelo, aspícite religatum ásperis
vinctúmque saxis, návem ut horrisonó freto
noctém paventes tímidi adnectunt návitae.
Satúrnius me síc infixit Iúppiter
Iovísque numen Múlciberi adscivít manus.
hos ílle cuneos fábrica crudeli ínserens
perrúpit artus. quá miser sollértia
transvérberatus cástrum hoc Furiarum íncolo.
iam tértio me quóque funestó die

tristi ádvolatu adúncis lacerans únguibus
Iovís satelles pástu dilaniát fero.
tum íecore opimo fárta et satiata ádfatim
clangórem fundit vástum, et sublime ávolans[1]
pinnáta cauda nóstrum adulat sánguinem.
cum véro adesum inflátu renovatum ést iecur,
tum rúrsum taetros ávida se ad pastús refert
sic hánc[2] custodem maésti cruciatús alo,
quae[3] mé perenni vívum foedat míseria,
namque, út videtis, vínclis constrictús Iovis
arcére nequeo díram volucrem a péctore.
sic me ípse viduus péstis excipio ánxias,
amóre mortis términum anquiréns[4] mali,
sed lónge a leto númine aspellór Iovis.
atque haéc vetusta saéclis glomerata hórridis
luctífica clades nóstro infixa est córpori,
e quó liquatae sólis ardore éxcidunt
guttaé, quae saxa adsídue instillant Caúcasi.

Cicero, *Tusculan Disputations* ii. 10. 23-25 ; ll. 14-15 *sublime — sanguinem* in Nonius Marcellus, *Compendiosa Doctrina* 17. 9 M.

[1] *advolans* : Lambinus. [2] *hunc* : Bentley.
[3] *qui* : Bentley. [4] *inquirens* : Victorius.

Ye race of Titans, offspring of Uranus, blood-kinsmen mine ! Behold me fettered, clamped to these rough rocks, even as a ship is moored fast by timid sailors, fearful of night because of the roaring sea. Thus hath Zeus, the son of Cronus, fastened me, and to the will of Zeus hath Hephaestus lent his hand. With cruel art hath he riven my limbs by driving in these bolts. Ah, unhappy that I am ! By his skill transfixed, I tenant this stronghold of the Furies. And now, each third woeful day, with dreadful swoop, the minister of Zeus with his hooked talons rends me asunder by his cruel repast. Then, crammed and glutted to the full on my fat liver, he utters a prodigious scream and, soaring aloft, with winged tail fawns upon my gore. But when my gnawed liver swells, renewed in growth, greedily doth he return anew to his fell repast. Thus do I feed this guardian of my awful torture, who mutilates me living with never-ending pain. For fettered, as ye see, by the bonds of Zeus, I have no power to drive from my vitals the accursed bird. Thus, robbed of self-defence, I endure woes fraught with torment: longing for death, I look around for an ending of my misery; but by the doom of Zeus I am thrust far from death. And this my ancient dolorous agony, intensified by the dreadful centuries, is fastened upon my body, from which there fall, melted by the blazing sun, drops that unceasingly pour upon the rocks of Caucasus.

108 (194)

ἵππων ὄνων τ' ὀχεῖα[1] *καὶ ταύρων γένος*[2]
δοὺς ἀντίδουλα[3] *καὶ πόνων ἐκδέκτορα*[4].

Plutarch, *On Fortune* 3. 98 c (cp. *On the Craftiness of Animals* 7. 965 A), Porphyry, *On Abstinence* 3. 18.

[1] *ὀχείαν* Plut. 965 A, Porph. [2] *γονὰς*: Wilam.
[3] *ἀντίδωρα* Plut. 98 c. [4] *ἀνδέκτορα* Plut. 965 A.

Giving to them stallions—horses and asses—and the race of bulls to serve them as slaves and to relieve them of their toil.

109 (195)

εὐθεῖαν ἕρπε τήνδε·[1] καὶ πρώτιστα μὲν
Βορεάδας ἥξεις πρὸς πνοάς, ἵν'[2] εὐλαβοῦ
βρόμον καταιγίζοντα, μή σ' ἀναρπάσῃ
δυσχειμέρῳ πέμφιγι συστρέψας ἄφνω[3].

Galen, *Commentary on Hippocrates' Epidemics* vi, vol xvii. 1. p. 879 (ἐν Προμηθεῖ δεσμώτῃ corr. H. Stephanus).

[1] ἑρπετὴν δὲ: Stephanus.
[2] πνοαῖσιν: Stephanus.
[3] ἄνω: Stephanus.

Follow this straight road; and, first of all, thou shalt come to the north winds, where do thou beware the roaring hurricane, lest unawares it twist thee up and snatch thee away in wintry whirlwind.

110 (196)

ἔπειτα δ' ἥξεις[1] δῆμον ἐνδικώτατον
<βροτῶν>[2] ἁπάντων καὶ φιλοξενώτατον,
Γαβίους, ἵν' οὔτ' ἄροτρον οὔτε γατόμος
τέμνει δίκελλ'[3] ἄρουραν, ἀλλ' αὐτόσποροι[4]
γύαι φέρουσι βίοτον ἄφθονον βροτοῖς.

Stephen of Byzantium, *Lexicon* 7. 5 (s.v. Ἄβιοι) on *Iliad* N 6 (cp. Scholiasts AT). Homer calls the Ἄβιοι the "most just of men."

[1] ἥξει: Stanley.
[2] < > Hermann.
[3] δικέλλης: Holsten.
[4] αὐτοσπόροι R, αὐτόσποροι other MSS.

Thereafter thou shalt come unto a people of all mortals most just and most hospitable, even unto the Gabians; where nor plough nor mattock, that cleaves the ground, parteth the earth, but where the fields, self-sown, bring forth bounteous sustenance for mortals.

111 (198)

ἀλλ' ἱππάκης βρωτῆρες εὔνομοι Σκύθαι

Strabo, *Geography* vii. 3. 7. p. 301.

But the well-ordered Scythians that feed on mares' milk cheese

In *Iliad* N 5 Homer mentions Ἱππημολγοί, who drink mares' milk.

112 (199)

ἥξεις δὲ Λιγύων εἰς ἀτάρβητον στρατόν,
ἔνθ' οὐ μάχης, σάφ' οἶδα, καὶ θοῦρός περ ὤν,
λίψῃ·[1] πέπρωται γάρ σε καὶ βέλη λιπεῖν
ἐνταῦθ'· ἑλέσθαι δ' οὔτιν' ἐκ γαίας λίθον
ἕξεις, ἐπεὶ πᾶς χῶρός ἐστι μαλθακός·
ἰδὼν δ' ἀμηχανοῦντά σ' οἰκτιρεῖ πατήρ,[2]
νεφέλην δ' ὑπερσχὼν[3] νιφάδι γογγύλων[4] πέτρων
ὑπόσκιον θήσει χθόν', οἷς ἔπειτα σὺ
βαλὼν[5] διώσῃ[6] ῥᾳδίως Λίγυν στρατόν.

Strabo, *Geography* iv. 1. 7. p. 183; ll. 1-3 Dionysius of Halicarnassus, *Early History of Rome* i. 41.

[1] μέμψῃ or πέμψῃ Strabo, μέμψιν Dion. B: Diels.
[2] σ' ὁ Ζεὺς οἰκτερεῖ πατήρ: Cobet (οἰκτιρεῖ Nauck).
[3] ὑποσχὼν: Casaubon. [4] στρογγύλων nog^{2}k^{2}.
[5] συμβαλὼν: Salmasius.
[6] δηώσει (δηώσεις s^{2}): διώσει Dobree, διώσῃ Wilam.

Thou shalt come to the dauntless host of the Ligurians, where, full well I know, thou shalt not be eager for battle, impetuous though thou art; for it is fated that even thy arrows shall fail thee there; and thou shalt not be able to take from the ground any stone, because the whole place is smooth. But the Father, beholding thy helplessness, shall pity thee, and, holding above thee a cloud, shall overshadow the land with a shower of round stones. Hurling these, thou shalt easily drive back the Ligurian host.

According to Strabo, Prometheus here gives directions to Heracles concerning the road he is to take on his journey from the Caucasus to the Hesperides.

Strabo states that the place was called the Stony Plain, and was situated between Marseilles and the outlets of the Rhone, about a hundred stades distant from the sea. It is now identified with " la plaine de la Crau " near Arles.

113 (200)

ἀγρεὺς δ' Ἀπόλλων ὀρθὸν ἰθύνοι βέλος.

Plutarch, *On Love* 14. 757 E. Ascribed to this play by Schütz.

May Hunter Apollo speed my arrow straight!

The prayer of Heracles as he bends his bow against the eagle that rends Prometheus (Plutarch).

114 (201)

ἐχθροῦ πατρός μοι τοῦτο φίλτατον τέκνον

Plutarch, *Life of Pompey* 1.

Of his sire, mine enemy, this dearest son

Prometheus addresses Heracles as the author of his deliverance (Plutarch).

ΠΡΟΜΗΘΕΥΣ ΠΥΡΚΑΕΥΣ [1]

To *Prometheus the Fire-Kindler* has been referred Fragment 156; to the " satyric Prometheus," 169, 170, 171, 172.

115 (205)

λινᾶ δὲ[1] πεσσὰ[2] κὠμολίνου μακροὶ τόνοι

Pollux, *Vocabulary* 10. 64.

[1] λινάδες P, λίνα δὲ other MSS.: Dindorf.
[2] πίσσα: Wilam.

And linen-lint and long bands of raw flax

[1] See appendix, p. 562.

116 (206)

ἐξευλαβοῦ δὲ μή σε προσβάλῃ[1] στόμα
πέμφιξ· πικρὰ γὰρ κοὐλιαζόεις ἀτμοί[2].

Galen, *Commentary on Hippocrates' Epidemics* vi, vol. xvii. 1. 880.

[1] προσβάλλῃ: Casaubon.
[2] κοὐ διὰ ζόης ἀτμοί: Headlam. The Fragment was referred to the Πυρκαεύς by Conington.

And do thou guard thee well lest a blast strike thy face; for it is sharp, and deadly-scorching its hot breaths.

117 (207)

τράγος γένειον ἆρα πενθήσεις σύ γε.

Plutarch, *How to Profit by our Enemies* 2. 86 F, Eustathius on *Iliad* 415. 7.

Like the goat, you'll mourn for your beard, you will.

Spoken, says Plutarch, by Prometheus to the satyr who desired to kiss and embrace fire on seeing it for the first time. Eustathius took τράγος to be the nominative used for the vocative; and the passage thus interpreted has been regarded as a proof that the satyr of the satyr-play was addressed as "goat." The translation assumes the existence of a proverb about a goat that burnt his beard (Shorey in *Classical Philology* iv. (1904) 433).

ΠΡΟΜΗΘΕΥΣ ΠΥΡΦΟΡΟΣ

Apart from Fragment 118, the only extant reference to *Prometheus the Fire-Bearer* is contained in the scholium on *Prom.* 94, where the statement is made that, in the Πυρφόρος, Prometheus declared that he had been bound (δεδέσθαι) thirty thousand years (to the same effect, Hyginus, *Astronomy* 2. 15, but without naming the play). On the assumption that the Πυρφόρος preceded the Δεσμώτης and that the Titan was prophesying the duration of his bondage, Hartung conjectured δεδήσεσθαι, Cobet δεθήσεσθαι. Welcker proposed to refer the utterance of Prometheus to the Λυόμενος; in Δεσμώτης l. 774 the hero says to Io that he shall be released by her descendant in the thirteenth generation.

118 (208)

σιγῶν θ' ὅπου δεῖ καὶ λέγων τὰ καίρια

Gellius, *Attic Nights* xiii. 19. 4.

Both silent, when there is need, and speaking in season

Cp. *Seven against Thebes* 619, *Libation-Bearers* 582, Euripides, Frag. 413.

ΠΡΩΤΕΥΣ

The satyr-play of the *Orestea* and dealing with the fortunes of Menelaüs in Egypt, whither he seems to have been carried by the storm described in *Agam.* 674. In the fourth book of the *Odyssey*, Menelaüs relates his encounter with the " deathless Egyptian Proteus," whom he compelled to disclose how he might find his way home from the island of Pharos.

119 (210)

σιτουμένην δύστηνον ἀθλίαν φάβα
μέσακτα πλευρὰ πρὸς πτύοις[1] πεπληγμένην[2]

Athenaeus, *Deipnosophists* ix. 50. p. 394 A.

[1] προσπτύοις A: Casaubon.
[2] πεπλεγμένην: Schweighäuser.

A wretched piteous dove, in quest of food, dashed amid the winnowing-fans, its breast broken in twain

ΣΑΛΑΜΙΝΙΑΙ

In Aristophanes, *Frogs* 1040, Aeschylus declares that his spirit, taking its impress from Homer, created many types of excellence, such as Patroclus and Teucer, the lion-hearted. It is highly probable that *The Women of Salamis*, the third play of the Ajax-trilogy, had as its theme the fortunes of Teucer, Ajax' half-brother, after his return from Troy with Eurysaces, the son of Ajax. Tradition reports Teucer's repudiation by his father Telamon, inconsolable at the loss of Ajax, for whose death he held Teucer responsible; Teucer's expulsion from his home; and his founding a new Salamis in Cyprus. The Chorus probably consisted of women of Salamis, who joined with their mistress Eriboea in lamenting the death of her son. The drama may have ended with the inauguration of the annual festival in honour of Ajax, whose virtues and unhappy fate were thus commemorated by his aged father.

The play is entitled Σαλαμίνιαι in Herodian (see Frag. 120), Σαλαμίνιοι in the Medicean Catalogue.

To *The Women of Salamis* have been referred Fragments 157, 167, 196, 232, 263.

120 (216)

εἴ μοι γένοιτο φᾶρος ἶσον[1] οὐρανῷ.

Herodian, *On Peculiar Words* ii. 942. 4 (Lentz), *On Words of Two Quantities* in Cramer, *Anecdota Graeca Oxoniensia* iii. 295. 15. Pseudo-Draco, *On Metres* 35. 12 (= Grammaticus Hermanni) derives from Herodian.

[1] ἶσον *Anecd. Oxon.*, Pseudo-Draco: ἴσον ἐν Herod. ii. 942. 4 (ἶσον ἐν Hermann).

Would that I might get a mantle like unto the heavens!

Mantles and curtains were often embroidered with stars among many ancient peoples: Eurip. *Ion* 1147, Nonnus, *Dion.* xl. 578; cp. Psalm civ. 2.

ΣΙΣΥΦΟΣ

Σίσυφος δραπέτης, *Sisyphus the Runaway*, is named only in the Medicean Catalogue; Σίσυφος πετροκυλιστής, *Sisyphus the Stone-Roller*, is mentioned twice in grammarians; elsewhere the form of citation is simply Σίσυφος.

The first-named drama was satyric; its theme, the escape from Hades of the crafty Corinthian king. According to the fabulous story told by Pherecydes (Frag. 78 in Müller, *Fragmenta Historicorum Graecorum*, i. p. 91) Sisyphus made known to Asopus that it was Zeus who had carried off his daughter Aegina; in punishment for which offence the god sent Death against the babbler; but Sisyphus bound Death fast, so that men ceased to die, until Ares came to the rescue, released Death, and gave Sisyphus into his power. Before he died, however, Sisyphus directed his wife Merope to omit his funeral rites, so that Hades, being deprived of his customary offerings, was persuaded by the cunning trickster to let him go back to life in order to complain of his wife's neglect. But, once in the upper world, he refused to return, and had to be fetched back by Hermes.—The Satyrs forming the Chorus were probably represented as initiates if the play was a parody of the Dionysiac-Orphic mysteries. (*Sisyphus the Stone-Roller* is one of the six dramas mentioned by the ancients in connexion with the charge of impiety brought against the poet.)

Σίσυφος πετροκυλιστής is probably identical with the Σίσυφος δραπέτης (at least Frag. 127 savours of a satyr-play); and the conclusion of the single drama may have been the famous punishment inflicted on the " craftiest of men " (cp. λ 593).

121 (225)

καὶ νίπτρα δὴ χρὴ θεοφόρων ποδῶν φέρειν.
λεοντοβάμων ποῦ σκάφη χαλκήλατος;

Pollux, *Vocabulary* 10. 78 (cp. 7. 40).

And now it behooves to bring water for feet that bear a god. Where is the bronze-wrought tub with lion-base?

Returning to Corinth from his journey from Hades, Sisyphus orders a bath for his feet, that bear one more than mortal. Cp. Horace, *Satires* ii. 3. 20

olim nam quaerere amabam,
quo vafer ille pedes lavisset Sisyphus aere.

122 (226)

σὺ δ' ὁ σταθμοῦχος εὖ κατιλλώψας ἄθρει.

Pollux, *Vocabulary* 10. 20.

Do thou, the master of the house, leer well and mark!

123 (227)

ἀλλ' ἀρουραῖός τίς ἐστι σμίνθος ὧδ' ὑπερφυής;

Aelian, *On Animals* xii. 5.

Nay, is it some field-mouse so monstrous large?

From a description of Sisyphus emerging from the earth.

124 (228)

Ζαγρεῖ τε νῦν με[1] καὶ πολυξένῳ ‹πατρὶ›[2] χαίρειν.

Etymologicum Gudianum 227. 40, Cramer, *Anecdota Graeca Oxoniensia* ii. 443. 11.

[1] μοι *Anecd. Oxon.* [2] ‹ › Hermann.

Now [I came] to bid farewell to Zagreus and to his sire, the hospitaler.

Sisyphus describes his departure from the lower world. Dionysus, viewed by the Orphics as the child of Zeus and Persephone, received the name Zagreus, the " great hunter." At times he was thus identified with Hades, at times made the son of the " hospitaler of the dead " (*Suppliant Maidens* 157).

125 (229)

καὶ ‹κατ›θανόντων[1] ἰσὶν οὐκ ἔνεστ' ἰκμάς[2].

Etymologicum Gudianum 321. 58, Cramer, *Anecdota Graeca Parisiensia* iv. 35. 22.

[1] θανόντων : Bamberger.

[2] εἰσὶν οὐκ ἐνεστιγμάσει, τὰ-σοὶ δ' οὐκ ἔνεστι κίκις οὐδ' αἱμόρρυτοι φλέβες *Et. Gud.*, εἰσιν οὐκέτι ἰμά[illegible] τὰ σοὶ δ' οὐκ ἔστι κίκυς κτλ. *Anecd. Par.* : ἰσὶν Nauck, οὐκ ἔνεστ' ἰκμάς Boeck, σοὶ . . . κῖκυς Boeckh.

And in the sinews of the dead there is no blood.

126 (230)

σοὶ δ' οὐκ ἔνεστι κῖκυς οὐδ' αἱμόρρυτοι φλέβες.

Etymologicum Gudianum 321. 58, Cramer, *Anecdota Graeca Parisiensia* iv. 35. 23.

See under Frag. 125.

But in thee there is no vigour nor veins that flow with blood.

127 (233)

Αἰτναῖός ἐστι κάνθαρος βίᾳ πονῶν[1].

Scholiast on Aristophanes, *Peace* 73 (ἐν Σισύφῳ πετροκυλιστῇ).

[1] πόνων: Dindorf.

'Tis a beetle of Aetna, toiling violently.

The ancients explained a "beetle of Aetna" either as a comic exaggeration ("as huge as Aetna") or as referring to the actual size of the beetles on the mountain. Epicharmus mentions (Frag. 76) a report that these beetles were of vast size. Pearson, *Class. Rev.* 28 (1914) 223, sees here a jest due to the verbal similarity of κάνθων "pack-ass" and κάνθαρος. Cp. Sophocles frag. 162.

ΣΦΙΓΞ

The *Sphinx* was the satyr-play of the Oedipus-trilogy. See Fragment 155.

128 (235)

τῷ δὲ ξένῳ γε στέφανος,[1] ἀρχαῖον στέφος,
δεσμῶν ἄριστος ἐκ Προμηθέως[2] λόγου.

Athenaeus, *Deipnosophists* xv. 16. p. 674 D.

[1] στέφανον: Grotius (λύγινον Weil). [2] προμηθέος A.

For the stranger a garland, an ancient crown, the best of bonds, as Prometheus said.

Athenaeus (xv. 13. p. 672 E-F) cites Menodotus of Samos to the effect that, after Zeus had freed Prometheus from his bonds and the Titan had professed himself willing to make a "voluntary and painless" expiation for his theft of fire, Zeus ordered him to wear a garland as a symbolic punishment; and that the Carian custom of wearing garlands of osier was a memorial of the shackles once worn by Prometheus, the benefactor of mankind. Athenaeus himself (xv.

16. p. 674 D) states that Aeschylus, in the *Prometheus Unbound*, distinctly says: "In honour of Prometheus we place garlands on our heads as an atonement for his bonds."

ἐκ Προμηθέως λόγου may signify either (1) that in τῷ δὲ ξένῳ . . . λόγου the (unknown) speaker is simply referring to the "story of Prometheus"; or (2) that the words δεσμῶν ἄριστος were spoken by the Titan in the *Prometheus Unbound* as an indication of his satisfaction with the form of retribution imposed on him after his release from the torture of his bonds. The latter explanation would dispose of the inconsistency thought by Athenaeus to exist between the utterance of Prometheus quoted above (674 D) and Fragment 128: namely, that a garland, which in later times was worn as a symbol of the agony of Prometheus, could not have been praised by the sufferer himself. If the second interpretation is correct, the Prometheus-trilogy is earlier than 467 B.C., the date of the production of the *Sphinx*.

The "stranger" is probably Oedipus; but the situation is unknown.

129 (236)

Σφίγγα δυσαμεριᾶν[1] πρύτανιν κύνα

Aristophanes, *Frogs* 1287 with Scholiast.

[1] δυσαμερίαν: Dindorf.

The Sphinx, the Watch-dog that presideth over evil days

ΤΗΛΕΦΟΣ

According to the Cyclic epic, the *Cyprian Lays*, Telephus, king of Mysia, having been wounded by the lance of Achilles in the first expedition of the Greeks against Troy, had recourse to the Delphic oracle, which returned the answer ὁ τρώσας καὶ ἰάσεται, "he who wounded, he shall also heal." The drama may also have adopted the legend that Telephus went to Argos, where, by the counsel of Clytaemestra, he seized the infant Orestes, whom he threatened to kill unless Agamemnon persuaded Achilles to heal him of his wound. The Scholiast on Aristophanes, *Acharnians* 323, says that, in Aeschylus, Telephus, in order to secure his safety among the Greeks, laid hold of Orestes. Since it is the *Telephus* of Euripides that is ridiculed by Aristophanes, it is supposed by many scholars that "Aeschylus" is an error for "Euripides" in the statement of the Scholiast.

See Fragment 198.

130 (238)

κύδιστ' Ἀχαιῶν Ἀτρέως πολυκοίρανε μάνθανέ μου παῖ.

Aristophanes, *Frogs* 1270. The Scholiast on the passage declares that, whereas Timachidas referred the verse to the *Telephus*, Asclepiades ascribed it to the *Iphigenia* of Aeschylus.

Most glorious of the Achaeans, wide-ruling son of Atreus, learn of me!

131 (239)

. . . ἁπλῆ[1] γὰρ οἶμος εἰς Ἅιδου φέρει.

Plato, *Phaedo* 108 A, Clement of Alexandria, *Miscellanies* iv. 7. p. 583; cp. Dionysius of Halicarnassus, *Art of Rhetoric* 6. 5 (Reiske v. 265).

[1] ὁ Αἰσχύλου Τήλεφος . . . ἁπλῆν οἶμόν φησιν εἰς Ἅιδου φέρειν Plato, μία γὰρ καὶ ἡ αὐτὴ οἶμος . . . εἰς Ἅιδου φέρουσα Dion. Hal.

For a single path leads to the house of Hades.

Cp. Cicero, *Tusculan Disputations* i. 43. 104 *undique enim ad inferos tantundem viae est*, referring the sentiment to Anaxagoras: πανταχόθεν ὁμοία ἐστὶν ἡ εἰς Ἅιδου κατάβασις (Diogenes Laertius ii. 3. 11).

ΤΟΞΟΤΙΔΕΣ

Actaeon, the hunter, turned into a deer, was torn asunder by his dogs, who did not recognize their master. The common version of the legend—that he was thus punished by Artemis for having seen her bathing—seems to have been adopted by Aeschylus. The Chorus of "Archer-Maidens" were nymphs, attendants of Artemis in the chase.

132 (241)

οὔπω τις Ἀκταίων' ἄθηρος ἡμέρα
κενὸν πόνου πλουτοῦντ' ἔπεμψεν ἐς δόμους.

Bekker, *Anecdota Graeca* 351. 9; cp. Photius, *Lexicon* 41. 10 (Reitzenstein) s.v. ἄθηρος ἡμέρα.

Not yet has any day, without its game, sent Actaeon homeward empty-handed, only rich in toil.

133 (242)

αἰδοῖ <γὰρ> ἁγναῖς[1] παρθένοις γαμηλίων
λέκτρων ἀπείροις[2] βλεμμάτων ῥέπει βολή[3].

Antigonus of Carystus, *Incredible Tales* 115.

[1] ἅδων ταῖς ἁγναῖς: Bothe.
[2] λέκτρων αστει μὴ: Heath.
[3] ρεπιβουλη: Salmasius.

For in pure maidens, knowing not the marriage-bed, the glance of the eyes sinks from shame.

134 (243)

νέας γυναικὸς οὔ με μὴ λάθῃ φλέγων
ὀφθαλμός, ἥτις ἀνδρὸς ᾖ γεγευμένη·
ἔχω[1] δὲ τούτων θυμὸν ἱππογνώμονα.

Antigonus of Carystus, *Incredible Tales* 115; ll. 1-2, Plutarch, *On Love* 21. 767 B; l. 2 Plutarch, *On Progress in Virtue* 10. 81 D. In Antigonus these lines follow Fragment 133 after a short interval.

[1] ἔχων: Salmasius.

The burning gaze of a young woman, such as hath tasted man, shall not escape me; for I have a spirit keen to mark these things.

135 (244)

κύνες διημάθυνον ἄνδρα δεσπότην.

Scholiast A on *Iliad* I 593.

The dogs destroyed their master utterly.

ΦΙΛΟΚΤΗΤΗΣ[1]

The story of Philoctetes, king of Malis, touched upon in *Iliad* B 721, was narrated at length in two Cyclic epics—the *Little Iliad* by Lesches and the *Destruction of Ilium* by Arctinus. On their expedition to Troy, the Greeks abandoned Philoctetes on the island of Lemnos because, having been bitten in the foot by a poisonous snake, his screams of pain and the odour from his wound rendered his presence intolerable. In the tenth year of the war, when the Greeks were despairing of victory, they learned from the seer Helenus that Troy could not be taken without the aid of Philoctetes and his bow and

[1] See appendix, p. 584.

arrows, weapons given him by the dying Heracles, who had himself received them from Apollo. Diomedes was accordingly sent to Lemnos, and fetched thence the hero and his arms.

In his fifty-second *Discourse* (4-10), Dion of Prusa, surnamed the "golden-mouthed," gives a brief comparison of the *Philoctetes* of Aeschylus, Sophocles, and Euripides. In the Aeschylean play, instead of the noble Diomedes, the "shrewd and crafty" Odysseus was the envoy. Unchanged in aspect and voice by Athena, he appeared before Philoctetes, but was unrecognized because the powers of the sufferer had been impaired by his disease, his hardships, and his solitary life. The Chorus consisted of men of Lemnos, who had left Philoctetes unvisited until then—a more tragic and a simpler device (says Dion) than the excuse proffered by them according to Euripides—so that the hero could with good reason set forth to them, as something new, the story of his desertion by the Greeks and the cause of his distress. Odysseus sought to cheer Philoctetes and to gain his confidence by a false tale—disaster had befallen the Greeks; Agamemnon was dead; Odysseus had been put to death by reason of some shameful crime; and the Greeks at Troy were in desperate case. Dion omits to tell how Odysseus secured the arms—whether this was done first by treason (as was done by Neoptolemus in Sophocles) and then by persuading the hero that his bow was necessary to the success of the Greeks. But Odysseus' deception and his pleas were seemly (Dion says), suited to a hero, and convincing—it needed no great skill or plot to contend against a sick man and that a simple bowman.

The drama of Aeschylus was distinguished, according to Dion, by simplicity, absence of complicated plot, and dignity ; by its antique air and its rugged boldness of sentiment and diction, so that it was well suited to express the nature of tragedy and to body forth the ancient manners of the heroic age.

Aspasius on Aristotle's *Nicomachean Ethics* 1150 b 6 states that in Aeschylus, as in Sophocles, Philoctetes endeavoured to conceal his agony but was finally forced to give it utterance.

See Fragments 163, 180, 185, 190, 191, 198.

136 (249)

Σπερχειὲ ποταμὲ βούνομοί τ' ἐπιστροφαί

Aristophanes, *Frogs* 1383 with Scholiast.

O Spercheus' stream and cattle-grazing haunts!

137 (250)

ἔνθ' οὔτε μίμνειν ἄνεμος οὔτ' ἐκπλεῖν[1] ἐᾷ.

Cited as a proverb by Suidas, *Lexicon* s.v. ἔνθ' οὔτε, Plutarch, *On the Tranquillity of the Mind* 18. 476 B, Aristaenetus, *Letters* i. 27, Pseudo-Diogenianus, *Proverbs* iv. 88, etc.

[1] οὔτ' ἐκπλεῖν Suid., Pseudo-Diogen., οὔτε πλεῖν the rest.

Where the wind suffers neither to remain nor to sail forth.

138 (251)

κρεμάσας τὸ τόξον[1] πίτυος ἐκ μελανδρύου

Scholiast on *Odyssey* ξ 12, Eustathius on *Odyssey* 1748. 57.

[1] κρεμάσασα τόξον Schol. *Od.*, κρεμάσας τόξον Eust. : Bothe.

Having hung the bow on a black pine-tree

139 (252)

οὐ γὰρ δράκων ἀνῆκεν, ἀλλ' ἐνῴκισεν
δεινὴν †στομάτων ἔκφυσιν, ποδὸς βλάβην[1].

Plutarch, *On the Impossibility of living happily by following Epicurus* 3. 1087 F.

[1] λαβεῖν or λάβεν : Schneidewin.

For the snake let not go its hold, but fixed in me its dreadful . . ., the ruin of my foot.

Hermann would read στομωτὸν ἔκφυσιν, which is supposed to mean "hard outgrowth," "outgrowth with a mouth-shaped cavity," "sharp projection." But we expect something like ὀδόντων (Nauck) ἔκπτυσιν (Herwerden), "venom spat from its teeth."

140 (253)

φάγεδαιν' ἀεί[1] μου σάρκας ἐσθίει ποδός.

Aristotle, *Poetics* 22. 1458 b 23.

[1] φαγέδαινα ἤ : Boissonade.

The ulcer ever feeds on my foot's flesh.

141 (255)

ὦ θάνατε παιάν, μή μ' ἀτιμάσῃς μολεῖν·
μόνος γάρ[1] εἶ σὺ τῶν ἀνηκέστων κακῶν
ἰατρός, ἄλγος δ' οὐδὲν ἅπτεται νεκροῦ.

Stobaeus, *Anthology* iv. 52. 32 (Hense v. 1082). Attributed to this play by Maximus of Tyre, *Dissertations* 7. 5.

[1] γὰρ om. SA. Plutarch, *Consolation to Apollonius* 10. 106 D, has ὦ θάνατε παιάν, <πῶς ἂν suppl. Cobet> ἰατρὸς μόλοις and 15. 109 F ἄλγος γὰρ ὄντως οὐδὲν ἅπτεται νεκροῦ, Theodorus Metochita, *Miscellan.* 347 ὦ θάνατε παιάν, ἰατρὸς μόλε.

O death, the healer, reject me not, but come! For thou alone art the mediciner of ills incurable, and no pain layeth hold on the dead.

On death as the deliverer cp. Sophocles, *Philoctetes* 797, *Trachinians* 1209, *Oedipus Coloneus* 1220, *Ajax* 854, Frag. 698, Euripides, *Hippolytus* 1373, *Heracleidae* 595, Diphilus, Frag. 88. With l. 3 cp. Sophocles, *Oedipus Coloneus* 955, Euripides, *Alcestis* 937, *Women of Troy* 642.

ΦΙΝΕΥΣ

The *Phineus* preceded *The Persians* in the tetralogy produced in 472 B.C. (see p. 377).

Apollodorus, *Library* i. 9. 21, relates the story of Phineus as follows : "Thence the Argonauts put out to sea and landed at Salmydessus in Thrace, where dwelt the seer Phineus, who had lost the sight of his eyes. . . . The gods also sent Harpies against him. These were winged female creatures, and when a table was spread for Phineus, they flew down from the sky and snatched away most of the food, but the little they left smelled so foul that no one could come near it. And when the Argonauts wished to learn about their voyage, he said that he would advise them about it if they would free him from the Harpies. So the Argonauts placed beside him a table of eatables, and the Harpies with a cry flew down and snatched the food. Seeing this, Zetes and Calaïs, the sons of Boreas, who were winged, drew their swords and chased them through the air. . . . Being freed from the Harpies, Phineus revealed their course to the Argonauts, and advised them concerning the Clashing Rocks on the sea."

142 (258)

καὶ ψευδόδειπνα πολλὰ μαργώσαις γνάθοις[1]
ἐρρυσίαζον[2] στόματος ἐν πρώτῃ χαρᾷ[3].

Athenaeus, *Deipnosophists* x. 18. p. 421 F.

[1] μαργώσης γνάθου : Hartung.
[2] ἐρρυσιας οἷον A : Lobeck. [3] πρωτιοχαραι A : Musurus.

And many a deceitful meal with greedy jaws did they snatch away amid the first delight of appetite.

143 (258 B)

. . ἄνηστις δ' οὐκ ἀποστατεῖ γόος.

Etymologicum Genuinum s.v. ἄνηστις.

Hungry wailing standeth not aloof.

144 (259)

πέλλυτρ' ἔχουσιν εὐθέτοις ἐν ἀρβύλαις.

Pollux, *Vocabulary* 7. 91 ; cp. 2. 196.

They wear socks in their well-fitting shoes.

Perhaps from a description of the sons of Boreas.

ΦΟΡΚΙΔΕΣ

The Daughters of Phorcys was a part of the trilogy containing *The Net-Draggers* (Δικτυουλκοί) and *Polydectes*. In the first of these plays, fisher folk of Seriphus rescued Danaë and her infant son Perseus, who had been placed in a chest and cast into the sea by her father Acrisius. In the second, Polydectes, king of Seriphus, in order the better to effect his purpose of marrying Danaë, sent her son, now grown to manhood, to fetch the head of Medusa, the one of the three Gorgons who was mortal. In pursuit of this quest, Perseus encountered the three daughters of Phorcys, old women from their birth, who possessed between them a single eye and tooth, which they passed to each other in turn, and also the cap of Hades. These women, the Graeae, were sisters and guardians of the Gorgons, who dwelt in a cave by the ocean. On his return, Perseus changed Polydectes into stone by displaying Medusa's head, which he had cut off with an adamantine sickle that he had received from Hephaestus. In *Poetics* 18. 1456 a 2, Aristotle regards as a distinct species of tragedy such plays as *The Phorcides*, *Prometheus*, and those whose scene was laid in the lower world. *The Phorcides* may be a satyr-drama.

145 (261)

. . ἔδυ δ' ἐς ἄντρον ἀσχέδωρος ὥς.

Athenaeus, *Deipnosophists* ix. 65. p. 402 B, Eustathius on *Odyssey* 1872. 5.

Into the cave he rushed like a wild boar.

Perseus enters the cave of the Gorgons. ἀσχέδωρος is called by the ancient grammarians a Sicilian word for σύαγρος.

ΦΡΥΓΕΣ ἢ ΕΚΤΟΡΟΣ ΛΥΤΡΑ

The scene of *The Phrygians* or *The Ransom of Hector* was the tent of Achilles, as in the twenty-fourth book of the *Iliad*, which the poet here dramatized.

Hermes, the divine guide of Priam and his escort of Phrygians, preceded the entrance of the embassy to regain the body of Hector. Except at the beginning, and then only in few words, Achilles refused to speak to the god, but sat in silence, his head veiled in token of his grief for Patroclus. The gold brought as ransom was actually represented as weighed out in sight of the audience (Scholiast on *Iliad* X 351). To the peculiar dance-figures designed by the poet for the Chorus, allusion is probably made in a passage of a lost play of Aristophanes (Frag. 678): "I remember seeing the Phrygians, when they came in order to join with Priam in ransoming his dead son, how they often danced in many postures, now this way, now that."

See Fragments 155, 158, 180, 255, 267, 268.

146 (263)

ἀλλὰ ναυβάτην
φορτηγόν, ὅστις ῥῶπον ἐξάγει χθονός

Pollux, *Vocabulary* 7. 131.

[Not a king,] but a trafficker by sea, one who takes petty wares from out a land

147 (264)

ἀνὴρ δ' ἐκεῖνος ἦν πεπαίτερος μόρων.

Athenaeus, *Deipnosophists* ii. 36. p. 51 c, Eustathius on *Iliad* 211. 16.

But that man was gentler than mulberries are soft.

The verse refers to Hector and was probably spoken by Priam.

148 (266)

καὶ τοὺς θανόντας εἰ θέλεις[1] εὐεργετεῖν
εἴτ' οὖν[2] κακουργεῖν, ἀμφιδεξίως ἔχει
τῷ[3] μήτε χαίρειν μήτε λυπεῖσθαι φθιτούς[4].
ἡμῶν γε μέντοι Νέμεσίς ἐσθ' ὑπερτέρα,
καὶ τοῦ θανόντος ἡ Δίκη πράσσει κότον.

Stobaeus, *Anthology* iv. 57. 6 (Hense v. 1138).

[1] εἰ θέλεις SM, om. A.
[2] δ γοῦν : Hermann.
[3] καὶ : Salmasius.
[4] βροτούς : Hermann.

And if unto the dead thou art fain to do good, or if thou wouldst work them ill—'tis all one, since they feel not or joy or grief. Nevertheless our righteous resentment is mightier than they, and Justice executeth the dead man's wrath.

Elsewhere Aeschylus declares that the dead possess consciousness and are wroth with those who have done them injury (*Libation-Bearers* 324, 41). Here, where Hermes has in mind the outrage done by Achilles to Hector's corpse, his utterance is intended to console Priam and rebuke Achilles with the thought that, though the dead are insensible and cannot avenge themselves, their cause is in the divine keeping. It is the gods alone who have power to do that which is commonly ascribed to the spirits of the dead.

149 (267)

Ἀνδραίμονος γένεθλον <ὦ>[1] Λυρνησσίου,
ὅθεν περ Ἕκτωρ[2] ἄλοχον ἤγαγεν φίλην.

Scholiast on Euripides, *Andromache* 1.

[1] < > Hermann.
[2] περ ἕκτωρ M, παρ' ἕκτορος GT.

Hail, offspring of Andraemon of Lyrnessus, whence Hector brought his dear wife.

The statement of the Scholiast that Andromache is addressed is the sole warrant for the interpretation of the action that supposes her to have accompanied Priam to the tent of Achilles. Since her father was Eëtion from Hypoplacian Thebe according to Homer, and since Chrysa and Lyrnessus were both in the plain of Thebe, the Scholiast seems to have confused Andromache with Briseïs, though he properly remarks on the strangeness of the name given to her father.

ΨΥΧΑΓΩΓΟΙ

The ancients, says Phrynichus (Bekker, *Anecdota Graeca* 73. 10), used the word ψυχαγωγός to denote one who by spells brought to life the spirits of the dead. *The Spirit-Raisers* was connected with the *Penelope* and *The Bone-Gatherers*, and included Teiresias' prophecy to Odysseus concerning that hero's death (cp. λ 100-137). In λ 134 the seer obscurely declares that " from out the sea thine own death shall come " (cp. Fragment 152).

150 (273)

Ἑρμᾶν μὲν πρόγονον τίομεν γένος οἱ περὶ λίμναν ‹οἰκοῦντες›.

Aristophanes, *Frogs* 1266 with Scholiast.

We, who dwell by the lake, honour Hermes as our ancestor.

Hermes was born on Mt. Cyllene, not far from Lake Stymphalis.

151 (274)

καὶ σκευοθηκῶν ναυτικῶν τ' ἐρειπίων

Pollux, *Vocabulary* 10. 10.

Arsenals and wreckage of ships

152 (275)

ἐρῳδιὸς[1] γὰρ ὑψόθεν ποτώμενος
ὄνθῳ σε πλήξει νηδύος[2] κενώμασιν[3]·
ἐκ τοῦδ' ἄκανθα ποντίου βοσκήματος
σήψει παλαιὸν βρέγμα[4] καὶ τριχορρυές.

Scholiast Vulg. on *Odyssey* λ 134.

[1] ἐρρωδιὸς: Herodian spelled the word ἐρῳδιός.
[2] ὄν θ' ὡς ἔπληξεν ἡ δ' υἱὸς: ὄνθῳ σε πλήξει Valckenaer, νηδύος Meursius.
[3] χειλώμασιν: Nauck. [4] δέρμα: Crusius.

For a heron, in its flight on high, shall smite thee with its dung, its belly's emptyings; a spine from out this beast of the sea shall rot thy head, aged and scant of hair.

Spoken by Teiresias. In Sophocles' Ὀδυσσεὺς ἀκανθοπλήξ, which took the story from the Cyclic epic *Telegonia*, the hero was killed by his son Telegonus, who smote him with a spear tipped with the spike or fin of a roach.

ΩΡΕΙΘΥΙΑ

According to the legend probably followed by Aeschylus, Boreas, being enamoured of Oreithyia, daughter of Erechtheus, king of Athens, sought her in marriage from her father; repulsed by him, he laid hold of the girl by violence and carried her off as she was sporting by the Ilissus. She bore him two daughters, Chione and Cleopatra, the latter of whom became the wife of Phineus; and two sons, Zetes and Calaïs, who rescued Phineus from the Harpies. In the two extant fragments, which are cited as examples of pseudo-tragic diction, Boreas, enraged at the rejection of his suit, threatens to display his power in its full force.

153 (281)

. . καὶ καμίνου σχῶσι μάκιστον σέλας·
εἰ γάρ τιν' ἑστιοῦχον ὄψομαι ψόλον[1]
μίαν παρείρας πλεκτάνην χειμάρροον
στέγην πυρώσω καὶ κατανθρακώσομαι.
νῦν δ' οὐ κέκραγά πω τὸ γενναῖον μέλος.

Pseudo-Longinus, *On the Sublime* 3. 1 (after a lacuna of two leaves); cp. John of Sicily, *On Hermogenes'* "*Kinds of Style*" in *Rhetores Graeci* vi. 225.

[1] μόνον: Salmasius.

. . . and check the oven's soaring blaze; for let me but behold some soot, the tenant of the hearth, weaving in a single wreath of torrent flame, I'll fire the roof and cinder it. But now—not yet have I blared my noble strain.

154 (281 A)

ταῖς δυσὶν σιαγόσι
φυσῶν κυκῶ θάλασσαν[1].

John of Sicily, as under Frag. 163.

[1] κυκῷ τὴν θάλασσαν: Sidgwick, who, reading σιαγόσιν διασαῖσιν ἐκφυσῶν ἐγὼ before κυκῶ, adds ἐξεμεῖν πρὸς οὐρανόν from Pseudo-Longinus.

With my two jaws I blow a blast and confound the main.

FRAGMENTS OF UNCERTAIN PLAYS

Under each Fragment are added ancient or modern conjectures as to its source. [Fragments 23, 65, 88, 95, 113, 130 have been transferred from this section.]

155 (282)

κυρεῖν παρασχὼν ἰταμαῖς κυσὶν ἀεροφοίτοις

Aristophanes, *Frogs* 1291. Ascribed to Aeschylus because ll. 1264-1288 contain quotations from him.

Giving him (?) as booty to the eager hounds that range the air

Ἀγαμέμνων Scholiast, Μέμνων Bergk, Σφίγξ Fritzsche, Ἀργεῖοι Hartung, Μυρμιδόνες or Φρύγες Rogers.

The "eager hounds" are eagles or vultures. Who or what is their booty is unknown.

156 (288)

δέδοικα μῶρον[1] κάρτα πυραύστου μόρον.

Aelian, *On Animals* xii. 8, Zenobius. *Proverbs* v. 79, Suidas, *Lexicon* s.v. πυραύστου μόρον.

[1] μωρὸν Aelian, μόρον Suidas.

Verily I do fear the stupid death of the moth.

Προμηθεὺς πυρκαεύς Bothe, Σεμέλη ἢ Ὑδροφόροι Hartung.

πυραύστου μόρος was a proverbial expression for the brevity of life (Eustathius on *Iliad* 1304. 8, etc.).

157 (289)

βοᾷς τοιοῦδε πράγματος θεωρὸς ὤν.

Ammonius, *On Words of like Form but different Meaning* 59 (Valckenaer).

Thou criest aloud, thou who art but a spectator of such a deed as this.

Ὑψιπύλη Valckenaer, Σαλαμίνιαι Hartung.

157 A (291)

θρηνεῖ δὲ γόον τὸν ἀηδόνιον[1]

Bekker, *Anecdota Graeca* 349. 7.

[1] ἀηδόνειον : Blomfield.

She waileth the nightingale's lament.

Compare *Agam.* 1146.

158 (296)

πᾶσα γὰρ Τροία δέδορκεν[1] Ἕκτορος τύχης διαί

Cramer, *Anecdota Graeca Oxoniensia* i. 119. 12.

[1] For δέδορκεν conjectures are δέδοικεν, δέδυκεν, δέδουπεν.

For all Troy hath beheld by reason of Hector's fate

Νηρεΐδες, or a connected play, Welcker, Φρύγες Hermann.

159 (298)

ἐτονθόρυζε[1] ταῦρος <ὡς>[2] νεοσφαγής.

Cramer, *Anecdota Graeca Oxoniensia* ii. 414. 13.

[1] ἐτονθώρυζε : Cramer. [2] < > Cramer.

He bellowed like a bull whose throat has just been cut.

Θρῇσσαι Hartung.

160 (299)

οὔτ' εἰμ' ἄπειρος[1] τῆσδε τῆς προσῳδίας.

Cramer, *Anecdota Graeca Oxoniensia* iv. 315. 28.

[1] οὔτι μ' ἄπειρον : Herwerden.

Neither am I without experience of this manner of address.

161 (300)

γένος μὲν αἰνεῖν ἐκμαθὼν[1] ἐπίσταμαι
Αἰθιοπίδος γῆς, Νεῖλος ἔνθ'[2] ἑπτάρροος[3]
γάνος[4] κυλίνδει[5] πνευμάτων ἐπομβρίᾳ[6],
ἐν δ'[7] ἥλιος πυρωπὸς[8] ἐκλάμψας χθονὶ[9]
τήκει πετραίαν[10] χιόνα· πᾶσα δ' εὐθαλὴς
Αἴγυπτος ἁγνοῦ νάματος πληρουμένη
φερέσβιον Δήμητρος ἀντέλλει[11] στάχυν.

Anonymous, *On the Swelling of the Nile*, quoted from cod. Laurentianus lvi. 1 (F) by H. Stephanus in *Appendix ad Aristotelis et Theophrasti scripta quaedam*, and inserted in Parisinus C in the Epitome of the second book of Athenaeus, *Deipnosophists* (Dindorf i. 165) ; cp. Aristeides, *Or.* 48, *On Egypt* (vol. ii. 443, 460).

[1] καὶ μαθὼν F, ἐκλαθὼν C : Schweighäuser.
[2] ἔνθα F (ἐντάδε C) νεῖλος : Dindorf.
[3] ἐπάρρους F, ἑπτάρρους C : Dindorf.
[4] γαῖαν : Hermann.
[5] κυλίνδων : Salmasius.
[6] ἐπομβρίαις F.
[7] ἐν ᾗ : Hermann.
[8] πυρωπὸς ἥλιος C, πυρωτὸν μηνὸς F : Hermann.
[9] ἐκλάμψαν φλόγα F.
[10] πετραίην F.
[11] ἀγγέλλει F.

Knowing full well, I can laud the race of the Aethiopian land, where seven-channelled Nile rolleth its refreshing tide, fed by abundant, wind-born rain, and therein the fire-eyed sun, beaming forth upon the earth, melteth the snow amid the rocks ; and all luxuriant Egypt, filled with the sacred flood, maketh to spring up Demeter's life-giving grain.

Μέμνων Butler, Ψυχοστασία Welcker.

162 (301)

ἀπάτης δικαίας[1] οὐκ ἀποστατεῖ θεός.

Anonymous in Orelli, *Opuscula Graecorum veterum sententiosa et moralia* ii. 222, Stobaeus, *Anthology* iii. 3. 13 (Hense iii. 195), Scholiast on *Iliad* B 114, Eustathius on *Iliad* 188. 43, 480. 43.

[1] ἀγαθῆς Eust. 480. 33.

From righteous deception God standeth not aloof.

Δαναΐδες Hermann, Αἰγύπτιοι Hartung, Θαλαμοποιοί Oberdick.

163 (302)

ψευδῶν δὲ καιρὸν ἔσθ' ὅπου τιμᾷ[1] θεός.

Anonymous in Orelli (as under Frag. 162).

[1] ὅποι τιμῇ (Doric) so Gale's MS. (?) : ὅπου Nauck, τιμᾷ Orelli.

But times there are when God honoureth the season for untruth.

Δαναΐδες Hermann, Φιλοκτήτης Hartung, Θαλαμοποιοί Wecklein.

164 (303)

μήτ' οὖν παρασπιστὴς ἐμοὶ
μήτ' ἐγγὺς εἴη[1].

Aristeides, *In Defence of the Four Statesmen* 46 (vol. ii. 379).

[1] Aristeides has μὴ μὲν οὖν ἔμοιγε κατ' Αἰσχύλον μήτε παρασπιστὴς μήτ' ἐγγὺς εἴη ὅστις μὴ φίλος τῷ ἀνδρὶ τούτῳ μηδὲ τιμᾷ τὰ πρέποντα : Butler.

Nor companion in arms, nor neighbour, let him be to me!

'Αργώ Wagner, Οἰδίπους Hartung, Κάβειροι Bergk.

165 (304)

τοῦτον δ' ἐπόπτην ἔποπα τῶν αὑτοῦ κακῶν
πεποικίλωκε κἀποδηλώσας ἔχει
θρασὺν πετραῖον ὄρνιν ἐν παντευχίᾳ·
ὃς ἦρι μὲν φανέντι[1] διαπαλεῖ[2] πτερὸν
κίρκου λεπάργου· δύο γὰρ οὖν μορφὰς φανεῖ[3]
παιδός τε χαὐτοῦ[4] νηδύος μιᾶς ἄπο·
νέας δ' ὀπώρας ἡνίκ' ἂν ξανθῇ[5] στάχυς,
στικτή νιν αὖθις ἀμφινωμήσει[6] πτέρυξ.
ἀεὶ δὲ μίσει[7] τῶνδ'[8] ἀπαλλαγεὶς τόπων[9]
δρυμοὺς ἐρήμους καὶ πάγους ἀποικιεῖ[10].

Aristotle, *Natural History* ix. 49. p. 633 a 20 ; cp. Pliny, *Natural History* x. 86 (44).

[1] φαίνονται A[a], C[a], φαίνοντι other MSS. : Nauck.
[2] διαπάλλει MSS. except A[a] C[a] D (διαβάλλει) : Gilbert.
[3] φαίνει A[a] C[a] D[a].
[4] καὐτοῦ : Sylburg.
[5] ἵνα καταξανθῇ : Camot.
[6] ἀμφινομήσῃ A[a] C[a], ἀμφινομήσει D[a], ἀμφινωμήσῃ PE[a].
[7] μίσει D[a], μισεῖ C[a], μισεῖ PA[a].
[8] τὸν δὲ PE[a] C[a].
[9] ἀπ' ἄλλον εἰς τόπον (ἀπάλλου E[a], ἀσπάλλον P, ἀπαλῶν A[a]) : Heath.
[10] ἀποικίσει : Salmasius.

This hoopoe, spectator of his own distress, hath Zeus bedecked in various hue and showed him forth a bird courageous in his full armour, tenanting the rocks. With the new-come spring he will ply the pinion of the white-feathered hawk—for he will display two forms from a single egg, his offspring's and his own—; but when the grain is threshed in early harvest-time, a parti-coloured wing will direct his course to this side or that. But ever quitting these haunts in loathing he will seek a new home amid the solitary woods and hills.

Now generally referred, with Welcker, to the Τηρεύς of Sophocles (Frag. 581 Jebb-Pearson); Κρῆσσαι Hartung.

When Procne had served to Tereus the flesh of their son Itys in revenge for his violation of her sister Philomela, Tereus pursued them with an axe; and when the sisters were overtaken, the gods in pity turned Procne into a nightingale and Philomela into a swallow. Tereus became a hoopoe, or a hawk, according to a variant version of the legend. The poet seems to have assimilated the two legends by making the young hoopoe resemble a hawk.

Before speaking of the hoopoe's change in colour and appearance, Aristotle remarks that the cuckoo changes its colour. "On the zoological side," says D'Arcy Thompson, "the myth is based on the similarity of note in the hoopoe and cuckoo, and on the hawk-like appearance of the latter bird." In l. 1 the ἔποψ is called ἐπόπτης "spectator" by word-play; and similarly Tereus was "the watcher" (τηρέω).

166 (305)

τὸ συγγενὲς γὰρ καὶ φθονεῖν ἐπίσταται.

Aristotle, *Rhetoric* ii. 10. p. 1388 a 7 with Scholiast.

For kinsfolk know well to envy too.

167 (307)

<ἄκμων>[1]
σφύρας δέχεσθαι κἀπιχαλκεύειν[2] μύδρους,
ὃς ἀστενακτὶ θύννος ὣς[3] ἠνείχετο[4]
ἄναυδος[5].

Athenaeus, *Deipnosophists* vii. 66. p. 303 c.

1 < > Blaydes.
2 κἀπιχαλκεύει λέγων A : Jacobs. 3 ὡς : Dindorf.
4 ἠνίχετο A : Hermann. 5 ἂν λυδός : Musurus.

An anvil to receive the hammer's blows and to forge the red-hot ore, he, without a groan, endured in silence, like a tunny-fish.

Tunnies, when netted, were killed by blows (*Pers.* 424). As fish, they are "mute" (cp. *Pers.* 575).

Σαλαμίνιαι Hartung.

168 (308)

τὸ σκαιὸν ὄμμα[1] προσβαλὼν θύννου δίκην

Athenaeus, *Deipnosophists* vii. 66. p. 303 c, Plutarch, *On the Craftiness of Animals* 29. 979 E, Aelian, *On Animals* ix. 42, Scholiast on Oppian, *On Fishing* iv. 504, Eustathius on *Iliad* 994. 52.

1 οὗτος καὶ ὄνομα Athen. A (ὄμμα C).

Squinting his left eye, like a tunny-fish

Κήρυκες Droysen.

169 (309)

ἐγὼ δὲ χοῖρον καὶ μάλ' εὐθηλούμενον
τόνδ' ἐν ῥοθοῦντι[1] κριβάνῳ θήσω. τί γὰρ
ὄψον γένοιτ' ἂν ἀνδρὶ τοῦδε βέλτερον[2];

Athenaeus, *Deipnosophists* ix 17. p. 375 E.

1 νοτοῦντι : Dindorf. 2 βέλτιον : Burney.

But this pig—and a well-fatted pig it is—I will place within the crackling oven. For what daintier dish could a man get than this?

Κίρκη E. A. J. Ahrens, Προμηθεὺς σατυρικός Hartung.

170 (310)

λευκός, τί δ' οὐχί; καὶ καλῶς ἠφευμένος
ὁ χοῖρος. ἕψου, μηδὲ λυπηθῇς πυρί.

Athenaeus, *Deipnosophists* ix. 17. p. 375 E; cp. Eustathius on *Iliad*, 1286. 21.

White, of course, and rarely singed, the pig. Boil him and don't be troubled by the fire.

Κήρυκες E. A. J. Ahrens, Προμηθεὺς σατυρικός Hartung.

171 (311)

θύσας δὲ χοῖρον τόνδε τῆς αὐτῆς ὑός,
ἣ πολλά μ'[1] ἐν δόμοισιν εἴργασται κακὰ
δονοῦσα καὶ στρέφουσα[2] τύρβ' ἄνω κάτω

Athenaeus, *Deipnosophists* ix. 17. p. 375 E.

[1] γ': Porson.
[2] τρέπουσα: Blaydes (cp. *Eum.* 651).

But having killed yon pig from the same sow, the sow that had worked me much havoc in the house, pushing and turning everything upside down pell-mell

Κήρυκες E. A. J. Ahrens, Προμηθεὺς σατυρικός Hartung.

172 (312)

αἱ δ' ἑπτ' Ἄτλαντος παῖδες ὠνομασμέναι
πατρὸς μέγιστον ἆθλον οὐρανοστεγῆ
κλαίεσκον, ἔνθα νυκτέρων φαντασμάτων
ἔχουσι μορφὰς ἄπτεροι πελειάδες.

Athenaeus, *Deipnosophists* xi. 80. p. 491 A; cp. Scholiast A on *Iliad* Σ 486, Eustathius on *Odyssey* 1713. 4.

And they who bear the name of Atlas' daughters seven oft bewailed their sire's supremest labour of sustaining heaven, where as wingless Peleiades they have the form of phantoms of the night.

Ἡλιάδες Butler, Προμηθεὺς σατυρικός Hartung.

The daughters of Atlas and Pleione, transformed by Zeus into the constellation of the Πλειάδες, were often regarded as doves (πελειάδες) by poetic fancy and popular mythology. The epithet "wingless" is corrective, because the maidens are not real birds.

173 (313)

χλιδῶν τε πλόκαμος, ὥστε παρθένοις ἁβραῖς·[1]
ὅθεν καλεῖν Κουρῆτα λαόν[2] ᾔνεσαν.

Athenaeus, *Deipnosophists* xii. 37. p. 528 C; cp. Eustathius on *Iliad* 1292. 53.

[1] παρθένου ἁβρᾶς Athen. C, Eust. [2] λοιπὸν Athen. E.

And luxurious locks, like those of delicate maidens; wherefore they approved the name Curetes for the folk.

The Κουρῆτες in question were the earliest inhabitants of Pleuron in Aetolia (cp. *Iliad* I 529; κούρητες in T 193 are "youths," κοῦροι). That the Greeks were hopelessly confused as to the meaning of the name is clear from the lengthy discussion in Strabo, *Geography* x. 3. 6-8, p. 466-467. Apart from other explanations, the word was derived now from κουρά, properly "clipping" of the hair; now from κοῦρος "boy" or κούρη "girl" (the Homeric forms of κόρος and κόρη), and with reference either to hair or to dress. The historian Phylarchus (third century B.C.) declares that Aeschylus here says that the Κουρῆτες got their name from their luxury; and the Fragment certainly implies that, like girls, they wore their hair long (cp. Scholiast on I 529 παρὰ τὸ μὴ κείρεσθαι τὰς κόμας, Scholiast L ἢ ἐπεὶ κόμας κορᾶν εἶχον). But in Agathon's *Thyestes* certain suitors say that they wore their hair long (κομῶντες) until they had been rejected by their lady-love, when they cut off their locks, "the witnesses of their luxury," and by reason of their shorn hair (κούριμος θρίξ) gained the glory of being Κουρῆτες. Archemachus of Euboea (see Strabo) had the notion that the Κουρῆτες, before they removed to Aetolia, wore their hair long behind, but cut it short in front in order that their enemies might not seize them there. Strabo himself attaches no little probability to the opinion of those who sought to reconcile the different accounts of the name; for he says that the application of art to the hair consists in attending to its growth and κουρά, and that both are the peculiar care of κόραι and κόροι. To render κουρά by "hair-dressing," "coiffure," with the implication that the reference is to long hair, is opposed to the etymology (from κείρω "cut"). Relationship between κουρά and κούρη, κόρη, accepted by Curtius, is altogether improbable.

Κρῆσσαι Butler, Ἠδωνοί Hartung.

174 (314)

εἶτ' οὖν σοφιστὴς καλὰ παρῆν παίων[1] χέλυν

Athenaeus, *Deipnosophists* xiv. 32. p. 632 c.

[1] παραπαίων: παρῆν παίων Herwerden.

Or the master of his craft was present, deftly striking the lyre

Athenaeus says that σοφιστής was anciently used of musicians.

175 (315)

τῷ πονοῦντι δ' ἐκ θεῶν
ὀφείλεται τέκνωμα τοῦ πόνου κλέος.

Clement of Alexandria, *Miscellanies* iv. 7. p. 586.

To him that toileth God oweth glory, child of his toil.

Κᾶρες ἢ Εὐρώπη Hartung.

176 (316)

ἀλλ' ἔστι κἀμοὶ κλῇς[1] ἐπὶ γλώσσῃ φύλαξ.

Clement of Alexandria, *Miscellanies* v. 5. p. 661.

[1] κλεὶς L.

But I too have a seal, as a guard, upon my lips.

"My lips were lock'd upon me," Beaumont and Fletcher.

Ἐπίγονοι Hartung.

177 (317)

οἴκοι μένειν χρὴ τὸν καλῶς εὐδαίμονα.
[καὶ τὸν κακῶς πράσσοντα καὶ τοῦτον μένειν]

Clement of Alexandria, *Miscellanies* vi. 2. p. 739; l. 1 Pseudo-Diogenianus *Proverbs* vii. 35 (without naming the poet); with δεῖ for χρή, attributed to Sophocles (Frag. 934 Jebb-Pearson) by Stobaeus, *Anthology* iii. 39. 14 (Hense iii. 724).

He who is truly happy should bide at home [and he who fares ill, he too should bide at home]

Ll. 1-2 Δαναΐδες Hermann, l. 1 Ἡλιάδες Hartung.

Nauck regards l. 2 as a tag by a comic poet: "And he who fares ill? He too should bide at home." The comic poets were fond of describing "the truly happy man."

178 (318)

τοσαῦτα, κῆρυξ, ἐξ ἐμοῦ διάρτασον.

Etymologicum Magnum 149. 57.

So much, Herald, do thou set forth from me point by point.

Ἱκέτιδες l. 953 A Burges, Ἐλευσίνιοι Hartung, Κήρυκες Droysen, Θαλαμοποιοί Wecklein.

179 (319)

εἴ‹τ'› οὖν ἀσαλὴς θεόθεν μανία[1]

Etymologicum Genuinum s.v. ἀσαλής (*Etymologicum Magnum* 151. 49 s.v. ἀσαλὴς μανία).

[1] τουνσαλῆς θεόθεν μανίαο: εἴτ' οὖν Nauck, the rest Reitzenstein.

Or reckless madness from the gods

Νεανίσκοι Hartung.

180 (322)

. . . κάπηλα προσφέρων τεχνήματα

Etymologicum Magnum 490. 12, *Etymologicum Gudianum* 298. 9, Cramer, *Anecdota Graeca Oxoniensia* ii. 456. 6, Suidas, *Lexicon* s.v. κάπηλος.

Applying huckster tricks

Φρύγες Welcker, Φιλοκτήτης Hartung.

181 (326)

ὃς εἶχε πώλους τέσσαρας ζυγηφόρους
φιμοῖσιν αὐλωτοῖσιν ἐστομωμένας

Eustathius on *Iliad* 1157. 36; cp. Pollux, *Vocabulary* 10. 56, Hesychius, *Lexicon* i. 323.

Who had four fillies under yoke, their nostrils bound with fluted muzzles.

Ψυχοστασία Butler, Γλαῦκος Ποτνιεύς Hermann, Μέμνων Kausche.

To produce a terrifying effect by a horse's breathing or trumpeting, its bronze muzzle was pierced with holes, through which the sound issued, as through the pipes of a flute. Cp. *Seven against Thebes* 461 ff.

182 (327)

πρὶν ἂν παλαγμοῖς αἵματος χοιροκτόνου
αὐτός σε χράνῃ[1] Ζεὺς καταστάξας χεροῖν

Eustathius on *Iliad* 1183. 18.

[1] χρᾶναι: Porson.

Until Zeus, letting fall the drops from his hands, himself shall purify thee with sprinklings of the blood of a slain swine

Ἰξίων Pauw, Περραιβίδες Hermann.

183 (329)

πότερα γυνή τις Αἰθίοψ φανήσεται;

Eustathius on *Odyssey* 1484. 48.

Is it some Aethiopian dame that shall appear?

Μέμνων Hermann.

184 (330)

λεοντόχορτον[1] βούβαλιν νεαίρετον[2]

Eustathius on *Odyssey* 1625. 44.

[1] λεοντοχόρταν: L. Dindorf. [2] νεαίτερον: W. Dindorf.

A newly caught antelope, a lion's food

Γλαῦκος Ποτνιεύς Hermann, Ξάντριαι Hartung.

185 (332)

ἕλα, δίωκε, μή τι[1] μαλκίων[2] ποδί.

Harpocration, *Glossary of the Ten Attic Orators* 198. 3.

[1] ἐλλαδίῳ (ἐλαδίω AQ) κεκμῆτι: ἕλα Valesius, δίωκε μή τι Lobeck. [2] μαλακίων BCN.

Push on, pursue, in no wise faint of foot!

Λάϊος Gronovius, Ἡλιάδες Gataker, Φιλοκτήτης Hermann.

186 (337)

ἀπτῆνα[1], τυτθόν, ἄρτι γυμνὸν ὀστράκων

Hesychius, *Lexicon* s.v. ὀστράκων; cp. Photius, *Lexicon* 353. 17.

[1] ἀπτὴν ἄτυτθον: Salmasius.

Wingless, tiny, but just now bare of the egg-shell

Οἰδίπους Hartung.

187 (341)

ὁ κισσεὺς Ἀπόλλων, ὁ βακχεύς,[1] ὁ μάντις

Macrobius, *Saturnalia* i. 18. 6.

[1] καβιας P, βακσιος B: Nauck.

Apollo, the ivy-crowned, the reveller, the seer

Νεανίσκοι Hartung, Βασσάραι Nauck.

The ecstatic mantic art of Apollo assumes a Bacchic character.

188 (342)

δέσποινα νύμφη, δυσχίμων[1] ὀρῶν[2] ἄναξ

Orion, *Etymologicum* 26. 5.

[1] δυσχείμων: Nauck. [2] ὀρῶν: Sturz.

Mistress maiden, ruler of the stormy mountains

Ἠδωνοί Hermann, Καλλιστώ Hartung.

189 (350)

ὁ δ' ἐνδατεῖται[1] τὰς ἐμὰς[2] εὐπαιδίας
νόσων τ' ἀπείρους καὶ μακραίωνας βίου,[3]
ξύμπαντά τ' εἰπὼν θεοφιλεῖς ἐμὰς τύχας
παιᾶν'[4] ἐπηυφήμησεν[5] εὐθυμῶν ἐμέ.
κἀγὼ τὸ Φοίβου θεῖον ἀψευδὲς στόμα
ἤλπιζον εἶναι μαντικῇ βρύον τέχνῃ·
ὁ δ'[6] αὐτὸς ὑμνῶν, αὐτὸς ἐν θοίνῃ[7] παρών,
αὐτὸς τάδ' εἰπών, αὐτός ἐστιν ὁ κτανὼν
τὸν παῖδα τὸν ἐμόν.

Plato, *Republic* ii. 383 B, whence Eusebius, *Preparation for the Gospel* xiii. 3. p. 647 A; ll. 5-9 Athenagoras, *Apology* 21. 104; ll. 7-8 attributed to Sophocles by Phoebammon, *On Figures*, in *Rhetores Graeci* viii. 518; cited, without naming the author, by Plutarch, *How a Young Man ought to hear Poems* 2. 16 E. Plato has οὐδ' [ἐπαινεσόμεθα τοῦτο] Αἰσχύλου ὅταν φῇ ἡ Θέτις τὸν Ἀπόλλω ἐν τοῖς αὐτῆς γάμοις ᾄδοντα ἐνδατεῖσθαι (ἐνδαιτεῖσθαι Euseb.) τὰς ἑὰς εὐπαιδίας . . . ἐμόν.

[1] ὃ δ' ἐνδατεῖται Hermann. [2] ἐμὰς Grotius.
[3] μακραίωνας βίους Plato, μακραίωνος βίου Euseb.: Stephanus (conj.).
[4] παιᾶνα F, παιῶν' AM, παιὼν D, Euseb.
[5] ἐπευφήμησεν MSS. [6] ὃν Plut.
[7] δαίτῃ Plut., γάμοις Phoebammon.

He dwelt on my happiness in my children, whose days were to be many and unacquainted with disease; and, comprising all, in triumph-strain that cheered my soul, he praised my lot, blest of the gods. And so I deemed that falsehood sat not upon Phoebus' lips divine, fraught with the prophet's art. But he, who raised this song himself, he who himself was present at my marriage-feast, he who himself spake thus, he it is who himself hath slain my son.

Ψυχοστασία Butler, Welcker (or from another play of the same group), Ὅπλων κρίσις Ern. Schneider, Θαλαμοποιοί Wagner, Νηρεΐδες Hartung.

Thetis contrasts Apollo's prophecy of her happy motherhood, uttered at her marriage to Peleus, with his deed in guiding the shaft of Paris that killed her son.

190 (352)

θάρσει· πόνου γὰρ τἄκρον[1] οὐκ ἔχει χρόνον.

Plutarch, *How a Young Man ought to hear Poems* 14. 36 B.

[1] ἄκρον: Burges.

Courage! Suffering, when it climbs highest, lasts not long.

Φιλοκτήτης Hartung.

191 (353)

ὡς οὐ δικαίως θάνατον ἔχθουσιν βροτοί,
ὅσπερ μέγιστον ῥῦμα τῶν πολλῶν κακῶν.

Plutarch, *Consolation to Apollonius* 10. 106 C.

Since unjustly men hate death, which is the greatest defence against their many ills.

Φιλοκτήτης Hartung.

192 (354)

ἀποπτύσαι δεῖ καὶ καθήρασθαι στόμα.[1]

Plutarch, *Of Isis and Osiris* 20. 358 E; cp. *Etymologicum Genuinum* and *Etymologicum Magnum* s.v. ἀπάργματα.

[1] τὸ στόμα: Reiske.

Thou needs must spit it out and make clean thy mouth.

Περραιβίδες or Λάϊος *Etymologicum Genuinum*.

Those who committed murder by treachery sought to purify themselves by tasting, and then spitting out, the blood of their victims.

193 (355)

. μειξοβόαν[1] πρέπει
διθύραμβον ὁμαρτεῖν
σύγκωμον[2] Διονύσῳ.

Plutarch, *On the* E *at Delphi* 9. 389 A.

[1] μιξόβοαν: Nauck (*Suppl.*). [2] σύγκοινον: Tyrwhitt.

'Tis meet that the dithyramb, his fellow-reveller, half song, half shout, attend on Dionysus.

Νεανίσκοι Hermann, 'Ηδωνοί Hartung.

194 (356)

λαβὼν γὰρ αὐτόθηκτον Εὐβοικὸν ξίφος

Plutarch, *On the Cessation of Oracles* 43. 434 A.

For seizing a self-sharpened Euboean sword

Θρῆσσαι Osann.

"Self-sharpened" is supposed to mean "cold-forged," not "fire-forged" (cp. *Seven against Thebes* 942). ἀρτίθηκτον "just sharpened," Sidgwick (after ἄρτι θηκτὸν Blaydes) is the best of the many conjectures.

195 (357)

ὑψηλὸν ἡβήσασα[1] τεκτόνων πόνον
<συνεῖλεν>.[2]

Plutarch, *On the Restraint of Anger* 4. 454 E.

[1] ἡβάσασα: Heath. [2] < > Hartung, from Plutarch.

[The flame,] come to its youthful strength, consumed the lofty labour of the carpenters.

196 (358)

†οὐδὲ ἀπο. . . αὐτόν· οὐ γὰρ ἐγγύθεν
. . . γέρων δὲ γραμματεὺς γενοῦ σαφής†

Plutarch, *Table Talk* i. 8. 1. p. 625 D.

. . . But when old show thyself a clear scribe (?)

Σαλαμίνιαι Hartung.

Cited by Plutarch to illustrate his remark that old men can read only when a book is held at a distance. The mangled passage eludes satisfactory emendation: σὺ δὲ (so Heath) | ἄπωθεν εἶδες αὐτόν· οὐ γὰρ ἐγγύθεν | ὁρᾷν· γέρων κτλ. Dindorf; and so E. A. J. Ahrens, but reading ὁρᾷς. σὺ δ' ἐξ ἀπόπτου (cp. Sophocles, *Philoctetes* 446) Headlam. The second line seems to mean "when old, write a large, clear hand," remembering that the aged read with difficulty.

197 (359)

σύ τοί μ' ἔφυσας,[1] σύ με[2] καταφθερεῖν[3] δοκεῖς.

Plutarch, *On Monarchy, Democracy, Oligarchy* 4. 827 C, *Life of Demetrius* 35.

[1] με φυσᾷς 827 c, *Dem.* PηRV, μ' ἔφυσας vulg.
[2] σύ με 827 c, *Dem.* PLDA², σύ μοι *Dem.* A¹BC, σύ με καταίθειν μοι *Dem.* cod. 1679, vulg.
[3] καταίθειν: καταφθέρειν Hartung, καταφθερεῖν Wecklein.

Thou indeed didst give me life, thou dost think to destroy me.

Πενθεύς Anonymous reported by Stanley, Ξάντριαι Stanley, Νιόβη Hartung, a satyr-play Gomperz.

The reading σύ τοι με φυσᾷς, σύ με καταίθειν δοκεῖς, adopted by Perrin, means "Thou fannest indeed my flame, methinks thou dost quench me too."

Demetrius Poliorcetes quoted the verse in addressing Fortune.

198 (361)

ἐξ ὀσφυαλγοῦς κὠδυνοσπάδος[1] λυγροῦ
γέροντος

Plutarch, *That the Stoics speak greater Improbabilities than the Poets* 2. 1057 F.

[1] καὶ ὀδυνοσπάδος : Dübner.

[Changed from] a piteous old man with a stitch in his back and cramped by pain

Τήλεφος Schütz, Φιλοκτήτης Butler, Διονύσου τροφοί Hartung.

199 (362)

ἀλλ' οὔτε πολλὰ τραύματ' ἐν στέρνοις λαβὼν
θνήσκει τις, εἰ μὴ τέρμα συντρέχει βίου,
οὔτ' ἐν στέγῃ τις ἥμενος παρ' ἑστίᾳ
φεύγει τι μᾶλλον τὸν πεπρωμένον μόρον.

Plutarch, *Life and Poetry of Homer* 157 (Wyttenbach v. 1196). In l. 2 Wecklein read μοῖρα for τέρμα.

A man dies not for all the many wounds that pierce his breast, unless it be that life's end keep pace with death, nor by sitting on his hearth at home doth he the more escape his appointed doom

Ἐλευσίνιοι Hartung.

This is perhaps the nearest approach to pure fatalism in Greek tragedy. Cp. Demosthenes, *On the Crown* (18. 97) πέρας μὲν γὰρ ἅπασιν ἀνθρώποις ἐστὶ τοῦ βίου θάνατος, κἂν ἐν οἰκίσκῳ τις αὐτὸν καθείρξας τηρῇ, "for all men's lives have a fixed limit in death, even though a man shut himself in a chamber and keep watch."

200 (363)

ὀξυγλύκειάν τἄρα κοκκιεῖς ῥόαν.

Cited from Aeschylus by Aristophanes, Fragment 610 (Pollux, *Vocabulary* 6. 80).

Truly then thou shalt pick the seeds from out the bitter-sweet pomegranate.

Ἐλευσίνιοι Butler.

201 (364)

Λιβυρνικῆς μίμημα μανδύης χιτών

Pollux, *Vocabulary* 7. 60; cp. Stephen of Byzantium, *Lexicon* 415. 10.

A frock that copies the Libyrnic cloak

Ἠδωνοί Hartung, Οἰδίπους others.

202 (365)

σὺ δὲ σπαθητοῖς τριμιτίνοις ὑφάσμασιν

Pollux, *Vocabulary* 7. 78.

And thou in a well-woven robe of drill

Ἠδωνοί Hartung.

τρίμιτος, "three-threaded," having three threads in the warp.

203 (366)

ἀλλ' ἐκ μεγίστων εὐμαρῶς λουτηρίων

Pollux, *Vocabulary* 7. 167, cp. 10. 46.

But easily from baths exceeding large

Γλαῦκος πόντιος Hermann.

204 (369)

ἐκ[1] πηλοπλάστου σπέρματος θνητὴ γυνή

Proclus, *Commentary on Hesiod's Works and Days* 156.

[1] ἐκ cod. Casanatensis, τοῦ vulg.

A mortal woman from out a seed moulded of clay

Προμηθεὺς λυόμενος Butler, a Προμηθεύς Hermann.

After Prometheus had stolen fire, Zeus in revenge bade Hephaestus fashion Pandora out of earth.

205 (372)

ἀφρὸς
βορᾶς[1] βροτείας ἐρρύη κατὰ[2] στόμα.

Scholiast Ravennas on Aristophanes, *Lysistrata* 1257.

[1] βορρᾶς Put., βορῆς K. [2] ἐρρυηκότα : Porson.

Froth from human food streamed over their jaws.

Γλαῦκος Ποτνιεύς Hartung.

206 (373)

δεινοὶ πλέκειν τοι μηχανὰς Αἰγύπτιοι.

Scholiast on Aristophanes, *Clouds* 1130, on Theocritus, *Idyll* xv. 48 ; and in collectors of proverbs : Zenobius iii. 37, Pseudo-Diogenianus iv. 35, Gregory of Cyprus (cod. Leid. 1. 88, Mosq. 2. 84), Macarius, *Rose-bed* iii. 21, and other late writers.

Truly at weaving wiles the Egyptians are clever.

Δαναΐδες Hermann, Θαλαμοποιοί Oberdick.

207 (375)

ἀμήχανον τέχνημα[1] καὶ δυσέκδυτον[2]

Scholiast on Euripides, *Orestes* 25.

[1] τεύχημα: Nauck. [2] δυσέκλυτον: Dindorf.

A device, irresistible and inextricable

In place of Χοηφόροι l. 999 Wecklein, Πρωτεύς Wilamowitz.

208 (379)

ὑμεῖς δὲ βωμὸν τόνδε καὶ πυρὸς σέλας
κύκλῳ περίστητ'[1] ἐν λόχῳ τ' ἀπείρονι
εὔξασθε.

Scholiast B on *Iliad* Ξ 200, Scholiasts DE on *Odyssey* α 98.

[1] περίσταρ' or περίστατε Schol. *Od.*

Take ye your stand in a ring about yon altar and its gleaming fire, and with your band grouped in a circle offer up your prayers.

Ἱκέτιδες (after l. 232) Burges, Δαναΐδες Hermann, Προμηθεὺς λυόμενος Hartung, Μυσοί Droysen.

209 (381)

ὅπου γὰρ ἰσχὺς συζυγοῦσι καὶ δίκη,
ποία ξυνωρὶς τῆσδε[1] καρτερωτέρα;

Scholiasts BLT on *Iliad* Π 542.

[1] τῶνδε: Grotius.

For where might and justice are yoke-fellows—what pair is stronger than this?

Προμηθεὺς λυόμενος Hartung.

210 (382)

πάτερ Θέοινε, Μαινάδων ζευκτήριε

Scholiast and Tzetzes on Lycophron's *Alexandra* 1247; cp. Harpocration, *Glossary of the Ten Attic Orators* 151. 5, Hesychius, *Lexicon* s.v. Θεοίνια.

Father Theoinos, thou subduer of the Maenads!

From a Dionysiac drama, possibly the Ξάντριαι, Butler; Νεανίσκοι Hartung.

211 (383)

Ἥρα τέλεια, Ζηνὸς εὐναία δάμαρ

Scholiast on Pindar, *Nemean* 10. 31 (18).

Hera, the Perfecter, wedded wife of Zeus

Compare *Eumenides* 214.

212 (384)

ἐναγώνιε Μαίας καὶ Διὸς Ἑρμᾶ

Scholiast on Pindar, *Pythian* 2. 18 (10).

O Hermes, lord of games, son of Maia and Zeus!

213 (385)

οἵ τοι[1] στεναγμοὶ τῶν πόνων ἐρείσματα.[2]

Scholiast on Sophocles, *Electra* 286, and Scholiasts TV on *Iliad* Ψ 10.

[1] οἵ τοι Schol. *Il.*, οἵ τε, οἱ γὰρ, or οἱ δὲ Schol. *El.*
[2] ἐρείσματα Schol. *El.*, ἰάματα Schol. *Il.*

Truly lamentation is a prop of suffering.

214 (386)

λαμπραῖσιν ἀστραπαῖσι λαμπάδων σθένει

Scholiast on Sophocles, *Oedipus Coloneus* 1047.

With bright flashes, the torches' might

'Ελευσίνιοι Pauw, Οἰδίπους Lobeck, 'Ιφιγένεια or 'Ιέρειαι Fritzsche.

Aeschylus may be speaking of Eleusis, where the initiates bore torches. But cp. *Eumenides* 1022.

215 (387)

ἔφριξ' ἔρωτι[1] τοῦδε μυστικοῦ τέλους.

Scholiast on Sophocles, *Oedipus Coloneus* 1049.

[1] ἔρως δὲ: Jacobs, Brunck.

I thrill with the rapture of this mystic rite.

'Ελευσίνιοι Pauw, Βάκχαι (= Βασσάραι) Hartung.

216 (388)

δέσποιν' Ἑκάτη,
τῶν βασιλείων πρόδομος[1] μελάθρων

Scholiast on Theocritus, *Idyll* ii. 36; cp. Aristeides, *Athena* 17 (vol. i. 27).

[1] πρόδομος Theocr. (cod. Canon. 86), πρόδρομος Theocr. vulg., Arist.

Lady Hecate, before the portal of the royal halls

Αἰγύπτιοι Tittler, Διονύσου τροφοί Hartung.

217 (389)

κοινὸν[1] τύχη, γνώμη δὲ τῶν κεκτημένων.

Stobaeus, *Anthology* ii. 8. 10 (Wachsmuth ii. 155), Menander, *Single-verse Maxims* 679.

[1] καινὸν Stob. P.

Fortune is for all, judgment is theirs who have won it for themselves.

218 (390)

ὁ χρήσιμ' εἰδώς, οὐχ ὁ πόλλ' εἰδώς, σοφός.

Stobaeus, *Anthology* iii. 3. 11 (Hense iii. 194) MA, om. S.

Who knows things useful, not many things, is wise.

219 (391)

ἁμαρτάνει τοι[1] καὶ σοφοῦ σοφώτερος.

Stobaeus, *Anthology* iii. 3. 14 (Hense iii. 195) MA, om. S.

[1] τοι A, τι M.

Truly even he errs that is wiser than the wise.

220 (392)

ἦ βαρὺ φόρημ' ἄνθρωπος εὐτυχῶν ἄφρων.

Stobaeus, *Anthology* iii. 4. 18 (Hense iii. 223).

Verily a prosperous fool is a heavy load.

221 (393)

κάτοπτρον εἴδους χαλκός ἐστ',[1] οἶνος δὲ νοῦ.

Stobaeus, *Anthology* iii. 18. 12 (Hense iii. 515); cp. Athenaeus, *Deipnosophists* x. 31. p. 427 F omitting the source.

[1] ἐστ' Athen., ἐστι Stob.

Bronze is a mirror of the face, wine of the mind.

'Αργώ Hartung.

222 (394)

οὐκ ἀνδρὸς ὅρκοι πίστις,[1] ἀλλ' ὅρκων ἀνήρ.

Stobaeus, *Anthology* iii. 27. 2 (Hense iii. 611), Arsenius, *Violet-bed* in *Paroemiographi Graeci* i. 579. 25.

[1] πίστις Stob. LA, πίστεις Stob. SMd, Ars.

Oaths are not surety for a man, but the man for the oaths.

Περραιβίδες Hartung.

223 (395)

φιλεῖ δὲ τῷ κάμνοντι συσπεύδειν θεός.[1]

Stobaeus, *Anthology* iii. 29. 31 (Hense iii. 630).

[1] φιλεῖ (φιλοῖ first hand) δέ τοι δαιμόνιε . . . θεοῖς M.

God loves to help him who strives to help himself.

From Euripides, according to Arsenius, *Violet-bed* in *Paroemiographi Graeci* ii. 712. 13.

224 (396)

καλὸν δὲ καὶ γέροντα[1] μανθάνειν σοφά.

Stobaeus, *Anthology* iii. 29. 24 (Hense iii. 632), Menander, *Single-verse Maxims* 297.

[1] γέροντι Men.

'Tis seemly that even the aged learn wisdom.

225 (397)

πρὸ τῶν τοιούτων χρὴ λόγων δάκνειν στόμα.

Stobaeus, *Anthology* iii. 34. 5 (Hense iii. 683) SM, om. A.

Ere thou utterest words such as these, thou must bite thy lips.

226 (398)

κακοὶ γὰρ εὖ πράσσοντες οὐκ ἀνασχετοί.

Stobaeus, *Anthology* iv. 4. 14 (Hense iv. 187).

For successful rascals are insufferable.

227 (399)

τὸ γὰρ βρότειον σπέρμ᾽ ἐφ᾽ ἡμέραν[1] φρονεῖ,
καὶ πιστὸν οὐδὲν μᾶλλον ἢ καπνοῦ σκιά.

Stobaeus, *Anthology* iv. 34. 44 (Hense v. 838), Apostolius in *Paroemiographi Graeci* ii. 686. 3.

[1] ἐφημέρια Stob. S, Apost., ἐφήμερα Stob. MA: Dindorf.

For mortal kind taketh thought only for the day, and hath no more surety than the shadow of smoke.

Νιόβη Hartung.

228 (400)

γῆρας γὰρ ἥβης ἐστὶν ἐνδικώτερον.

Stobaeus, *Anthology* iv. 50. 7 (Hense v. 1022).

For age is more just than youth.

229 (401)

ζόης[1] πονηρᾶς θάνατος αἱρετώτερος·[2]
τὸ μὴ γενέσθαι δ᾽ ἐστὶν ἢ[3] πεφυκέναι
κρεῖσσον κακῶς πάσχοντα.[4]

Stobaeus, *Anthology* iv. 53. 17 (Hense v. 1102) SA, om. M, Menander, *Single-verse Maxims* 193.

[1] ζωῆς: Dindorf.
[2] εὐπορώτερος Stob., αἱρετώτερος Men.
[3] ἐστὶ μᾶλλον ἢ: Grotius.
[4] κρεῖσσον . . . πάσχοντα A, om. S.

Death is rather to be chosen than a toilsome life; and not to be born is better than to be born to misery.

Οἰδίπους Hartung; Euripides, L. Dindorf.

230 (402)

. . ἀφ' οὗ Ῥήγιον κικλήσκεται

Strabo, *Geography* vi. 6. p. 258.

Whence it shall bear the name Rhegium

Γλαῦκος πόντιος Hermann, Προμηθεὺς λυόμενος Schütz.

At Rhegium Sicily was broken off (ἀπορρήγνυμι) from the mainland by an earthquake.

231 (403, 403 A, 284)

Βοῦράν θ' ἱερὰν καὶ κεραυνίας Ῥύπας
Δύμην ‹θ'›[1] Ἑλίκην ἠδ' Αἴγειραν
τήν τ' αἰπεινὴν[2] ζαθέαν[3] Ὤλενον

Strabo, *Geography* viii. 7. 5. p. 387 (ll. 2-3 in the Cozza-Luzzi MS.); l. 3 Stephen of Byzantium, *Lexicon* 707. 13; cp. Photius, *Lexicon* 492. 10.

[1] ‹ › Wilam.
[2] ἢ δ' αἰγέα ραν τὴν ταπεινὴ : Wilam.
[3] ζαθέαν τ' Paris.

Hallowed Bura and thunder-smitten Rhypae, and Dyme, Helice and Aegeira and precipitous, sacred Olenus

All these places are in Achaea.

Γλαῦκος πόντιος Hartung, Κᾶρες ἢ Εὐρώπη Meineke, Δαναΐδες M. Schmidt.

232 (404)

Αἴγινα δ' αὕτη πρὸς νότου κεῖται πνοάς.

Strabo, *Geography* ix. 1. 9. p. 393.

Aegina yonder lies towards the southern blasts.

Σαλαμίνιαι Wagner. A description of the position of the ancient city of Salamis.

233 (451 G)

ἀκμὴν δ᾽ ὅσα
τὰ κύμβαλ᾽ ἠχεῖ

Anonymous Grammarian in *Lexicon Vaticanum* (cod. Vaticanus Graecus 12) s.v. ἀκμήν.

But as yet all the cymbals that raised a din

DOUBTFUL OR SPURIOUS FRAGMENTS

234 (452)

οὐ χρὴ λέοντος σκύμνον ἐν πόλει τρέφειν·[1]
[μάλιστα μὲν λέοντα μὴ 'ν πόλει τρέφειν][2]
ἢν δ' ἐκτραφῇ τις, τοῖς τρόποις ὑπηρετεῖν.

Aristophanes, *Frogs* 1431, *Palatine Anthology* x. 110, Suidas, *Lexicon* s.v. οὐ χρή and σκύμνος; l. 1 Macarius, *Rose-bed* vi. 71; ll. 2-3 quoted by Plutarch in reference to Alcibiades in his *Life* 16.

[1] Rejected by Dindorf.

[2] Rejected by J. H. Voss (the verse is absent in Aristoph Ven. ACD).

One must not rear a lion's whelp in the State [best of all not to rear a lion in the State]; but if one be reared to his full growth, we must humour his ways.

Compare *Agam.* 717 ff.

Ll. 1 and 3 Δαναΐδες Hermann.

235 (453)

καλῶς τεθνάναι[1] κάλλιον ἂν μᾶλλον ἢ σεσῶσθαι.

Thomas Magister, *Collection of Attic Nouns and Verbs* 238. 8.

[1] τεθνᾶναι GB.

Nobly to die were better than to save one's life.

Ἑπτὰ ἐπὶ Θήβας Thomas Magister, but μᾶλλον ἐνδικώτερος (cp. l. 673) is lacking in his citation.

DOUBTFUL OR SPURIOUS FRAGMENTS

236 (456)

δράσαντι γάρ τοι[1] καὶ παθεῖν ὀφείλεται.

Stobaeus, *Anthology* i. 3. 24 (Wachsmuth i. 56), Theophilus, *To Autolycus* ii. 37. p. 176.

[1] τι Stob. A.

For, of a truth, the doer is bound to suffer.

Probably from Sophocles (Fragment 229 Jebb-Pearson), but ascribed to Aeschylus because of *Choëph.* 313.

237 (462)

ψυχὰς ἔχοντες κυμάτων ἐν ἀγκάλαις

Aristophanes, *Frogs* 704 with Scholiast.

With our lives in the clasp of the waves

Archilochus 25, but ascribed to Aeschylus by Didymus.

238 (463)

Κύπρου Πάφου τ' ἔχουσα πάντα κλῆρον

Strabo, *Geography* viii. 3. 8. p. 341, Eustathius on *Iliad* 305. 34.

Possessing as their allotted share all Cyprus and Paphos

Δαναΐδες or Θαλαμηπόλοι (*sic*) Hartung ; from Archilochus according to Meineke.

239 (464)

χώριζε θνητῶν τὸν θεὸν καὶ μὴ δόκει
ὅμοιον αὐτοῖς[1] σάρκινον καθεστάναι.
οὐκ οἶσθα δ'[2] αὐτόν· ποτὲ μὲν ὡς πῦρ φαίνεται
ἄπλατος ὁρμῇ,[3] ποτὲ δ' ὕδωρ, ποτὲ[4] γνόφος·
καὶ θηρσὶν αὐτὸς γίνεται παρεμφερής,

ἀνέμῳ νεφέλῃ τε, κἀστραπῇ,[5] βροντῇ, βροχῇ.
ὑπηρετεῖ δ' αὐτῷ θάλασσα καὶ πέτραι
καὶ πᾶσα πηγὴ χὔδατος[6] συστήματα·
τρέμει δ' ὄρη καὶ γαῖα καὶ πελώριος
βυθὸς θαλάσσης κὠρέων[7] ὕψος μέγα,[8]
ὅταν[9] ἐπιβλέψῃ γοργὸν ὄμμα δεσπότου.
πάντα δύναται[10] γάρ· δόξα δ'[11] ὑψίστου θεοῦ.

Clement of Alexandria, *Miscellanies* v. 14. p. 727, Eusebius, *Preparation for the Gospel* xiii. 13. p. 689 B, [Justin Martyr,] *On Monarchy* 2. 130.

[1] ὅμοιον αὑτῷ or ἑαυτῷ Clem., ὅμοιον ἑαυτῷ or σαυτῷ Just., ὅμοιον σαυτῷ IO*, σαυτῷ ὅμοιον (three MSS.), ὅμοιον αὐτῷ O[2], Eus.: Blaydes.

[2] οἶσθα δ' Clem., οἶσθά γ' or οἶσθας Eus., οἶσθας or οἶσθα δ' Just. [3] ὁρμῇ Eus., ὁρμή Clem., Just.

[4] ποτὲ δὲ Clem., Just.

[5] καὶ ἀστραπῇ Clem., Eus. IO. [6] καὶ ὕδατος : Sylburg.

[7] κὠρέων or καὶ ὀρέων Just., καὶ ὀρέων Clem., Eus.

[8] ἐπὶ μέγα Eus. [9] ὅταν Just., ἐπὰν Clem., Eus.

[10] δύναται Clem., Just., δυνατὴ Eus.

[11] δόξα δὲ Just., δόξα Clem., Eus.

Set God apart from mortal men, and deem not that he, like them, is fashioned out of flesh. Thou knowest him not; now he appeareth as fire, unapproachable in his onset, now as water, now as gloom; and he, even himself, is dimly seen in the likeness of wild beasts, of wind, of cloud, of lightning, thunder, and of rain. Ministers unto him are sea, and rocks, and every spring, and gathered floods; before him tremble mountains and earth and the vast abyss of the sea and the lofty pinnacles of the mountains, whensoever the flashing eye of their lord looketh on them. For all power hath he; lo, this is the glory of the Most High God.

Aeschylean authorship has generally been rejected since Grotius.

The Fragment was ascribed to Aeschylus in antiquity probably because of its lofty conception of God.

240 (Wecklein 478)

ἀνδρῶν τάδ'[1] *ἐστὶν ἐνδίκων*[2] *τε καὶ σοφῶν,*
κἀν τοῖς κακοῖσι[3] *μὴ τεθυμῶσθαι θεοῖς.*

Plutarch, *Consolation to Apollonius* 29. 116 F, Stobaeus, *Anthology* iv. 4. 36 (Hense v. 967).

[1] *τάδ'* Stob., *γὰρ* Plut.
[2] *ἐνδίκων* Stob., *ἐναρέτων* Plut.
[3] *ἐν τοῖς κακοῖσι* (or *κακίστοις*) Plut., *κἀν τοῖς δεινοῖσι* Stob.

This is the mark of men just and wise as well—even in calamity not to cherish anger against the gods.

From Aeschylus (Plutarch), Μυρμιδόνες E. A. J. Ahrens. Νιόβη Burmeister; from Euripides (Stobaeus: Nauck Frag. 1078).

241 (Wecklein 479)

Δήμητερ ἡ θρέψασα τὴν ἐμὴν φρένα
εἶναί με τῶν σῶν ἄξιον μυστηρίων.

Spoken by Aeschylus in Aristophanes. *Frogs* 886-7 (see Scholiast); l. 1 assigned to Aeschylus in inferior MSS. (not in Ven. or Rav.).

O Demeter, thou that didst nourish my soul, grant that I be worthy of thy Mysteries!

Ἐλευσίνιοι Butler.

242 (Anon. 97, Wecklein 467)

λαβὼν ἀριστόνικον ἐν μάχῃ κράτος

Athenaeus, *Deipnosophists* x. 85. p. 457 B.

Having won a glorious victory in battle

Assigned to Aeschylus by Nauck.

243 (Anon. 208, Wecklein 468)

ἐν πέδαις[1] ‹σε›[2] γαμόρος
μάρψειεν[3] Ἅιδης.

Hesychius, *Lexicon* s.v. ἐμπεδής.

[1] ἐμπεδὴς: ἐν πέδῃς M. Schmidt (πέδαις Wecklein).
[2] ‹ › Burges. [3] μάρψεν: Burges.

May Hades, whose portion is the earth, seize and fetter thee!

Assigned to Aeschylus by Burges.

Text and application are uncertain. Possibly Hades is called "landowner" to contrast his distinctive domain from that of Zeus and of Poseidon.

244 (Anon. 269, Wecklein 470)

Τιρύνθιον πλίνθευμα,[1] Κυκλώπων ἕδος

Hesychius, *Lexicon* s.v. Τιρύνθιον πλίνθευμα and Κυκλώπων ἕδος.

[1] πλίνθεμα: Musurus.

Walled Tiryns, the Cyclopes' seat

Assigned to Aeschylus by Nauck. The two glosses were joined by Meineke.

245 (Anon. 295, Wecklein 471)

δεινόν γε τὴν μὲν μυῖαν ἀλκίμῳ σθένει
πηδᾶν ἐπ' ἀνδρῶν σώμαθ', ὡς πλησθῇ φόνου,
ἄνδρας δ' ὁπλίτας πολέμιον ταρβεῖν δόρυ.

Lucian, *The Fly* 11 (Sommerbrodt iii. 121).

Shameful is it that the fly, with courageous might, should leap upon men's bodies to glut itself with blood, yet men-at-arms should dread the foeman's spear.

Assigned to Aeschylus by Bergk.

246 (Anon. 303)

θεόθεν δὲ πνέοντ' οὖρον ἀνάγκη
τλῆναι καμάτοις ἀνοδύρτοις.

Marcus Antoninus, *Meditations* 7. 51.

When a storm bloweth, sent of the gods, we needs must endure it, toiling without complaint.

Assigned to Aeschylus by Wagner.

247 (Anon. 358)

ΑΛΚ. ἀνδροκτόνου γυναικὸς ὁμογενὴς ἔφυς.
ΑΔΡ. σὺ δ' αὐτόχειρ γε μητρὸς ἥ σ' ἐγείνατο.

Plutarch, *How a Young Man ought to hear Poems* 13. 35 E, *How to Profit by our Enemies* 5. 88 F.

ALC. Thou art near akin to a woman that brought death upon her husband.

ADR. And thou, with thine own hand, didst slay the mother that bare thee.

'Επίγονοι Wagner. Brunck and Hermann ascribed the verses to Sophocles' 'Επίγονοι.

L. 1 spoken by Alcmeon, son of Amphiaraüs and Eriphyle, l. 2 by Adrastus, brother of Eriphyle. Eriphyle had been bribed by Polynices with the necklace of Harmonia to influence Amphiaraüs against his better judgment to join the first expedition against Thebes, from which he knew that he should not return alive (cp. *Seven against Thebes* l. 587). In the second expedition the most important person was Alcmeon, who killed his mother and went mad.

248 (Anon. 2)

ὀλόμενε παίδων, ποῖον εἴρηκας λόγον;

Athenaeus, *Deipnosophists* xiii. 14. p. 584 D.

Cursed boy! What word is this that thou hast uttered?

From the Ἐπίγονοι of Aeschylus or of Sophocles (Wagner).

249 (Anon. 375, Wecklein 472)

ἀλλ' εἴτ' ἔνυπνον φάντασμα φοβῇ
χθονίας θ' Ἑκάτης κῶμον ἐδέξω

Plutarch, *On Superstition* 3. 166 A.

But either thou art frightened of a spectre beheld in sleep and hast joined the revel-rout of nether Hecate

Assigned to Aeschylus by Porson.

250 (Anon. 405, Wecklein 473)

οὐ γάρ με Νὺξ ἔτικτε δεσπότην λύρας,
οὐ μάντιν, οὐδ' ἰατρόν, ἀλλ' εὐνάτορα[1]
ψυχαῖς.

Plutarch, *On Love* 15. 758 B.

[1] ἀλλὰ θνητὸν ἅμα: Jacobs ἀλλ' εὐνήτορα (εὐνάτορα Nauck).

For Night brought me not forth to be the lord of the lyre, nor to be seer or leech, but to lull to rest men's souls.

Assigned to Aeschylus by Hermann.
Spoken by Sleep.

251 (Anon. 446, Wecklein 474)

<ὁ>[1] Ζεὺς κατεῖδε χρόνιος εἰς[2] τὰς διφθέρας.

Scholiast B on *Iliad* A 175, and cited by collectors of proverbs: Zenobius iv. 11, Gregory of Cyprus (cod. Leid. 2. 19, Mosq. 3. 53), Pseudo-Diogenianus iv. 95 a.

[1] < > Valckenaer. [2] ἐπὶ Pseudo-Diogen.

Zeus looked late into his book.

Assigned to Aeschylus by Valckenaer.

A proverb concerning the delayed punishment of the wicked. The "book of Zeus" is the "book of life." Cp. *Eum.* 275.

252 (Anon. 470)

ἔπειτα πάσης Ἑλλάδος καὶ ξυμμάχων
βίον διῴκησ' ὄντα πρὶν πεφυρμένον
θηρσίν θ' ὅμοιον. πρῶτα μὲν τὸν πάνσοφον
ἀριθμὸν ηὕρηκ'[1] ἔξοχον σοφισμάτων.

Stobaeus, *Anthology* i., proem. 1 a (Wachsmuth 1. 15); cp. Plato, *Republic* vii. 522 D.

[1] εὕρηκ': Nauck.

Thereafter I ordered the life of all Hellas and of the allies, the life aforetime confused and like to that of wild beasts. First I invented number, all-wise, chiefest of sciences.

Παλαμήδης Wachsmuth. Cp. Frag. 96, from that play.

253 (Anon. 493, Wecklein 475)

ὁρᾷ Δίκη σ' ἄναυδος οὐχ ὁρωμένη
εὕδοντα καὶ στείχοντα καὶ καθήμενον.
ἑξῆς δ' ὀπαδεῖ δόχμιον, ἄλλοθ' ὕστερον.

Stobaeus, *Anthology* i. 3. 28 (Wachsmuth i. 57), Theophilus, *To Autolycus* ii. 37. p. 178.

ὁρᾷ δίκην ἄναυδον (Theoph., Stob. P[2], ἄνανδον F, ἄναβδον

P[1]) οὐχ ὁρωμένην εὕδοντι καὶ στείχοντι καὶ καθημένῳ (στίχοντι καθημένῳ Theoph.)· ἑξῆς δ' ὀπηδεῖ (ἑξῆς ὀπάζει Theoph.) δόχμιον (δόγμιον Theoph.) ἄλλο δ' (δὲ Theoph.) ὕστερον: Herwerden (ὀπαδεῖ Nauck, ἄλλοθ' Grotius).

Justice, voiceless, unseen, seeth thee when thou sleepest and when thou goest forth and when thou liest down. Continually doth she attend thee, now aslant thy course, now at a later time.

Assigned to Aeschylus by Hermann.

254 (Anon. 506, Wecklein 476)

πάντων τύραννος ἡ τύχη 'στὶ τῶν θεῶν,
τὰ δ' ἄλλ'[1] ὀνόματα ταῦτα προσκεῖται μάτην·
μόνη διοικεῖ[2] γοῦν[3] ἅπανθ' ᾗ[4] βούλεται.

Stobaeus, *Anthology* i. 6. 16 (Wachsmuth i. 87).

[1] ἄλλα FP.
[2] διοικεῖν: Jernstedt.
[3] οὖν: Nauck.
[4] ἅπαντα: Jernstedt.

Sovereign of all the gods is Fortune, and these other names are given her in vain; for she alone disposeth all things as she wills.

Assigned to Aeschylus by Wachsmuth.

Some "other names" of Tyche are πρακτήριος *Suppliant Maidens* 523, σωτήρ *Agam.* 664, ἡ εὖ διδοῦσα Sophocles, *Oedipus Tyrannus* 1080.

255 (Anon. 519)

οὐ χρὴ πόδωκη τὸν τρόπον λίαν φορεῖν.

Stobaeus, *Anthology* iii. 4. 16 (Hense iii. 223).

One must not have a manner too swift-paced.

Assigned to Φρύγες ἢ Ἕκτορος λύτρα by Hermann, who made Priam speak this verse, followed (as in Stobaeus) by σφαλεὶς γὰρ οὐδεὶς εὖ βεβουλεῦσθαι δοκεῖ

("For none who hath been overthrown deems that he has been counselled well");

and let Priam, after two verses by Achilles, continue his reproach with the lines:

τὸ δ' ὠκὺ τοῦτο καὶ τὸ λαιψηρὸν φρενῶν
εἰς συμφορὰν καθῆκε πολλὰ δὴ βροτούς.

("For this hastiness and lightness of mind hath oft brought mortals to misery").

Nauck ascribed σφαλεὶς γὰρ κτλ. to Chaeremon (Frag. 26), the two verses to Euripides (Frag. 1032).

256 (Anon. 238, Wecklein 480)

ὡς οἰνοπλῆγες <καὶ>[1] μεθυστάδες γάμων

Hesychius, *Lexicon* s.v. μεθυστάδες.

[1] < > Salmasius.

Like maids, wine-stricken and drunk with love

Λυκούργεια Hermann, Νεανίσκοι Hartung.

257 (Anon. 261, Wecklein 481)

<νοτὶς>[1] προσαυρίζουσα χερσαίᾳ †τροχῇ

Hesychius, *Lexicon* s.v. προσαυρίζουσα.

[1] < > Salmasius.

Moisture meeting a current from dry land (?)

Assigned to Aeschylus by Dindorf.

258 (Anon. 260, Wecklein 482)

. . προσαιθρίζουσα[1] πόμπιμον φλόγα

Hesychius, *Lexicon* s.v. προσαιθερίζουσα.

[1] προσαιθερίζουσα: Alberti.

Raising to the skies the missive flame

Intruded into *Agam.* 301 by Dindorf.

259 (483 Wecklein)

ᾄσσουσα δ' ἐξέλαμψεν ἀστραπῆς δίκην.[1]

Aelian, *Historical Miscellanies* xiii. 1.

[1] ὥσπερ ἀστὴρ διᾴττουσα ἐξέλαμπεν (of Atalante) ἀστραπῆς δίκην : Cobet.

Shooting upward, [the flame] flashed forth like lightning.

Placed after *Agam.* 301 by Meineke, after l. 307 by Wecklein.

260 (485 Wecklein)

ὀργῆς ματαίας εἰσὶν αἴτιοι λόγοι.

Stobaeus, *Anthology* iii. 20. 13 (Hense iii. 541).

Words do provoke to senseless wrath.

A corruption or variation of *Prom.* 380.

261 (487 Wecklein)

<τὸ>[1] μελαμβόρεον <δὲ> καταιγίζει[2]
πνεῦμα βίαιον καὶ φρικῶδες.

Strabo, *Geography* iv. 1. 7. p. 182.

[1] < > Coray.
[2] μελαμβόριον καταιγίζει : Teuffel (-βόρεον Sidgwick).

The black North, a blast violent and chilling, descends in a tempest.

Προμηθεὺς λυόμενος Teuffel.

Probably from a description of the Λιθῶδες, the Stony Plain ; cp. Frag. 112.

262 (488 Wecklein)

λέληθεν οὐδὲν τῶνδέ μ' ὧν[1] σὺ νουθετεῖς·
γνώμην δ' ἔχοντά μ' ἡ φύσις βιάζεται.

Clement of Alexandria, *Miscellanies* ii. 15. p. 462: l. 2 cited, without the poet's name, by Plutarch, *On Moral Virtue* 6. 446 A, Stobaeus, *Anthology* ii. 7. 10ᵃ (Wachsmuth ii. 89).

[1] λέληθε δέ με οὐδὲν τῶνδε ὧν L, λέληθε δέ μ' οὐθὲν τῶνδ' V: Sylburg.

Naught escapes me whereof thou admonishest me; yet, for all my resolve, Nature constrains me.

Λάϊος Gataker, Euripides' Χρύσιππος Valckenaer.

263 (Anon. 569, Wecklein 489)

Τεῦκρος δὲ τόξου χρώμενος φειδωλίᾳ
ὑπὲρ τάφρου πηδῶντας ἔστησεν[1] Φρύγας.

Trypho, *On Tropes* in *Rhetores Graeci* viii. 738, who says that φειδωλία (which generally means "sparing") is here used in the sense of ἀκρίβεια, "accuracy"; cp. Gregory of Corinth, *Tropes* viii. 767, Moschopulus, *Opuscula Grammatica* 76.

[1] ἔστησε: Nauck.

Teucer, plying his bow with sure aim, stayed the Phrygians as they would overleap the foss.

Σαλαμίνιαι Hermann, Μυρμιδόνες Anon. in Welcker; Sophocles' Τεῦκρος Blomfield. From a description of the battle in Θ 266 ff.

264 (Anon. 110)

οὐκ ἦν ἄρ' οὐδὲν πῆμ' ἐλευθέραν[1] δάκνον
ψυχὴν ὁμοίως ἀνδρὸς ὡς ἀτιμία.

οὕτως πέπονθα καί με συμφορᾶς ἀεὶ[2]
βαθεῖα κηλὶς ἐκ βυθῶν ἀναστρέφει
λύσσης πικροῖς κέντροισιν ἠρεθισμένον.

Clement of Alexandria, *Miscellanies* ii. 15. p. 462; ll. 1-2 Letronne, *Les Papyres grecs* p. 96.

[1] ἐλευθέρου: Clem. [2] συμφοροῦσα: Süvern.

So then 'tis true—no misery gnaws a free man's soul like dishonour. Thus do I suffer, and the deep stain of my calamity ever stirs me from the depths, agitated as I am by the piercing goads of frenzy.

Θρῇσσαι Süvern.

Spoken by Ajax before his suicide (Clement).

265 (486 Wecklein)

ἄλλον ἄλλῃ πρὸς πόλει τεταγμένον

Plato, *Republic* viii. 550 c.

Another man stationed against another State

Quoted by Plato as from Aeschylus, but probably a playful allusion to *Seven against Thebes* (cp. ll. 451, 570). From a lost play, Herwerden.

266

βέβληκ' Ἀχιλλεὺς δύο κύβω καὶ τέσσαρα.

Aristophanes, *Frogs* 1400.

Achilles has thrown two aces and a four.

Of unknown source (Aristarchus), Μυρμιδόνες (a late Scholiast). Now generally assigned to Euripides (Frag. 888), whose *Telephus* is said, on poor authority, to have represented the heroes as dicing. Dionysus, who quotes the verse in Aristophanes, implies that the verse is as bad as the throw. Three dice were used, the highest cast being a triple six (*Agam.* 33).

DOUBTFUL OR SPURIOUS FRAGMENTS

267 (Anon. 560)

χωρὶς τὰ Μυσῶν καὶ Φρυγῶν ὁρίσματα.

Strabo, *Geography* xii. 8. 2. p. 572, and in collectors of proverbs: Gregory of Cyprus iii. 99, Macarius, *Rose-bed* viii. 83, and other late writers.

The boundaries of the Mysians and the Phrygians are distinct.

Assigned to Aeschylus by Hermann.

268 (Anon. 162)

Κίλιξ δὲ χώρα καὶ Σύρων ἐπιστροφαί

Eustathius on *Odyssey* 1484. 49.

The Cilician country and the haunts of the Syrians

Φρύγες Bergk (ἐπιστροφαί occurred in this play according to Hesychius, *Lexicon* s.v.).

Frag. 267 may have been followed immediately by Frag. 268 (Nauck).

ELEGIAC FRAGMENTS

269 (492 Wecklein)

Τυρσηνῶν[1] γενεάν, φαρμακοποιὸν ἔθνος

Theophrastus, *History of Plants* ix. 15; cp. Pliny, *Natural History* xxv. 11 (5).

[1] Τυρρηνὸν: Bergk.

The race of the Tyrrhenes, a nation that maketh drugs

270 (493 Wecklein)

βριθὺς ὁπλιτοπάλας, δάϊος ἀντιπάλοις

Plutarch, *Concerning the Fortune or Virtue of Alexander the Great* ii. 2. p. 334 D, cp. *Table Talk* ii. 5. 2. p. 640 A; and, without naming the poet, *Concerning the Fortune of the Romans* 3. 317 E, *Comparison of Cicero and Demosthenes* 2, Eustathius on *Iliad* 513. 33.

[A warrior,] sturdy, heavy-armed, terrific to the foe

271 (494 Wecklein)

Εἰς ἑτέρους προμάχους Θεσσαλῶν.

κυανέη καὶ τούσδε μενέγχεας[1] ὤλεσεν ἄνδρας
μοῖρα, πολύρρηνον πατρίδα ῥυομένους.
ζωὸν δὲ φθιμένων πέλεται κλέος, οἵ ποτε γυίοις
τλήμονες Ὀσσαίαν ἀμφιέσαντο κόνιν.

Palatine Anthology vii. 255.

[1] μενεγχέας P Pl^w, μενέγχεας Pl^m.

On other Thessalian champions.

Dark Fate likewise laid low these valiant spearmen defending their fatherland, rich in sheep. But living is the glory of the dead who of old, steadfast in battle, clothed themselves in Ossa's dust.

272 (495 Wecklein)

Αἰσχύλον Εὐφορίωνος Ἀθηναῖον[1] τόδε κεύθει
μνῆμα καταφθίμενον πυροφόροιο[2] Γέλας·[3]
ἀλκὴν δ' εὐδόκιμον Μαραθώνιον ἄλσος[4] ἂν εἴποι[5]
καὶ βαθυχαιτήεις[6] Μῆδος[7] ἐπιστάμενος.[8]

Life of Aeschylus in the Medicean and many other MSS., ll. 1-2 Plutarch, *Of Banishment* 13. 604 F, Eustratius on Aristotle, *Nicomachean Ethics* iii. 2. p. 1111 a; ll. 3-4 Athenaeus, *Deipnosophists* xiv. 23. p. 627 c.

[1] ἀθηναίων M, ἀθηναῖον recc. Plut. Eustr.

[2] πυροφόροιο Plut.: παραφόροιο M[1]P Flor. 28. 25: παραφόροις Flor. 31. 8 R: πυραφόροιο M[2]VK: πυροφόρου Pal. 139: πυροφόρον Lips. 1, Mon. 486, Eustr. (who has τόδε σῆμα κεύθει ἀποφθινόμενον).

[3] γέλας Plut., πέλας MQP Paris. 2785, 2786 and very many other recc.: σέλας VBK[2]R Ottob. 210, Pal. 139, Flor. add. 98, etc.

[4] ἄλλος MPγρ. Paris. 2785, Ottob. 346, Pal. 139: ἄλσος M, Athen.

[5] εἴπη Athen., Flor. 31. 8, 91. 5. Flor. Add. 7, etc.

[6] βαθυχαιτήης (M[1]: -ήεις M[2] then erasure of six letters), βαθυχαιτείης Flor. 28. 25, Flor. add. 98, Vat. 57 R., βαθυχαῖταί κεν Athen. (χεταικεν A).

[7] μῆδοι Athen., δῆμος Baroc. 231.

[8] ἐπιστάμενοι Athen., Paris. 3521, ἐπιστάμενον G.

This tomb hideth the dust of Aeschylus, an Athenian, Euphorion's son, who died in wheat-bearing Gela; his glorious valour the precinct of Marathon may proclaim, and the long-haired Medes, who knew it well.

Athenaeus and Pausanias (i. 14. 5) state that the epigram was written by Aeschylus himself. The *Life* states that it was inscribed by the Geloans on the public tomb in which he was buried with splendid honours at the cost of their city.

APPENDIX

EDITED BY

HUGH LLOYD-JONES, M.A.

FELLOW OF CORPUS CHRISTI COLLEGE, OXFORD

CONTENTS OF APPENDIX

		PAGE
	PREFATORY NOTE	526
	AIDS TO THE READER	528
273.	GLAUCUS MARINUS	529
274–5.	DICTYULCI	531
276.	THEORI OR ISTHMIASTAE	541
277.	NIOBE	556
278.	? PROMETHEUS THE FIREKINDLER	562
279.	? SEMELE OR HYDROPHORI	566
280.	UNKNOWN PLAY (I) (P. Oxy. no. 2251)	571
281.	UNKNOWN PLAY (IIa) (P. Oxy. no. 2256, fr. 8)	573
282.	UNKNOWN PLAY (IIb) (P. Oxy. no. 2256, fr. 9a)	576
283.	UNKNOWN PLAY (III) (P. Oxy. no. 2253)	582
284.	UNKNOWN PLAY (IV) (P. Oxy. no. 2256, fr. 71)	584
285.	[? CHILDREN OF HERACLES]	586
286.	[? MYRMIDONS]	590
287.	HYPOTHESIS TO WOMEN OF AETNA [1]	593
288.	HYPOTHESIS TO UNKNOWN PLAY (P. Oxy. no. 2256, fr. 3)	595

[1] Illogical as it doubtless is, I think it is convenient to print these two hypotheses and to include them in the serial numbering.

PREFATORY NOTE

So far as possible, the new fragments are here presented by the method devised by Professor D. L. Page for his *Greek Literary Papyri* in this series, and explained by him in the preface to that book. I do not claim that my bibliographies are complete ; but I have referred to all works dealing with the fragments which I have consulted while preparing this edition, not excluding those in which I failed to discover anything of value.

I began the work wishing to practise the severest austerity with regard to supplements ; but soon came to realise that what is proper in an *editio princeps* is impracticable in an edition designed for the purposes of the Loeb Library. Where I have thought the general sense of a mutilated passage reasonably clear, I have printed supplements ; where I have not, I have abstained. The supplements are meant simply to show the reader how I think the complete text may have run. If any reader thought I meant them more seriously than that, no one would be more distressed than I.

According to Weir Smyth's principle (see p. 374), I print only the fragments of which " at least one entire verse, or two connected half-verses, is preserved." Thus I omit many fragmentary papyrus texts, including, for example, the piece lately published by E. Siegmann as P. Heidelberg 185 and assigned by him, with some probability, to the *Pro-*

metheus Lyomenos. Some readers will be surprised to find here no text of the piece published from a Milan papyrus by W. Buchwald in his *Studien zur Chronologie der attischen Tragödie,* 455 *bis* 431, Diss. Koenigsberg, 1939, p. 57, and assigned to Aeschylus by him and H. J. Mette, *Nachtrag zum Supplementum Aeschyleum,* p. 33. Through the kindness of Professor R. Cantarella I have obtained a photograph of this crabbed and mutilated text ; which, with great good nature, Mr. E. Lobel has inspected for me. Mr. Lobel has shown me that there is reason to doubt whether the disjoined fragments have been properly put together : after *Καπανέ*[*ωσ*] in l. 4, for instance, there is a gap in the text which the metre does not allow to contain anything at all. But even if we could trust a text based upon the papyrus in its present condition, I can see no positive reason whatever for ascribing this piece to Aeschylus.[1]

I am grateful to those friends who have discussed the problems of these texts with me, and whose suggestions are acknowledged in the apparatus criticus ; in particular, to Professor P. Maas. Above all, I must thank Professor Page, who with a willingness no less than his capacity to help has read through the manuscript and made a great number of valuable suggestions. Mr. T. C. W. Stinton has very kindly corrected the proofs.

Corpus Christi College, Oxford H. Ll.-J.
August, 1956

[1] I learned only late, and at second hand (*L'Année Philologique,* 1954, p. 3) of E. Eichgruen's article at *Prolegomena* II, 1953, 9 f. He thinks the piece consists of three separate fragments, one of which he assigns to Aeschylus' *Eleusinioi.* The language of the fragment in question suggests to me rather that of an Euripidean prologue.

AIDS TO THE READER

Π throughout in notes = the original papyrus of the text.

Dates at the head of each piece refer to the century within which the papyrus is thought to have been written.

Square brackets [ ] enclose letters lost in gaps in the original papyrus and conjecturally restored by modern scholars. Round brackets ( ) indicate the omission in the original of the letters enclosed, either by accident or through abbreviation (as in fr. 287).

Dots under letters signify that the letters are not certainly read. Dots inside square brackets signify the approximate number of missing letters. A dash (paragraphus) in the margin denotes change of speaker or the beginning of a new choral stanza; where the paragraphus is omitted or is not visible in the text, but a change of speaker is inferred, I have printed a dash inside square brackets.

Where no indication of their authorship is given, supplements are those of the first editor.

The Byzantine practice of using a different form of sigma at the end of a word is not followed in this Appendix. It is particularly unsuitable in texts printed from papyri, since the editor may not always wish to commit himself as to whether a sigma is final or not.

ΓΛΑΥΚΟΣ ΠΟΝΤΙΟΣ (see p. 388) A.D. 2

273

Ed. pr. Lobel, *P. Oxy.*, vol. 18, no. 2159 with Plate I; cf. Siegmann, *Philologus* 97, 59; Mette, *Nachtrag zum Suppl. Aesch.*, 1949, 5; Cantarella, *I nuovi frammenti eschilei di Ossirinco*, 1949, 9; Steffen, *Satyrographorum Graecorum Fragmenta*², 1952, 119; Mette, *Gymnasium* 62, 1955, 402; Lesky, *Die Tragische Dichtung der Hellenen*, 1956, 85. Cf. Snell, *Gnomon* 25, 1953, 437.

Lobel suggests that this is part of a speech by Glaucus himself describing the miracle of the ἀείζωοσ πόα (cf. fr. 15, 16). But Glaucus before his transformation was a fisherman, not a cowherd as the speaker seems to be; l. 6 looks as if the speaker is protesting that the oddness of his story must not be set down to his blindness or frivolity; and Siegmann seems likely to be right in suggesting that an old herdsman is here describing to an incredulous listener an appearance of the transformed Glaucus. Siegmann and Cantarella think we have first part of a dialogue, then a continuous speech; Siegmann begins the latter at l. 5, Cantarella at l. 8. But ἴσθι in l. 4 is no certain evidence for this, and for all we know the whole fragment may belong to a single speech by a single speaker.

]αυτα μωρο[
]τιν η θύελ[λα
]ν παύρουσ[
]ν μὲν ἴσθι σ[

καὶ τ]ῷνδ' ἔτ' ἐστὶ π[ί]στισ ὀμμ[άτων σαφήσ.
οὐδ' ἀ]μβλυώσσων οὐδὲ μὰψ αὔ[τωσ βλέπων
ἤθρη]σα δεῖμα καὶ περισπερ[χὲσ πάθοσ.
οἶσθ' ὡ]σ ἄγραυλόσ τ' εἰμι κἀπιχ[ώριοσ,
ἀεὶ θ]αμίζων τῇδε Χαλκίδ[οσ πέραν
Μεσσ]απίου τ' ἄφυλλον ὑψηλὸ[ν πάγον
φοιτῶ]ν ἀπ' αὐ[λῆσ] βουσὶ φορ[βάσιν μέτα.
κεῖθ]εν κατεῖδον θαῦμα· π[ροσμολόντι γὰρ
Εὐβο]ίδα καμπήν, ἀμφὶ Κηνα[ίου Διὸσ
ἀκτή]ν, κατ' αὐτὸν τύμβον ἀθ[λίου Λίχα
]νταπερ τέθριππον[

5, 6 Siegmann. 7 beginning Siegmann, end Ll.-J. (cf. Soph., *Aj.* 982, with *Σ*). 8 beginning Page, end Siegmann. 9 Ll.-J. (cf. *Ag.* 190). 10 Ed. Fraenkel (πάγον Ll.-J.). 11–12 Ll.-J. 13–14 = fr. 17, q.v. 14 MSS. of Strabo: αὐτὴν *Π*.

. . . foolish . . . whirlwind . . . few . . be sure. . . . And I still believe the certain witness of my own eyes. I was not blear-eyed or peering vainly to no purpose when I saw this fearful thing, this awful happening. You know, I am a countryman and of these parts; and I am always about the land here opposite Chalcis, and am used to accompany the grazing cattle from the byre to Messapion's[1] leafless lofty crag. And it was from here that my eye lit upon the miracle. When I had come to the bend of Euboea, about the headland of Cenaean Zeus, right by unhappy Lichas' tomb . . . four-horse chariot. . . .

[1] Mt. Messapion is near Anthedon on the Boeotian shore of the Euripus; this is where the Glaucus legend is localised by Strabo 9, 405, and Pausanias 9, 22, 5 f.

DICTYULCI

ΔΙΚΤΥΟΥΛΚΟΙ A.D. 2

274–5

(*a*) 274 : ed. pr. Vitelli-Norsa, *Bulletin de la société royale d'archéologie d'Alexandrie*, no. 28, 1933, 115, with Plate ; cf. ibid., no. 29, 1934, 247 ; *Mélanges Bidez* 3, 1934, 66 ; Körte, *Hermes* 68, 1933, 267 ; id., *Archiv für Papyrusforschung* 11, 1935, 249 ; Goossens, *Chronique d'Égypte* 19, 1935, 120 ; Vitelli-Norsa, *Papiri Greci e Latini* 11, 1935, no. 1209, 97, with Plate ; Fritsch, *Neue Fragmente des Aischylos und Sophokles*, Diss. Hamburg, 1936, 7 ; Pfeiffer, *S.B. Bayer. Akad.*, 1938, 2, 3 ; Olivieri, *Dioniso* 6, 1938, 314 ; Morel, *Bursians Jahresb.* 259, 1938, 29 ; Untersteiner, *Boll. di Filol. Class.* 45, 1939, 199 ; Mette, *Supplementum Aeschyleum*, 1939, 178 ; Page, *Greek Literary Papyri*, 1941, 8 ; Cantarella, *Eschilo* I, 1941, 343 ; Lesky, *Philol. Wochenschr.*, 61, 1941, 129 ; Goossens, *Chronique d'Égypte* 16, 1941, 127 ; ibid. 17, 1942, 113.

(*b*) 275 : ed. pr. Lobel, *P. Oxy.*, vol. 18, 1941, no. 2161, 9, with Plate III ; Ed. Fraenkel, *Proc. Brit. Acad.*, 1942, 240 ; Snell, *Die Antike* 20, 1944, 119 ; Siegmann, *Philologus* 97, 1948, 71 ; Setti, *Ann. Scu. N.S. di Pisa* ser. 2, 17, 1948, 2 ; Mette, *Nachtrag zum Suppl. Aesch.*, 1949, 24 ; Cantarella, *I nuovi frammenti eschilei di Ossirinco*, 1949, 36 ; Steffen, *Journal of Juristic Papyrology* 3, 1949, 121 ; id., *Sat. Gr. Frag.*², 1952, 123 ; Lesky, *Gymnasium* 61, 1954, 298 ; Kamerbeek, *Mnemosyne* ser. 4, 7, 1954, 89 ; Mette, *Gymnasium* 62, 1955, 402 ; Pohlenz, *Die Griechische Tragoedie* ii², 1955, 66 ; Pfeiffer, *Corolla Linguistica* (Festschrift Sommer), 1955, 177 ; Webster, *Greek Theatre Production*, 1955, 17 ; Lesky, *TDH*, 1956, 83. See also Snell, *Gnomon* 25, 1953, 440.

This was the satyr-play that accompanied Aeschylus' trilogy about Perseus. Two of the plays were called *Phorcides* and *Polydectes* (see p. 469) ; the name of the third is not known. If it was the first of the trilogy, it presumably described the cruel treatment of Danaë by her father Acrisius ; if it was the third, it may have described Perseus' coming to

Argos and Acrisius' death (see Pfeiffer, l.c., 20; Howe, *A.J.A.* 57, 1953, 269).

Fr. 274 describes how two people catch sight of the chest containing Danaë and the infant Perseus as it appears near the shore of the small Aegean island of Seriphos. The usual legend was that it was fished up by Dictys, the brother of Polydectes, king of that place; considering the proverbial insignificance of Seriphos there is nothing odd in the king's brother being a fisherman. Dictys must be one of the speakers; who is the other? Possibly it is a companion or a slave of his; but the limitation on the number of the actors makes against this. Setti thinks that the Chorus of satyrs is already on the stage, and that one or more of its members speaks during this scene; but it seems likelier that the Chorus arrives in answer to the call for help in ll. 17 f., just as the Chorus of Aristophanes' *Peace* is summoned by a very similar appeal (296 f.). Perhaps the likeliest companion for Dictys during this scene is the father of the satyrs, Silenus.

What are the satyrs doing on Seriphos? Perhaps Aeschylus accounted for their presence by the legend of their pursuit of the pirates who carried off Dionysus (cf. Euripides' *Cyclops*). It may be that they are temporarily enslaved there, perhaps to Polydectes, as they are to Polyphemus in the *Cyclops*. Dictys' companion seems to be there to help him; and it may be that Silenus has come fishing with him as his assistant.

There is no certain means of knowing which lines are spoken by Dictys and which by his companion. Like all others except Setti, I have assumed that there are only two speakers; but I have preferred to make Dictys the second, not the first, of these. The chest is said to have been fished up by Dictys, and the first speaker has been identified with Dictys on the ground of l. 12, where the net is called his. But it is doubtful if the ethic dative shows that the net is regarded as the special property of either speaker; they may well have one net between them, and the words may simply mean, "What have you there in the net?" I suspect that Dictys was the more observant and less excitable of the two companions; but there is no knowing which he really was. If the other speaker really is Silenus, and if the net was in any sense his, he may have based his claim to Danaë later on this fact; compare the behaviour of Gripus in Plautus' *Rudens*.

Fr. 275 begins with a solemn offer of protection made to Danaë by an unknown speaker. Danaë's response is to appeal to the gods for help. There follow 14 lines of what look to have been choriambic dimeters, spoken by the Chorus. Next comes a passage of glyconics and pherecrateans 22 lines long, in which the unknown speaker tries to captivate the child by describing the delights of hunting that he will enjoy when he, the speaker, is his stepfather. The Chorus next calls, in anapaestic dimeters, for the immediate conclusion of the marriage.

Who is the unknown speaker of 765–72 and of 798–820? If Lobel is right in suggesting that 799–800 may have meant "Damme if I am not glad . . .", with the speaker referring to himself, as people sometimes do in utterances of this kind, 798–820 will have been spoken by Dictys. But as Lobel says (p. 9), one need only reject this suggestion to make it possible to assign the parts differently. And the suggestion is a very long way from being certain. It may be that the speaker is expected to say " If . . . , damn me," but gets a comic effect by saying instead, " If . . . , damn *Dictys* " (Dictys being his rival) ; or it may be that the apodosis to the " if " clause came in the lost portion of the text that precedes it, and that a new sentence begins at the beginning of l. 800. Now whoever speaks these lines is evidently in close collusion with the satyrs, as their following anapaests show. Can the person thus closely associated with the satyrs have been Dictys? Nothing can be more unlikely. A reliable clue to his identity is given by his holding out to the child the delights not of fishing, but of hunting. There cannot have been much game on Seriphos ; but the description of the woodland life is just what might be expected from the other obvious possible speaker, Silenus, father of the satyrs.

It is reasonable to suppose, with Siegmann, that Dictys' call for help in hauling in the heavy chest was answered by the satyrs ; that they helped him bring his catch to land ; that Dictys and the satyrs quarrelled over what should be done with Danaë ; and that Dictys went off to get help. Who will have spoken 765–72? These cannot be the last words of Dictys before departing, for we could not then understand why instead of answering Danaë implores the gods for help. They must have been spoken by Silenus ; 770–2 looks like a piece of the same grotesque wheedling as Silenus' later speech contains.

We know from a stichometrical mark opposite l. 800 that the first line of this fragment was l. 765 of the play. Kamerbeek insists that an Aeschylean satyr-play cannot have had many more than 800 lines ; and that since other plays by Aeschylus ended with marching anapaests, therefore this one must have ended with the marching anapaests that begin at 821. As we have no idea of the average length of an Aeschylean satyr-play, and as we have no possible ground for insisting that the marching anapaests must have brought the play to a close, his argument lacks cogency. And if the conclusions drawn above are not hopelessly wrong, we must infer that Dictys returned with a party of his friends and forced Silenus to give up his booty.

The view of Mette and Kamerbeek that Dictys and Silenus are somehow one and the same person seems to me very improbable indeed.[1] The rescue of a distressed beauty from the satyrs was a not uncommon theme of satyric drama; Amymone, Iris and even Hera were all beset by satyrs (see Guggisberg, *Das Satyrspiel*, Diss. Zürich, 1947, 63). And the red-figure lecythos illustrated in *Ath. Mitt.* 1891, plate IX (cf. Buschor, ibid., 1927, 230, and *Satyrtänze und Frühes Drama* 105, with Abb. 80) illustrates what may happen when an unprotected female arrives at a lonely island where there are satyrs who in Buschor's words "are suffering severely from the lack of nymphs."

[1] I suppose they, like Webster (l.c.), feel themselves obliged to assume that in a satyr-play Aeschylus can never have used more than two actors, so that Dictys, Silenus and Danaë can never all have been upon the stage at once. How do they know that in his later satyr-plays Aeschylus did not use three actors? It seems probable that this play requires three; which may indicate that it belongs to Aeschylus' later period, after Sophocles had introduced the third actor.

274

—ξυνῆκ[ασ ;
[ΔΙΚΤΥΣ]—ξυνῆκα·[
? —τί σοι φυλάσσω ;[
[ΔΙ.]—εἴ που θαλάσσησ[
? —ἄσημα· λεῖοσ πόν[τοσ ὄμμασίν γ' ἐμοῖσ.
[ΔΙ.]—δέρκου νυν ἐσ κευ[θμῶνασ ἀκταίων πετρῶν.
? —καὶ δὴ δέδορκα τωιδετ[
ἔα· τί φῶ τόδ' εἶναι ; πότερα [πόντιον τέρασ,
φάλαιναν ἢ ζύγαιναν ἢ κῆ[τοσ, βλέπω ;
ἄναξ Πόσειδον Ζεῦ τ' ἐνά[λι', οἷον τόδε
δ]ῶρον θαλάσσησ πέμπετ' [
[ΔΙ.]—τί] σοι θαλάσσησ δίκτυον δ[ῶρον στέγει ;
π]εφυκ[ίωτ]αι δ' ὥστε δαγνο[
ἆρ' ἔστ']ἔναιμον ; [ἤ τι] χ[ρῆμ'] ἐν [λάρνακι
πέμπει] γέρων νησαῖοσ ; ὡσ [ὑπερφυῶσ
ἐμβριθέσ] ἐστι. τοὖργον οὐ χωρεῖ πρόσω.
καὶ δὴ β]οὴν ἵστημι τοῖσδ' ἰύγμασιν.
ἰού· π]άντεσ γεωργοὶ δεῦτε κἀμπελοσκάφοι,
βοτήρ τ]ε ποιμήν τ' εἴ τίς ἐστ' [ἐ]γχώριοσ,
πάραλ]οί τε κἄλλο [πᾶν ἁλιτ]ρύτων ἔθνοσ
]ἐναντιωτάτησ

5 Page. 6 Pfeiffer. 9 κῆ[τοσ Lobel. 10 οἷον τόδε Page. 12 Schadewaldt. 13 Goossens, Page. 14 beginning and end Ll.-J. [ἤ τί] χ[ρῆμ'] Kamerbeek. 15, 16 Ll.-J. 18 ἰού Beazley. 17–20 Pfeiffer.

? —Can you see . . .?
DICTYS.—I can see. . . .
? —What do you want me to look out for? . . .
DICTYS.—In case anywhere . . . in the sea. . . .

—Not a sign ; so far as I can see, the sea's a millpond.

DICTYS.—Look now at the crannies of the cliffs by the shore.

? —All right, I'm looking. . . . Good Lord, what am I to call this! Is it a monster of the sea that meets my eyes, a grampus or a shark or a whale? Lord Poseidon and Zeus of the deep, a fine gift to send up from the sea . . .!

DICTYS.—What gift of the sea does your net conceal? It's covered with seaweed like. . . . Is it some warm-blooded creature? Or has the Old Man of the Islands [1] sent us something in a chest? How tremendously heavy it is! the work's not going ahead! I'll shout and raise an alarm. HALLO THERE! Farmers and ditchers, this way, all of you! Herdsmen and shepherds, anyone in the place! Coastal folk and all you other toilers of the sea! . . .

[ΣΙΛΗΝΟΣ.]

]αν καὶ θεοὺσ μαρτύρομαι
κλυεῖν ἃ νῦν ἄπ]αντι κηρύσσω στρατῶι.
σὺ δ' οὖν ἀφ' ἡμῶν] παντάπασι μὴ φθαρῆισ,
ἀλλ' ὀψέ περ μα]θοῦσα πρόξενόν θ' ἅμα
μάλ' εὐμενῆ δέχ]ου με καὶ προπράκτορα.

[1] The context suggests that γέρων νησαῖοσ, "the Old Man of the Islands," may have been identical with the ἅλιοσ γέρων, "the Old Man of the Sea." But the text is partly conjectural, and the assumption is not a safe one.

Pfeiffer (l.c. 18, cf. ibid. 11) thinks the words γέρων νησαῖοσ refer to Dictys' companion. If so, why is he referred to in the third person, as their being in the nominative case seems to imply?

καὶ μὴν ὁ παῖσ γ]ε μαῖαν ὥσ γερασμίαν
σαίνει προσαυδῶν] ἠπίοισ προσφθέγμασιν.
οὔκουν ὅδ᾽ αἰὲν αὐτὸ]σ ἐν χρόνωι μενεῖ ;

ΔΑΝΑΗ.

Ἄργουσ τε κρῆναι] καὶ γενέθλιοι θεοὶ
καὶ Ζεῦ τελευτ]ὰσ τάσδε μοι πόνων τιθείσ,
ἦ δῆτα τοῖσ]δ[ε] κνωδάλοισ με δώσετε,
ὧν προσβολαῖσ μάρ]γοισι λυμανθήσομαι
ἢ τἄσχατ᾽ αἰχ]μάλωτοσ οὖσ᾽ ἕξω κακά ;
ἐκφεύξομ]αι γοῦν· ἀγχόνην ἄρ᾽ ἅψομαι
τῆσ αἰκί]ασ τεμοῦσα κωλυτήριον
ἄκεσμ᾽, ὅπ]ωσ μὴ ποντίσηι τισ αὖ πάλιν,
ἢ θὴρ ὑβρισ]τὴσ ἢ πατήρ ; δέδοικα γάρ.
Ζεῦ, τῶνδε] πέμπ᾽ ἀρωγόν, εἰ δοκεῖ, τινά·
σὺ μὲν γὰρ] εἶχεσ αἰτίασ τῆσ μείζονοσ
βλάβησ, δίκη]ν δὲ πᾶσαν ἐξέτεισ᾽ ἐγώ.
θεῖναι τάδ᾽] εὖ σ᾽ ἔλεξα· πάντ᾽ ἔχεισ λόγον.

ΧΟΡΟΣ.

ἡδὺ] γελᾶι μου προσορῶν,
ἦν, τόδ᾽] ὁ μικκὸσ λιπαρὸν
τὸ μιλτόπρεπτον φαλακρόν. . . .

(Fragments of ten lines. L. 795 ends *ΠΟΣΘΟΣΦΙΛΗΣΟΝΕΟΣΣΟΣ*, which Lobel suggests may be a mistake for ὥσ ποσθοφιλὴσ ὁ νεοσσόσ).

766 Cantarella. 767–9 Ll.-J. 770–2 Page. 773 Ll.-J. (cf. Soph., *O.C.* 1333). 774 Maas. 775 Siegmann. 776 Ll.-J. 777 τἄσχατ᾽ Ll.-J. 778–9 Siegmann. 780 Snell. 781 Ll.-J. 782 Mette. 783 Ll.-J. (for acc. pl. αἰτίασ cf. *Suppl.* 229). 784 beginning Ll.-J., δίκη]ν Pfeiffer. 785, 787 Ll.-J.

SILENUS. . . . I call upon . . . and the gods to witness what I now proclaim to the whole company. But whatever you do, don't rush recklessly away from us ; understand at last and accept me as a most kindly protector and supporter. Why, look, the boy is greeting me with friendly words, as he would his respected grandmother. Won't he always be the same towards me, as time goes on?

DANAË. Rivers of Argos and gods of my fathers, and you, Zeus, who bring my ordeal to such an end! Will you give me to these beasts, so that they may outrage me with their savage onslaughts, or so that I endure in captivity the worst of tortures? Anyhow, I shall escape. Shall I then knot myself a noose, applying a desperate remedy against this torture, so that no one may put me to sea again, neither a lascivious beast nor a father? No, I am afraid to! Zeus, send me some help in this plight, I beg you! for you were guilty of the greater fault, but it is I who have paid the full penalty. I call upon you to set things right! You have heard all I have to say.

CHORUS. Look, the little one is smiling sweetly as he looks on this shining raddled bald pate. . . . Qualis vero amator mentularum est hic pusillus!

ΣΙΛ. . . . . . .
εἰ μὴ σε χαίρω π[ροσορῶν.
ὄλοιτο Δίκτυσ, κρ̣[υφάδην
τῆσδέ μ' ἄγρασ ἀ̣[ποστερῶν.
ὦ φίντων, ἴθι δε[ῦρο.
ποππυσμόσ.
θάρσει δή· τί κινύρηι ;
δεῦρ' ἐσ παῖδασ ἴωμεν, ὡσ [τάχιστα

ἴξηι παιδοτρόφουσ ἐμάσ,
ὦ φίλοσ, χέρασ εὐμενοῦσ,
τέρψηι δ' ἴκτισι κα[ὶ] νεβρο[ῖσ
ὑστρίχων τ' ὀβρίχοισ[ι],
κοιμήσηι τε τρίτοσ ξὺν
μητρὶ [καὶ π]ατρὶ τῶιδε.
ὁ πάπα[σ δ]ὲ παρέξει
τῶι μικκῶι τὰ γελ[οῖ]α
καὶ τροφὰσ ἀνόσουσ, ὅπωσ π[οτ' ἰσχὺν
ἀλδὼν αὐτὸσ, ἐ[πεὶ πατὴρ
χαλᾶι νεβροφόν[ου] ποδ[όσ],
μάρπτων θῆρασ ἄνευ δ[ορόσ
θῶσθαι μητρὶ παρέξεισ
κ]ηδεστῶν τρόπον οἷσιν
ἔ]ντροφοσ πελατεύσεισ.

ΧΟ.—ἀλλ'] εἶα, φίλοι, στείχωμεν, ὅπωσ
γ]άμον ὁρμαίνωμεν, ἐπεὶ τέλεοσ
καιρὸσ ἄναυδοσ τάδ' ἐπαινεῖ,
καὶ τήνδ' [ἐ]σορῶ νύμφην ἤ[δ]η
πάνυ βουλομένην τῆσ ἡμετέρασ
φιλότητοσ ἄδην κορέσασθαι.
καὶ θαῦμ' οὐδέν· πολὺσ ἦν αὐτῆι
χρόνοσ ὃν χήρα κατὰ ναῦν ὕφαλοσ
τείρετο. νῦν δ' οὖν
ἐ]σορῶσ' ἥβην τὴν ἡμετέραν
γαθ]εῖ, γάνυται, νυμφ[ί]ον [ο]ἷον
δαι]σὶν λαμπραῖσ τῆσ 'Α[φ]ροδίτησ. . . .

799 Siegmann. 800 Page. 801 Ll.-J. 805 Ed. Fraenkel. 807 εὐμενοῦσ Page: εὐμενὴσ *Π*. 814–15 Page. 820 ἔ]ντροφοσ E. Harrison:]ντροπος *Π*. 831 Kamerbeek (γηθεῖ Siegmann).

[SILENUS.] . . . if I don't rejoice in the sight of you. Damnation take Dictys, who is trying to cheat me of this prize behind my back! [To Perseus] Come here, my dearie! [He makes clucking noises.] Don't be frightened! Why are you whimpering? Over here to my sons, so that you can come to my protecting arms, dear boy—I'm so kind—, and you can find pleasure in the martens and fawns and the young porcupines, and can make a third in bed with your mother and with me your father. And daddy shall give the little one his fun. And you shall lead a healthy life, so that one day, when you've grown strong, you yourself —for your father's losing his grip on his fawn-killing footwork—you yourself shall catch beasts without a spear, and shall give them to your mother for dinner, after the fashion of her husband's family, amongst whom you'll be earning your keep.

CHORUS. Come now, dear fellows, let us go and hurry on the marriage, for the time is ripe for it and without words speaks for it. Why, I see that already the bride is eager to enjoy our love to the full. No wonder : she spent a long time wasting away all lonely in the ship beneath the foam. Well, now that she has before her eyes our youthful vigour, she rejoices and exults ; such is the bridegroom that by the bright gleam of Aphrodite's torches. . . .

ΘΕΩΡΟΙ Η ΙΣΘΜΙΑΣΤΑΙ (see p. 406) A.D. 2

276

Ed. pr. Lobel, *P. Oxy.*, vol. 18, no. 2162, with Plates IV and V (cf. id. ibid., vol. 20, p. 167) ; cf. Ed. Fraenkel, *Proc. Brit. Acad.* 28, 1942, 244 ; Mette, *Nachtrag zum Suppl. Aesch.*, 1949, 27 ; Untersteiner, *Dioniso* n.s. 14, 1951, 19 ; Steffen, *Sat. Gr. Frag.*², 1952, 128 ; Setti, *Ann. Scu. N.S.*

di Pisa 21, 1952, 3 ; Snell, *Gnomon* 25, 1953, 436 ; Goerschen, *Dioniso* n.s. 17, 1954, 3 ; Mette, *Gymnasium* 62, 1955, 403 ; Pohlenz, *Die Griechische Tragoedie* ii[1], 1955, 66 ; Kamerbeek, *Mnemosyne* s. 4, vol. 8, 1955, 1 ; Snell, *Hermes* 84, 1956, 1 ; Terzaghi, *Studi in onore di U.E. Paoli*, 1956, 685 ; Lesky, *TDH*, 1956, 85: Barigazzi, *Ann. Scu. N.S.*, 23, 1954, 338.

These fragments are preserved on two sheets of papyrus (1 and 2), each containing two columns of writing ; of these columns, 1 (i) and 2 (ii) are mostly readable, but only the bottom part of 1 (ii) and only the top part of 2 (i) are preserved. Were the two sheets in fact consecutive, so that 2 (i) supplies the top and 1 (ii) the bottom of the same column, a column that stood in the text between 1 (i) and 2 (ii)? Lobel says that this cannot be determined, but that the possibility cannot be excluded ; Snell (in *Hermes*, l.c.) boldly assumes that it is so. The sense yielded by the text at the three points where the fragments would join one another ought to resolve this question; these points fall between lines 35 and 36, between lines 53 and 61 and between lines 72 and 73 in the text printed below. At the first two points, the text is too deficient for the sense to furnish any evidence either way ; but at the third the sense given by the join is good. I have therefore followed Snell in printing the text in accordance with this suggestion, but not without considerable misgivings. If 1 (ii) and 2 (i) really belonged to the same column, one would expect the pattern of the fibres to make this clear ; but it does not. There is a small fragment (1 (*b*)) which if this is right must come from the middle of the column containing 1 (ii) and 2 (i) ; but it cannot be fitted to either of these fragments.

In view of the length of these fragments, it is

remarkable that we can make out so little of the subject-matter. θεωροί could mean " spectators " or " members of a sacred embassy " ; and since the text shows that the satyrs of the Chorus mean to compete in the Isthmian games, the title probably indicates that they came there as members of a sacred embassy, presumably sent or conducted by Dionysus in honour of Poseidon.

Our portion of the text begins with the satyrs thanking someone for exact likenesses of themselves, which they then proceed to nail up upon the temple of Poseidon Isthmios, with the remark that they will frighten away strangers. The strangers will presumably be frightened, as Snell suggests, because they will think they have come to a place like the palace of Oenomaus with its display of severed human heads. We are told that the likenesses are painted (l. 12) ; but that does not rule out their being sculptures rather than pictures. Eduard Fraenkel has suggested that they are antefixes, the upright ornaments placed along the cornices of Greek temples, originally in order to mask the ends of the covering tiles that protected the joints between the rain-tiles, and customarily shaped like masks. Satyr-masks were sometimes used as antefixes, and the practice may well have suggested this scene ; it is not, of course, meant that the satyrs' portraits *are* antefixes, since antefixes cannot be nailed up or taken down at will. The fright which the portraits are likely to give to the satyrs' mother or to any strangers makes it likely that such portraits, and probably the art of portraiture itself, are thought of as being unusual or even new at the time in question.

A new character now enters the stage ; he has

been looking for the satyrs, and grimly remarks that he has known where to find them. He remarks on them what are probably the effects of the practice known as *ligatura praeputii*, one which was often adopted by Greek athletes in training and which satyr-athletes on several vases are shown as adopting ; on this and on the similar but distinct Roman practice of *infibulatio*, see Dingwall, *Male Infibulation*, London, 1925, and Brommer, *Satyrspiele* 74. The satyrs should be giving their minds to the dance, says this personage, but instead they have learned new habits, and are exercising their arms and wasting his money (or " ruining his property "?). Between lines 35 and 65 very little can be made out ; but it looks as if either the Choragus or a Silenus like those of the *Ichneutae* and the *Cyclops* replied to this speech with one in which he complained of the discomforts which the satyrs have endured while in the other speaker's service and declared that they would no longer obey his orders. Lines 53–60 are missing. When we pick up the thread, the other speaker is replying. " You say I am no good at iron-work", he says, " but am a cowardly, womanish creature " ; then he repeats his former reproaches, and threatens to be avenged. Finally he draws the attention of the satyrs to somebody or something near at hand.

The satyrs now repeat their refusal to leave the temple (80–4). L. 85 seems to be addressed to a new character, who has brought with him, he says, newly-made objects straight from adze and anvil. He offers the first of these to the satyrs, who refuse it with alarm. " What am I to do with this? " they ask, and are told in reply that they are to use it in practising the new craft that they have adopted (91–2). This presumably means athletics (cf. 35). A dangerous object which might come in useful to athletes and which is made with an adze may well be a javelin, as Snell suggests.

Silenus (or the Choragus) now says to the other person, " What will you do in return if I let you sail? " (l. 93 : Lobel's suggested restoration of this line, which Snell ignores, seems almost unavoidable). The other replies that he will be a good comrade to him at the Isthmian games. Then Silenus may have said that the other character " will go on board " (l. 95). Soon after that, the text breaks off.

The character who quarrels with the satyrs is very probably Dionysus, their usual master. It might be Silenus, in which case the part which I have suggested might belong to Silenus would belong to the Choragus ; but Snell rightly observes that the reproach of being a *γύννισ* is much more appropriately levelled against Dionysus (cf. fr. 31, etc.). It seems that the satyrs have been brought by Dionysus to the Isthmus as members of a sacred embassy to the Isthmian games. Once arrived, they have decided to compete in the games themselves, and have slipped off to practise for them instead of dancing. Perhaps Dionysus had meant them to give a display of their usual dances or to enter for the choral contest. They are encouraged in this behaviour by a character who first brings them their portraits meant apparently to scare off rival competitors, and then implements, very likely javelins, that will be useful in the games. (If the javelin-throwing competition was already in existence, the javelin could not be a new invention ; but perhaps these were the first javelins equipped with the ἀγκύλη (Lat. *amentum*), a device which makes them a good deal easier to aim ; see Saglio in *Daremberg-Saglio* i, 226.)

Who can this other character be? Snell suggests that it is Sisyphus, the crafty king of Corinth, who figured in satyr-plays by all the three great tragedians (see p. 457 f.). Sisyphus, according to one story, founded the Isthmian games, and Snell thinks the play may have dealt with their foundation. Corinth was a famous centre of craftsmanship ; Sisyphus himself is credited with φιλοτεχνία as well as with πανουργία by Diodorus 6, fr. 6, 3 and is coupled with the famous smiths, the Cercopes and the Telchines, by Aelian, *De nat. anim.* 6, 58. Snell also suggests that a fragmentary text (*P. Oxy.* 2250, in vol. xx, 12) in which a rich king is addressed in marching anapaests, may come from an address to Sisyphus by the Chorus of this play.

This suggestion might possibly be right, but there is very little positive evidence in its favour. There is no suggestion in the text that this is the first performance of the Isthmian games : if it were, Aeschylus as an Athenian might be thought likely to prefer the legend that made Theseus their founder. Nor is there any real evidence for Sisyphus as a craftsman. φιλοτεχνία in Diodorus must mean much the same as πανουργία, and Aelian compares Sisyphus to the Cercopes and Telchines in point of cunning, not of craftsmanship. No tradition connects Corinth with the origins of representative art or of weapons ; its fame as a centre of craftsmanship belongs to historic rather than to heroic times. A more positive objection to the theory is the difficulty of reconciling it with Lobel's very probable restoration of l. 93. Why should Sisyphus ask the satyrs " to let him sail " or " to take him on board "? As for P. Oxy. 2250, it might have occurred in any number of different contexts, and there is no substantial reason for connecting it with this play.

It is worth exploring other possibilities, provided one remembers that certainty is not likely to be attainable. It seems likely that the maker of the portraits and the weapons may be one of the great artificers of mythology. At l. 7 one of the likenesses is called *τὸ Δαιδάλου μίμημα*. This has been taken to mean " the likeness like one by Daedalus." But a more natural sense would be " the likeness by Daedalus." Can Daedalus be the maker of the portraits and the javelins?

Daedalus is often said to have invented the art of sculpture (see Apollodorus 3, 15, 9, Hyginus, *Fab.* 274). He was also the inventor of carpentry and several of its instruments, including the adze (Pliny, *N.H.* 7, 198). He was by origin a noble Athenian, a kinsman of Theseus (Cleidemus ap. Plutarch, *Theseus* 19, etc.), and had to leave Athens because he killed his nephew out of jealousy at his superior skill. Is Daedalus at the Isthmus, trying to persuade the satyrs to take him on their ship, perhaps so that he can get to Crete? Daedalus certainly figured in the *Daedalus* and *Camici* of Sophocles, either or both of which may have been satyric, apart from the comedies by Plato and Aristophanes called after him.

But there is a sculptor and smith even more renowned than Daedalus who is constantly portrayed on vases in the company of satyrs. This is Hephaestus. In spite of Wilamowitz (*Kleine Schriften* v, 11), there is good reason to believe that Hephaestus was sometimes referred to as *Δαίδαλοσ* (see Pearson, *Fragments of Sophocles* i, 110 and literature there quoted). No legend about satyrs is more commonly depicted on vases than that of the Return of Hephaestus; of how Hera slighted her deformed son; of how he made for her a marvellous throne, which when she tried to rise from it held her fast bound; of how Ares tried to overcome Hephaestus by force and failed miserably; of how Hephaestus vanished from Olympus, so that no one was able to release his mother; and of how he was finally brought back by Dionysus and his satyrs, who had made him drunk (see Beazley, *Development of Attic Black-Figure* 31, 44; Brommer, *Jahrbuch des Deutschen Instituts* 52, 1937, 198; id., *Satyrspiele* 23, 68, etc.). Wilamowitz' guess that it formed the subject of a lost Homeric Hymn rests on insufficient evidence; but it was handled by Alcaeus (see Page, *Sappho and Alcaeus* 258 f.) and by Epicharmus in his *Κωμασταὶ ἢ Ἅφαιστοσ*. The earliest Athenian work that we know to have treated this theme is the satyr-play *Ἥφαιστοσ* of the tragedian Achaeus; but there must have been other satyr-plays that had the exile and return of Hephaestus as a principal or as a subsidiary theme.

Dionysus complains (l. 66 f.) that the satyrs reproach him with being no good at work in iron. This suggests that he may be being unfavourably contrasted with some other possible patron who *is*. It reminds us that there are several legends in which the satyrs figure as Hephaestus' workmen (see Pearson, op. cit., ii, 136). And it recalls the problem set by a fairly numerous group of vases which feature what at first sight seems to be the Return of Hephaestus: only the figure on the ass and holding the smith's tools that we should expect to be Hephaestus turns out on closer inspection to be Dionysus (see Brommer, *Jahrb. des Deut. Inst.* l.c., 206, with literature there quoted). It has already been suggested that there may have been a story of Dionysus stealing Hephaestus' tools. I cannot help suspecting that the giver of the portraits and the javelins may have been the exiled Hephaestus, eager for a lift on the satyrs' ship to escape those who are trying to fetch him back to Olympus ; that Dionysus may have tried to punish Hephaestus for stealing his retainers by stealing his tools ; and that finally Dionysus may have learned that Hephaestus was wanted on Olympus and have made the return of the tools conditional upon his surrender. But I put this forward only as a guess at the nature of facts that are not known.

I add brief remarks on some of the problems of this perplexing piece.

5–6. No suitable supplement occurs to me. One might make reasonable sense and at the same time do justice to the traces by writing: *ἄθρησον εἰ π[άρε]σ̣θ̣' [ὁμὸν] εἴδωλον, κτλ.* But *ὁμόσ* is not found in tragedy ; and I mention the suggestion only to show what I suspect the general sense to have been.

9–10. One might read *χωρεῖ, χωρεῖ μάλα* in the sense of " Ça va! " ; cf. fr. 274, 16 ; Ar., *Peace* 472, 509. But I have preferred a different view.

15. The middle of *αἰάζω* occurs nowhere else ; but cf. *ὀλολυζομένη* at Soph. fr. 534, 6 Pearson, etc.

22. *ἐπίτροπόσ [θ' ἡμῖν γενοῦ* Snell, *ἐπίτροποσ [τῶν 'Ισθμίων* Goerschen.

26–7. *πλησιοσφ[* is written in the papyrus with a grave accent on the *O*, implying that it is part of a single compound word. The only compound I can think of that seems as if it might be suitable is *πλησιόσφυροσ*. If *ὁμόσφυροσ* can mean “ companion ” (see Hesych. and Suid. s.v.), this word might have a similar sense ; one might supplement, e.g. :

.....] *ὁρῶντα τούσδε πλησιοσφ[ύρουσ*
ἤγγειλε] ταῦτα καὶ σαφῶς ἡγεῖτό μοι.

But this is very speculative ; and Page may be right in suspecting that the grave accent over the *O* of *πλησιοσφ[* arose from a *Υ* omitted by mistake and written in above the line. Then the right reading would be *πλησίουσ φ[*.

80. *τοῦ ἱεροῦ*. The synizesis seems to be unique ; but since in l. 50 we find *]ωι ἱερῶι*, it would be unwise to conjecture *τοῦ <δ’> ἱεροῦ*.

[?]—*ὁρῶντεσ εἰκοὺ[σ] οὐ κατ’ ἀνθρώπουσ[⏑–.*
ὅπηι δ’ ἂν ἔ[ρ]δηισ, πάντα σοι τάδ’ εὐσεβῆ.
[*ΧΟ.*]—*ἦ κάρτ’ ὀφείλω τῶνδέ σοι· πρόφρων γὰρ εἶ.*
ἄκουε δὴ πᾶσ, σῖγα δ’ ειθ . λειδ[. .].
ἄθρησον ει π[. .]. .[. . .]
εἴδωλον εἶναι τοῦτ’ ἐμῆι μορφῆι πλέον,
τὸ Δαιδάλου μίμημα· φωνῆσ δεῖ μόνον.
τάδ’ [ἀθρ]εῖ[σ;
ὁρᾶ[ισ ; χ]ώρ[ει,
χώρει μάλα.
—*εὐκταῖα κόσμον ταῦτ[α] τῶι θεῶι φέρω,*
καλλίγραπτον εὐχάν.
[—] *τῆι μητρὶ τὴιμῆι πράγματ’ ἂν παρασχέθοι.*
ἰδοῦσα γάρ νιν ἂν σαφῶσ
τρέποιτ’ ἂν αἰάζοιτό θ’ ὡσ
δοκοῦσ’ ἔμ’ εἶναι τὸν ἐξ-
έθρεψεν· οὕτωσ ἐμφερὴσ ὅδ’ ἐστίν.

εἶα δὴ σκοπεῖτε δῶμα ποντίου σεισίχθο[νοσ,
κἀπιπασσάλευ' ἕκαστοσ τῆσ κ[α]λῆσ μορφῆσ
σ̣[αφῆ
ἄγγελον, κήρυκ' [ἄ]ναυδον, ἐμπόρων κωλύ-
τορ[α,
ὅσ γ'] ἐπισχήσει κελεύθου τοὺσ ξένο[υσ], φό̣[βον
βλέπων.
χαῖρ', ἄναξ, χαῖρ', ὦ Ποσεῖδον, ἐπίτροπο[σ . .[
[ΔΙΟΝΥΣΟΣ]--ἔμελλον εὑρήσειν ἄρ' ὑμᾶσ, ὠγαθο[ί.
οὐ τοῦτ' ἐρῶ σ', "οὐ δῆλοσ ἦσθ' ὁδοιπο[ρῶν."
αὐ[τὴ] κέλευθοσ ταῦτά μοι προσεν[νέπει,
]ο̣ρῶντα τούσδε πλησ[ι]οσφ[
]τ̣αῦτα καὶ σαφῶσ ἡγεῖτό μο[ι
]η̣τα. δω[.]μη . . δωι πατ[
ὁ̣ρ̣ῶν μύουρα καὶ βραχέα τὰ φ[αλλί]α,
ὡς ἐξέτριβεσ Ἰσθμιαστικὴν [τριβὴ]ν,
κοὐκ ἠμέλησασ, ἀλλ' ἐγυμνάζ[ου κα]λῶσ.
εἰ δ' οὖν ἐσώζου τὴν πάλαι παρο̣[ιμία]ν,
τοὔρχημα μᾶλλον εἰκὸσ ἦν σ' ἐπ̣[ισκοπ]εῖν.
σὺ δ' ἰσθμιάζεισ καὶ τρόπουσ και[νοὺσ μ]αθὼν
βραχίο̣[ν' ἀ]σκεῖσ, χρήματα φθείρων ἐμά.
κτεα[ν]ε ταῦτ' †ἐπη̣ρανωιπονων†.
οὐκοῦν] ἔ̣ν̣[ο]ρ̣κόν ἐστί σοι κα[τα]φρονεῖν
ἐμοῦ ;] κακῶσ ὄλοιο καὶ τρ̣ε . . . . . . ε

(Fragments of fifteen lines, including δ]οῦλον ἢ τρίδουλον 41, ἄν]αξ δίκα[ιοσ 42, κακ]ῶι τε κο̣[ί]τωι καὶ κακαῖσ δ[υσ]α̣υ̣λ̣ί̣α̣ι̣σ 43,]ει παλαιοῦ τοῦδ' ἐν οἰκτ[44,]ασ π̣ο̣λύπ̣[ο]δ̣ο̣[σ x – ᴗ – | φ]εύγω 45–6, π]ο̣τερα παθὼν τι δε[ινόν. . . . . . [κο]ὐ πολλὰ δράσασ . . . . ; 47–8, ε]ἶα θαρσῶν λέξ[ον

49, τ[ῶι ἱερῶι μεν[50. Lines 53–60 are missing altogether ; fragments of two lines follow.)

. . . . [.]ṭạδ' ἤ̣δη δ.[
σάκει καλύψασ[. . .]εν
σπείρεισ δὲ μῦθον τ[ό]νδε.[
καὶ ῥηματίζεισ, εἰσ ἔμ' ẹ̣κτρέπ̣[ων κότον,
ὡσ οὐδέν εἰμι τὴν σιδηρῖτι[ν τέχνην,
γύννισ δ' ἄναλκισ, οὐδ' ἔνειμ[' ἐν ἄρσεσιν.
καὶ νῦν τάδ' ἄλλα καὶ ποταίṇ[ι' ὄργανα,
ἔχθιστα πάντων τῶ[ν ὅπλων, ἕτοιμά σοι.
πλύνεισ τ' ἔμ' αὐτὸν [τήν τ' ἐμὴν χορό-
στασιν,
ἐφ' ἣν ἀγείρω πλ[ῆθοσ 'Ισθμίασ χθονόσ,
κοὐδεὶσ παλαιῶν οὐδὲ τῶν νεωτέρω[ν
ἑκὼν ἄπεστι τῶνδε διστοίχω[ν χορῶν.
σὺ δ' ἰσθμιάζεισ, καὶ πίτυοσ ἐστ[εμμένοσ
κλάδοισι κισσοῦ γ' οὐδ[α]μοῦ τιμὴ[ν νέμεισ.
ταῦτ' οὖν δακρύσεισ οὐ καπνῶ[ι δεδηγμένοσ.
παρόντα δ' ἐγγὺσ οὐχ ὁρᾷισ τὰ [φίλτατα ;

—ἀλλ' οὔποτ' ἔξειμ' ἐ[γὼ
τοῦ ἱεροῦ, καὶ τί μοι̣
ταῦτ' ἀπειλεῖσ ἔ̣χ[ων ;
"Ισθμιον ἀντε[ισέρχομαι
Ποσειδᾶνοσ ο[ἶκον.
σὺ δ' ἄλλοισ ταῦτ[α π]έμπε[δῶρα.
[?]—ἐπεὶ τ]ὰ καινὰ ταῦτα μα[νθά]νειν φιλεῖ[σ,
ἐγὼ [φέ]ρω σοι νεοχμὰ [ταῦτ'] ἀθύρματα
ἀπὸ [σκε]πάρνου κἄκμ[ονοσ ν]ẹόκτ[ιτα.
τουτ[ὶ τὸ] πρῶτον ἐστί σοι τῶν π̣αι̣[γνίω]ν.
—ἐμοὶ μὲν οὐχί· τῶν φίλων νεῖμόν τινι.

—μὴ ἄπειπε μηδ' ὄρνιθοσ οὕνεκ', ὠγαθέ.
—τί δεῖ γανοῦσθαι τοῦτο ; καὶ τί χρήσομαι ;
—ἥνπερ μεθεῖλ[εσ τὴ]ν τέχνην, ταύτῃ[ι]
        πρέπ[ει.
—τί δ' ἀντιποιεῖν [δόν]τι πλοῦν μοὐ[φ]αν-
        δάν[ει ;
—ξυνισθμιάζειν, [ἔργον] ἐμμελέστατον.
—φέρω[   ]ἐμβήσεται.
—ἐπισ[   ]βάδην ἐλ[αι]σ.

(Fragments of two more lines, including φ . μων σφυρά 98.)

8–9 Page. 15 Page : ἀξιάζοιτό θ' Π. 19 Page (cf. *Th.* 82). 20 Dodds, Ed. Fraenkel : ἔμπορον Π. 21 Ll.-J. 29 Maas. 30 Ll.-J. 37 beginning Ll.-J., ἔνορκόν Kamerbeek. 66 end Ll.-J. (cf. *Ag.* 1464). 68 Ll.-J. 69–70 Snell. 71–2 Ll.-J. 76 κἄλλοισι : γ' Page : δ' Π. 77 Maas. 78 Ll.-J. 81 Kamerbeek. 82–5 Snell. 86 (ταῦτ'), 88 Siegmann. 91 δεῖ Ll.-J. : δὴ Π. 92 πρέπ[ει Page. 94 Ll.-J.

[?] . . . seeing the portraits, wrought by superhuman skill. And however you may act, you won't be guilty of irreverence.

[CHORUS.] I'm very grateful to you for this : you're most obliging. Listen, all of you, and . . . in silence. Look and see whether this image could [possibly] be more [like] [1] me, this likeness by the Skilful One ; it can do everything but talk! Look at these! You see? Yes, come! Come! I bring this offering to the god to ornament his house, my lovely votive picture. It would give my mother a bad time! If she could see it, she'd certainly run shrieking off, thinking it was the son she brought up : so like me is this fellow.

Ho there! look upon the house of the Lord of the Sea, the Shaker of Earth! and let each fasten up the

[1] Text very doubtful : see Summary.

likeness of his handsome face, a truthful messenger, a voiceless herald to keep off travellers ; he'll halt strangers on their way by his terrifying look. Hail, King, hail, Poseidon . . . protector. . . .

[DIONYSUS.] I knew I'd find you, my good fellows! I won't apply to you the words, " I couldn't see that you were on your way." [1] The road itself tells me this, and [the . . . . , seeing these companions of yours],[2] warned me of this and set me on the right track . . . cum decurtatas, tanquam murium caudas, mentulas vobis video. You've practised hard for the Isthmia ; you haven't been slack but have trained properly. Well, if you'd been loyal to the old saying,[3] you might have seen to your dancing instead. But you're playing the Isthmian competitor ; you've learned new ways, and are keeping your arm-muscles in trim and wasting my money. . . . So aren't you breaking your oath when you flout me? a curse on you . . . .

(Fifteen lines unintelligible, including " a slave or thrice a slave," " rightful master," " miserable bed and miserable sleepings-out," " in the (? wretched) . . . of this old . . . ," " running away from . . . of a polyp," " Did I do anything . . . to you? Didn't I do you many . . .? " " Well, then, be brave and speak . . . ," " . . . stay in the temple." Eight lines missing ; fragments of two lines.)

[1] *ΟΥΤΟΥΤΕΡΩΣΟΥΔΗΛΟΣΗΣΘΟΔΟΙΠΟΡΩΝΠ*: other editors read this as οὔτοι ἑτέρωσ', οὔ, δῆλοσ, κτλ. Prof. K. J. Dover makes the very attractive suggestion that the words I have put in inverted commas may be a quotation from one of Archilochus' beast-fables. But I can find no evidence to substantiate this.

[2] Text very doubtful: see Summary.

[3] Doubtless ἔρδοι τισ ἣν ἕκαστοσ εἰδείη τέχνην: " Let each practise the craft he knows " (Lobel).

. . . covering with a shield . . . and you spread this story . . . and let loose a spate of words, venting your fury against me, saying that I'm no good at work in iron, but am a cowardly, womanish creature, not to be counted as a male. And now you have to hand these other new implements, the most detestable of all tools. And you abuse me and my dancing, for which I'm summoning together the people of the Isthmian land, and no one, young or old, stays away from these double rows of dancers if he can help it. But you are playing the Isthmian competitor, and with your wreath of pine-leaves [1] you refuse the ivy [2] its due honour. Well, you'll weep for this, you'll weep tears that are not stung from you by mere smoke. But don't you see your darling close at hand?

CH. No, I will never leave the temple! Why do you keep threatening me so? I enter my new home, the Isthmian house of Poseidon. But you must direct these gifts to others.

[?] Since you like to learn of novelties like these, I'm bringing these new toys, freshly made, straight from adze and anvil. Here's the first plaything for you.

[CH.] No, not for me! Give it to one of my friends!

[?] Don't refuse, my dear fellow! Why, think of the evil omen!

[CH.] How can one enjoy this thing? and how shall I use it?

[?] It is suited to the new craft which you've taken up.

[CH.] But what are you willing to do in return, if I let you sail?

[1] Worn by competitors at the Isthmian games in early times.
[2] Emblem of Dionysus.

[?] To be your comrade at the Isthmian games, a most agreeable pursuit.

[CH.] . . . bring . . . shall go on board . . . you shall go on foot . . . ankles.

NIOBH (see p. 430) A.D. 2

277

Ed. pr. Vitelli-Norsa, *Bulletin de la société royale d'archéologie d'Alexandrie* 28, 1933, 108, with Plate ; republished, ibid. 29, 1934, 229 ; cf. Körte, *Hermes* 68, 1933, 249, and *Archiv für Papyrusforschung* 11, 1935, 248 ; Latte, *Goett. Nachr.*, 1933, 22 ; Maas, *Gnomon* 9, 1933, 289 ; Cazzaniga, *Rend. Ist. Lomb.* 66, 1933, 843 ; Pfeiffer, *Philologus* 89, 1934, 1 ; Schadewaldt, *S.B. Heidelberg* 1933–4, Abh. 3 ; Reinhardt, *Hermes* 69, 1934, 233, and *Sophokles*, 1933, 246 ; Rostagni, *Riv. di Fil.* 62, 1934, 117 ; Lesky, *Wiener Studien* 52, 1934, 1 ; Schmid-Stählin, *Gr. Lit.* I, ii, 1934, 117, 2 ; Pickard-Cambridge, *Greek Poetry and Life*, 1936, 106 ; Lesky, *R.E.* xvii, 1, 649 : Fritsch, *Neue Fragmente des Aisch. und Soph.*, Diss. Hamburg, 1936, 25 ; Morel, *Bursian* 259, 1937, 30 ; Zimmermann, *Phil. Woch.* 57, 1937, 743 ; Kloesel, *Hermes* 72, 1937, 466 ; Cazzaniga, *Athenaeum* n.s. 17, 1939, 49 ; Mette, *Suppl. Aesch.*, 1939, 47 ; Page, *G.L.P.* no. 1, p. 2 ; Cantarella, *Eschilo* 1, 1941, 327 ; Cataudella, *Riv Fil.* 69, 1941, 34 ; Ed. Fraenkel, *Proc. Brit. Acad.*, 1942, 238 ; Fitton Brown, *Cl. Qu.* n.s. 4, 1954, 175 ; Wycherley, *Classical Philology* 49, 1954, 38 ; Pohlenz, *Die Griechische Tragoedie* ii^2, 1955, 65 ; Lloyd-Jones, *J.H.S.* 76, 1956, 63 ; Lesky, *TDH*, 1956, 82.

The papyrus gives no direct indication of speaker or speakers. Are the words preserved spoken by one speaker or no? And is all or part of the fragment spoken by Niobe herself?

Let us first consider ll. 1–9. We know from Aristophanes (*Ran.* 911 f.) and from the ancient *Life of Aeschylus* (quoted below) that for the whole of the early part of the play Niobe remained veiled and silent. Do these lines come from a speech made by her, after she has at last broken her silence, or do they come from a description of her behaviour by some other character? Three passages look as though, if their text was complete, they would supply an answer to this question. But of these three passages two (1–4, 10–11) are mutilated at the vital point, and might be supplemented in accordance with either view. In l. 1, we might read either *ἀναστέν[ειν ἔχω* or *ἀναστέν[ειν ἔχει*. L. 11 would be most naturally filled in by a participle (e.g. *ζητῶν, ἄγων*) ; but one cannot rule out the possibility that the poet wrote, e.g., *ψυχῆς] κόμιστρα τῆσδε, κτλ* : in which case Niobe would after all have been the speaker. Ll. 6–8 should furnish a more certain indication, especially since they are quoted, or rather paraphrased by Hesychius (cf. fr. 78). But unfortunately the text of the papyrus is almost certainly corrupt, nor does Hesychius help us to amend it with certainty.

Hesychius explains the word *ἐπώζειν* as follows : *ἐπικαθῆσθαι τοῖς ᾠοῖσ. Αἰσχύλος Νιόβῃ μεταφορικῶς· ἐφημένη τάφον τέκνοις ἔπωζε τοῖς τεθνηκόσιν.* From this scholars have inferred that the *ἐποιμώζουσα* of the papyrus in l. 7 is corrupt. Those who think Niobe is not the speaker mostly suppose that the corruption arose from *ἐπώζε⟨ι ζῶσα⟩* (Latte), and in l. 8 supply a participle ; those who think she is in l. 7 read *ἐπωάζουσα* and in l. 8 supply an aorist indicative.

The verbs *ἐπώζω* and *ἐπωάζω* can both mean " to sit on eggs " ; but also both can mean " to utter cries," one deriving from *ὤ* and the other from *ᾠά*.

(When they mean "to sit on eggs," they should properly be written with adscript iota after the ω, but adscript iotas are so often omitted in papyri that the absence of this is of no significance.) Hesychius, or rather his authority, clearly thought that Niobe was compared to a hen; and some of those who share his view argue against Niobe's being the speaker on the ground that she herself can hardly have made such a comparison. But the argument has no force, since Hesychius is unlikely to be right. The sense of "utter cries of lamentation" is far better suited to the context; nor is it reasonable to insist that Niobe's silence must exclude the uttering of cries of lamentation. See Kloesel's excellent treatment of this point.

Page rightly says that it would have been far easier for the MS. reading to be displaced by a paraphrasing word that would not destroy the sense than by a word that would destroy it; and this makes in favour of ἐποιμώζουσα as against ἐπώζει ζῶσα. But it is still unlikely that those who supply an aorist in l. 8 are right. Wolff's τριταῖ]ον at the beginning of l. 6 is generally accepted. He compares *Vita Aeschyli* s. 6, where in all MSS. except M we read ἐν γὰρ τῆι Νιόβηι ἕωσ τρίτησ ἡμέρασ ἐπικαθημένη τῶι τάφωι τῶν παίδων οὐδὲν φθέγγεται. The words τρίτησ ἡμέρασ may be a mere corruption of M's reading τρίτου μέρουσ. But even if it is, τριταῖον or some other ordinal number is very probably right. Is it possible for τριταῖον ἦμαρ . . . ἐφημένη, "I have been sitting . . . for two days," to be followed by a main verb that is not present but aorist? Page explains his reading ἔκλαυσα as being an instantaneous aorist, of the kind which in English is properly rendered by a present.

But I know of no case of a present participle that is used closely with an indication of time, as ἐφημένη is used with τριταῖον ἦμαρ, being followed by an aorist main verb. Instantaneous aorists of this sort may be equivalent in sense to English presents, but they are not treated as presents in Greek syntax. I therefore think it likely that whatever was displaced by ἐποιμώζουσα must have included a main verb in the present tense and that at the beginning of l. 8 we should supply a participle.

The favourite supplement of those who insist that Niobe must be the speaker is therefore unlikely to be right; but their main contention is not necessarily wrong. For ἐποιμώζουσα did not necessarily arise from ἐπώζει ζῶσα. It may equally well have arisen from ἐπώζω ζῶσα; and though the ugly repetition of ζω may be thought to make against this reading, it is somewhat likelier to have given rise to the corruption in the papyrus than is ἐπώζει ζῶσα. Hesychius, it is true, puts the verb in the third person; but since he is probably paraphrasing the text rather than quoting it, this consideration has little weight.

We are forced to conclude that the text as it stands offers no reliable means of determining whether Niobe speaks the lines or no. Those who argue that she does not contend that their tone is too calm and reflective to be suitable to her. I feel some sympathy with this argument, but it is not one that can be pressed far; though it may derive some strength from the reflection that ll. 10–11 look as if they are not spoken by or to Niobe. Not that this is certain.

Some scholars think the fragment is part of a dialogue, ll. 1–9 being spoken by an actor, 10–13 by the Chorus and the rest by the actor again. This cannot be ruled out, but is unlikely to be right. The question in ll. 12–13 looks like a rhetorical question of the kind that the asker himself at once proceeds to answer; for such a question and answer in Aeschylus compare, for instance, *P.V.* 500–4.

If the speaker is not Niobe, who else may it be? Latte suggested Niobe's nurse; others refuse to credit a nurse with so much *σεμνότησ* and suggest Niobe's mother-in-law, Antiope. There is some reason to suspect that a nurse was mentioned in this play (see Lesky, l.c., p. 7); and as the single instance of the *Choephoroe* does not prove that all Aeschylean nurses were incapable of *σεμνότησ*, the nurse has a shade the better claim. But we cannot know which of them it was, if it was either.

To sum up, we have not sufficient evidence to know whether Niobe is the speaker or no. Nor can we be quite sure that they belong to a single speaker, though it is likelier than not that this is so. I suspect, although I cannot prove, that this speaker was not Niobe, and my supplements are made accordingly. But I offer them with very little confidence.

1–3. The speaker does *not* mean to say: "She can only weep for Tantalus." The speaker means to say: "She can only weep for the disastrous marriage which Tantalus made for her"; but this is expressed by means of the common construction exemplified, e.g., by Eur., *Med.* 37: *δέδοικα δ' αὐτὴν μή τι βουλεύηι νέον.*

ἡ δ' οὐ]δὲν εἰ μὴ πατέρ' ἀναστέν[ειν ἔχει,
τὸν δ]όντα καὶ φύσαντα Ταντάλου β[ίαν,
εἰσ οἷ]ον ἐξώκειλεν ἀλίμενον γάμον.

παντ]ọσ κακοῦ γὰρ πνεῦμα προσβ[άλλε]ι δόμοισ·
αὐταὶ] δ' ὁρᾶτε τοὐπιτέρμιον γάμου.
τριταῖ]ον ἦμαρ τόνδ' ἐφημένη τάφον
τέκν]οισ ἐπώζει ζῶσα τοῖσ τεθνηκόσιν,
θρηνο]ῦσα τὴν τάλαιναν εὔμορφον φυήν.
βροτὸ]σ κακωθεὶσ δ' οὐδὲν ἄλλ' εἰ μὴ σκιά.
αὖθισ] μὲν ἥξει δεῦρο Ταντάλου βία,
ἐπ' ἀγ]κόμιστρα τῆσδε καὶ πεφạ[σμένοσ.
πατὴρ] δὲ μῆνιν τίνα φέρων Ἀμφίονι
πρόρρι]ζον αἰνῶσ ἐξεφύλλασεν γένοσ ;
ἐγὼ πρ]ὸσ ὑμᾶσ, οὐ γάρ ἐστε δύσφρονεσ,
λέξω·] θεὸσ μὲν αἰτίαν φύει βροτοῖσ,
ὅταν κα]κῶσαι δῶμα παμπήδην θέληι.
ὅμωσ δ]ὲ θνητὸν ὄντα χρὴ τὸν ἐ[κ θεῶν
ὄλβον π]εριστέλλοντα μὴ θρασυστομ[εῖν.
ἀλλ' οἱ μέγ'] εὖ πράσσοντεσ οὔποτ' ἤλπισα[ν
σφαλέντ]εσ ἐκχεῖν ἣν ἔχουσ[ι πλησμονήν.
αὕτη γ]ὰρ ἐξαρθεῖσα καλλισ[

1 beginning Maas, ἔχει Pohlenz. 3 beginning Schadewaldt: βίον corrected to γάμον in *Π*. 4 beginning Pfeiffer, end Latte. 5 Schadewaldt. 6 E. Wolff. 7 τέκνοισ Hesych. (see fr. 78) ἐπώζει ζῶσα Latte: ἐποιμώζουσα *Π*. 8 Ll.-J. 9 Ed. Fraenkel. 10 Page. 11 Page (*G.L.P.*, p. 7, where he also suggested τῆσδ' ἑκὰσ: if ἀγ] is right, the space suggests that ἀνα[was written in *Π*). 12 Lesky. 13 αἰκῶσ corrected to αἰνῶσ in *Π*. 15–16 = fr. 77. 18 ὄλβον Latte. 19 μέγ' Ll.-J. 20 beginning Ed. Fraenkel, end Page. 21 καλλισ[τεύματι ed. pr., καλλισ[τεύμασι Lobel: "or some form of κάλλιστοσ ?" Page.

But she can only lament over the luckless marriage, one that proved no haven, into which mighty Tantalus, the father that begot her and gave her away, forced her fortune's ship. For the blast of all manner of evil is striking against her house, and you yourselves can see the conclusion of the marriage. This is the third day she has sat by this tomb, wailing over her children, the living over the dead, and mourning the misfortune of their beauty. Man brought to misery is but a shadow. Mighty Tantalus will in due course come here ; to bring her home will be the purpose of his coming. But what cause of wrath had the Father against Amphion, that he has thus ruthlessly destroyed his family, root and branch? Loyal as you are, I will tell you. A god causes a fault to grow in mortals, when he is minded utterly to ruin their estate. But none the less, a mortal must abstain from rash words, carefully nursing the happiness that the gods give him. But in great prosperity men never think that they may stumble and spill the full cup of their fortune. So it was that this woman, exultant in . . . beauty. . . .

? ΠΡΟΜΗΘΕΥΣ ΠΥΡΚΑΕΥΣ (see p. 453) A.D. 2

278

Ed. pr. Lobel, *P. Oxy.*, vol. 20, no. 2245, with Plate I ; cf. Ed. Fraenkel, *Proc. Brit. Acad.*, 1942, 246 ; Snell, *Gnomon* 25, 1953, 435 ; Mette, *Aischylos' Prometheia*, 1953, 59 ; Terzaghi, *Riv. di Filol.* n.s. 32, 1954, 337 ; Murray, *Aeschyli Fabulae*[2], 1955, 99 ; Mette, *Gymnasium* 62, 1955, 396 : Stark, *Maia* n.s. 2, 1956, 89 ; Lesky, *TDH*, 1956, 63.

Aeschylus wrote certainly three and probably four plays about Prometheus ; the extant *Prometheus Desmotes*, the *Prometheus Lyomenos* (see p. 446), the *Prometheus Pyrphoros*, which was probably either the first or the third play of the trilogy that contained the former two, and the *Prometheus Pyrkaeus* (see the discussion on pp. 454–5). The last-mentioned play was probably the satyr-play produced in 472 together with the *Persae*, the *Phineus* and the *Glaucus Potnieus* : see the hypothesis to the *Persae*. The play probably dealt with the bringing of fire to earth by Prometheus ; and the numerous vases that show satyrs carrying fire in fennel-stalks, sometimes accompanied by Prometheus himself, are likely to be connected with it ; see Beazley in *A.J.A.* 43, 1939, 618 ; ibid., 44, 1940, 212 ; Brommer, *Satyrspiele* 44, 79. Fraenkel is almost certainly right in assigning this fragment to this play. Its subject-matter accords well with what is known of the *Pyrkaeus* (see fr. 117 with note) ; and both the dance and the allusion to the nymphs suggest satyric drama rather than tragedy. The lines may belong to the chorus of satyrs ; but the reference to Prometheus in the third person does not preclude their belonging to Prometheus himself.

Terzaghi's case for attributing the fragment to the *Pyrphoros* rests on the word χιτῶνα in l. 3. Satyrs, he says, do not wear χιτῶνεσ and therefore the text cannot belong to a satyr-play. But even if we could be sure that this word referred to the dress of the Chorus, which we cannot, vases not infrequently show satyrs dressed like ordinary people. Of course we do not *know* to which play the fragment belongs ; but there is no positive evidence in favour of Terzaghi's view.

Previous editors have assumed that the first occurrence of the refrain (ll. 6–7) is preceded by a strophe whose first line is missing, the second (ll. 15–18) by the antistrophe. This is by no means certain. Mette analyses the alleged strophe and antistrophe as follows :

$$2\delta + 2\text{ia} + \text{cr} + \delta + \text{ia} + 2\text{ba} \;;\;\; 2\text{ia} + \text{cr}[=2\delta?] + 2\delta$$

This involves assuming (1) that *πῠροσ ᾰκᾰμᾰ-*[1] in l. 3 responds with what seems likely to have been a normal bacchius in l. 12 ; (2) that the normal iambic metron (*κλῠοῡσ' ἓμο̄υ*) in l. 4 responds with the bacchius *χ̆ορεῡσεῑν* in l. 13 ; (3) in l. 13 the syllable *νι̣* is long.

(1) is undeniably awkward. True, the text of l. 12 is uncertain ; Lobel points out that [*τε καὶ*] does not suit the remaining traces or fill the space after *φερέσβιοσ* and that *σπευσίδωροσ* is a strange word. But an acute accent on the *O* of *φερέσβιοσ* shows that an enclitic must have followed it, and as Lobel says [*τε καὶ*] seems unavoidable ; nor is *σπευσίδωρ*[*οσ* much easier to avoid. And a resolved bacchius of the kind supposed, while in theory conceivable, would in practice be unique. (2), again, is a serious difficulty. The responsion of a pure iambic metron to a bacchius is found in tragedy only at *Agam.* 195–208, where since Porson editors have been accustomed to emend. Nor is the dochmiac form ⏑ – ⏑ – ⏑ – found responding with ⏑ – – ⏑ –.[2] (3) is less formidable, for it is not certain that the *N* was followed by an *I* ; see the facsimile.

[1] The first *a* of this word is marked as short in the papyrus.

[2] See Dale, *Lyric Metres of Greek Drama*, 113. This colon certainly occurs in dochmiac contexts ; but it is not certain that it is dochmiac, and in any case it is not found in Aeschylus.

I do not think it is certain that the two stanzas correspond. But if they do not, they will be the only two known to us which are followed by an identically worded *ἐφύμνιον* without corresponding; and I would not dare to assert that Aeschylus could not possibly have allowed the licences in question. Nor can the possibility of corruption be altogether ruled out. I suspect that the two stanzas *did* originally correspond; but without new evidence the question cannot be decided.

If it is not certain that the stanzas correspond, is it safe to assume, as previous editors have done, that a dissyllable is missing after φ[α]ενν[ὸ]ν in l. 2? I think it is, since sense as well as metre seems to suggest that this is so. Not that I feel confident that Snell's supplement, which I print, is necessarily right.

. . . .

—σι[α] δέ μ' εὐμενὴσ χορεύει χάρισ.
φ[α]ενν[ὸ]ν [βάλε
χιτῶνα πὰρ πυρὸσ ἀκάματον αὐγάν.
κλυοῦσ' ἐμοῦ δὲ Ναΐδων τισ παρ' ἑστιοῦχον σέλασ πολλὰ διώξεται.
—νύμφασ δέ τοι πέποιθ' ἐγώ ἐφυμν.
στήσει[ν] χορούσ
Προμηθέωσ δῶ[ρ]ον ὥσ σεβούσασ.
—κα̣λ̣[ὸ]ν̣ δ' ὕμνον ἀμφὶ τὸν δόντα μολ-
πάσειν [ἔ]ολ[π' ἐγ]ὼ λεγούσασ τόδ' ὥσ
Προμηθε[ὺσ βρο]τοῖσ
φερέσβιόσ [τε καὶ] σπευσίδωρ[οσ].
χορεύσειν .[. . . . . .]ν̣ι̣' ἐλπὶσ ὠ-
ρίου χε̣[ίμ]ατ[οσ . . .]ερ . ιχ̣[. .]α̣.
[—] νύμφ]ασ δέ τ[οι] πέπ[ο]ιθ' ἐγώ ἐφυμν.

στήσε]ιν χοροὺσ 16
Προμ]η[θ]έωσ δῶρον ὣσ σεβοῦσα[σ.

(Fragments of six more lines, including ποιμέν[.]σ πρέπειν 18, τὸ νυκτίπλαγ[κτον] ὄρχημα . . . . . .]σιν ἐπιστεφεῖσ φύλλοισ 19-21, [βα]θυξυλο[24.

2 end Snell.

. . . and . . . gracious kindness sets me dancing. [Throw down] your bright cloak by the unwearying light of the fire. Often shall one of the Naiads, when she has heard me tell this tale, pursue me by the blaze within the hearth.

The nymphs, I know full well, shall join their dances in honour of Prometheus' gift!

Sweet, I think, will be the song they sing in honour of the giver, telling how Prometheus is the bringer of sustenance and the eager giver of gifts to men.

The nymphs, I know full well, shall join their dances in honour of Prometheus' gift!

(Fragments of six more lines, including " . . . shine . . . shepherd's (shepherds?)," " night-wandering dance . . . crowned with . . . leaves," " deep thicket.")

? ΣΕΜΕΛΗ Η ῾ΥΔΡΟΦΟΡΟΙ A.D. 2

279

Ed. pr. Lobel, *P. Oxy.*, vol. 18, no. 2164, with Plate I; cf. Latte, *Philologus* 97, 1948, 47; Mette, *Nachtrag zum Suppl. Aesch.*, 1949, 14; Lobel, *P. Oxy.*, vol. 20, p. 10; Lasserre, *Mus. Helv.* 6, 1949, 140; Cantarella, *I nuovi frammenti eschilei di Ossirinco*, 1949, 108; Snell, *Gnomon* 25, 1953, 436; Mette, *Gymnasium* 62, 1955, 401; Nilsson, *L'Antiquité Classique* 24, 1956, 336; Lesky, *TDH*, 1956, 85.

Ed. pr. assigned this fragment to the *Xantriae*, because ll. 16–17 coincide with a quotation assigned by one of its quoters to that play. This quotation is fr. 84, which is presented in the following manner by the authors who preserve it: (1) Plato, *Rep.* 381 D: *μήδ' ἐν τραγωιδίαισ μήδ' ἐν τοῖσ ἄλλοισ ποιήμασιν μηδεὶσ εἰσαγέτω Ἥραν ἠλλοιωμένην, ὡσ ἱέρειαν ἀγείρουσαν Ἰνάχου Ἀργείου ποταμοῦ παισὶν βιοδώροισ.* (2) Diogenes, *Epist.* 34, 2: *τῶν τραγωιδοποιῶν οἵτινεσ Ἥραν τὴν Διὸσ παράκοιτιν ἔφασαν εἰσ ἱέρειαν μεταμορφωθεῖσαν τοιοῦτον βίου σχῆμα ἀναλαβεῖν νύμφαισ κρηνιάσιν* (Meineke: *κρήναισιν*) *κυδραῖσ θεαῖσ ἀγείρουσαν Ἰνάχου Ἀργείου* (*Ἀργείαισ* codd.) *ποταμοῦ παισὶν βιοδώροισ.* (3) Scholiast on Aristophanes, *Frogs* 1344: *νύμφαι ὀρεσσίγονοι· ἐκ τῶν Ξαντριῶν Αἰσχύλου φησὶν Ἀσκληπιάδησ. εὗρε δὲ Ἀθήνησι ἔν τινι τῶν διορθωθέντων* (Latte: *διαθέντων*) *νύμφαισ θεαῖσιν ἀγείρω, Ἰνάχου Ἀργείου ποταμοῦ παισὶν βιοδώροισ.* These authorities, in Lobel's words, "diverge strangely from each other and from the papyrus."

Only the scholion on Aristophanes names the *Xantriae*. Latte points out that we have good reason to think this play contained an account of the tearing to pieces on Mt. Cithaeron of Semele's nephew, Pentheus; the testimony of a scholion on *Eum.* 26, is borne out by fr. 85, whose words were spoken by Lyssa, the goddess of madness (see Dodds on Eur., *Bacchae* 977). It is hard to see how a play that contained this can also have contained a scene in which Hera appeared disguised as a begging priestess. But such a scene would fit well into another play which was part of the same trilogy, the *Semele*. Semele's ruin, according to the usual story, was brought about by Hera, who disguised as an old woman induced her to persuade Zeus to appear before her armed with his thunder. The versions of this legend known to us make Hera disguise herself as an old nurse. But these are all of much later date. In Aeschylus she may well have disguised herself as a priestess; and such a priestess may well have claimed to have arrived in Thebes from Argos, the great centre of Hera's worship. (Nilsson's assumption that the invocation of the Argive nymphs proves that the scene of the play was Argos seems to me unsafe.) Latte points out that Asclepiades was a careless writer, and gives several examples of a quotation being mistakenly assigned to a play belonging to the same trilogy as that to which it really belongs. He rightly concludes that the balance of probability is in favour of the *Semele*, and not the *Xantriae*, being the play to which this fragment belongs.

Ll. 1–11 seem to consist of choriambic dimeters, 12–15 of marching anapaests, 16–30 of lyric hexameters. The general sense of 1–15 cannot be guessed at with any certainty; but it seems reasonable to guess that the Chorus is describing the favours conferred by Zeus on Semele and praying that her good fortune may continue.

At 16–17, the reading of the papyrus seems to confirm the opinion of the commentator on Aristophanes that ὀρεσσίγονοι was not in the text, as Asclepiades supposed it was. Diogenes' κρήναισ may be an explanatory gloss; and Latte's suggestion (printed below) is likely to be right. The nymphs of the Argive rivers were four of the daughters of Danaus, Hippe, Automate, Amymone and Physadeia. Danaus was descended from Inachus; and this, together with the fact that Inachus was the principal river of Argos, makes it natural for the nymphs to be called "daughters of Inachus." The nymphs were patronesses of marriage and childbirth (see Latte, p. 54). This is why brides and women who had just given birth performed a ceremonial ablution in the water of the particular spring consecrated by their city to this purpose. At Athens this was Enneakrounos (Thuc., 2, 15), at Thebes Ismenus (Eur., *Phoen.* 347), at Argos Automate (see Callim., fr. 65 Pfeiffer).

ἔχ]ραιν' ἀλοιφᾶ[ι
]δ' οὐ πλέον Ἥρας
]ὑπεροπλότεροι
. . .[. .] . . θεκ[. .]α μιγνύμεναι
. πωθόνειρα[ ]θη . [
—μένο[ι θ]εῶν [ ]όσιμοσ βιοτὰ
φίλοισιν ἐν μ . κεσι . [. ὅ]στις
φθονερ[ὸσ δ' ἀπέστω
δόξα τ' ἀεικήσ. [Σ]εμέλασ δ' ε[ὐ-
χόμεθ' εἶναι διὰ πᾶν
εὐθύπορον λά[χοσ ὄλβου.
—τὰ γὰρ ἄλλα τάδ[
Κάδμῳ Σεμέ[λα
τῷ] παντοκρα[τ
Ζηνί, γάμων δ'[

[ἭΡΑ.]

[—] νύμφαι ναμερτεῖσ, κ[υδραὶ θεα]ί, αἷσιν
ἀγείρω,

Ἰνάχου Ἀργείου ποταμοῦ παισὶν βιο-
δώροι[σ,
αἴτε παρίστανται πᾶσιν βροτέοισιν ἐπ' ἔργ[οισ,
εἰ̣[λαπίναισ θαλίαισ] τ̣ε̣ καὶ εὐμόλποισ ὑμ[εναίοισ
καὶ τ[ελέουσι κόρασ ν]εολέκτρους ἀρτι-
γάμ[ουσ τε
λευκο. [ ]μ̣μασιν ἐ[ῦ]φρονες[
φῶσ δεκ[ο]περ ὄμματοσ ἐστ[
αἰδὼς γὰρ καθαρὰ καὶ ν[υ]μφοκόμοσ μέ[γ]' ἀρί[στα,
παίδων δ' εὔκαρπον τε[λ]έθει γένοσ, οἷ̣σ̣[ιν ἐκεῖναι
ἵλαοι ἀντιάσουσι μελίφ[ρονα θυμὸν ἔχουσαι
ἀμφότεραι σύμεναι μ[
τραχεῖαι στυγεραί τε καὶ[
ἀ]γχίμολοι· πολλὰσ μὲν[
]γον εὐναίου φωτὸ̣[σ
]ε̣λ̣ασίν τε μίτραισ[

8 "Or φιλοῦσιν" Lobel: end Latte. 11 λά[χοσ Latte: end Ll.-J. 16 Lobel warns that this supplement seems too long for the gap. 19 Cantarella. 20 Lasserre. 24 end Ll.-J. 25 ἔχουσαι Ll.-J.

. . . anointed with unguents . . . not more than Hera . . . more arrogant . . . mighty . . . from afar. May there abide . . . life . . . the gods . . . among friendly . . . But may all the envious be absent, and all unseemly rumour. We pray that Semele's good fortune may ever steer a straight course. For . . . this other . . . Semele . . . Cadmus . . . the all-powerful Zeus . . . marriage.

[HERA.] Nymphs that speak the truth, honoured goddesses are they for whom I collect offerings, the life-giving children of Inachus the river of Argos. They are present at all the actions of men, at feasts and banquets and the sweet songs of marriage, and they initiate maidens lately wedded and new to love. . . . kindly . . . eyes . . . of the eye. . . . For unsullied modesty . . . is by far the best of adorners for a bride. And fruitful in children are the families of those to whom the nymphs shall come in kindness, with sweet disposition, . . . coming . . . both . . . harsh and hateful . . . when they come near. Many . . . husband . . . girdles. . . .

UNKNOWN PLAY (1) A.D. 2

280

Ed. pr. Lobel, *P. Oxy.*, vol. 20, no. 2251, with Plate III; cf. Snell, *Gnomon* 25, 1953, 436; Cunningham, *Rhein. Mus.* 96, 1953, 223; Mette, *Gymnasium* 62, 1955, 402; Pohlenz, *Die Griechische Tragoedie* II², 1955, 21; Lesky, *TDH.*, 1956, 69; Kakridis, *Acme* 8, fasc. 2–3, 1955(?), 91.

A Chorus composed of female persons is lamenting for a hospitable person (or for such a person's house), one who (or which) has been visited by some grievous and, in their opinion undeserved, fate. Miss Cunningham thinks the fragment belongs to the *Αἰγύπτιοι*, the second play of the trilogy about the Danaids (see vol. 1, p. 3); she recalls the conjecture (see Hermann, *Opusc.*, ii, 323 f.) that the Argive king Pelasgus was killed in battle while protecting the Danaids against the sons of Aegyptus. But for all we know many hospitable persons may have suffered destruction in lost plays of Aeschylus; and there are positive objections to Miss Cunningham's view. One is that the name of the play *Αἰγύπτιοι* indicates that the sons of Aegyptus formed the Chorus ; this compels Miss Cunningham to suggest that the Danaids may have formed an additional Chorus. There is an extra Chorus of handmaidens in the *Supplices*, and it is not impossible that there may have been an extra Chorus in the *Αἰγύπτιοι*. But the necessity of supposing that there is does not recommend the theory which involves it. Further, the letters *κατασκ̣[* in l. 3 are most easily explained by Snell's supplement, printed below ; Miss Cunningham in the interests of her theory is driven to conjecture that *κατασκαφέντα* was written by mistake for *κατασφαγέντα*. The verdict must be that the evidence is wholly insufficient to assign this piece to the *Αἰγύπτιοι* or to any other play.

L. 8 : " the metaphor in *ἄναυλον βρέγμα* is not appreciably odder than in *καὶ ψάλλ' ἔθειραν* (*Persae* 1062) " : Lobel. One may speak of " plucking " the string of a musical instrument ; and to speak of " plucking " one's hair is a not unnatural extension of this usage. But is it as easy to speak of the front of one's head as being " without the pipe "? Since the pipe was associated with joyful occasions, " without the pipe " might be used as equivalent to " joyless ". (But Stinton suggests *ἄναυδον*, which may be right).

χειρ.[
ἰδὲ γάρ, ὦ Ζ[εῦ] ξέ[νιε], ν[ῦν δόμον
τ]ὸν ξενοδόκον κατασκ̣[αφέντα.
ἆρ' ἐ]στὶν χάρισ ἐν θεοῖσ
ἀνδρά]σι τοῖσ δικαίοισ ;

UNKNOWN PLAY (I)

τοίγαρ κ[ατα]πρισσομ[ένα
κόμασ [ἀ]φειδεῖ χερ[ί,
τόδ' ἄνα[υ]λον βρέγμα π[ατά]σ[σω
δυρομ[έν]α σὸν πότμον γό[οισιν.

(Scraps of five more lines.)

2, 3 ends Snell. 4 Page. 8 ἄνα[υ]λον *Π*. end Snell.

For look now, Zeus, lord of the law of host and guest, upon the destruction of the hospitable house! What kindness do the gods show to righteous men? Therefore I tear my hair with unsparing hand and beat my crown with joyless sound, lamenting with wailing your fortune. . . .

UNKNOWN PLAY (II a)

281

Ed. pr. Lobel, *P. Oxy.*, vol. 20, no. 2256, fr. 8, with Plate V. For bibliography, see next fragment.

This piece is written in the same hand as No. 282. In itself, this need mean no more than that both are by the same author (see Lobel in *P. Oxy.*, vol. 20, p. 29); but the content indicates that they may well come from the same scene of the same play. If so, it seems rather likelier than not that this piece came before the other; but one cannot be sure of this. The text presents several difficult problems of interpretation.

5. ἐκπαγλούμενον. This verb is nowhere else a passive; and the apparent quasi-adjectival use of the participle is curious. In the three other tragic examples of its use, the verb is in the middle and

means " magnify " in the sense of " admire " or " exalt." It seems possible that it could also mean " magnify " in the sense of " make great " ; and I suspect that ἐκπαγλουμένη with this meaning may be the right reading here. If so, the termination was mistakenly assimilated to that of the preceding word.

6. Ed. pr. renders : " so that in competition they surpass their neighbours in prosperity," ἅμιλλαν being taken as accusative of respect. I have preferred to make ἅμιλλαν the direct object of κρατεῖν, which regularly governs an accusative when it means " surpass."

7–8. (1) How are we to divide, and how interpret, *ΓΗΣΕΠΕΜΒΟΛΑΣ* (*B* is corrected to *Π* in the papyrus)? (2) Is λέληνται from λανθάνω? Or from λαμβάνω? Or from what verb is it? (3) What is the right restoration of the first word of l. 8? There is room in the gap for only two letters. I can return no satisfactory answer to any of these questions , and if I explain here the solution I have adopted in the text, it is not because I am convinced it is the right one.

The context leads us to expect a mention of what the citizens do now that they have given up warfare. We should therefore expect the verb in l. 8 to mean " turn towards " or " wish for." Lobel points out that, if this could be done, a natural supplement would be θυ]μῶι. In two passages (*Th.* 355, 380) Aeschylus uses in the sense of " desiring " a perfect participle which is written λελιμμένοσ in the MSS. except by the Medicean codex in the former passage, which has λελημμένοι. A scholion on the second passage derives the participle from λίπτω, from which is formed *λιψουρία* (*Ch.* 756) and which is used in the active in the sense of " desire " in Hellenistic poetry. Can these two passages (and possibly *Ag.* 876, where Blomfield conjectured *λελιμμένη* and Ahrens *Ἅιδου . . . λελιμμένη*) be relevant to *λέληνται* here? If they are, it is unlikely that they come from *λίπτω*. For if the verb here came from *λίπτω*, we should have to read *λέλινται* : and from this verb with its consonantal stem we should expect not this but *λελίφαται* (see Kühner-Blass, ii, p. 75). But I do not feel certain that the ancient grammarian was right in referring these participles to *λίπτω*, and suspect that they may be instances of a use of the middle of *λαμβάνω*, not so different from, say, that found at Soph., *O.C.* 373.

Supposing this were right, we could restore *θυ]μῶι* and translate : " And they eagerly desire (or perhaps ' have seized upon ') land for. . . ." For what purpose will they have desired land? If we read *ἐμπολάσ* it will be for trade ; but since they are likelier to have desired land for ploughing, *ἀμπολάσ* (already mentioned as one possibility by Lobel) is attractive. But the whole line of argument is very hazardous.

]. σ ζῳννῦσα μὴ σπείρειν κακ[
( ]ν τ[ό]τ' ἐστὶν εἰρήνη βροτοῖσ.
θεὸν δ' ἐπ]αινῶ τήνδε. τιμᾶι γὰρ πόλιν
ἐν ἡσύ[χοισ]ι πράγμασιν καθημένην,
δόμων τ' ἀέξει κάλλοσ ἐκπαγλού[μ]ενον
ἅ]μιλλαν ὥστε γειτόνων ὄλβωι κρατεῖν)
μη]δ' αὖ φυτεύειν. οἱ δὲ γῆσ ἐπ' ἀμπολὰσ
θυ]μῶι λέληνται, δαίασ πεπαυμένοι
σάλ]πιγγοσ, οὐδὲ φρουρί[.] . εξ . . . [.].

(Scraps of two more lines.)

3 Ll.-J. 7, 8–9 see Summary above: εμβολασ corrected nto εμπολασ in *Π*.

. . . girdling (?) . . . not to sow evil . . . (Then Peace is . . for mortals. And I praise this goddess; for she honours a city that reposes in a life of quiet, and augments the admired beauty of its houses, so that they surpass in prosperity the neighbours who are their rivals), nor yet to engender it. And they earnestly desire land for ploughing,[1] abandoning the martial trumpet, nor do . garrisons. . . .

[1] Translation very dubious; see Summary above.

UNKNOWN PLAY (II b) A.D. 2

282

Ed. pr. Lobel, *P. Oxy.*, vol. 20, no. 2256, fr. 9a, with Plate VI; cf. Robertson, *Class. Rev.*, n.s. 3, 1953, 79; Ed. Fraenkel, *Eranos* 52, 1954, 61; Pohlenz, *Die Griechische Tragoedie* ii², 1955, 198; Mette, *Gymnasium* 62, 1955, 405; Goerschen, *Dioniso*, n.s. 18, 1955, 139; Lloyd-Jones, *J.H.S.*, 76, 1956, 59; Stark, *Maia*, n.s. 2, 1956, 83; Lesky, *TDH.*, 1956, 85; Kakridis, *Acme* 8, fasc. 2–3, 1955(?), 92.

This fragment is shown to be Aeschylean by the coincidence of l. 28 with fr. 377 Nauck ²; the occurrence in l. 9 of the word ὀτιή (found at Eur., *Cycl.* 643, but nowhere in tragedy) points to its coming from a satyr-play. Clearly one of the speakers is the goddess Dike, Justice, who is explaining how she came by her prerogatives and what they are. It is likely, though not certain, that she is conversing with the Chorus. Dike is the πάρεδροσ of Zeus as early as Hesiod (Op. 259); but in Hesiod it is not she herself, but thirty thousand δαίμονεσ who are appointed by

Zeus to keep a watch upon men. On the notion of the "book of Zeus," in which men's crimes are recorded, see Solmsen, *Class. Quart.*, 58, 1944, 27. It looks as if Euripides had this play in mind when, in a famous passage from one of his two plays about Melanippe (fr. 506 Nauck[2]) he ridiculed this belief.

Ll. 30 ff. raise awkward problems. Is the persecutor of travellers, who is cited as a classic instance of injustice punished, Ares himself, or another? The only person connected with Ares who is known to have behaved in this fashion is Cycnus, not the king of Tenedos, but the Cycnus of the Hesiodic *Shield of Heracles* who persecuted visitors to Delphi and was slain by Heracles. Aeschylus certainly wrote a play in which a Cycnus was a character (see Ar., *Frogs* 963), though this may have been the other Cycnus. Ares is surely the subject of ll. 31 f.: and perhaps Ares' support of Cycnus is the subject lower down.

Another explanation is offered by Robertson, who thinks the speaker is leading up to an account of the trial of Ares before the court of Areopagus for the murder of Poseidon's son Halirrhothius ; and he explains the behaviour attributed to Ares by supposing that he may have been represented as having been a difficult child at this time (cf. the Hermes of the Homeric Hymn and the *Ichneutae* of Sophocles). Yet in the usual version of this story, Ares was not an aggressor, but was defending the virtue of his daughter Alcippe (see Frazer, *Apollodorus*, ii, p. 81).

We cannot be sure that this narration relates to the main theme of the play, and there seems to be nothing to indicate the name of the play this fragment comes from. Eduard Fraenkel has inferred from the apparent importance of Dike in the plot that it is the *Aetnaeae* (or *Aetnae*), which Aeschylus wrote to celebrate Hieron's foundation of the city of Aetna, *οἰωνιζόμενοσ βίον ἀγαθὸν τοῖσ συνοικίζουσι τὴν πόλιν* (*Vita Aeschyli*, p. 371, Murray[2], i, 8 ; see p. 381). A play that celebrates Dike might be thought appropriate to the foundation of the city which Pindar hopes will conduce *σύμφωνον ἐσ ἀσυχίαν* (*Pyth.* 1, 71) ; and the presence among these fragments of a hypothesis of the Aetna-play (p. 593) shows that it would not be surprising if they contained also a portion of its text. But these considerations fall a very long way short of being concrete evidence.[1]

In *J.H.S.*, l.c., I have tried to show how this fragment stands in relation to Aeschylus' theology.

18. *καλόν γε θ]εῖσα θέσμιον τόδ' ἐν βροτοῖσ* Ed. Fraenkel : but this does not accord with the traces. The letter before *σα* might be *η* or *ι* ; but if the latter, it was preceded by an upright stroke. If *η* is right, then 18–20 will presumably have formed a continuous speech of three lines interrupting the stichomythia. Such an interruption is possible, but unlikely (Gross, *Die Stichomythie*, 25 f.).

30. *φέρε[ι* if right, will be 2nd sing. pres. indic. middle. *φέρε[ισ* might give a similar sense ; and one might also read *φέρε[ιν*, epexegetic infinitive with *λέξω*. None of these readings is really satisfactory ; " one would expect *πρέπει* " : Ed. Fraenkel, l.c., 67.

32. *θυμοίδησ* is unique ; we should expect *θυμώδησ*. The suffix - *ώδησ* derives from the root of *οἰδάνω*

[1] [I do not think the theory is refuted by Grassi, *La Parola del Passato* 48, 1956, 208, whose article I saw while this Appendix was in proof.]

(Wackernagel, *Das Dehnungsgesetz der griechischen Komposita*, 1889, 44 f. = *Kl. Schr.* II 940 f.) But by Aeschylus' time the suffix was in general use, and its derivation no doubt forgotten. Aeschylus probably preferred θυμοίδησ because he meant not simply " full of θυμόσ " but " having a swelling θυμόσ, as the writer of *Com. Adesp.* 1111 preferred πεοίδησ.

(Fragments of four lines, the two first beginning μακάρων and αὐτὴ (αὕτη?) θεῶν.)

ἵζει δ' ἐν αὐτῶι τ[οῦ πατρὸσ θρόνωι, Κρόνον
δίκηι κρατήσασ· τῶι̣δε ν̣[ῦν αὐχεῖν πάρα,
πατὴρ γὰρ ἦρξεν, ἀνταμ[είψασθαι δίκηι.
ἐκ τοῦδέ τοί με Ζεὺσ ἐ̣τί̣μ̣[ησεν μέγα,
ὁτιὴ παθὼν ἠμ̣[είψατ' οὐκ ἄνευ δίκησ.
ἵζω Διὸσ θρόνοισιν [ἠγλα]ισμένη̣.
πέμπει δέ μ' αὐτὸσ οἷσιν εὐμεν[ὴσ πέλει
Ζ[ε]ύσ, ὅσπερ ἐσ γῆν τήνδ' ἔπεμψέ μ' ε̣ὐ̣[φρόνωσ.
ὄψ]εσθε δ' ὑμεῖσ, εἴ τι μὴ μά[την] λέγω.
— τί σ'] οὖ[ν προ]σεννέποντεσ εὖ π̣[οι]ήσομεν ;
— Δίκην, με̣[γιστ]ον πρέσβοσ ἣ[σ] ἐ[ν οὐ]ρα̣[νῶι.
— ποίασ δὲ τ[ιμ]ῆσ ἀρχι[τεκ]τ̣[ο]ν̣εῖσ, λ̣[έγε.
[—]τοῖσ μὲν δ[ι]καίοισ ἔνδικον τίν[ω βί]ο[ν.
]η̣σα θε̣[σ]μ[ι]ον τόδ' ἐν βρ[ο]το[ῖσ·
τοῖσ δ' αὖ μα]ταίοισ [σώφρονασ φύω]φ[ρένας.
[—] πειθοῦσ ἐ]πωιδαῖσ ἢ κατ' ἰσχύοσ τρόπο[ν] ·
[—] γράφουσα] τἀμπλακήματ' ἐν δέλτωι Διό̣[σ.]
[—] ποίωι χρόν]ωι δ̣ὲ̣ πίνακ' ἀναπτύσσει[σ] κακ[ῶν ;
[—] εὖτ' ἂν τελ]ῆι σφιν ἡμέρα τὸ κύριον.
[—] οὔκουν προθύμωσ εἶ σὺ δ]εκτέα στρατῶι ;

[—] καὶ κάρτ' ὄναιτ' ἄν, εἰ δ]έχοιτό μ' εὔφρ[όν]ωσ.
]. [. . . . . . .]ησᾶτα[. .]εχω
]ν[. . . . . .]ο ἐπισπέ . . .[. . . .]. .[.] [.
πό]λισ τισ οὔτε δῆμοσ οὔτ' ἔτησ ἀνὴρ
τοιάνδε μοῖραν π[αρ]ὰ θεῶν καρπουμένη[σ.
τέκμαρ δὲ λέξω τῶι τόδ' εὐδερκὲ[σ] φέρε[ι.
ἔθρε[ψε] παῖδα μάργον ὃν τίκτει [ποτέ
Ἥρα μιγεῖσα Ζηνί, θυμοίδ[η θεόν,
δ]ύσαρκτ[ο]ν, αἰδὼσ δ' οὐκ ἐνῆ[ν]
φρ[ον]ήματι,
ἱεὶσ δ' ἄφ]υκτα τῶν ὁδοιπόρων βέλη
λόγχαισ τ' ἀναι]δῶσ ἀγκύλαισιν ἀρταμῶν
] ῖ̣ν ἔχ[αι]ρε κἀγέλα κακὸν
]ν ὄζοι φόνοσ
]μουμένη
. ιπρ[. . . . .]γον χέρα
]οῦν ἐνδίκωσ κικλήσκεται
]νιν ἔνδικ[. . . . .] . οσ.

5–7 Ll.-J. 8 μέγα, 9, 16, Page. 17 τείνω Π. 19 Ll.-J. 20 Maas. 24 οὔκουν . . . ; Ll.-J. (οὐκοῦν ed. pr.). 28 = fr. 377 Nauck². 31–2, 34 ἱεὶσ δ'., 35 Ll.-J. 37 στά[ζοι variant in margin.

DIKE. And he has his seat upon his father's very throne, having overcome Kronos by means of Justice; for Zeus can now boast, since his father began the quarrel, that he paid him back with Justice on his side. That is why Zeus has done me great honour, because after being attacked he paid him back, not unjustly. I sit in glory by the throne of Zeus, and he of his own will sends me to those he favours; I mean Zeus, who has sent me to this land with kind intent. And you shall see for yourselves whether my words are empty.

CH. How then shall we rightly address you?

DIKE. By the name of Dike, her who is greatly revered in heaven.

CH. And of what privilege are you the mistress?

DIKE. As for the just, I reward their life of justice.

[CH.?] . . . this ordinance among mortals.

DIKE. But in the reckless I implant a chastened mind.

CH. By Persuasion's spells, or in virtue of your might?

DIKE. I write their offences on the tablet of Zeus.

CH. And at what season do you unroll the list of crimes?

DIKE. When the proper time brings the fulfilment of what is theirs by right.

CH. Eagerly, I think, should the host[1] welcome you.

DIKE. Much would they gain, should they receive me kindly.

(*Two lines unintelligible*).

. . . no city or people or private man, since such is the god-sent fortune she enjoys. And I will tell you a proof which gives you this clearly. Hera has reared a violent son whom she has borne to Zeus, a god irascible, hard to govern, and one whose mind knew no respect for others. He shot wayfarers with deadly arrows, and ruthlessly hacked . . . with hooked spears . . . he rejoiced and laughed . . . evil . . . scent of blood. . . .

(*Two lines unintelligible*) . . . is therefore justly called . . . just.[2]

[1] Perhaps " the people ".

[2] Clearly this passage contained one of those etymologisings of proper names which are not rare in Aeschylus. Lobel suggests that the name " Ares " may have been derived from ἀρή, " bane," " ruin."

UNKNOWN PLAY (III) A.D. 2

283

Ed. pr. Lobel, *P. Oxy.*, vol. 20, no. 2253, with Plate III; cf. Snell, *Gnomon* 25, 1953, 437; Stark, *Hermes* 82, 1954, 372; Mette, *Gymnasium* 62, 1955, 401; Lesky, *TDH*, 1956, 86; Kakridis, *Acme* 8, fasc. 2–3, 1955(?), 91.

This looks very like the beginning of a prologue of a play; it recalls *Eum.* 1 ff. Clearly it comes from a play "about the matter of Troy." The word *συναλλαγή* (l. 7) can mean "relations", "dealings", "visitation" or it can mean "reconciliation"; in this context, it is likeliest to have the latter meaning. At what stage of the Trojan war can a Greek have prayed for "friendly reconciliation"? If reconciliation with the Trojans is meant, we think of the early stages, of the time before and just after the arrival of the Greeks at Troy: Stark has suggested that the play may be the *Iphigeneia*, but without adducing any substantial evidence. *P. Oxy.* 2254 seems to come from a play that dealt with the fight at Tenedos which preceded the siege, and it is possible that both come from the *Iphigeneia* or from some play unknown to us which described an early stage in the history of the war: e.g., Aeschylus *may* have written a *Cycnus*, and the Cycnus in question *may* have been the king of Tenedos killed by Achilles.

But the "reconciliation" may easily have been a reconciliation between the Greek chiefs themselves. A famous Aeschylean trilogy (*Myrmidones*, *Nereides*, *Phryges or Ἕκτορος Λύτρα*) is known to have dealt with the most notorious of their quarrels (see pp. 422, 429, 470). The speaker seems to be praying for a friendly reconciliation " for the chieftains of Greece ". This *might* mean " a reconciliation with the Trojans "; but it more probably means " a reconciliation with each other." It is therefore likelier than not to come from the Achillean trilogy ; and the likelihood is strengthened by the fact that very minute scraps, proved by a coincidence with a quotation (fr. 59) to come from the *Myrmidones* and probably by the same copyist as the Aeschylean fragments in vol. 20, have already been published (vol. xviii, 2163 ; Snell, l.c., has shown that another small fragment in vol. 20 —2256, fr. 55—probably coincides with a quotation, fr. 65 in this book). Further, the formal stateliness and the impression which it gives of introducing the audience to a new situation makes somewhat in favour of its belonging to the first play of a trilogy ; though here the similarity with the opening of *Eum.* should put us on our guard. And who is the speaker likely to be? Maas has thought of Calchas ; but Agamemnon has at least as good a claim. The range of possibilities here is very wide ; and the supplements are more than usually uncertain.

Ζηνὸσ μ]ὲν εὐχαῖσ πρῶτα πρεσβεύων σέβ[ασ
ἱκέτησ ἱ]κνοῦμαι, φέγγοσ ἡλίου τὸ νῦν
πόνουσ ἀμ]εῖψαι ξὺν τύχαισ εὐημέρ[οισ,
καὶ γῆσ ἁπάσησ] Ἑλλάδοσ λοχαγέταισ,
οἳ σὺν Με]νέλεωι τὴν βίαιον ἁρπαγὴν
γυναικὸσ ἐκ]πράσσουσι Πριαμίδην Πάριν,
νείκησ βαρεία]σ εὐμενῆ συναλλαγήν.

1 Snell. 2 Ll.-J. 3 πόνουσ Snell. 4–5 Ll.-J. 6 γυναικὸσ Snell. 7 Ll.-J.

To Zeus' majesty I first do reverence, and with supplication I beseech him that this day's light may see us exchange our labours for prosperous fortune; and for the chieftains of all the land of Greece, who with Menelaus demand vengeance of Paris, son of Priam, for the violent rape of Helen, I pray for a friendly reconciliation of their grievous quarrel.

UNKNOWN PLAY (IV) A.D. 2

284

Ed. pr. Lobel, *P. Oxy.*, vol. 20, no. 2256, fr. 71, with Plate VIII; cf. Snell, *Gnomon* 25, 1953, 439; Mette, *Gymnasium* 62, 1955, 399; Kakridis, *Acme* 8, fasc. 2–3, 1955(?), 92.

"The subject of this fragment of a chorus is evidently the death of Ajax consequent on the award of the arms of Achilles": Lobel. This was the subject of Aeschylus' Ajax-trilogy (see pp. 438, 456, 407); and Lobel suggests that this may come from the *Ὅπλων Κρίσισ,* Mette preferring the *Σαλαμίνιαι.* But the lines contain a *summary* account of the end of Ajax, not at all what we should expect to find in a play of which this formed the main subject, but very much what might be given if the story of Ajax is being cited as a parallel to a similar episode that has occurred or seems likely to occur in some different play. This impression is strengthened by the occurrence of *ὥσπερ καὶ* at the beginning of l. 16. As Snell (l.c., 440) has noticed, this can hardly introduce a theme for comparison; for a mention of Ajax follows, and Ajax has been the subject of the preceding stanza. The obvious inference is that after briefly narrating the death of Ajax the Chorus said: "Just as the noble son of Telamon perished by his own hand . . . so will (someone else) perish."

In what lost play of Aeschylus might this have

happened? Several of them may have contained characters who threatened suicide (the *Oedipus*, for example, comes to mind); but there are slight indications in favour of the *Philoctetes*. Philoctetes threatens suicide in Sophocles' play; his suicide and that of Ajax would have had this in common, that in both cases Odysseus was responsible; and among the Aeschylean fragments in *P. Oxy.*, vol. 20, is a fragmentary hypothesis to the *Philoctetes* (no. 2256, fr. 5).[1] But these indications do not amount to anything like a proof.

] . [. .] . [
τ̣ά̣ξομα[ι
τίσ τάδ[ ] . [
πήματ[.] . [.]δ̣έ̣χο̣ιτ̣[
ἀντ . [. .]ιμ . . . [
—τὸν δὴ περιρρύ[τ]α̣σ̣ [χθονὸσ στραταγὸν στρ.
ὤλ[εσ]αν ῥυσίπτολ[ιν
π[οι]μανδρίδαι[
ὄρχαμοί τ' ἐπίσκο[ποι
τευχ[έω]ν [ἐ]πε̣[λ]π̣ι̣σαντ[α. . . . .
—δίκαι δ' Ὀδυσσῆϊ ξυνῆισαν [ἀρχοὶ ἀντιστρ.
ο]ὐκ ἰσορρόπωι φρενί
—]σφιν εὐθυν[. . .]. .
φρὴν μελ]α̣γχίτων[
μ̣[αχα]ναῖσ ξιφοκτόν[οισι . . . . .
—ὥσπερ καὶ Τελαμῶ[νοσ ἐσθλὸσ υἱὸσ
αὐτ]οκτόνοσ ὤλετο[
]. . . . πρ[

6 Ll.-J. 10 Snell. 11 Ll.-J. 15 Snell. 16 ἐσθλὸσ υἱὸσ Ll.-J.

I will dissolve in tears (?) . . . who . . . these . . . sufferings . . . receive. . . . He, the city-guarding chieftain of the seagirt land, was brought to ruin by the shepherds of the people, the chieftains and commanders of the host, after he had set his heart upon the arms. And in the judgment the generals connived with Odysseus, with no impartial mind . . guide . . . his mind cloaked in darkness . . contrivance of the fatal sword.

Even as the noble son of Telamon perished by his own hand. . . .

[1] Too fragmentary for inclusion in this volume. The only feature of the scraps that may be important is that Neoptolemus, Philoctetes and Odysseus are mentioned as *dramatis personae* in that order, and so are likely to have appeared on the stage in that order; see Snell in *Gnomon*, l.c., p. 439.

[ʽΗΡΑΚΛΕΙΔΑΙ?] (see p. 404) A.D. 2–3

285

Ed. pr. Lefebvre, *Bulletin de la société royale d'archéologie d'Alexandrie*, no. 14, 191, 192, with Plate IX, 3; cf. Körte, *Archiv für Papyrusforschung*, no. 7, 1924, 141; Fritsch, *Neue Fragmente des Aisch. und Soph.*, Diss. Hamburg, 1936, 14; Mette, *Suppl. Aesch.*, 1939, 22; Cantarella, *Eschilo* i, 1941, 323; Page, *Greek Literary Papyri*, no. 35, p. 188; Srebrny, *Eos* 45, 1951, 41; Lesky, *TDH*, 1956, 87.

Körte assigned this fragment to Aeschylus on the score of his supplement ἀμφιμήτ[ορεσ in l. 4. This adjective occurs in extant literature only at Eur., *Andr.* 466; but Hesychius says that Aeschylus used it in his *Heracleidae* (fr. 76 Nauck). Page (l.c.) has pointed out that this supplement is far from certain, since in l. 4 ἀμφὶ μητ[έρα is an obvious possibility.

And even if it were certain, it would not prove that this fragment came from Aeschylus' *Heracleidae*; since we have no reason to assume that the word occurred *only* in that play. We know that it occurred also in the *Andromache*; and it may easily have occurred elsewhere also. We must therefore recognise at the outset that it is very doubtful whether this fragment is from the *Heracleidae* or is by Aeschylus at all.

But several scholars have maintained that the action which the fragment describes can be shown to be one likely to have been described in the *Heracleidae*. If this is true, the possibility that this fragment belongs to that play becomes greater; and this claim must therefore be investigated.

Körte, Fritsch and Mette all assume that the *Heracleidae* of Aeschylus, like the play of the same name by Euripides, dealt with the persecution of the Heraclids, after their father's death, by Eurystheus. They take ἀμφιμήτορες to mean "children by different mothers", as it does in the *Andromache* and as Hesychius says it meant in Aeschylus; this description, they say, is true of the children of Heracles. They think this passage came from part of the play in which Eurystheus or one of his adherents (perhaps the herald Copreus) is threatening the Heraclids with burning, and supplement accordingly.

Lycus threatens to burn the children of Heracles by Megara in the *Heracles* of Euripides; but we are nowhere told that Eurystheus did the same. Heracles certainly had children by many different mothers (though it is doubtful whether the description ἀμφιμήτορεσ applies to the children who survived to be persecuted by Eurystheus; according to the usual legend, all these were his children by Deianeira). In l. 3, Körte and his followers read θα[λαμ]ούχοι[σ δόμοισ, but [*ΛΑΜ*] is too long for the gap ; and in l. 6 they presumably take *φαρμάκου* to refer to fire, which it can scarcely do.

This attempt to show that the fragment fits the plot of the *Heracleidae* scarcely stands up to examination. Srebrny has made another on quite different lines. He calls attention to the bold attempt of Zielinski (*Eos* 25, 57 ; cf. *Tragodumenon libri tres*, 3, 90) to show that Aeschylus' *Heracleidae* dealt with the same subject as Sophocles' *Trachiniae*, the death of Heracles. Zielinski's arguments fall a long way short of proving his case ; but they certainly show that it is just as likely that the play was about this as that it was about the same subject as Euripides' play of the same name. Accepting this thesis, Srebrny offers a restoration of this fragment based upon it. In itself, this restoration is less open to objection than are those of Körte and his followers. In l. 3 the word θα[μν]ούχοι[σ (for which cf. the sense of δρύοχα at Eur., *Electra* 1163), though it occurs nowhere else, seems to be the only conceivable word that will fit the space ; and in l. 6 *φαρμάκου* can refer to the poison in the blood of Nessus. Leaving aside any considerations based on the conjecture ἀμφιμήτ-[ορεσ, Srebrny's hypothesis seems to explain the fragment more satisfactorily than any other assumption I have been able to think of, and after considerable hesitation I have decided to print the text with supplements along the lines he indicates. But the considerations I have set out above oblige us to recognise that any such hypothesis is anything but certain.

Suppose Srebrny is right, the fragment seems to describe the circumstances of Heracles' death in too summary a manner for it to be the principal account given in the play of an important episode in the action ; contrast the elaborate instructions which Heracles gives to Hyllus in the *Trachiniae*. The tense of ἦν in l. 2 is surprising. Can the whole narration have been in the past tense? If so, the fragment teaches us nothing about the plot of Aeschylus' *Heracleidae*, even if we suppose Srebrny's whole argument to be correct ; for even a play that dealt with the same subject as Euripides' *Heracleidae*, or with a different subject altogether, might have included a description of the death of Heracles in the past tense.

The possibility that this is so is somewhat strengthened if one considers the problem of the letter missing in l. 4 between οἵδε and the *A* of ἀμφιμήτορεσ or ἀμφί. Only a vertical stroke is preserved ; *Γ*, *M*, *N* are possible. No supplement seems suitable except γε or a pronoun ; and γε neither suits the sense nor fits the space. What would fit the space would be this writer's broad *M*.

]λι[ ]νκαι[
πυρὰ]ν γὰρ αὐτ̣ό̣τευκ[τον]ἦν ἐν[ταῦθ' ἰδεῖν,
Οἴτη]σ ἐν ὑψηλοῖσι θα[μν]ούχοι[σ τόποισ
εἰσ τή]νδε παῖδεσ οἵδε[. ἀ]μφιμή[τορεσ
ἤνεγκο]ν ἄρδην καυσίμοισ ἐν δ[ένδρεσιν
οἰδοῦν]τα καὶ λοπῶντα φαρμάκου [μένει.

2 Ll.-J. 3 Srebrny. 4 beginning Ll.-J., end Körte ; see Summary. 5 Ll.-J. 6 beginning Nisbet, end Latte.

For in those parts was visible a place designed by Nature for a pyre, in the lofty, bush-covered country of Oeta. To this did [? my] children by different mothers raise [? me] aloft, encompassed with trees for fuel, flesh swollen and skin peeling beneath the strong poison.

[?ΜΥΡΜΙΔΟΝΕΣ] (see p. 422) A.D. 1–2

286

Ed. pr. Vitelli-Norsa, Mélanges Bidez, *Annuaire de l'institut de philologie et d'histoire orientales*, ii, 1934, 968, with Plate; cf. Körte, *Archiv für Papyrusforschung* 11, 1935, 250; Sulzberger, *L'Antiquité Classique* 3, 1934, 447; Vitelli-Norsa, *Papyri Greci e Latini* 11, 1935, no. 1211, p. 102, with Plate; Kalén, *Eranos* 33, 1935, 39; Pfeiffer, *Deutsche Literaturzeitung*, 1935, 1133; Schadewaldt, *Hermes* 71, 1936, 25; Fritsch, *Neue Fragmente des Aischylos und Sophokles*, Diss. Hamburg, 1936, 16; Zimmermann, *Phil. Woch.* 57, 745; Stella, *Rend. dell' Ist. Lomb.* 69, 1936, 553; Frico, *Phil. Woch.* 57, 1937, 478; Page, *Greek Literary Papyri*, 1942, no. 20, p. 136; Kenner, *Wiener Jahreshefte* 33, 1941, 1; Ed. Fraenkel, *Proc. Brit. Acad.*, 1942, 239; Lasserre, *Bulletin des études littéraires et linguistiques*, Lausanne, 1946, 133; Cantarella, *I nuovi frammenti eschilei di Ossirinco*, 1949, 99; Goerschen, *Dioniso* 13, 1950, 179; Pohlenz, *Die Griechische Tragoedie* ii², 64; Lesky, *TDH*, 1956, 84.

Page rightly points out that earlier writers were over-confident in their assignation of this fragment to Aeschylus' *Myrmidones*. The only expression in the fragment which they were able to claim was peculiarly Aeschylean was διαί in l. 8; and even this piece of evidence has no value, as these forms of the disyllabic prepositions occur in Sophocles and in paratragedic passages of comedy (see Page, l.c.). Further, the style of the fragment is simpler and plainer than that of Aeschylus commonly is; though I do not think this argument can be pressed. Page also contends that the Achilles of this piece is " psychologically more advanced, more sophisticated and argumentative, more interested in himself and his own motives and actions, than we expect in Aeschylus ". I cannot share this opinion ; to me this Achilles seems very like Homer's and therefore very like the Achilles we might expect from Aeschylus.

It is true that the content of the scene is what we might expect to have occurred somewhere in Aeschylus' Achilles trilogy, and that there is nothing in it that we can positively state to be unaeschylean : it is also true that we do not know Sophocles or Euripides to have written on this theme. But, as Page points out, Achilles was the hero of plays by Astydamas, Carcinus and others ; and there is not sufficient evidence to conclude that this must be Aeschylean. The writing of the exiguous fragments printed in *P. Oxy.* 2163, and shown by coincidence with a quotation (fr. 59) to be from the *Myrmidones* is like that of *P.S.I.* 1208–10 (Lobel, *P. Oxy.*, vol. 18, p. 23), but not like that of this piece. Neither does the writing of *P. Oxy.* 2256, fr. 55 (plausibly assigned to the *Myrmidones* by Snell, *Gnomon* 25, 1953, 437) nor that of fr. 283 resemble the writing of this fragment.

The situation in which the speech is delivered must be quite clear to anyone who knows the *Iliad* ; the Greeks are suffering grievous losses through Achilles' refusal to fight, and Achilles is being unsuccessfully implored to return to the battle.

[*'ΑΧΙΛΛΕΥΣ*]

λεύσουσι τοὐμὸν σῶμα· μὴ δόκει ποτε
πέτρ[ο]ισ καταξανθέντα Πηλέωσ γόνον

Δαναοὺσ ὀ]νήσειν Τρωικὴν ἀνὰ χθόνα·
ἀλλ᾽]ἡμένοισι Τρωσὶ τὴν ἄ[ν]ευ δορὸσ
νικᾶ]ν γένοιτ᾽ ἄν, εὐπετέστερον δ᾽ ἔχοισ
. . . .]τοῦτο δὴ βροτοῖσιν ἰατρὸν πόνων.
φόβῳ]ι δ᾽ Ἀχαιῶν χεῖρ᾽ ἐφορμήσω δορὶ
μαιμ]ῶσαν ὀργῆι ποιμένοσ κακοῦ διαί ;
ἀλλ᾽ εἴ]περ εἶσ ὤν, ὡσ λέγουσι σύμμαχοι,
τροπὴ]ν τοσαύτην ἔκτισ᾽ οὐ παρὼν μάχηι,
οὐκ εἰ]μ᾽ ἐγὼ τὰ πάντ᾽ Ἀχαικῶι στρατῶι;
τοιόν]δ᾽ ἀφεῖναι τοὔποσ οὐκ αἰδώσ μ᾽ ἔχει·
τίσ γὰρ] τοιούτουσ εὐγενεστέρουσ ἐμοῦ
ἀγοὺσ ἂ]ν εἴποι καὶ στρατοῦ ταγεύματα ;
]ύμᾶσ εἶσ ἀνὴρ ἠικίζετο
τ]αράσσων καὶ πολυσκεδεῖσ [τιθείσ
]τεύχη περὶ νέοισ βραχίοσιν.

πάνθ᾽ ὑμῶν στρατόν 18, *εὐμαρῶσ ἐτ[ρέ]ψατο* 19, *ἀ]νδ[ρ]ὸσ προδοσίαν* 20, *ἄ]νδρα τόνδ᾽ α[ἰσχρῶσ] θανεῖν* 21, *τόνδ᾽ ἀπολλυ-* 25, *]ασ εἶπον οὐ ψευδῆ λέγων* 26, *τόνδ᾽ ἀποφθερεῖ στρατόν* 27, *μ]ῆνισ ὡσ ὁρᾶν πάρα* 28, *ἐμ]φανῶσ κατήγοροσ* 30, *ἐλε[ύ]θερον λέγεισ* 31, *ο]ὐδαμῶσ πρέπει τάδε* 34, *]αι διαλ[λα]γαί* 35, *]υχω μειλί[γ]ματι* 36.

3–4 Page. 7, 11 Schadewaldt. 12 Körte. 13 Fritsch. 14 Schadewaldt.

ACHILLES. . . . they will stone me! The torturing of Peleus' son with stones will prove no blessing—never think it!—to the Greeks in the land of Troy. No, then the Trojans could sit at their ease and win the victory without a fight ; and you would more easily meet . . the healer of mortal sorrows. Shall fear of the Achaeans force me to lay my hand upon my spear, a hand now quivering with anger through the doing of a cowardly leader? Why, if I alone by my absence from the battle caused this great rout, as my comrades say, am I not all in all to the Achaean host? Respect forbids me not to utter such words; for who could say such chieftains, such commanders of the army, were nobler than I? . . . one man has stricken you . . . shaken and scattered you . . . armour on youthful shoulders. . . .

(Fragments of nineteen more lines.)

HYPOTHESIS I (AITNAIAI) (see p. 381) A.D. 2

287

Ed. pr. Lobel, *P. Oxy.*, vol. 20, no. 2257, fr. 1, with Plate IX; Snell, *Gnomon* 25, 1953, 440; Mette, *Gymnasium* 62, 1955, 395; for further bibliography see under fr. 282.

This seems likely to come from a hypothesis of the play mentioned in *Vita Aeschyli*, ch. 9, p. 371, Murray: *ἐλθὼν τοίνυν ἐσ Σικελίαν, Ἱέρωνοσ τότε τὴν Αἴτνην κτίζοντοσ, ἐπεδείξατο τὰσ Αἴτνασ* [*Αἰτναίασ* BRTr.] *οἰωνιζόμενοσ βίον ἀγαθὸν τοῖσ συνοικίζουσι τὴν πόλιν.* Ll. 6–7 seem to refer to the *Eumenides*; the *Ἀχιλλέωσ ἐρασταί*, mentioned in l. 8, was a satyr-play of Sophocles (see Pearson, *Fragments of Sophocles*, I, 103 f.). The *Eumenides* contains a change of scene from Delphi to Athens, and it is therefore likely that these two plays are cited as containing changes of scene, and so helping to render less surprising the numerous changes of scene that are attributed to the play in question. Lobel suggests that the letters *τρωι* in l. 7 may indicate a reference to another Sophoclean play, the *Troilus* (see Pearson, op. cit.,

II, 253 f.). " I could reconcile the remaining ink in l. 7," he writes, " with]δυ^{μ} . . . τρωι . κεφα^{λ}." The *Troilus* may have been cited as another instance of a change of scene ; though Snell thinks this line may have described the 'Αχιλλέωσ ἐρασταί as containing a change of scene from some unknown place (]δυμ) to Troy and again to another unknown place](.) . . φα̣λ̣( ). On the suggestion that frs. 281–2 may belong to this play, see the Summary prefixed to fr. 282.

(Scraps of five lines.)

. εἰσ 'Α]θήν[ασ] ἐ̣κ̣ [Δελ]φῶν μ(ε)τ[α-
βιβ]άζε[ται . [. . .] . . . . τρωι . . φ .
]ο̣ἱ 'Αχιλ(λέωσ) ἐρα[σ]ταί. κ(ατὰ) μ(ὲν) γ(ὰρ) τὸ πρῶτον μ(έροσ)
αὐτοῦ ἡ σκηνὴ ὑ(πό)κε[ι]τ(αι) Αἴτνῃ, κ(ατὰ) δ(ὲ) τὸ δεύτ(ερον)
Ξουθία, κ(α)τ(ὰ) δὲ [τ]ὸ τρίτον πάλιν Αἴτνῃ, εἶτ' ἀ-
πὸ ταύτησ εἴ[σ Λε]οντίνουσ μ(ε)τ(α)βάλλει καὶ γί(νεται) ἡ
σκηνὴ Λεον[. .], μ(ε)τ(ὰ) δ' αὐτὸν Συρακοῦσσαι
καὶ τὰ λοιπὰ [   ] . ηι δ(ια)περαίνετ(αι)
ὅσ (ἐστι(τοπ̣(   ).

12 λεον[. . .] : " This must be presumed to represent a proper name (since with a common noun the article would be expected) and to specify some spot in or about Leontini. The name might, of course, consist of two words, in which case λεον[might be and perhaps is likely to be λεον[τ(ίνων), followed perhaps by a (masculine) common noun " : ed. pr.

. . . is transferred from Delphi to Athens . . . the

Lovers of Achilles. For during the first act the scene is Aetna, in the second Xuthia,[1] in the third Aetna again; then it shifts from here to Leontini and the scene is Leon . . . , and after that it is Syracuse and the rest is concluded at[2] . . . , which is a place. . . .

[1] This is the name of ἡ περὶ Λεοντίνουσ χώρα, according to Diodorus 5, 8.

[2] Pfeiffer suggests that in l. 13 we might read [ἐν τῶι Τεμενί]τηι (cf. Thuc., vi 75, 1).

HYPOTHESIS II (UNKNOWN PLAY)

A.D. 2

288

Ed. pr. Lobel, *P. Oxy.*, vol. 20, no. 2256, fr. 3, with Plate V; cf. Pieraccioni, *Maia* 5, 1952, 288; Snell, *Gnomon* 25, 1953, 438; Mette, *Aischylos' Prometheia*, 1953, 6; Davison, *Class. Rev.* n.s. 3, 1953, 144; Kakridis, *Hellenika* 13, 1954, 165; Lesky, *Gymnasium* 61, 1954, 304; Yorke, *Class. Rev.* n.s. 4, 1954, 10; *Class. Quart.* n.s. 4, 1954, 183; Turner, *Class. Rev.* n.s. 4, 1954, 21; Pohlenz, *Die Griechische Tragoedie* ii[2], 22; Murray, *Aeschyli Fabulae*[2], 1955, v; Lesky, *Hermes* 82, 1954, 1; Mette, *Gymnasium* 62, 1955, 397; Freymuth, *Philol.* 99, 1955, 64, n.l.; Lesky, *TDH*, 1956, 59; Orgels, *Bull. de l'Acad. Roy. de Belg.* (Cl. des Lettres), 41, 1955, 528; Lasserre, *Hermes* 83, 1955, 128.

This fragment must come from a hypothesis to one of the plays of the trilogy about the Danaids (see vol. i, p. 3). Before its publication, it had been generally believed on grounds of style and language that the *Supplices* was an early work of Aeschylus, produced perhaps about 500 B.C. But we have here a record of its production at a festival in which Sophocles was a competitor. Sophocles is said to have won his first victory in 468 (*Parian Marble* 56; Plutarch, *Cimon* 8); Plutarch says that this was his first appearance in the competition. Eusebius indicates that he competed first in 470 or 469 but even if this earlier date is right, this fragment indicates that the *Supplices* was not produced before 470. There is some ground for suspecting that the date was 464, for though the letters *AP* in l. 1 may be part of the word ἄρχοντοσ, it is possible that they are the beginning of an archon's name, and the only archon falling within the relevant period whose name begins with these two letters is Archedemides, who held office in 464–3. We know of several instances of sons entering for the competition the works of their deceased fathers ; Aeschylus' sons are known to have done this ; and it has been suggested that the competition here recorded may have taken place after Aeschylus' death. But in such cases it was customary for the fact to be recorded in the didascalia , see, for example, the hypothesis to the *Seven Against Thebes* and the similar hypothesis to the *Laius* published as P. Oxy 2256, fr. 2. Nor can the notice refer to a revival (see Lesky, *Hermes*, l.c., 2–3) ; and Krause's suggestion (ap. Lesky) that the trilogy may have been written long before 464, but acted only then, is not likely to be right.

Even before the publication of this text, Walter Nestle (first in 1934) and Yorke (1936) had argued for a date in the sixties. In the light of the evidence as it now stands, it is perverse to proceed on any other assumption. The belief that in the *Supplices* the fifty Danaids were represented by the unusual number of fifty χορευταί has, I think, owed much of its popularity to the assumption that the play is of very early date. It will be interesting to see if it continues to be popular.

Of the titles in ll. 6 ff., *Κωφοί* and *Ποιμένεσ* are Sophoclean (see Pearson, *Fragments of Sophocles*, ii, 31 f., and 147 f.). We do not know that Sophocles wrote a *Βάκχαι*, but, as Lobel points out, the mark before this title in the papyrus probably means that it has been deleted. Nor do we know Sophocles to have written a *Κύκνος* or a *Κύκλωψ*, though we cannot rule out the possibility that he did. The presence of two distinctively Sophoclean titles in the list makes it almost certain that it gives the names of the plays exhibited in this year by Sophocles. What, then, is the word *μέσατοσ* doing between the name of Sophocles and the list of the plays exhibited by him? *μέσατοσ* as an equivalent to *μέσοσ* was a poetic word, and cannot possibly have stood here. The word must therefore be a proper name, and there is good ground for believing that it was in fact the name of a fifth-century tragic poet (Schol. V Ar., *Wasps* 1502, Pseudo-Euripides, *Epist.* 5 ; cf. *I.G.* ii, 2325). Yorke and Lesky suggest that Mesatus won the third prize on this occasion, that the writer of our text went by mistake straight from the name of Sophocles to the name of Mesatus, and that he therefore had to write in the name of Sophocles' plays after, instead of before, the name of Mesatus, the third competitor. Yorke thinks the note of cancellation before *Βάκχαισ* is meant to apply to all the four plays. But the most natural way of accounting for what stood after *μέσατοσ* is to suppose that it was the title of another play, and if it was, *Βάκχαισ* must have been deleted, or we should have a list of five plays instead of four. Snell suggests that the Sophoclean title *Ν̣α̣υ̣π̣[λιωι* was written (see Pearson, l.c., ii, 80) ; but I cannot see *α̣υ̣π̣* in the facsimile.

ἐπὶ ἄρ[
ἐνίκα [Αἰ]σχύλο[σ Ἱκέτισι Αἰγυπτίοισ
Δαν[αί]σι Ἀμυ[μώνηι σατυρικῆι.
δεύτ[ε]ρ[ο]σ Σοφοκλῆ[σ
Μέσατοσ[[ν . [ ] [
[[Βάκχαισ Κωφοῖ[σ
Ποι]μέσιν Κυκν̣[ω̣ι
σατυ(ρικῶ̣ι).

1 ἐπὶ Ἀρ[χεδημίδου? Lobel. 7 Pieraccioni · Κύκλ̣[ωπι Lobel.

In the archonship [? of Archedemides? : 464–3] Aeschylus won the prize with the [*Supplices*, *Aegyptioi*,] *Danaides* and the satyr-play *Amymone*. Sophocles was second . Mesatos . . . *Bacchae*, *Kophoi*, *Poimenes*, *Cycnus* [1] . . . satyr-play . . .

[1] or *Cyclops*.

ADDENDUM : NEW TEXT OF FR. 50

(see p. 414)

Ed. pr. Weil, *Un papyrus inédit : nouveaux fragments d'Euripide et d'autres poètes grecs* : Monuments Grecs publiés par l'association pour l'encouragement des études grecques en France, no. 8, 1879, with Plate ; id., *Rev. de Phil.* 4, 1880, 145 ; Blass, *Rhein. Mus.* 35, 1880, 84 ; Bücheler, ibid., 93 ; Bergk, ibid., 248 ; Kock, ibid., 272 ; Gomperz, *Wiener Studien* 2, 1880, 16 ; Cobet, *Mnemosyne* n.s. 8, 1880, 64 ; Schenkl, *Zeitschr. f. öster. Gymn.*, 1880, 75 ; Herwerden, *Versl. d. Koninkl. Akad. d. Wetenschap. d. Nederl.* n.s. 2, 10, 1881 ; Ellis, *J. Phil.* 19, 1882, 27 ; Wecklein, *Bursians Jahresb.* 1879 (publ. 1881) 44 ; id., *Philol.*, 39, 1880, 414 ; id., *Aeschyli Fabulae I* (1885) 521 ; ibid.[2] (1893), 297 ; Nauck, *T.G.F.*[2], 1889, p. 32 ; Sidgwick, *Aeschyli Tragoediae*, 1899, fr. 99 ; Wilamowitz, *Aischylos : Interpretationen*, 1914, 234 ; Messerschmidt, *Mitt. d. D. Inst.* (Rom. Abt.) 47, 1937, 139 ; Ed. Fraenkel, *Proc. Brit. Acad.*, 1942, 237.

M. Paul Barguet, of the Egyptian Department of the Louvre, has with great kindness supplied me with an excellent photograph, which everywhere confirms the accuracy of Nauck's transcription. The papyrus is full of mistakes ; many letters are almost indistinguishable from other similarly shaped letters, and vowels are constantly confused with one another in a way that suggests that the text was dictated. Wilcken (*Urkunde der Ptolemäerzeit* 115) has shown that it was written down by Apollonius, the young brother of Ptolemaeus, the recluse of the Serapeum ;

Apollonius at the time was thirteen or fourteen years of age.

1. The text is not recoverable with certainty. Weil's reading *ταύρωι δὲ λειμὼν ξένια πάμβοτοσ παρῆν* has been universally accepted. But the placing of *ξένια* between *λειμὼν* and *πάμβοτοσ* is peculiar, so is the application of the word *ξένια* to a meadow; and though neither of these things is in itself impossible, the two together in a conjectural restoration render it unconvincing. The right reading may have been something like . *ταύρωι δ' ἐκείνωι ξένια· πᾶν ποδὸς πάρα* (cf. Pind. *Pyth.* 3, 60 ; 10, 62 , *παρὰ πόδα* Soph., *Ph.* 838).

2. For this use of *μέν* see Denniston, *Greek Particles*, 364 ; Schenkl's conjecture *τοιόνδ' ἐμὲ* destroys the sense. Wilamowitz' emendation *ἄμοχθοσ* might be right, but is not necessary.

4. *τί οὖν ;* cf. *Th.* 208. Blass rightly pointed out that the reading *τί οὖν τὰ πολλὰ κεῖνα* gives unsatisfactory sense. But his own emendation of *τει* to *ἵν'* is unnecessary.

5–6. For this use of *ἀμείβειν*, cf *P.V.* 23. *παρθένου σέβασ = παρθενία* : cf. Homer's *παρθένοσ αἰδοίη*.

6. Blass's *ξυνάονι* is preferable to Weil's *ξυνωνίαι*. He compares Kaibel, *Epigrammata* 241 a 3, p. 521, *δυσὶν ζευχθεῖσα φίλοισ ξυνάοσι τέκνων*.

8–9. The two lines (correctly construed by Blass) yield a sense which is certainly harsh but I find the harshness wholly Aeschylean (for the use of *μέμφομαι*, cf. *Th.* 560, *Suppl.* 774).

13. *αὐγαῖσ* is the best suggestion made ; but it is a long shot.

15. For *νοῦσ* in such a context, Page compares

Eur., fr. 964, 2, *εἰσ φροντίδασ νοῦν . . . ἐβαλλόμην.*

17–18. These lines cannot be restored with anything like certainty.

20. The antecedent of *οὗ* is presumably *κλέοσ*. *δόρει* : cf. fr. 129 N[2]. The MSS. of Aeschylus always have *δορί* : but at *Th.* 347 and *Supp.* 846 *δόρει* has to be restored (see Fraenkel, *Agamemnon*, p. 538, n.1).

22. Hope cannot be poised on a razor's edge lest Europa should lose all ; but Europa herself can. I write *ἐπὶ ξυροῦ μένω*, but with little confidence.

23. For the image of the reef, cf. *Agam.* 1004, *Eum.* 564, and *P.V.* 885, and see also Anacreon 31 D. and Alcaeus 73, 6 L.-P. And yet for 76 years editors have rejected Blass's certain emendation in favour of Bücheler's poor one.

. . . . †ΤΑΥΡΩΤΕΛΙΜΩΞΕΝΙΑΠΑΜΠΟΔΟΣΠΑΡΗΝ†
τοιόνδε μὲν Ζεὺσ κλέμμα πρεσβυτοῦ πατρὸσ
αὐτοῦ μένων ἄμοχθον ἤνυσεν λαβεῖν.
τί οὖν ; τὰ πολλὰ κεῖνα διὰ παύρων λέγω·
γυνὴ θεῶι μειχθεῖσα παρθένου σέβασ
ἤμειψα, παίδων δ' ἐζύγην ξυνάονι.
καὶ τρισὶν ἀγῶσι τοὺσ γυναικείουσ πόνουσ
ἐκαρτέρησ'· ἄρουραν οὐκ ἐμέμψατο,
τοῦ μὴ 'ξενεγκεῖν, σπέρμα γενναῖον πατρόσ.
ἐκ τῶν μεγίστων δ' ἠρξάμην φυτευμάτων,
Μίνω τεκοῦσα. . . . .
'Ραδάμανθυν, ὅσπερ ἄφθιτοσ παίδων ἐμῶν.
ἀλλ' οὐκ ἐν αὐγαῖσ ταῖσ ἐμαῖσ ζόη σφ' ἔχει,
τὸ μὴ παρὸν δὲ τέρψιν οὐκ ἔχει φίλοισ.
τρίτον δέ, τοῦ νοῦσ φροντίσιν χειμάζεται,
Σαρπήδον', αἰχμὴ μὴ 'ξ Ἄρεωσ καθίκετο.

κλέοσ γὰρ ἥκειν Ἑλλάδοσ λωτίσματα
πάσησ, ὑπερφέροντασ ἀλκίμωι σθένει,
αὐχεῖν δὲ Τρώων ἄστυ πορθήσειν βίαι.
πρὸσ οὗ δέδοικα μή τι μαργαίνων δόρει
ἀνυπέρβατον δράσηι τε καὶ πάθηι κακόν.
λεπτὴ γὰρ ἐλπὶσ ἡδ' ἐπὶ ξυροῦ μένω
μὴ πάντα παίσασ' ἐκχέω πρὸσ ἕρματι.

2 *ΤΟΙΟΝΤΕ . . . ΠΡΟΣΒΥΤΟΥ Π.* 3 Blass : *ΗΝΟΣΟΝ Π.* 4 Question-mark after τί οὖν Ll.-J. *ΤΕΙ . . . . ΠΑΥΡΩ Π.* 5 *ΘΕΟΥ Π.* 6 *ΕΜΙΨΕ . . . ΕΣΥΓΗ Π.* Blass: *ΞΥΝΑΓΩΕΙ Π.* 7 *ΤΡΙΑΙΓΩΝΕΙΣΤΟΥΣ Π.* 8 Gomperz, Schenkl : *ΕΚΑΡΤΕΡΗΣΑΑΡΟΥΡΑΚΑΙ Π.* 9 *ΤΟΥΜΕΝΞΕΝΑΙΚΕΙΝ Π.* Schenkl : *ΓΕΝΑΙ Π.* 10 *ΕΡΞΑΜΗΝΦΥΔΕΥΜΑΤΩΝ Π.* (φιτευμάτων Bergk). 11 Lacuna after τεκοῦσα indicated by Bücheler. 12 *ΡΑΔΑΜΑΝΘΟΝΩΣΠΕΡΑΦΘΙΔΟΣ Π.* 13 αὐγαῖσ Gomperz, Kock, Wecklein : *ΑΛΛΑΚΕΜΑΓΑΙΣ Π.* *ΖΟΑΣΕΧΕΙΝ Π.* 14 *ΠΑΡΩΝΤΕ . . . ΦΙΛΟΥΣ Π.* 15 Page: *ΝΟΥΝ Π.* *ΦΡΟΝΤΙΖΕΙΝ Π.* 16 μὴ 'ξ Herwerden : *ΣΑΛΦΗΔΟΝΑΙΑΧΜΗΣΔΕΞΑΡΕΟΣ Π.* 17 Ἑλλάδοσ Blass λωτίσματα Gomperz : *ΚΛΕΟΓΑΡΗΚΕΙΕΝΛΟΤΙΣΛΟΤΙΣΜΑΤΟΣ Π.* 18 ὑπερφέροντασ Wilamowitz (ὑπερφέροντοσ Weil) ἀλκίμωι σθένει Gomperz, Bergk : *ΥΠΕΡΠΕΡΩΝΤΑΣΑΛΧΙΜΟΥΣΤΕΝΗΣ Π.* 19 αὐχεῖν Wilamowitz *ΑΥΧΕΙΔΕΤΡΩΑΝΑΣΤΥΠΑΡΘΗΣΗΒΙΟΝ Π.* 20 *ΔΕΔΩΚΑΜΗΤΕΙΜΑΡΓΑΙΑΝ Π.* 21 *ΑΣΤΥΠΕΡΒΑΤΟΝ Π.* 22 μένω Ll.-J.: *ΕΠΙΞΥΡΗΜΕΝΗΙ Π.* 23 Blass: *ΑΙΜΑΤΕΙ* or *ΑΡΜΑΤΕΙ Π.*

(First line unintelligible.) Such was the trick which Zeus devised to steal me from my aged father, effortlessly, without leaving his place.[1] What then? my whole long story I tell you in few words. A mortal woman united with a god, I exchanged the honoured state of maidenhood, and was joined with the begetter of my children. And in three travails I endured the pains of women ; the noble seed of

[1] Cf. *Suppl.* 101 f. (p. 11).

the father could not reproach the field he sowed, that it did not bring it forth. And I began with the greatest of my offspring, giving birth to Minos. . . . Rhadamanthys, the immortal one among my children. But though he still lives, he lives out of my sight, and they that are absent give no delight to those that love them. And third I bore Sarpedon, for whom my mind is storm-tossed, for fear the spear of Ares may have smitten him. For it is famed abroad that the flower of all Hellas is come, men supreme in warlike strength, and that they are confident that they will destroy by violence the city of the Trojans. It is this news makes me afraid that with rash valour he may do and suffer [1] the extreme of ill. Slender is my hope, and I stand balanced on the edge of doom, lest I strike against a reef and lose all I have.[2]

[1] "The doer must suffer"; the common doctrine expressed at *Cho.* 313–14 (p. 189), Pindar, *Nem.* 4, 32, and elsewhere makes it clear why doing is mentioned here.

[2] For similar mixed metaphors in Aeschylus, cf. *Agam.* 218 f., 1178 f., etc: cf. Stanford, *Aeschylus in his Style*, 94–5.

INDEX OF PROPER NAMES

[*A.*=*Agamemnon* *Ch.*=*Choēphoroe* ; *E.*=*Eumenides* ; *P.*=*Persians* . *Pr.*=*Prometheus* ; *S.*=*Suppliant Maidens* ; *Th.*=*Seven against Thebes* ; *Fr.*=*Fragment*. *The name of a country commonly includes references to that of its inhabitants.*]

ACHAEA *A*. 108, 185, 189, 269, 320, 538, 624, 649, 660 ; *P*. 488 ; *Th*. 28, 324 ; *Fr*. 130, 286
Acheloan cities, *P*. 869
Acheron *A*. 1160 ; *Th*. 856
Achilles *Fr*. 59, 60, 266, 286
Achillis Amatores of Sophocles, p. 594
Actaeon *Fr*. 132
Actor *Th*. 555
Adeues *P*. 312
Adrastea *Pr*. 936 ; *Fr*. 79
Adria *Fr*. 35
Aegean sea *A*. 659
Aegeira *Fr*. 231
Aegeus *E*. 683
Aegina *Fr*. 232
Aegiplanctus, *A*. 303
Aegisthus *A*. 1436, 1612 ; *Ch*. 111 134, 482, 570, 656, 734, 877, 893, 989, 1011
Aegyptii p. 598
Aegyptus *Fr*. 161. See Egypt
Aeschylus *Fr*. 272
Aethiopia, *S*. 286 . *Fr*. 105, 161, 183
Aethiops, a mythical river, *Pr*. 809
Aetna *Pr*. 367 ; *Fr*. 127, 287 ; *The Women of Aetna*, p. 381, 593
Agamemnon *A*. 26, 42, 523, 1246, 1314, 1404, 1499 ; *Ch*. 861, 937 ; *E*. 456
Agbatana *P*. 16, 535, 961
Agdabatas *P*. 959
Aïdoneus P. 649, 650
Aisa *Ch*. 647
Aischyne *Th*. 409
Ajax *Fr*. 284 ; island of (Salamis). *P*. 307, 368, 596, *Fr*. 284
Alcmene *A*. 1040
Alexander (Paris) *A*. 61, 363
Amazons *E*. 628, 685 ; *Pr*. 723 *S*. 287
Amistres *P*. 21
Amistris *P*. 320
Amphiaraüs *Th*. 569
Amphion, son of Zeus and Antiope, husband of Niobe, *Th*. 528 ; *Fr*. 81, 277
Amphistreus *P*. 320
Amymone p. 382
Anchares *P*. 994
Andraemon *Fr*. 149
Andros *P*. 886
Anticleia *Fr*. 90
Antigone *Th*. 862
Antilochus *Fr*. 62
Aphrodite *A*. 419 ; *S*. 555, 664, 104 ; *Fr*. 275
Apia, an older name of the Peloponnesus, *A*. 256 ; *S*. 117 = 128, 260, 777
Apis, a mythical person of early Peloponnesian history, son of Apollo, *S*. 262, 269
Apollo *A*. 55, 513, 1073, 1077, 1080, 1085, 1202, 1257, 1269 *Ch*. 559, 1057 ; *E*. 85, 198, 299, 574, 610 ; *S*. 214 ; *Th*. 159, 745, 859 ; *Fr*. 113, 187 (Apollo-Dionysus) ; "Commander of Sevens" *Th*. 801 ; Lycean *A*. 1257, *S*. 686, *Th*. 145. See Loxias, Phoebus.
Ara, Arae curse (sometimes per-

sonified) *A*. 309 ; *E*. 417 ; *Th*. 70, 695, 833, 894, 952
Arabia (?) *Pr*. 420
Arabus *P*. 318
Arachnaeus *A*. 309
Arcadian *Th*. 547, 553
Arcteus *P*. 44, 312
Ares *A*. 48, 78, 437, 642, 1235, 1511 ; *Ch*. 162, 462, 938 ; *E*. 355, 689, 862, 918 ; *P*. 86, 952, *Pr*. 861 ; *S*. 636, 665, 702, 749, 935 ; *Th*. 45, 53, 64, 105, 115, 135, 244, 344, 412, 414, 469, 497, 943 ; hill of *E*. 685, 690 ; *Fr*. 37. 7, 50. 16, 51, 282 (?)
Argestes *P*. 308
Argive *A*. 45, 198, 267, 503, 506, 573, 577, 652, 824, 855, 1393, 1633, 1665 ; *Ch*. 1041, 1046 *E*. 290, 455, 757 ; *S*. 269, 274, 278, 290, 299, 605, 621, 739, 980 ; *Th*. 59, 120, 679 ; *Fr*. 84, 279. See Argos
Argive, p. 383.
Argo *Fr*. 8
Argo, p. 385
Argolic *S*. 236
Argos *A*. 24, 810 ; *Ch*. 676, 680 ; *E*. 654 ; *Pr*. 854, 869 ; *S*. 15 ; *Th*. 548, 573. See Argives
Argus *Pr*. 567, 578 ; *S*. 305
Arian *Ch*. 423
Arimaspi, a Scythian people, *Pr*. 805
Ariomardus *P*. 38, 321, 968
Arsaces *P*. 995
Arsames *P*. 37, 308
Artabes *P*. 318
Artaphrenes *P*. 21, 776, [778]
Artembares *P*. 29, 302, 972
Artemis *A*. 135, 202 ; *S*. 1030 ; *Th*. 154, 450 ; *Fr*. 43 ; Artemis Hecate *S*. 676. cp. *Fr*. 87
Asia *P*. 12, 57, 61, 73, 249, 270, 549, 584, 763, 929 ; *Pr*. 412, 735 ; *S*. 547 ; *Fr*. 106
Asopus *A*. 297 ; *P*. 805
Astacus *Th*. 407
Astaspes *P*. 22
Ate *A*. 770, 1230, 1433 ; *P*. 112, 1007 ; *Th*. 954
Athamas *P*. 70. See Helle
Athamas p. 380
Athena *E*. 235, 288, 299, 443, 614, 892 ; *Th*. 487. See Onca. Pallas
Athenians *P*. 355
Athens *P*. 231, 285, 348, 474, 716, 824, 976 ; *Fr*. 18 (in Euboea), 272
Athos *A*. 285
Atlas *Pr*. 350, 428 ; *Fr*. 172
Atossa, wife of Darius, and mother of Xerxes
Atreidae *A*. 3, 44, 123, 204, 310, 400, 451, 1088 ; *Ch*. 322, 407
Atreides *A*. 530, 1371
Atreus *A*. 60, 784, 1502, 1583, 1591 ; *Ch*. 745 ; *Fr*. 130
Attic *E*. 681
Aulis *A*. 191
Axius *P*. 493

Babylon *P*. 52
Bacchae *E*. 25
Bacchae p. 385 ; of Sophocles (?), p. 598
Bactria *P*. 306, 318, 732
Bassarae p. 386
Batanochus *P*. 981
Belus *S*. 319
Berecynthian *Fr*. 79
Bia *Pr*. 12
Bibline mountains *Pr*. 811
Boeotians *P*. 482, 806
Bolbe, a lake in Macedonia, *P*. 494
Boreas *Fr*. 109. See on *Oreithyia* p. 474
Borrean gate of Thebes, *Th*. 527
Bosporus *P*. 723, 746 ; *Pr*. 733
Bromius *E*. 24
Bura *Fr*. 231

Cabiri p. 412
Cadmus (Cadmeans) *Th*. 1, 9, 39, 47, 74, 120, 136, 303, 531, 548, 679, 823, 1012, 1021, 1031, 1032
Caïcus *Fr*. 67, 68
Calchas *A*. 156, 249
Canobus, a town situated (in classical times) near Alexandria *Pr*. 846 ; *S*. 311
Capaneus *Th*. 423, 440 ; *Fr*. 7
Carians or *Europe* p. 414, 599
Cassandra *A*. 1035
Caucasus *Pr*. 422, 719 ; *Fr*. 107. 28
Cegdadatas *P*. 997
Cenean promontory *Fr*. 17, 273
Cerchnea, a spring near Lerna in Argolis, *Pr*. 676
Ceryces p. 419
Cercyon p. 418

INDEX OF PROPER NAMES

Chalcis *A*. 190, 273
Chalybes, workers in iron, dwelling near the east coast of the Euxine, *Pr*. 715 ; *Th*. 728
Chios *P*. 883
Chrysa, a city of Asia Minor, *P*. 314
Chryseïs *A*. 1439
Chthon *E*. 6 ; *Pr*. 207. See Gaia
Cilicia *P*. 327 ; *Pr*. 353 ; *S*. 551 ; *Fr*. 268
Cilissa *Ch*. 732
Cissia, a district of Susiana in which the city of Susa was situated, *Ch*. 423 ; *P*. 17, 120
Cisthene *Pr*. 793
Cithaeron *A*. 298
Clytaemestra (so written in the MSS., not -mnestra) *A*. 84, 258, 585 ; *Ch*. 882 ; *E*. 116
Cocytus *A*. 1160 ; *Th*. 690
Colchis *Pr*. 415
Corycian cave *E*. 22
Cotyto *Fr*. 27. 1
Cranaüs *E*. 1011
Cratos *Ch*. 244 ; *Pr*. 12
Creon *Th*. 474
Cretan *Ch*. 616 ; *Fr*. 102
Cretan Women p. 419
Cronus *E*. 641 ; *Pr*. 187, 203, 222, 577 ; *Fr*. 107. 5, 282
Curetes *Fr*. 173
Curse personified, see Ara
Cychrea, a name of the island of Salamis, *P*. 570
Cyclopes *Fr*. 244
Cyclops of Sophocles (?), p. 598
Cycnus of Sophocles (?), p. 598
Cypris *E*. 215 ; *S*. 1034 ; *Th*. 140
Cyprus *P*. 892 ; *S*. 282 ; *Fr*. 238
Cyrus *P*. 768, 773
Cytherea *S*. 1032

DADACES *P*. 304
Danaans *A*. 66, 149, 1466 ; *Fr*. 59
Danaïds p. 393, 598
Danaüs *S*. 11, 321, 969, 979
Darian *P*. 651, 663
Darius *P*. 6, 156, 164, 554, 713, etc.
Daulian *Ch*. 674
Delos *E*. 9
Delphi, *Fr*. 287
Delphus *E*. 16
Demeter *Fr*. 25, 161, 241
Diaexis *P*. 995
Dike *A*. 250, 383, 772, 1432 ; *Ch*. 148, 244, 311, 461, 641, 646, 949 ; *E*. 511 ; *S*. 709 ; *Th*. 415, 646, 662, 667, 671 ; *Fr*. 148, 253, 282
Dion *Fr*. 18
Dionysus *Fr*. 193, 276 (?)
Dirce, a stream close to Thebes on the west, *Th*. 273, 307
Dodona *Pr*. 658, 830 ; *S*. 258
Dorian *P*. 183, 817
Doris *P*. 486
Dotamas *P*. 959
Dyme *Fr*. 231

EARTH, see Gaia
Edonians *P*. 495
Edonians p. 398
Egypt *P*. 35, 311 ; *S*. 873 ; *Fr*. 206 ; see Aegyptus
Electra *Ch*. 16, 252
Electran gate of Thebes *Th*. 423
Eleusinians p. 396
Enyo *Th*. 45
Epaphus *Pr*. 851 ; *S*. 48, 315, 589
Epigoni p. 396
Erasinus, a river of Argolis, *S*. 1020
Erechthens *E*. 855
Erinys, Erinyes *A*. 59, 463, 645, 749, 991, 1119, 1190, 1433, 1580 ; *Ch*. 283, 402, 577 ; *E*. 331, 344, 512, 951 ; *Pr*. 516 ; *Th*. 70, 574, 700, 723, 791, 867, 887, 979=993, 1061
Eteocles *Th*. 6, 39, 1013
Eteoclus *Th*. 458
Etruscan *E*. 567 ; *Fr*. 269
Euboea *Fr*. 17, 194, 273
Euphorion *Fr*. 272
Euripus *A*. 292
Europe *P*. 799 ; *Fr*. 106
Europe or Carians p. 414, 599
Eurymachus *Fr*. 94
Eye of the Persians *P*. 979

FATES, see Moerae
Furies, see Erinyes

GABIANS *Fr*. 110
Gaia, Ge *Ch*. 148, 399, 489 ; *E*. 2 ; *P*. 220, 523, 629, 640 ; *Pr*. 90, 212 ; *S*. 305, 890 ; *Th*. 16, 69. See Chthon
Gela *Fr*. 272
Geryon *A*. 870, *Fr*. 37. See p. 388
Glaucus Pontios p. 388, 529

INDEX OF PROPER NAMES

Glaucus Potnieus p. 391
Gorgons *Ch.* 1048; *E.* 48; *Pr.* 793, 799
Gorgopis *A.* 302
Grypes, a fabulous, bird-like species of animal, *Pr.* 804

Hades *A.* 667, 1115, 1235, 1291, 1528; *E.* 273; *P.* 923; *Pr.* 152, 238, 433, 1029; *S.* 228, 416, 791; *Th.* 322, 868; *Fr.* 131, 243
Halys, the chief river of Asia Minor and forming the boundary between the Lydian and the Persian empire, *P.* 865
Harmonia, daughter of Aphrodite, *S.* 1041
Hecate *Fr.* 216, 249. See Artemis
Hector *Fr.* 149, 158
Hector's Ransom or The Phrygians p. 470
Helen *A.* 687, 800, 1455, 1464; *Fr.* 283
Heliades p. 402
Helice *Fr.* 231
Helios *A.* 633; *Ch.* 986; *P.* 232; *Fr.* 105
Hellas *A.* 109, 578; *P.* 2, 186, 234, 271, 758, 796, 809, 824; *S.* 237, 243; *Fr.* 50. 17, 252, 283
Helle, daughter of Athamas (*P.* 70) and Nephele, an immortal. When she and her brother Phrixus were persecuted by their stepmother, Ino, Nephele appeared and carried off her children on a golden ram, but Helle, falling into the sea, was drowned; whence it was called Hellespont
Hellene, Hellenic *A.* 429, 1254; *E.* 31, 756, 920; *P.* 334, 338, 362, 409, etc. *S.* 220, 914; *Th.* 269
Hellespont *P.* 745, cp. 875
Hephaestus *A.* 281; *E.* 13; *Pr.* 3, 369, 619; *Fr.* 33. 3, 107. 6
Hera *Pr.* 592, 704, 900; *S.* 291, 586, 1035; *Th.* 152; *Fr.* 26; Hera, "the Fulfiller," *E.* 214, *Fr.* 211, 279, 282
Heracleidae p. 404, 586
Heracles, references to *A.* 1040; *Pr.* 872; *Fr.* 109-116, 285 (?)
Hermaean crag *A.* 283
Hermes *A.* 515; *Ch.* 1, 124a, 622, 727; *E.* 90; *P.* 629; *Pr.* 1036; *S.* 305; *Th.* 508; *Fr.* 150, 212
Hesione, daughter of Oceanus, *Pr.* 559
Himeras *Fr.* 19
Hippomedon *Th.* 488
Homoloïd gate of Thebes *Th.* 570
Hybristes *Pr.* 717
Hyperbius *Th.* 504, 512, 519
Hystaechmas *P.* 972

Icarus *P.* 890
Ida *A.* 281, 283, 311, 564; *Fr.* 79, 83
Ἱέρειαι p. 408
Ilium *A.* 29, 406, 440, 453, 457, 589, 626, 699, 747, 814, 860, 882, 907, 968, 1227, 1287, 1439; *Ch.* 345; *E.* 457
Imaeus *P.* 31
Inachus, the most ancient hero or god of Argos, father of Io, *Ch.* 6; *Pr.* 590, 663, 705; *S.* 497; *Fr.* 84, 279
Io *Pr.* 635, 788, 815; *S.* 292, 535, 573, 1064
Ionian, Ionians *P.* 178, 563, 771, 899, 950, 951, 1011, 1025
Ionian sea *Pr.* 840
Iphigenia *A.* 1526, 1555
Iphigenia p. 411
Ismene *Th.* 862
Ismenus, a stream close to Thebes on the east, *Th.* 273, 378
Ister *Fr.* 76
Isthmiastae or Theoroi p. 406, 541
Itys *E.* 1144
Ixion *E.* 441, 718
Ixion p. 409

Keres, vengeful spirits of the dead, *Th.* 1061
Kophoi of Sophocles, p. 598

Laius *Th.* 691, 745, 802, 842
Lasthenes *Th.* 620
Leda *A.* 914
Lemnos *A.* 284; *P.* 890; the "Lemnian horror" *Ch.* 631, 634
Leon p. 420
Leontini, *Fr.* 287
Lerna, a marshy district near the sea, on the south-west of the Argolic Plain, *Pr.* 652, 677

INDEX OF PROPER NAMES

Lesbos *P.* 882 ; Lesbian moulding *Fr.* 39
Leto *E.* 323, *Th.* 147, *Fr.* 87
Libya *E.* 292 ; *S.* 279, 316 ; Libyan fables *Fr.* 63
Libyrnia *Fr.* 201
Lichas *Fr.* 17, 273
Ligurians *Fr.* 112. 1, 9
Lilaeus *P.* 308, 970
Loxias *A.* 1074, 1208, 1211 ; *Ch.* 269, 558, 900, 952, 1030, 1036, 1039, 1059 ; *E.* 19, 35, 61, 235 ; 241, 465, 758 ; *Pr.* 669 ; *Th.* 618 ; *Fr.* 42
Lyceüs (Apollo) *A.* 1257, *S.* 686, *Th.* 145
Lycia *Ch.* 346
Licurgus p. 420
Lydia *P.* 41, 770 ; *S.* 550 ; *Fr.* 29
Lyrna, a city in the Troad, *P.* 324
Lyrnessus *Fr.* 149
Lyssa *Fr.* 85
Lythimnas *P.* 997

Macedonia *P.* 492
Macistus *A.* 289
Maeotic lake, the sea of Azov, *Pr.* 418, cp. 731
Magnesia *P.* 492
Magus *P.* 318
Maia *Ch.* 813, *Fr.* 212
Maraphis [*P.* 778]
Marathon *P.* 475, *Fr.* 272
Mardi, a Persian tribe, *P.* 993
Mardon *P.* 51
Mardus *P.* 774
Mariandynians *P.* 938
Masistes *P.* 30
Masistras *P.* 971
Matallus *P.* 314
Medes *P.* 236, 791, *Fr.* 272
Medus *P.* 765
Megabates *P.* 22, 982
Megareus *Th.* 474
Melanippus *Th.* 414
Melian gulf *P.* 486
Memnon p. 421
Memphis (1) the city *P.* 36 ; *S.* 311 ; (2) a general under Xerxes *P.* 971
Menelaüs *A.* 42, 617, 674 ; *Fr.* 283
Messapius *A.* 294 ; *Fr.* 273
Metis, wife of Tereus, commonly called Procne ; she killed her son Itys, *S.* 60
Metrogathes *P.* 43
Minos *Ch.* 618, *Fr.* 50. 11 ; p. 601
Moera, Moerae *A.* 130, 1451, 1537 ; *Ch.* 306, 910, 911 ; *E.* 172, 335, 724, 961, 1046 ; *Pr.* 511, 516 ; *Th.* 977 = 991
Molassian plains, in Epirus, *Pr.* 829
Myconos *P.* 884
Myrmidons p. 422, 582 (?), 590 (?)
Mysia *P.* 52, 322, 1054 ; *S.* 549 ; *Fr.* 67, 267
Mysians p. 427

Naiads *Fr.* 278
Naupactus *S.* 262
Naxos *P.* 884
Neaniskoi p. 428
Neïstan gate of Thebes, *Th.* 460
Nemesis *Fr.* 148
Nereids *Fr.* 89
Nereïds p. 429
Nile *P.* 34, 311 ; *Pr.* 812, 847, 852 ; *S.* 4, 71, 281, 308, 561, 880, 922, 1024 ; *Fr.* 161
Nilotis *Pr.* 814
Niobe p. 430, 556
Nisus *Ch.* 619
Northern gate of Thebes *Th.* 527
Nyx *E.* 322, 416, 745, 792 = 822, 845 = 877, 1034 ; *Fr.* 250

Oceanus *Pr.* 140, 298, 531, *Fr.* 105
Odysseus *A.* 841 ; *Fr.* 284
Oebares *P.* 983
Oedipus *Th.* 203, 372, 654, 677, 709, 725, 752, 775, 801, 806, 833, 886, 978 = 992, 1061
Oedipus p. 437
Oenops *Th.* 504
Oeta *Fr.* 285 (?)
Olenus *Fr.* 231
Olympus (Olympians) *Ch.* 784 ; *E.* 73, 618, 664 ; *Pr.* 149 ; *S.* 161, 981, 1014
Onca *Th.* 164; Onca Pallas *Th.* 501
Ὅπλων κρίσις p. 438
Oreithyia p. 474
Orpheus *A.* 1629
Ossa *Fr.* 271
Ostologoi p. 440

Paeones *S.* 257
Paian the healer, a name of Apollo, *A.* 146

INDEX OF PROPER NAMES

Palaechthon *S.* 250, 348
Palamedes p. 441
Palici *Fr.* 3
Pallas *E.* 10, 21, 79, 224, 629, 667, 754, 758, 772, 916, 1001, 1017, 1045 ; *P.* 347 ; *Th.* 130 ; Pallas Pronaia *E.* 21 ; Onca Pallas *Th.* 501, cp. 164
Pamphylians *S.* 552
Pan *A.* 56 ; *P.* 449
Pangaeus *P.* 494, *Fr.* 12
Paphus *P.* 892, *Fr.* 238
Paris *A.* 399, 532, 712, 1156 ; *Fr.* 283
Parnassus *Ch.* 563, 952 ; *E.* 11
Paros *P.* 884
Parthenopaeus *Th.* 547
Parthus *P.* 983
Pegastagon *P.* 35
Peitho *Ch.* 726 ; *E.* 885, 970 ; *S.* 1040 ; *Fr.* 82
Pelagon *P.* 959
Pelasgia *Pr.* 860 ; *S.* 253, 328, 349, 616, 624, 634, 912, 967, 1023
Pelasgus *S.* 251, 1010
Peleus, *Fr.* 286
Pelops *E.* 703 ; Pelopidae *A.* 1600 ; *Ch.* 503
Penelope p. 445
Pentheus *E.* 26
Pentheus p. 443
Perrhaebians *S.* 256
Perrhaebians p. 444
Persephassa (Persephone) *Ch.* 490
Perseus *Ch.* 831 ; *Fr.* 274-5
Persia *P.* 1, etc.
Pharandaces *P.* 31, 958
Pharnuchus *P.* 313, 967
Phasis *Fr.* 76, 106
Pheres *E.* 723
Philoctetes p. 464, 584 (?)
Phineus *E.* 50
Phineus p. 468
Phlegraean plain *E.* 295
Phobos *Th.* 45
Phocis *A.* 881 ; *Ch.* 564, 674, 679 ; *P.* 485
Phoebe *E.* 7, 8
Phoebus *E.* 8, 283 ; *P.* 206 ; *Th.* 691 ; *Fr.* 189. 5 ; Phoebus Apollo *E.* 744
Phoenicians *P.* 410
Phorcides, the Gorgons and Graeae, daughters of Phorcys, *Pr.* 794
Phorcides p. 469
Phrygia *P.* 770 ; *S.* 548 ; *Fr.* 262, 267
Phrygians or Hector's Ransom p. 470
Phthia *Fr.* 60
Pindus *S.* 257
Pista, Pistoi, name of the Persian Council, *P.* 1, cp. 528, 681
Plataea *P.* 817
Pleiads *A.* 826, *Fr.* 172
Pleisthenes, - dae *A.* 1569, 1602
Pleistus *E.* 27
Pluton, a mythical river, *Pr.* 806
Poimenes of Sophocles, p. 598
Polynices *Th.* 577, 641, 658, 1019, 1073
Polyphontes *Th.* 448
Poseidon *E.* 27 ; *P.* 750 ; *Pr.* 925 ; *Th.* 131, 309 ; *Fr.* 274, 276
Pothos *S.* 1039
Potniae *Fr.* 88
Priam *A.* 40, 127, 267, 710, 935, 1336 ; sons of Priam *A.* 537, 747 ; *Ch.* 935 ; *Fr.* 283
Proetid gate of Thebes *Th.* 377
Proetus *Th.* 395
Prometheus 66, etc., *Fr.* 104, 128, 278 ; the name etymologized, *Pr.* 85 ; *Λυόμενος* p. 446 : *Πυρκαεύς* p. 453, 562 *Πυρφόρος* p. 454
Propontis *P.* 876
Proteus p. 455
Psammis *P.* 960
Psychagogoi p. 473
Pylades *Ch.* 20, 562, 899
Pytho, Pythian *A.* 509 ; *Pr.* 658 ; *Th.* 747

Rhadamanthys *Fr.* 50. 12 ; p. 601
Rhea, gulf of, *Pr.* 837
Rhegium *Fr.* 230
Rhodes *P.* 891
Rhypae (or -es) *Fr.* 231

Salamis (1) the island *P.* 273, 284, 447, 965 ; *Fr.* 284 ; (2) a city in Cyprus *P.* 893 ; *The Women of Salamis* p. 456
Salmydessus, a district in Thrace, on the Euxine, north-west from the entrance of the Bosporus, *Pr.* 726
Samos *P.* 883
Sardis, the ancient capital of Lydia, at the foot of Mt. Tmolus, *P.* 45, 321

Saronic gulf *A.* 306
Sarpedon, a Lycian prince, slain by Patroclus, *S.* 869, *Fr.* 50. 16 ; p. 601
Scamander *A.* 511, 1157; *Ch.* 366 ; *E.* 398
Scylla *A.* 1233
Scythia *Ch.* 161 ; *E.* 703; *Pr.* 2, 417, 709 ; *Fr.* 111
Seisames *P.* 322
Semele, p. 566
Sesames *P.* 982
Seualces *P.* 969
Sicily *Pr.* 371
Sidon *S.* 122=133
Sileniae, a part of the coast of Salamis, *P.* 303
Silenus *Fr.* 274-5, 276 (?)
Simoïs *A.* 696
Sisyphus *Fr.* 90 ; p. 546
Sisyphus p. 457
Soli, a city in Cyprus, *P.* 893
Sophocles, p. 594, 598
Sosthanes *P.* 32
Spercheus *P.* 487, *Fr.* 136
Sphinx *Th.* 541, *Fr.* 129
Sphinx p. 460
Strophius *A.* 881 ; *Ch.* 679
Strymon *A.* 192 ; *P.* 497, 867 ; *S.* 255
Supplices, *Fr.* 288
Susa *P.* 16, 119, 535, 557, 644, 730, 761
Susas *P.* 959
Susicanes *P.* 34, 960
Syennesis *P.* 326
Syracuse *Fr.* 287
Syria *A.* 1312 ; *P.* 84 ; *S.* 5 ; *Fr.* 268

Tantalus *Fr.* 277
Tantalidae *A.* 1469
Tartarus *E.* 72 ; *Pr.* 154, 221, 1029, 1051
Telamon *Fr.* 284
Telephus p. 461
Tenagon *P.* 306
Tenos *P.* 885
Tereus *S.* 60
Tethys Pr. 137 ; *Th.* 311
Teucer *Fr.* 263
Teucrian *A.* 112
Teuthras, an ancient king of Mysia, *S.* 549
Thalamopoioi p. 406
Thanatos *Fr.* 82
Tharybis, *P.* 51, 323, 971
Thebes, in Egypt, *P.* 38
Themis *E.* 2 ; *Pr.* 18, 211, 874 . *S.* 360
Themiscyra, a city in Pontus at which the Thermodon flows into the Euxine, *Pr.* 724
Theoinos *Fr.* 210
Theoroi or Isthmiastai p. 406
Thermodon *Pr.* 725
Theseus *E.* 402, 686. 1026
Thesprotia *Pr.* 831
Thessaly *P.* 489
Thestius, father of Althaea, mother of Meleager, *Ch.* 605
Thrace *A.* 654, 1418 ; *P.* 509, 566, 870 ; *The Women of Thrace* p. 407
Thyestes *A.* 1242, 1584, 1588 ; [*Ch.* 1069)
Thyiad, a female follower of Dionysus, *Th.* 498, 836
Tiryns *Fr.* 244
Titan *E.* 6 ; *Pr.* 207, 427, 874 ; *Fr.* 107. 1
Tmolus *P.* 49
Tolmus *P.* 998
Toxotides p. 463
Triton *E.* 293
Troy *A.* 9, 67, 132, 316, 320, 334, 357, 525, 529, 577, 591, 783, 1457 ; *Ch.* 303, 363 ; *E.* 457 ; *Fr.* 50. 19, 158 ; 286
Tydeus *Th.* 377, 380, 407, 571
Tyndareus *A.* 83
Typho, Typhos *Pr.* 356, 372 ; *S.* 560 ; *Th.* 493, 511, 517
Tyrian *P.* 963
Tyrrhene *E.* 567, *Fr.* 268

Uranus *Pr.* 207 ; *Fr.* 108. 2

Xantriae p. 435, 566
Xerxes *P.* 144, 299, 356, 550, 551, etc.

Zagreus *Fr.* 124
Zeus, often in all the plays, except *Pers.* (532, 740, 762, 827, 915) ; son of Cronus *Pr.* 578, *Fr.* 282 ; son of Earth *S.* 892 = 901 ; the father *Pr.* 17, 40, 53, 947, 969, 984, 1018, *S.* 139, 592, *Th.* 116, 512, *Fr.* 42 ; father of the Olympians *Ch.* 784, *E.* 618 ; father of Dike *Ch.* 949, *Th.* 662, cp. *A.* 526, *Fr.* 282 ; father of Themis *S.* 360 ; the averter *Th.*

8; the apportioner *S.* 360; the awarder *Th.* 485; the fulfiller, accomplisher *A.* 973, 1486, *E.* 28, *S.* 264, *Th.* 116, cp. *Fr.* 211; the purifier *E.* 718 (cp. 441), *Fr.* 182; the Saviour *S.* 26, *Th.* 520, *Fr.* 26. 4; the third *Ch.* 244, *S.* 26; protector of host and guest *A.* 61, 362, 703, 748, *S.* 627, *Fr.* 280; protector of household wealth *S.* 445; protector of suppliants *E.* 92, *S.* 1, 192, 347, 385, 478, 616, 653, *Fr.* 283; a deity of nature *Pr.* 360, 374, 667, *S.* 780, *Fr.* 34; fosters the life of animals and fruit *S.* 689; harmony of *Pr.* 551; inspirer of eloquence *E.* 973, of prophecy *E.* 17; king *A.* 355, *P.* 532, 762; libations to *Fr.* 26; his might *A.* 1485, *Ch.* 245, *E.* 28, 918, 1045, *S.* 816, 1052, *Th.* 822, *Fr.* 34; Nether Zeus *S.* 158, 231, cp. *Ch.* 382; 2. of the Sea. *Fr.* 274; and Hera *E.* 214, *S.* 1035, *Fr.* 26, 211, 282; and Hermes *Fr.* 212; p. 601 and Europe *Fr.* 50 and Danae, *Fr.* 275; and Ixion *E.* 441, 718; and the Moerae *E.* 1045, and the Moerae and the Erinyes *Pr.* 516; and the Palici *Fr.* 3; and Semele, *Fr.* 279; the recording book of *Fr.* 251, 282; worshipped on the Cenean promontory *Fr.* 17, 273, on Mt. Ida *Fr.* 83; chief celebration of *S.* 524, 592, *Fr.* 34.